Hans-J. Engelke

Dassault Systèmes
3DEXPERIENCE©
SOLIDWORKS 2026

Parts and Components
Create and Customize

1st Edition 2026

Publisher: BoD · Books on Demand GmbH, Überseering 33, 22297 Hamburg, bod@bod.de
Print: Libri Plureos GmbH, Friedensallee 273, 22763 Hamburg
ISBN: 978-3-6963-7487-7

Bibliography information's published by the German National Library.
The German National library lists this publication in t he National Bibliography.
Detailed bibliographic data are available on the Internet http://dnb.dnb.de.

Hans-J. Engelke was responsible for the training of technical product designers and technical draftsmen as a teacher and also worked as a CAD lecturer in adult education and continuing education.

Verlag: BoD · Books on Demand GmbH, Überseering 33, 22297 Hamburg, bod@bod.de

Druck: Libri Plureos GmbH, Friedensallee 273, 22763 Hamburg

ISBN: 978-3-6963-7487-7

Bibliografische Information der Deutschen Nationalbibliothek

Die Deutsche Nationalbibliothek verzeichnet diese Publikation in der Deutschen Nationalbibliografie; detaillierte bibliografische Daten sind im Internet über dnb.d-nb.de abrufbar.

Der Autor:

Hans- J. Engelke war als Lehrkraft für die Ausbildung Technischer Produktdesigner und Technischer Zeichner zuständig, außerdem als CAD-Dozent in der Erwachsenenbildung- und Weiterbildung tätig.

Hans-J. Engelke

Dassault Systèmes
3DEXPERIENCE©
SOLIDWORKS 2026

Parts and Components
Create and Customize

Contents

Table of Contents
Chapters 1 to 10

1	**Technical Drawings a Cultural History**	**2**
1.1	Older than paper	2
1.2	The history of geometry	2
1.3	The "Technical Drawing"	4
1.3.1	The history of drawing as a design template	4
1.4	The perspective representation	5
1.4.1	The history of perspective	5
1.4.2	The master of the impossible perspective	5
1.4.3	The drawing as a design template in technology	6
1.4.4	The drawing as a construction template, historical representation rules	6
1.4.5	Drawing methods in mechanical engineering	7
1.4.6	The history of technical standardization	8
1.5	3D Solids, an introduction	9
1.5.1	Platonic solids	9
1.5.2	Kepler-Poinsot Solids	10
1.5.3	Archimedean Solids	10
1.5.4	Catalan Solids	10
1.5.5	Johnson Solids	10
1.6	3D Solids and Solid Edge 2026	11
1.6.1	Creating 3D volume primitive solids	11
1.6.2	Creating Solids from 2D geometry	11
1.6.3	3D Solids based on other objects, examples	11
1.7	Geometric Primitive Solids and SOLIDWORKS 2026	12
1.7.1	Basic solid "Cuboids", geometric description	12
1.7.2	Basic solid "Cube", geometric description	12
1.7.3	Basic solid "Cylinder", geometric description	12
1.7.4	Basic solid "Sphere", geometric description	13
1.7.5	Basic solid "Cone", geometric description	13
1.7.6	Basic solid "Truncated Cone", geometric description	13
1.7.7	Basic solid "Ellipsoid of revolution", geometric description	13
1.7.8	Basic solid "Torus", geometric description	13
1.7.9	Basic solid "Pyramid", geometric description	14
1.7.10	Basic solid "Truncated Pyramid", geometric description	14
2	**SOLIDWORKS© Design 2026, Program basics**	**16**
2.1	SOLIDWORKS Design 2026, the program start	16
2.1.1	Introduction to design concepts and SOLIDWORKS terms, basics, an overview	16
2.1.1.1	Parts	16
2.1.1.2	Assemblies	16
2.1.1.3	Drawings	16
2.1.1.4	Technical tasks	16
2.1.2	SOLIDWORKS Design 2026, program startup	16
2.1.2.1	SOLIDWORKS Design 2026, program startup 3DEXPERIENCE© SOLIDWORKS 2026 for Makers	16
2.1.2.2	SOLIDWORKS Design 2026, program startup	17
2.1.3	SOLIDWORKS Design 2026, the start screen	17
2.1.3.1	SOLIDWORKS Design 2026 start screen "Home", "Recent", "Learn" and "Alerts"	17
2.1.3.2	SOLIDWORKS Design 2026, start screen "Learn"	17
2.1.4	The template files, basics	18
2.1.4.1	SOLIDWORKS Design 2026, start screen New SOLIDWORKS Document "Standard"	18
2.1.4.2	SOLIDWORKS Design 2026, start screen New SOLIDWORKS Document "Advanced"	18
2.1.5	New SOLIDWORKS Document, program functions	19
2.1.5.1	New SOLIDWORKS Document, symbolism	19
2.1.5.2	Component files	19
2.1.5.3	Assembly files, assemblies	19
2.1.5.4	Drawing files	19
2.2	SOLIDWORKS Design 2026, Component files User Interface Overview	20
2.2.1	Open the working file, select the component from the book's DVD	20
2.2.2	SOLIDWORKS Design 2026, the part user interface	20
2.2.2.1	SOLIDWORKS Design 2026, the part user interface, preliminary remarks	20
2.2.2.2	User interface, overview	20
2.2.3	SOLIDWORKS 2026, the user interface, definitions of terms	22
2.2.3.1	Windows Functions	22
2.2.3.2	SOLIDWORKS Document Window	22
2.2.3.3	PropertyManager	22
2.2.3.4	FeatureManager	22
2.2.3.5	ConfigurationManager	22
2.2.3.6	SOLIDWORKS Document, Window Extensions	22
2.2.3.7	Menus	22
2.2.3.8	Toolbars	22
2.2.3.9	CommandManager	23
2.2.3.10	Shortcut bars	23
2.2.3.11	Context Toolbars	23
2.2.3.12	Callouts and Handles	23
2.2.3.13	Selection Breadcrumbs	23
2.2.4	SOLIDWORKS Design 2026, the user interface, advanced views, definitions of terms	24
2.2.4.1	The "Menu bar", "Quick Access Tools"	24
2.2.4.2	SOLIDWORKS menus, excerpts	24
2.2.5	CommandManager for components, excerpt	24
2.2.5.1	CommandManager "Features"	25
2.2.5.2	CommandManager "Sketch"	25
2.2.5.3	CommandManager "Surfaces"	25
2.2.5.4	CommandManager "Sheet Metal"	25
2.2.5.5	CommandManager "Weldments"	25
2.2.5.6	CommandManager "Direct Editing"	25
2.2.5.7	CommandManager "Evaluate"	25
2.2.5.8	CommandManager "SOLIDWORKS Add-Ins"	25
2.2.6	The toolboxes, component features, excerpt	26
2.2.6.1	Feature toolbars	26
2.2.6.2	Selectable flyouts in the "Features" toolbar, excerpt	26
2.2.7	"FeatureManager", "Transparent Flyout FeatureManager" and "PropertyManager"	27
2.2.7.1	Display of Managers	28
2.2.7.2	Der FeatureManager	28
2.2.7.3	Der PropertyManager	28
2.2.7.4	Transparent Flyout FeatureManager	28
2.2.7.5	ConfigurationManager	29
2.2.7.6	DimXpertManager	29
2.2.7.7	DisplayManager	29
2.2.8	Task Window Area	29
2.2.8.1	Command "SOLIDWORKS Welcome dialog"	29
2.2.8.2	Task Pane Tabs	29
2.2.8.3	The "Help" window area	30
2.2.9	Heads-Up View Toolbar	31
2.2.9.1	Flyout "View Settings", excerpt	31
2.2.9.2	Flyout "Heads-Up View Toolbar"	31
2.2.9.3	Flyout "Display Style"	32
2.2.9.4	Flyout "Section View"	32

2.2.9.5 Flyout "Previous View" 32
2.2.9.6 Flyout "Zoom to Area" 32
2.2.9.7 Flyout "Zoom to Fit" 32
2.2.9.8 Flyout "View Orientation" 33
2.2.10 Error message 34
2.2.10.1 Error description 34
2.2.10.2 Error messages and possible solutions 34
2.2.11 SOLIDWORKS main window 38
2.2.11.1 Split document window 38
2.3 Creating a new template file for components 39
2.3.1 SOLIDWORKS Design 2026, program startup 39
2.3.2 Opening the SOLIDWORKS template file for parts 39
2.3.3 Customizing the CommandManager 39
2.3.3.1 Adjusting the Button Size, Command Bar 39
2.3.3.2 Setting the Button Size using Options/Customize 40
2.3.4 Adjusting the graphics area 40
2.3.4.1 Color assignment of the graphics area, suggestion 40
2.3.4.2 Activating the work planes 41
2.3.4.3 Switching on the isometric view 41
2.3.4.4 Assigning a background display 41
2.3.4.5 View Orientation im Bauteil-Modus 42
2.3.5 Adjusting system properties, suggestions 42
2.3.5.1 Inherited default settings 42
2.3.5.2 Festlegen von System options, Sketch / Relation / Snap 42
2.3.5.3 Setting the options from the "General" tab 43
2.3.5.4 Setting the options from the "Performance" tab 43
2.3.5.5 Setting the options from the "FeatureManager" tab 43
2.3.5.6 Setting the options from the "Default Templates" tab 43
2.3.6 Adjusting document properties, suggestions 44
2.3.6.1 Setting the "Image Quality" for the active document 44
2.3.6.2 Setting the "Detailling" for the active document 44
2.3.6.3 Setting "Units" for the Active Document 44
2.3.6.4 Setting "Plane Display" for the Active Document 44
2.3.7 Data backup of the customized template file 45
2.3.8 Assistant for Copying User Settings, Basics 45
2.3.8.1 Saving system settings 46
2.4 Mouse Functions 47
2.4.1 Mouse with three buttons 47
2.4.2 Mouse with wheel 47
2.4.3 2.4.3 SOLIDWORKS users and 3Dconnexion 3D Mouse 48
2.4.3.1 Access to all SOLIDWORKS functions at the touch of a button 48
2.4.3.2 Part Modeling Mode 48
2.4.3.3 Assembly mode 48
2.4.3.4 Drawing Mode 48
2.4.3.5 Access to special additional functions 48
2.4.4 Mouse Gestures 49
2.4.4.1 Using Mouse Gestures 49
2.5 Command input using the keyboard 50
2.5.1 Command shortcuts, excerpt 50
2.6 Instant3D Features, excerpt 51
2.6.1 Overview of Instant3D Functionality 51
2.6.2 Modifying Features in Instant3D 51
2.6.3 Instant3D Rulers 52
2.6.4 Instant3D Live Section Planes 52

Rules for written execution in the book, how do I use the book 54

3 Views and Settings 55

3.1 SOLIDWORKS Design 2026© controls, functions, and customization 55
3.1.1 Starting SOLIDWORKS Design 2026, Open the working file, select the component from the book's DVD 55
3.1.2 Heads-up View Toolbar 56
3.1.3 RealViewGraphics, Heads-up View Toolbar 56
3.1.4 View Setting "Shadows", Heads-up View Toolbar 56
3.1.4.1 View mode "Shadow", settings using "Edit Scene" 57
3.1.5 View Setting "Perspective", Heads-up View Toolbar 57
3.1.5.1 Changing the Perspective 58
3.1.5.2 Resetting the Perspective 58
3.1.6 View size changes 58
3.1.6.1 Zoom to Area 58
3.1.6.2 Zoom to Fit 59
3.1.6.3 Zooming in and out 59
3.1.7 Magnified Selection 60
3.1.7.1 Magnified Selection, access using the context menu 60
3.1.7.2 Magnified Selection, accessed using the keyboard 60
3.1.8 View position changes 61
3.1.8.1 Move display 61
3.1.9 View changes, rotating position 61
3.1.9.1 Rotate view 61
3.1.9.2 Rotate view around one edge 61
3.1.9.3 View changes, "Roll View" 62
3.1.10 View Orientations, according to DIN ISO 128-30, excerpt 63
3.1.11 Axonometric representations according to DIN ISO 5456-3 64
3.1.12 Displaying models in "Normal To" view 65
3.1.12.1 Select "View Orientations" using "Normal To" 65
3.1.12.2 Select View Orientations "Normal To" using the CTRL key 65
3.1.13 Multiple Views 66
3.1.13.1 Multiple Views, Viewports 66
3.1.13.2 Multiple Views, linking orthogonal views 66
3.1.13.3 Changing orthogonal views together 66
3.1.14 "Section Views" in models 67
3.1.14.1 "Section View" on Plane 67
3.1.14.1 Checking the data backup of the created "Section View" 67
3.1.14.2 "Section View" adjust the level variably 68
3.1.14.3 Activate created "Section Views" 68
3.1.15 Display Style 69
3.2 Allocation of materials to components 70
3.2.1 Materials Overview 70
3.2.2 Material allocation 70
3.2.2.1 Component Preparation 70
3.2.2.2 Reassign component material 70
3.2.2.3 Reassigning component material, examples 71
3.2.2.4 Data backup 71
3.3 Surface finish for components 72
3.3.1 Surface finish "Machined" und "Burnished" 72
3.3.2 Surface finish "Sandblasted" und "Casted" 72
3.4 Changing the component color 73
3.4.1 Appearance on components 73
3.4.2 Appearance select "Feature" 73
3.4.3 Appearance select "Faces" 74
3.4.3.1 Data backup 74
3.5 Assigning a "Decal" 75
3.5.1 Turn on the "Decal element" 75
3.5.2 Assigning an element "Decal" 75
3.5.2.1 Data backup 75
3.6 Assigning a background image 76
3.6.1 Changing the background of a scene 76
3.6.1.1 Data backup 76

4	**Geometric Fundamentals**	**78**
4.1	Geometric Fundamentals, basics	78
4.2	Design fundamentals	78
4.2.1	Sketches	78
4.2.2	Planes	79
4.2.3	Dimensions	79
4.2.3.1	Dimensions, basics	79
4.2.3.2	Dimensioning methods	79
4.2.4	Relationships	80
4.2.5	Creating a feature, rules and options	80
4.2.5.1	Coordinate systems	80
4.2.5.2	Color tones for highlighting	80
4.2.5.3	Sketch Snap Functions, excerpt	81
4.2.5.4	Selection Tools	82
4.2.5.5	Highlight object selection	82
4.2.5.6	Dynamic Preview	83
4.2.5.7	End condition for Extrude Boss/Base	83
4.3	Sketch creation, an overview	86
4.3.1	Line construction, sketch snap function "Point"	86
4.3.2	Line construction, sketch snap function, "Point-Midpoint"	86
4.3.3	Line construction, sketch snap function, "Point-Centerpoint"	87
4.3.4	Line construction, sketch snap function, "Point-Tangent Point"	87
4.3.5	Line construction, sketch snap function, "Tangent"	87
4.3.6	Line construction, sketch snap function, "Point-Perpendicular"	87
4.4	Sketch Relationships	90
4.4.1	Sketch definitions	90
4.4.1.1	Fully defined sketches are black	90
4.4.1.2	Underdefined sketches are blue	90
4.4.1.3	Overdefined sketches are yellow	90
4.4.1.4	No solution found	90
4.4.1.5	Invalid solution found	90
4.4.2	Assigning relationships in sketches	91
4.4.2.1	Relationship assignment "Horizontal or Vertical"	91
4.4.2.2	Relationship assignment "Points merge"	91
4.4.2.3	Relationship assignment "Concident"	92
4.4.2.4	Relationship assignment Parallel“	92
4.4.2.5	Relationship assignment "Midpoint“	93
4.4.2.6	Relationship assignment "Perpendicular“	93
4.4.2.7	Relationship assignment "Equal"	94
4.4.2.8	Relationship assignment "Symmetric"	94
4.4.2.9	Relationship assignment "Tangent“	95
4.4.2.10	Relationship assignment "Concentric“	96
4.4.2.11	Relationship assignment "Collinear“	96
4.4.2.12	Relationship assignment "Intersection“	97
4.4.3	3D Sketching Functions	98
4.4.3.1	3D Sketching Functions, basics	98
4.4.3.2	Sketch relationships in 3D sketches	99
4.4.3.3	Dimensioning in 3D sketches, a selection	99
4.5	Sketch Dimensions	102
4.5.1	Sketch Dimensions, basics	102
4.5.2	Dimensioning in 2D sketches	103
4.5.2.1	Dimension in 2D sketches, horizontal and vertical	103
4.5.2.2	Dimensioning in 2D sketches, angular dimensioning	104
4.5.2.3	Dimensioning in 2D sketches, distance dimensioning	104
4.5.2.4	Dimensioning in 2D sketches, circular dimensioning	105
4.5.2.5	Dimensioning in 2D sketches, radius dimensioning	105
4.5.2.6	Dimensioning in 2D sketches, quadrant-circle distance dimensioning Dimensioning in 2D sketches, Diameter dimension using center	105
4.5.2.7	Dimensioning in 2D sketches, Radian measure	106
4.5.2.8	Dimensioning in 2D sketches, Diameter dimensioning across centerline	106
4.5.2.9	Dimensioning in 2D sketches, Baseline Dimension	107
4.6	Fundamentals for basic constructions, "Work Planes"	110
4.6.1	Working Planes, basics	110
4.6.1.1	Basic planes	110
4.6.1.2	Automatic adjustment of planes and axes	110
4.6.2	Creating Work Planes	111
4.6.2.1	Open working file, component from the book DVD	111
4.6.2.2	Creating work planes, "Parallel Plane"	111
4.6.2.3	Data backup	111
4.6.2.4	Creating work planes, "Mid Plane"	112
4.6.2.5	Data backup	112
4.6.2.6	Creating work planes, "Plane through Point"	113
4.6.2.7	Data backup	113
4.6.2.8	Creation of work planes, "Plane with defined Offset"	114
4.6.2.9	Data backup	114
4.6.2.10	Creating work planes, "Plane centered between two Sides"	115
4.6.2.11	Data backup	115
4.6.2.12	Creation work planes, "Plane with Angle input"	116
4.6.2.13	Data backup	116
4.6.2.14	Creation work planes, "Plane with multiple defined Offsets"	117
4.6.2.15	Data backup	117
4.6.3	Creating work plane, "Plane on a cylindrical Surface"	118
4.6.3.1	Creating the work plane on a cylindrical surface, by selecting a sketch line	118
4.6.3.2	Data backup	118
4.6.3.3	Creating the work plane on a cylindrical surface, by selecting a sketch point	119
4.6.3.4	Data backup	119
4.6.3.5	Creation work planes, „Angular Plane axis-related“	120
4.6.3.6	Data backup	120
4.6.3.7	Creation work planes, „Angular plane offset distance“	121
4.6.3.8	Data backup	121
5	**Geometric basics, Primitives bodies**	**124**
5.1	Creating 3D solid primitive body	124
5.1.1	Creating solids from 2D geometry	124
5.1.2	Feature-based solids	124
5.2	Geometric basics, Primitives bodies SOLIDWORKS 2026	125
5.2.1	Geometric basics, Primitives bodies SOLIDWORKS 2026, basics	125
5.2.2	Basics of construction	125
5.2.2.1	Sketches	125
5.2.2.2	Planes	126
5.2.2.3	Dimensions	126
5.2.2.4	Basics of construction, geometric relationships	126
5.3	Basic geometric primitiv body "Cuboid"	129
5.3.1	Basic geometric primitiv body "Cuboid", geometric description	129
5.3.2	Geometric basic primitive body "Cuboid" Sketch function "Center Rectangle", using "Extrude"	130
5.3.2.1	Sketch function "Center Rectangle"	130
5.3.2.2	Opening your own template file	130
5.3.2.3	The basic sketch construction	130
5.3.2.4	Creating an "Extrude" feature	131
5.3.2.5	Data backup	131

5.3.3 Geometric basic primitive body "Cuboid" Sketch function "Corner Rectangle", using "Extrude" 132
5.3.3.1 Opening your own template file 132
5.3.3.2 Cuboid using "Corner Rectangle", sketch construction 132
5.3.3.3 Sketch dimensioning, horizontal 132
5.3.3.4 Sketch dimensioning, vertical 133
5.3.3.5 Create "Extrude" feature with depth change 133
5.3.3.6 Data backup 133
5.3.4 Geometric basic primitive body "Cuboid "Line" sketch construction with dimension entries 134
5.3.4.1 Opening your own template file 134
5.3.4.2 "Cuboid" construction using a line sketch Outline basics for guidelines and relationships 134
5.3.4.3 The basic sketch construction 134
5.3.4.4 Sketch dimensioning, horizontal and vertical 136
5.3.4.5 Create "Extrude" feature, change length 136
5.3.4.6 Data backup 136
5.4 Geometric basic primitive body "Cube" 139
5.4.1 Geometric basic primitive body "Cube", geometric description 139
5.4.2 Geometric basic primitive body "Cube" Sketch function "Center Rectangle", using "Extrude" 140
5.4.2.1 Opening your own template file 140
5.4.2.2 Creating the basic sketch 140
5.4.2.3 Creating an "Extrude" feature 141
5.4.2.4 Data backup 141
5.5 Geometric basic primitive body "Cylinder" 142
5.5.1 Geometric basic primitive body "Cylinder", geometric description 142
5.5.2 Basic shape "cylinder" using circular area Sketch creation within volume generation 143
5.5.2.1 Opening your own template file 143
5.5.2.2 Creating the basic sketch 143
5.5.2.3 Volume Generation 144
5.5.2.4 Data backup 144
5.5.3 Geometric basic primitive body "Cylinder" Rotation over a stationary rectangular area Sketch creation within volume generation 145
5.5.3.1 Opening your own template file 145
5.5.3.2 Creating the basic sketch 145
5.5.3.3 Revolve volume creation 146
5.5.3.4 Data backup 146
5.6 Geometric basic primitive body "Sphere" and "Spherical Cap" 147
5.6.1 Geometric basic primitive body "Sphere", geometric description 147
5.6.2 Geometric basic primitive body "Hemisphere" and "Spherical Cap", geometric description 147
5.6.3 Geometric basic primitive body "Sphere", using a rotation of a halved circular area 148
5.6.3.1 Opening your own template file 148
5.6.3.2 Creating the basic sketch 148
5.6.3.3 Creating the halved circular area 149
5.6.3.4 Revolved volume creation 149
5.6.3.5 Data backup 149
5.6.4 "Spherical Cap" using rotation of a circular segment area, sketch creation 150
5.6.4.1 Opening your own template file 150
5.6.4.2 Creating the basic sketch 150
5.6.4.3 Creating the circular area 151
5.6.4.4 Revolved volume creation 152
5.6.4.5 Data backup 152
5.7 Geometric basic primitive body "Cone" and "Truncated Cone" 153
5.7.1 Geometric basic primitive body "Cone", geometric description 153
5.7.2 Geometric basic primitive body "Truncated Cone", geometric description 153
5.7.3 Geometric basic primitive body "Cone", using rotation of a triangular area made of lines 154
5.7.3.1 Opening your own template file 154
5.7.3.2 Creating the basic sketch 154
5.7.3.3 Revolved volume creation 155
5.7.3.4 Data backup 155
5.7.4 Geometric basic primitive body "Truncated Cone" using feature "Extrude" and "Draft" 156
5.7.4.1 Opening your own template file 156
5.7.4.2 Creating the basic sketch 156
5.7.4.3 "Draft" Volume Generation 157
5.7.4.4 Data backup 157
5.8 Geometric basic primitive body " Pyramid" and "Truncated Pyramid" 158
5.8.1 Geometric basic primitive body "Pyramid", geometric description 158
5.8.2 Geometric basic primitive body "Truncated Pyramid", geometric description 158
5.8.3 Geometric basic primitive body "Pyramid" using "Extrude" and "Draft" feature 159
5.8.3.1 Opening your own template file 159
5.8.3.2 Creating the basic sketch 159
5.8.3.3 Extrude" and "Draft" volume creation 160
5.8.3.4 Create a "Pyramid" using "Draft" 160
5.8.3.5 Data backup 161
5.8.4 Geometric basic primitive body "Truncated Pyramid" using "Extrude" feature option "Draft" 162
5.8.4.1 Opening your own template file 162
5.8.4.2 Creating the basic sketch 162
5.8.4.3 "Draft" volume generation 163
5.8.4.4 Data backup 163
5.9 Geometric basic primitive body "Rotational ellipsoid" 164
5.9.1 Geometric basic primitive body "Rotational ellipsoid", geometric description 164
5.9.2 Geometric basic primitive body "Rotational ellipsoid" Rotation of half an elliptical surface 165
5.9.2.1 Opening your own template file 165
5.9.2.2 Creating the basic sketch 165
5.9.2.3 Revolved volume creation 166
5.9.2.4 Data backup 166
5.10 Geometric basic primitive body "Torus" 167
5.10.1 Geometric basic primitive body "Torus", geometric description 167
5.10.2 Geometric basic primitive body "Torus" Rotation of a circular area around a central axis 168
5.10.2.1 Opening your own template file 168
5.10.2.2 Erstellung der Basisskizze 168
5.10.2.3 Revolved volume creation 169
5.10.2.4 Data backup 169

6 Powerful commands, optimized constructions 172

6.1 Powerful commands, optimized constructions, basics 172
6.2 Technical principles for basic constructions, drilling 173
6.2.1 Drilling, technical basics 173
6.2.1.1 Simple Hole 173
6.2.1.2 Threaded Hole 173

6.2.1.3 Countersink DIN 974-1, for cylinder head screws 173
6.2.1.4 Countersink DIN 974-2, for hexagon head screws 173
6.2.1.5 Countersink DIN 74 and DIN EN ISO 15065, for countersunk screws 173
6.2.2 Holes as a SOLIDWORKS "Hole Wizard" function 173
6.2.2.1 SOLIDWORKS „Hole Wizard“ feature, hole types 173
6.2.2.2 SOLIDWORKS „Hole Wizard“ feature, "End condition" 173
6.2.2.3 The "Hole Wizard", basics 174
6.2.2.4 Threaded Holes 174
6.2.2.5 End Condition 175
6.2.2.6 "Hole Wizard" edit feature for holes 175
6.2.2.7 "Advanced Hole" tool 175
6.2.2.8 The thread as a "cosmetic thread" 175
6.2.2.9 The "Stud Wizard" 175
6.2.2.10 The physical thread with the function "Thread" 175
6.2.2.11 Keyway slot according to DIN 6885-1 175
6.3 Basic constructions of the shaft element 178
6.3.1 Shaft element using a line construction 178
6.3.1.1 The basic geometry 178
6.3.1.2 Opening your own template file 178
6.3.1.3 A closed surface of rotation using lines with vector data 178
6.3.1.4 Revolved volume creation 179
6.3.1.5 Material assignment, default settings 179
6.3.1.6 Reassigning component material 179
6.3.1.7 Data backup 179
6.3.2 Basic constructions of the shaft element with a line construction using "SmartDimension" 180
6.3.2.1 Opening your own template file 180
6.3.2.2 A closed surface of Rotation using command "Line" 180
6.3.2.3 "SmartDimension" with resizing 180
6.3.2.4 Revolved volume creation 181
6.3.2.5 Material assignment, default settings 181
6.3.2.6 Reassigning component material 181
6.3.2.7 Data backup 181
6.4 Basic constructions of the shaft element "Holes and Threadings" 182
6.4.1 Drilling the through hole 182
6.4.1.1 Open the working file 182
6.4.1.2 The "Through hole" using the "Hole Wizard" 182
6.4.2 The "Threaded base hole", using the "Hole Wizard" 183
6.4.2.1 The "Threaded base hole", the creation 183
6.4.2.2 Adjusting the thread representation 183
6.4.2.3 Data backup 183
6.4.3 Basic constructions of the shaft element, external thread 184
6.4.3.1 External thread using "Stud Wizard", position change 184
6.4.3.2 External thread using "Stud Wizard", the creation 184
6.4.4 Basic constructions of the shaft element, "Chamfers" and "Fillets" 185
6.4.4.1 Edge breaking using "Chamfer", the creation 185
6.4.4.2 Edge breaking using "Fillet", the creation 185
6.4.4.3 Data backup 185
6.4.5 "Section View" for design control 186
6.4.5.1 Data backup 186
6.4.6 Basic constructions of the shaft element, Keyway slot, the creation 187
6.4.6.1 Create tangential working plane for the basic sketch of the keyway 187
6.4.6.2 Creating the basic sketch 187
6.4.6.3 Keyway slot, the creation 188
6.4.6.4 Data backup 188
6.5 Creating a drill plate 189
6.5.1 Creating a drill plate, basics 189
6.5.2 The basic geometry, drawing representation 189
6.5.3 Creating a drill plate, the basic body 190
6.5.3.1 Opening your own template file 190
6.5.3.2 The basic sketch construction 190
6.5.4 The basic sketch for the drilling, version 1 191
6.5.4.1 Basic sketch, center axes 191
6.5.4.2 Basic sketch, vertical, parallel lines 191
6.5.4.3 Basic sketch, horizontal, parallel lines 192
6.5.4.4 Overview of sketch construction for parallel lines 192
6.5.4.5 Data backup 192
6.5.5 Basic sketch with function "Rectangle over center", v ersion 2 193
6.5.5.1 Open the working file 193
6.5.5.2 Basic sketch with function "Rectangle over center" 193
6.5.5.3 Data backup 194
6.5.6 The "Dowel hole" in the center of the component 195
6.5.6.1 The Dowels hole 195
6.5.6.2 Data backup 195
6.5.7 Four M10 threaded holes, axle element 1 196
6.5.7.1 Adjusting the thread representation 196
6.5.7.2 Data backup 196
6.5.8 Four countersunk holes DIN 74, axle element 2, reverse side 197
6.5.8.1 Edit sketch plane, reverse side 197
6.5.8.2 Four countersunk holes DIN 74, the ceation 197
6.5.8.3 Data backup 197
6.5.9 Four countersunk holes DIN 974-1, axle element 3 198
6.5.9.1 Edit sketch plane, reverse side 198
6.5.9.2 Four counterbore holes DIN DIN 974-1, the ceation 198
6.5.9.3 Data backup 198
6.5.10 Assigning component material 199
6.5.10.1 Material assignment, default settings 199
6.5.10.2 Assigning component material, the creation 199
6.5.10.3 Data backup 199
6.6 Powerful commands, optimized constructions, Form element features 202
6.6.1 List of form element functions, basics 202
6.6.1.1 Form element function "Fillet" 202
6.6.1.2 Form element function "Chamfer" 202
6.6.1.3 Form element function "Draft" 202
6.6.1.4 Form element function "Shell" 203
6.6.1.5 Form element function "Linear Pattern" 203
6.6.1.6 Form element function "Circular Pattern" 203
6.6.1.7 Form element function "Rib" 203
6.6.1.8 Form element function Helix / Spiral 203
6.6.1.9 Form element function "Thread" 203
6.6.1.10 Form element function "SOLIDWORKS Toolbox" 204
6.6.1.11 Form element function "Loft" 204
6.6.1.12 Form element function "Sweep" 204
6.6.1.13 Form element function curved construction "Dome" 205
6.6.1.14 Form element function curved construction "Freeform" 205
6.6.1.15 Form element function curved construction "Deform" 205
6.6.1.16 Form element function curved construction "Flex" 205
6.7 Basic construction "Cuboid with top" Form element feature "Draft", "Shell", "Fillet" 206
6.7.1 The basic geometry, specifications 206
6.7.2 Conical adaptations 206
6.7.2.1 Open the working file 206
6.7.2.2 Draft angle for the cylinder using "Manual Draft" 206
6.7.2.3 Draft angle for the base cuboid using "Manual Draft" 207
6.7.3 "Shell" Feature, the creation 207
6.7.4 "Fillet" Feature, the creation 208
6.7.4.1 Data backup 208
6.8 Basic construction "Drill plate" Form element feature "Hole Wizard", "Linear Pattern" 209

6.8.1 The basic geometry, specifications 209
6.8.2 Creating the basic body 209
6.8.2.1 Opening your own template file 209
6.8.2.2 The “Cuboid” as a basic geometry, using feature “Extrude” 209
6.8.3 “Hole wizard” feature, type “Counterbore”, the creation 210
6.8.4 “Linear Pattern” feature, the creation 211
6.8.4.1 Data backup 211
6.9 Basic construction “Flange ring with mounting holes” Form element feature “Hole Wizard”, “Cicular Pattern” 212
6.9.1 The basic geometry, specifications 212
6.9.2 Creating the basic body 212
6.9.2.1 Opening your own template file 212
6.9.2.2 The ring cylinder as the basic geometry 212
6.9.3 “Hole wizard” feature, type “Counterbore”, the creation 213
6.9.4 “Circular Pattern” feature, the creation 214
6.9.4.1 Data backup 214
6.10 Basic construction “Cuboid with top” Form element feature “Rib”, “Mirror”, “Cicular Pattern” 215
6.10.1 The basic geometry, specifications 215
6.10.2 Basic body processing 215
6.10.2.1 Open the working file 215
6.10.2.2 Create a central plane between planar surfaces 215
6.10.2.3 Data backup 215
6.10.3 “Rib” feature, one rib, the creation 216
6.10.3.1 The basic sketch construction 216
6.10.3.2 “Rib” feature, the basic rib 216
6.10.4 “Rib” feature, mirrored rib construction, the creation 217
6.10.5 “Rib” feature, multiple ribs over “Circular pattern”, the creation 217
6.10.5.1 Data backup 217
6.11 Basic construction “Compression spring” Form element feature “Helix/Spiral”, “Swept Boss” 218
6.11.1 The basic geometry, specifications 218
6.11.2 Creating basic body 218
6.11.2.1 Opening your own template file 218
6.11.3 The “Helix/Spiral” feature 218
6.11.3.1 The basic sketch construction 218
6.11.3.2 The Helix/Spiral feature, the creation 219
6.11.4 The Compression spring, a “Swept/Boss” feature 219
6.11.4.1 The profil sketch construction 219
6.11.4.2 The Compression spring, a “Swept/Boss” feature, the creation 220
6.11.4.3 Assigning component material 220
6.11.4.4 Data backup 220
6.12 Basic construction “Trapezoidal thread” Form element feature “Helix/Spiral”, “Cut/Sweep” 221
6.12.1 The basic geometry, specifications 221
6.12.2 Creating basic body 221
6.12.2.1 Opening your own template file 221
6.12.2.2 Creating basic cylinder 221
6.12.3 Basic body processing, the “Helix/Spiral” feature 222
6.12.4 The “Trapezoidal thread”, the creation 223
6.12.4.1 Basic body processing, the revolve sketch 223
6.12.4.2 The Trapezoidal thread using the feature “Cut Sweep” 224
6.12.5 The final “Chamfer”, the creation 224
6.12.5.1 The final “Chamber”, the basic sketch 224
6.12.5.2 The final “Chamfer”, using the feature “Cut Revolve” 225
6.12.6 Assigning component material 225
6.12.6.1 Data backup 225
6.13 Basic construction “Physical Thread Profile” Form element feature “Thread” 226
6.13.1 Simple hole with physical thread profile, specification 226
6.13.2 Form element feature “Thread” using core diameter 226
6.13.2.1 Open the working file 226
6.13.2.2 Change the specified bore diameter to the core diameter 226
6.13.2.3 Form element feature “Thread”, the creation 226
6.13.2.4 Data backup 227
6.13.3 Form element feature “Thread” with physical thread, using outer diameter 228
6.13.3.1 Open the working file 228
6.13.3.2 Change the specified bore diameter to the core diameter 228
6.13.3.3 Form element feature “Thread”, the creation 228
6.13.3.4 Data backup 228
6.13.4 External thread with physical thread profile, specification 229
6.13.5 Form element feature “Stud Wizard” using outer diameter 229
6.13.5.1 Open the working file 229
6.13.5.2 External thread using “Stud Wizard”, the creation 229
6.13.5.3 Data backup 229
6.13.5.4 Form element feature “Thread”, the creation 230
6.13.5.5 Data backup 230
6.14 Basic construction “Gear Shaft” Creation using the SOLIDWORKS toolbox 233
6.14.1 Basic construction “Gear Shaft”, specification 233
6.14.1.1 The design sketch for component production 233
6.14.1.2 Basic construction “Gear Shaft”, component representations 233
6.14.2 Gear creation using the SOLIDWORKS toolbox 234
6.14.2.1 Opening your own template file 234
6.14.2.2 Gear creation 234
6.14.2.3 Assigning component material 235
6.14.3 Basic construction “Gear Shaft”, editing of the basic geometry 235
6.14.3.1 Insert cylindrical countersink 235
6.14.3.2 Creating drive shaft attachments 235
6.14.4 Basic constructions of the shaft element, Keyway slot, the creation 236
6.14.4.1 Construction point for the working plane 236
6.14.4.2 Create tangential working plane for the basic sketch of the keyway 236
6.14.4.3 Basic sketch for the keyway slot 237
6.14.4.4 Keyway slot, the creation 237
6.14.5 Basic constructions of the shaft element Edge breaking using “Chamfer”, the creation 238
6.14.5.1 Edge breaking using “Chamfer”, value 2 mm x 45°, the creation 238
6.14.5.2 Edge breaking using “Chamfer”, value 1 mm x 20°, the creation 238
6.14.5.3 Data backup 238
6.15 Basic construction “Internally toothed Spur Gear” Creation using the SOLIDWORKS toolbox 239
6.15.1 The design sketch for component production 239
6.15.2 Basic construction “Internally toothed Spur Gear”, component representations 239
6.15.3 Gear creation using the SOLIDWORKS toolbox 240
6.15.3.1 Opening your own template file for assemblies 240
6.15.3.2 Gear creation 240
6.15.3.3 Assigning component material 241
6.15.4 Basic construction “Internally toothed Spur Gear” the outer contour editing 241
6.15.4.1 Create cut rotation 241

6.15.4.2 Edge breaking using "Chamfer", value 1 mm x 45°, the creation 242
6.15.5 Creating mounting holes 242
6.15.5.1 Creating M4 threaded hole 242
6.15.5.2 Threaded hole M4, creating "Circular Pattern" feature 243
6.15.5.3 Data backup 243
6.16 Basic construction "Bevel Gear" Creation using the SOLIDWORKS toolbox 244
6.16.1 The design sketch for component production 244
6.16.2 Basic construction "Bevel Gear", component representations 244
6.16.3 Gear creation using the SOLIDWORKS toolbox 245
6.16.3.1 Opening your own template file 245
6.16.3.2 Gear creation 245
6.16.3.3 The "Bevel gear", the creation 245
6.16.3.4 Assigning component material 245
6.16.4 Basic construction "Bevel Gear", the outer contour editing 246
6.16.4.1 Outer contour editing, length change 246
6.16.4.2 Outer contour editing, diameter change of the attachment cylinder 246
6.16.4.3 Data backup 247
6.17 Basic construction "Cone element with draft angle" Form element feature "Chamfer", "Draft", "Shell" 250
6.17.1 The basic geometry, specifications 250
6.17.2 Open the working file and make adjustments 250
6.17.2.1 Open the working file 250
6.17.2.2 Edge breaking of the base body, the creation 250
6.17.3 Draft angle for the basic body, the creation 251
6.17.4 Creating a cone element, using "Shell" 252
6.17.4.1 Data backup 252
6.18 Basic construction "Rectangular cone element" Form element feature "Planes", Lofted-Boss", "Shell" 253
6.18.1 The basic geometry, specifications 253
6.18.2 Creating the basic sketch 253
6.18.2.1 Opening your own template file 253
6.18.2.2 Basic sketch, the creation 253
6.18.2.3 Additional work plane above 253
6.18.2.4 Final sketch, the creation 254
6.18.3 The transitional body 254
6.18.3.1 The transitional body, using "Lofted Boss", the creation 254
6.18.3.2 Creation of the hollow body, using "Shell" 255
6.18.3.3 Data backup 255
6.19 Basic construction "Round to Square" Form element feature "Planes", Lofted-Boss", "Shell" 256
6.19.1 The basic geometry, specifications 256
6.19.2 Creating the basic body 256
6.19.2.1 Opening your own template file 256
6.19.2.2 Basic sketch, the creation 256
6.19.2.3 Additional work plane above 256
6.19.2.4 Additional sketch, "Circle" on the upper work "Plane1" 257
6.19.2.5 Additional work plane below 257
6.19.2.6 Additional sketch, "Circle" on the lower working "Plane2" 257
6.19.3 Basic construction "Round to Square", the creation 257
6.19.3.1 The upper basic body 257
6.19.3.2 The lower basic body 258
6.19.4 Creation of the hollow body, using "Shell" 258
6.19.4.1 Data backup 258
6.20 Basic construction "3D Piping" Form element feature "Planes, "3D Sketch", Lofted-Boss" 259
6.20.1 The basic geometry, specifications 259
6.20.1.1 2D sketch cannot be converted to 3D sketch 259
6.20.2 The 2D-basic sketch, the creation 259
6.20.2.1 Opening your own template file 259
6.20.2.2 The rectangular basic sketch 259
6.20.3 Additional work planes 260
6.20.3.1 Additional work plane, reference Plane "Right" 260
6.20.3.2 Additional work plane, reference Plane "Front" 260
6.20.4 "3D Sketch" for the pipeline path, the creation 260
6.20.4.1 The basic sketch for the lower pipeline 260
6.20.4.2 The basic sketch, line extensions on "Plane2" 261
6.20.4.3 The basic sketch, line extensions on "Front Plane" 261
6.20.4.4 The basic sketch, "Sketch Fillet" 261
6.20.5 The cross-sectional area for the pipe body 262
6.20.5.1 Additional work plane, reference Plane "Right" 262
6.20.5.2 The cross-sectional area, the creation 262
6.20.6 Basic construction "3D Piping" with "Thin feature" 262
6.20.6.1 Basic construction "3D Piping", view settings 262
6.20.6.2 Basic construction "3D Piping" with "Thin feature", the creation 263
6.20.6.3 Data backup 263
6.21 Basic construction "Pipe Bend" Form element feature "Planes", "3D Sketch","Lofted-Boss" 264
6.21.1 The basic geometry, specifications 264
6.21.2 The 2D-basic sketch, the creation 264
6.21.2.1 Opening your own template file 264
6.21.2.2 The basic sketch, transition guidelines 264
6.21.3 "3D Sketch" for the "Pipe Bend path", the creation 265
6.21.3.1 Additional work plane, reference Plane "Top" 265
6.21.3.2 The basic sketch for the end circles, using "3D Sketch" 265
6.21.4 The "Pipe Bend" creation, using feature "Lofted-Boss" 266
6.21.4.1 Data backup 267
6.22 Basic construction "Hollow body" Form element feature "Curve through XYZ Points" 268
6.22.1 The basic geometry, specifications 268
6.22.2 Creating the curve sketch 268
6.22.2.1 Opening your own template file 268
6.22.2.2 The text file for the XYZ points 268
6.22.2.3 Curve line as "Curve through XYZ Points" from a text list 268
6.22.3 The basic sketch, the creation 269
6.22.3.1 The hollow body axis, as an alignment element of the base surface 269
6.22.3.2 The hollow body base, using sketch feature "Polygon" 269
6.22.3.3 The orientation, "Polygon to Curve", relation "Pierce" 269
6.22.3.4 The orientation, center of polygon to the main axis, Relation "Coincident" 270
6.22.4 Creating a hollow body, using "Shell" 271
6.22.4.1 Axis of rotation as a line sketch 271
6.22.4.2 The hollow body, the creation 271
6.22.4.3 Creation of the hollow body, using "Shell" 272
6.22.4.4 Data backup 272
6.23 Surface modeling „Rectangular funnel element" Form element feature "Lofted Surface ", "Thicken" 275
6.23.1 "Lofted Surface", the creation 275
6.23.1.1 Open the working file 275
6.23.1.2 Basic profile curves for a "Lofted Surface", the creation 275
6.23.2 Apply wall thickness, using the "Thicken" feature 276
6.23.2.1 Data backup 276
6.24 Surface modeling "Boundary Surface" Different profile surfaces, corner-determined 277
6.24.1 "Boundary Surface", the creation 277
6.24.1.1 Open the working file 277
6.24.1.2 Basic profile curves for a "Boundary Surface", the creation 277

6.24.2 Closing the base area using "Planar surface" 278
6.24.3 Apply wall thickness, using the "Thicken" feature 278
6.24.3.1 Data backup 278
6.25 Surface modeling "Molded surfaces" Differentiate curve surface over trim surface 279
6.25.1 "Trim Surface", the creation 279
6.25.1.1 Open the working file 279
6.25.1.2 Create a basic sketch for "Trim Surface" 279
6.25.1.3 Create a "Trim Surface" using "Surface-Extrude" 280
6.25.2 Differentiating surface bodies using "Trim Surface" 280
6.25.2.1 Create the differentiating surface bodies 280
6.25.2.2 Disable "Trim Surface" 281
6.25.3 Apply wall thickness, using the "Thicken" feature 281
6.25.3.1 Data backup 281
6.26 Surface modeling "Freeform Editing" Form element feature "Surface Extrude", "Freeform" 282
6.26.1 "Freeform Surface", the creation 282
6.26.1.1 Open the working file 282
6.26.2 The "Freeform Fittings" adjustments 282
6.26.2.1 The "Freeform", adjustment of the cover surface 282
6.26.2.2 Data backup 283
6.26.2.3 The "Freeform", adjustment of the front surface 284
6.26.2.4 Apply wall thickness, using the "Thicken" feature 284
6.26.2.5 Data backup 284
6.27 Surface modeling "Molded surfaces" "3D-Sketch", basic profile curves 285
6.27.1 "Molded surfaces", basics 285
6.27.2 Creating sketches of the three basic profile curves 285
6.27.2.1 Opening your own template file 285
6.27.2.2 Basic sketch, the creation 285
6.27.2.3 Additional work plane above 285
6.27.2.4 Additional work plane above 285
6.27.2.5 Creating the frame geometry 286
6.27.2.6 Creating the basic profile curves 286
6.27.3 Generating basic profile curves for a surface shape 287
6.27.4 Apply wall thickness, using the "Thicken" feature 288
6.27.4.1 Data backup 288

7 Boolean form elements 290

7.1 Boolean form elements, basics 290
7.1.1 Commands for "Boolean operations" 290
7.1.2 "Boolean operation" dynamic preview mode 290
7.1.3 "Boolean operations" 291
7.1.3.1 "Boolean Union", operation type "Add" 291
7.1.3.2 "Boolean Difference", operation type "Subtract" 291
7.1.3.3 "Boolean Intersection", operation type "Combine" 291
7.1.3.4 "Boolean Split" 291
7.2 Boolean Operations for Surfaces Base Areas using "Trim" feature 294
7.2.1 Creating the basic sketch 294
7.2.1.1 Opening your own template file 294
7.2.1.2 Boolean operations for surfaces, basic sketch 294
7.2.1.3 Resizing circular objects to the same size 294
7.2.1.4 Data backup 294
7.2.2 Boolean Operations for Surfaces Editing with Sketch functions 295
7.2.2.1 "Boolean Union", operation type "Add", using "Trim" function 295
7.2.2.2 "Boolean Difference", operation type "Subtract", using "Trim" function 295
7.2.2.3 "Boolean Intersection", operation type "Combine", using "Trim" function 296
7.2.2.4 Data backup 296
7.3 "Boolean Difference", operation type "Subtract", Rectangle-Circle-Difference using "Extrude" feature 297
7.3.1 Creating the base surface for differential extrusion 297
7.3.1.1 Opening your own template file 297
7.3.1.2 Base area using function "Center Rectangle" 297
7.3.1.3 Creating volumes using the "Extrude" feature 297
7.3.1.4 Data backup 297
7.4 Boolean Operations for basic bodies Operation type "Add" and "Subtract" Converting " Features to Bodies" 298
7.4.1 Boolean Operations for basic bodies, Operation type "Add", using "Extruded-Boss" 298
7.4.1.1 Open the working file 298
7.4.1.2 Operation type "Add", using "Extruded-Boss", the creation 298
7.4.1.3 Data backup 298
7.4.2 "Converting Features to Bodies" 299
7.4.2.1 Converting "Features to Bodies", the creation 299
7.4.2.2 Data backup 299
7.4.3 Boolean Operations for basic bodies Operation type "Subtract", using "Extruded Cut" 300
7.4.3.1 Open the working file 300
7.4.3.2 Create basic component 300
7.4.3.3 Operation type "Subtract", using "Extruded Cut", the creation 300
7.4.3.4 Data backup 300
7.4.3.5 Converting "Features to Bodies", the creation 301
7.4.3.6 Data backup 301
7.5 Boolean Operation "Combine Bodies" Operation type "Add", "Subtract" and "Common" 302
7.5.1 Boolean Operations "Combine Bodies" Cuboid and cylinder operation type "Add" 302
7.5.1.1 Adjusting the basic body, open the working file 302
7.5.1.2 Create basic component 302
7.5.1.3 "Combine Bodies" "Add", basics 302
7.5.1.4 "Combine Bodies" "Add", the creation 303
7.5.2 "Combine Bodies" "Subtract", the creation 303
7.5.2.1 Data backup 303
7.5.3 "Combine Bodies" "Common", the creation 304
7.5.3.1 Data backup 304
7.6 Boolean Operation "Combine Bodies" Distance Shaft, using "Combine Bodies" feature 305
7.6.1 Positioning basic sketches 305
7.6.1.1 Positioning the basic sketches, open the working file 305
7.6.1.2 Positioning the basic body, moving the "Sketch2" 305
7.6.2 Distance Shaft, volume creation 306
7.6.2.1 Creating the inner body 306
7.6.2.2 Length adjustment of the inner body 306
7.6.2.3 Creating the outer body 306
7.6.3 Boolean Operations "Combine Bodies" operation type "Subtract" 307
7.6.3.1 Data backup 307
7.7 Boolean Operation "Combine Bodies" using "Split" 308
7.7.1 Boolean Operation "Combine Bodies" using feature "Split" 308
7.7.1.1 Open the working file 308
7.7.1.2 Splitting the Base Body 308
7.7.1.3 Data backup 309
7.8 Boolean Operation "Multibody Part" Creating one part using "Combine Bodies" feature 310
7.8.1 Boolean Operation "Multibody Part" 310
7.8.1.1 Boolean Operation "Multibody Part", basics 310
7.8.1.2 Open the working assembly file 310
7.8.1.3 Boolean Operation "Multibody Part", the creation 310

7.8.1.4 Data backup 310
7.8.2 Creating one part using "Combine Bodies" feature 311
7.8.2.1 Data backup 311

8 Model Changes 314

8.1 Model Changes, basics 314
8.1.1 Instant3D 314
8.1.1.1 Modifying sketches, geometry changes, an excerpt 314
8.1.1.2 Modifying sketches, changing positions, an excerpt 314
8.1.1.3 Modifying sketches, changes in position regarding relationship, an excerpt 314
8.1.1.4 Model Changes, example lists 314
8.2 Modifying sketches, geometry changes 316
8.2.1 Dimensional change, a selection 316
8.2.1.1 Dimensional change for a sketch "Circle" using "SmartDimension" 316
8.2.1.2 Dimensional change of a sketch "Center Rectangle" using SmartDimension 316
8.2.1.3 Dimensional change for a sketch "Centerpoint Straight Slot" using "SmartDimension" 316
8.3 Modifying sketches, changing positions 317
8.3.1 Modifying sketches, changing positions, a selection 317
8.3.1.1 Position change for "Circles" 317
8.3.1.2 Position change for a "Center Rectangle" 317
8.3.1.3 Position change for a "Centerpoint Straight Slot" 317
8.4 Modifying sketches, Changes in position regarding relationship 318
8.4.1 Changes in position regarding relationship, a selection open the working file 318
8.4.1.1 Change of position using the "Merge" relation 318
8.4.1.2 Change of position using the "Horizontal" relation 318
8.4.1.3 Change of position using the "Parallel" relation 319
8.4.1.4 Change of position using the "Symmetric" relation 319
8.4.1.5 Change of position using the "Tangent" relation 320
8.4.1.6 Rectangle position change, alignment to center line, using the "Collinear" relation 320
8.4.1.7 Rectangle position change, alignment to a guideline, using the "Parallel" relation 321
8.5 Model changes, modifying features 324
8.5.1 Cube over geometry changes, the creation 324
8.5.1.1 Open the working file 324
8.5.1.2 Changing the dimensions of the basic sketch 324
8.5.1.3 Feature "Extrude-Boss" change dimension assignment 324
8.5.1.4 Data backup 324
8.5.2 Basic body "cube", change of position 325
8.5.2.1 Open the working file 325
8.5.2.2 The sketch position change 325
8.5.2.3 Data backup 325
8.5.3 Changing the polygon prism 326
8.5.3.1 Open the working file 326
8.5.3.2 Feature "Extrude Boss", change polygon height 326
8.5.3.3 Changing the polygon size using the base sketch 326
8.5.3.4 Sketch geometry "Polygon", change number of corners 326
8.5.3.5 Data backup 327
8.5.4 Draft angle adjustment by entering the angle value 328
8.5.4.1 Open the working file 328
8.5.4.2 Modifying the basic body using the "Extrude" option "Draft" 328
8.5.4.3 Data backup 328
8.6 Feature "Hole Wizard" Change "Hole size" and "Hole type" 329
8.6.1 Feature "Hole Wizard" change "Hole size" 329
8.6.1.1 Open the working file 329
8.6.1.2 Feature "Hole Wizard" Change hole size, the creation 329
8.6.1.3 Data backup 329
8.6.2 Feature "Hole Wizard", change „Hole type" 330
8.6.2.1 Open the working file 330
8.6.2.1 Feature "Hole Wizard", change "Hole type", the creation 330
8.6.2.2 Assign display filter "Shaded cosmetic threads". 330
8.6.2.3 Data backup 330
8.7 Pattern Arrangement Changing "Linear Pattern" and "Circular Pattern" 331
8.7.1 Changing "Linear Pattern" 331
8.7.1.1 Open the working file 331
8.7.1.2 Feature "Linear Pattern", pattern change 331
8.7.1.3 Data backup 331
8.7.2 Changing "Circular Pattern" 332
8.7.2.1 Open the working file 332
8.7.2.2 Feature "Circular Pattern", pattern change 332
8.7.2.3 Data backup 332
8.8 Changing edge breaking "Chamfer" and "Thread Stud" 333
8.8.1 Changing the edge breaking "Chamfer" 333
8.8.1.1 Open the working file 333
8.8.1.2 Feature "Chamfer", change distance assignment 333
8.8.1.3 Feature "Thread Stud", set a "Undercut" 333
8.8.1.4 Data backup 333
8.9 "Instant3D" model changes 336
8.9.1 Dynamic Feature Editing 336
8.9.2 "Instant3D", Unit Adjustment 336
8.9.3 "Instant3D", Cube over geometry changes 337
8.9.3.1 Open the working file 337
8.9.3.2 Adjusting the basic dimensions, assigning "Driven" 337
8.9.3.3 "Instant3D", changing the dimension of the cuboid height 337
8.9.3.4 "Instant3D", changing the dimensions of the cuboid surfaces 337
8.9.3.5 Data backup 338
8.9.4 Hole changes in the component 339
8.9.4.1 Open the working file 339
8.9.4.2 Changing the position of the hole, shifting the center point 339
8.9.4.3 Changing the position of the hole, shifting the center point using sketch 339
8.9.4.4 Changing the hole size using "Instant3D" 340
8.9.4.5 Changing the position of the hole, shifting the center point 340
8.9.4.6 Change the position of the hole, center point on corner point 341
8.9.4.7 Copy hole in component 341
8.9.4.8 Copying the hole to front side of the cuboid 342
8.9.4.9 Data backup 342
8.9.5 Changing the rotation angle using "Instant3D" 343
8.9.5.1 Open the working file 343
8.9.5.2 Changing the rotation angle using "Edit Feature" 343
8.9.5.3 Changing the rotation angle using "Instant3D", the creation 343
8.9.5.4 Data backup 343
8.9.6 Geometry changes using "Instant3D", Truncated cone to cone 344
8.9.6.1 Open the working file 344
8.9.6.2 Truncated cone to cone, adapting the base body 344
8.9.6.3 Data backup 344
8.9.7 Geometry changes using "Instant3D", Truncated pyramid to pyramid 345
8.9.7.1 Open the working file 345
8.9.7.2 Truncated pyramid to pyramid, adapting the base body 345
8.9.7.3 Data backup 345

8.9.8 Component adjustments using "Triad" 346
8.9.8.1 Open the working file 346
8.9.8.2 Adjusting the angle of the base body 346
8.9.8.3 Data backup 346
8.9.8.4 Adjusting the high of the base body 347
8.9.8.5 Data backup 347
8.9.8.6 Adjust the position of the cone attachment 348
8.9.8.7 Data backup 348
8.9.8.8 Adjusting the hollow body height 349
8.9.8.9 Data backup 349
8.10 Deformation functions on a basic body, using feature „Flex" 353
8.10.1 Feature "Flex", basics 353
8.10.1.1 Feature "Flex", option "Bending" 353
8.10.1.2 Feature "Flex", option "Twisting" 353
8.10.1.3 Feature "Flex", option "Tapering" 353
8.10.1.4 Feature "Flex", option "Stretching" 353
8.10.2 Model changes using feature "Flex", option "Bending" 354
8.10.2.1 Open the working file 354
8.10.2.2 Editing a component using the "Bending" option 354
8.10.2.3 Data backup 355
8.10.3 Model changes using feature "Flex", option "Twisting" 356
8.10.3.1 Open the working file 356
8.10.3.2 Editing a component using the "Bending" option 356
8.10.3.3 Data backup 356
8.10.4 Model changes using feature "Flex", option "Tapering" 357
8.10.4.1 Open the working file 357
8.10.4.2 Editing a component using the "Tapering" option 357
8.10.4.3 Data backup 357
8.11 Deformation functions on a basic body, using feature "Deform" 358
8.11.1 Feature "Deform", basics 358
8.11.2 Model changes using feature "Deform", option "Point" 358
8.11.2.1 Open the working file 358
8.11.2.2 Editing a component using the "Point" option 358
8.11.2.3 Data backup 358
8.11.3 Model changes using feature "Deform" Option "Point", selection "Edge" 359
8.11.3.1 Open the working file 359
8.11.3.2 Editing a component using the "Point" option, selecting "Edge" 359
8.11.3.3 Data backup 359
8.11.4 Model changes using feature "Deform" Option "Curve to Curve" 360
8.11.4.1 Open the working file 360
8.11.4.2 Create a new work plane 360
8.11.4.3 Construction of a transition curve 360
8.11.4.4 Editing a component using the "Point" option, selecting "Edge" 360
8.11.4.5 Data backup 361

9 Create Components 364

9.1 Parts and Components, preliminary remarks 364
9.1.1 Dimensions, an overview 364
9.1.2 Parametric dimensions 364
9.1.3 Creation of components, command selection for creation 365
9.1.4 Creation of the components manufacturing fundamentals 365
9.2 Component creation "Coupling bolt" 368
9.2.1 The design sketch for the component creation 368
9.2.2 The coupling bolt, the creation 368
9.2.2.1 Opening your own template file 368
9.2.2.2 Creating the basic component 368
9.2.2.3 The coupling bolt, assign material 369
9.2.3 The coupling bolt, using "Stud Wizard" 369
9.2.3.1 External thread assignment, long extension M16 using "Stud wizard" 369
9.2.3.1 External thread assignment, long extension M10 using "Stud wizard" 370
9.2.3.2 The coupling bolt, using feature "Fillet" 370
9.2.3.3 Data backup 370
9.3 Component creation "Drive Shaft" 371
9.3.1 The design sketch for the component creation 371
9.3.2 The "Drive Shaft", the creation 371
9.3.2.1 Creating the basic sketch 371
9.3.2.2 Revolved volume, the creation 372
9.3.2.3 Assigning component material 372
9.3.2.4 Chamfers for edge breaking 1 mm x 45° 372
9.3.3 Creating the keyway slot 373
9.3.3.1 Tangential working plane for the basic sketch of the keyway slot 373
9.3.3.2 Basic sketch for the keyway slot 373
9.3.3.3 Keyway slot, the creation 373
9.3.4 Creating center holes 374
9.3.4.1 Create centering hole on the keyway side 374
9.3.4.2 Create centering hole on the other shaft side 374
9.3.4.3 Data backup 374
9.4 Component creation "Mounting bolts" 375
9.4.1 The design sketch for the component creation 375
9.4.2 Creating the base body 375
9.4.2.1 Opening your own template file 375
9.4.2.2 The basic sketch construction 375
9.4.2.3 The creation of the basic body, using feature "Revolve" 376
9.4.3 Edge breaking using "Chamfer", the creation 376
9.4.3.1 Creating the thread end chamfer 376
9.4.3.2 Creating the chamfers for the wave shoulder 377
9.4.4 The central counterbore 377
9.4.5 Creating a keyway slot 378
9.4.5.1 Creating a tangent plane 378
9.4.5.2 Creating the basic sketch for the keyway slot 378
9.4.5.3 Keyway slot, the creation 378
9.4.6 Physical thread assignment 379
9.4.6.1 Physical external thread, using feature "Thread" 379
9.4.6.2 Physical internal thread, using feature "Thread" 380
9.4.7 Assigning component material 380
9.4.7.1 Data backup 380
9.5 Component creation "Drive Shaft" 381
9.5.1 The design sketch for the component creation 381
9.5.2 The drive shaft, component creation 381
9.5.2.1 Opening your own template file 381
9.5.2.2 Creating the basic sketch 381
9.5.2.3 Revolved volume, the creation 381
9.5.2.4 Assigning component material 382
9.5.2.5 Edge breaking using feature "Chamfer" 382
9.5.2.6 Edge breaking using feature "Fillet" 382
9.5.3 Locking plate slot, the creation 383
9.5.3.1 Basic sketch for locking plate slot 383
9.5.3.2 Locking plate slot using feature „Extruded Cut" 383
9.5.4 Shaft grooves, the creation 384
9.5.4.1 Basic sketch for shaft groove 384
9.5.4.2 Shaft grooves using feature „Extruded Cut" 384
9.5.4.3 Distribution of shaft groove using "Circular Pattern" 384
9.5.4.4 Distribution of shaft groove using feature "Mirror" 385
9.5.5 Inserting a tangential transverse bore 385
9.5.5.1 Creating an additional tangential work plane 385
9.5.5.2 Basic sketch for the transverse drilling 386

9.5.5.3 Inserting a tangential transverse bore, the creation 386
9.5.6 External thread assignment using the "Thread" function 386
9.5.6.1 Data backup 386
9.6 Component creation "Gear Shaft" 387
9.6.1 The design sketch for the component creation 387
9.6.2 Gear creation using the SOLIDWORKS toolbox 387
9.6.2.1 Opening your own template file 387
9.6.2.2 Gear creation 387
9.6.2.3 Assigning component material 388
9.6.2.4 Creating drive shaft attachments 388
9.6.3 Edge break using "Chamfer", the creation 389
9.6.3.1 Data backup 389
9.7 Component creation "Worm Shaft" 390
9.7.1 The design sketch for the component creation 390
9.7.2 "Worm Shaft", the basic creation 390
9.7.2.1 Opening your own template file 390
9.7.2.2 A closed surface of Rotation using command "Line" 390
9.7.2.3 Revolved volume creation 391
9.7.2.4 Assigning component material 391
9.7.2.5 Edge breaking using feature "Chamfer" 391
9.7.2.6 Edge breaking using feature "Fillet" 392
9.7.3 External thread assignment using the "Thread" function 392
9.7.4 Worm Shaft using "Helix/Spiral" and "Cut Sweep" 392
9.7.4.1 "Helix" construction as a basis 392
9.7.4.2 Sketch for circumferential worm shaft profile 393
9.7.4.3 Creating a worm shaft structure using "Cut Sweep" 393
9.7.5 Relief groove for the physical thread 393
9.7.6 Break more edges 394
9.7.7 Central mounting hole 394
9.7.8 Groove for locking plate 395
9.7.8.1 Create work plane for groove 395
9.7.8.2 Groove for locking plate, the creation 395
9.7.8.3 Data backup 395
9.8 Component creation "Housing Dome" 398
9.8.1 The design sketch for the component creation 398
9.8.2 Creating the basic component 398
9.8.2.1 Opening your own template file 398
9.8.2.2 Creating and adapting basic body 398
9.8.3 Creating flange holes 399
9.8.4 Creating mounting holes 400
9.8.4.1 Data backup 400
9.9 Component creation "Bearing Housing" 401
9.9.1 The design sketch for the component creation 401
9.9.2 Creating the basic component 401
9.9.2.1 Opening your own template file 401
9.9.2.2 Creating and adapting basic body 401
9.9.3 Creating flange holes 402
9.9.4 Insert threaded connection as an attachment 403
9.9.4.1 Data backup 404
9.10 Component creation "Housing for Bevel Gear" 405
9.10.1 The design sketch for the component creation 405
9.10.2 The component representation for component creation 405
9.10.3 Bevel gear housing, the creation 406
9.10.3.1 Opening your own template file 406
9.10.3.2 Creating the basic component 406
9.10.4 Creating housing holes 406
9.10.5 Create the inner body 407
9.10.5.1 Create the main inner body 407
9.10.5.2 Inner attachment surfaces, the creation 408
9.10.6 Creating connection holes 409
9.10.7 Edge breaking using feature "Fillet" 410
9.10.7.1 Data backup 410
9.11 Component creation "Bearing Cover" 413
9.11.1 The design sketch for the component creation 413
9.11.2 Bearing Cover, the creation 413
9.11.2.1 Opening your own template file 413
9.11.2.2 Creating the basic component 413
9.11.2.3 Creating connection holes 414
9.11.2.4 Data backup 414
9.12 Component creation "Bearing Base Part" 415
9.12.1 The design sketch for the component creation 415
9.12.2 Bearing base part, the creation 415
9.12.2.1 Opening your own template file 415
9.12.2.2 Creating the basic component 415
9.12.2.3 Create central hole 417
9.12.2.4 Create mounting holes 417
9.12.2.5 Assigning component material 418
9.12.2.6 Physical thread unsing feature "Thread" 418
9.12.2.7 Data backup 419
9.13 Component creation "Base Plate" 420
9.13.1 The design sketch for the component creation 420
9.13.2 Base plate, the creation 420
9.13.2.1 Opening your own template file 420
9.13.2.2 Creating the basic component 420
9.13.3 Edge Breakings 422
9.13.3.1 Edge Breakings using features "Chamfer" 422
9.13.3.2 Edge Breakings using features "Hole Wizard" 422
9.13.4 Create mounting holes 423
9.13.4.1 Mounting holes on the top side of the component 423
9.13.4.2 Mounting holes on the front side of the component 423
9.13.4.3 Mounting holes on the back side of the component 424
9.13.4.4 Assigning component material 424
9.13.4.5 Data backup 424
9.14 Component creation "Gear Switching Element" 425
9.14.1 The design sketch for the component creation 425
9.14.2 Interlocking tooth row, the creation 425
9.14.2.1 Opening your own template file 425
9.14.2.2 Basic sketch for the interlocking tooth 425
9.14.2.3 Create the left interlocking tooth row using the "Circular Sketch pattern" 426
9.14.2.4 Creating the right interlocking tooth row using "Mirror Entities" 426
9.14.2.5 Completing the sketch construction 427
9.14.3 Volume generation of the „Gear switching element“ 427
9.14.4 Drilling the central hole in the gear switching element 428
9.14.5 Edge breaking using feature "Fillet" 428
9.14.6 Assigning component material 428
9.14.6.1 Data backup 428
9.15 Component creation "Housing Cover" 429
9.15.1 The design sketch for the component creation 429
9.15.1.1 "Housing Cover", component representations 429
9.15.2 "Housing Cover", the creation 429
9.15.2.1 Opening your own template file 429
9.15.2.2 Creating the basic component 429
9.15.2.3 Assigning component material 430
9.15.2.4 Attachment surfaces, the creation 430
9.15.2.5 Creating Housing Holes 431
9.15.2.6 Creating a lubricating oil bore 432
9.15.2.7 Creating connection holes 433
9.15.2.8 Component creation "Housing Cover", final edits 434
9.15.2.9 Data backup 435
9.16 Component creation "Brake Disc" 436
9.16.1 The design sketch for the component creation 436
9.16.2 The basic body, the creation 436
9.16.2.1 Opening your own template file 436
9.16.2.2 Creating cylindrical basic bodies 436

9.16.2.3 Assigning component material 437
9.16.3 Creating central bore 437
9.16.4 Creating connection holes 438
9.16.5 Creating central counterbore 438
9.16.6 Creating vent holes 439
9.16.7 Edge rounding on the base body 439
9.16.8 Data backup 440

10 The book DVD, order option 442

10.1 The book DVD, basics 442
10.2 The book DVD, price and ordering options 442
10.3 The book DVD, contents at a glance 442
10.3.1 The book DVD, SOLIDWORKS Design 2026, files for the learning units 442
10.3.2 The Book DVD, SOLIDWORKS Design 2026, PDF file 442
10.3.3 The book DVD, list of contents, short overview 442

"By immediately considering the surface, we let the bodies in motion follow, before considering the bodies merely in isolation,

whereas it would be proper to let the third extension follow after the second."

- Plato "The Republic" -

- Socrates laments the state of spatial geometry -

(c. 375 BC)

"Geometry predates the creation of things, as eternal as the Spirit of God itself, and in it it provided the archetypes for the creation of the world."

- Johannes Kepler, Harmonices Mundi, 1619 -

Prolog

3D CAD, or three-dimensional computer-aided design, is a design and development technology that replaces manual drawing with an automated process.

This process creates objects in three dimensions. 3D modeling involves creating and saving geometric objects in three-dimensional form.

On the one hand, this allows for a realistic representation and better spatial perception of the body, while on the other hand, the three-dimensional representations such as cross-sectional and elevation views can be automated.

This book is aimed at beginners who want or need to take their first steps with the new Solid Edge. Program steps, customizations, and command functions are presented in detail and supported by explanatory image sequences. The content is based on Solid Edge 2026, but is largely version-neutral.

The second chapter covers the basic installation, the complex program customization, and the required additional application installations.

The third chapter provides an introduction to the application of various representation techniques based on a ready-made template.

Chapter four to nine demonstrate the various solutions for creating components using the customized Solid Edge commands.

For purchasers of this book, I offer the opportunity to order a free DVD upon presentation of the purchase confirmation. Please see Chapter 10 for details.

The book DVD contains the component files described in Chapters 2 to 9, the required templates, and a selection of standard parts from the StandardPart library. The component files were created using the academic version of Solid Edge.

Furthermore, the complete book is included in a color edition in PDF format to mitigate the disadvantages of the BOD grayscale edition.

If you'd like to support the author, please order directly from BOD Publishing:
https://www.bod.de/buchshop/

Special thanks go to my wife Birgit, who once again excelled as an editor.

Hans-J. Engelke, April 2026

1

Dassault Systèmes 3DEXPERIENCE©
SOLIDWORKS Design 2026

Parts and Components
Create and Customize

Technical Drawings
Cultural History

1 Technical Drawings a Cultural History

1.1 Older than paper

The word "map" comes from the Greek word chartes, meaning "sheet of paper." The first surviving graphic representations of the environment, reminiscent of our modern maps, date back to 2300 BC. At that time, the Babylonians scratched route lines into clay tablets and burned them.

The knowledge thus collected converged in the city of Miletus, which became a center of geography by 600 BC. The term "geometry" (earth mapping) also originates from this period.

During this time, quite different hypotheses emerged. Hecataeus of Miletus (c. 550–480 BC), author of the first geography book around 500 BC, argued that the Earth was indeed flat.

A few decades later, Herodotus saw things quite differently, having more data from a Phoenician circumnavigation of Africa.

However, increasingly precise observations led to a consensus that the Earth must be spherical. A detailed explanation for this was provided by Aristotle around 350 BC. The Greeks, the last and most important being Ptolemy (90–168 BC), were so good at their subject that even their errors persisted for a very long time.

For example, it was partly thanks to the fact that Ptolemy greatly underestimated the Earth's radius that Columbus, with widely known results, set out westward to find India.

China had a highly developed surveying system, and the Greek tradition was still maintained in the Ottoman Empire. Parallel to this new precision, a new desire to decorate and color maps emerged well into modern times. Many areas were literally blank spaces waiting to be filled with imagination; soon, sea monsters, dragons, and the like roamed there, often depicted in copperplate engravings or woodcuts.

1.2 The history of geometry

Geometry, the measurement of the earth, is certainly one of the oldest sciences. Wherever excavations allow stories of prehistoric cultures to speak to our time, they also tell a story of geometry: regularly or symmetrically shaped, painted, or arranged every day, utilitarian, or ritual objects testify to the recognition and transfer of geometric structures found in many different ways in nature.

Spherical clay vessels can be produced with less material and are more stable, while maintaining the same capacity, than cuboids-shaped ones, which are easier to smooth.

People can orient themselves using the stars, and in cave paintings and on clay, people, animals, and landscapes can be recognized if they are depicted in such a small scale that their proportions are preserved.

The written languages that emerged with the first advanced civilizations also transmit geometric knowledge from architecture, crafts, agriculture, and astronomy.

In Egypt, not only could rectilinear surfaces be converted into right-angled triangles, and these in turn into rectangles of equal area, but the formula for the volume of general truncated pyramids was also known. The implementation of this knowledge in buildings such as the Pyramids of Giza (ca. 2900 BC) is still impressive today.

The origins of geometry can also be found among the Chaldeans. The Phoenician Tales went to Egypt to study and subsequently settled in Miletus, where he founded the Ionian School, from which emerged the Greek philosophers to whom we owe the first advances in geometry.

Pythagoras of Samos, a student of Thales, first went to Egypt and India, like Thales, then withdrew to Italy and founded his school there, which has become far more famous than the one from which it emerged. To this philosopher and his students belongs the fame of the first discoveries in geometry, among the most outstanding of which are the theory of incommensurability, the incommensurability of certain lines, such as the diagonal of a square compared to its side, and the theory of regular solids.

These first steps in the science of extended quantities present only a few elementary theorems relating to the straight line and the circle, among which the most remarkable are those of Pythagoras.

The impossibility of measuring the diagonals of a square or a regular pentagon using numerical ratios, as well as the paradoxes of Zeno of Elea with moving objects (around 450 BC), contributed to Greek mathematics focusing more on geometry.

The impossibility of measuring the diagonals of a square or a regular pentagon using numerical ratios, as well as Zeno of Elea's paradoxes involving moving objects (around 450 BC), contributed to Greek mathematics focusing more on geometry.

In the Middle Ages, the term "Perspectiva corporum regularium" was coined by Wentzel Jamnitzer. This term referred to geometric chains of reasoning derived from strict logic and translated into cut images by the etcher Jost Amman.

These rules are the result of his intensive study of the problems of perspective representation. However, his paintings not only express the skillful use of compass and ruler according to Euclid's rules, but also view the five regular solids and their metamorphoses in a metaphysical context.

A number of other mathematicians, philosophers, and artists have explored geometry, volume, and perspective in the past. These include:

Michelangelo, Kant, Hilbert, William Hogarth, Oscar Reutersvärd, B. Kruse, T. Olsson, János Bolyai, Nikolai Ivanovich Lobachevsky, Carl Friedrich Gauss, Bernhard Riemann, Roger Penrose, George Polya, F. Haag, and others.

The knowledge of space, geometry, and perspective is considered complete today, yet there are still performing artists who explore new, often surprising, and fascinating aspects of perspective representation in their works.

Tales

Pythagoras

Title page of 5 series of 5 copperplate engravings each on the REGULAR BODIES of the "Perspectiva corporum regularium

1.3 The "Technical Drawing"

Before we can use innovative products and technical developments, they must be designed. This is the job of a technical draftsman.

For a new building, the engine for a vehicle, or a production facility for a company, architects, engineers, or graphic designers compile measurement data and ensure the correct arrangement of dimensions.

Even though their drawings are now largely created on computers using CAD programs, working with paper and traditional equipment is essential.

The first technical drawings were created with a thin stick in fine sand. A little later, drawing boards were used, on which drawings were scratched with a so called drawing board. Then, pencils were used, which were then over painted with Chinese ink to make the drawings indelible.

The pencil was the perfect tool for precise work with scribes, squares, and compasses. This equipment has essentially proven its worth for technical drawings on paper to this day, supplemented by a few additional tools for drawing in ink.

Filippo Brunelleschi

Michelangelo Buonarotti

Leonardo Da Vinci

Albrecht Dürer

1.3.1 The history of drawing as a design template

The geometric description of perspective (central projection) begins at the end of the 13th century. Italian painters, in particular, began to explore perspective depiction during this period.

The true era of perspective, however, began with the artist and architect Filippo Brunelleschi (1377-1446), who's most famous building is the Cathedral of Santa Maria del Fiore in Florence.

Brunelleschi already used the principle of two vanishing points in his drawings and sketches; during the Italian High Renaissance, many renowned artists explored perspective, such as Michelangelo Buonarotti (1475-1564) and Leonardo da Vinci (1452-1519). For example, Michelangelo designed the dome of St. Peter's Basilica in Rome.

The planning of such gigantic projects revitalized many scientific disciplines. Mathematics, physics, statics, and, above all, geometry, where perspective became the center of Renaissance geometry. One of the most famous examples is Leonardo da Vinci's painting "The Last Supper."

The German painter Albrecht Dürer (1471-1528) explored perspective in a very special way. The following paintings show how Dürer created his perspective in practice. Albrecht Dürer also explored many other areas of natural science. For example, Dürer explored the creation of magic squares and the theory of Platonic and Archimedean solids.

Such objects appear in some of his wood engravings. Albrecht Dürer described perspective in a book so precisely that this text was considered the standard work on perspective geometry until the early 20th century. The method used by Albrecht Dürer is now known in descriptive geometry as the piercing method.

1.4 The perspective representation

1.4.1 The history of perspective

The search for the correct rules for the graphic execution of central projection has occupied numerous artists and mathematicians since the late Middle Ages, some of whose important works are mentioned in the following description:

Leon Battista Alberti, 1435 De pictura, Piero della Francesca ca. 1450 De prospetiva pingendi, Luca Pacioli 1494 Summa de arithmetica, 1509 De divina proportione with drawings by Leonardo da Vinci, Albrecht Dürer from 1495 four books on geometry, Leonardo da Vinci 1514 De ludo geometrico, Sebastiano Serlio 1545 Libro di geometria e di prospettiva, Wentzel Jamnitzer 1568 Perspectiva corporum regularium, Daniele Barbaro 1568/69 La practica della perspettiva, Guidobaldo del Monte 1600 Perspectivae libri sex, Johannes Kepler 1604 Ad Vitellionem paralipomena quibus astronomiae pars optica traditur, René Descartes 1637 Geometry.

M. C. Escher

M. C. Escher „Relativity"

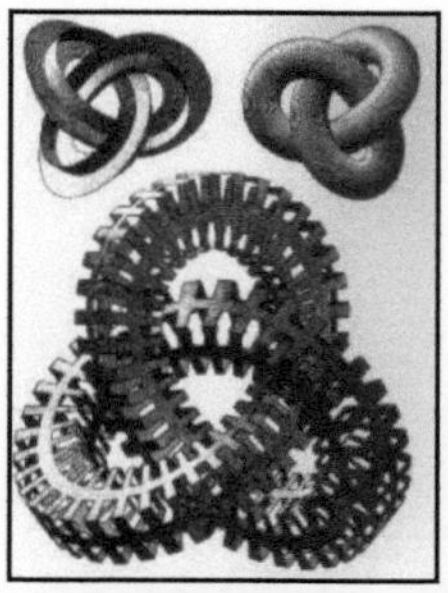

1.4.2 The master of the impossible perspective

M. C. Escher has always remained a problem for art history. His exploration of perspective impossibilities and optical illusions differs greatly from the classic themes of fine art and cannot be categorized. Thus, for a long time, Escher was not accepted by the art world as an artist in the classic sense.

In contrast, Escher was highly valued by scientists and mathematicians from an early age, as his clean, precise works approach mathematical topics in an intuitive and sensual way and illustrates scientific problems.

Escher was often invited to give mathematics lectures, even though he himself claimed to know nothing about mathematics. He also gave well-attended lectures on his work throughout Europe.

The paradoxical and often mystical quality of his mysterious images also resonated with esotericisms and 20th-century pop culture. His images were printed as posters and used as record covers. In 2002, a special Escher Museum was established in the former palace of Queen Emma, displaying his graphic work as well as private photographs and working sketches.

According to his own statements, despite not having much mathematical talent, Escher nevertheless succeeded in translating some abstract geometric ideas into graphically appealing forms in his artistic work, making his paintings extremely well-known and popular, especially among mathematicians, but by no means exclusively among them.

In a whole series of works, M. C. Escher also depicted individual mathematical objects, such as spirals, knots, Möbius strips, and regular solids.

1.4.3 The drawing as a design template in technology

Technology, from the Greek for art, generally refers to artificial objects created by humans that fulfill a useful function. A person skilled in technology was called techmites in Greek. Today, the term technology also encompasses the knowledge and experience required to use the objects. To examine constructive drawing in technology, it is sufficient to consider the period from the early Renaissance, i.e. from around 1400. In previous eras, no distinction was made between artistic drawings and technical ones. Furthermore, the depictions were strongly characterized by individual differences. With the onset of the early Renaissance, constructive drawings became increasingly clearer and more precise.

The perspective ends around 1930. With the development of general drawing rules and the near completion of drawing standardization, constructive drawing had evolved into technical drawing. Subsequent developments concerned only details. In the linear drawings of the Renaissance, particularly in technical sketches, the relationships to classical draftsmanship are still clearly visible. Through the use of similar drawing techniques and comparable design elements, such as hatching, dot grids, partial sections, changing viewing directions, and various views, the differences were minimal. Over time, however, the representation of the function and precise geometry of objects came to the fore.

The problem that vivid representations could achieves a comprehensible visual impression, but not dimensional accuracy had to be solved. Some solutions were already known from antiquity. In the drawings, perspective representation and projection with different directions were replaced by an oblique parallel projection with a single viewing direction.

Many of the early modern technical illustrated manuscripts and collections of illustrations were used only to a very limited extent for constructive drawing. Due to their inaccurate and incomplete representation, they were generally unsuitable as a basis for the constructional realization of an object.

Even the incorporated written explanations did not change this. The drawings contained various allegorical elements, curiosities, and technical gadgets, often without reference to the object's function. The drawings were used by educated people for pleasure and to learn about mechanical features. Due to the artisanal production and the considerable cost of the drawings, their distribution was limited.

1.4.4 The drawing as a construction template, historical representation rules

In practice, the rules for producing technical drawings were still very inconsistent, even varying from individual to individual. Although free-form drawings in an individual style were on the decline, bound drawings still retained allegorical and personal stylistic elements for a long time.

If the transformation from idea to object was in one hand, this diversity of representation was not a problem. With increasing trade and the division of production among different trades in different locations, the need for clear and uniform representation became ever more urgent.

In France, the mathematician and engineer Girard Desargues (1591–1661) addressed the problem. He attempted to summarize the various drawing constructions and visual representations in a coherent approach. A.-F. Frezier (1682–1773) wrote a detailed three-volume work on the ground plan and elevation method.

These approaches, along with the work of other mechanics, instrument makers, and engineers, led to the beginnings of an independent machine drawing technique in the 17th century. Gaspard Monge (1746–1818) analyzed the individual approaches in his work *Geometrie descriptive* and placed them on a precise scientific basis, including the translation of the graphic representations into mathematical functional equations of analytic geometry.

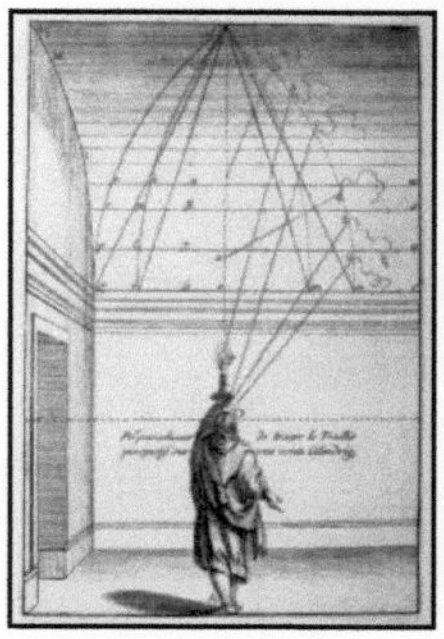

Girard Desargues

Now function, precise geometric representation, and dimensional accuracy came to the fore. Technical drawing had definitively become the connecting element between the idea and its realization through manufacturing techniques. The first specialist books dealing exclusively with the problems of technical drawing appeared at the beginning of the 19th century.

Gaspard Monge

The titles used the terms "Constructive Drawing, "Machine Drawing," and "Technical Drawing." One of the first was Le Blanc's "Choix de Modeles, Dessin des Machines," published in Paris in 1830. It included projection theory, penetrations, the representation of different machine parts, descriptive drawing, various types of perspective, and instructions on the procedure for creating a technical drawing.

Choix de Modeles, Dessin des Machines

1.4.5 Drawing methods in mechanical engineering

In the 19th century, graphical methods for solving a wide variety of design problems were widespread. Particularly well-known from this period are the methods of graph statics and graph dynamics for solving load and motion problems. Closed-form mathematical solutions were often available only for simple problems that rarely occurred in practice.

While technical problems could often be formulated mathematically, solving complex integral and differential equations was impossible. The extremely high demands on mathematical background also posed a barrier for many engineers.

Approximate graphical solutions were sufficient for solving most technical problems. Graphical methods also had the advantages of leading to results quickly, the solution process was immediately understandable, and, in many applications, a check for correctness was already built into the method.

The graphic representations of the processes did not place high demands on the actual drawing technique. Understanding the processes was much more difficult. These were taught in all engineering training programs. Intensive practice was mandatory. The course on constructive drawing also included the graphic processes of mechanical engineering, or more precisely, the graphic results of the processes, since the corresponding representations had to be created by engineers.

Almost all of these methods have been forgotten today. They have been replaced by numerical methods. The new methods are more accurate because, thanks to the use of electronic data processing and corresponding programs, they also lead to rapid results and allow for a wide range of variations and optimizations for design problems.

Screw as a picture drawing

1.4.6 The history of technical standardization

As the name suggests, technical drawings are to be seen in connection with technical machines, devices or apparatus or with their technical drawings are, as the name suggests, in connection with production.

For one thing, there were no regulations yet, and for another, there was no well-developed division of labor. The designer was more or less also the producer, and the screws were manufactured for this one machine and only fit that machine.

The creation of standards should also be understood in this context. This allowed a screw manufactured according to standards to be used everywhere.

At the same time, a common language for visualization had to be created: the standardized technical drawing, with almost no artistic additions.

The fact that this happened early on is still evident today in the low DIN number of the standards.

The German Institute for Standardization (DIN) was founded in 1917. The first German industrial standard referred to taper pins.

This standardization led to a progressive abstraction and reduction of representation. Details disappeared, and the screw as an image is now represented almost symbolically.

Technical drawings are based on a standardized set of rules. This describes the basic building blocks and systematic of a drawing set, although DIN standards do not necessarily lead to the same results in implementation.

Although a number of standards regulate drawing creation, these should not necessarily be viewed as negative or restrictive.

Rather, they form a meaningful framework while still allowing the drawing creator some constructive freedom. Qualifying descriptions such as "preferred" or "predominantly" are found in many places, allowing for deviations from these if necessary.

1.5 3D Solids, an introduction

In geometry, a solid is a three-dimensional, bounded geometric figure that can be described by boundaries. A geometric figure is said to be three-dimensional if it is not completely contained in any plane, and bounded if there is a sphere that completely contains this shape.

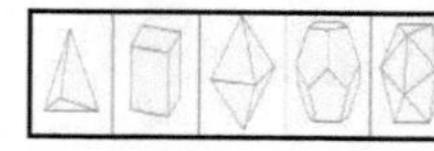

Platonische Körper

Kepler-Poinsot-Körper

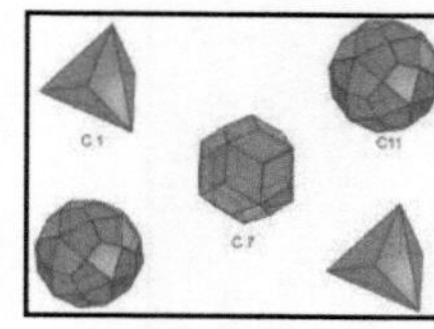

Catalanische Körper

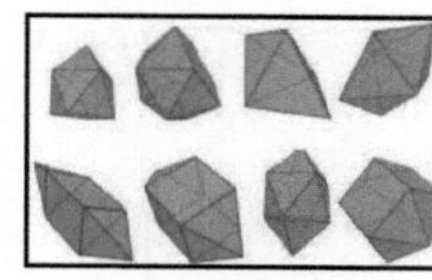

Johnson-Körper

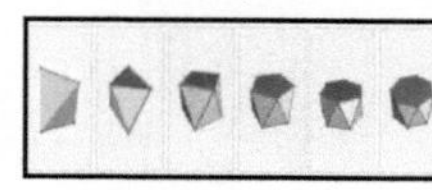

Antiprismen

Three-dimensional bodies have flat, circular, or spherical interfaces. Examples of bodies in general include: cube, tetrahedron, pyramid, prism, deltahedron, cylinder, cone, sphere, parabolic, hyperboloid, and torus.

Among the most well-known geometric solids are regular polyhedral. These are three-dimensional polyhedrons bounded by regular polygons, whose edges point only outwards and are not infinitely large, thus also being convex and bounded, such as the cube, the tetrahedron, or the so-called football.

There are only five types of these solids:

- Platonic solids that is dual to themselves or to each other.
- Archimedean solids
- Kepler-Poinsot solids
- Dual Catalan solids
- Johnson solids
- Prisms and antiprisms

These types usually only include a limited number of solids. For example, there are 5 Platonic solids, 13 Archimedean solids, 13 Catalan solids, and 92 Johnson solids, making a total of 123. The maximum possible number of vertices of the bounding polygons is 10. The number of prisms and antiprisms, however, is unlimited, since the base can, in principle, have any number of vertices.

However, if the number of vertices of the base is also limited to 10, 8 solids each result, of which the cube and the octahedron are already contained in other types, thus resulting in 7 more solids each, making a total of 137 solids. However, there are only 5 regular polyhedral, which alone can fill space without gaps.

1.5.1 Platonic solids

In geometry, the Platonic solids, named after the Greek philosopher Plato, are perfectly regular polyhedral, three-dimensional bodies bounded by polygons as their sides.

Every Platonic solid has an inner sphere, on which the centers of all faces of the body lie, and an outer sphere, on which all vertices of the body lie.

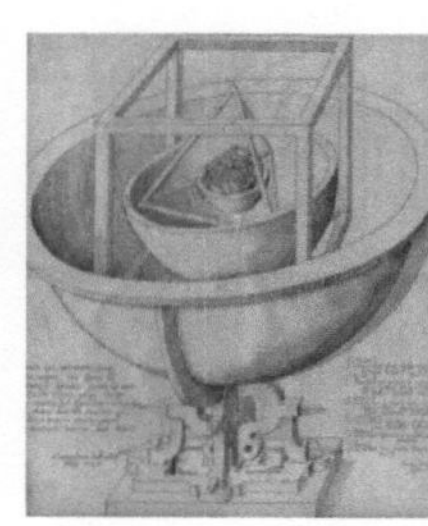

The Greek philosopher Plato (c. 428-348 BC), whose name they bear today, describes these bodies in his work Timaeus and also calls them cosmic bodies, assigning them the elements from which the world is constructed:

- Fire tetrahedron
- Water icosahedrons
- Air octahedron
- Earth cube (hexahedron)
- Ether dodecahedron

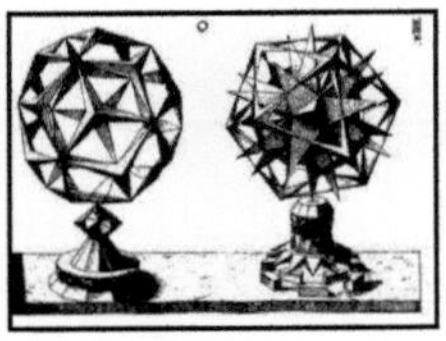

1.5.2 Kepler-Poinsot Solids

Kepler-Poinsot solids are regular, non-convex polyhedral and are classified as stellar bodies. These include the dodecahedron and icosahedrons, as well as the great dodecahedron and the great icosahedrons.

They are named in honor of Johannes Kepler (1571–1630) and Louis Poinsot (1777–1859).

1.5.3 Archimedean Solids

Archimedean solids are a class of regular geometric solids. They are characterized by the fact that their vertices cannot be distinguished from one another. There are 13 such solids.

They are named after the Greek mathematician Archimedes, who presumably discovered them all as early as the third century BC.

Archimedes' writings have not survived; only a summary by the Alexandrian mathematician Pappus (4th century AD) has survived.

1.5.4 Catalan Solids

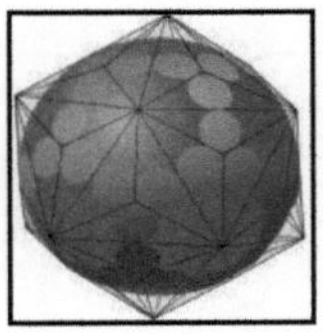

A Catalan solid, or dual Archimedean solid, is a solid that is dual to an Archimedean solid. For example, the rhombic dodecahedron is dual to the cuboctahedron. The Catalan solids, of which there are thirteen, are named after the Belgian mathematician Eugène Charles Catalan.

All Catalan solids have in common that they have an insphere that touches all faces from the inside. There is also an edge sphere that touches all edges from the inside. All torsion angles of a Catalan solid are equal.

1.5.5 Johnson Solids

Johnson solids are strictly convex polyhedral composed exclusively of regular polygons, but there are neither Platonic solids, Archimedean solids, prisms nor antiprisms.

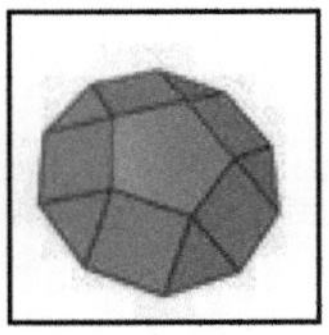

They share the same property as Catalan solids, the vertices of a Johnson solid are not identical. In 1966, Norman Johnson published a list of 92 such polyhedral, which he assumed to be complete.

1.6 3D Solids and Solid Edge 2026

1.6.1 Creating 3D volume primitive solids

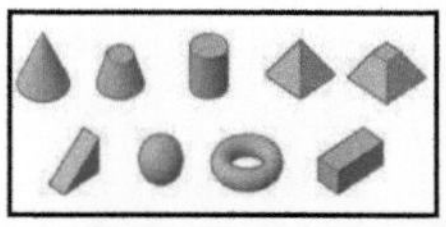

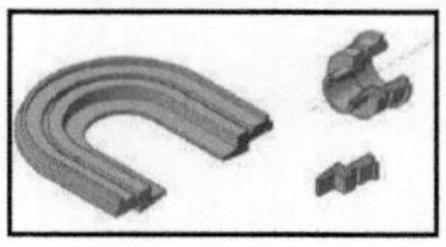

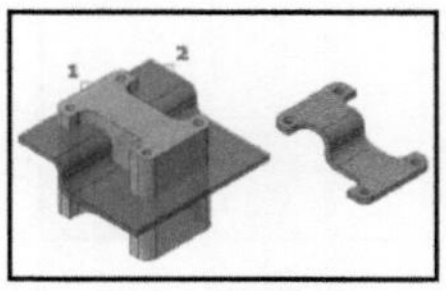

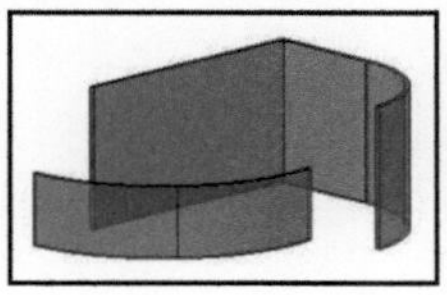

3D solid objects can start from simple primitives or from extruded, swept, revolved, or lofted profiles. You can combine these using Boolean operations, and you can also create various simple 3D shapes using basic solid commands.
You can also create 3D solids by performing operations such as extruding, rotating, or sweeping closed 2D objects.
In the illustration, the same closed 2D polyline is drawn along a path, rotated about an axis, and extruded in a specified direction.
By combining 3D solids with Boolean operations such as union, subtraction, and intersection, you can create a composite solid.
A quick way to create 3D solids in the shape of walls is to use the Polysolid command. The process is similar to creating a polyline with straight and curved segments, except that you can specify a default value for the height, width, and orientation of the resulting 3D solid.

1.6.2 Creating Solids from 2D geometry

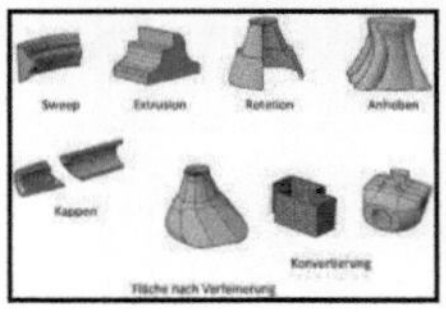

You can construct surfaces and 3D solids by extruding, sweeping, lofting, and revolving.

When you create an extrusion, revolving, sweeping, or lofting from curves, you can create both solids and surfaces.

Open curves always create surfaces, but closed curves can generate either solids or surfaces, depending on certain settings.

1.6.3 3D Solids based on other objects, examples

You can also create 3D solids from 2D geometry or other 3D objects. For example, 3D solids can also be based on extruding a 2D shape along a specified path in 3D space.

The following methods are available:

- Sweep: Extends a 2D object along a path.
- Extrude: Extends the shape of a 2D object perpendicularly into 3D space.
- Rotate: Sweeps a 2D object around an axis.
- Draft: Extends the contours of a shape between one or more open or closed objects.
- Intersect: Splits a solid object into two separate 3D objects.
- Hole: A hole is a circular feature created by removing material from a part. When constructing holes in the surrounding
- Offset Surface: Converts mesh objects and planar objects to solids and surfaces using the object height.

Sweep

Extrude

Revolve

Loft

Intersect

Hole

Offset Surface

1.7 Geometric Primitive Solids and SOLIDWORKS 2026

1.7.1 Basic solid "Cuboids", geometric description

A three-dimensional body with six pairs of parallel faces is called a parallelepiped, regardless of their perpendicularity. Thus, every cuboid is a right-angled parallelepiped.

A parallelepiped is a geometric body bounded by six pairs of congruent parallelograms lying in parallel planes.

Every cuboid is a prism with a rectangular base.

A cuboid is a body with six rectangular faces, all of which are right angles, eight right-angled corners, and twelve edges, four of which are equal lengths and parallel to each other.

In geometry, extrusion refers to the dimensional increase of an element by parallel translation in space. Extruding a face produces a body with the cross-section of the face; extruding a polygon creates a prism.

The geometric data, dimensions for the length and width of the rectangle base, are defined during sketch construction; the construction command is Rectangle Center.

1.7.2 Basic solid "Cube", geometric description

The cube (from Latin cubus, "cube") is one of the five Platonic solids, more precisely a three-dimensional polyhedron (polyhedron) with six congruent squares as boundary faces, twelve equal edges, and eight vertices, each of which has three congruent faces.

The cube is a special three-dimensional parallelepiped, a special equilateral cuboid, and a special right square prism. The size of a cube is determined by the edge length.

Because of its high symmetry all vertices, edges, and sides are identical the cube is a regular polytypic and has point symmetrical points about its center.

1.7.3 Basic solid "Cylinder", geometric description

According to the general definition, a finite cylinder (from rolling, rolling) is bounded by two parallel, flat surfaces, a base and a top surface, and a peripheral or cylindrical surface formed by parallel lines.

If the lines are perpendicular to the base and top surfaces, it is called a right cylinder. The height of the cylinder is given by the distance between the two planes in which the base and top surfaces lie.

When a cylinder is mentioned in geometry, it is often a right circular cylinder.

1.7.4 Basic solid "Sphere", geometric description

The spherical surface is the surface created by the rotation of a circle around a diameter, also called the surface of revolution. The sphere has the smallest surface area of all bodies with a given volume. Of all bodies with a given surface area, it encloses the largest volume.

The sphere has an infinite number of planes of symmetry, namely the planes through the sphere's center. Furthermore, the sphere is rotationally symmetric with respect to every axis through the center and every angle of rotation, and point-symmetric with respect to its center.

Both a spherical surface and a spherical body are often referred to simply as a sphere; the union of a spherical surface and its interior is called a spherical body or solid sphere.

1.7.5 Basic solid "Cone", geometric description

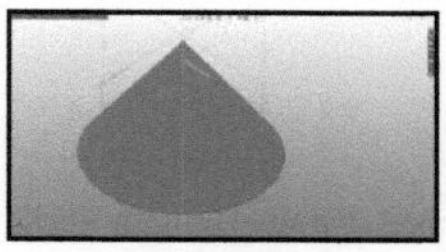

A cone is a geometric solid created by connecting all points of a bounded circular surface lying in a plane with a straight line to a vertex outside the plane. The surface is called the base, its boundary line is the directory, and the point is called the apex or vertex of the cone.

The distance between the apex and the base is the height of the cone; the lines connecting the apex to the directory are called generatrix lines; their union forms the surface of the cone.

When a cone is mentioned in geometry, the special case of a right circular cone is often meant. Especially in engineering, the word "cone" (from Latin "conus") is also used for a cone of revolution.

1.7.6 Basic solid "Truncated Cone", geometric description

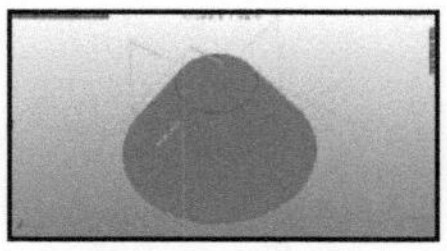

In geometry, a truncated cone is the name given to a special solid of revolution. A truncated cone is created by cutting a smaller cone from a right circular cone parallel to the base. This smaller cone is called the complementary cone of the truncated cone.
The height of a truncated cone is the distance between the base and the top.

1.7.7 Basic solid "Ellipsoid of revolution", geometric description

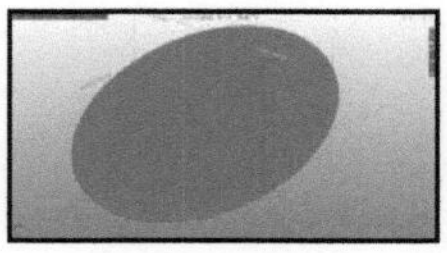

An ellipsoid of revolution is an ellipsoid created by rotating an ellipse around one of its axes. Unlike a general ellipsoid, two axes are of equal length.
Depending on the length of the axis of rotation, a distinction is made between an elongated ellipsoid, which rotates around the semi-major axis, and an oblate ellipsoid, which rotates around the semi-minor axis.

1.7.8 Basic solid "Torus", geometric description

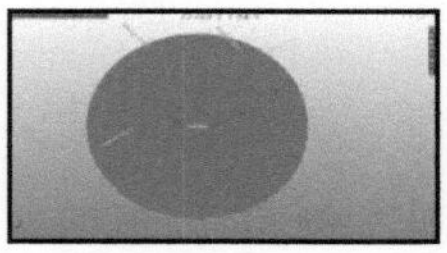

The torus is a special surface of revolution and tube, or also a tubular ring-shaped mathematical body, created by rotating a circle around an axis lying in its plane but not intersecting it. Depending on its position relative to the axis of rotation, the torus appears in the forms of a ring torus, a thorn torus, or a spindle torus. In mathematics, the torus is also called a ring body or a circular bulge.

1.7.9 Basic solid "Pyramid", geometric description

The pyramid is a geometric solid, more precisely a polyhedron, whose base is a polygon and whose side faces are triangles that are adjacent to the polygon on one side and meet at a point, the so-called apex of the pyramid, on the other. The polygon is also called the base of the pyramid. The triangles together form the surface of the pyramid.

From a particular point, the apex of the pyramids emanates a bundle of rays whose rays intersect a plane at the vertices of the pyramid's base. For example, with four rays of a certain inclination in space, one obtains a square base, thus forming the square pyramid.

One can also start the construction with any base of a polygon in the plane and choose a point outside this plane, which then becomes the apex of the pyramid. By connecting each vertex of the base to the apex, the aforementioned bundle of rays is created. The points of each base edge are connected to the pyramid apex via the triangular surface.

1.7.10 Basic solid "Truncated Pyramid", geometric description

A truncated pyramid is a term from geometry that describes a special type of polyhedron. A truncated pyramid is created by cutting off a smaller, similar pyramid (a supplementary pyramid) from a pyramid parallel to its base.

The two parallel faces of a truncated pyramid are similar to each other. The larger of these two faces is called the base, and the smaller is called the vertex. The distance between the base and vertex is called the height of the truncated pyramid.

2

Dassault Systèmes
3DEXPERIENCE©
SOLIDWORKS Design
2026

Parts and Components
Create and Customize

Program Basics
Program Adjustments

2 SOLIDWORKS© Design 2026, Program basics

2.1 SOLIDWORKS Design 2026, the program start

2.1.1 Introduction to design concepts and SOLIDWORKS terms, basics, an overview

SOLIDWORKS© CAD software is a design application for mechanical engineering that allows designers to quickly translate their ideas into sketches, experiment with features and dimensions, and create models and detailed drawings.

2.1.1.1 Parts

Demonstration of the design methods, tools and features commonly used to create parts.

2.1.1.2 Assemblies

Adding parts to an assembly, setting mates, and using in-context design methods

2.1.1.3 Drawings

Drawing sheet formats, views, dimensions, labels and parts lists.

2.1.1.4 Technical tasks

Description of additional applications, utilities, and other resources needed for demanding tasks.

2.1.2 SOLIDWORKS Design 2026, program startup

2.1.2.1 SOLIDWORKS Design 2026, program startup 3DEXPERIENCE© SOLIDWORKS 2026 for Makers

Compass

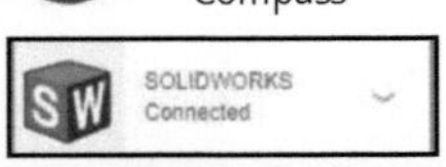

- Log in to the 3DEXPERIENCE platform using the launcher.

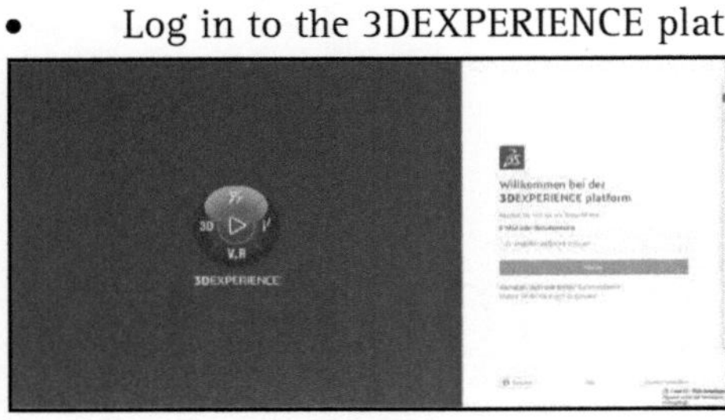

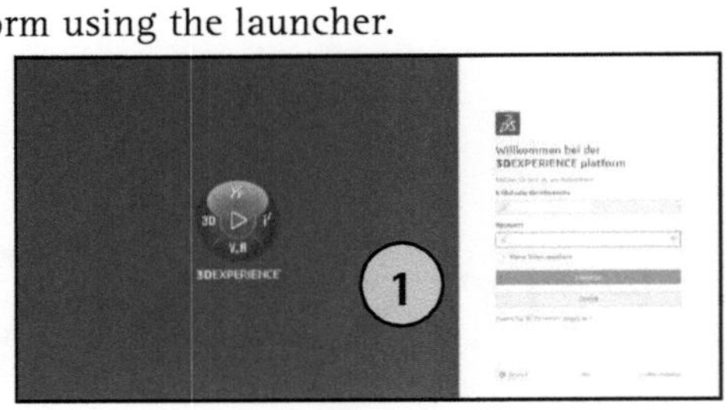

- Click on the Compass in the top bar of the **3DDashboard**.
- Click Open SOLIDWORKS Connected (2).

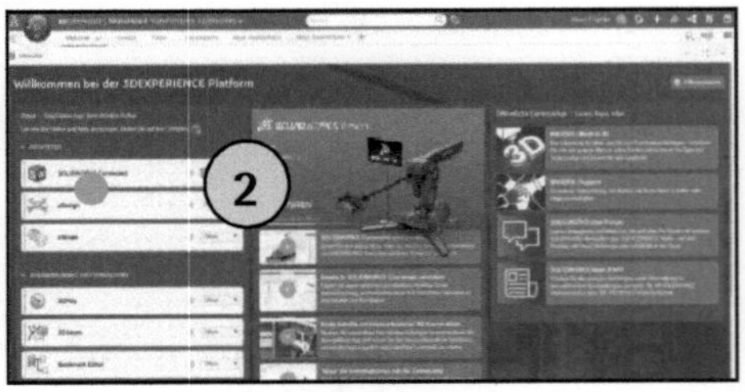

2.1.2.2 SOLIDWORKS Design 2026, program startup

Start SOLIDWORKS Design 2026 by double-clicking the desktop icon. Alternatively, you can start it using the Windows Start icon in the lower left corner of the screen.

Start / Programme / SOLIDWORKS 2026 / SOLIDWORKS Design 2026

When you first start SOLIDWORKS Design 2026, several status messages appear, which can simply be acknowledged with **Yes**.

2.1.3 SOLIDWORKS Design 2026, the start screen

The following illustration shows the start screen of SOLIDWORKS Design 2026.

2.1.3.1 SOLIDWORKS Design 2026 start screen "Home", "Recent", "Learn" and "Alerts"

Home

Recent

Learn

Alerts

2.1.3.2 SOLIDWORKS Design 2026, start screen "Learn"

Getting Started Guide

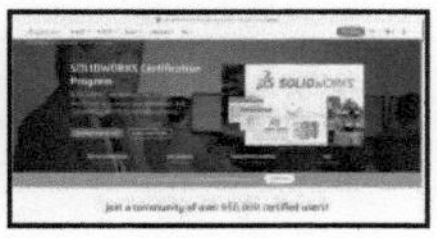

My Training

Certification

Curriculum

2.1.4 The template files, basics

Templates are part, drawing, and assembly documents with user-defined parameters and form the basis for new documents. You can manage many different document templates. For example, you can create the following templates:

One document template uses millimeters, and another uses inches.

One document template uses the ANSI dimension standard, and another uses the ISO standard.

You can organize and access your document templates by placing them on different tabs. The templates can contain settings for the following document properties:

Grid spacing, overhang line and break edge spacing, length of the bent leader line for parts list symbols, text scale and size of the text display, material density, etc.

Templates are used as the basis for the format and properties of new documents. Templates contain user-defined document properties, such as units of measurement or other levels of detail. Templates allow for the storage of many different document styles.

A document template can be a part, drawing, or assembly that you have saved as a template. You can create different types of model files with SOLIDWORKS 2026. Part files contain only one part, while assembly files always consist of multiple parts.

2.1.4.1 SOLIDWORKS Design 2026, start screen New SOLIDWORKS Document "Standard"

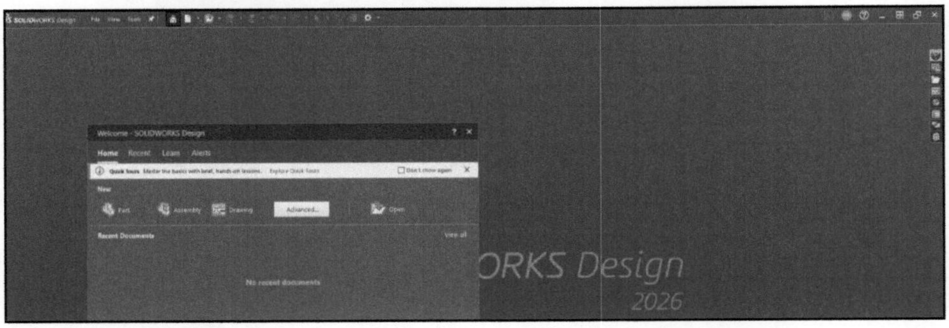

2.1.4.2 SOLIDWORKS Design 2026, start screen New SOLIDWORKS Document "Advanced"

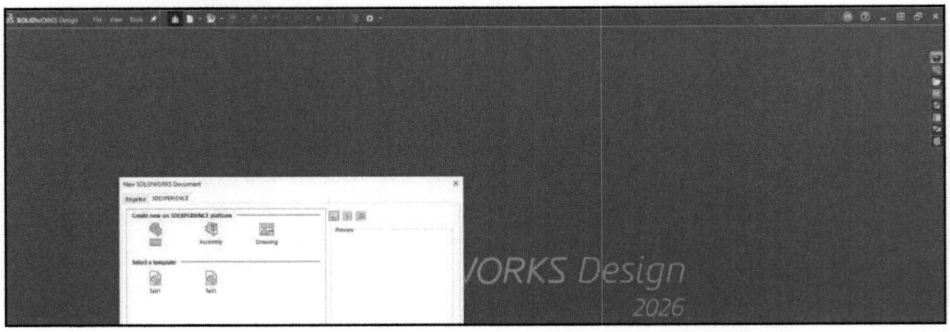

2.1.5 New SOLIDWORKS Document, program functions

The SOLIDWORKS-specific method of selecting these options does not involve individual program modules, as in comparable CAD programs, but rather template files.

The following pages provide an overview of the requirements for working with part and assembly files.

2.1.5.1 New SOLIDWORKS Document, symbolism

2.1.5.2 Component files

A part file can contain only one part.

Part

Use part files to control the individual design of a single part, create standard parts for use in assemblies, construct 2D geometries for sketches and work features as the basis for an assembly layout, or create sheet metal parts.

Part files are saved with the **.PRTDOT** file extension.

2.1.5.3 Assembly files, assemblies

Assembly files can contain one or more parts or subassemblies.

Assembly

You can assign any number of external parts and subassemblies to an assembly file. To create a new part within an assembly, the Create Component function is available.

Assembly files are saved with the **.ASMDOT** extension.

2.1.5.4 Drawing files

Drawing

Drawing files contain the drawing views of your parts and assemblies, displayed across any number of sheets. You can create drawings from open part, assembly, and presentation files.

Drawing files are saved with the **.DRWDOT** extension.

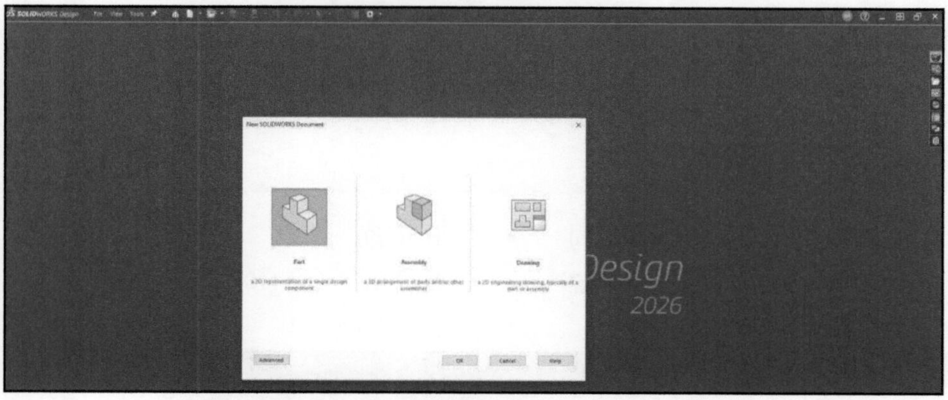

2.2 SOLIDWORKS Design 2026, Component files User Interface Overview

Start SOLIDWORKS Design 2026 by double-clicking the desktop icon. Alternatively, you can start it via the Windows Start icon in the lower left corner of the screen.

2.2.1 Open the working file, select the component from the book's DVD

Open

Open (Menu bar) (A) / Component from the book-DVD / **OK** (B)

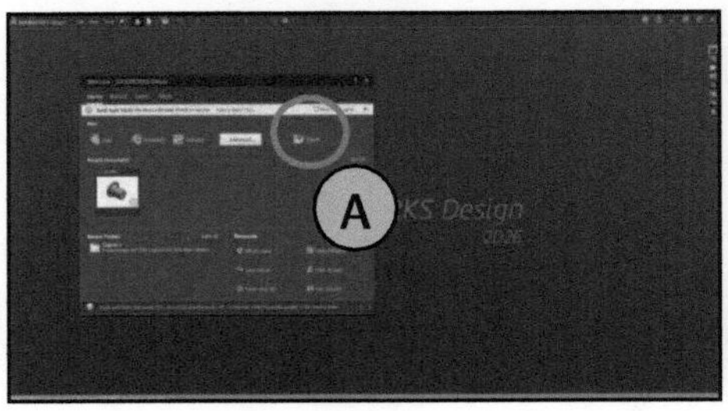

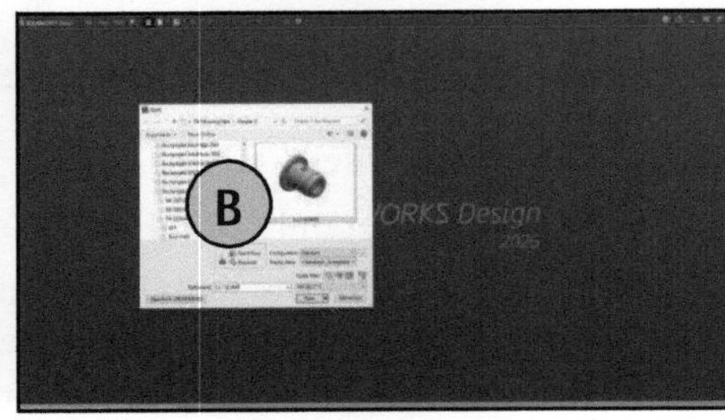

2.2.2 SOLIDWORKS Design 2026, the part user interface

2.2.2.1 SOLIDWORKS Design 2026, the part user interface, preliminary remarks

The user interface of the SOLIDWORKS software contains various tools and functions that allow you to create and edit your models efficiently.

2.2.2.2 User interface, overview

- Menu Bar (1)
- CommandManager (2)
- PropertyManager (3)
- ConfigurationsManager (4)
- FeatureManager Design Tree (5)

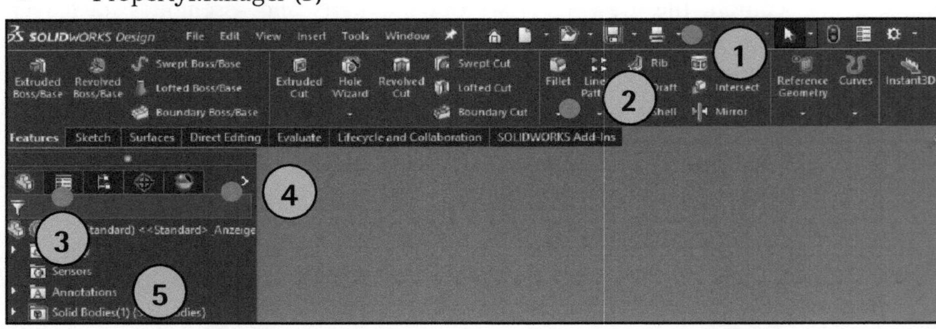

- Selection Breadcrumbs (6)
- Heads-up View Toolbar (7)
- Search (8)
- Help (9)
- Feature Select (10)
- Task Pane (11)

- Status Bar (12)
- Reference Triad (13)
- Unit System (14)

- Feature selection (17)
- Selection Breadcrumbs (16)
- PropertyManager (19)
- Menu Bar (15)
- Context menus (18)

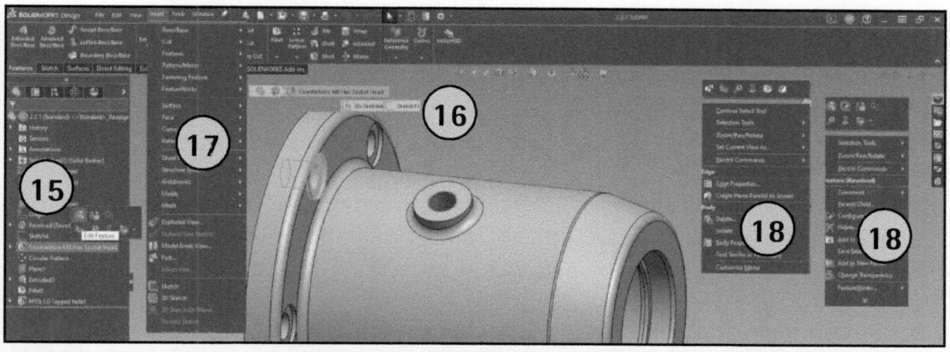

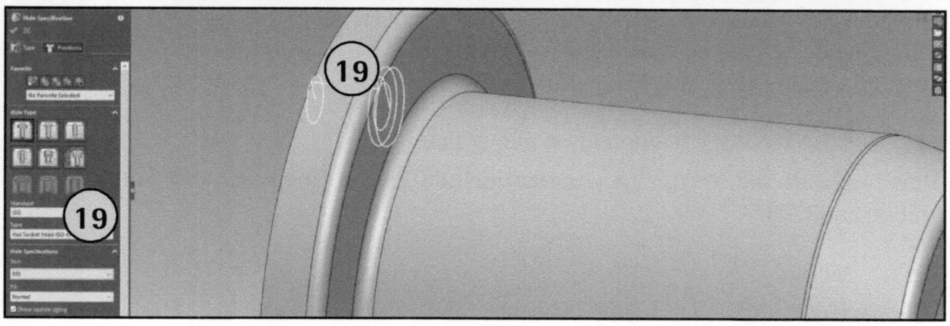

- Callouts (20)
- Handles (21)

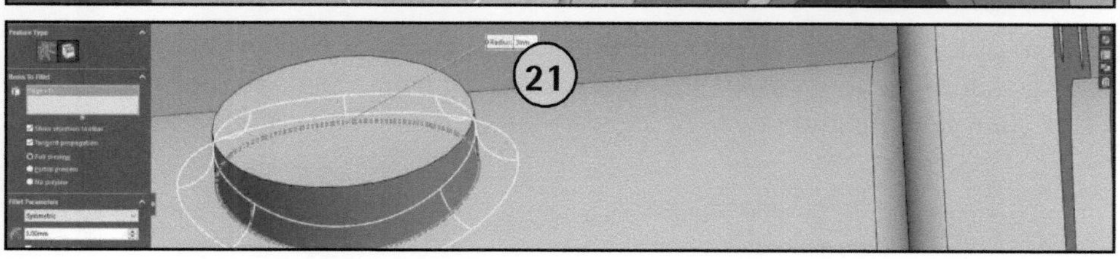

2.2.3 SOLIDWORKS 2026, the user interface, definitions of terms

2.2.3.1 Windows Functions

SOLIDWORKS software can be used with familiar Windows functions, such as dragging and resizing windows. Many identical icons, printing, opening, saving, cutting, and pasting are also parts of the SOLIDWORKS application.

2.2.3.2 SOLIDWORKS Document Window

SOLIDWORKS document windows have several panes. The left pane, or Manager pane, contains the FeatureManager, PropertyManager, and ConfigurationManager. The right pane is the graphics area where the part or drawing is created or edited.

2.2.3.3 PropertyManager

The PropertyManager provides settings for many functions such as sketches, fillet features, and assembly mates.

2.2.3.4 FeatureManager

Display the structure of the part, assembly, or drawing. Select an element from the FeatureManager to, for example, edit the anderlying sketch or feature and suppress or unsuppress the feature or component.

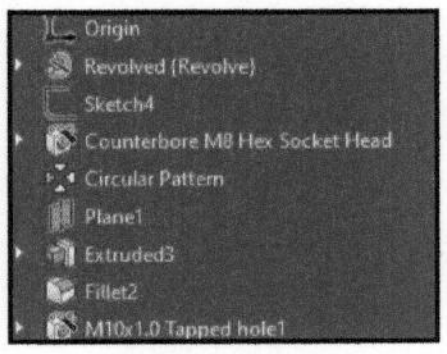

2.2.3.5 ConfigurationManager

The ConfigurationManager helps you create, select, and view multiple configurations of parts or assemblies within a document. Configurations are variations of a part or assembly in a single document.

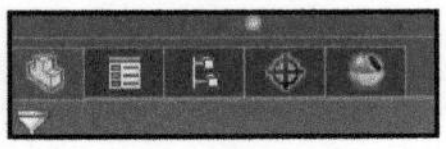

2.2.3.6 SOLIDWORKS Document, Window Extensions

Other areas of the document window include menus, toolbars, shortcut bars, and context toolbars.

2.2.3.7 Menus

All SOLIDWORKS commands can be accessed via menus. The menus in SOLIDWORKS follow Windows conventions. They include, for example, submenus and checkboxes to indicate an active menu item. You can also use context-sensitive menus by right-clicking.

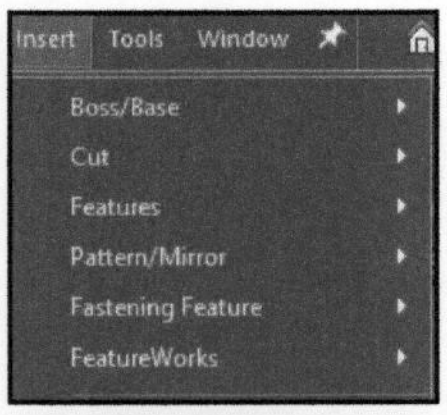

2.2.3.8 Toolbars

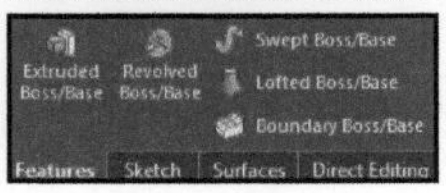

You can access SOLIDWORKS functions using toolbars. The toolbars are structured by function, such as the Sketch or Assembly toolbars. Each toolbar contains individual icons for specific tools. Toolbars can be shown or hidden, docked to the four edges of the SOLIDWORKS window, or freely positioned anywhere on the screen.

SOLIDWORKS software registers the state of the toolbars at each session. You can also customize the toolbars by adding or removing icons. Tooltips appear when you hover your mouse pointer over an icon.

2.2.3.9 CommandManager

The CommandManager is a context-sensitive toolbar that is dynamically updated based on the active document type.

2.2.3.10 Shortcut bars

Customizable shortcut bars let you create your own command sets for part, assembly, drawing, and sketch modes. To access the bars, press a user-defined key combination, the default being the S key.

2.2.3.11 Context Toolbars

Context toolbars appear when you select items in the graphics area or FeatureManager design tree. They provide access to frequently performed actions in that context. Context toolbars are available for parts, assemblies, and sketches.

2.2.3.12 Callouts and Handles

- **Callouts**

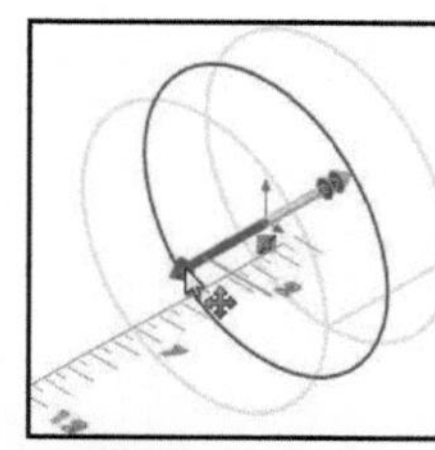

Callouts are text-filled boxes that appear in the graphics area when you use certain tools. Handles allow you to dynamically click, move, and set certain parameters without leaving the graphics area. Callouts help you easily distinguish between different entities. For example, these callouts show the sweep profile and the sweep path. You can drag these callouts to reposition them, but you cannot use them to change any properties of the entity to which they refer.

- **Handles**

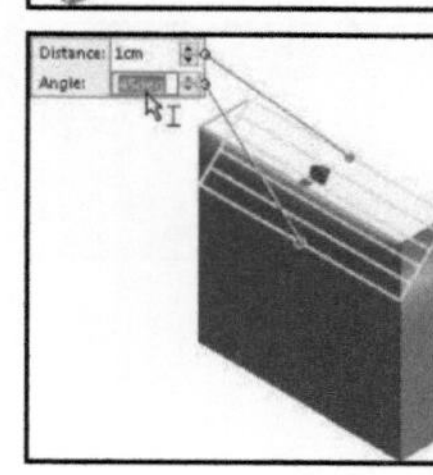

Handles spant the length of extrusions. Drag the handle to the desired extrude depth, and the handle spans that length. You can also drag the pointer (instead of the handle) to the desired extrude depth. Click the handle, then drag the pointer in either direction. In the example below, the pink handle is active and the gray handle is inactive. One handle has one arrow head, and the other handle has two arrow heads, to help you see which direction the handle applies to.

2.2.3.13 Selection Breadcrumbs

Selection breadcrumbs are a context-based view of the current selection. They show related elements in the hierarchical tree for parts and assemblies.

You can select an item in the graphics area and refine that selection through the context-based representation of the item by using breadcrumbs. For example, in an assembly, when you select a face, you can see all the mates of the component that the face belongs to.

Use breadcrumbs to access the hierarchical chain of entities from the item that you selected up through the top-level assembly or part. Breadcrumbs provide access to common selections that are near the entities in the breadcrumb, like the anderlying sketch of a feature or the mates of a component.

2.2.4 SOLIDWORKS Design 2026, the user interface, advanced views, definitions of terms

2.2.4.1 The "Menu bar", "Quick Access Tools"

The menu bar contains a set of the most frequently used tool buttons from the standard toolbar. Clicking the down arrow next to a tool button expands it and displays a flyout menu with additional functions.

This allows you to access most commands in the File menu from the toolbar. For example, the Save flyout menu contains the **Save**, **Save As**, and **Save All** commands.

2.2.4.2 SOLIDWORKS menus, excerpts

The menus appear when you move the cursor over or click the SOLIDWORKS logo.

You can also pin the menus using the pushpin icon to keep them visible at all times. When the menus are pinned, the toolbar shifts to the right.

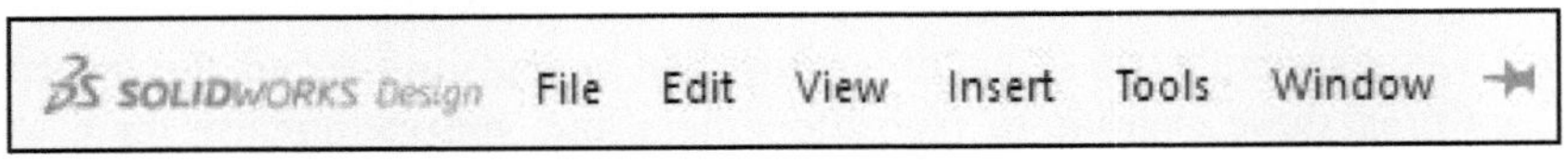

2.2.5 CommandManager for components, excerpt

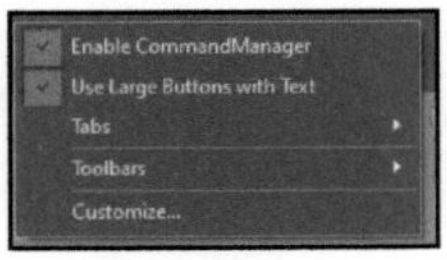

The **CommandManager** is a context-sensitive toolbar that dynamically updates depending on the toolbar you want to access. By default, certain toolbars are embedded in the CommandManager, depending on the document type.

When you click a tab ander the CommandManager, it updates and displays that toolbar. For example, clicking the Sketch tab displays the Sketch toolbar.

The **CommandManager** allows you to access centrally located toolbar buttons and save space in the graphics area.

To turn the descriptions and button size on or off, right-click on the CommandManager and select or deselect the **Use Large Buttons with Text** option.

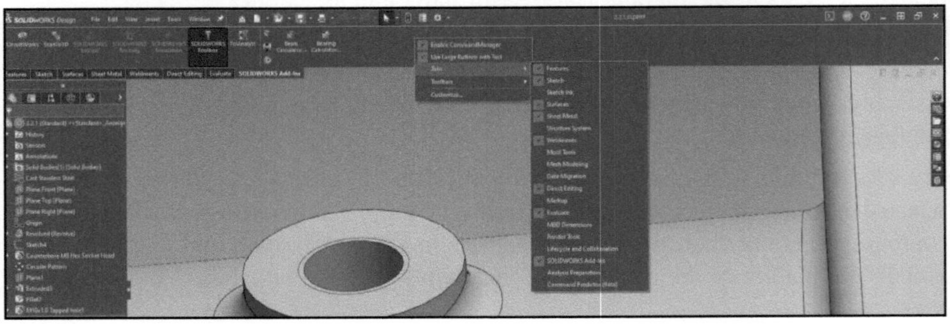

2.2.5.1 CommandManager "Features"

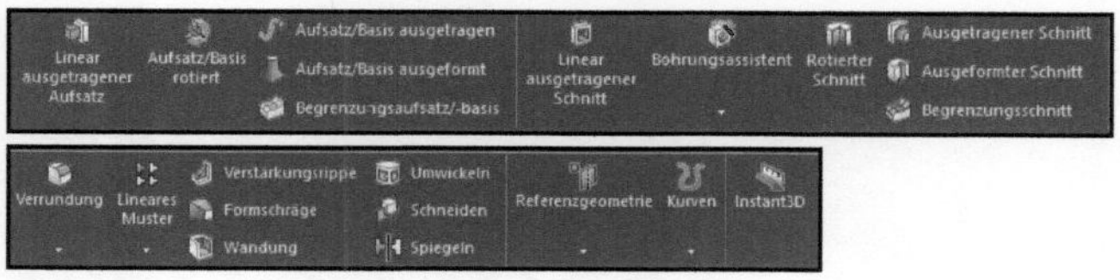

2.2.5.2 CommandManager "Sketch"

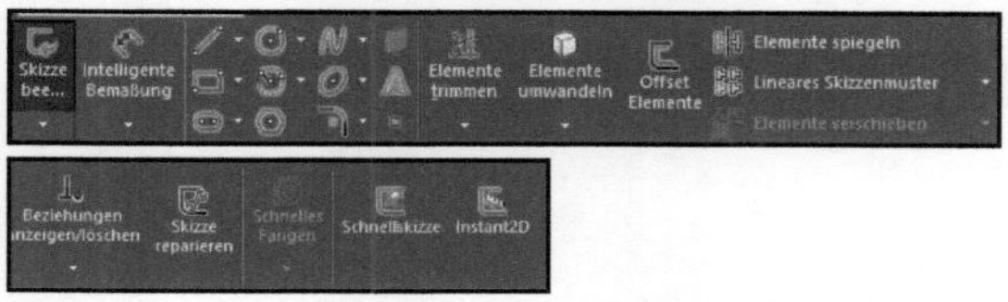

2.2.5.3 CommandManager "Surfaces"

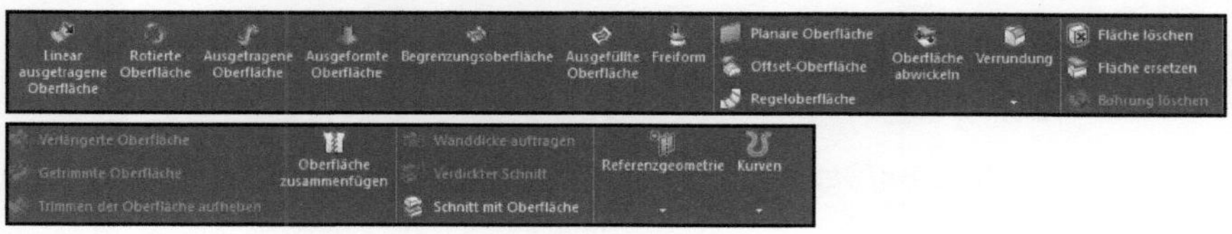

2.2.5.4 CommandManager "Sheet Metal"

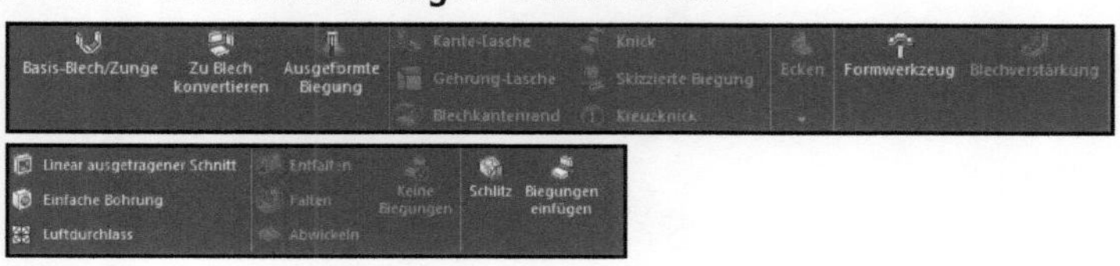

2.2.5.5 CommandManager "Weldments"

2.2.5.6 CommandManager "Direct Editing"

2.2.5.7 CommandManager "Evaluate"

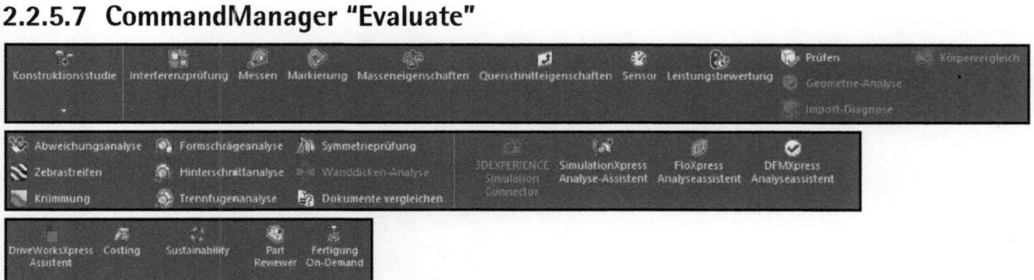

2.2.5.8 CommandManager "SOLIDWORKS Add-Ins"

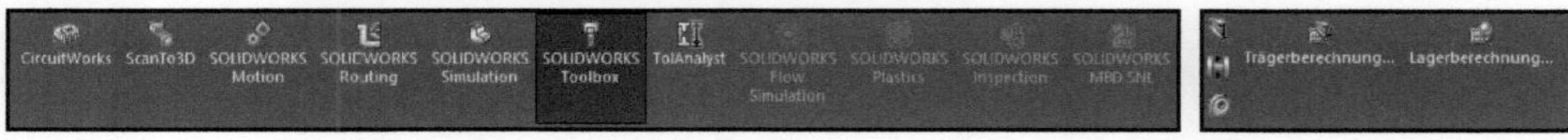

2.2.6 The toolboxes, component features, excerpt

Do a Right-click in the empty area next to the toolbar (1) and select a feature toolbar according to the following illustration of the toolbars (2).

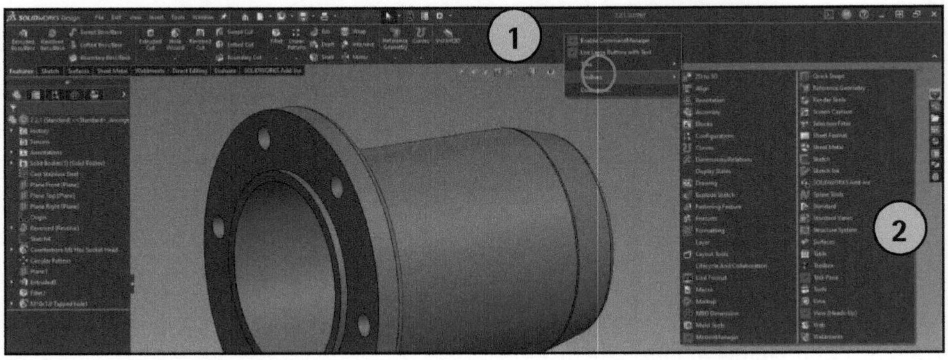

2.2.6.1 Feature toolbars

Possible function calls, excerpt:

 **Extrude Boss/Base**  **Extrude Cut**

 **Chamfer**  **Fillet**

 **Revolved Cut**  **Revolved Boss/Base**

 **Lofted Boss/Base**  **Rib**

 **Shell**  **Draft**

 **Hole Wizard**  **Linear Pattern**

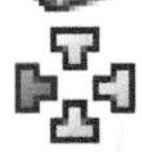 **Circular Pattern**  **Feature Mirror**

 **Reference-Geometry**  **Spline**

 **Instant3D**

2.2.6.2 Selectable flyouts in the "Features" toolbar, excerpt

Some selectable functions are implemented as flyouts.

 **Extrude Boss/Base**

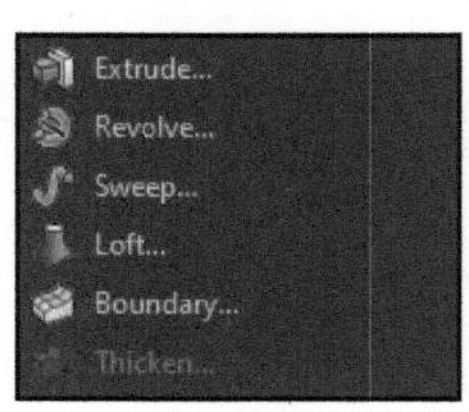

Extrude Cut

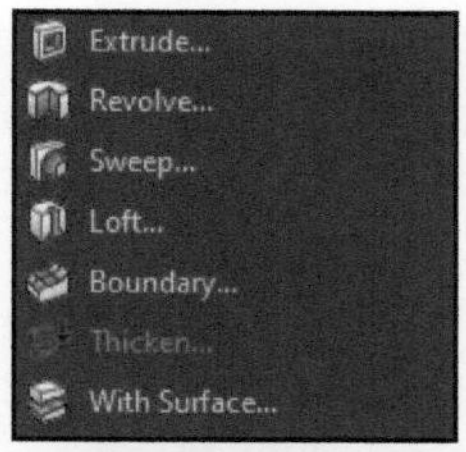

Fillet

Linear Pattern

Circular Pattern

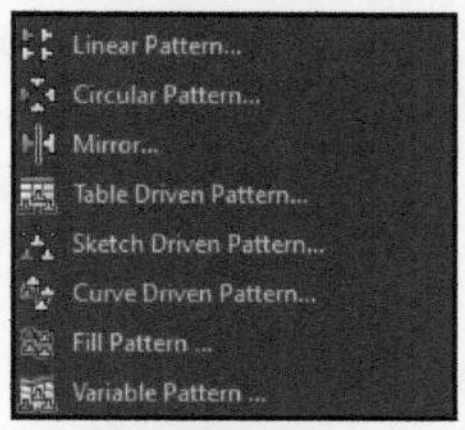

Reference-Geometry

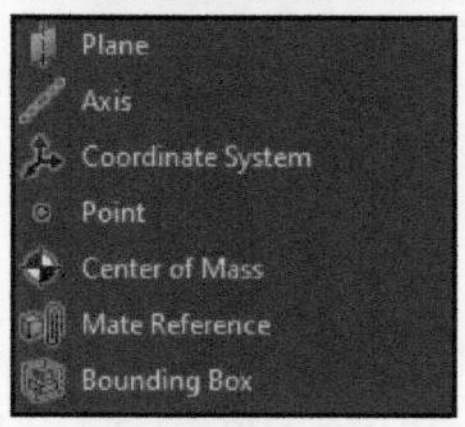

Spline

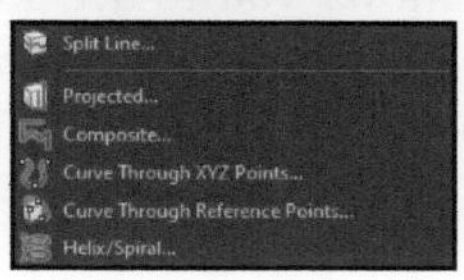

2.2.7 "FeatureManager", "Transparent Flyout FeatureManager" and "PropertyManager"

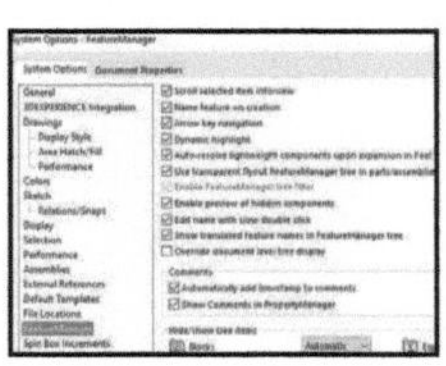

The **FeatureManager** on the left side of the SOLIDWORKS window gives you an overview of the active part, assembly, or drawing. This allows you to see how the model or assembly was constructed, or to examine the different sheets and views in a drawing.

The **FeatureManager** and the graphics area are dynamically linked. In both areas, you can select features, sketches, drawing views, and construction geometry.

You can split the **FeatureManager** and either display two instances of the **FeatureManager** or combine the **FeatureManager** with the **ConfigurationManager** or **PropertyManager**.

The **Transparent Flyout FeatureManager** (1) allows you to display the **FeatureManager** and the **PropertyManager** (2) simultaneously. Sometimes it's easier to select items in the **Swinging FeatureManager** than in the graphics area.

2.2.7.1 Display of Managers

You can switch between the **FeatureManager**, **PropertyManager**, **ConfigurationManager** and **DisplayManager** by clicking the tabs at the top of the left pane of the SOLIDWORKS window.

When a **PropertyManager** is active, the corresponding **FeatureManager** is automatically displayed.

Expand, options:
Click **+** next to the document name in the expanding **FeatureManager design tree**.

Click the name of the top-level item in the expanding **FeatureManager** design tree.
Press the **C** key.

2.2.7.2 Der FeatureManager

The **FeatureManager** (1) on the left side of the SOLIDWORKS window gives you an overview of the active part, assembly, or drawing. This allows you to gain insight into the design of the model or assembly, or to examine the different sheets and views in a drawing.

2.2.7.3 Der PropertyManager

The **PropertyManager** (2) allows you to set properties and other options for many SOLIDWORKS commands. The PropertyManager appears on the **PropertyManager** tab in the left pane of the window, adjacent to the graphics area. It opens when you select items or commands defined in the **PropertyManager**.

2.2.7.4 Transparent Flyout FeatureManager

The **Transparent Flyout FeatureManager** (3) lets you display the **FeatureManager** and **PropertyManager** simultaneously. Sometimes it's easier to select items in the expanding **FeatureManager** than in the graphics area.

You can also hide selected items, change their transparency, resize them, or call them up. However, you cannot suppress items or their layout.

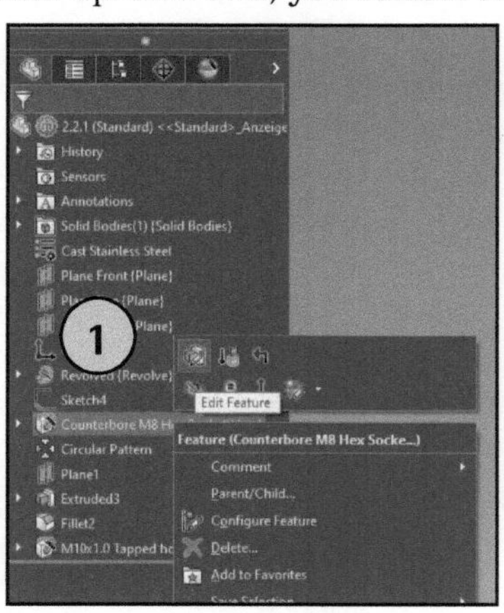

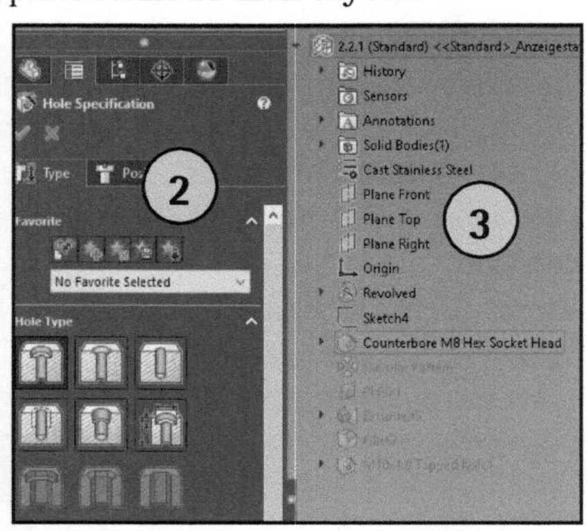

2.2.7.5 ConfigurationManager

ConfigurationManager:

The **ConfigurationManager** is a tool that allows you to create, select, and display multiple configurations of parts and assemblies.

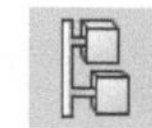

Configuration-Manager

2.2.7.6 DimXpertManager

DimXpertManager:

The **DimXpertManager** lists the tolerance features defined by DimXpert for parts. It also displays DimXpert tools that you use to insert dimensions and tolerances into parts. You can import these dimensions and tolerances into drawings.

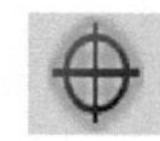

DimXpert-Manager

2.2.7.7 DisplayManager

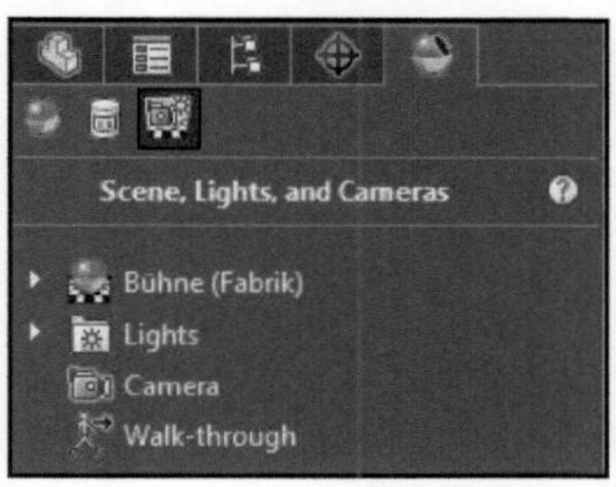

DisplayManager:

The Display Manager provides editing access to and lists appearances, decals, scenes, lighting fixtures, and cameras applied to the current model.

Display-Manager

2.2.8 Task Window Area

The Task Window Area provides access to SOLIDWORKS resources, libraries of reusable design elements, views that can be dragged onto a drawing sheet, and other useful elements and information. The Task Window Area appears when the SOLIDWORKS software is opened.

2.2.8.1 Command "SOLIDWORKS Welcome dialog"

The **SOLIDWORKS Welcome dialog** in the Task Window Area contains commands, links, and information.

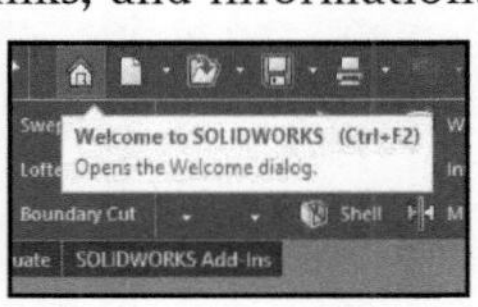

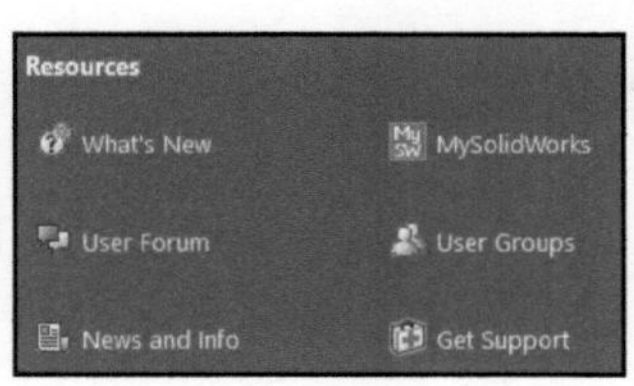

2.2.8.2 Task Pane Tabs

3DExperience:

The **3D**EXPERIENCE add-in provides access to all the **3D**EXPERIENCE services and apps that you are entitled to use based on your roles. If you are a member of your organization's **3D**EXPERIENCE platform, you can download and install add-in components that provide access to **3D**EXPERIENCE collaboration apps, file sharing.

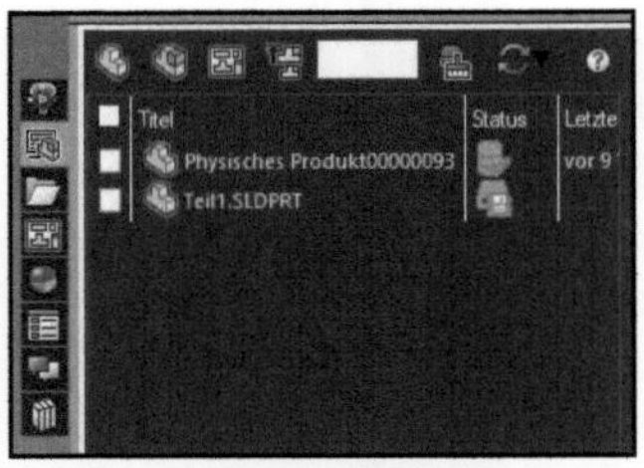

3DExperience:
Files on the PC save to **3DExperience.**

File Explorer

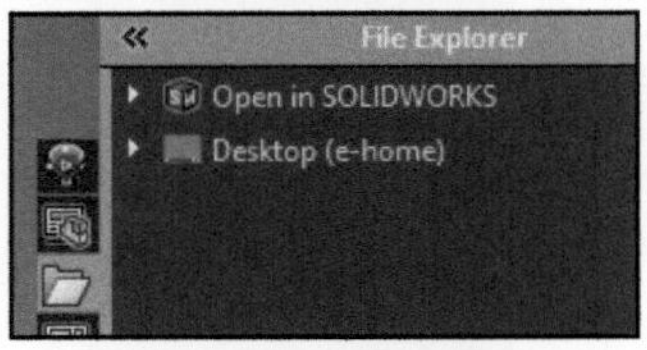

File Explorer:
The **File Explorer** tab in the task pane is a copy of Windows Explorer on your local computer and displays the directories.

Design Library

Toolbox

SOLIDWORKS Content

3D-Componets PartSupply

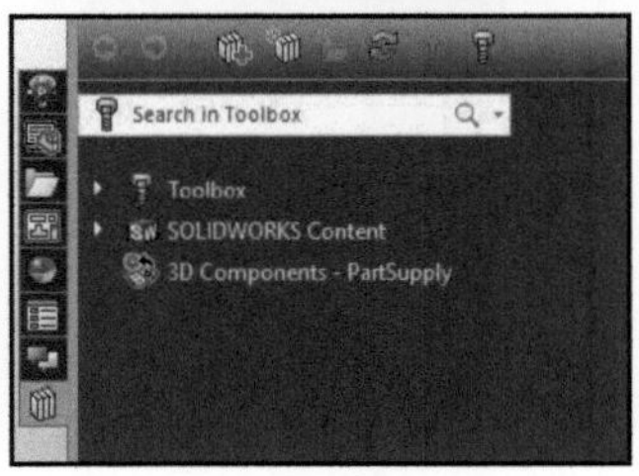

Design Library:
Subfolders that are filled by SOLIDWORKS with reusable elements such as parts, blocks, and annotations.

Toolbox:
To access the content, install the SOLIDWORKS Toolbox Browser and activate it as an add-on application.

SOLIDWORKS Content:
Additional SOLIDWORKS content for blocks, routing, CircuitWorks and weldments; Ctrl+click to download .zip files to your system.

PartSupply:
Here's how to access Part Supply via the 3DEXPERIENCE Marketplace.

Appearance

Scenes

Decals

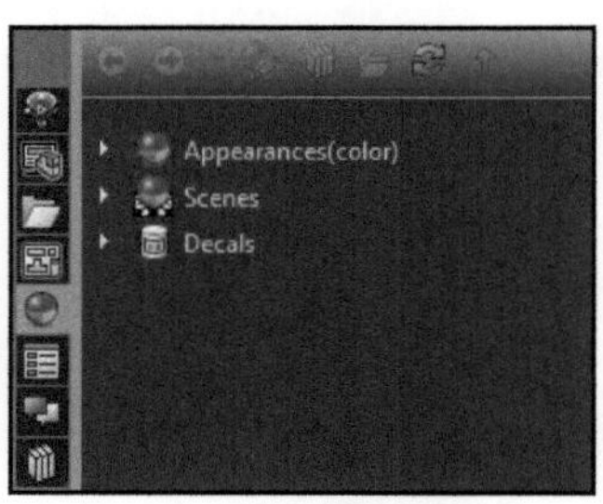

Appearance:
If you drag an Appearance, Scene, or Decal from the tab into the graphics area, you can apply it directly to the model.

Scenes:
Double-clicking Appearance or Stage on the Scenes tab will attach the elements to the active document.

Decals:
Double-clicking a decal opens the Decals PropertyManager. However, the decal is not inserted into the graphics area.

2.2.8.3 The "Help" window area

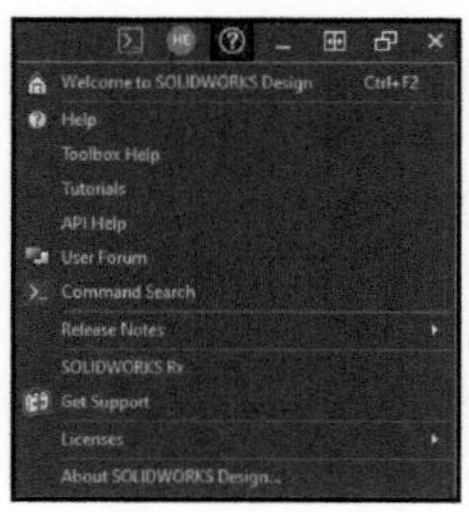

When accessing the help, a web version of the documentation is displayed in a web viewer. Identifying relevant topics using relevance lists, spell checkers, short descriptions in search result views, and guided navigation. Navigate through the help topics using the Next and Previous buttons and the path at the top.

2.2.9 Heads-Up View Toolbar

A transparent toolbar in each viewport provides all the standard tools used for view editing. The Display pane lets you view various display settings in part and drawing documents. For assemblies and parts, you can also change these settings. The arrow icons open the following flyouts:

Flyout **View Settings**, Flyout **Apply Scene**,
Flyout **Hide all Types**, Flyout **Display Style** and
Flyout **View Orientation**, Flyout **Section View**.
Previous View, **Zoom to Area**, **Zoom to Fit**.

2.2.9.1 Flyout "View Settings", excerpt

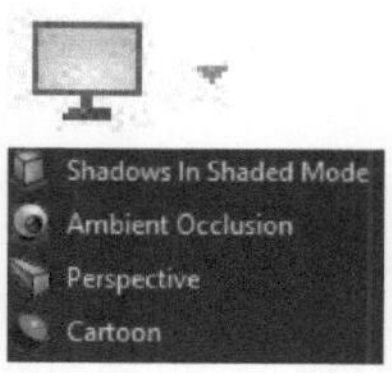

RealViewGraphics:
RealView Graphics is only available with graphics cards that support RealView Graphics display.

Shadows in Shaded Mode:
Displays a shadow ander the model. When shadows are displayed, the light falls from the highest point of the model in the current orientation. If you rotate the model, the shadow rotates with the model.

Ambient occlusion:
Ambient occlusion is a global lighting method that adds realism to models by controlling the attenuation of ambient light due to occluded areas.

Perspective:
Perspective relates to the size of the object being viewed and its distance from the viewer. You can modify the perspective by defining object sizes and distances. The smaller the value, the greater the perspective distortion.

Cartoon:
Cartoon rendering lets you add a non-photorealistic cartoon-like effect to your RealView models. Displays cartoon settings, cartoon edge color and cartoon edge thickness, defined in options.

RealView Graphics

Shadows in Shaded Mode

Ambient Occlusion

Perspective

Cartoon

2.2.9.2 Flyout "Heads-Up View Toolbar"

This function allows you to select which elements to show or hide.

On the View toolbar or the **Heads-Up View toolbar**, click **Hide/Show all Types**, and then select or deselect an item from the menu.

The tool is split into two sides. On the left side, you can toggle between hide all types and show the previous visibility state. On the right side, you can view the existing list of types to change visibility of one item at a time.

Hide/Show all Types

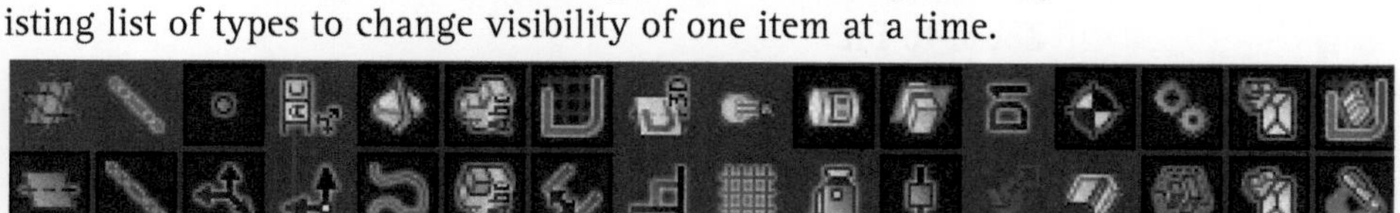

2.2.9.3 Flyout "Display Style"

You can specify options for the default edge display in all drawing documents. The specified display types apply to new drawing views, except for new views created from existing views. If you create a new view from an existing view, the display settings of the original view are used in the new view.

Flyout **Display Style**
Flyout control that allows you to select the display mode of the active document.

Shaded with Edges

Shaded with Edges:
Displays a shaded view of the model with edges visible.

Shaded

Shaded:
Displays a shadow ander the model. When shadows are displayed, the light appears from the top-most part of the model in the current orientation.

Hidden Lines Removed

Hidden Lines Removed:
Displays the model with all edges that are not visible from the current view angle removed.

Hidden Lines Visible

Hidden Lines Visible:
Displays the model with all edges that are not visible from the current view angle in gray.

Wireframe

Wireframe:
Displays all the edges of the model.

2.2.9.4 Flyout "Section View"

Flyout **Section View**:
In a section view in a part or assembly document, the model is displayed as if it has been cut through planes and surfaces that you specify, so that the internal structure of the model is revealed.

2.2.9.5 Flyout "Previous View"

Previous View
After moving the model to one or more views, you can revert the model or drawing to the previous view. The last 10 view changes can each be andone.

2.2.9.6 Flyout "Zoom to Area"

Zoom to Area:
Enlarges a section that you select by dragging a frame.

2.2.9.7 Flyout "Zoom to Fit"

Zoom to Fit:

Enlarged or reduced so that you can see the entire model, assembly, or drawing sheet.

2.2.9.8 Flyout "View Orientation"

You can rotate or zoom the model or drawing to a predefined view. Select one of the standard views or add your own custom views in the Orientation dialog box.
To return to the previous view, click **Previous View** in the Heads-Up View toolbar. The last 10 view changes can be andone. The standard Views toolbar provides the following tools:

To align the part and assembly in predefined standard view.
Viewports are used to view the model or drawing.
You can use the Views Selector to display and select model views.

View Orientation

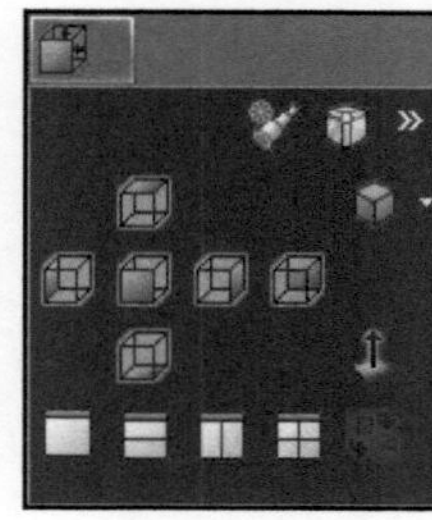

View Orientation DIN ISO 128-30:

Front **Back**

Left **Right**

Top **Bottom**

View Orientation Projektion DIN ISO **5456**

Isometric **Trimetric**

Dimetric

View Orientation, Display Viewports

Single View **Two View Horizontal**

Two View Vertical **Four View**

Normal To
With this method, the first face you choose is parallel to the screen and the second face you choose is at the top of the view.

View Orientation, Previous View

View Selector:

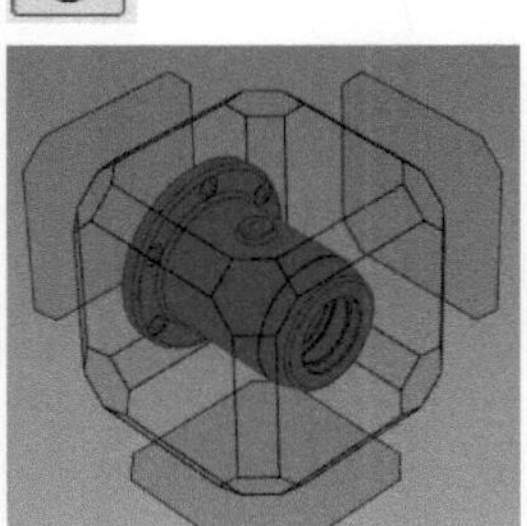

You can use the **View Selector** to display and select model views in context. The **View Selector** lets you see how the right, left, front, back, and top views, as well as the axonometric views, will appear. Click on a face of the **View Selector** to display a view.

2.2.10 Error message

2.2.10.1 Error description

You can identify rebuild errors and warnings using the symbols in the FeatureManager:

Indicates an error in the model. The symbol is located on the document name at the top of the FeatureManager and on the feature containing the error. The text of the part or feature is displayed in red.

Indicates an error with a feature. This symbol is located on the feature name in the FeatureManager. The feature text is displayed in red.

Displays a warning below the shown node. This symbol appears on the document name at the top of the FeatureManager design tree and on the parent feature whose child feature contains the error. The feature text is displayed in green.

A warning message regarding a feature or sketch. This symbol appears in the FeatureManager design tree on the feature containing the error. The feature or sketch text is displayed in green.

2.2.10.2 Error messages and possible solutions

Error messages and solutions for errors when creating SOLIDWORKS sketches and models:

- **Unsolvable sketch**

The Sketches with dimensions that the lead to impossible geometry.

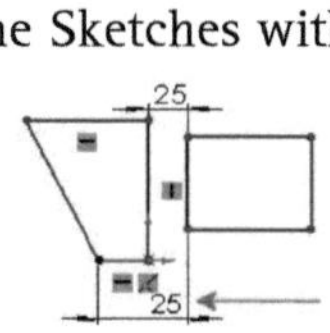

The dimension references a sketch element that is not valid for this dimension. The invalid sketch element is displayed in red. The dimension creates an invalid sketch because it creates a line with a length of **0**.

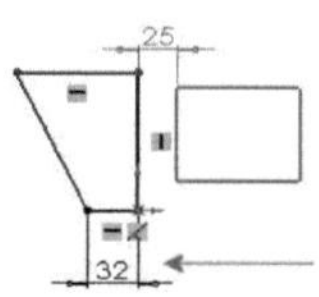

Possible solution 1:
The sketch is solved by dragging the dimension extension line to a valid element for this dimension.

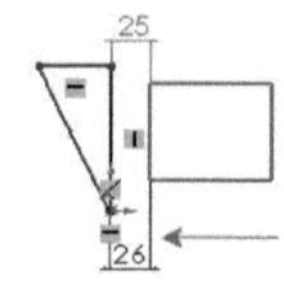

Possible solution 2:
The sketch is solved by changing the lower dimension to a value > 25, so that the lower horizontal line no longer has a length of 0.

- **Over-defined sketch**

Sketches with unnecessary dimensions or relationships.

A dimension of 100 creates an unsolvable sketch because this dimension cannot exceed the sum of the two other triangle sides. The unsolvable sketch is displayed in yellow.

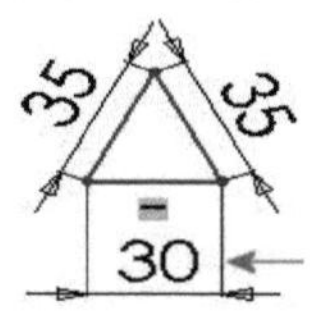

The sketch is solved by changing the dimension to a solvable value.

- **Sketch conflicts**

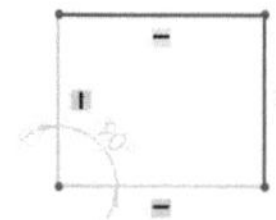

Over defined relations display the over defining sketch entities and relation callouts in yellow.

Over defined dimensions display in yellow.

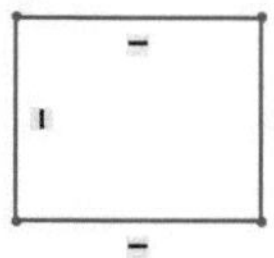

Sketch repaired by deleting the redandant 90° dimension.

You can also delete the redandant vertical or horizontal relation to repair the sketch.

- **Check sketch for feature usage**

Example of checking sketch contours for suitability for a Revolve feature.

Klicken Sie in einer offenen Skizze auf:
Tools / Sketch Tools / Check Sketch for Feature.

For feature usage, select the Basic Revolve option.

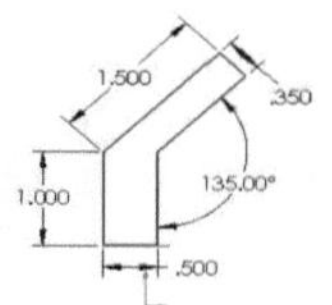

Multiple unconnected closed sections are displayed as the contour type.

Click Check.

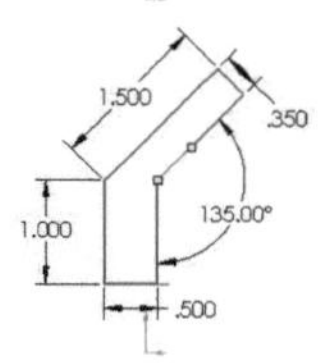

A diagnostic message appears, and the corresponding redandant edge is highlighted.
The sketch cannot be used for a feature because an endpoint is incorrectly shared by multiple elements. Delete the highlighted edge.
Click Check again.

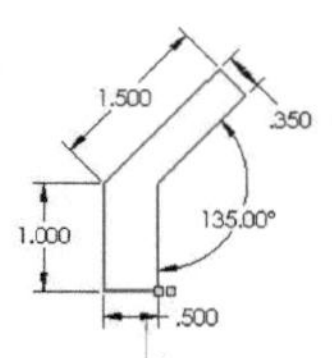

The same message appears, and another redandant edge is highlighted.
The sketch cannot be used for a feature because an endpoint is incorrectly shared by multiple elements. Delete the highlighted edge.
Click Inspect again. A new message indicates that the highlighted edge is not connected to the intersecting edges. The sketch has more than one open contour. Trim one end of the edge and extend it.

- **Freestanding geometry**

Dimensions or relationships to geometry, that no longer exists.

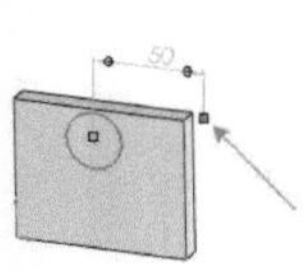

Freestanding dimensioning

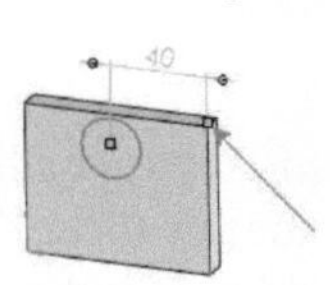

Possible solution: Dimensioning is repaired by dragging.

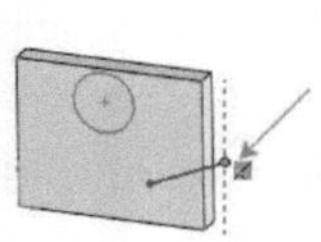

Freestanding relationship

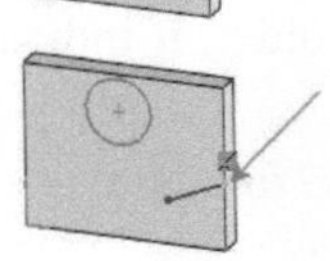

Possible solution: The relationship is repaired using the **Show/Delete** Relationships tool.

- **Wall defects**

Potential errors associated with wall operations.

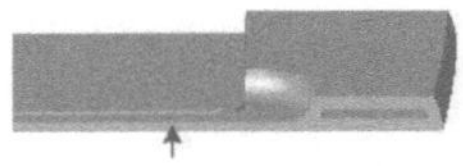

Surfaces extend into adjacent surfaces.
A wall cannot be created with a wall thickness of 1 mm. The model thickness at the indicated point is less than 1 mm. The inner surface penetrates the outer surface.

The wall thickness is greater than the minimum radius of curvature. The wall cannot be created because the wall thickness setting is greater than the minimum radius of curvature for the model.

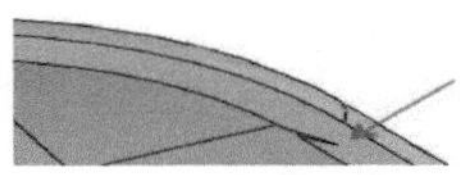

Some three-sided surfaces cannot be properly lined because there are problems with loosening walls at the corner point.

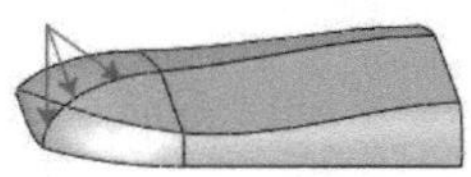

Walls can fail if extruded cuts using an existing model edge produce small areas along the resulting edge.

- **Geometry of thickness zero**

Solid edges, vertices, and tangential edges that result in a geometry with zero thickness.

Each edge of a solid body must have exactly two adjacent faces.

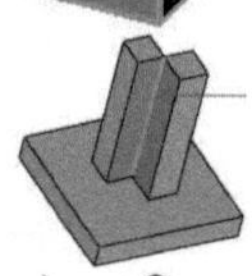

Corner points where geometry of thickness zero is located.

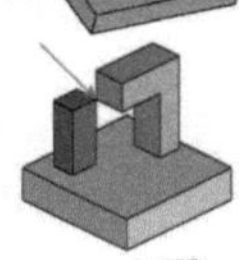

Corner points where geometry of thickness zero is located.

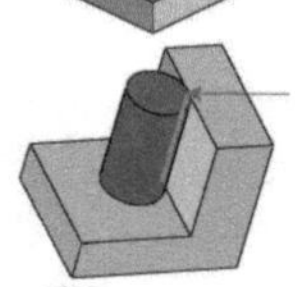

Tangential line with geometry of thickness zero.

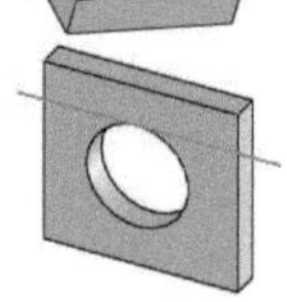

Zero-thickness geometry occurs when you attempt to extrude a section tangential to a hole.
This is a common cause of faulty section views in drawings.

- **Linking error**

Link displayed/ shown

Error messages, warnings, and error symbols related to assembly mates.
If it appears in the Mates folder, it means that at least one mate is not satisfied.
If it appears in the Mates folder, it indicates that all mates are satisfied, but at least one mate is overdefined.

In the following example, there is a concentric relationship between the right-hand holes of the two parts. If you attempt to add a second concentric relationship to the left-hand holes (shown in blue), the assembly becomes overdefined because the distance between the holes on one part is not identical to the distance between the corresponding holes on the other part.

Sometimes the geometry within or between components appears correct but is actually slightly incorrect.

For example, the following situations may occur:

- Two components appear parallel but diverge slightly.
- An imported block appears to have orthogonal faces, but the angle between the two faces is 90.1 degrees.
- Two components appear to be the same height but are slightly different.
- Screw holes in two components that are equidistant. However, one component uses roanded metric units, while the other uses roanded imperial units.

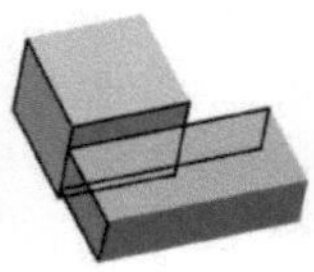

They align two blocks so that they are congruent on one side and one end, as shown in the illustration. Visually, the blocks appear to be orthogonal.

First, insert a link that matches the two pages.

Then add a coincident join between the ends.

Sometimes a link cannot be fulfilled because the components have constraints that make a link impossible. The components may be fixed or linked to other components.

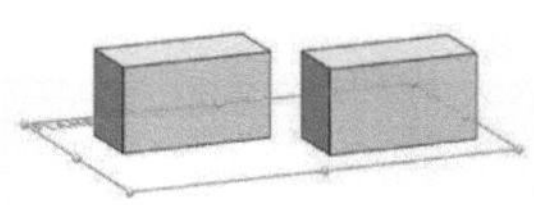

The lower surfaces of these two blocks are linked to the same plane.

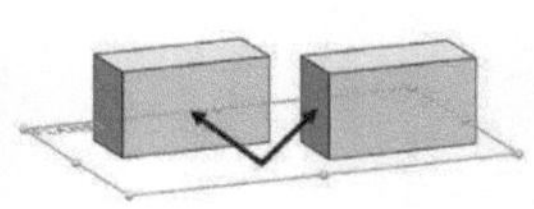

If you add a coincident link between the side of one block and the side of the other block.

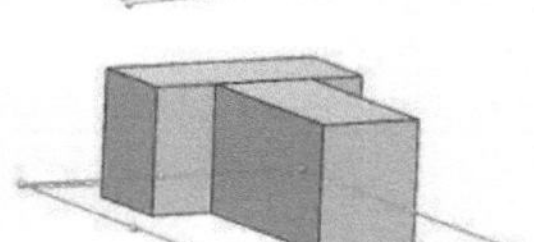

The blocks are moved into the link.

If you change the geometry of a component so that the link can no longer be satisfied, the links become unlinked.

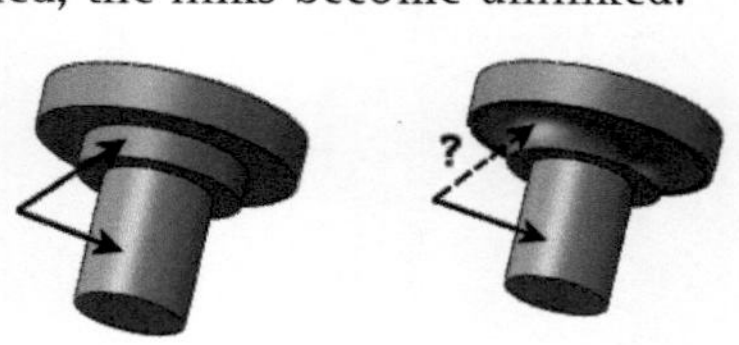

A concentric connection exists between the shaft and the smaller diameter on the cap. Later, you will add a fillet to the cap, which eliminates the smaller cylindrical surface. The concentric connection with this surface can no longer be satisfied.

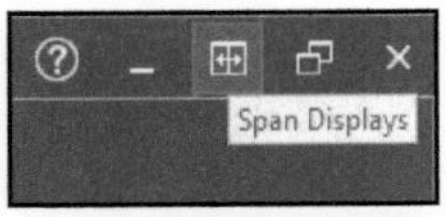

2.2.11 SOLIDWORKS main window

You can automatically position and resize the SOLIDWORKS main window to span two displays. You can also position and resize two document windows to span one or two displays.

If you have multiple displays, you can use displays to span two displays without having to manually resize the SOLIDWORKS window.

When two displays are configured side by side, the "Displays Across" function spans the two displays using the height of the display with the smallest vertical resolution, as shown in the figure.

When two displays are configured one above the other, the "Displays Spanned" function spans both displays using the width of the display with the smallest horizontal resolution, as shown in the illustration. With more than two displays, "Displays Spanned" only spans two of them, using the following priority order to determine which additional display is spanned: Right, Left, Bottom, Top.

2.2.11.1 Split document window

Tile Left

Tile Right

You can split a document window to occupy half of a display or all of the available space on one of two displays. You can also resize the SOLIDWORKS window to fill a single display or to create two displays simultaneously while splitting a document window.

This function is useful when arranging two document windows to make optimal use of the available display space. For example, you can split one document window containing an assembly on one display and another containing a part of that assembly on the other display. This also allows you to arrange two document windows even when more than two document windows are open.

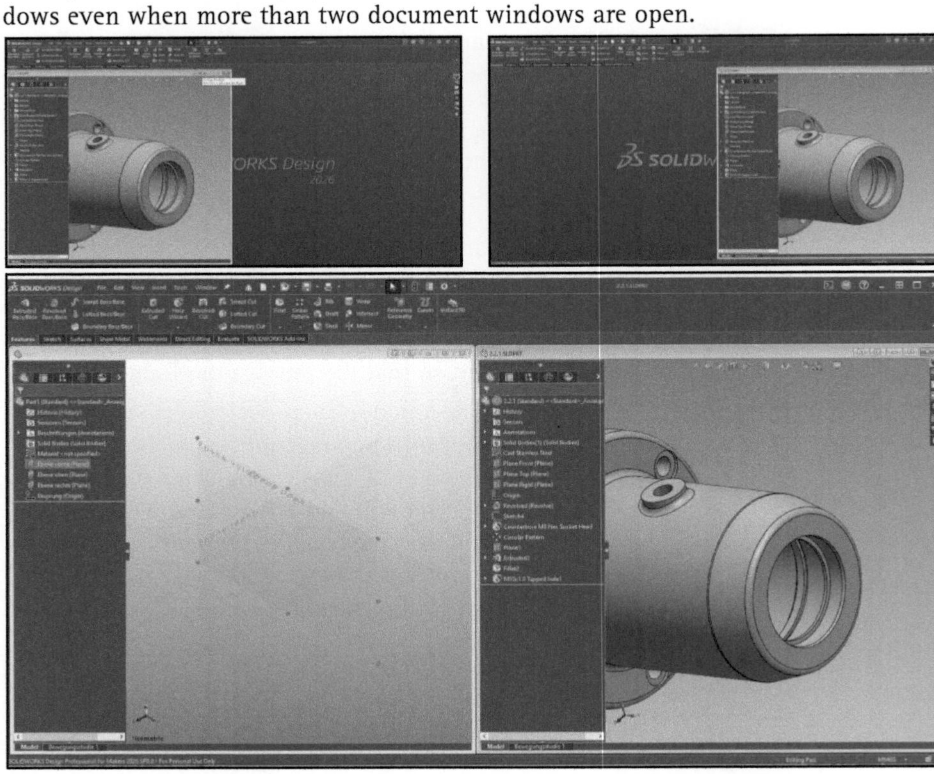

2.3 Creating a new template file for components

2.3.1 SOLIDWORKS Design 2026, program startup

Start SOLIDWORKS Design 2026 by double-clicking the desktop icon. Alternatively, you can start it using the Windows Start icon in the lower left corner of the screen.

Start / Programme / SOLIDWORKS 2026 / SOLIDWORKS Design 2026

2.3.2 Opening the SOLIDWORKS template file for parts

Neu

Teil.prtdot

- Menu Bar **New** (1) /  /  click **Part** (2) / **OK** (3, 4)

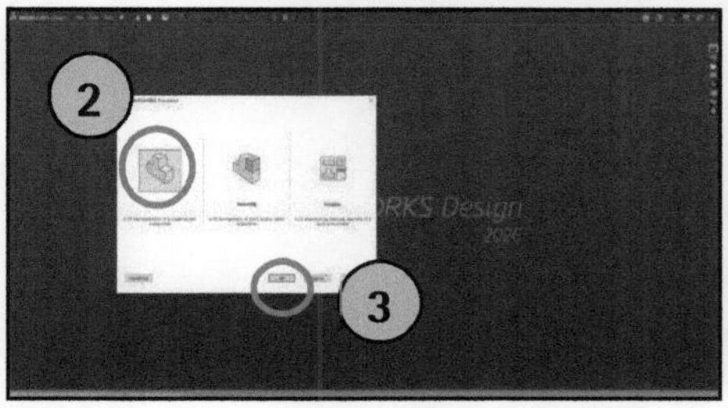

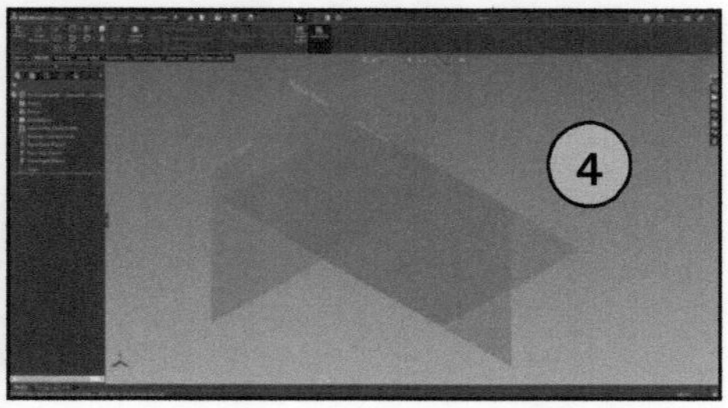

2.3.3 Customizing the CommandManager

2.3.3.1 Adjusting the Button Size, Command Bar

Options

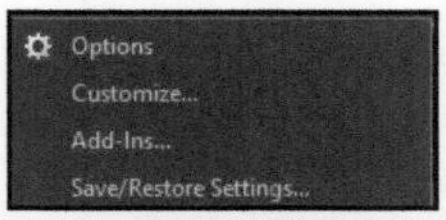

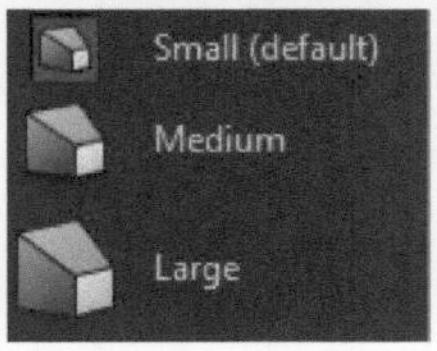

In the Options flyout (5), you can set the Button Size to small, medium, or large. You can select the larger size if you are running the SOLIDWORKS software on a computer with a high-resolution display or to make it easier to select tools when using a touch interface.

- Button Size **Small** (default):

- Button Size **Medium:**

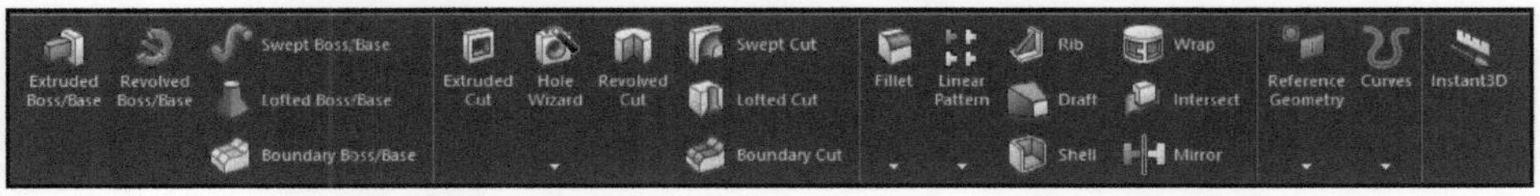

- Button Size **Large:**

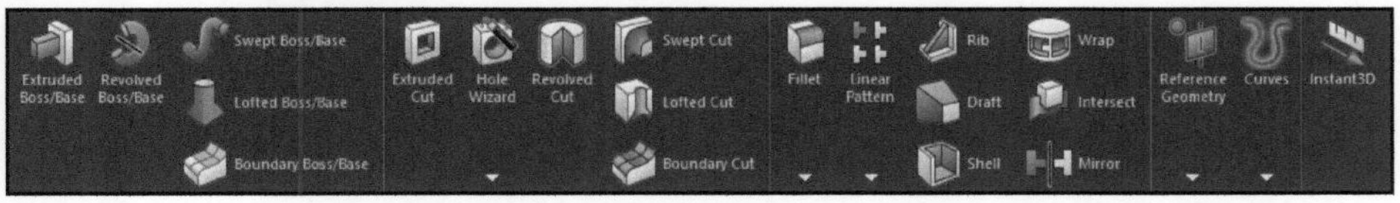

Optionen

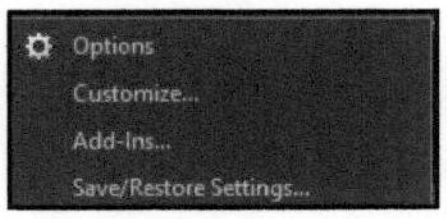

2.3.3.2 Setting the Button Size using Options/Customize

- In the Options flyout, you can choose **Customize**.
- On the Toolbars tab, you can optionally activate:

  Icon Size **small** (6)
  Enable CommandManager (7),
  Use large buttons with text (7).

  Show tooltips:
  Large tooltips with images (8).

  Context toolbar:
  Show on selection, show quick configurations, show in shortcut menu (8).

  Quick Access Tools:
  Show in the Menu Bar (10).

  Lock CommandManager and toolbars (11).

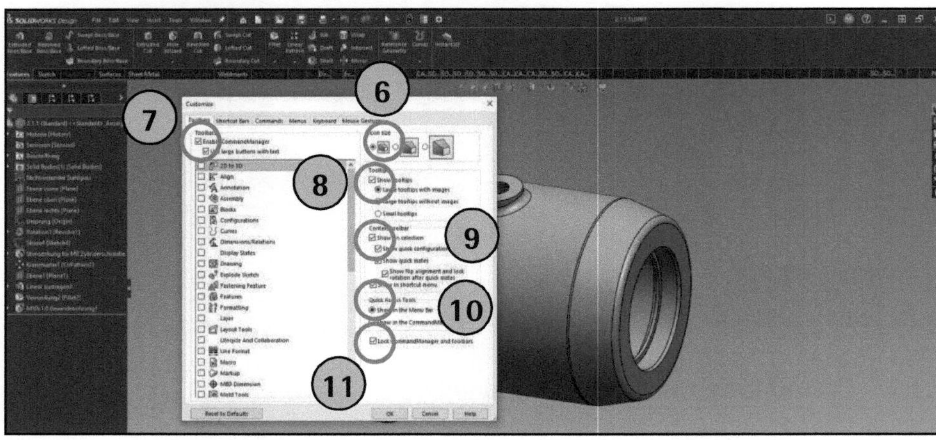

2.3.4 Adjusting the graphics area

2.3.4.1 Color assignment of the graphics area, suggestion

Options

Options / Register **System Options / Colors**
Backgroand **Dark**, Current color scheme **Default OK** (11)

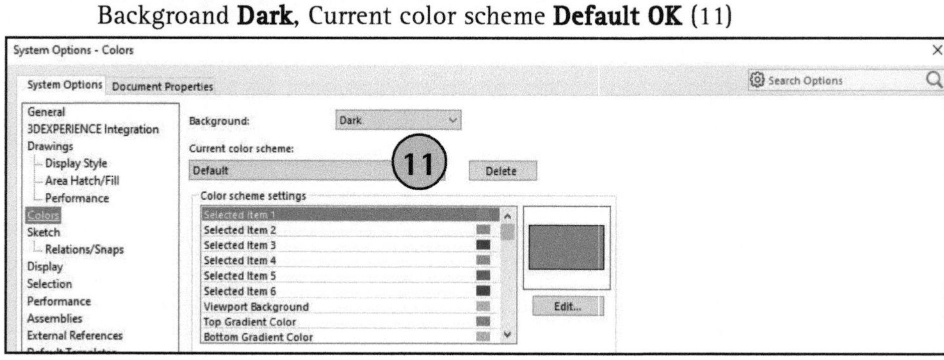

2.3.4.2 Activating the work planes

For constructing the first learning units, it is advisable to set an isometric view of the graphics area with the principal planes enabled.
In the FeatureManager (12), click on the following in sequence:

Plane **Top**, Plane **Front**, Plane **Right**

In the flyout that appears, select the **Show** option in each case.

Show

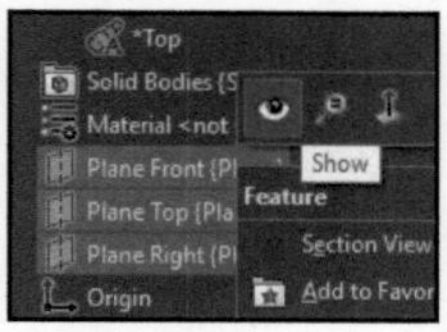

2.3.4.3 Switching on the isometric view

Flyout **View Orientation** (Heads-up View Toolbar)

Select **Isometric** view (12).

Flyout View Orientation

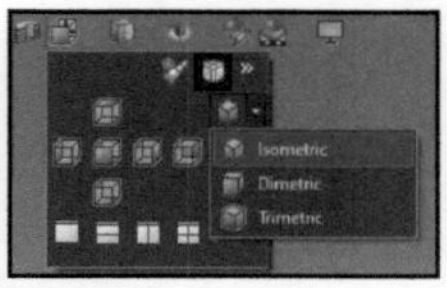

Isometric

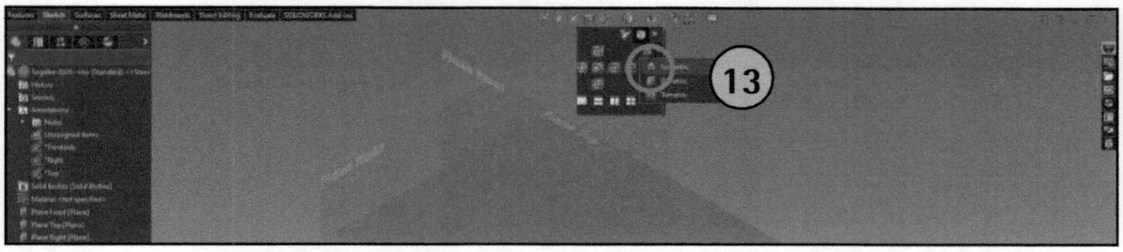

2.3.4.4 Assigning a backgroand display

Do a Right-click in the graphics area.
Select **Edit Scene** from the context menu (14).
Click on the **Basic** tab.
In the **Backgroand** option, select **Gradient**. (15).
Choose the colors according to the illustrations shown (16, 17).

Edit Scene

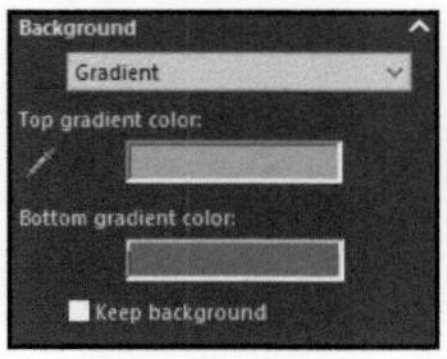

Close dialog box (18)

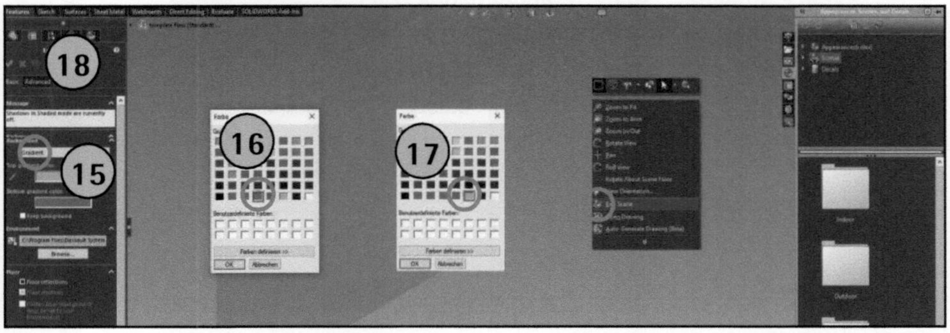

2.3.4.5 "View Orientation" in component Mode

The view preferences are suggestions; they can be changed during part and assembly generation.

View Orientation

Shaded with Edges

View Orientation (Heads-up View Toolbar)

View Orientation option **Shaded with Edges** (19).

2.3.5 Adjusting system properties, suggestions

Options

Adapt the template file according to its intended use. The settings shown are for the following learning units; different tasks will require changes to the template file. The various settings can be saved in template files if needed. The settings can be accessed in several ways:

- Using the **Menu bar** (20).

- Using the **SOLIDWORKS menus** (21).

2.3.5.1 Inherited default settings

No changes are made to the unmentioned registers for the initial setup, but this can be changed if necessary.

2.3.5.2 Setting System options "Sketch" "Relation / Snap"

Options

Options / System options / Sketch (22)
Select Register **Relation / Snap** (23)
Enable snapping, Snap to model geometry
Sketch snap, Selection of all snap elements
Grid, Snap only when grid is displayed / OK

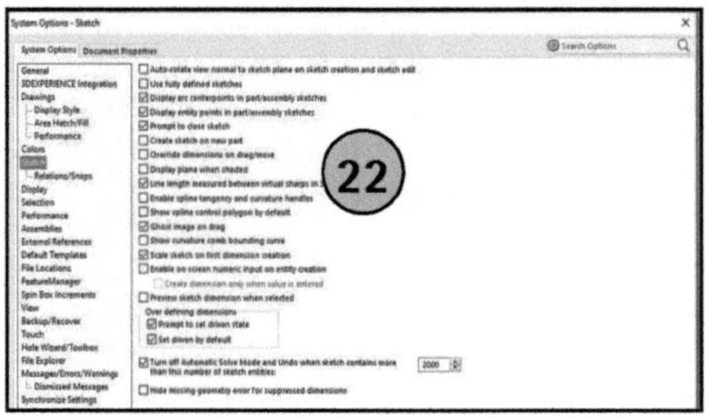

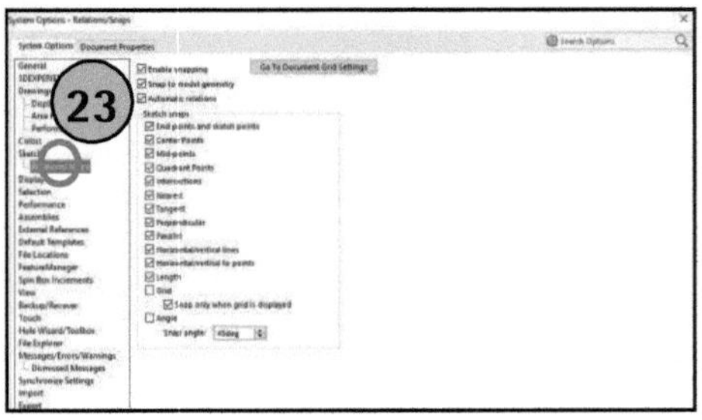

2.3.5.3 Setting the options from the "General" tab

Options / System options / General (24).
No changes are made to the unmentioned registers for the initial setup, but this can be changed if necessary (25).

Options

2.3.5.4 Setting the options from the "Performance" tab

Options / System options / Performance (26)
High quality (27) / Mate animation speed **Schnell** (28)

Options

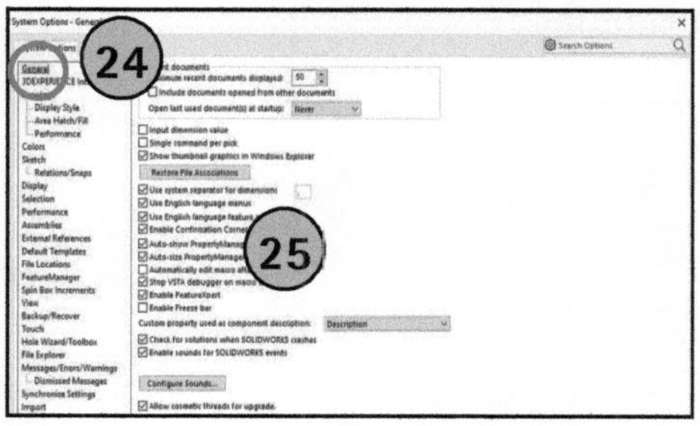

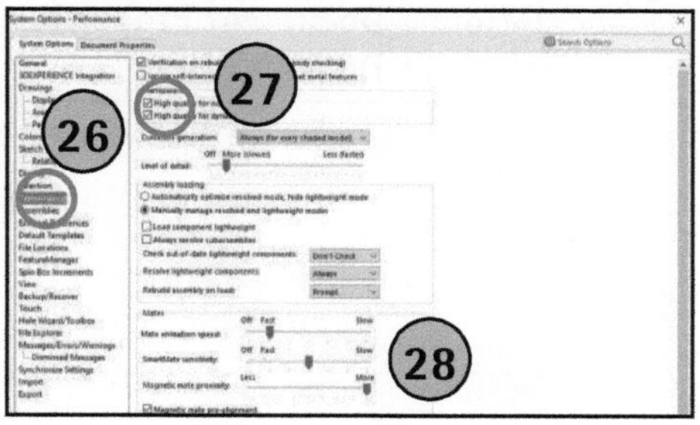

2.3.5.5 Setting the options from the "FeatureManager" tab

Options / System options / FeatureManager (29)
No changes are made to the unmentioned registers for the initial setup, but this can be changed if necessary.

2.3.5.6 Setting the options from the "Default Templates" tab

Options / System options / Default Templates (30)
No changes are made to the unmentioned registers for the initial setup, but this can be changed if necessary.

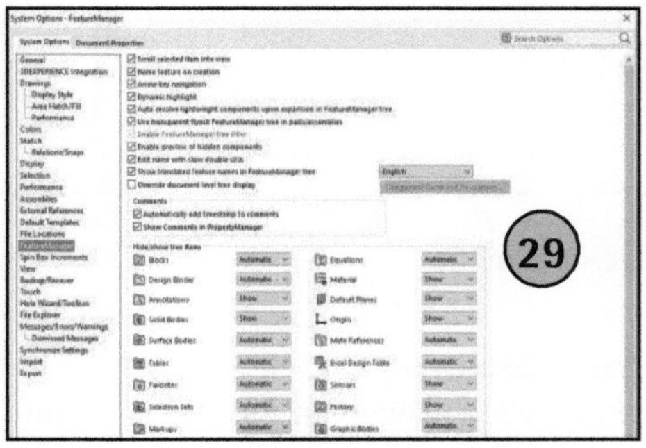

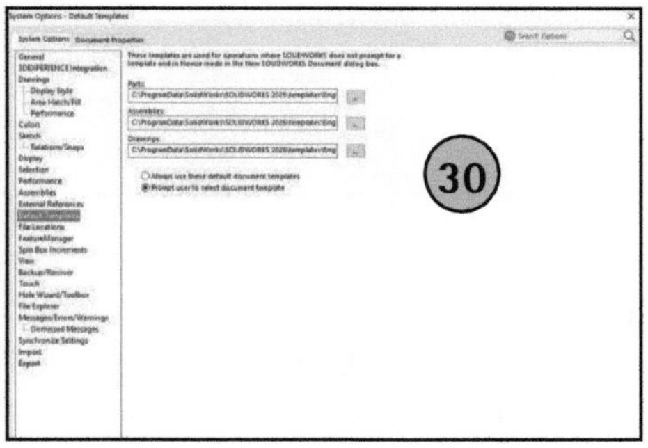

Options

2.3.6 Adjusting document properties, suggestions

2.3.6.1 Setting the "Image Quality" for the active document

Options / Document Properties / Image Quality
Set the settings shown, taking into account the performance reserves of the system unit (31).

2.3.6.2 Setting the "Detailing" for the active document

Options / Document Properties / Detailling
Select the **Display filters** (32).

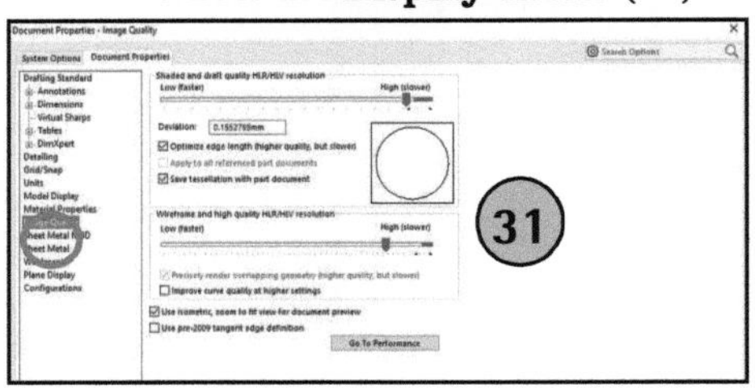

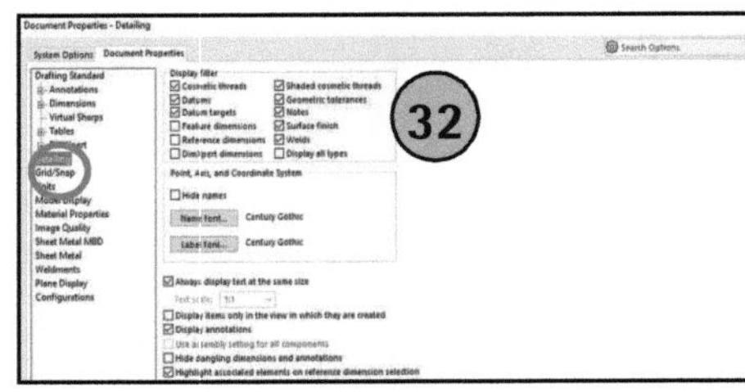

2.3.6.3 Setting "Units" for the active document

Options / Document Properties / Units
For the projects, set the following value types to
Unit system: **mm, gram, second,** (33)
no Decimals for **Angle** and **Time, one Decimal** for **Length** (34).

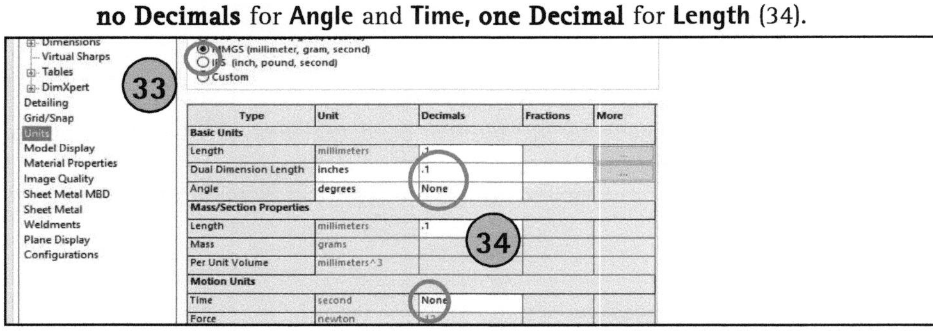

2.3.6.4 Setting "Plane Display" for the active document

Options / Document Properties / Plane Display
No changes are made to the unmentioned registers for the initial setup, but this can be changed if necessary.

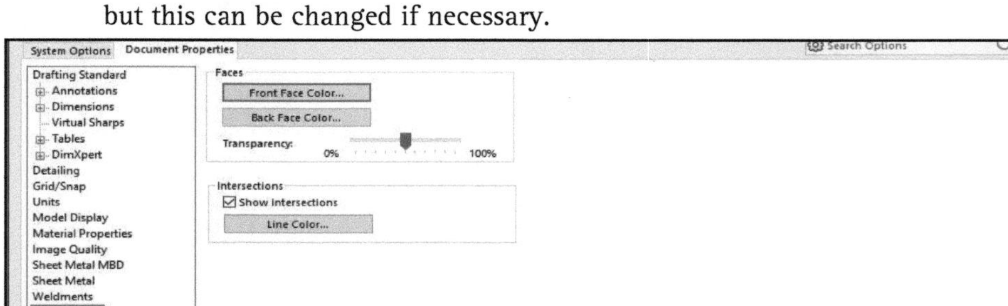

2.3.7 Data backup of the customized template file

You can save a template after modifying its details.

Only options on the **Document Properties** tab are saved in a document template.

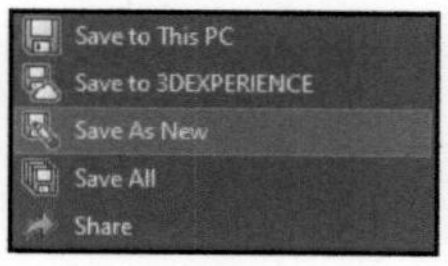

- Click **File / Save to This PC** (35).
- Select the template type for **Save as type**:
  Part Templates (*.prtdot) (36)
  The destination path automatically changes to the default template folder when you select a template type for **Save as type**.
- Type a name for **File name**.
- Click **Save**.

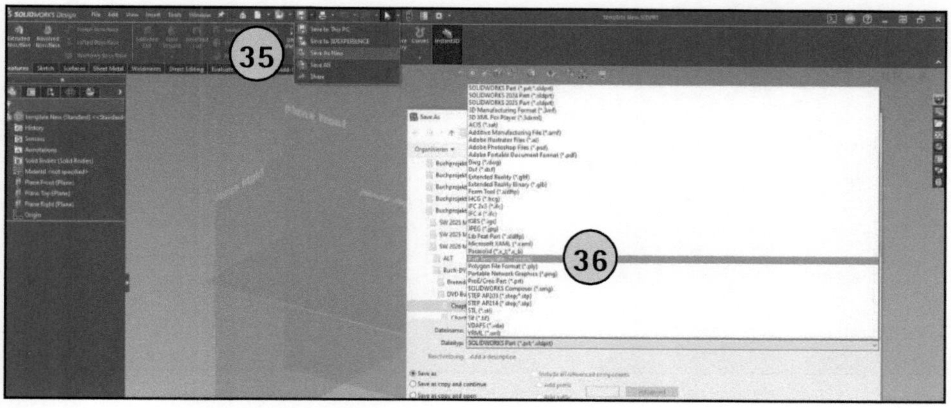

2.3.8 Assistant for Copying User Settings, Basics

The User Settings Copy Wizard allows you to save, restore, and distribute system settings to users, computers, or profiles.

When you select options for SOLIDWORKS software, these settings are saved in a registry file, and the software recognizes the settings from one SOLIDWORKS version to the next.

Most users don't need to do anything to maintain their settings. You can save or restore system settings for:

System options, all toolbars, keyboard shortcuts, mouse gestures,
Menu customization, and saved views.

When you select Restore Settings, the Copy Settings Wizard runs in a special mode where the SOLIDWORKS software continues to run while you save or restore the current user settings.

The settings files have a default extension of **.sldreg**. Double-clicking a file with this extension will display the wizard for copying user settings.

2.3.8.1 Saving system settings

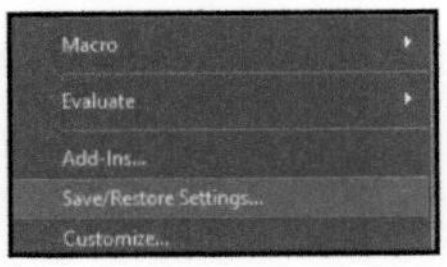

- Select the option **Save/Restore Settings** (2) using Command Tabs **Tools** (1) and click **Next**.
- Select a file name, file path and setting types (3).
- Click **Finish**.
  The assistant confirms that the settings have been written to the specified file.
- Click **OK**.

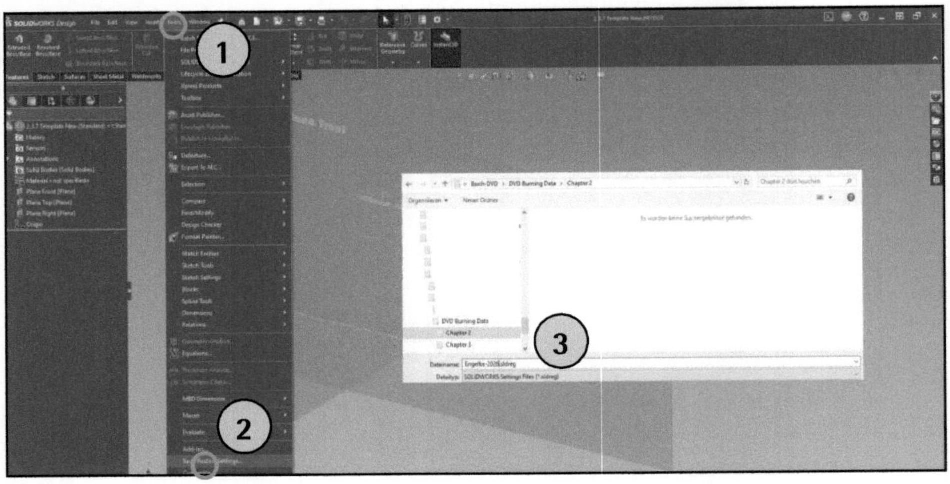

2.4 Mouse Functions

2.4.1 Mouse with three buttons

Use the middle mouse button for the following view commands:

Rotate view: (parts and assemblies only)	**Rotate model view**: Drag with the middle mouse button. Rotate aroand a vertex, edge, or face: Click with the middle mouse button on a vertex, edge, or face; then drag the cursor with the middle mouse button.
Move:	Hold down the **Ctrl** key and drag with the middle mouse button. You don't need to hold down the **Ctrl** key in an active drawing.
Zoom in / Zoom out:	Hold down the **Shift** key and drag with the middle mouse button.

2.4.2 Mouse with wheel

Use the wheel for the following view commands:

Rotate view: (parts and assemblies only)	**Rotate model view**: Hold down the wheel and move it to rotate. Rotate aroand a vertex, edge, or face: Click and hold the wheel on a vertex, edge, or face; then hold the wheel and drag.
Zoom in / Zoom out:	**Zoom to cursor position**: Scroll the wheel forward and backward. When scrolling the mouse wheel, the cursor must always be within the area you want to zoom to. If the cursor is outside the graphics area, the zoom will instead be to the center of the model. **Zoom to the center of the screen**: Click on: **View / Modify /** **Zoom to center of screen** Turn the wheel forwards and backwards.

2.4.3 SOLIDWORKS users and 3Dconnexion 3D Mouse

A groandbreaking navigation concept and sophisticated functionality: 3Dconnexion® 3D mice redefine the standards of 3D navigation. Using patented sensor technology, models or camera views can be rotated, panned, or zoomed simultaneously in a fluid motion with an incredible six degrees of freedom, intuitive, efficient, and with the highest precision.

Together with a conventional mouse, the 3D mouse enables a two-handed and synchronous workflow. One hand operates the 3D mouse to position a model or move aroand in virtual environments, while the other hand handles selection and editing on the mouse. This two-handed workflow saves clicks and time.

2.4.3.1 Access to all SOLIDWORKS functions at the touch of a button

By combining SOLIDWORKS with one of our 3D mice, you can optimize your entire workflow. From concept and sketch to part, assembly, and drawing, you'll be faster in all modes. A 3Dconnexion 3D mouse eliminates many mouse clicks compared to a conventional mouse.

3Dconnexion-CADMouse

Assign functions or keyboard commands to programmable shortcut keys. Create function sets for different document types, such as part assemblies or drawings. The commands are updated on the SpacePilot's LCD as soon as you switch document types.

2.4.3.2 Part Modeling Mode

View a model from different angles using the 3D mouse, and simultaneously make adjustments with the regular mouse. Benefit from easy access to functions such as toggle, Ctrl, Esc, zoom adjustment, top/front/left/right view, chamfer, and fillet.

3Dconnexion SpaceNavigator

2.4.3.3 Assembly mode

Create assemblies faster. Insert components while positioning the entire assembly at the best angle. Move existing components as needed. Find the optimal viewing angle to select component contact surfaces. Access functions like insert, join, or move components, exploded view, Ctrl, and Esc via the hotkeys.

3Dconnexion SpacePilot

2.4.3.4 Drawing Mode

Position the entire drawing sheet while creating and placing drawing views, dimensions, and annotations. The Quickly access zoom adjustment, measurement functions, center point markers, and all other drawing mode features.

2.4.3.5 Access to special additional functions

Zoom in on the cursor (quick zoom) by holding down the middle mouse button and simultaneously pressing the navigation cap. Set the center of rotation by selecting any face or vertex, or the axis of rotation by selecting a line or edge.

2.4.4 Mouse Gestures

You can use a mouse gesture, similar to a keyboard shortcut, as a shortcut to execute a command or macro. You can use mouse gestures by right-clicking and dragging the mouse pointer into the graphics area to access a pre-assigned tool or macro from a drawing, part, assembly, or sketch.

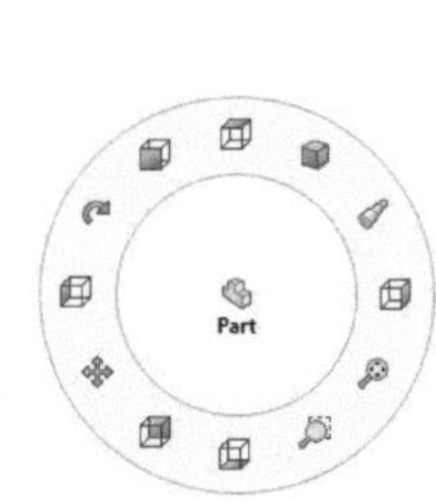

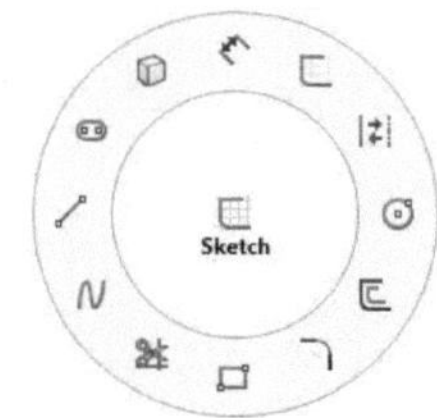

You can enable or disable mouse gestures and set the number of gestures shown in the mouse gesture guide to 2, 3, 4, 8 or 12.

If you set the number to 2 gestures, you can align them vertically or horizontally. By default, mouse gestures are enabled, and four gestures are displayed in the mouse gesture guide. To enable or disable mouse gestures while a document is open, click **Tools** > **Customize**. On the Mouse Gestures tab, select or clear the Enable Mouse Gestures option.

To specify the number of mouse gestures in the mouse gesture guide, in an open document, click **Tools** > **Customize**. On the Mouse Gestures tab, select the number of mouse gestures. You can also customize the mouse gesture assignments using a visual drag-and-drop interface. Drag tools from the list of commands onto any mouse gesture guide (1, 2).

2.4.4.1 Using Mouse Gestures

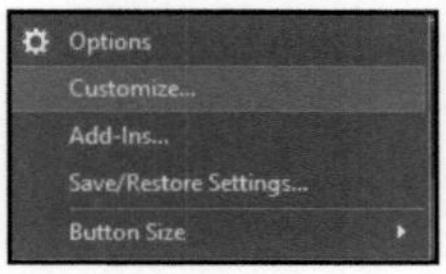

Make Right-click in the graphics area and drag in the direction corresponding to the tool or macro. The mouse gesture guide will appear, highlighting the icon for the tool or macro assigned to your mouse gesture direction. For example, in an open window, right-click and drag towards the lower right corner to the highlighted tool.

To use mouse gestures with assemblies, right-click and drag the mouse away from components in the graphics area to avoid component rotation, or press **Alt +**, right-click and drag (3).

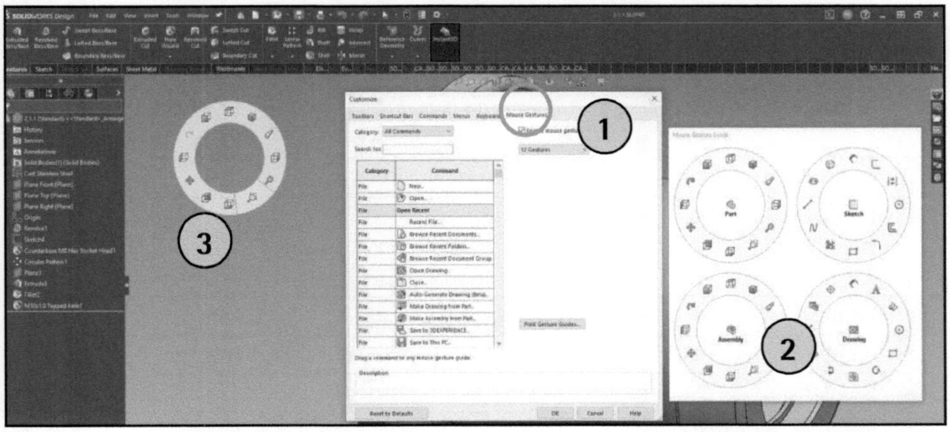

2.5 Command input using the keyboard

SOLIDWORKS offers many ways to customize the user interface and access various commands. Mouse gestures and the shortcut bar are shown. Even before these features were added to SOLIDWORKS, it was possible to use keyboard shortcuts, and this functionality is still available. In fact, SOLIDWORKS 2026 boasts an incredible 803 commands.

Keyboard shortcuts can be created using the command tab **Tools/Customize**.

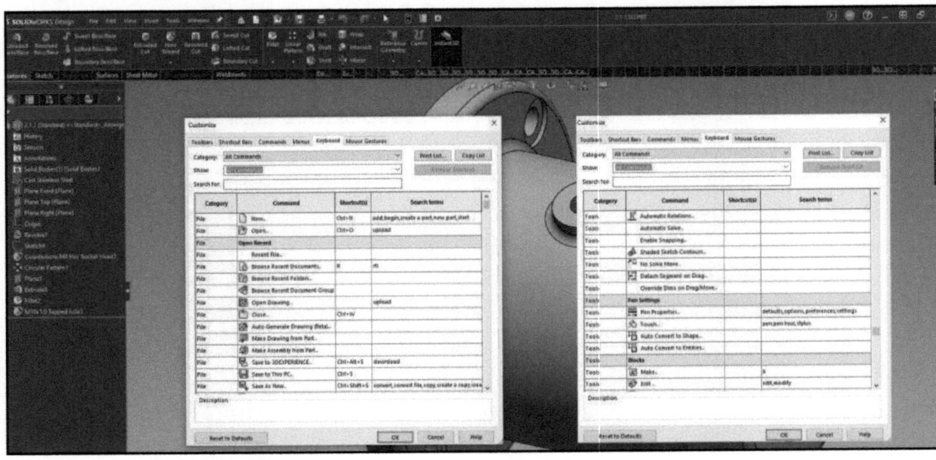

2.5.1 Command shortcuts, excerpt

New	Ctrl+N	Open	Ctrl+O	Close	Ctrl+W
Save	Ctrl+S	Print	Ctrl+P		
Ando	Ctrl+Z	Redo	Ctrl+Y	Repeat Commant	Enter
Cut	Ctrl+X	Copy	Ctrl+C	Paste	Ctrl+V
Delete	Entf	Rebuild	Ctrl+B	redraw	Ctrl+R
Orientation	Leer-taste	Zoom to Fit	F	Previous View	Ctrl +Shift+Z
Quick Snap	F3	Full Screen	F11		
FeatureManager Tree Area	F9	Toolbars	F10		
Front	Ctrl+1	Back	Ctrl+2	Left	Ctrl+3
Right	Ctrl+4	Top	Ctrl+5	Bottom	Ctrl+6
Isometric	Ctrl+7	Normal To	Ctrl+8		
Find/ Replace	Ctrl+F	Magnified Selection	G	Spell Checker	F7

2.6 Instant3D Features, excerpt

Instant3D allows you to quickly create and modify model geometry using handles and rulers. **Instant3D** is supported in parts and assemblies.

2.6.1 Overview of Instant3D Functionality

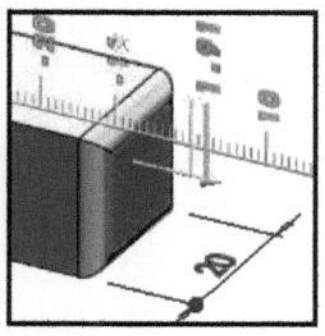

Drag geometry and dimension manipulators to adjust the size of features. You can also drag dimension handles to resize features.

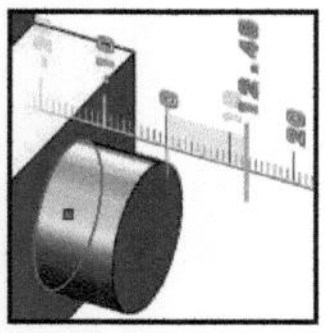

In assemblies, you can edit components within the assembly or sketches at the assembly level, assembly features, and mate dimensions. Use on-screen rulers to accurately measure modifications.

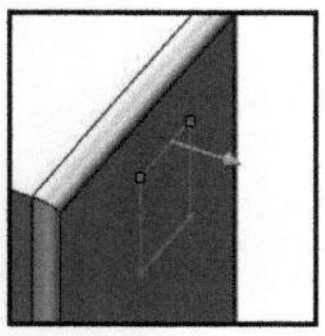

Create linearly extruded attachments and cuts based on selected contours or sketches.

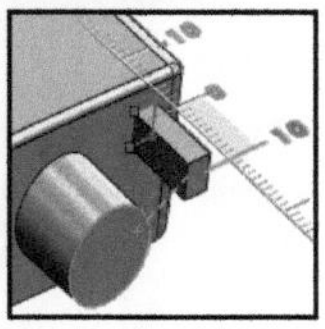

Capture geometry with handles.

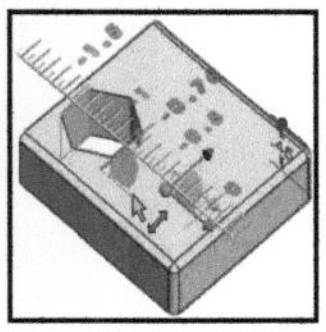

Edit internal sketch contours.

2.6.2 Modifying Features in Instant3D

Drag the dimension or arrow to offset or move surfaces.

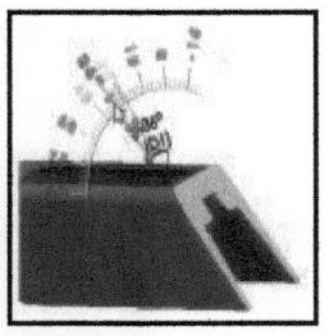

Drag the angular dimension to rotate surfaces.

Use the center point of the triad to drag or copy the entire feature to other faces. Hold down the **Ctrl** key while dragging to copy the feature.

2.6.3 Instant3D Rulers

Use on-screen rulers to precisely measure modifications.

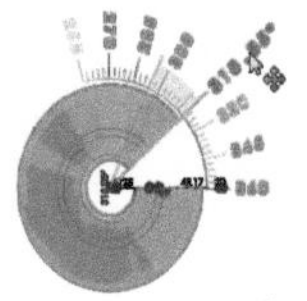

An angular ruler appears for revolves, drafts, and when you use the triad rings to rotate Live Section Planes

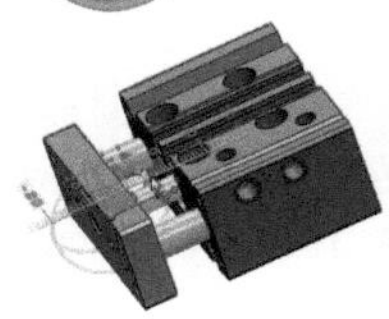

In assemblies, when you click Move with Triad from the shortcut menu, rulers appear with the triad so you can move components to a defined location.

2.6.4 Instant3D Live Section Planes

Select a planar face or a plane, right-click and select Live Section Plane.

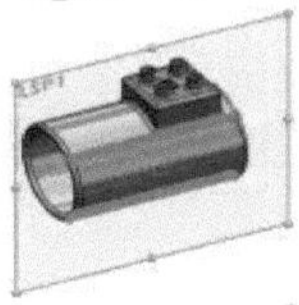

The plane size is based on the selected face. You can resize the plane by dragging its handles. The Live Section Planes folder, which stores all Live Section Planes, appears in the FeatureManager design tree.

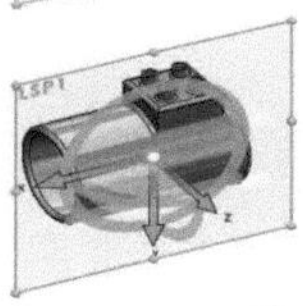

Right-click the plane's border again and select Show Triad.

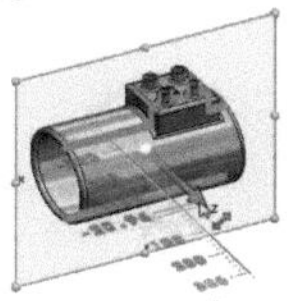

Drag the triad handle to dynamically section the model. The ruler appears for precise measurements.

You can use the triad rings to rotate the Live Section Plane to section the model from different angles. A protractor lets you set precise angles.

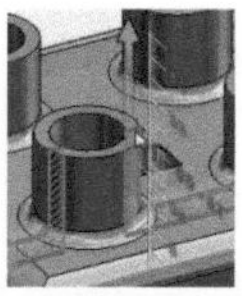

At any point, you can stop dragging the Live Section Plane, select a section contour to display a ruler, then modify that entity's model geometry

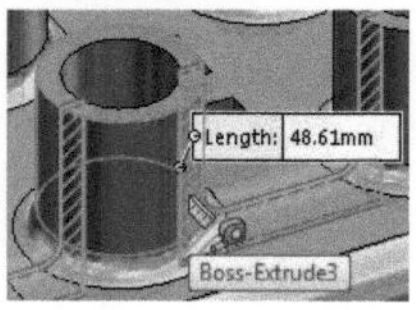

To measure entities, click Tools > Evaluate > Measure and select the entity

3

Dassault Systèmes

3DEXPERIENCE©

SOLIDWORKS Design

2026

Parts and Components

Create and Customize

Views and Settings

Rules for written execution in the book, how do I use the book

3 Views and Settings **6 Powerful commands, optimized constructions**	The chapter's main heading clearly state its content, examples.
Line (Sketch tab) **Edit Material (FeatureManager)**	Representation of a Solid Edge command in the subchapter heading, examples.
Menu Bar **New** / / click **Engelke2026.PRTDOT** **Revolved** (**Features** tab) **Hole Wizard** (**Features** tab) **Extrude** (**Features** tab) **Stud Wizard** (**Features** tab)	Command call using the display and position definition of the Solid Edge icon, examples.
Draft (**Features** tab) Set the **draft angle** to **10°** **Shell** (**Features** tab) Set the **Thickness** to **5** mm Option **Faces to Remove**	Representation of the Solid Edge command within a command call, examples.
Hole Wizard (**Features** tab) Click the **Type** tab. **DIN**, **Counterbore**, **M5**, depth: **Through all**. **Hex Socket Head Cap EN ISO 4672** Countersink-Ø **10** mm, **5.4** mm deep, through hole Ø **5.5** mm.	Display of the Solid Edge command **drill-hole** within a command call, examples.
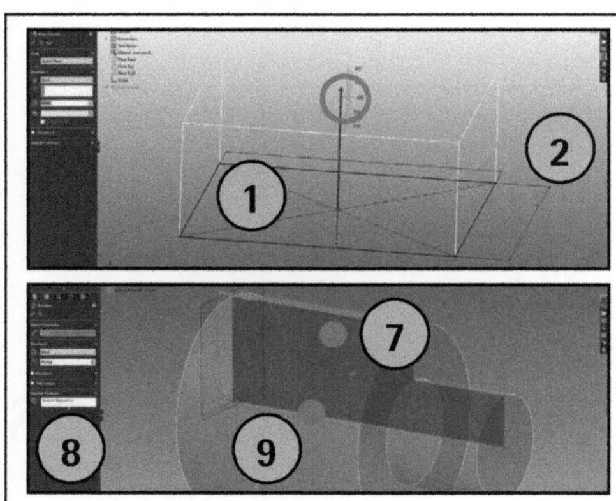	Sequence of individual steps in a complex command sequence, example.

3 Views and Settings

3.1 SOLIDWORKS Design 2026©
controls, functions, and customization

3.1.1 Starting SOLIDWORKS Design 2026,
Open the working file,
select the component from the book's DVD

- Launch the installed version of SOLIDWORKS Design2026 by double-clicking the desktop icon or by clicking the Windows start icon in the lower left corner of the screen.
- Open the component file provided on the DVD.
- To browse to a document to open, click the **Open** command.

Open (Menu bar) (1) / Component from the book-DVD / **OK** (2, 3)

Open

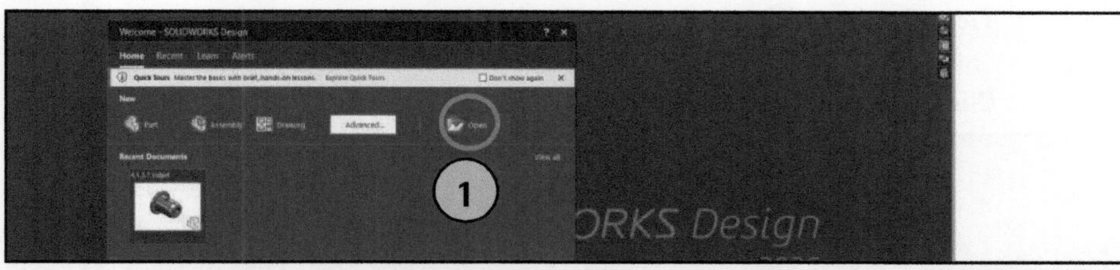

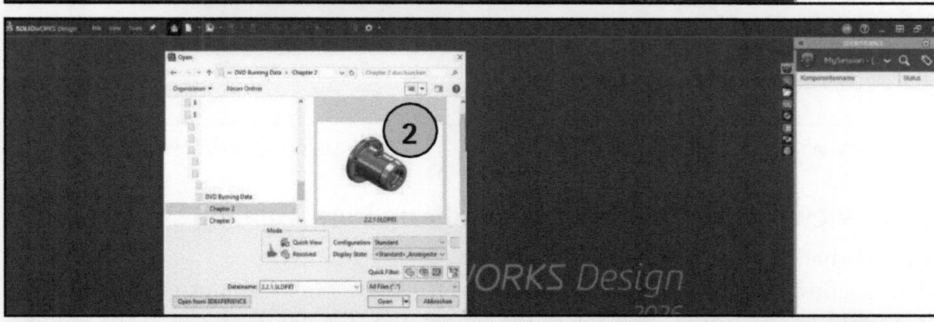

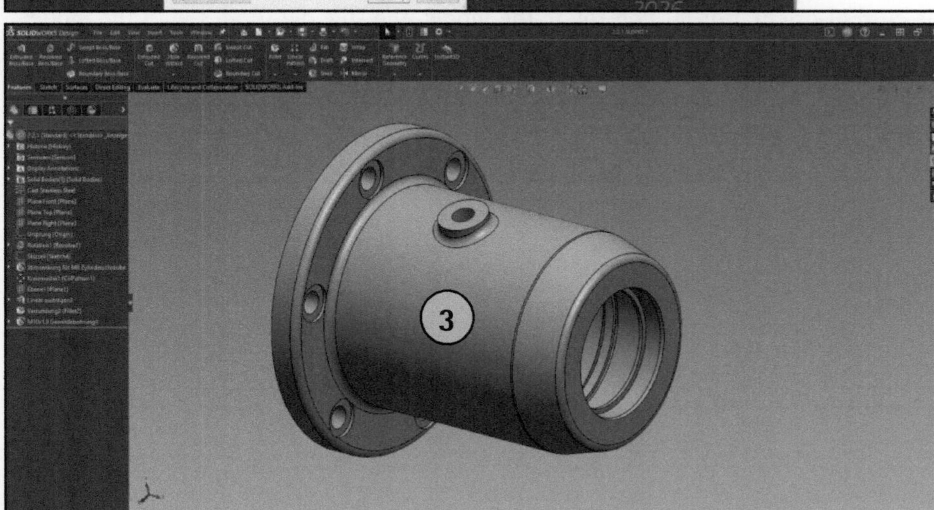

3.1.2 Heads-up View Toolbar

A transparent toolbar in each individual viewport provides all the usual tools for view editing.

3.1.3 RealViewGraphics, Heads-up View Toolbar

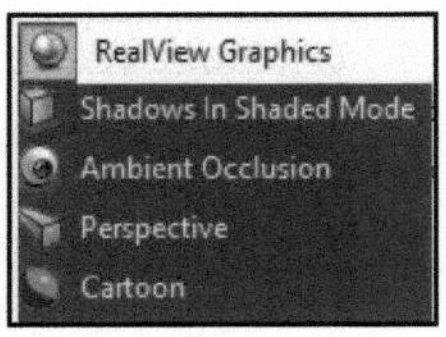

RealView-Graphics

When applying an appearance, use **RealViewGraphics** for a more realistic model display. **RealViewGraphics** is only available with supported graphics cards.
The **RealViewGraphics** setting is therefore dynamically adjusted based on the corresponding hardware.
Rendered views retain their appearance during movement; this setting also displays **Scene**, **Environmental reflections**, and **Self-shadowing** from the first directional light.

- Click on one of the following options:

View Settings (Heads-up View Toolbar)

Click on **RealView Graphics** button.

Display without **RealViewGraphics**

Display using **RealViewGraphics**

3.1.4 View Setting "Shadows", Heads-up View Toolbar

Shadows in Shaded Mode

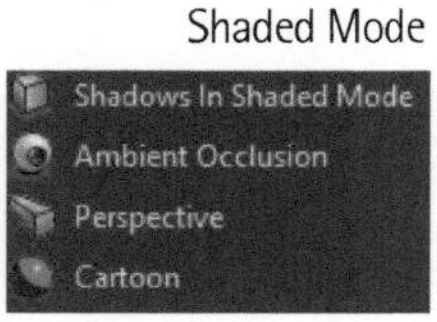

Displays shadows under the model.
When shadows are displayed, the light falls from the highest point of the model in the current orientation. If you rotate the model, the shadow rotates with the model.

View Settings (Heads-up View Toolbar)

Click on **Shadows in Shaded mode**

3.1.4.1 View mode "Shadow", settings using "Edit Scene"

To display different floor views, select from the context menu, right-click on the work plane:

Edit Scene (Context menu) (1)
Activate the **Floor** entry (2), the **Floor reflections** option and **Floor shadows** (3) as needed.

Finish with **OK** symbol (4).

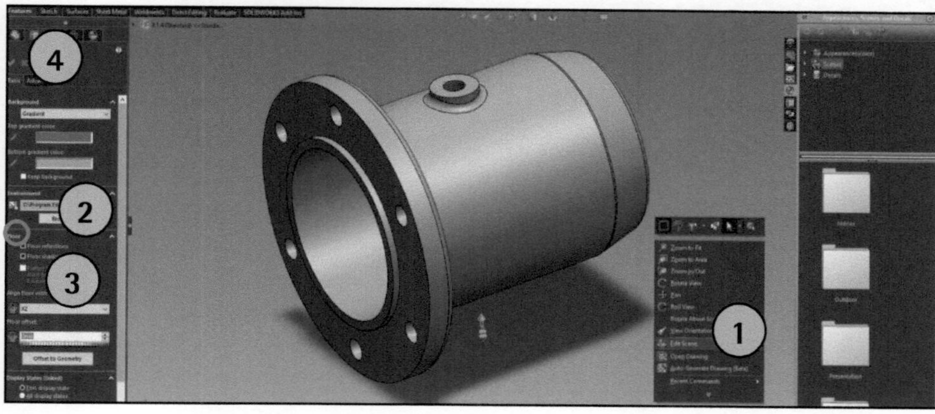

Edit Scene

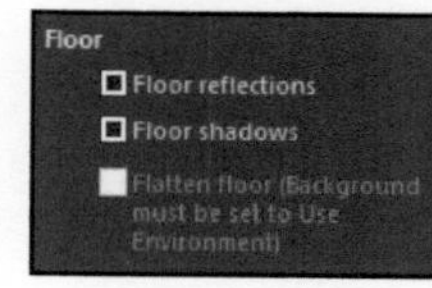

OK-symbol

3.1.5 View Setting "Perspective", Heads-up View Toolbar

The **Perspective** view mode displays a perspective view of the model. A perspective view is the natural view to the eye. Parallel lines converge at a vanishing point in the distance.

You can create a named view in a drawing from a perspective view of a model.

View Settings (Heads-up View Toolbar)

Click on **Perspective** button.

Perspective

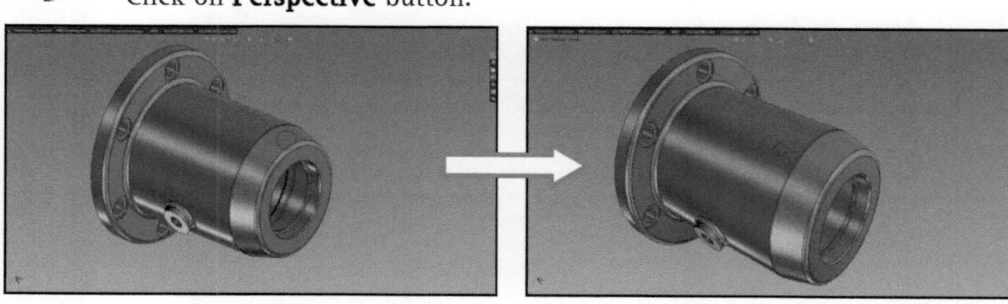

3.1.5.1 Changing the Perspective

Perspective

Perspective relates to the size of the object being viewed and its distance from the viewer. You can modify the perspective by defining object sizes and distances.

The smaller the value is, the greater the perspective distortion.

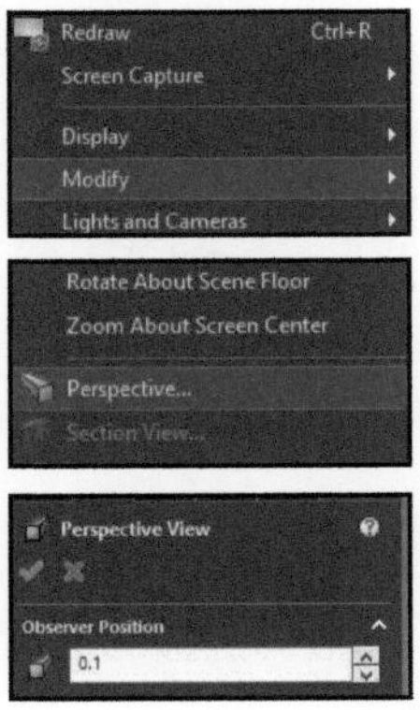

Select Command bar **View / Modify / Perspective** (1).
Enter the value **0.1** (no comma) (2).

Finish with **OK** symbol (3).

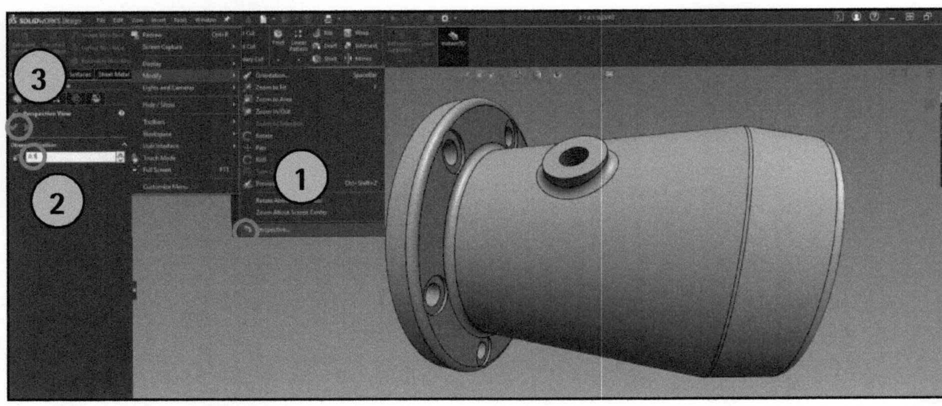

3.1.5.2 Resetting the Perspective

View Settings (Heads-up View Toolbar)

Previous View

Previous View

3.1.6 View size changes

3.1.6.1 Zoom to Area

Enlarge the section, which you select, by dragging a frame.

Zoom to Area

Zoom to Area (Heads-up View Toolbar)

Click and drag a diagonal rectangle around the area you want to enlarge (4, 5).
Release the mouse button; the selected area will be enlarged (6).

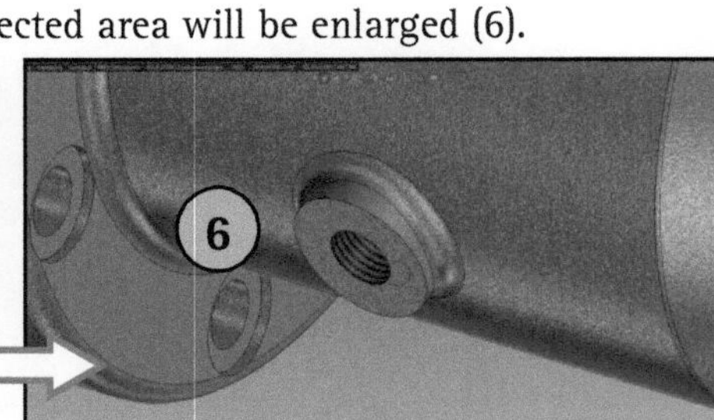

3.1.6.2 Zoom to Fit

This command allows you to display the entire model again.

Zoom to Fit (Heads-up View Toolbar) (7, 8)

Zoom to Fit

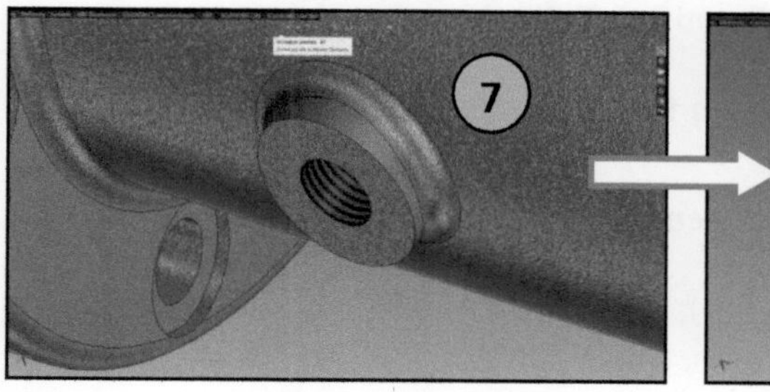

3.1.6.3 Zooming in and out

You have several options to change the size of the displayed image.

- Input device: **mouse, scroll wheel**:

Zooming in and out (Context menu) (9)

Drag the cursor up to zoom in and down to zoom out.

Turn the wheel forwards and backwards. When turning the mouse wheel, the cursor must always be in the area you want to zoom in on (10, 11).

Hold down the **Shift** key and drag with the **middle mouse button** (12).

Zooming in and out

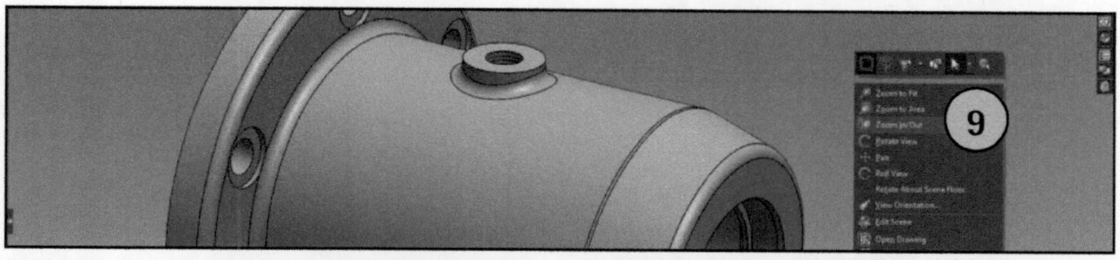

Previous View (Heads-up View Toolbar)

Previous View

Magnified Selection

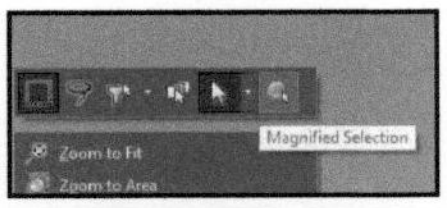

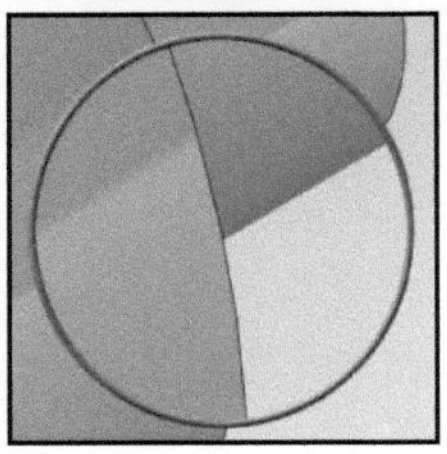

3.1.7 Magnified Selection

Magnified Selection allows you to examine a model and select elements without changing the overall view. This simplifies element selection during operations such as creating links.
There are several ways to access the **Magnified Selection** view shown.

3.1.7.1 Magnified Selection, access using the context menu

Magnified Selection (Context menu) (13)
Opens **Magnified Selection**.
Move the cursor within the model.
Magnified Selection also moves, but maintains the same zoom level; the model itself does not move (14).
To enlarge the contents of the selection, scroll the **mouse wheel**.

3.1.7.2 Magnified Selection, accessed using the keyboard

- Move the cursor over the area to be examined, and press the **G key**.
  Opens **Magnified Selection**.
  Move the cursor within the model.
  Magnified Selection also moves, but maintains the same zoom level; the model itself does not move (15).
  To enlarge the contents of the selection, scroll the **mouse wheel**.

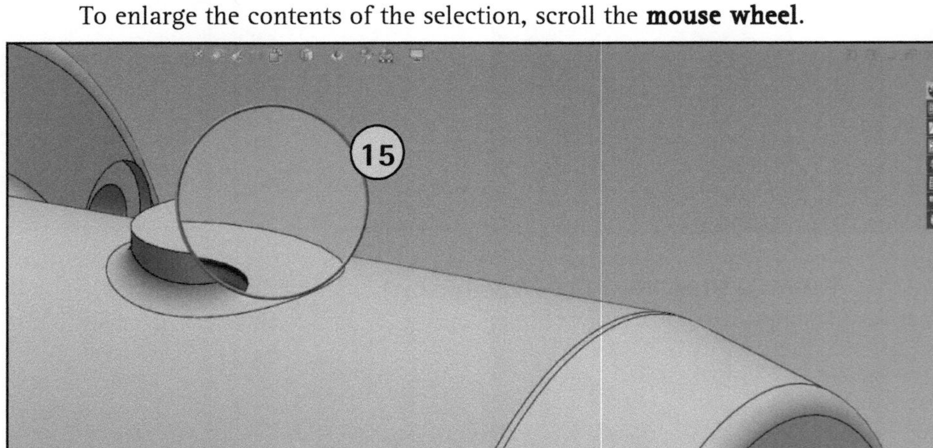

3.1.8 View position changes

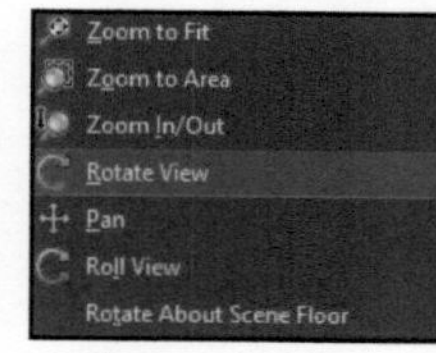

3.1.8.1 Move display

You have several options to change the size of the displayed image.

Pan (Context menu) (1)
Drag the view of the component over the work plane while holding down the left mouse button.
Input device mouse, **CTRL key** + **mouse wheel** (2)

Pan

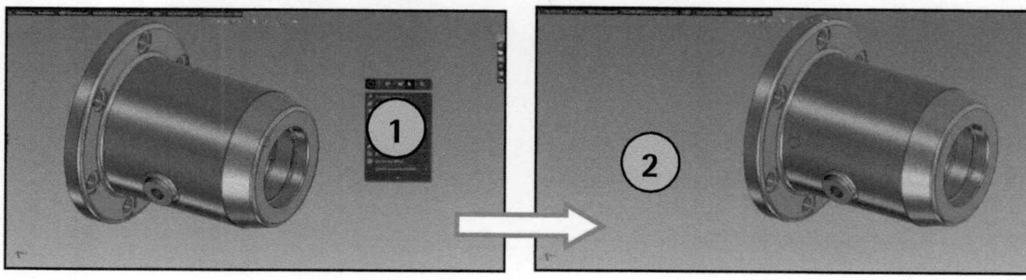

3.1.9 View changes, rotating position

3.1.9.1 Rotate view

This function rotates the model on the workspace.

Rotate View (Context menu) (3)
Rotate the view by holding down the left mouse button (4).

Rotate View

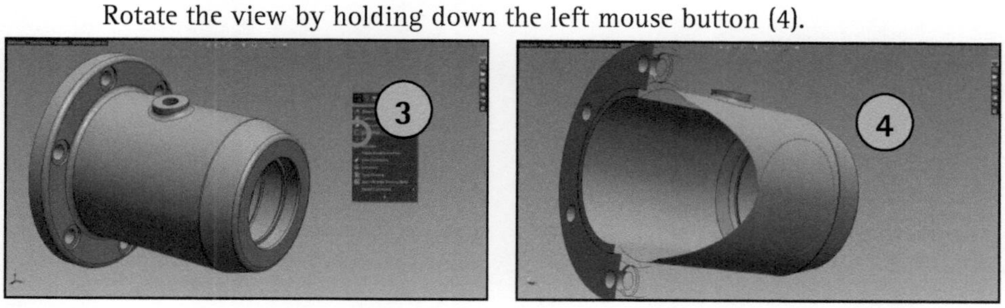

3.1.9.2 Rotate view around one edge

This function rotates the model along a selected edge on the workspace.

Rotate View (Context menu) (5)
Click an edge (6).
Rotate the view by holding down the **left mouse button**.

Rotate View

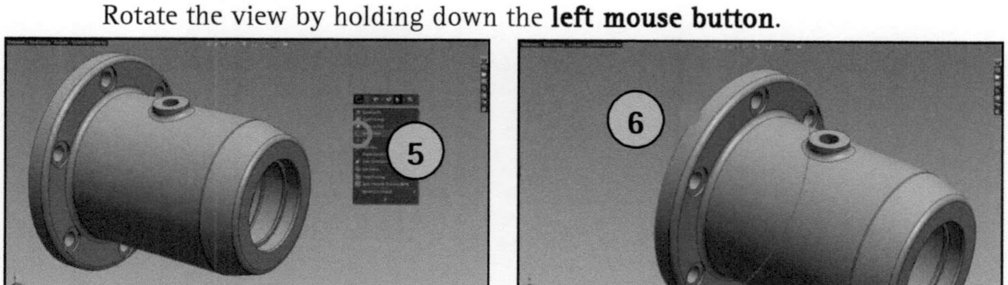

Previous View (Heads-up View Toolbar)

Previous View

3.1.9.3 View changes, "Roll View"

This function rolls the model around the workspace.

Roll View

Roll View (Context menu) (7)
Scroll the view by holding down the left mouse button (8).
Hold down the **ALT** key and scroll the mouse wheel while scrolling.

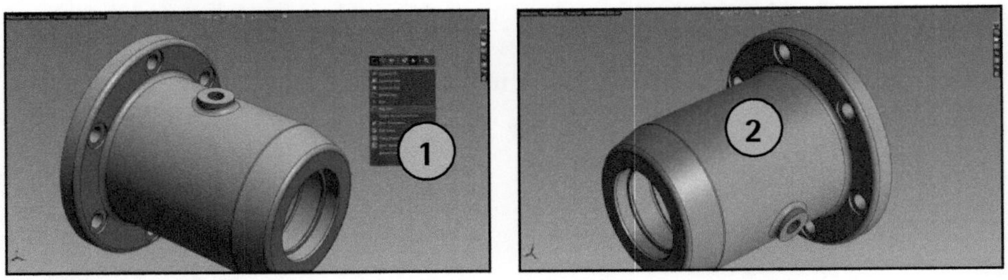

Previous View

Previous View (Heads-up View Toolbar)

3.1.10 View Orientations, according to DIN ISO 128-30, excerpt

View Selector

View Orientation

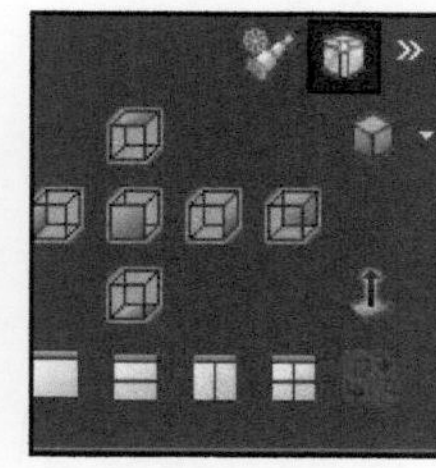

You can achieve view orientations in different ways; here are two possibilities:

- Possibility 1: Press the **spacebar** to access the symbol box.
- Possibility 2:

View Orientations (Heads-up View Toolbar) (3)

View Orientations **Top** (4):

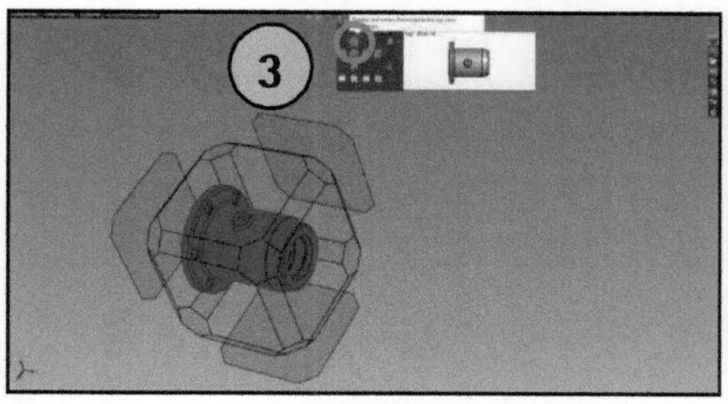

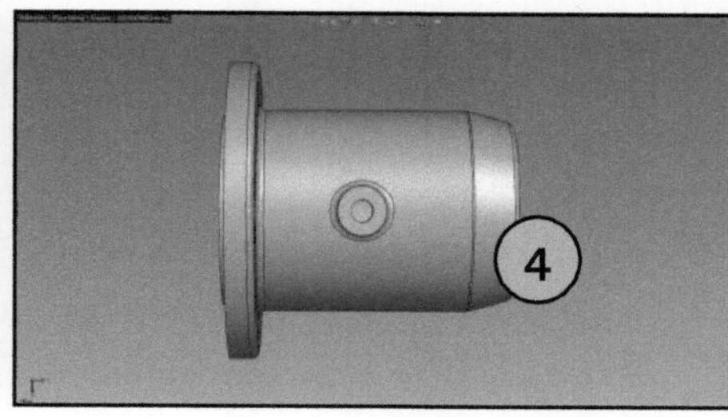

- View Orientations **Front** (5):

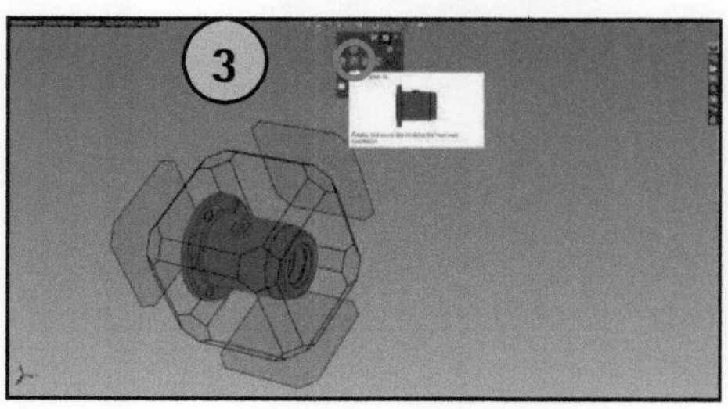

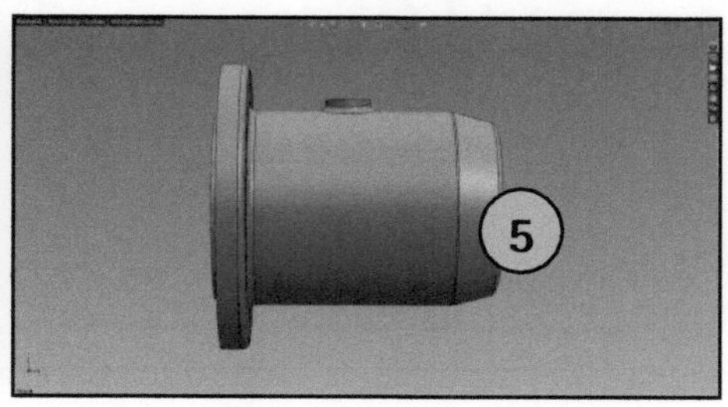

- View Orientations **Right** (6):

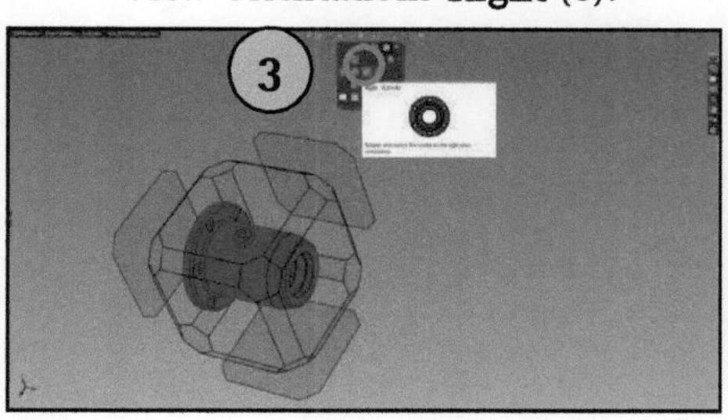

- View Orientations **Bottom** (7):

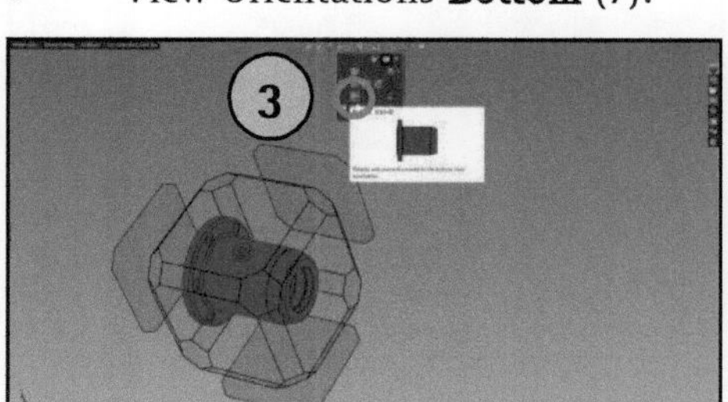

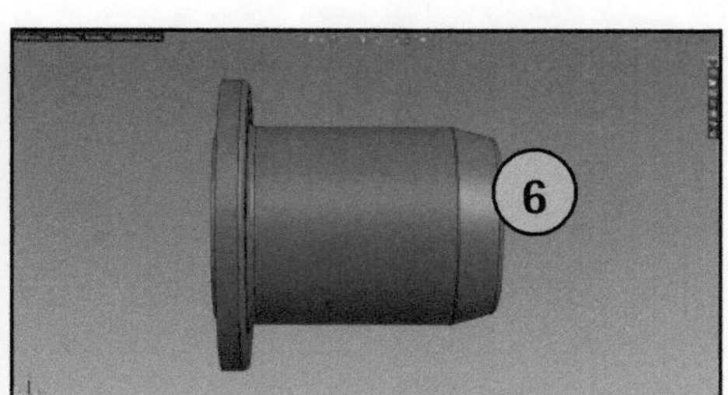

3.1.11 Axonometric representations according to DIN ISO 5456-3

Axonometric is the projection method that produces a parallel-perspective image of a body using the coordinates of its points. A distinction is made between rectangular and oblique axonometric, depending on whether the projecting rays are perpendicular to the image plane or not.

In both cases, the projection method is based on the coordinate systems whose coordinate planes are perpendicular to each other and correspond to the plan, elevation and side view planes of the ordinary orthogonal projection.

View Orientation

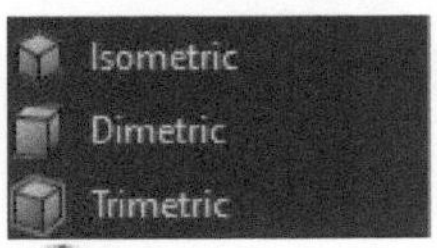

The three coordinate planes intersect along three mutually perpendicular lines, the coordinate axes; the latter forms the cross of axes.

View Orientations (Heads-up View Toolbar)

Select your preferred display method (1):

View Orientation **Isometric** (2):

Isometric

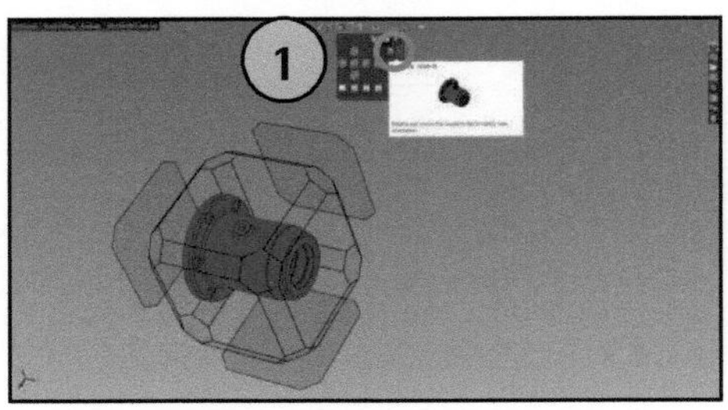

- View Orientation **Dimetric** (3):

Dimetric

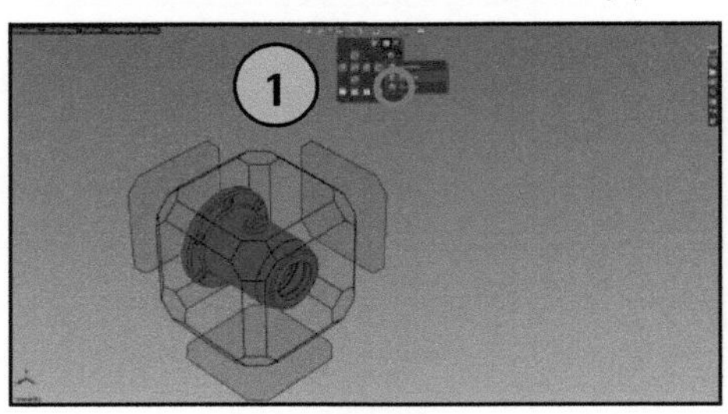

- View Orientation **Trimetric** (4):

Trimetric

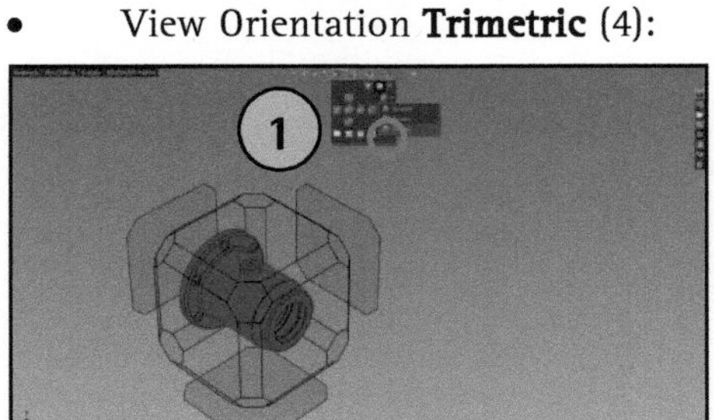

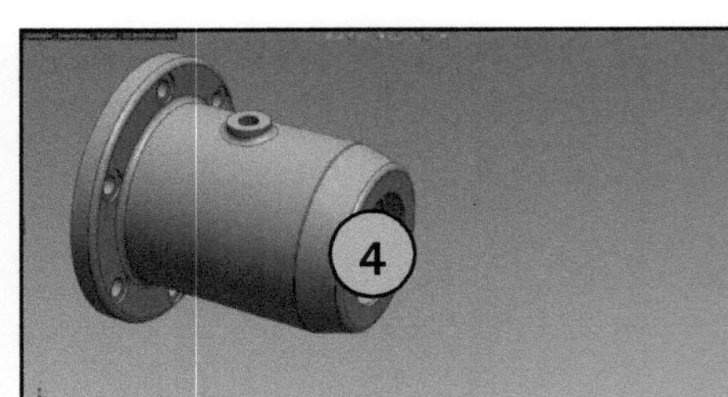

3.1.12 Displaying models in "Normal To" view

3.1.12.1 Select "View Orientations" using "Normal To"

- Possibility 1: Press the **spacebar** to access the symbol box.
- Possibility 2:

View Orientations (Heads-up View Toolbar)

View Orientation

Normal To (Heads-up View Toolbar) (1)
In the model, select the following elements:
Select a plane or planar surface (2, 3).

Normal To

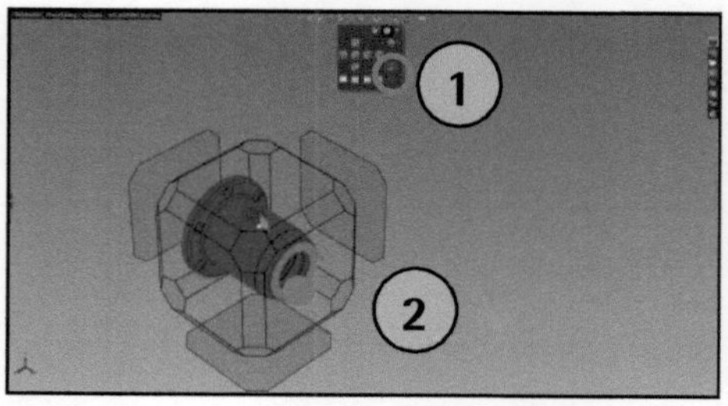

- If you click **Normal To** again on (4), the model will be rotated 180° (5).

Normal To

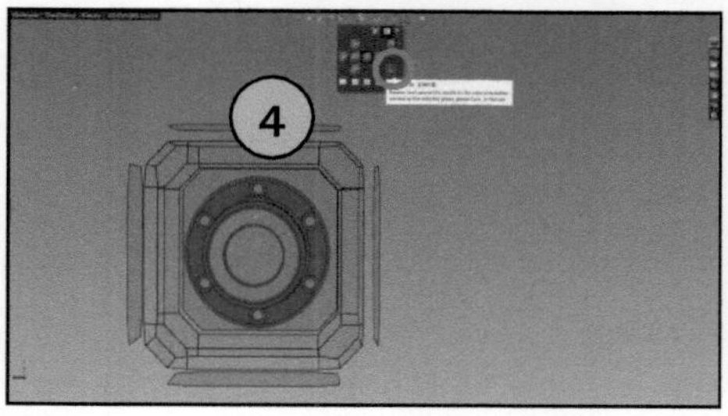

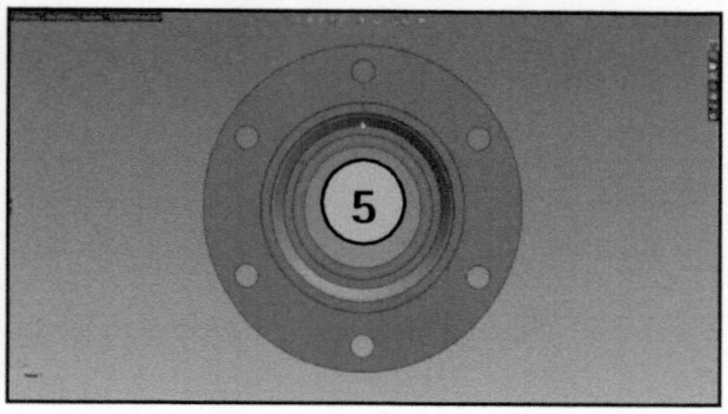

3.1.12.2 Select View Orientations "Normal To" using the CTRL key

Normal To (Heads-up View Toolbar)

Normal To

Hold down the **CTRL** key and select two planar surfaces (6, 7).

The second planar surface must not be parallel to the first.

With this method, the first surface you select is parallel to the screen, and the second surface you select is at the top of the view (8).

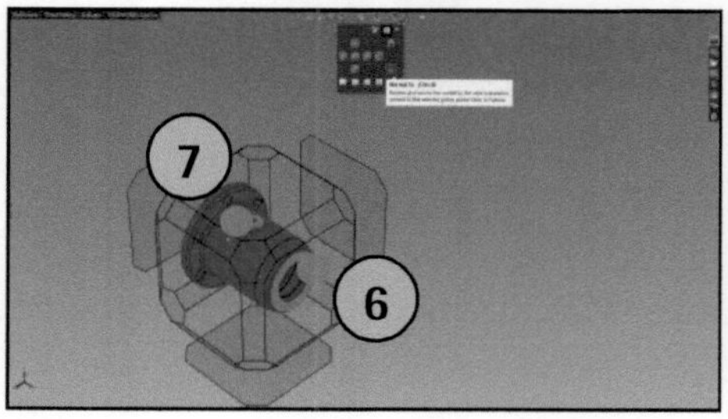

3.1.13 Multiple Views

View Orientation

3.1.13.1 Multiple Views, Viewports

Models can be displayed using one, two, or four viewports.

In the **Heads-Up View toolbar** or the Standard **Views toolbar**, you can select the following viewport layouts:

Einzelne Ansichten

Vierfach-Ansicht

- Multiple Views **Single View** (1) and **Four View** (2):

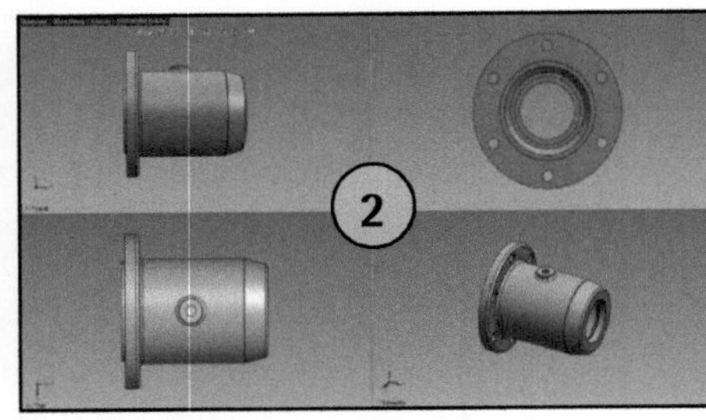

Doppelansicht Horizontal

Doppelansicht Vertikal

- Multiple Views **Two View Vertical** (3) and **Two View Horizontal** (4):

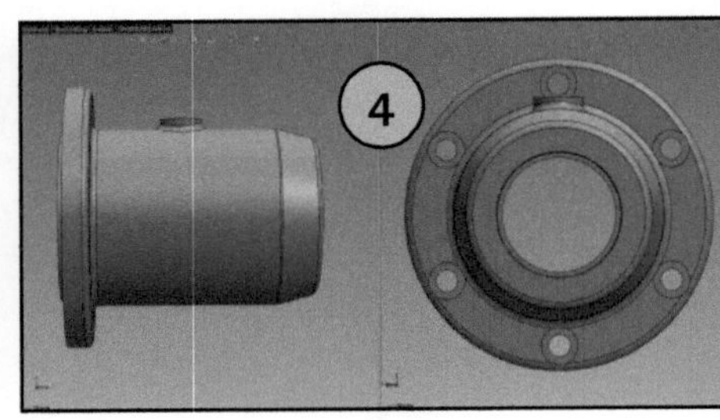

3.1.13.2 Multiple Views, linking orthogonal views

Orthogonal views can be linked. Linking is not possible with non-orthogonal views, isometric, trimetric, dimetric, or user-defined orientations.

3.1.13.3 Changing orthogonal views together

Link Views

Link Views (Heads-up View Toolbar)
Select the function (5).
The projections of the orthogonal views can be changed together (6).

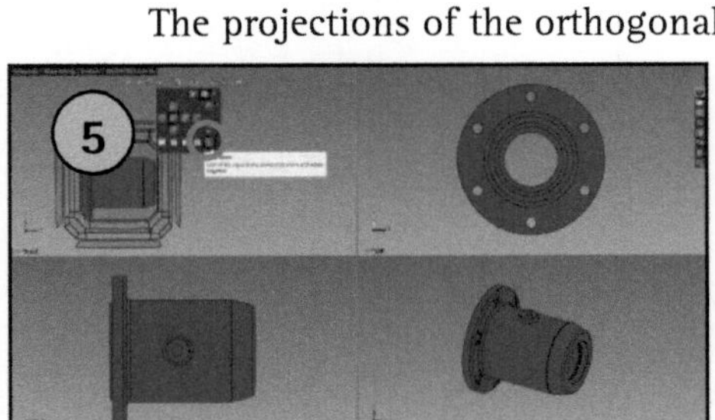

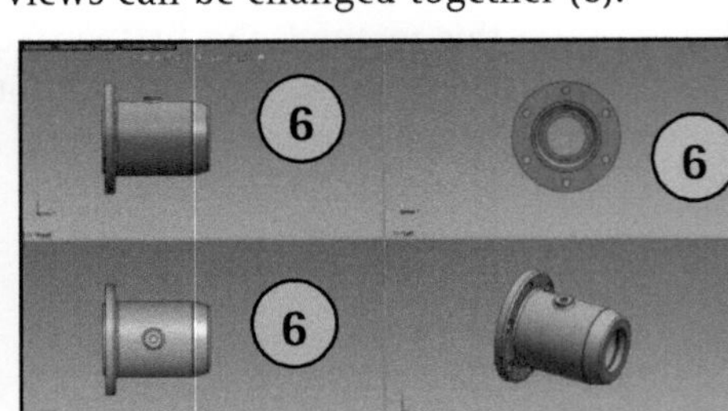

3.1.14 "Section Views" in models

In a **Section View** in a part or assembly document, the model is displayed as if it were cut through planes and surfaces that you define, so that the internal structure of the model is shown.

3.1.14.1 "Section View" on Plane

Section View (Heads-up View Toolbar) (1)
Section Options Reference **Plane Front** (2).

Click on **Plane Front** (3)

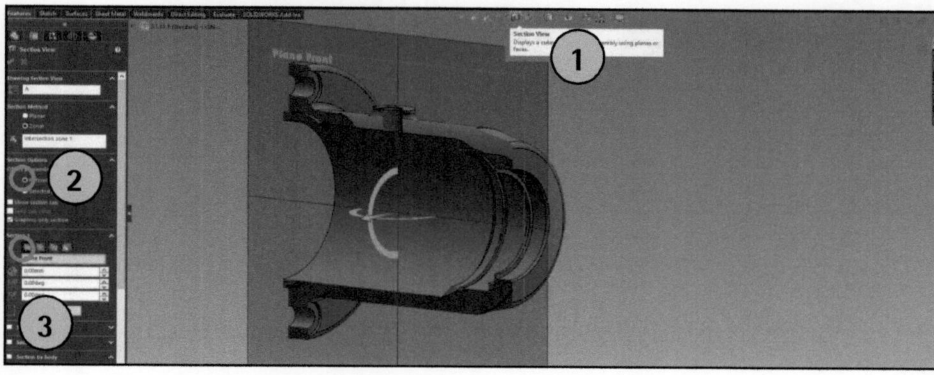

Section View

Front

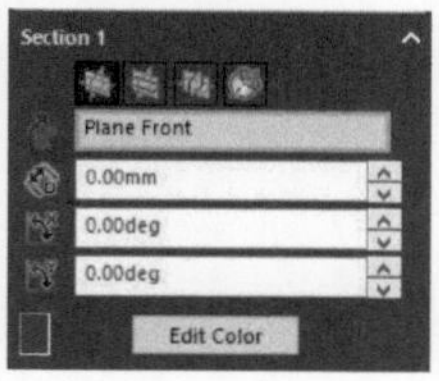

- **Save** (PropertyManager) (4)
  Save as a view orientation, give this view a name (5).

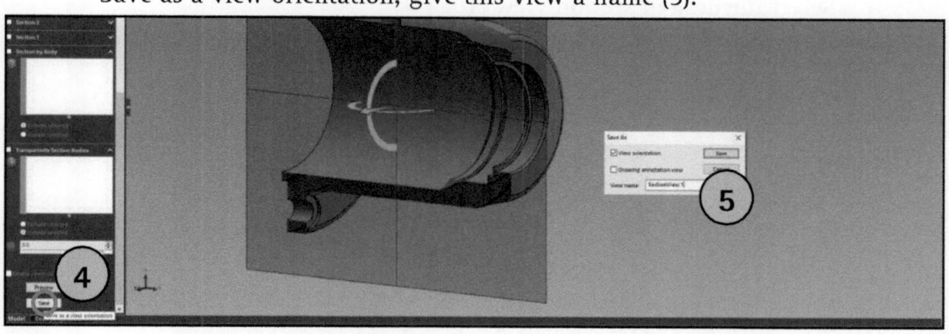

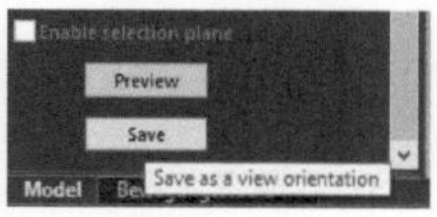

3.1.14.1 Checking the data backup of the created "Section View"

View Orientation (Heads-Up View toolbar)
The entry for the created **Section View** is displayed (6).

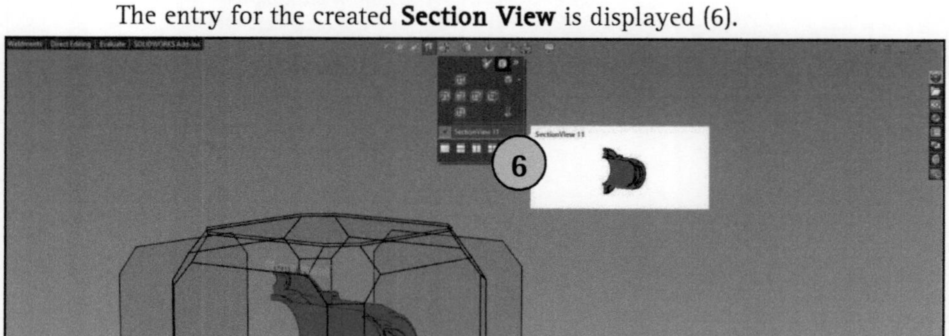

View Orientation

3.1.14.2 "Section View" adjust the level variably

Section View

Section View (Heads-up View Toolbar)
Section Options Reference **Plane Top** (7).

Top

Click on **Plane Top** (8)
Drag the triad arrow (9) to create the section view.

Save (PropertyManager)
Save as a view orientation, give this view a name (10).

3.1.14.3 Activate created "Section Views"

View Orientation

View Orientation (Heads-Up View toolbar)
Select the desired section view (10, 11)

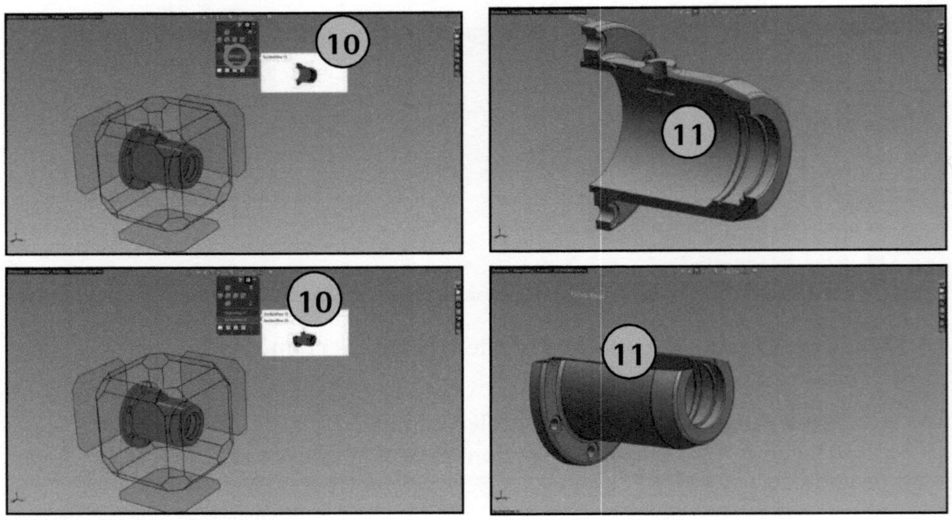

3.1.15 Display Style

The graphical display of your model is called the model view. Sometimes it is also called the scene. How the view is displayed depends on the settings applied. These include view types, the source plane, reflections and shadows on the source plane, lighting, and camera projection.

The view type controls the display of model faces and edges in the graphics window. The commands change the display mode of the view of the active part or assembly in the graphics window. View types determine how the model's faces and edges are displayed in the view. Several standard styles exist to meet a wide range of design requirements.

Display Style

Display Style (Heads-Up View toolbar)
Select your preferred display method:

Wireframe:
Display all edges of the model.

Wireframe

Hidden Lines Visible:
Display the model with all edges that are not visible from the current perspective shown in gray.

Hidden Lines Visible

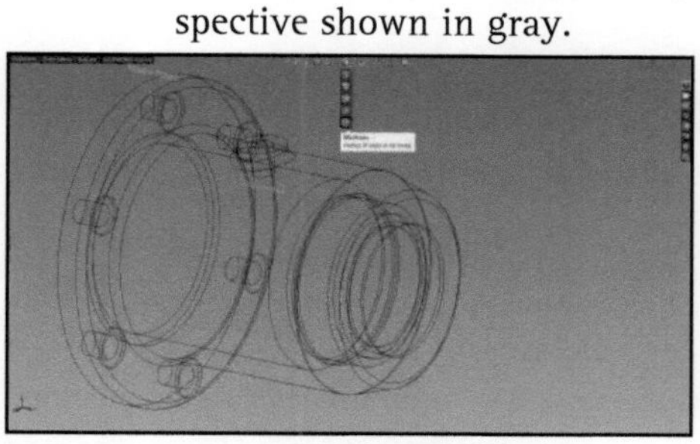

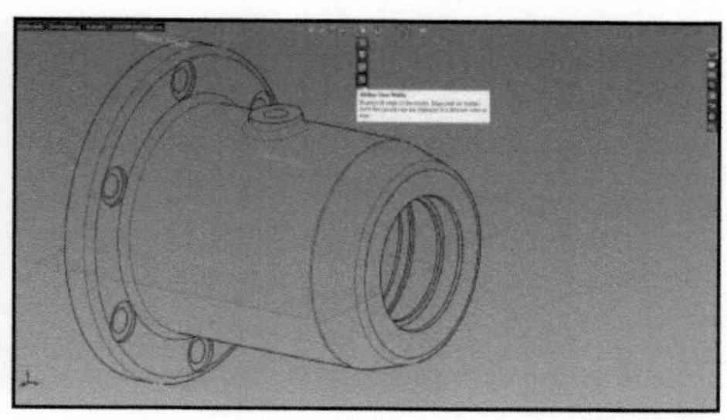

- **Hidden Lines Removed:**
  Display the model with all edges, hidden that are not visible from the current viewing angle.

Hidden Lines Removed

- **Shaded:**
  Display a shaded view of the model.

Shaded

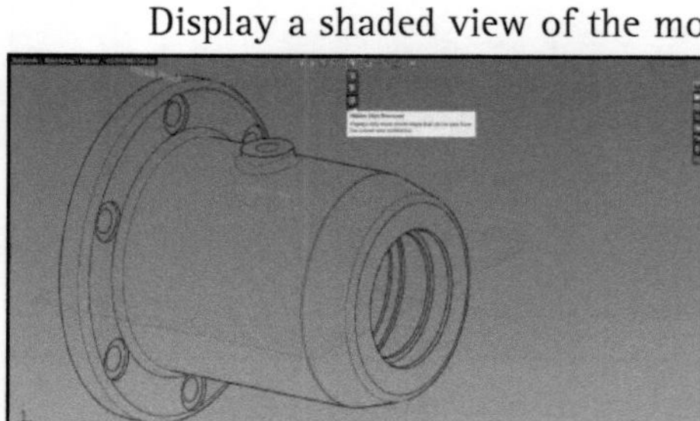

- **Shaded with edges:**
  Display a shaded view of the model with visible edges.

Shaded with edges

3.2 Allocation of materials to components

3.2.1 Materials Overview

Edit Material

Use the Material dialog box to create and edit custom materials or libraries, apply materials, or set material favorites. Materials summarize the physical properties of a part. SOLIDWORKS includes a library of predefined materials that are also used for SOLIDWORKS simulation. You can assign a material to a part or to one or more bodies of a multibody part in an assembly.

3.2.2 Material allocation

3.2.2.1 Component Preparation

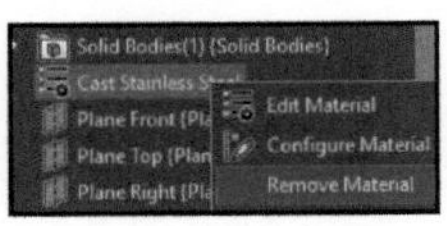

- Select the component to be edited from the assembly using the **FeatureManager design tree.**
- Switch to **RealViewGraphics** display mode if available.
- Remove the assigned material using the **Remove Material** option.

3.2.2.2 Reassign component material

Edit Material

Edit Material (FeatureManager)
In a subdocument, right-click on Material button to display the context menu for **Edit Material.**
Select **SOLIDWORKS Materials / Copper Alloys / Copper** from the favorites list.
Click **Apply** and then **Close.**

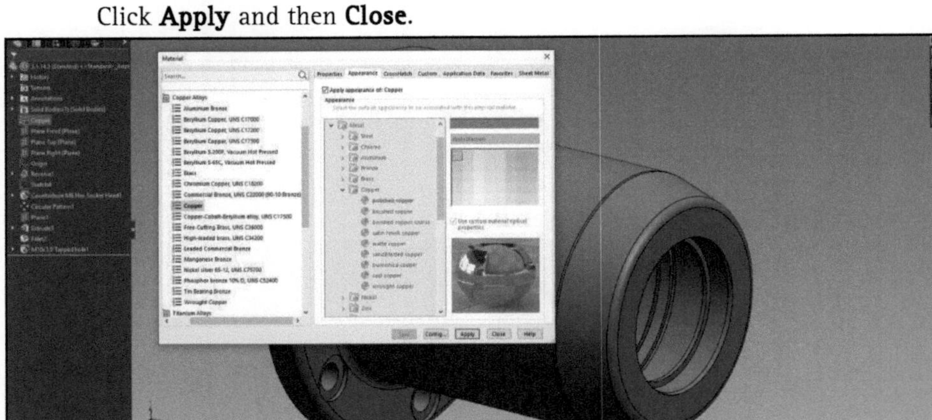

RealView-Graphics

- Display with or without **RealViewGraphics** display mode:

3.2.2.3 Reassigning component material, examples

- Material allocation SOLIDWORKS Materials **Brass**, context menu **Edit Material**
  Display with or without **RealViewGraphics** display mode:

Edit Material

RealView-Graphics

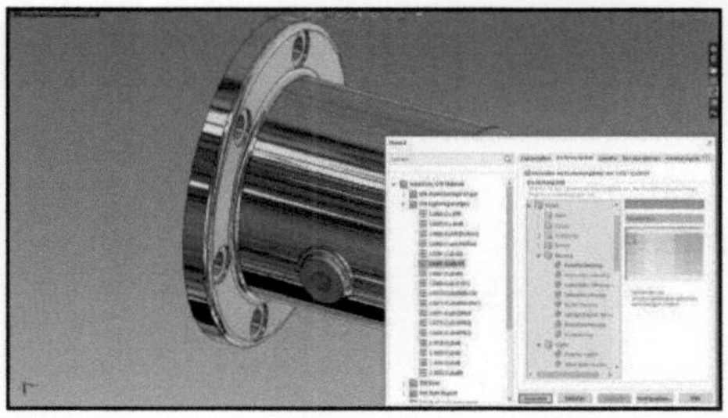
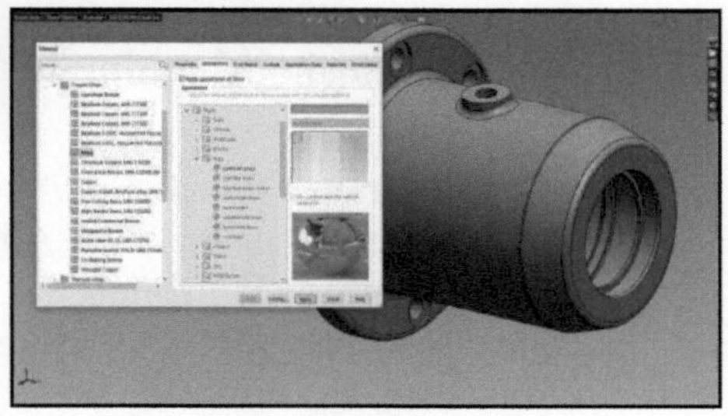

- Material allocation SOLIDWORKS Materials **Cast Stainless Steel**, context menu **Edit Material**
  Display with or without **RealViewGraphics** display mode:

Edit Material

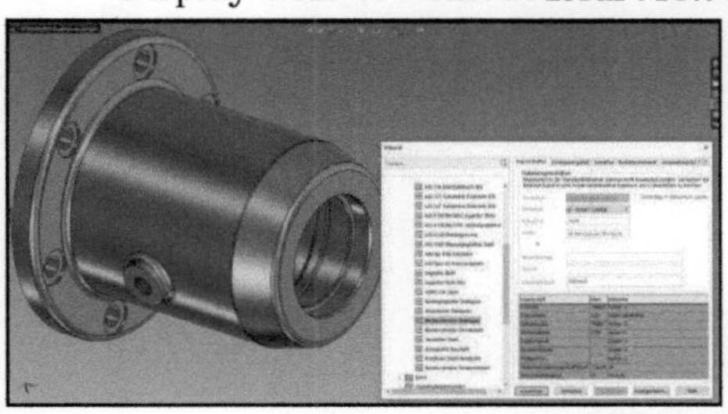
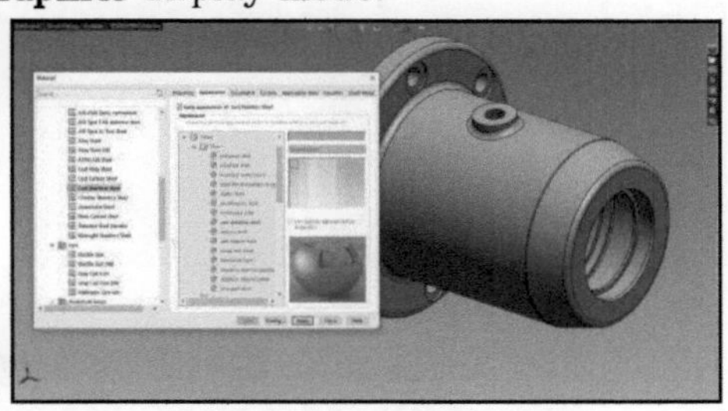

- Material allocation SOLIDWORKS-Materials **Acrylik** and **Neoprene,** context menu **Edit Material, d**isplay with standard display mode:

Edit Material

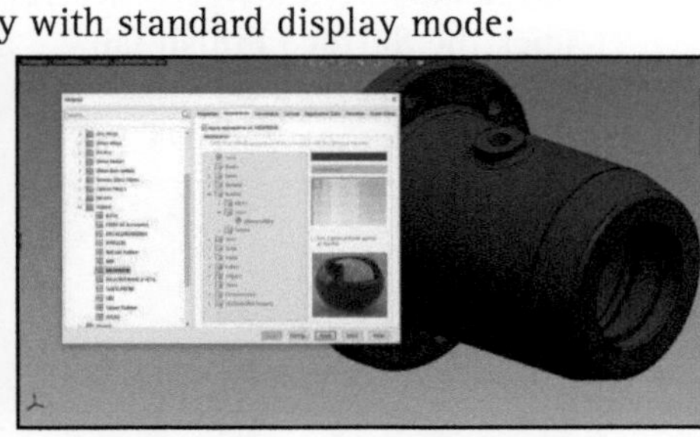

- Material allocation SOLIDWORKS-Material **Mahogany** and **1060-Alloy,** context menu **Edit Material, d**isplay with standard display mode:

Edit Material

3.2.2.4 Data backup

Save as new / Enter a filename of your choice.

Save as new

3.3 Surface finish for components

The PropertyManager **Appearance-Surface finish** defines the type of surface in the appearance. Display with **RealViewGraphics** display mode.

3.3.1 Surface finish "Machined" and "Burnished"

Edit Appearance

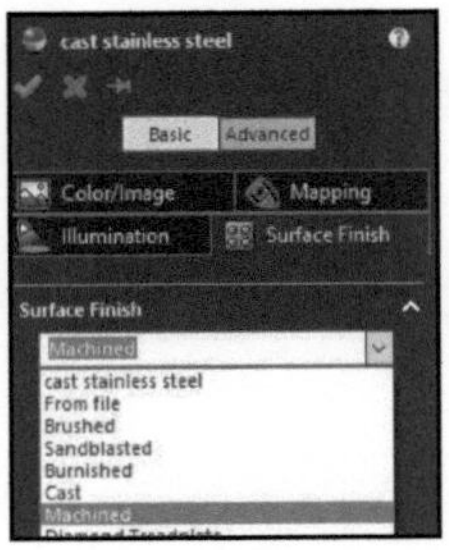

Edit Appearance (Heads-Up View toolbar)
In the PropertyManager, click **Advanced**.
Click the **Surface Finish** tab.
Select: **Machined** (1).
Close dialog box with **OK**.

Edit Appearance

Edit Appearance (**FeatureManager**, Context menu)
PropertyManager-menu **DisplayManager**.
In the PropertyManager, click **Advanced**.
Click the **Surface Finish** tab.
Select: **Burnished** (2).
Close dialog box with **OK**.

3.3.2 Surface finish "Sandblasted" and "Casted"

- **Edit Appearance** (Heads-Up View toolbar)
  In the **PropertyManager**, click **Advanced** and **Surface Finish** tab.
  Select: **Sandblasted** (3) and **Casted** (4).

3.4 Changing the component color

You can assign a color and optical properties to the entire part, selected faces or features (including surfaces or curves), or selected bodies. You can also modify the color by editing the shaded appearance of the model. The Edit Appearance command displays the colors of faces, features, bodies, or the part itself, providing a quick and easy way to edit appearances. You can view the color hierarchy by expanding the command. A color selection made using the PropertyManager takes precedence over colors set on the Document Properties tab.

3.4.1 Appearance on components

Edit Appearance (Heads-Up View toolbar)
In the PropertyManager, click **Basic** (1).
Click the **Color/Images** tab (1).
The selected Geometrie, select **Part** (2).
Choose a color of your choice, for example **Green** (3, 4).
Close dialog box with **OK**

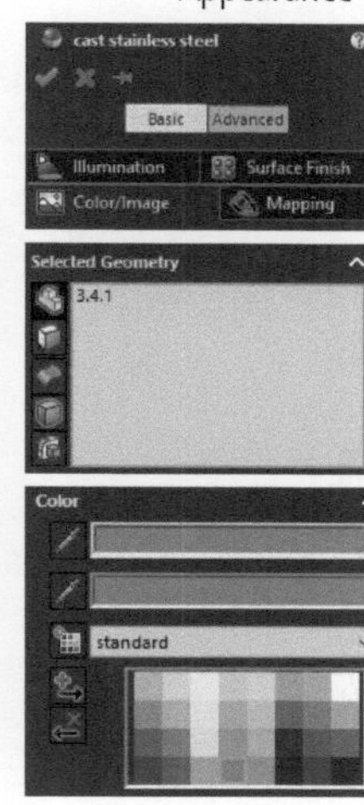

3.4.2 Appearance select "Feature"

Edit Appearance (Heads-Up View toolbar)
In the PropertyManager, click **Basic**.
Click the **Color/Images** tab.
Select **Feature, Counterbore, Circular Pattern** (5).
Choose a color of your choice, for example **Red** (6, 7).
Close dialog box with **OK**.

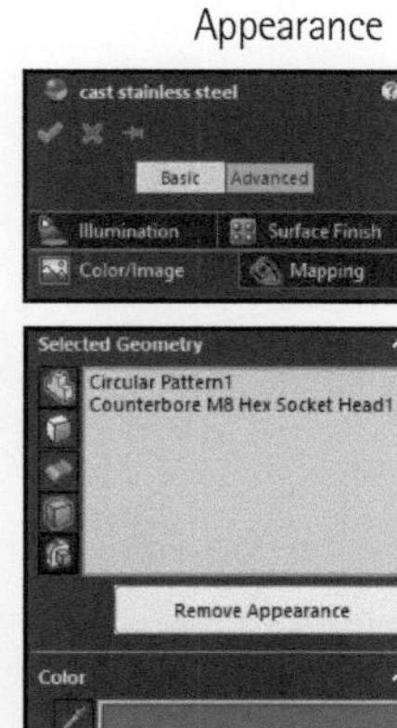

3.4.3 Appearance select "Faces"

Edit Appearance

Edit Appearance (Heads-Up View toolbar)
In the PropertyManager, click **Basic** (1).
Click the **Color/Images** tab (1).
Select **Faces** (7).
Choose a color of your choice, for example **Blue** (8, 9).
Close dialog box with **OK**.

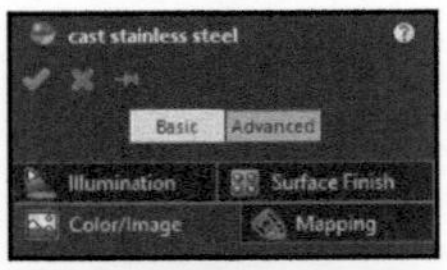

3.4.3.1 Data backup

Save as new

Save as new / Enter a filename of your choice.

3.5 Assigning a "Decal"

Control the surfaces of a component, to which the decal should be applied.
Display with **RealViewGraphics** display mode.

3.5.1 Turn on the "Decal element"

Visibility On / Off (Heads-Up View toolbar)

Click the **Visibilities Decals On**.

Visibility On / Off

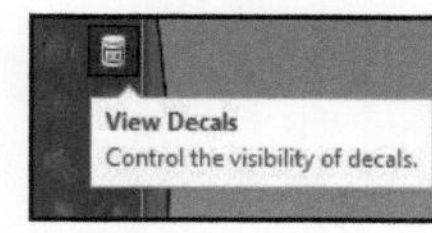

3.5.2 Assigning an element "Decal"

Edit Scene (Heads-Up View toolbar)

Decals
Click the **Decals** tab (1).
Double-click the decal shown (2).
Click the inner cylinder surface (3, 4).
Close dialog box with **OK**.

Edit Appearance

Decals

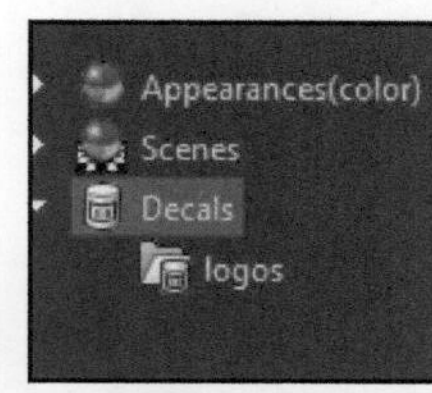

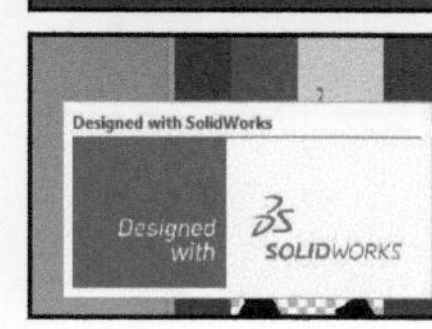

3.5.2.1 Data backup

Save as new / Enter a filename of your choice.

Save as new

3.6 Assigning a background image

Scenes form the visual background behind a model. In SOLIDWORKS, the visual background creates reflections on the model. When PhotoView 360 is enabled, scenes provide a realistic light source with illumination and reflections, reducing the need for lighting adjustments.

The objects and lights within a scene can represent reflections on the model and cast shadows on the ground.

A stage backdrop is a 2D image placed between the model and the stage environment. Even with a backdrop, the reflections on the model originate from the stage environment.

3.6.1 Changing the background of a scene

Edit Appearance

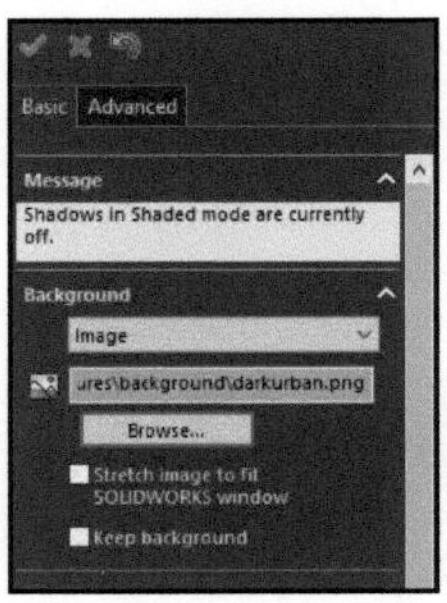

Right-click in the graphics area.
Select **Edit Scene** from the context menu.
Click the **Basic** tab.
In the **Background** option, select **Image** (1).
Image selection, example: **Darkurban.png / Open** (2)
Set option **Stretch image to fit SOLIDWORKS Windows** (3).
Close dialog box with **OK**.

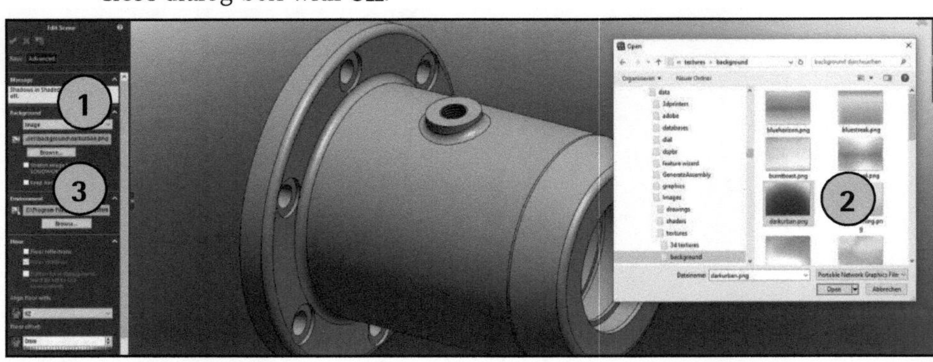

3.6.1.1 Data backup

Save as new

Save as new / Enter a filename of your choice.

4

Dassault Systèmes
3DEXPERIENCE©
SOLIDWORKS Design
2026

Parts and Components

Create and Customize

Geometric Fundamentals

4 Geometric Fundamentals

4.1 Geometric Fundamentals, basics

SOLIDWORKS consists of several components called environments. These environments were specifically created for generating individual parts, sheet metal parts, assemblies, and detailed drawings.

In the SolidWorks Part environment, you can design a basic feature and then modify it with additional features such as features, cutouts, and holes to create a complete solid model.

In SOLIDWORK, you use the following basic workflow to model parts:

- Identify model requirements
- Develop a model concept based on the identified requirements
- Analyze the model
- Construct the model
- Edit the model, if necessary

4.2 Design fundamentals

4.2.1 Sketches

Creating a model typically begins with a sketch. Features can then be created based on the sketch. A model usually contains at least one sketch and at least one feature.

A sketch is a 2D profile or cross-section. To create a 2D sketch, you use a plane or a flat surface. Besides 2D sketches, you can also create 3D sketches, which include a Z-axis in addition to the X and Y axes.

In many cases, you begin your sketch at the origin, which serves as an anchor for the sketch. Often, a centerline is sketched through the origin to establish the rotation. While a centerline isn't always necessary in a sketch, it does contribute to creating symmetry.

A centerline can also be used to apply a mirror relationship and to create equal and symmetrical relationships between sketch elements. Symmetry is an important tool for quickly creating axially symmetrical models.

Sketches can be fully defined, underdefined, or overdefined. In a fully defined sketch, all lines and curves in the sketch, as well as their positions, are described by dimensions, relations, or both.

Sketches do not need to be fully defined to be used for creating features. However, you should fully define sketches to maintain your design plan.

Fully defined sketches are black.

You can view the underdefined elements of a sketch to determine which dimensions or relations still need to be added to make the sketch fully defined.

Sub define sketches are blue.

Underdefined sketches are not only color-coded, but their elements can also be dragged, as they are not fixed within the sketch.

4.2.2 Planes

Planes can be created in part or assembly documents. You can sketch on layers using sketching tools such as line or rectangle and use the layers to create a section view of a model.

In some models, the plane on which you sketch only affects how the model is displayed in the isometric view. In other cases, models can be created more efficiently if you select the correct sketching plane right from the start.

Choose a plane on which to sketch. The default planes are forward, top, and right. You can also add new planes and position them as needed.

4.2.3 Dimensions

4.2.3.1 Dimensions, basics

Sketches are displayed in various states. To fully define the sketch, add relations and apply dimensions using the Smart Dimension tool (Dimensions/Relations toolbar).

Smart Dimension

The types of sketch entities also affect dimensioning functions. 2D or 3D sketch entities are dimensioned using the Smart Dimension tool. You can drag or delete a dimension while the tool is active.

Dimension types are determined by the sketch elements you select. For some dimension types (point-to-point, angular, circular), the location where the dimension is placed influences the dimension type that is added.

You can create features without adding dimensions to the sketches. However, it is generally recommended to dimension sketches. Dimension according to the design plan of the model. For example, you should place holes at a specific distance from an edge or at a specific distance from each other.

4.2.3.2 Dimensioning methods

You can specify dimensions between elements, such as lengths or radii. Changing the dimensions also changes the size and shape of the part. Depending on how you dimension the part, the design plan can be maintained. The software uses two types of dimensioning, driving dimensioning and controlled dimensioning.

- Driven dimensions

Controlling dimensions are created using the Dimension tool. They cause a change in the model size when the dimension values are modified.

- Controlled dimensions

Some dimensions belonging to the model are controlled. You can insert controlled dimensions or reference dimensions for informational purposes using the Dimension tool.

The value of driven dimensions changes when you modify the driving dimensions or ratios in the model. You cannot directly change the values of driven dimensions; they must be converted into driving dimensions.

4.2.4 Relationships

Relationships represent geometric relationships such as equality and tangents between sketch elements. While it is possible to dimension horizontal elements separately, adding an equal relationship between these two elements means you only need to update one dimension when the length changes.
The green symbols indicate a relationship between sketch objects.
You can also add relationships while creating individual sketch entities or when selecting two existing entities. The Existing Relationships and Add Relationships fields appear in each sketch entity's PropertyManager.
When creating relationships, at least one of the elements must be a sketch element. The other elements can be sketch elements, edges, faces, vertices, origins, planes, axes, or curves from another sketch that form a line or arc when projected onto the sketch plane.

4.2.5 Creating a feature, rules and options

4.2.5.1 Coordinate systems

SOLIDWORKS uses a system of coordinate systems with an origin. A part document has an origin by default. When you select a plane, face, or open a sketch, the origin is created in alignment with the plane or face.

An origin can be used as an anchor for sketch elements and helps with axis alignment. A three-dimensional reference triad helps you orient yourself in the X, Y, and Z directions in part and assembly documents.

The sketch origin is displayed in red in an open sketch. The sketch origin helps you orient yourself to the sketch's coordinates.

Component origin: One in each sub-document.

Isometric alignment: Derivation to an assembly origin.

Sketch origin: One for each new sketch.

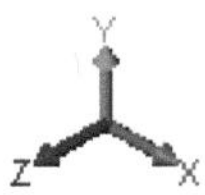

Reference triad: In component and assembly documents.

4.2.5.2 Color tones for highlighting

Geometric relationships, such as endpoints, midpoints, and vertices, are highlighted when the cursor moves towards them and their color changes when the cursor is stopped for selection.

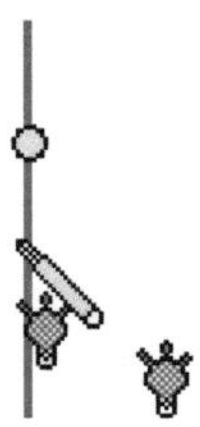

The center point is highlighted, and the cursor indicates that a coincident relationship is possible at the current position.

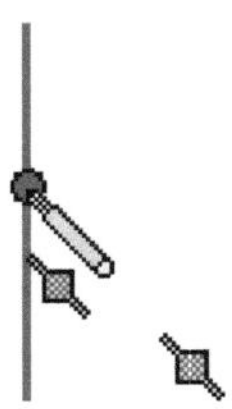

The color of the center point has changed, and the cursor indicates that it recognizes the center point.

4.2.5.3 Sketch Snap Functions, excerpt

Sketch snap functions simplify the selection of key points on sketch elements.

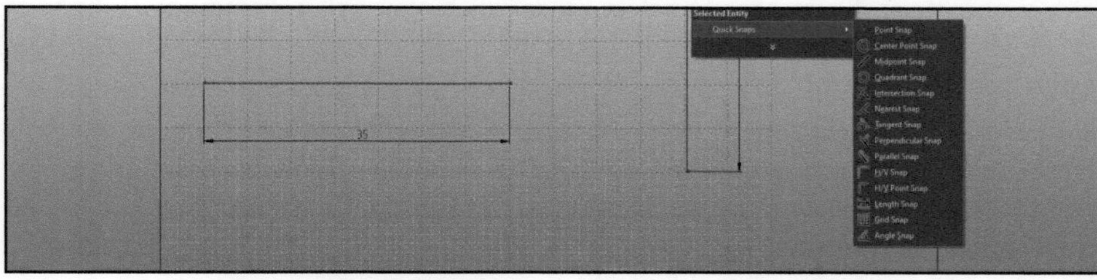

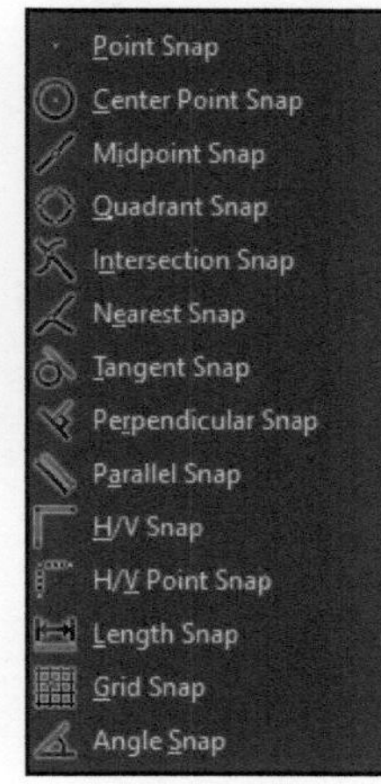

Endpoints and Sketch Points:
The following sketch elements are captured at their ends: lines, polygons, rectangles, parallelograms, fillets, arcs, parabolas, partial ellipses, splines, points, chamfers, and centerlines.

Mid Points:
The system snaps to the midpoints of lines, polygons, rectangles, parallelograms, fillets, arcs, parabolas, partial ellipses, splines, points, chamfers, and centerlines.

Tangent:
The scanner captures tangents to circles, circular arcs, radii, parabolas, ellipses, partial ellipses and splines.

Intersections:
The camera is caught at the intersection points of elements that touch or intersect.

Perpendicular:
It snaps to angles. To set the angle, click Relationships/Snap and specify a value for Angle Snap.

Parallel
Creates a parallel element to lines.

Center points:
The following sketch elements are captured at their center point: circles, arcs, radii, parabolas, and partial ellipses.

Quadrant Points:
The camera is captured at the quadrant points of circles, circular arcs, roundings, parabolas, ellipses and partial ellipses.

Grid:
Sketch elements are snapped to the vertical and horizontal grid lines.

Angle:
It snaps to angles. To set the angle, click Relationships/Snap and specify a value for Angle Snap.

Horizontal/verticale lines:

A line is snapped vertically to an existing horizontal sketch line and horizontally to an existing vertical sketch line.

Nearest
Supports all elements.
The cursor does not need to be in close proximity to another sketch element to indicate snapping to that point.

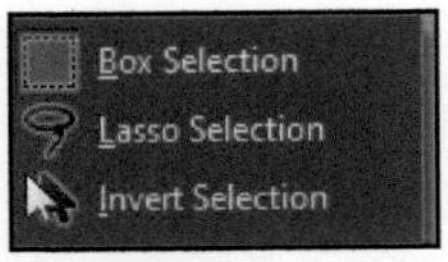

4.2.5.4 Selection Tools

Select mode is the default mode when you are not in a command. In most cases, the control automatically returns to select mode when you exit a command. When select mode is active, you can select items in the graphics area or the FeatureManager design tree using the pointer.

You can use the Select tool to end a command and return to Select mode, which is helpful with view tools and when working in sketches. Dynamic highlighting informs you which element can be selected as you move the cursor. You can set an option to enable or disable dynamic highlighting.

When selecting from the frame from left to right, only elements completely within the frame are selected. When selecting from the crossbar from right to left, elements that extend beyond the frame are also selected. When selecting from the window, the window is displayed with solid lines. When selecting from the crossbar, the window is displayed with dotted lines.

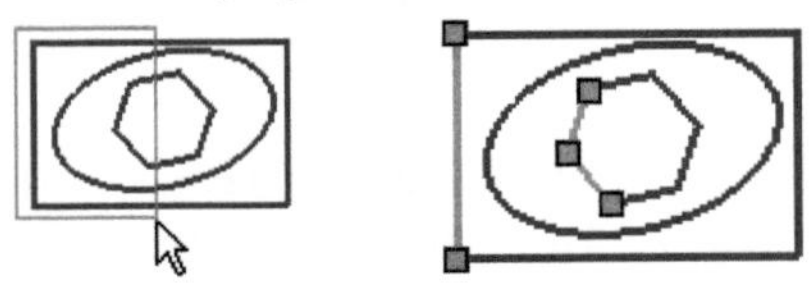

Window selection from left to right

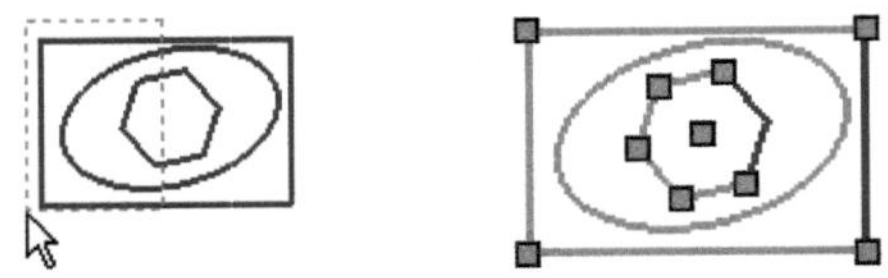

Window selection from right to left

4.2.5.5 Highlight object selection

Elements are highlighted in the graphics area when you select them, or dynamically highlighted when you hover the cursor over them. How selected elements are highlighted depends on the color settings, the selected display mode, and whether RealView is active.

RealView, shaded

Selected edges are highlighted as bright lines.

Selected areas are highlighted in a bright, solid color.

RealView disabled, shaded

Selected edges are highlighted as thick, continuous lines.

Selected areas are highlighted in a solid color.

Hidden edges hidden

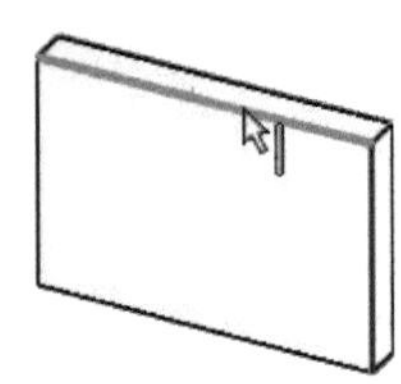

Selected edges are highlighted as thick, continuous lines.

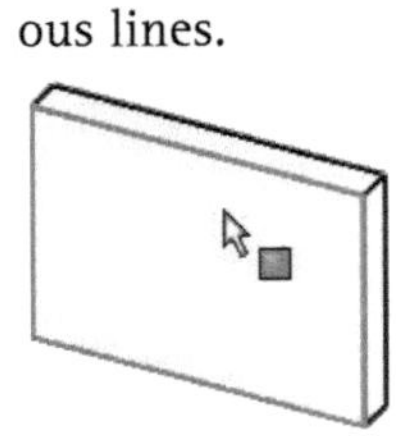

Selected surface edges are highlighted as thin, continuous lines.

4.2.5.6 Dynamic Preview

When you create or edit a feature that supports dynamic preview, a dynamic preview in the graphics area shows how the model changes as you move the cursor. First, a shaded preview is displayed.

Click a handle in the shaded preview and drag the cursor to display the dynamic preview. After saving the linearly extruded feature, you can use grips for the preview and modify dimensions that are not constrained. A scale bar indicates the dimension changes.

Preview the graphical representation. Handles appear, allowing you to drag the preview to the desired depth. Handles for the active direction are yellow, while those for the inactive direction are gray. A description displays the current depth value. Click on the screen to switch the preview to shaded mode.

The cursor changes to an arrow. If you want to create the feature now, make a right-click. Otherwise, you can make further changes to the settings. For example, the depth of the linear extrusion can be changed by dragging the dynamic handle with the mouse or by setting a value in the PropertyManager.

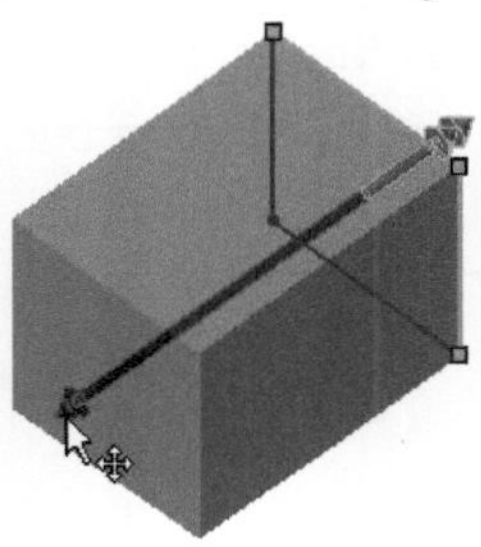

Click on the handle, as shown in the image.

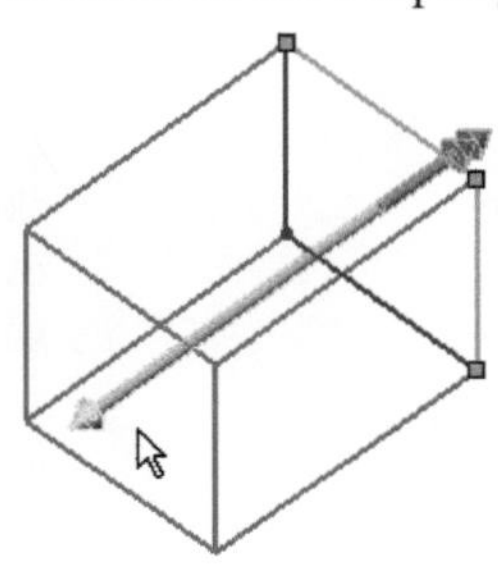

Drag the cursor to display the dynamic preview.

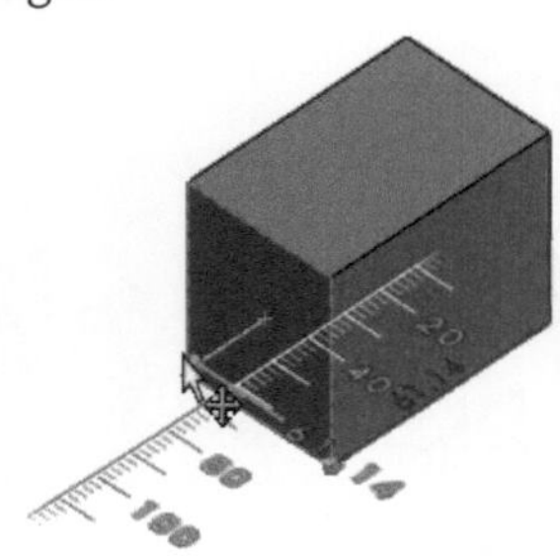

Use the scale to preview dimension changes.

4.2.5.7 End condition for Extrude Boss/Base

If you want to generate a solid from a sketch profile using the Extrude Boss/Base command, you must select an end condition for the solid boundary edge from the PropertyManager. The following images show the corresponding options to be entered:

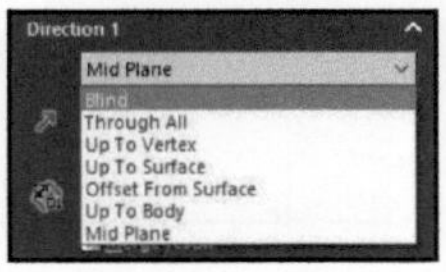

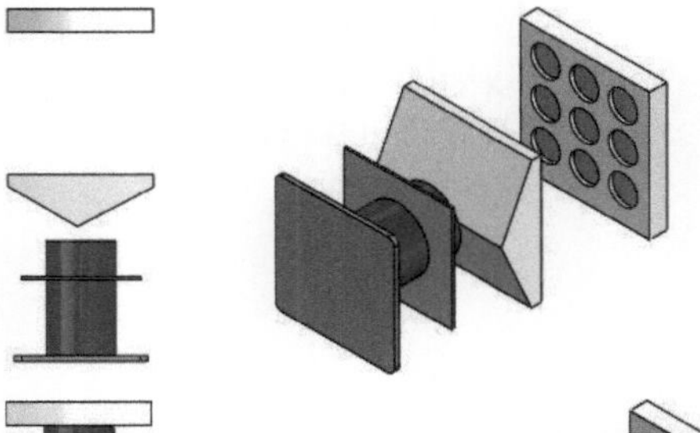

Blind:

Extends the feature from the sketch plane by a specified distance.

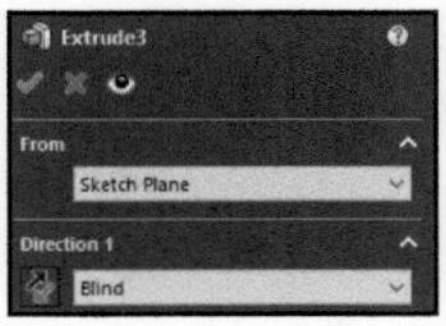

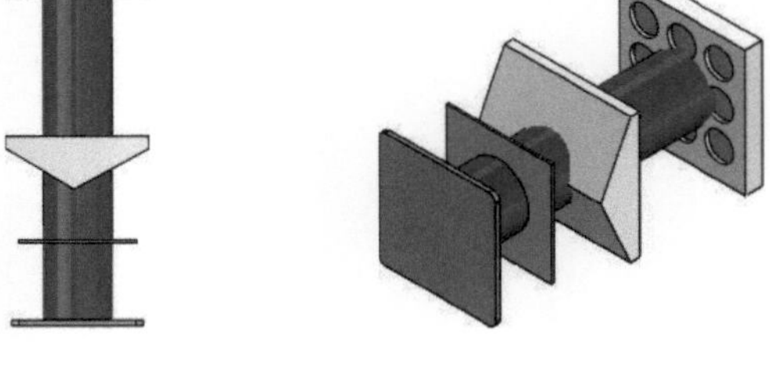

Through All:

Extends the feature from the sketch plane through the entire existing geometry.

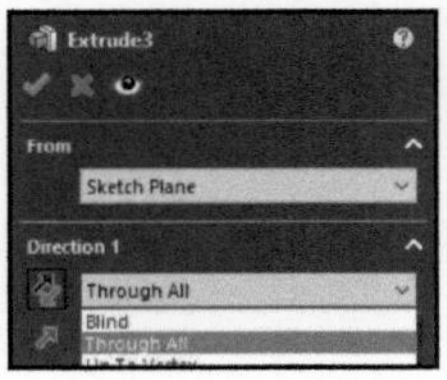

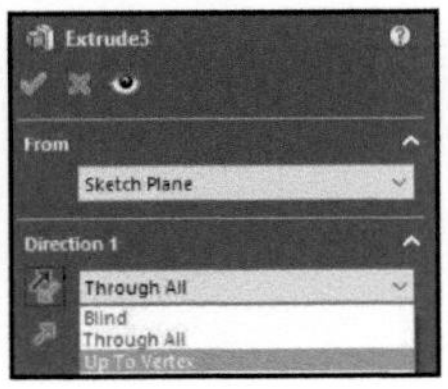

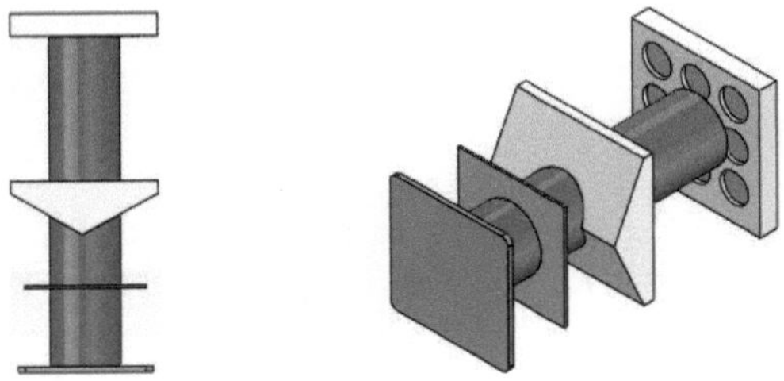

Up to Vertex:

Extends the feature from the sketch plane to a plane that is parallel to the sketch plane and passes through the specified vertex.

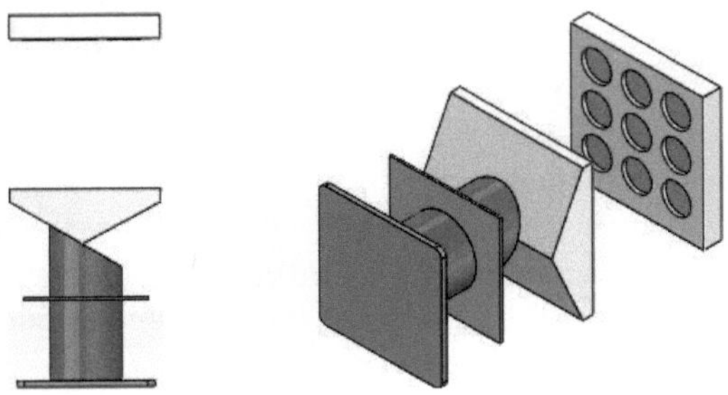

Up to Surface:

Extends the feature from the sketch plane to the selected surface.

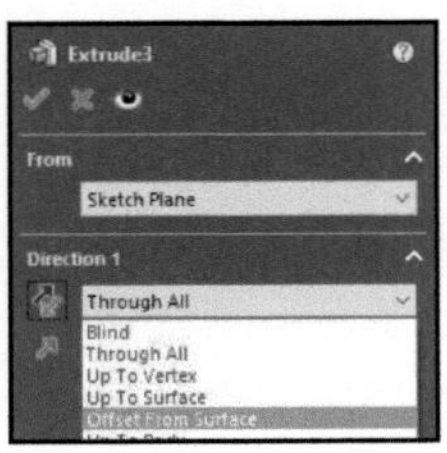

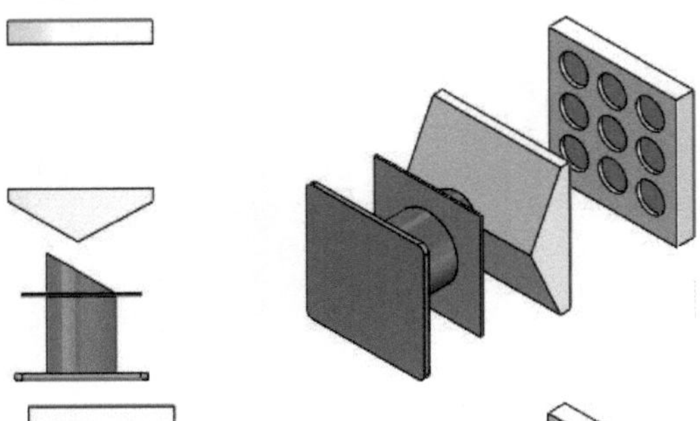

Offset from Surface:

Extends the feature from the sketch plane to a specified distance from the selected surface.

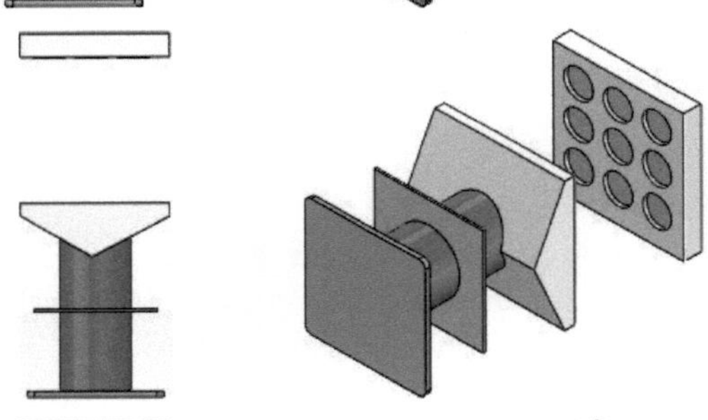

Up to Body:

Extends the feature from the sketch plane to a specified body. You can use the ”To Body” option with assemblies, castings, and multibody parts.

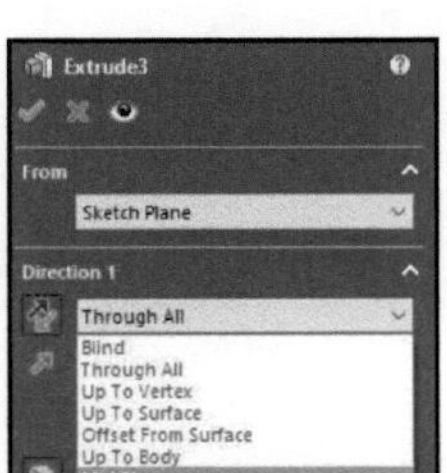

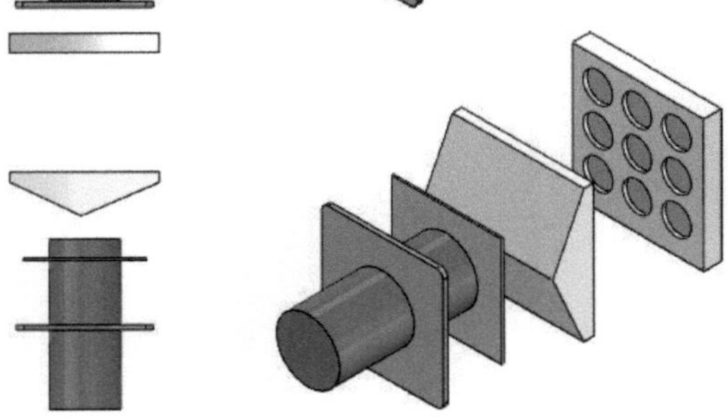

Mid Plane:

Extends the feature evenly in both directions from the sketch plane.

Project I

Sketch creation

Page 86 to 87

- Line construction, sketch snap function
  "Point Snap"
- Line construction, sketch snap function
  "Point Snap-Intersection Point Snap"
- Line construction, sketch snap function
  "Point Snap-Midpoint Snap"
- Line construction, sketch snap function
  "Point Snap-Tangent Snap"
- Line construction, sketch snap function
  "Tangent Snap"
- Linienkonstruktion, Skizzen-Fangfunktion
  "Point Snap-Perpendicular Snap"

4.3 Sketch creation, an overview

When you create a new part or assembly, the three default planes are aligned to specific views. The plane you select for the initial sketch determines the orientation of your part. When you create a new part and select a sketching tool, you will be prompted to choose a plane. There are two modes for sketching in 2D:

Click/drag mode and click mode.

SOLIDWORKS automatically detects which mode you want based on mouse pointer movements:

Clicking and dragging the first point puts you in **click-drag mode.**
Clicking and releasing the mouse button puts you in **click mode.**

In **click mode**, the Line and Arc tools create segment chains as you click. To complete a sketch chain, do one of the following:

Double-click to end the element chain and keep the tool active.
Right-click and select End Chain.
Press the Esc key to end the chain and deactivate the tool.
Move the cursor out of the viewport to stop dragging. You can then select a different tool to end the chain.

4.3.1 Line construction, sketch snap function "Point"

Line

Point

Line (Command Tab **Sketch** / **Geometric elements**)
from **Point** (1) to **Point** (2)

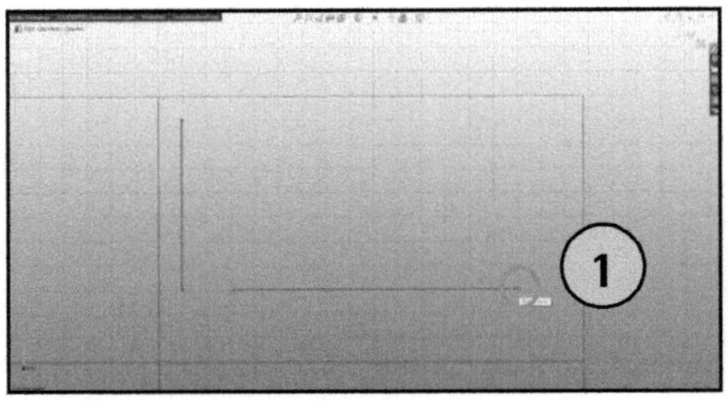

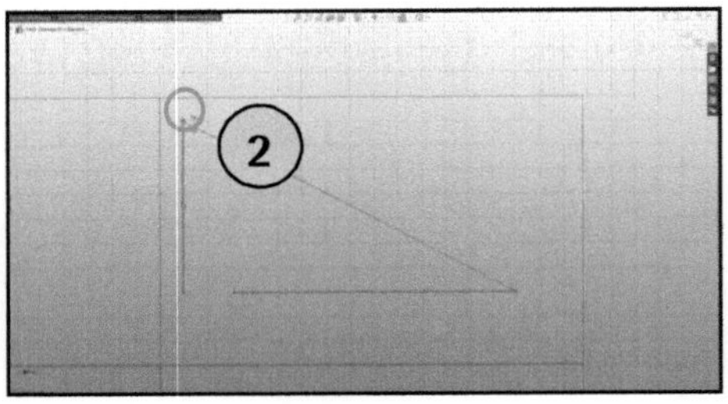

4.3.2 Line construction, sketch snap function, "Point-Midpoint"

Line

Point

Midpoint

Line (Command Tab **Sketch** / **Geometric elements**)
from **Point** (3) to **Midpoint** (4)

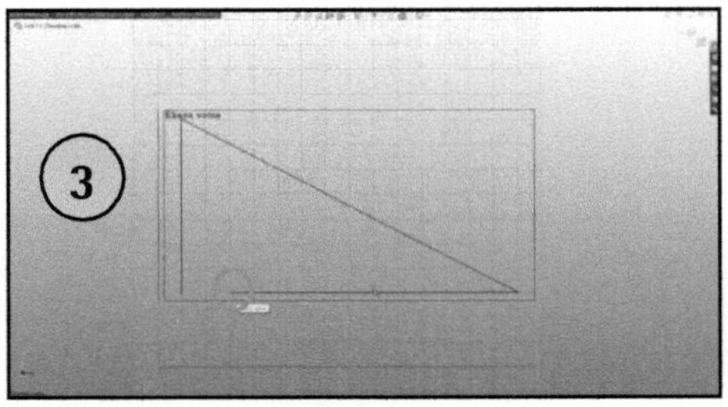

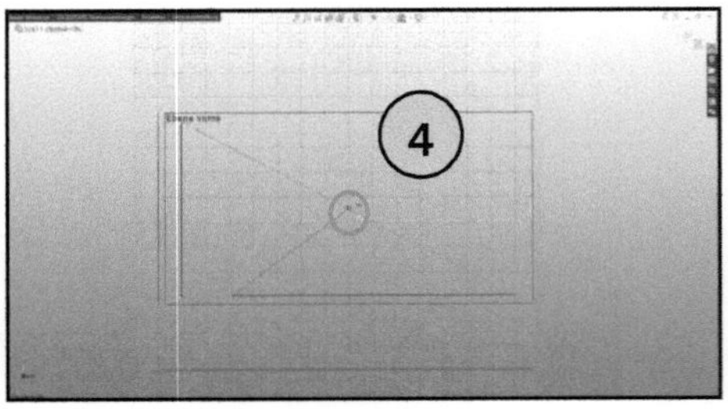

4.3.3 Line construction, sketch snap function, "Point-Centerpoint"

(Command Tab **Sketch** / **Geometric elements**)
from **Point** (5) to **Centerpoint** (6)

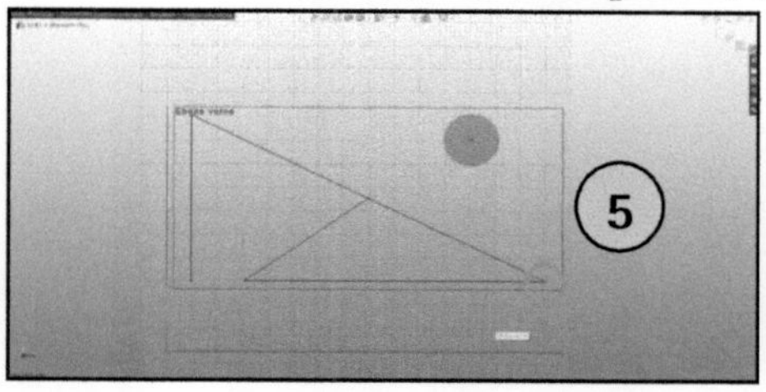

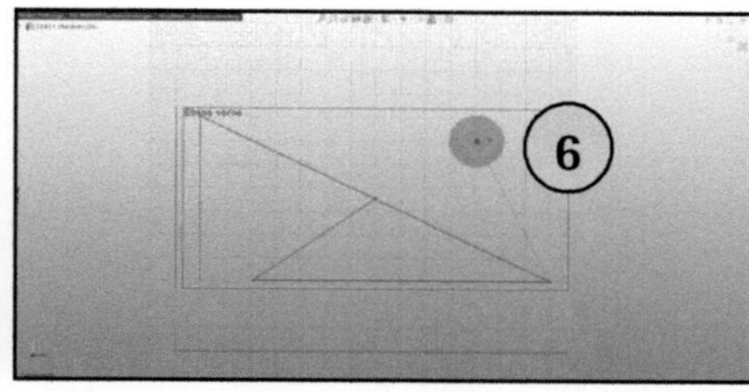

4.3.4 Line construction, sketch snap function, "Point-Tangent Point"

(Command Tab **Sketch** / **Geometric elements**)
from **Point** (7) to **Tangent Point** (8)

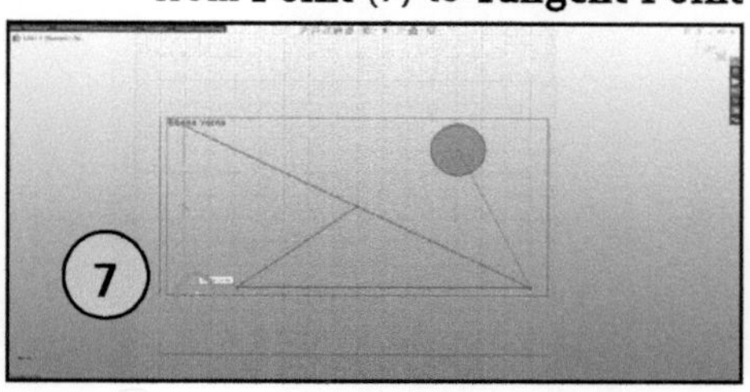

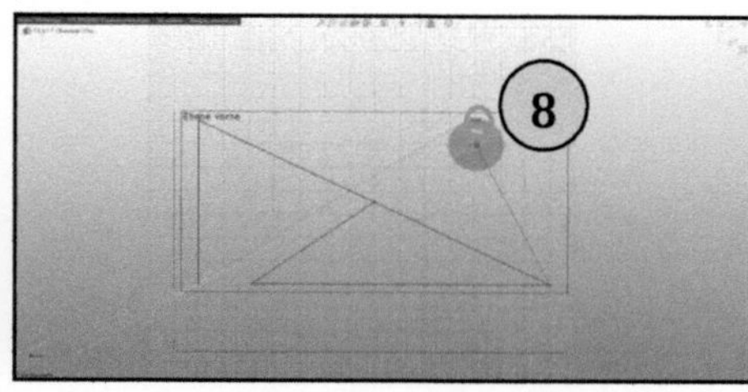

4.3.5 Line construction, sketch snap function, "Tangent"

(Command Tab **Sketch** / **Geometric elements**)
from **Tangent Point** (9) to **Tangent Point** (10)

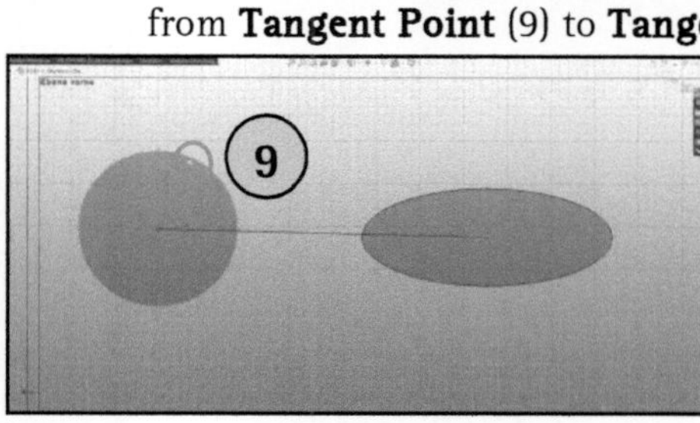

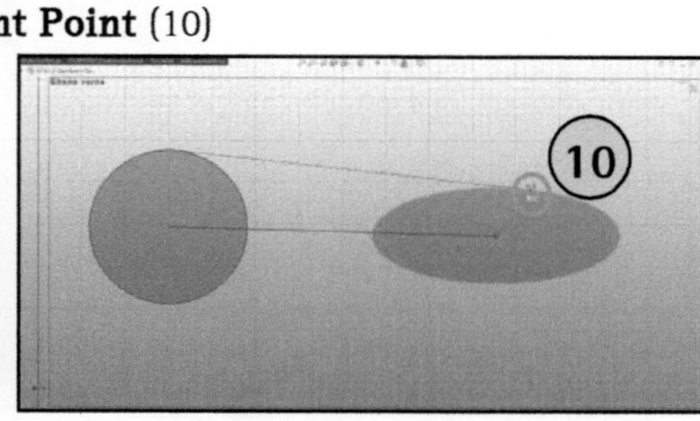

4.3.6 Line construction, sketch snap function, "Point-Perpendicular"

(Command Tab **Sketch** / **Geometric elements**)
from **Point** (11) to **Perpendicular Point** (12)

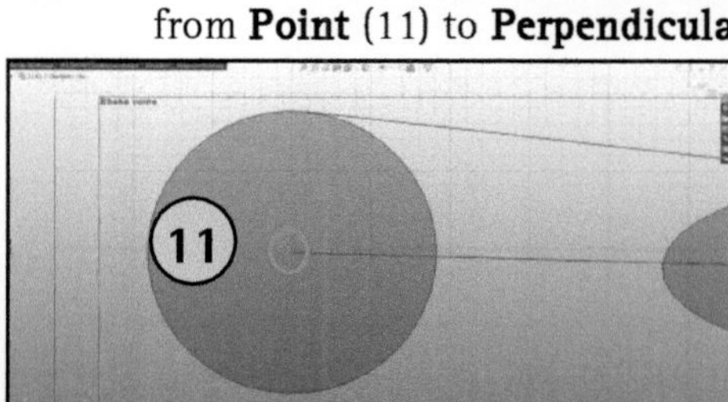

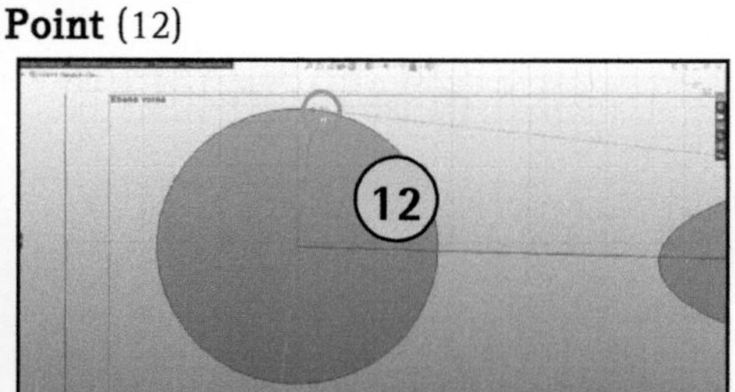

Project II

Sketch relationships
Page 90 to 99

- Relationship assignment
  “Horizontal or Vertical“
- Relationship assignment
  “Merge“
- Relationship assignment
  ”Concident“
- Relationship assignment
  ”Parallel“
- Relationship assignment
  ”Midpoint“
- Relationship assignment
  “Perpendicular“
- Relationship assignment
  ”Equal“
- Relationship assignment
  ”Symmetric“
- Relationship assignment
  ”Tangent“
- Relationship assignment
  ”Conzentric“
- Relationship assignment
  ”Collinear“
- Relationship assignment
  “Intersection“

4.4 Sketch Relationships

With SOLIDWORKS, it is not necessary to fully dimension or define sketches before using them to create features. However, you should fully define sketches before considering the part complete.

4.4.1 Sketch definitions

Sketches can be in one of five different states. The sketch's state is displayed in the status bar at the bottom of the SOLIDWORKS window.

4.4.1.1 Fully defined sketches are black

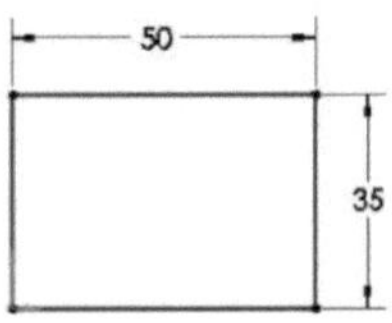

In a fully defined sketch, all lines and curves in the sketch, as well as their positions, are described by dimensions, relations, or both.

Sketches do not need to be fully defined to be used for creating features. However, you should fully define sketches to maintain your design plan.

4.4.1.2 Under defined sketches are blue

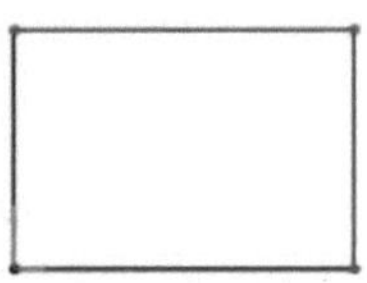

You can view the under defined elements of a sketch to determine which dimensions or relations still need to be added for the sketch to be fully defined. Color coding indicates whether a sketch is underdefined.

Underdefined sketches are not only color-coded, but their elements can also be dragged, as they are not fixed within the sketch.

4.4.1.3 Over defined sketches are yellow

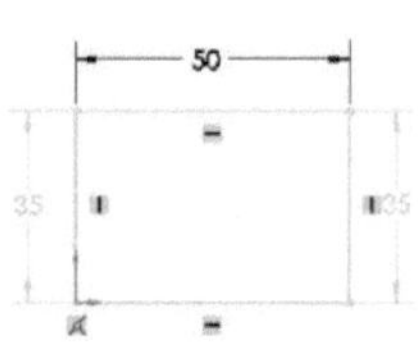

Over defined sketches contain redundant dimensions or conflicting relations. You can delete overdefined dimensions or relations, but you cannot edit them.

A sketch is over-dimensioned if both vertical lines of the rectangle are dimensioned. By definition, a rectangle has two sides of equal length; therefore, dimensioning the side length is only necessary once.

4.4.1.4 No solution found

The sketch is not solved. The geometry, relations, and dimensions that prevent the sketch from being solved are displayed.

This requires deleting some relations or dimensions, or revert the sketch element to its previous state.

4.4.1.5 Invalid solution found

The sketch is solved, but it results in invalid geometry, such as zero line length, zero arc radius, or a self-intersecting spline.

This indicates that the sketch geometry cannot determine the position of one or more sketch elements.

4.4.2 Assigning relationships in sketches

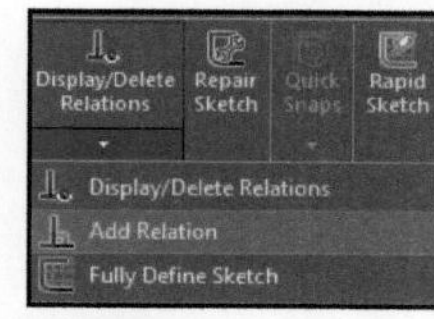

4.4.2.1 Relationship assignment "Horizontal or Vertical"

Horizontal or Vertical:

One or more lines or at least two points.

Lines are defined horizontally or vertically. Points are aligned horizontally or vertically.

Add Relation

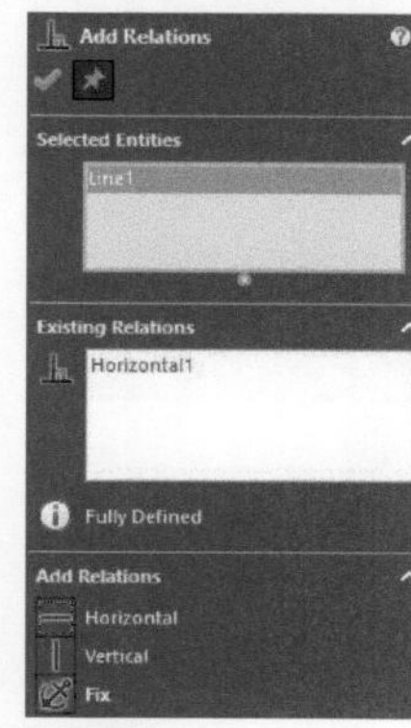

Add Relation (Command Tab **Sketch / Relation**)

Select the drawn line (1).

Activate **Horizontal** relationship (2).

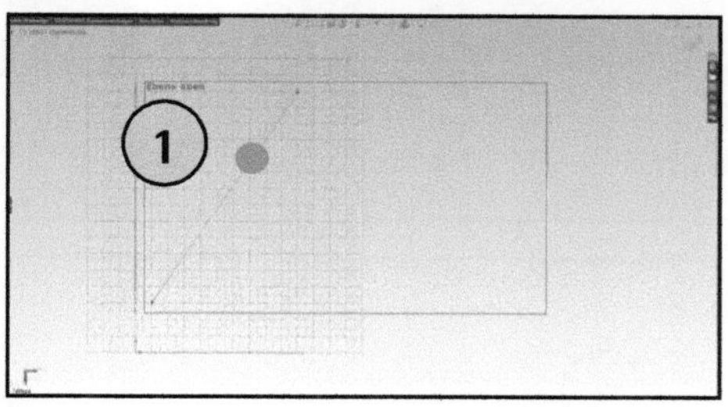

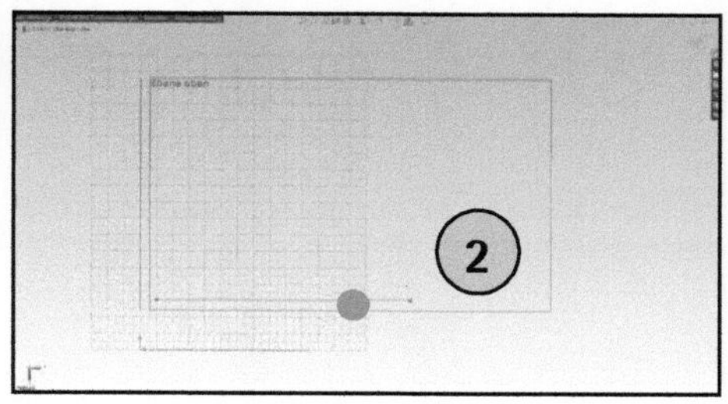

Relation Horizontal

4.4.2.2 Relationship assignment "Points merge"

Points merge:

Two sketch points or endpoints.

The two points are merged into one point.

Add Relation (Command Tab **Sketch / Relation**)

Select the shown endpoints of the lines (3, 4).

Add Relation

Activate **Merge** relationship (5).

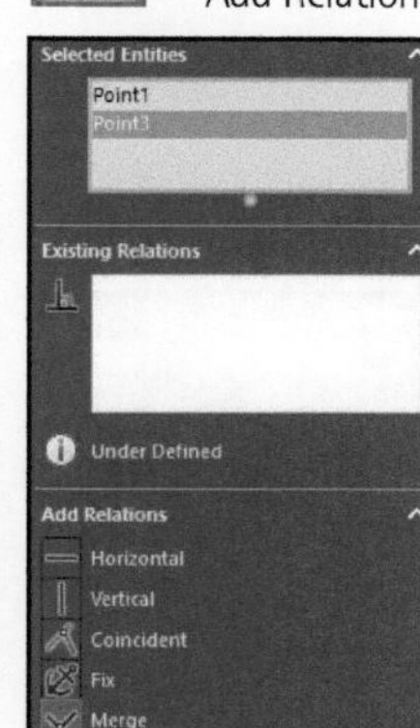

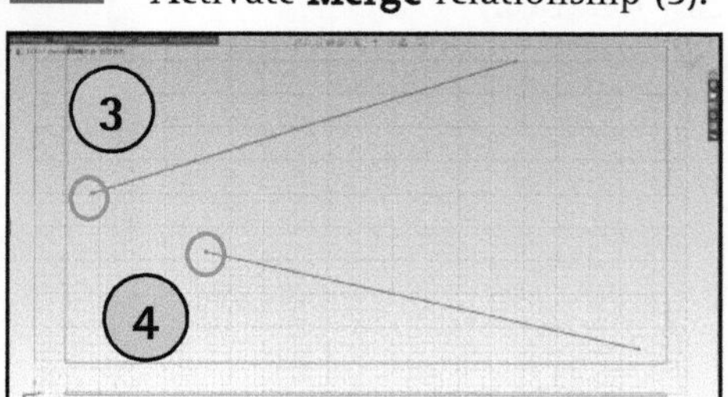

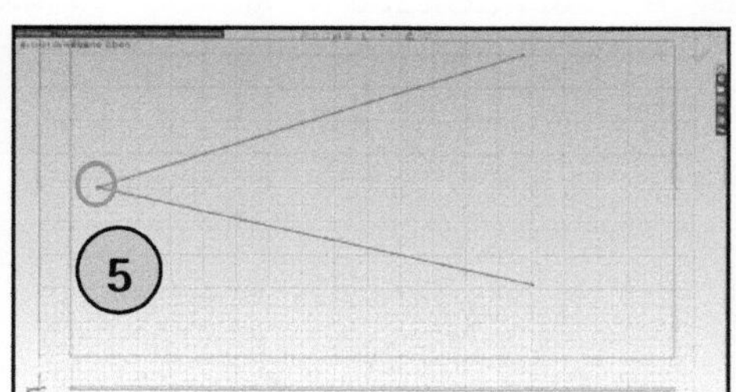

Relation Merge

4.4.2.3 Relationship assignment "Concident"

Concident:
A point on a line, rectangle, arc, ellipse, etc.
The target point lies at the intersection of the origin planes.

Add Relation

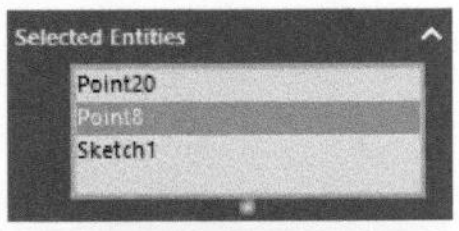

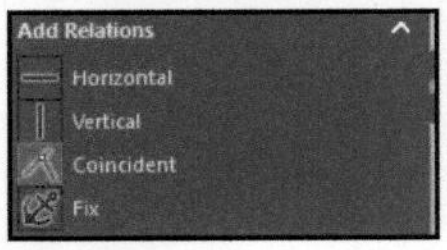

Relation Concident

Add Relation (Command Tab **Sketch** / **Relation**)
Select the center point of the rectangle center lines shown (1, 2).

Activate **Concident** relationship (3).

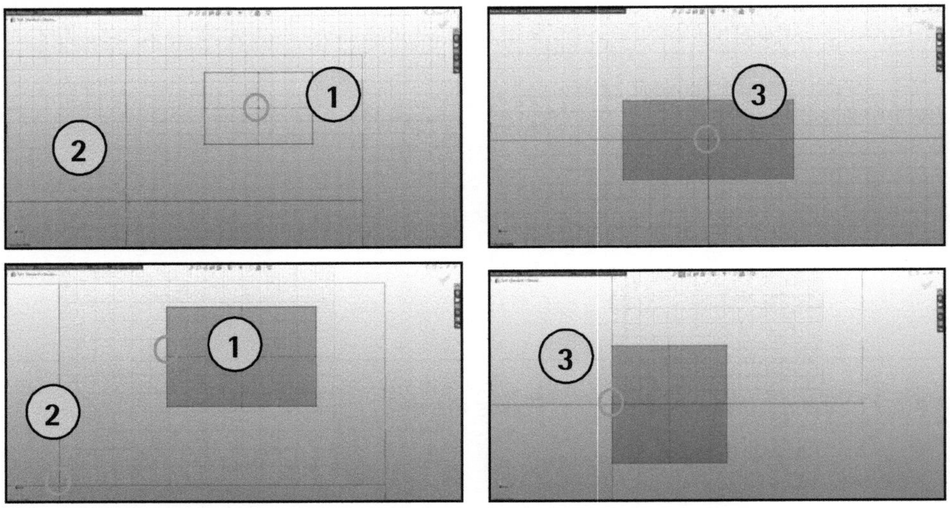

4.4.2.4 Relationship assignment "Parallel"

Parallel:
At least two lines.
The elements are parallel to each other.

Add Relation

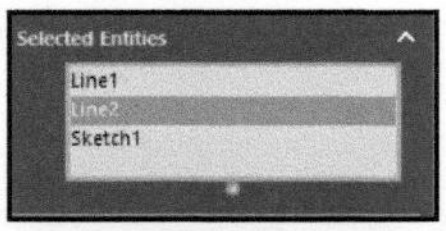

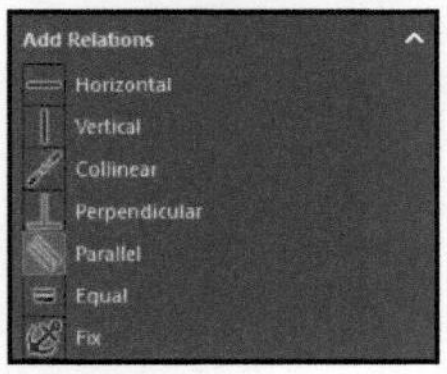

Relation Parallel

Add Relation (Command Tab **Sketch** / **Relation**)
Select the lines shown (4, 5).

Activate **Parallel** relationship (6).

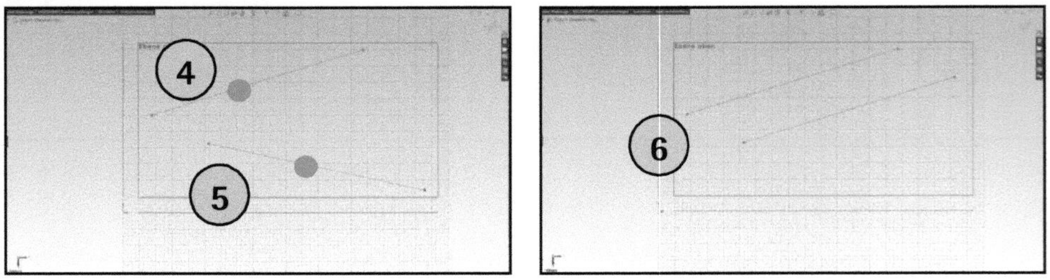

4.4.2.5 Relationship assignment "Midpoint"

Midpoint:
Two lines or a point and a line.
The point remains at the midpoint of the line.

Add Relation (Command Tab **Sketch** / **Relation**)
Select the lines shown (1, 2).

Activate **Midpoint** relationship (3).

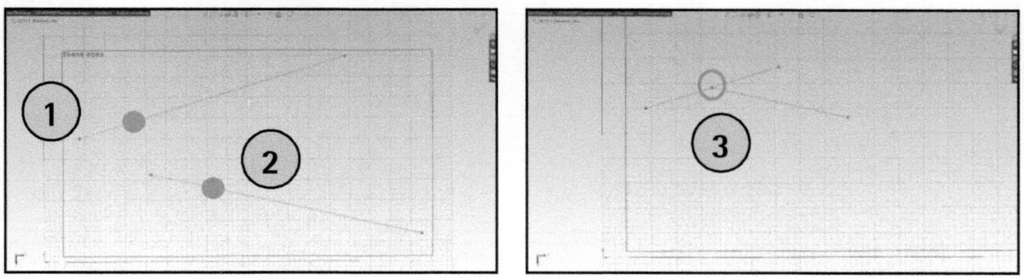

Add Relation

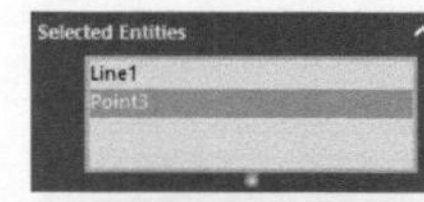

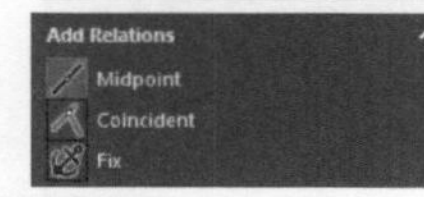

Relation Midpoint

4.4.2.6 Relationship assignment "Perpendicular"

Perpendicular:
The second line was sketched perpendicular to the first.
The sketching tool is active, and the sketch snap function at the midpoint is displayed on the line.

Add Relation (Command Tab **Sketch** / **Relation**)
Select the lines shown (4, 5).

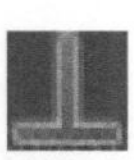

Activate **Perpendicular** relationship (6).

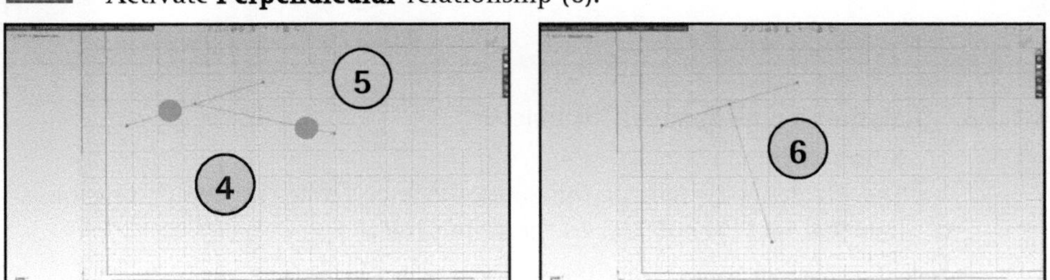

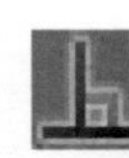

Add Relation

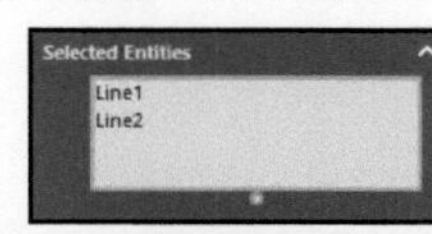

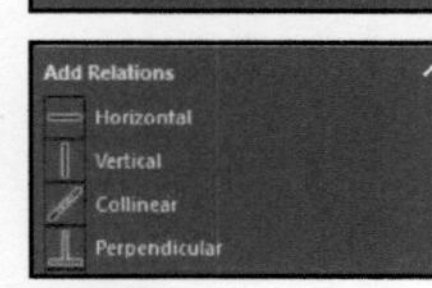

Relation Perpendicular

4.4.2.7 Relationship assignment "Equal"

Equal:
At least two lines or at least two arcs.
The line lengths and radii remain the same or become the same.

Add Relation

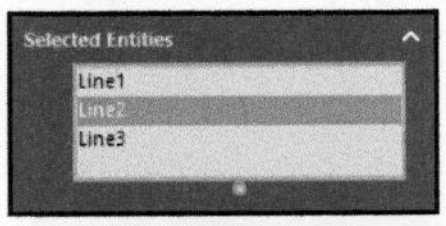

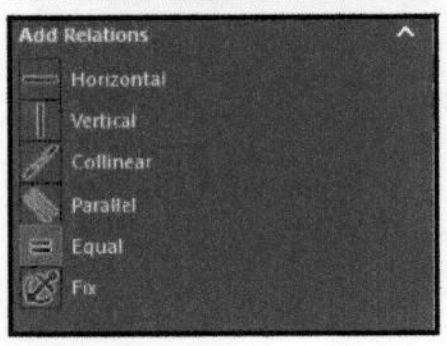

Relation Equal

Add Relation (Command Tab **Sketch / Relation**)
Select the geometry objects shown (1, 2, 3).

Activate **Equal** relationship (4).

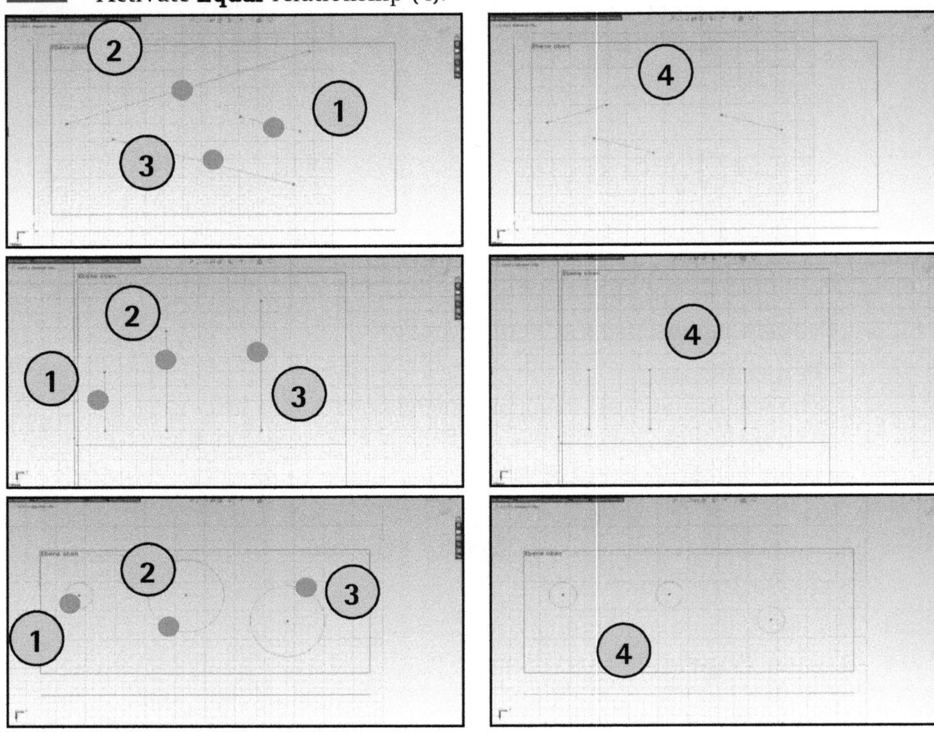

4.4.2.8 Relationship assignment "Symmetric"

Symmetric:
The elements remain at the same distance from the center line on a line that is perpendicular to the center line.

- Click the selected line and assign it the option **For construction** (1, 2).

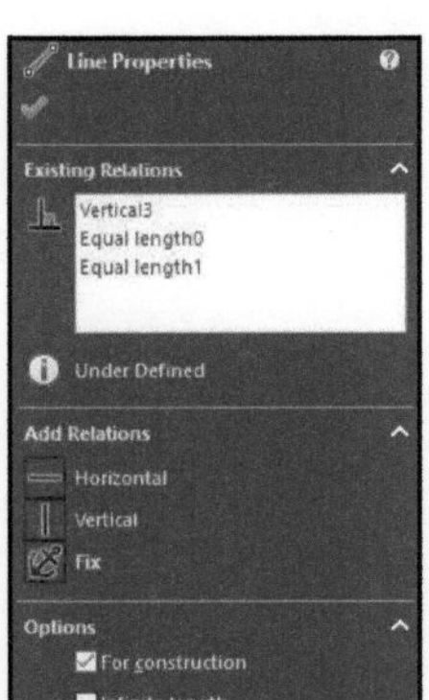

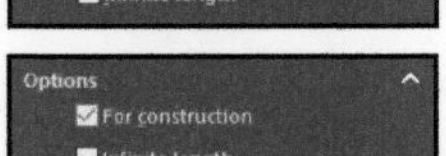

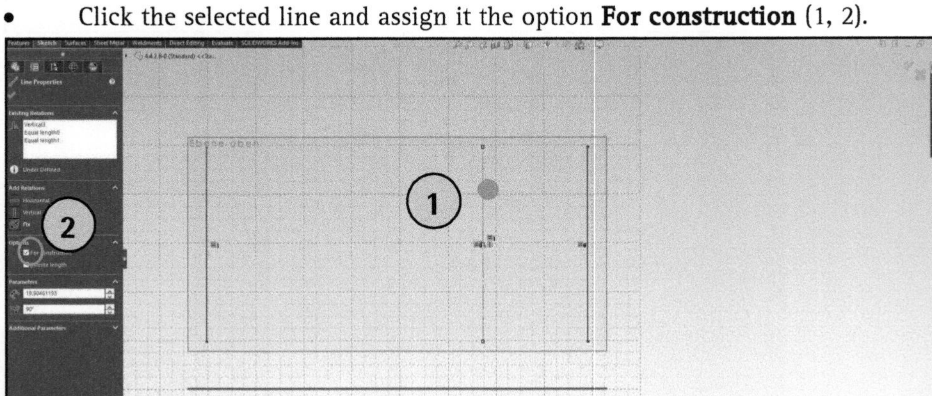

Add Relation (Command Tab **Sketch** / **Relation**)

Select the geometry objects shown (2, 3).

Activate **Symmetric** relationship (4).

Add Relation

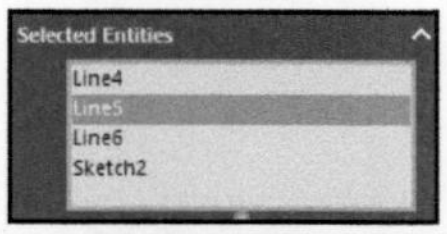

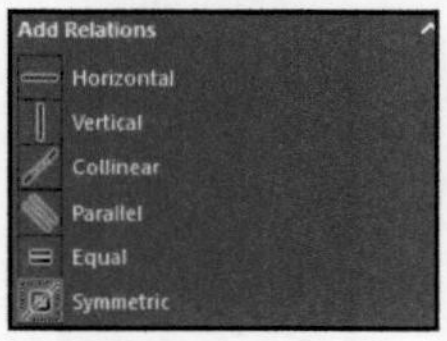

Relation Symmetric

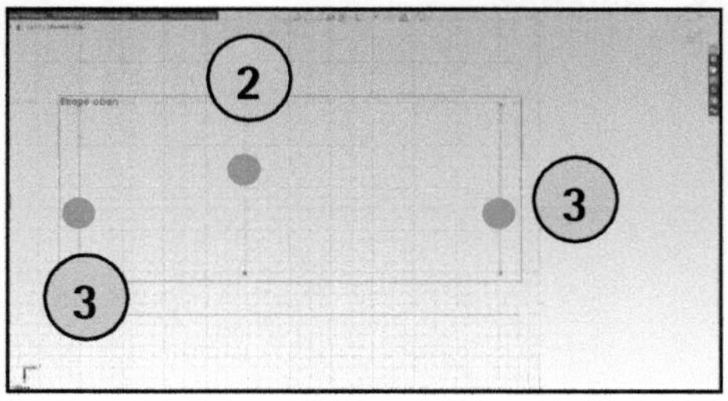

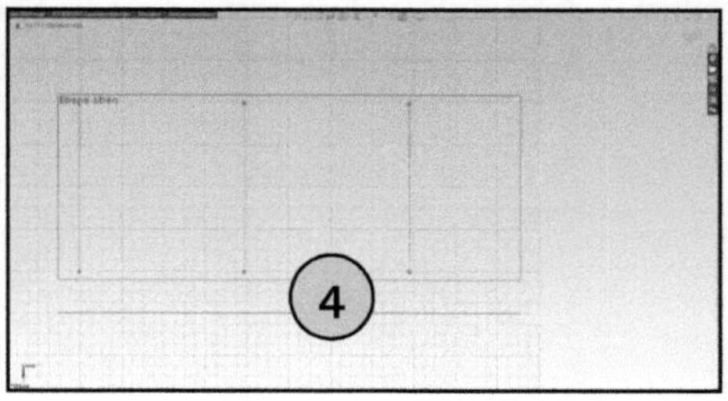

4.4.2.9 Relationship assignment "Tangent"

Tangent:

A circular arc, an ellipse, a spline, and a line or circular arc. The two elements remain tangential.

Add Relation (Command Tab **Sketch** / **Relation**)

Select the geometry objects shown (5, 6).

Activate **Tangential** relationship (7).

Add Relation

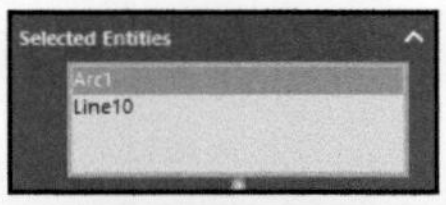

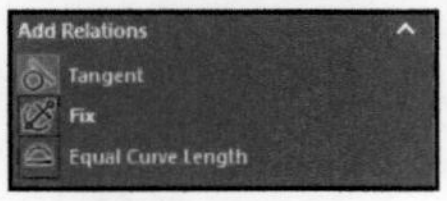

Relation Tangent

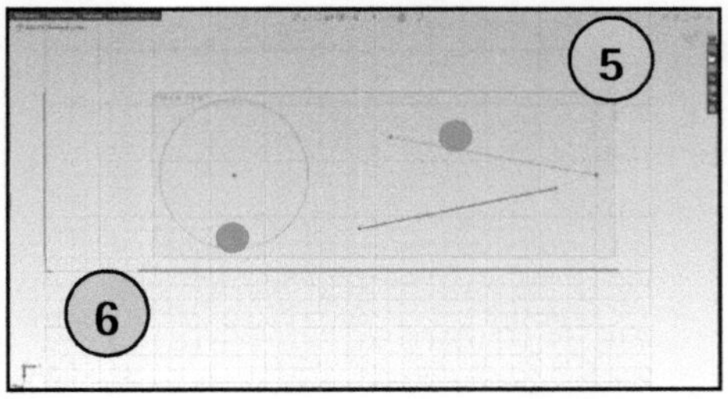

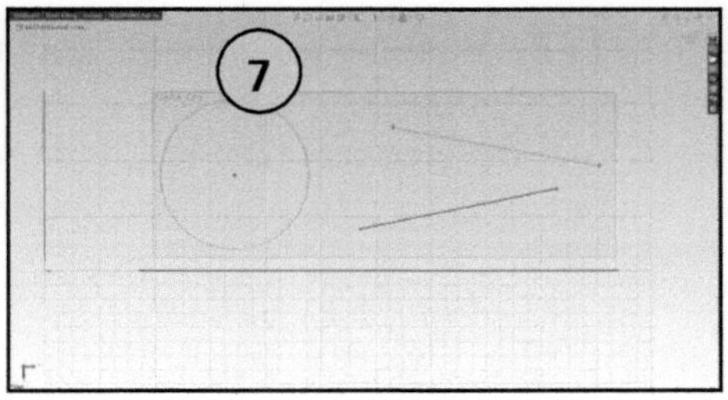

- Select the geometry objects shown (5, 6).

Activate **Tangential** relationship (7).

The first assigned relationship will be carried over.

Relation Tangent

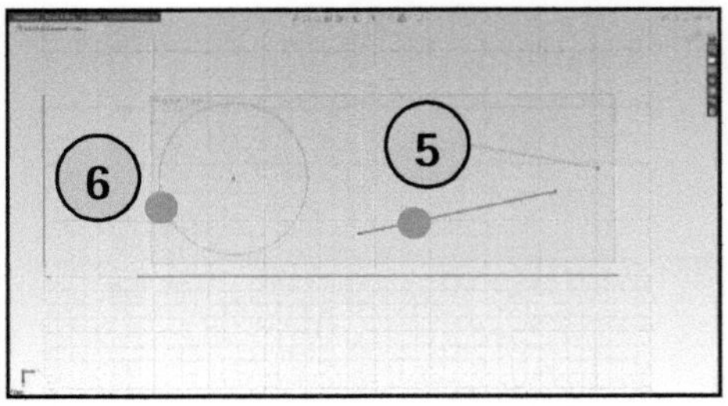

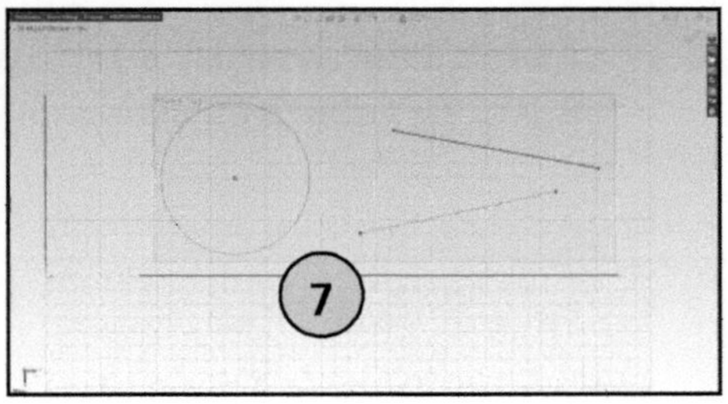

Add Relation

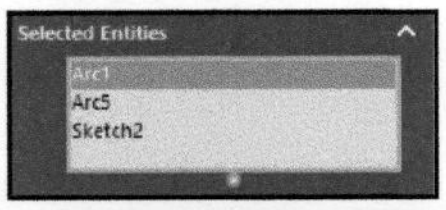

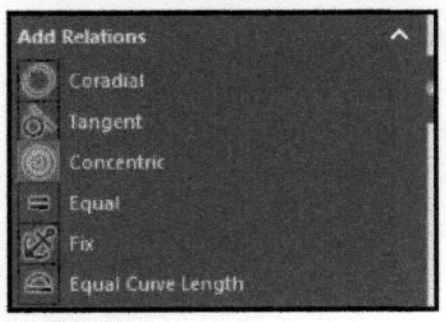

Relation
Concentric

4.4.2.10 Relationship assignment "Concentric"

Concentric:
Mindestens zwei Kreisbogen oder ein Punkt und ein Kreisbogen. Die Kreisbogen haben denselben Mittelpunkt.

Add Relation (Command Tab **Sketch** / **Relation**)
Select the geometry objects shown (1, 2).

Activate **Concentric** relationship (3).

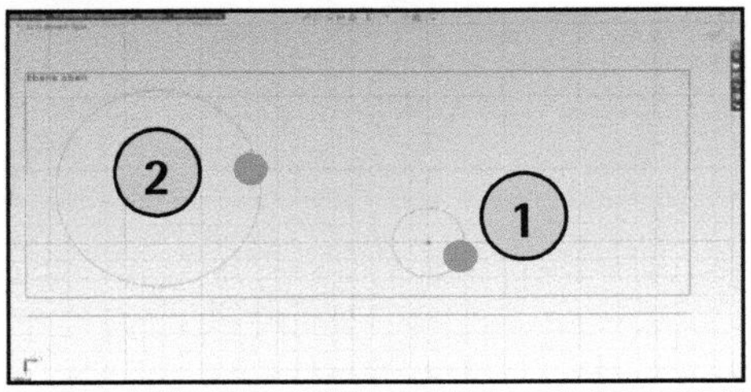

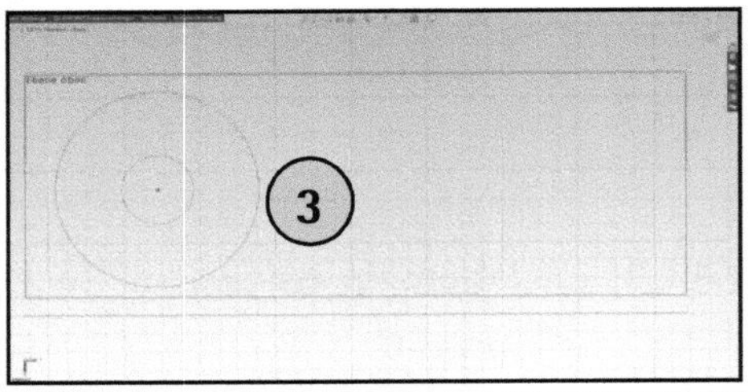

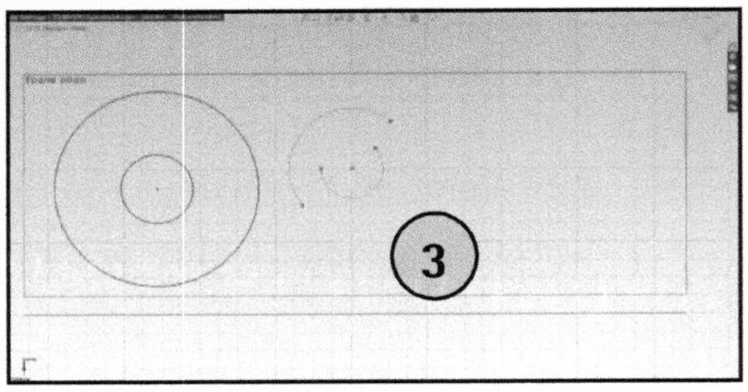

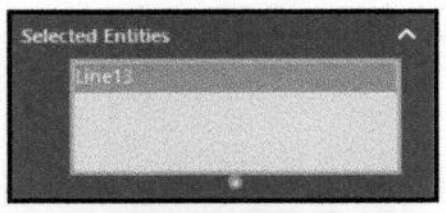

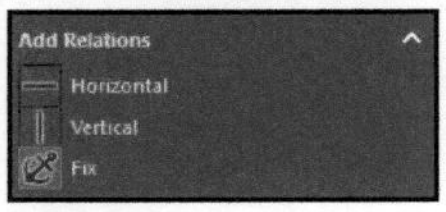

Relation
Fix

Add Relation

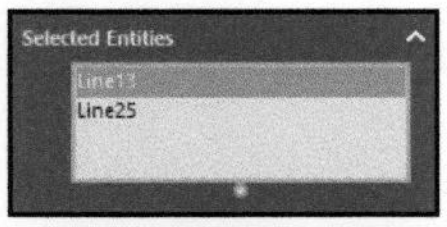

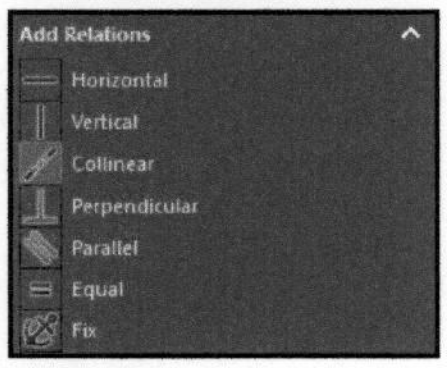

Relation
Collinear

4.4.2.11 Relationship assignment "Collinear"

Collinear:
The elements then lie on the same infinite line.

- Click the selected line, assign this relationship **Fix** to (4, 5).

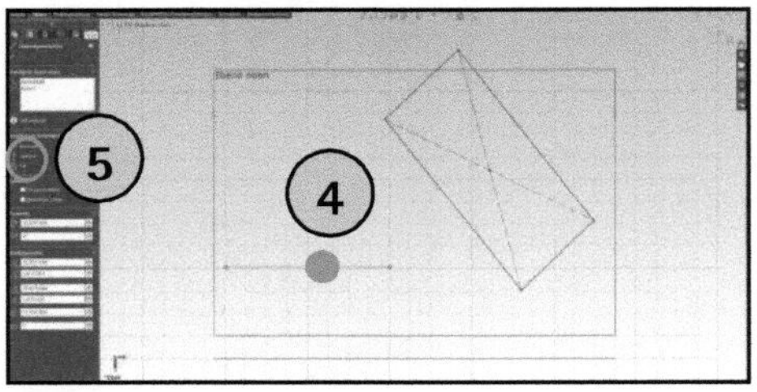

Add Relation (Command Tab **Sketch** / **Relation**)
Select the geometry objects shown (6, 7).

Activate **Collinear** relationship (8).

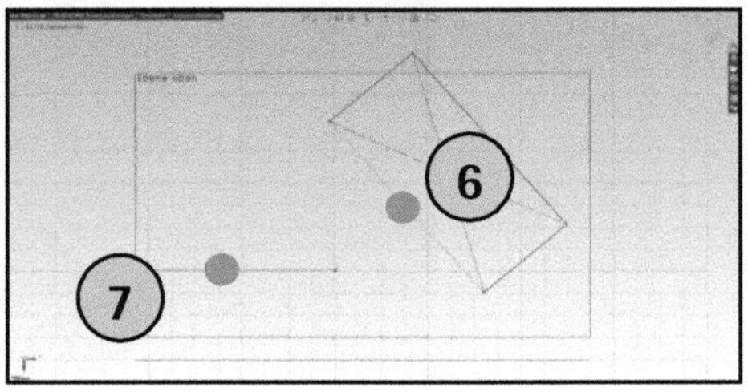

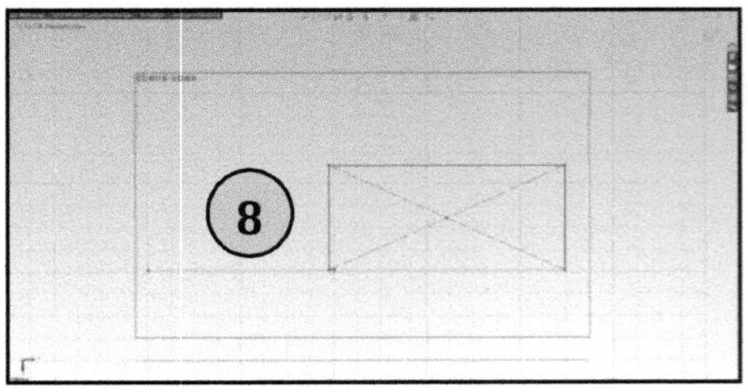

Add Relation (Command Tab **Sketch** / **Relation**)
Select the geometry objects shown (9).

Activate **Collinear** relationship (10).

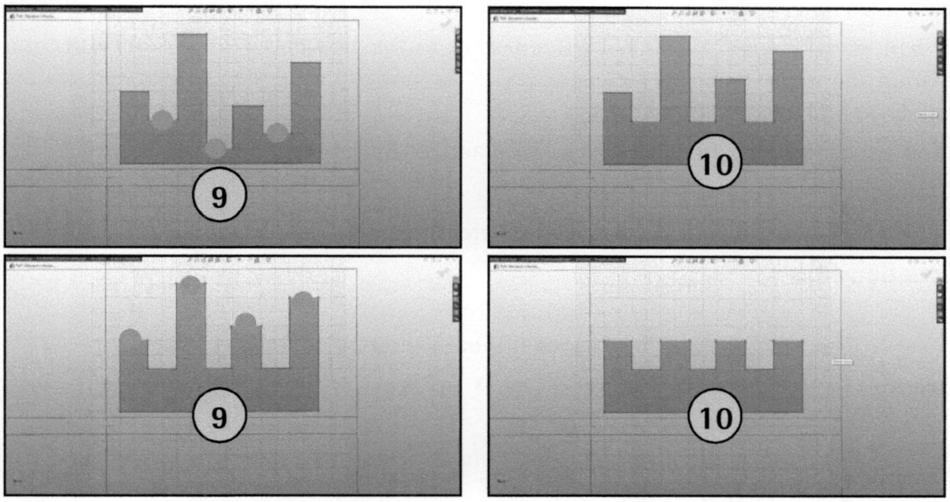

Add Relation

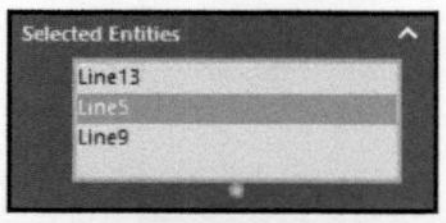

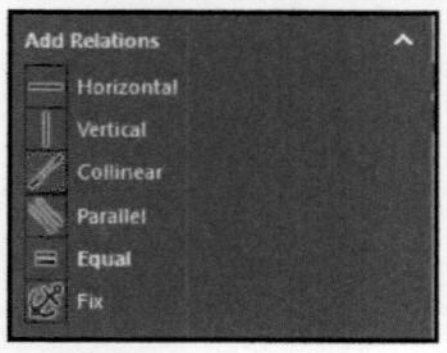

Relation
Collinear

4.4.2.12 Relationship assignment "Intersection"

Intersection:
Two lines and a line endpoint.
The line endpoint is located at the intersection of the lines.

Add Relation (Command Tab **Sketch** / **Relation**)
Select the shown endpoint of the line (11).
Select the intersecting lines (12, 13).

Activate **Intersection** relationship (14).

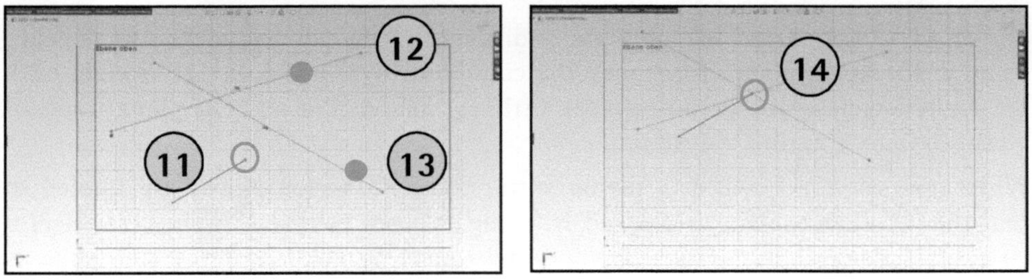

Add Relation

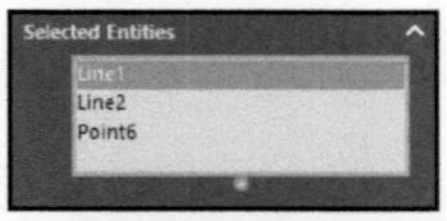

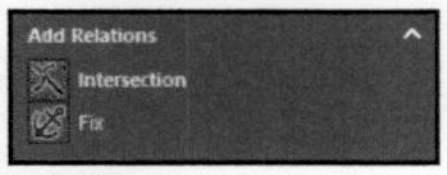

Relation
Intersection

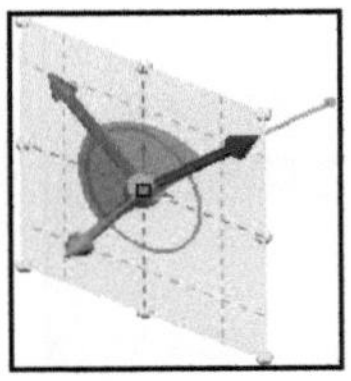

4.4.3 3D Sketching Functions

4.4.3.1 3D Sketching Functions, basics

When sketching in 3D, you can snap to the principal directions X, Y, or Z and apply constraints along X, along Y, and along Z. These constraints are based on the global coordinate system.

When sketching on a plane, you can snap to the horizontal or vertical direction within the plane and apply constraints to the horizontal/vertical. These constraints apply to a plane, a planar surface.

You can add planes to a 3D sketch. 3D plane attributes include:

Define:

Planes can be fully defined, underdefined, and overdefined.

Relationships:

Add or remove relationships to layers.
Use relationships to place additional geometry or the layer itself.

Move:

You can drag and move planes.
You can resize planes by dragging their corner handles or rotate them using the middle handles.

Aktivieren Activate:

Double-click a plane to activate it.

When you use Quick Sketch with an open sketch tool, a plane is created on a selected planar face.

In the **Properties** PropertyManager, you can hide dimensions, relations, or planes.

When sketching in 2D mode on a 3D plane, elements that are not on the active sketch plane are dimmed. Relations and dimensions that do not refer to the plane or elements on that plane are also hidden.

When you create a 3D sketch, you sketch by default relative to the model's default coordinate system. To switch to one of the other two default planes, click the desired sketching tool and press the **Tab** key.

The origin of the current sketch plane is displayed. You can also create 3D sketches using a 3D sketch plane. To change the coordinate system for the 3D sketch, click the desired sketch tool, hold down the Ctrl key, and click a plane, a planar face, or a user-defined coordinate system.

When you select a plane or a planar surface, the 3D sketch planes are rotated so that the XY sketch plane is aligned with the selected element. When you select a coordinate system, the 3D sketch planes are rotated so that the XY sketch plane is parallel to the XY plane of the coordinate system.

4.4.3.2 Sketch relationships in 3D sketches

Many relationships available in 2D sketches are also available in 3D sketches.

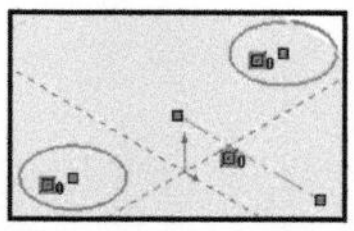

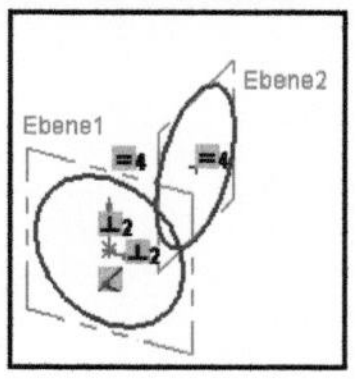

Additional sketch relationships are available for 3D sketching:

- Perpendicular relationships between lines through a point on a surface.
- Relationships between 3D sketch elements on the same and on different sketch planes.
- Symmetrical relationships around a line between 3D sketches created on the same plane.
- Relationships using spline handles, such as along an axis or between handles.
- Center-to-center relationships.
- Equal relationships.
- Tangential or equal curvature relationships between surfaces and splines.
- Relationships between circular arcs and other sketch elements.
- Relationships between circular arcs: concentric, tangential, or equal relationships.
- Normals between a line and a plane or between points and a plane.

4.4.3.3 Dimensioning in 3D sketches, a selection

Various dimension types are available in 3D sketches: absolute, along **X**, along **Y** and along **Z**:

Absolutely:

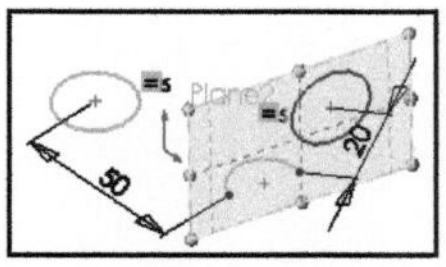

Measures the absolute distances between two points.
If you press the Tab key to dimension along an axis, press and hold the **Tab** key until the cursor changes shape to indicate an absolute measurement.

Along X:

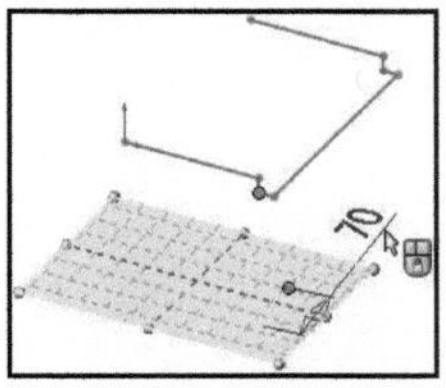

Measures the distances between two points along the X-axis.
Press the **Tab** key once to measure along the X-axis.

Along Y:

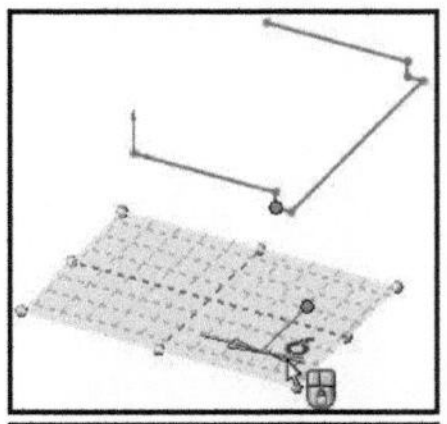

Measures the distances between two points along the Y-axis.
Press the Tab key twice to measure along the Y-axis.

Along Z:

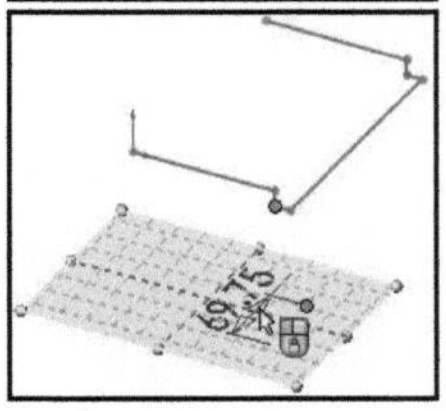

Measures the distances between two points along the Z-axis. Press the Tab key three times to measure along the Z-axis.

Project III

Sketch dimensions

Page 102 to 107

- Dimension entries in 2D sketches
  "Horizontal und Vertical"
- Dimension entries in 2D sketches
  "Angular dimensioning"
- Dimension entries in 2D sketches
  "Distance dimensioning"
- Dimension entries in 2D sketches
  "Circular dimensioning"
- Dimension entries in 2D sketches
  "Radius dimensioning"
- Dimension entries in 2D sketches
  "Quadrant-circle spacing dimensioning"
- Dimension entries in 2D sketches
  "Radian measure"
- Dimension entries in 2D sketches
  "Diameter dimensioning across centerline"
- Dimension entries in 2D sketches
  "Baseline Dimension"

4.5 Sketch Dimensions

4.5.1 Sketch Dimensions, basics

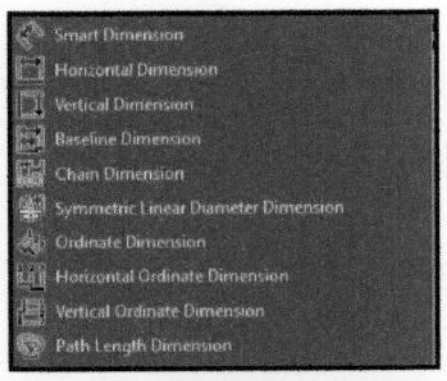

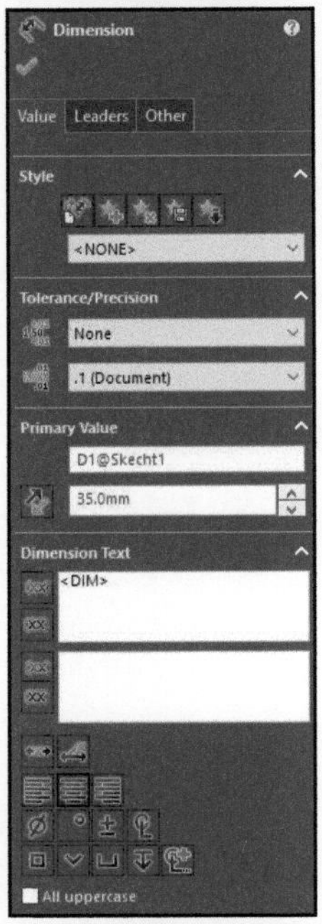

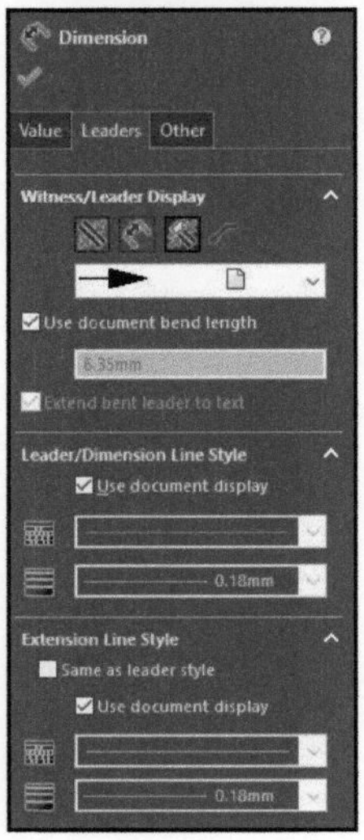

2D or 3D sketch elements are dimensioned using the Smart Dimension tool. You can drag or delete a dimension while the Smart Dimension tool is active.

Dimension types are determined by the sketch elements you select. For some dimension types (point-to-point, angular, circular), the location where the dimension is placed influences the dimension type that is added.

You can create features without adding dimensions to the sketches. However, it is generally recommended to dimension sketches. Dimension according to the design plan of the model.

For example, you should place holes at a specific distance from an edge or at a specific distance from each other; the default dimension type is parallel.

If you wish, you can also select a different dimension type from the context menu. Do the Right-click on the sketch and select **More Dimensions**.

Choose one of the following options:

Horizontal, vertical, ordinate, horizontal ordinate, or vertical ordinate. When editing a drawing view, you have the additional choice of dimension types datum and chamfer.

Select the elements to be dimensioned, as shown in the table below. As you move the cursor, the dimension will snap to the nearest orientation.

Click to place the dimension.

4.5.2 Dimensioning in 2D sketches

4.5.2.1 Dimension in 2D sketches, horizontal and vertical

Length of a line or edge. Select line (1) or
Select points (2).

Horizontal

Vertical

- Dimension entries in 2D sketches, **Horizontal**, select **Line**.

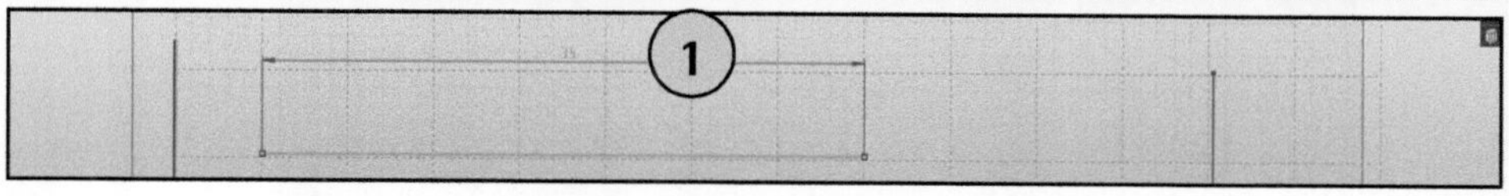

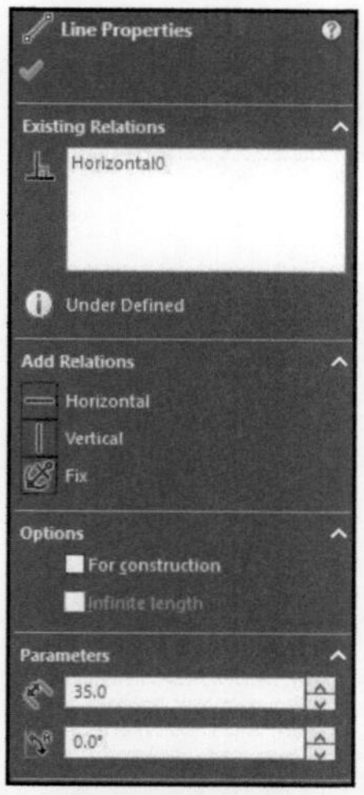

- Dimensioning in 2D sketches, **Horizontal**, select **Points**.

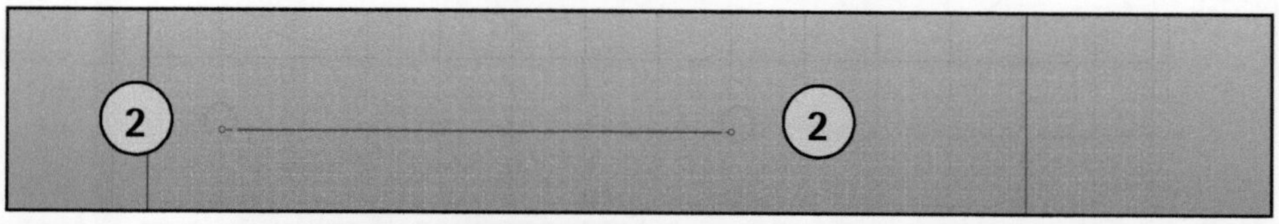

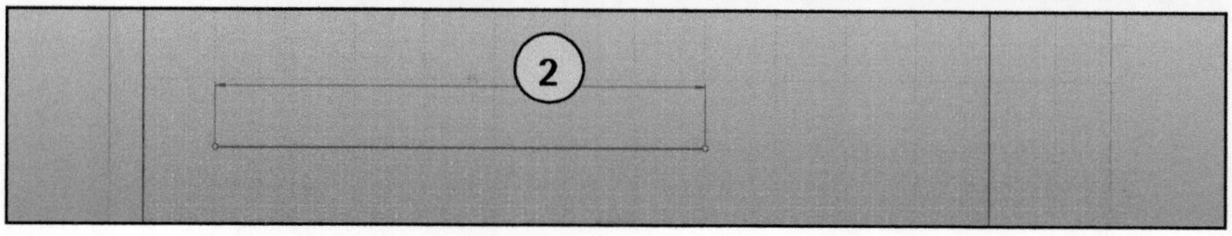

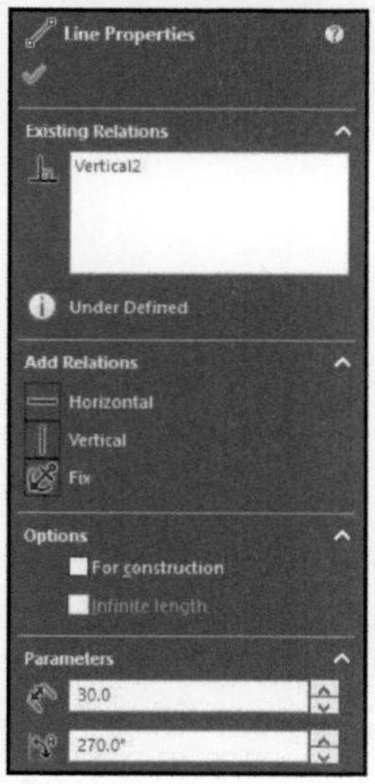

- Dimensioning in 2D sketches, **Vertical**.

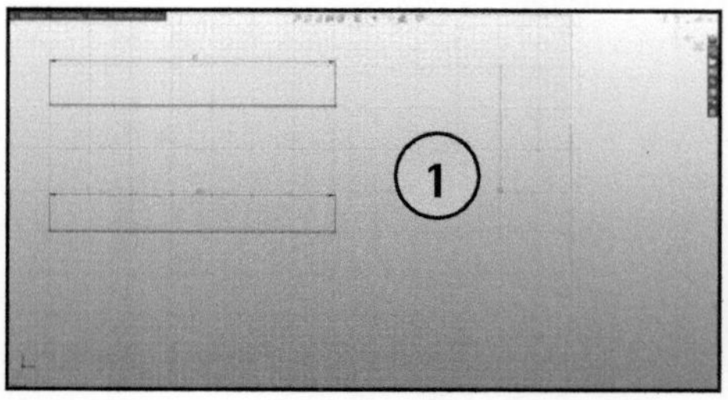

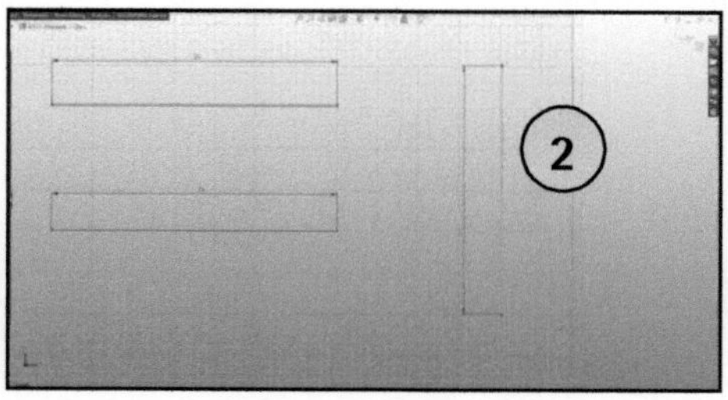

4.5.2.2 Dimensioning in 2D sketches, angular dimensioning

Smart Dimension

Angle between two lines.

Choose two lines or one line and one model edge; the position of the dimensions depends on the vector selection (1, 2, 3, 4).

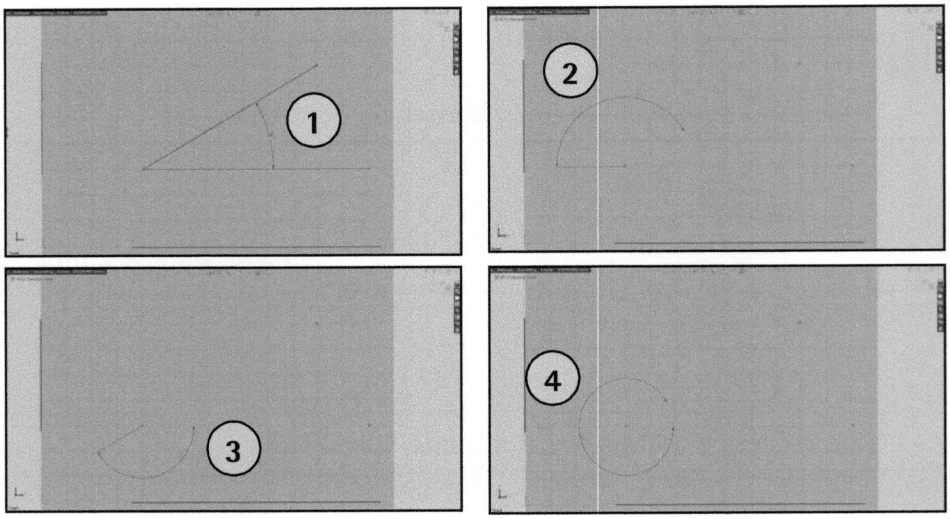

4.5.2.3 Dimensioning in 2D sketches, distance dimensioning

Smart Dimension

Distance between two lines.

Select two parallel lines.
Set the position. (5, 6).

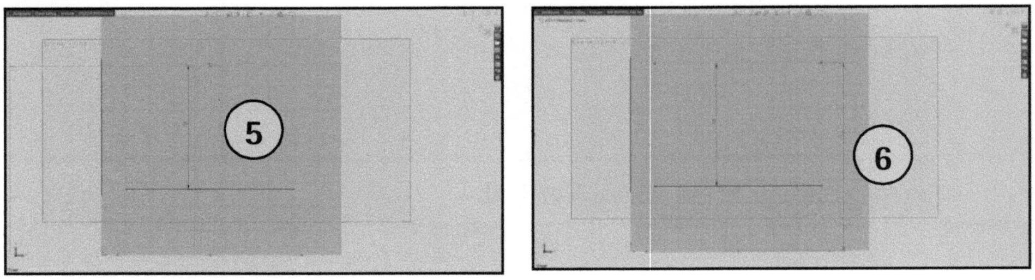

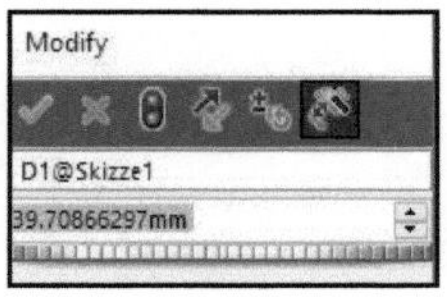

- Dimensional changes during dimension entry.
  Select the two lines to be dimensioned.
  Double-click on the dimension value (7).

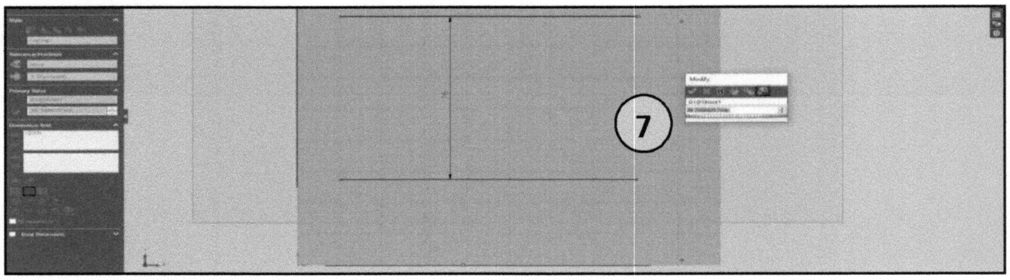

- Dimensional changes occur after entering the measurement.
  Double-click on the measurement value.

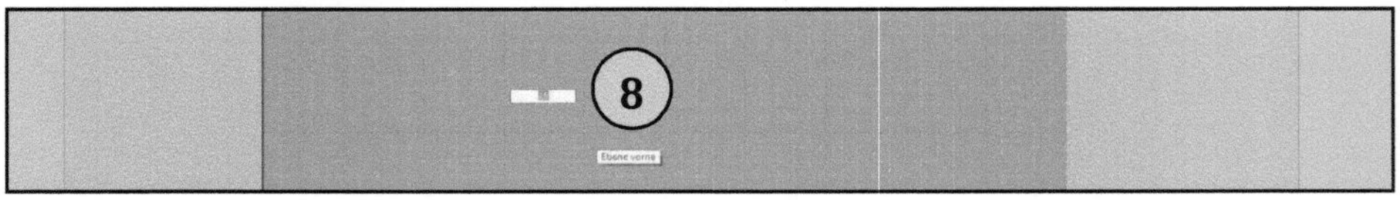

4.5.2.4 Dimensioning in 2D sketches, circular dimensioning

Circular dimensions

Apply the diameter of a circle.

Dimensions between arcs or circles, centering.

Smart Dimension

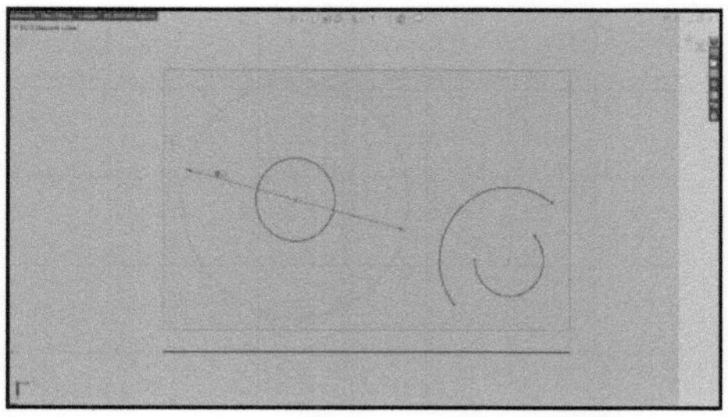

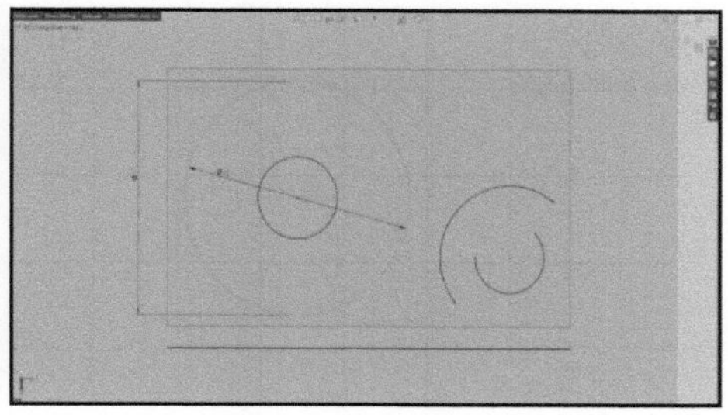

4.5.2.5 Dimensioning in 2D sketches, radius dimensioning

Arc dimensioning

Radius of a circular arc.

Linear center-to-center distances.

Smart Dimension

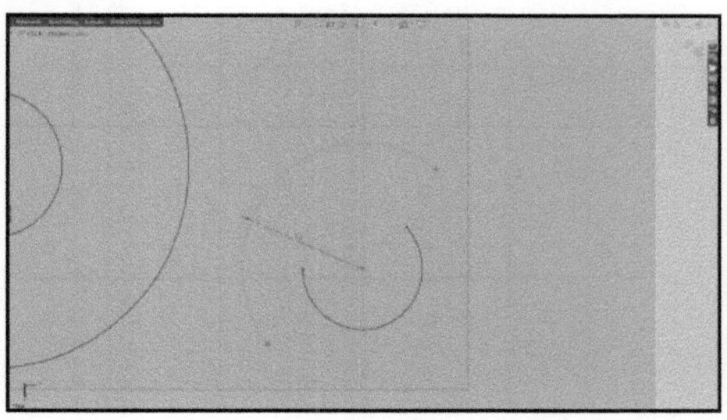

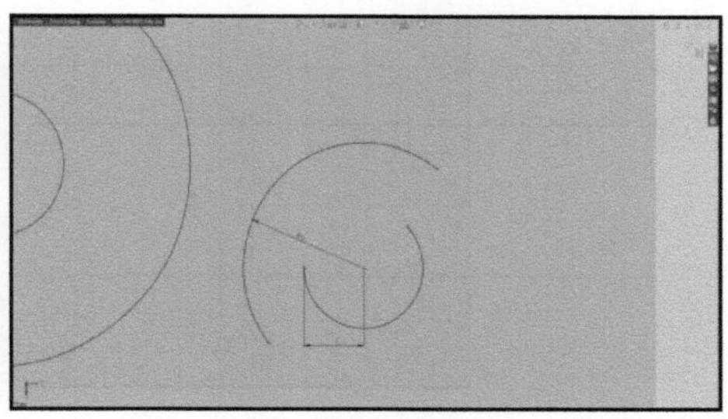

4.5.2.6 Dimensioning in 2D sketches, quadrant-circle distance dimensioning Dimensioning in 2D sketches, Diameter dimension using center

Circle center distance

Quadrant circle distance dimensioning

Dimensions between arcs or circles, center point application.

Select the circle. Hold down the **Shift** key and select the first quadrant of the arc and then the center point or the second quadrant.

Smart Dimension

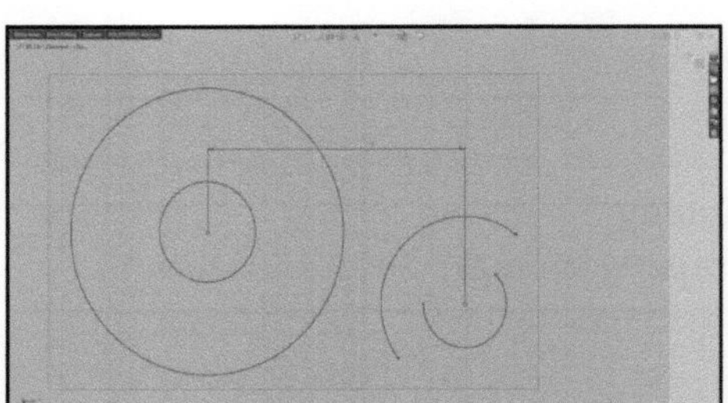

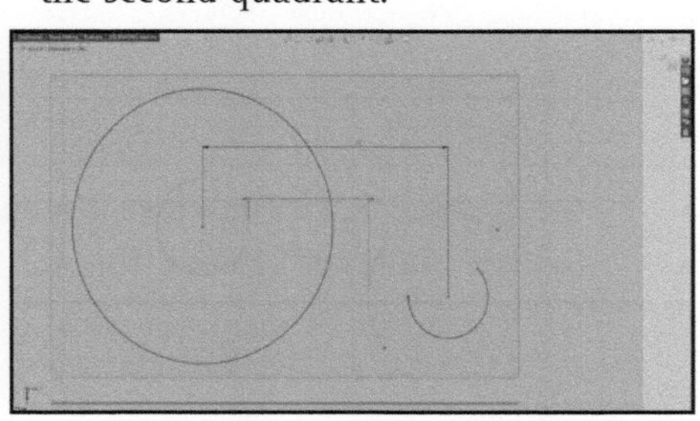

Smart
Dimension

4.5.2.7 Dimensioning in 2D sketches, Radian measure

Radian measure

Select the arc.
Press the **Ctrl** key and select the two endpoints of the arc.
Move the pointer to preview the dimension.

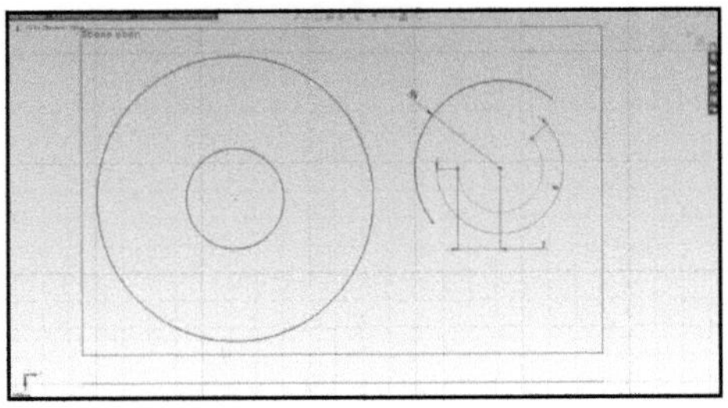

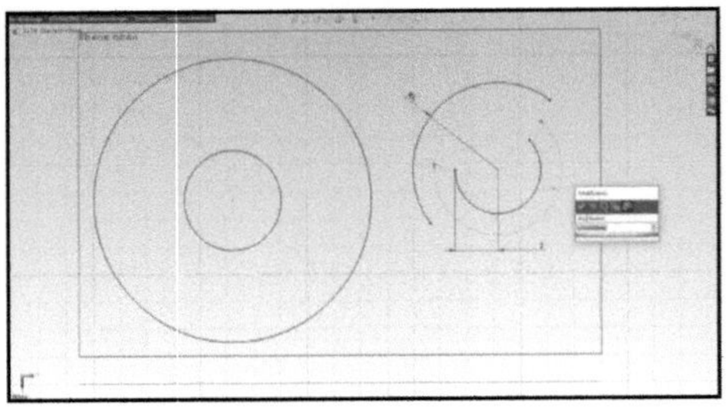

Smart
Dimension

4.5.2.8 Dimensioning in 2D sketches, Diameter dimensioning across centerline

Diameter dimensioning across centerline

The distance between a sketch element and a center line is twice that.

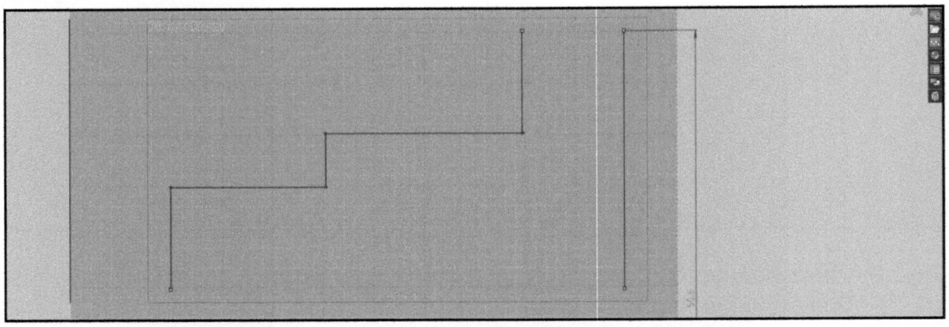

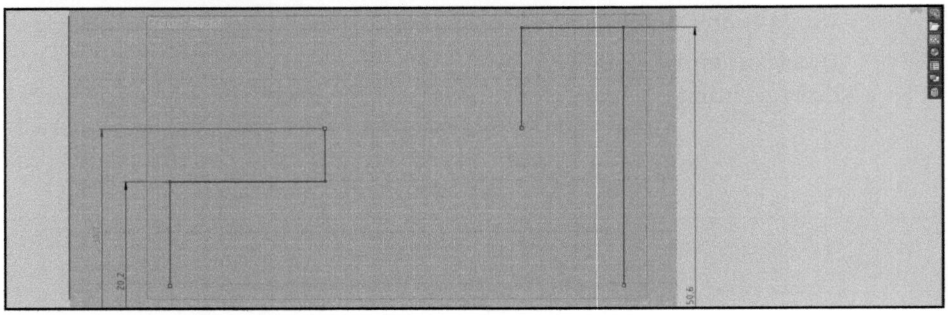

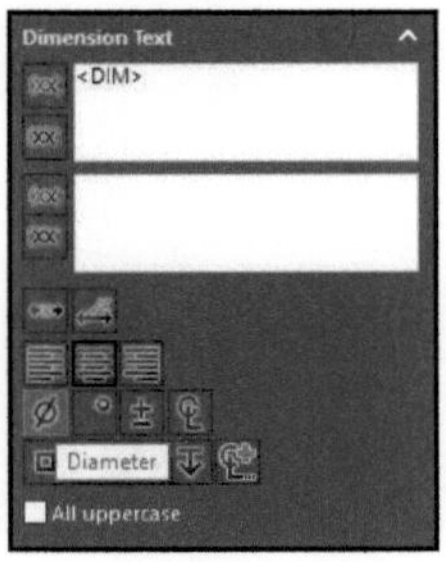

- Select the created **Diameter dimensioning**.
- Set the **Diameter** symbol from the **PropertyManager** for the dimensions.

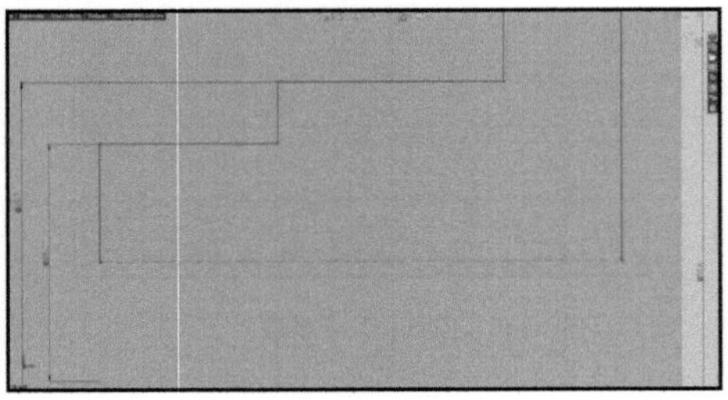

4.5.2.9 Dimensioning in 2D sketches, Baseline Dimension

Baseline Dimension

Click on the edge you want to use as a reference.

Click on each edge you want to dimension.

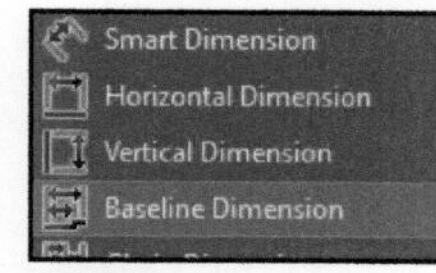

Baseline-Dimension

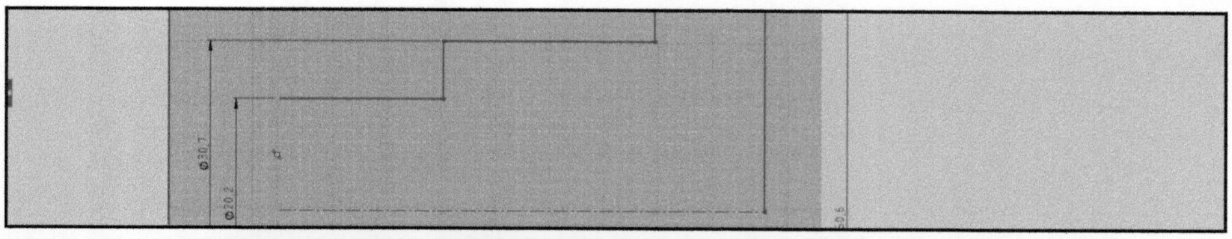

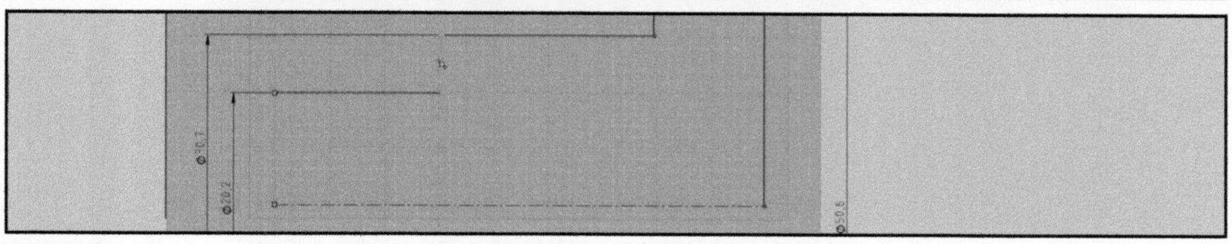

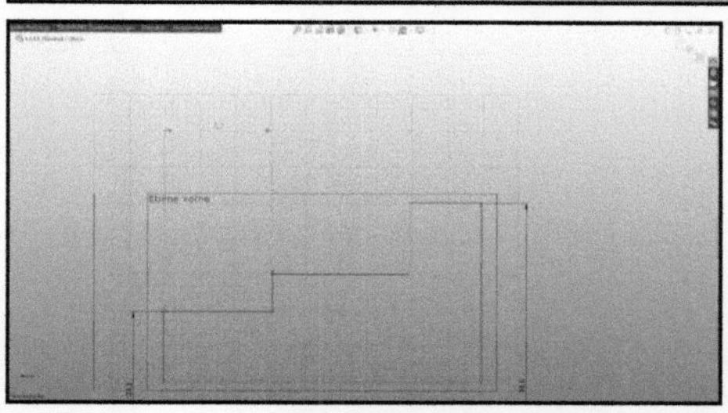

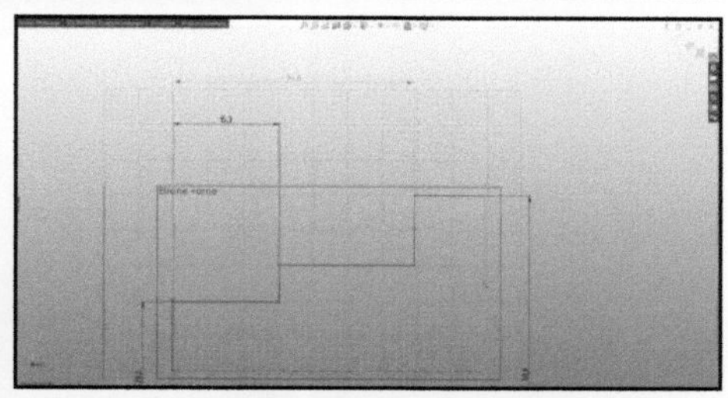

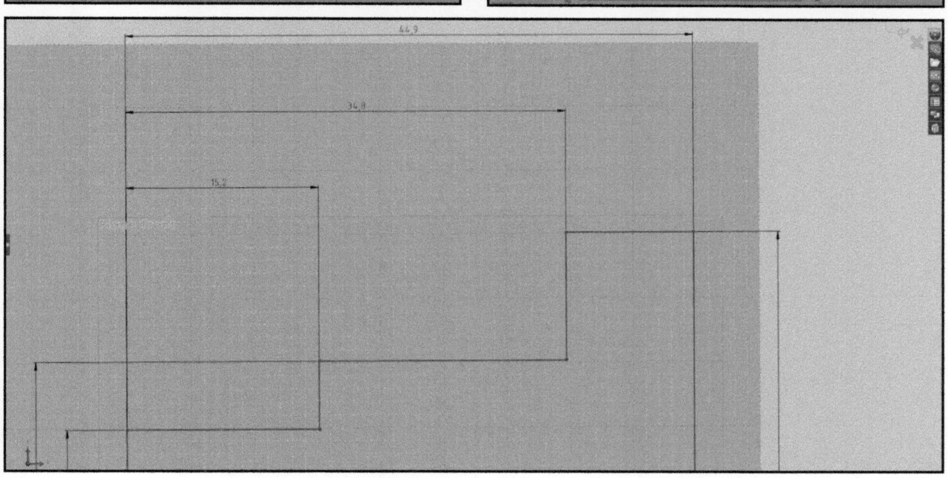

Project IV

Work Planes

Page 110 to 122

- Creation of work planes
  "Work plane Parallel"
- Creation of work planes
  "Mid plane"
- Creation of work planes
  "Work plane select Midpoint"
- Creation of work planes
  "Work plane with defined offset"
- Creation of work planes
  "Work plane centered between two sides"
- Creation of work planes
  "Work plane with angle input"
- Creation of work planes
  "Work plane with multiple defined offsets"
- Creation of work planes on a cylindrical surface
  "Tangent work plane by selecting a sketch line"
- Creation of work planes on a cylindrical surface
  "Tangent work plane by selecting a sketch point"
- Creation of work planes on a cylindrical surface
  "Work plane angular plane, axis-related"
- Creation of work planes on a cylindrical surface
  "Work plane offset distance"

4.6 Fundamentals for basic constructions, "Work Planes"

4.6.1 Working Planes, basics

Work planes can be placed in any orientation in space, offset from existing surfaces, or rotated around an axis or edge.

A work plane can be used as a sketch plane and defined with dimensions or constraints relative to other elements or components.

In an assembly, you can create a work plane between planar surfaces on separate components.

4.6.1.1 Basic planes

Plane Front

Plane Right

Plane Top

SOLIDWORKS offers Front, Top, and Right planes as default values. The three orthogonal reference planes located at the origin of a new part or assembly document are called base planes. They define the main planes Top, Right, and Front.

You can use the base planes to construct sketch-based features, to position a part in an assembly, or to define the X-axis for a new plane that you define with a partial surface. You can show and hide these planes individually or as a group in the FeatureManager.

In addition to the standard planes, you can create reference planes, and you can open sketches on planar model surfaces.

4.6.1.2 Automatic adjustment of planes and axes

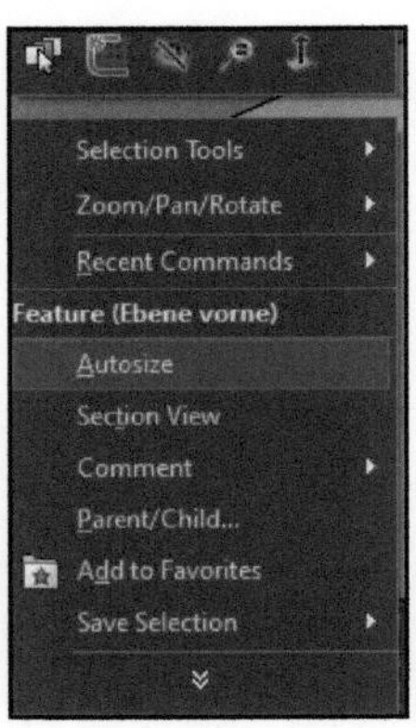

The size of the created planes and axes is automatically adjusted relative to the geometry on which they are created or relative to the model geometry's frame. If the geometry size changes, the planes and axes are updated accordingly.

You can override automatic adjustment by manually changing the size of the plane or axis. This will disable future automatic adjustment for that element. To re-enable automatic adjustment, select the Auto Adjust option from the context menu (1).

The created plane is 5% larger than the geometry on which it was created, or 5% larger than the frame. This minimizes selection problems when planes are created directly on surfaces or from orthogonal geometry.

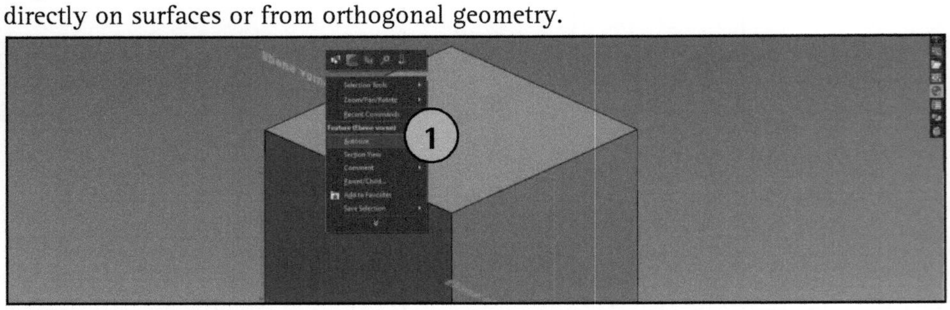

4.6.2 Creating Work Planes

4.6.2.1 Open working file, component from the book DVD

- **Open** the component file from the book DVD.

Open

4.6.2.2 Creating work planes, "Parallel Plane"

Follow the prompt to create a plane and view its status. The color of the message field, the layer's color, and messages in the **PropertyManager** will help you choose.

The layer must have a **Fully Defined** status before it can be created.

Plane (Command Tab **Feature / Reference Geometry**)

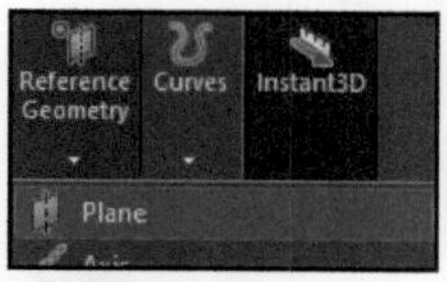

First Reference, select the fronts face of the cube (1).

Click the **Parallel** relationship in the **FeatureManager** (2).
Select **Invert Offset** for the plane in Cube (3).
Enter the distance **20** mm (4).
Close dialog box (5).

Plane

First Reference

Parallel

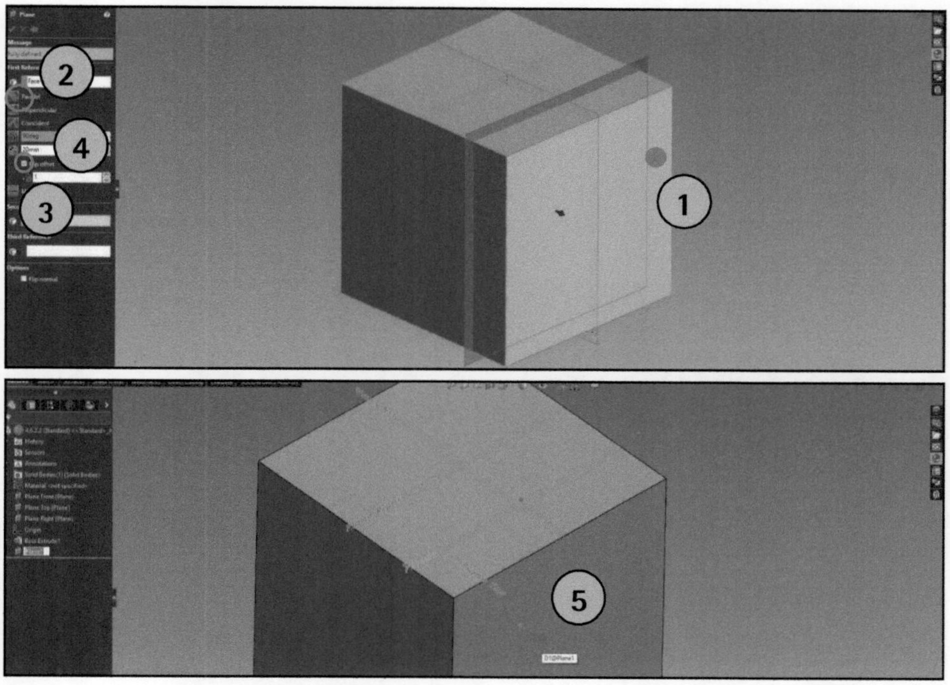

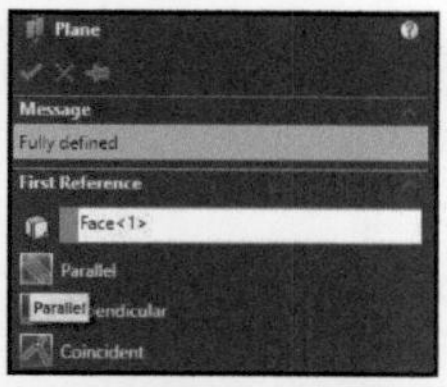

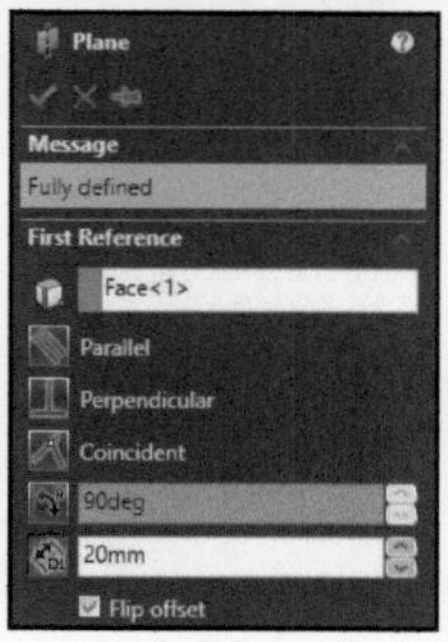

4.6.2.3 Data backup

Save as New / Enter a name of your choice.

Save as New

4.6.2.4 Creating work planes, "Mid Plane"

Open

Plane

First Reference

Mid Plane
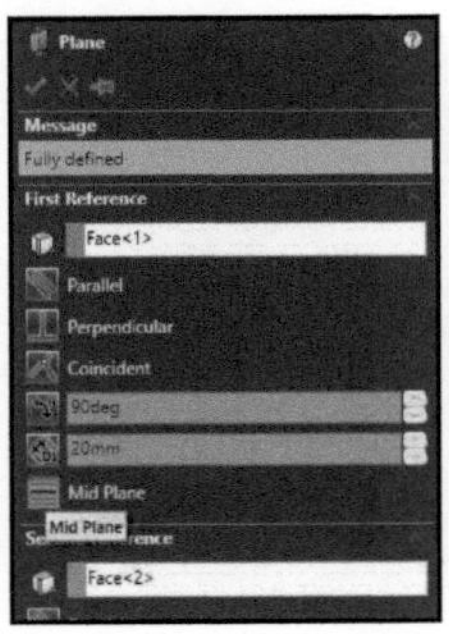

- **Open** the component file from the book DVD.

Plane (Command Tab **Feature / Reference Geometry**)

First Reference, select the fronts face of the cube (1).

Enable the **Mid Plane** option in the **FeatureManager** (2).
Select the back face of the cube (3).
Close dialog box.

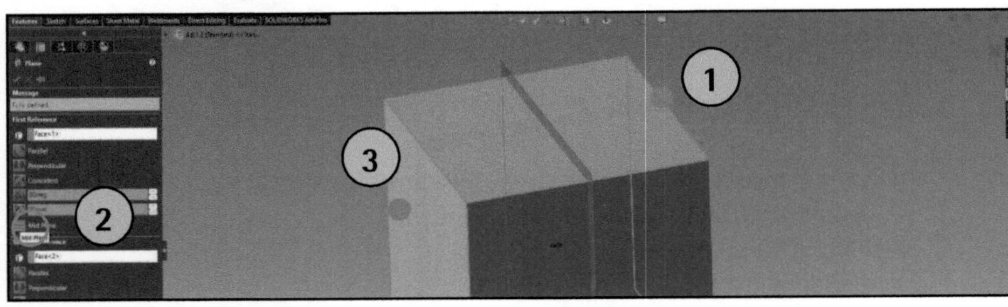

If the rear surface cannot be selected by rotating, there is the option of extended selection.

Plane

First Reference

Mid Plane
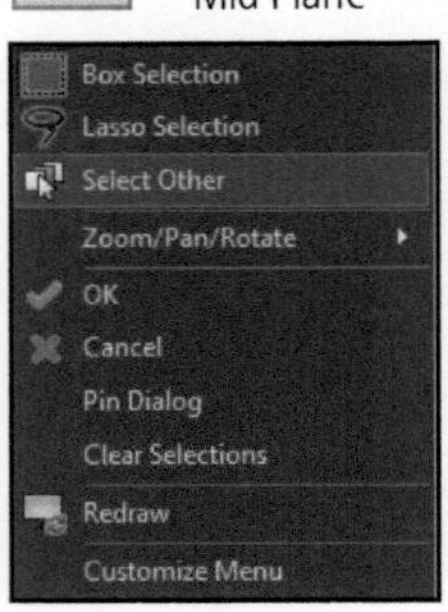

Plane (Command Tab **Feature / Reference Geometry**)
Select the front face of the cube (4).
Select **Select Other** from the **Context menu**. (5).
In the icon box that appears, click the illuminated, rear face of the cube. (6).

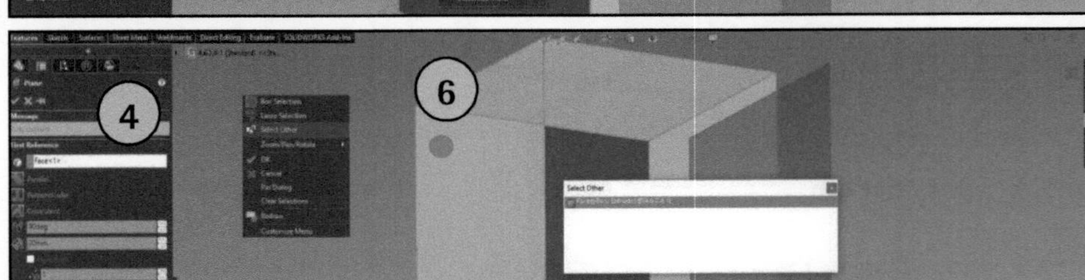

4.6.2.5 Data backup

Save as New

Save as New / Enter a name of your choice.

4.6.2.6 Creating work planes, "Plane through Point"

- **Open** the component file from the book DVD.
- Set the **Front** and **Right** planes to **Hide**.

Plane (Command Tab **Feature / Reference Geometry**)

First Reference, select the fronts face of the cube (1).

Enable the **Parallel** option in the **FeatureManager** (2).

Second Reference, Context menu **Select Midpoint** (3).
Select the center of the top edge of the cube (4).
Close dialog box.

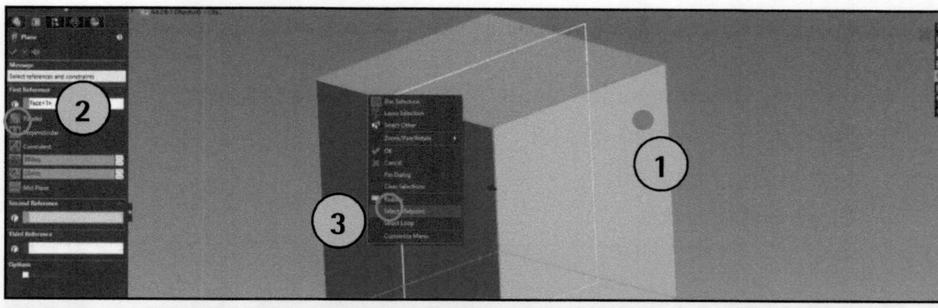

Open

Plane

First Reference

Parallel

Second Reference

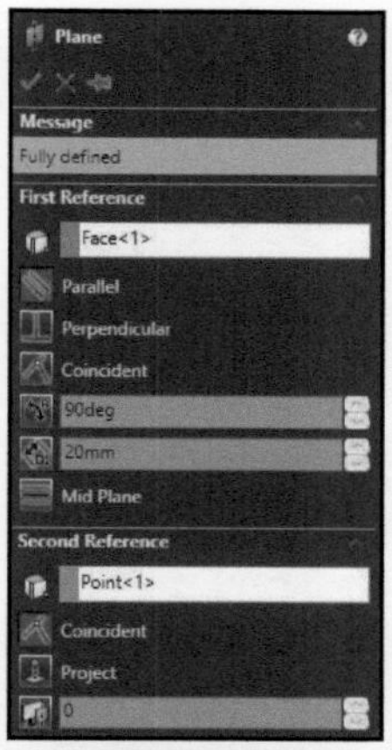

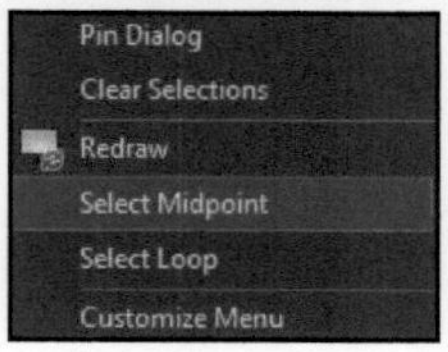

4.6.2.7 Data backup

Save as New / Enter a name of your choice.

Save as New

Open
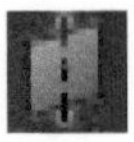
Plane

First Reference

4.6.2.8 Creation of work planes, "Plane with defined Offset"

- **Open** the component file from the book DVD.
- Set the **Front** and **Right** planes to **Hide**.

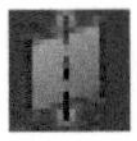

Plane (Command Tab **Feature / Reference Geometry**)

First Reference, select the bottoms face of the cube (1).

Offset distance
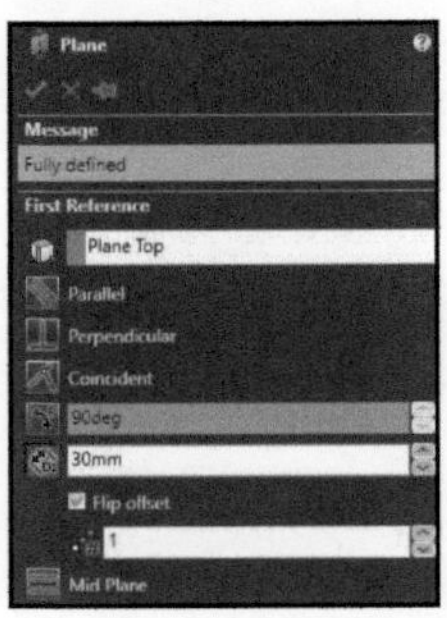

Click the **Offset distance** option in the **FeatureManager** (2).

Enter the distance **30** mm (2).

Option **Flip offset** (2).

Close dialog box.

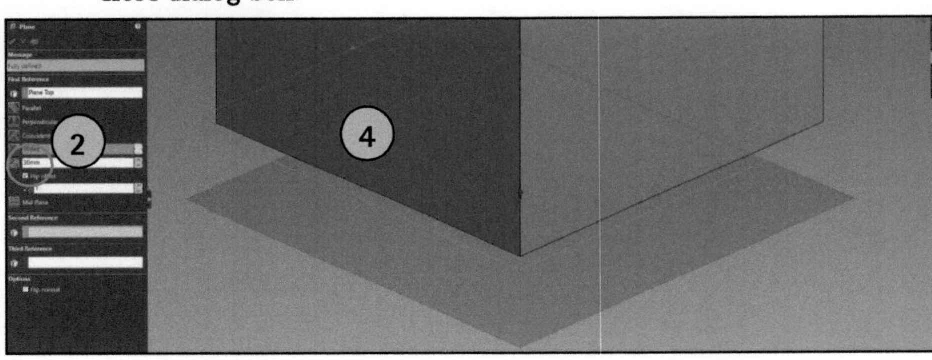

Save as New

4.6.2.9 Data backup

Save as New / Enter a name of your choice.

4.6.2.10 Creating work planes, "Plane centered between two Sides"

- **Open** the component file from the book DVD.
- Set the **Front**, **Top** and **Right** planes to **Hide**.

Open

Plane (Command Tab **Feature / Reference Geometry**)

Plane

First Reference, select the right face of the cube (1).

First Reference

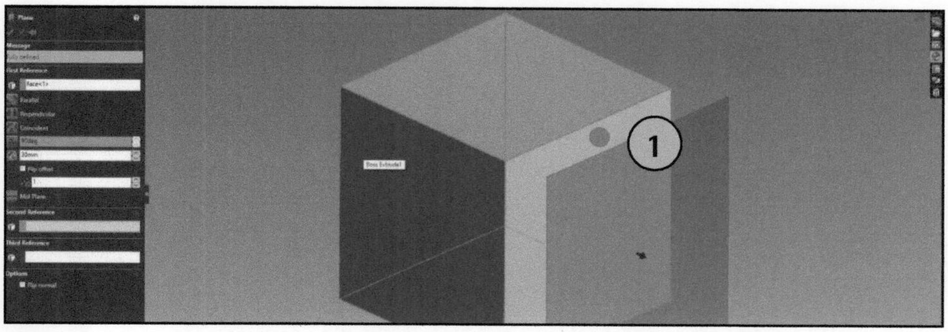

Second Reference, select the left face of the cube (2).

Second Reference

Activate the **Mid Plane** option in the **FeatureManager** (3).

Mid plane

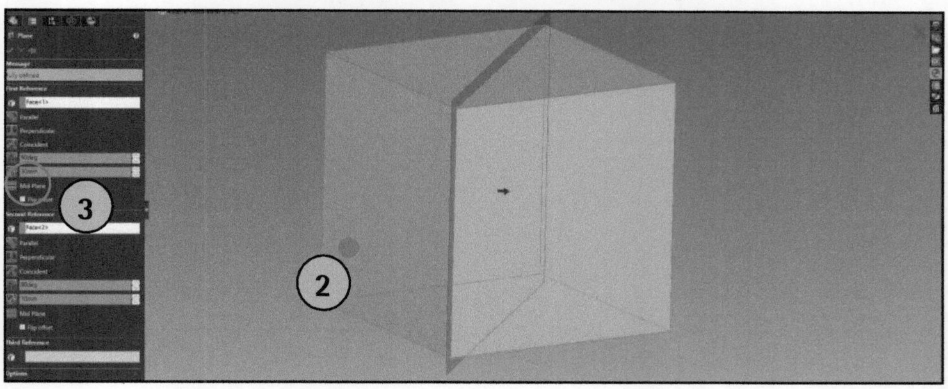

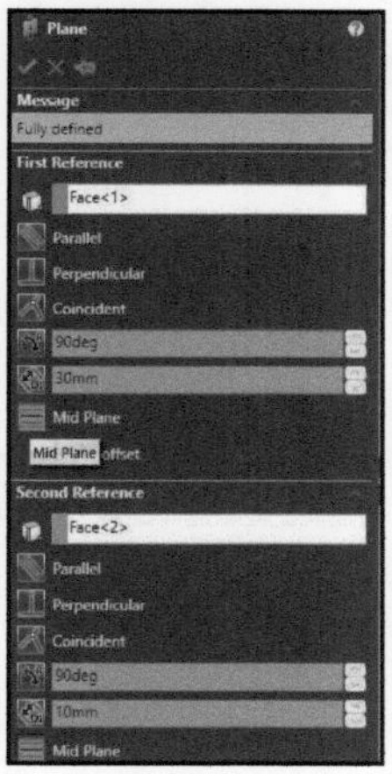

- Option **Flip offset** (4, 5).

- **Close dialog box.**

4.6.2.11 Data backup

Save as New / Enter a name of your choice.

Save as New

Open

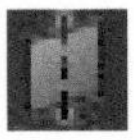
Plane

First Reference

Second Reference

At Angle

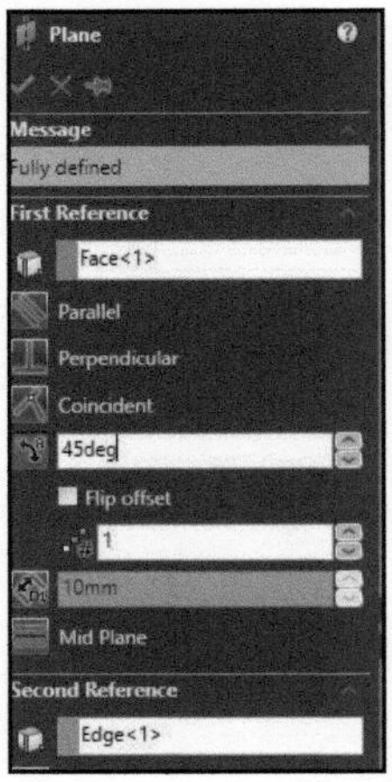

4.6.2.12 Creation work planes, "Plane with Angle input"

- **Open** the component file from the book DVD.
- Set the **Front**, **Top** and **Right** planes to **Hide**.

Plane (Command Tab **Feature / Reference Geometry**)

First Reference, select the fronts face of the cube (1).

Second Reference, select the bottom edge of the cube (2).

Click the **At Angle** option in the **FeatureManager** (3).
Enter the value **45°** (3).

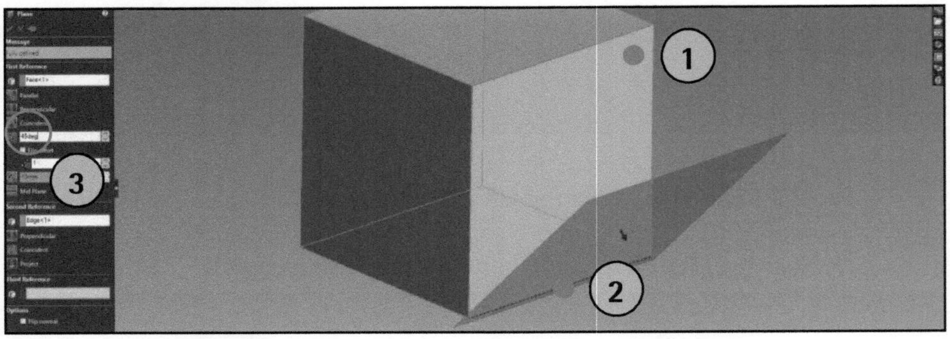

- The **Flip** Offset option flips the plane into a cube (5, 6).
- **Close dialog box**.

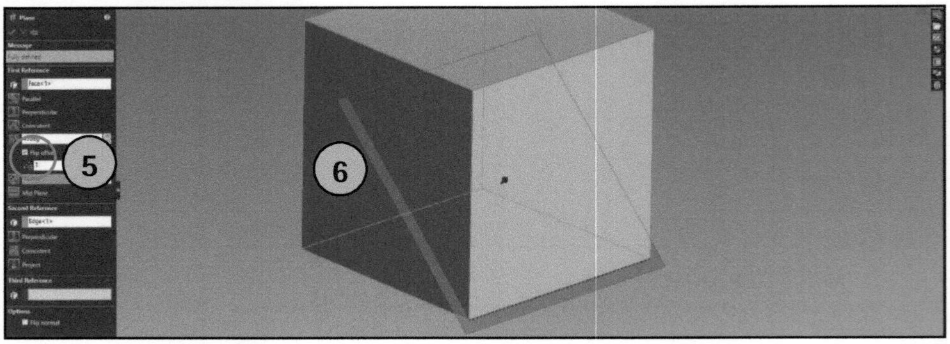

Save as New

4.6.2.13 Data backup

Save as New / Enter a name of your choice.

4.6.2.14 Creation work planes, "Plane with multiple defined Offsets"

- **Open** the component file from the book DVD.
- Set the **Front**, **Top** and **Right** planes to **Hide**.

Plane (Command Tab **Feature / Reference Geometry**)

First Reference, select the fronts face of the cube (1).

Click the **Offset distance** option in the **FeatureManager** (2).
Enter the distance **20** mm (2).
Option **Number of planes to create** enters the value **5** (3, 4).

Open

Plane

First Reference

Offset distance

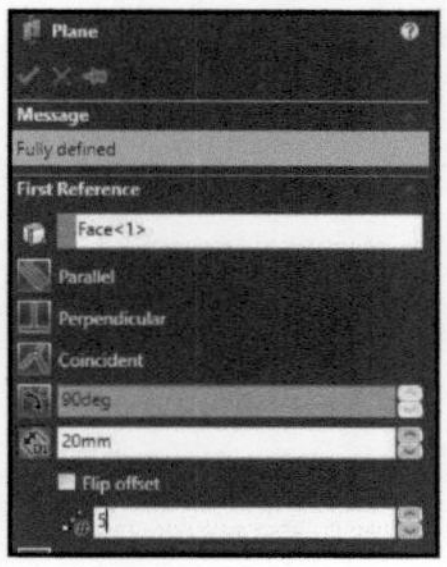

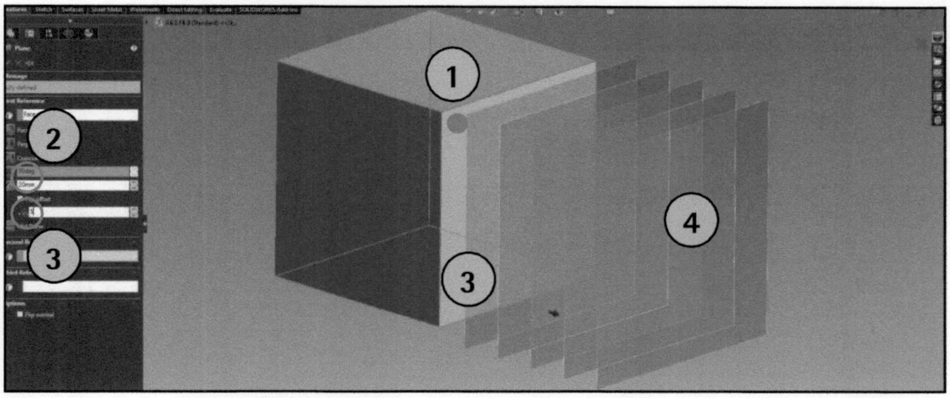

- Option **Flip offset** (5, 6).
- **Close dialog box**.

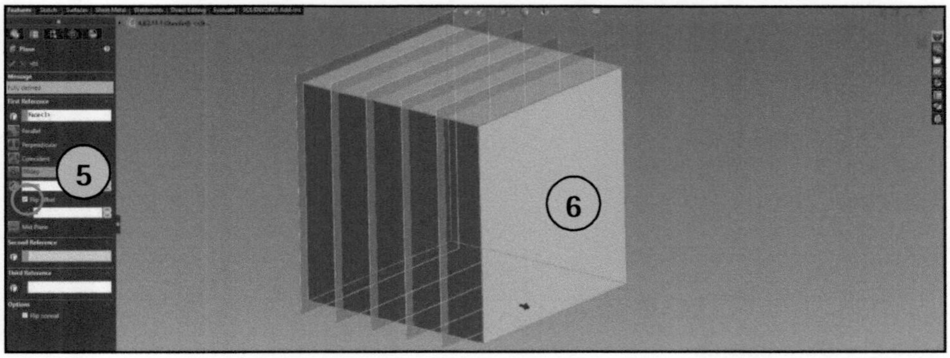

4.6.2.15 Data backup

Save as New / Enter a name of your choice.

Save as New

4.6.3 Creating work plane, "Plane on a cylindrical Surface"

4.6.3.1 Creating the work plane on a cylindrical surface, by selecting a sketch line

Open

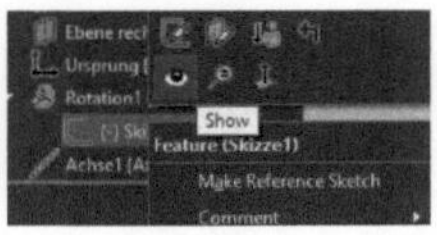

- **Open** the component file from the book DVD.
- Set the **Front, Top** and **Right** planes to **Hide**.
- Switch the rotation sketch to option **Show**.

Plane

First Reference

Tangent

Second Reference

Plane (Command Tab **Feature / Reference Geometry**)

First Reference, select the upper cylinder surface (1).

Click the **Tangent** relationship in the **FeatureManager** (2).

Second Reference, select the sketch line shown (3).

Close dialog box (4).

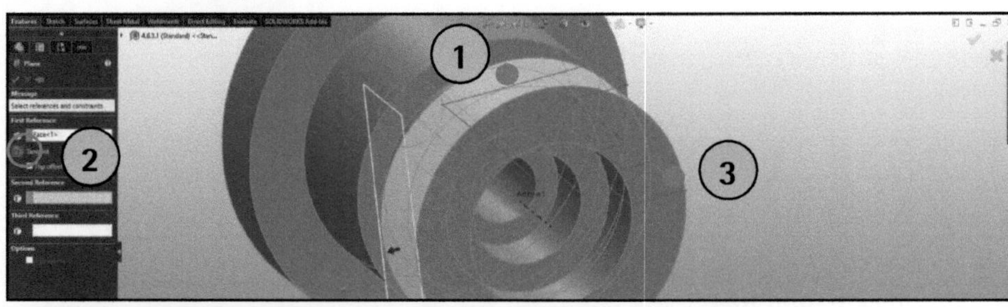

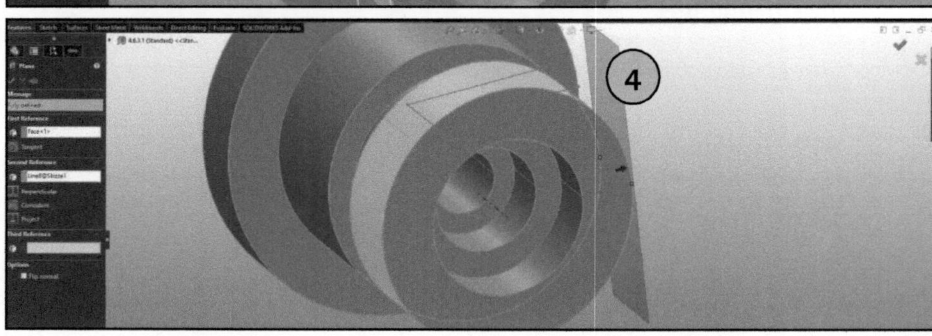

4.6.3.2 Data backup

Save as New

Save as New / Enter a name of your choice.

4.6.3.3 Creating the work plane on a cylindrical surface, by selecting a sketch point

- **Open** the component file from the book DVD.
- Set the **Front, Top** and **Right** planes to **Hide**.
- Switch the rotation sketch to option **Show**.

Open

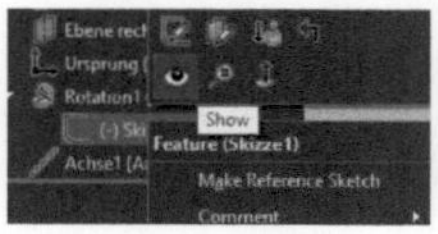

Plane (Command Tab **Feature / Reference Geometry**)

First Reference, select the upper cylinder surface (1).

Click the **Tangent** relationship in the **FeatureManager** (2).

Second Reference, select the sketch point shown (3).

Close dialog box (4).

Plane

First Reference

Tangent

Second Reference

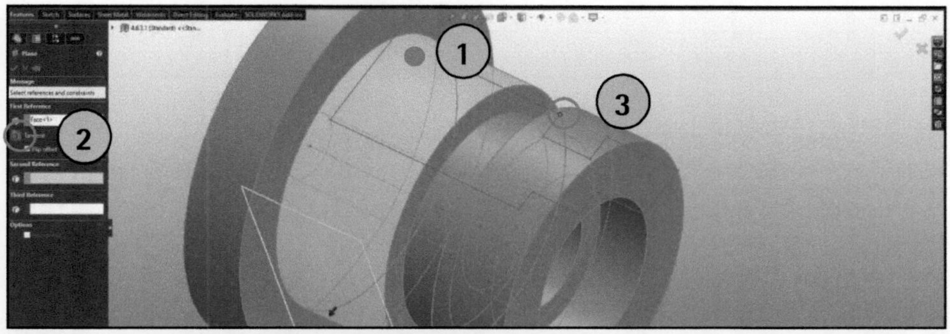

4.6.3.4 Data backup

Save as New / Enter a name of your choice.

Save as New

4.6.3.5 Creation work planes, „Angular Plane axis-related"

Open

- **Open** the component file from the book DVD.
- Set the **Front, Top** and **Right** planes to **Show**.

Achse

Axis (Command Tab **Feature / Reference Geometry**)

First Reference

First Reference, select the cylinder shown. (1).
Axis type: **Cylindrical surface** (2)
Close dialog box (3).

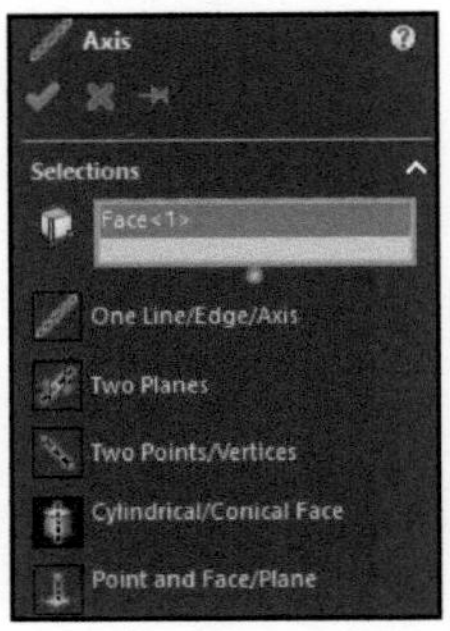

Plane

Plane (Command Tab **Feature / Reference Geometry**)

First Reference

First Reference, select the created cylinder axis (4).

Second Reference

Second Reference, select the origin plane **Top** (5).

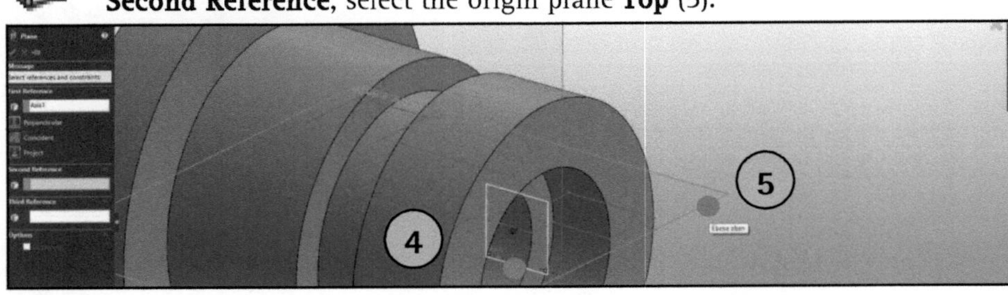

At Angle

Click the **At Angle** option in the **FeatureManager** (6).
Enter the value **90°** (6).
Close dialog box.

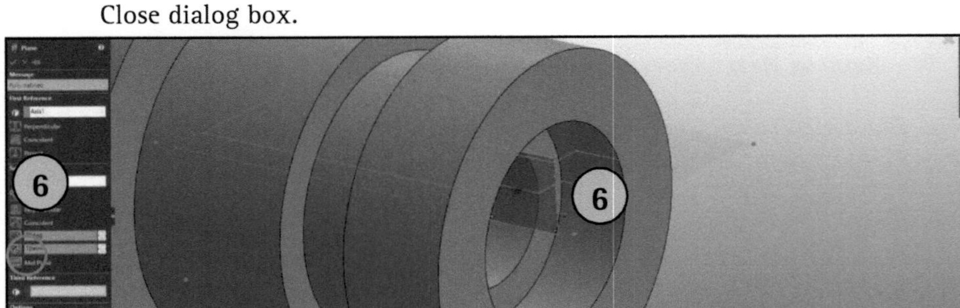

4.6.3.6 Data backup

Save as New

Save as New / Enter a name of your choice.

4.6.3.7 Creation work planes, „Angular plane offset distance"

- **Open** the component file from the book DVD.

Plane (Command Tab **Feature / Reference Geometry**)

First Reference, select the fronts face of the cylinder (1).

Click the **Offset distance** option in the **FeatureManager** (2).
Enter the distance **10** mm (2).
Option **Flip offset** (2).
Close dialog box (3).

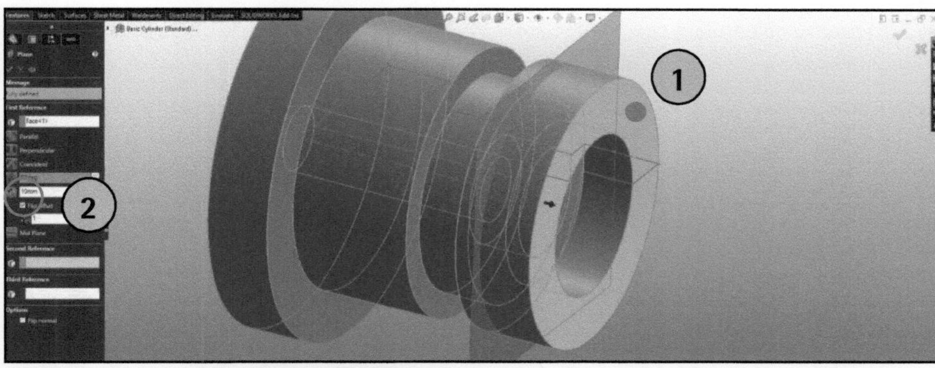

Open

Plane

First Reference

Offset distance

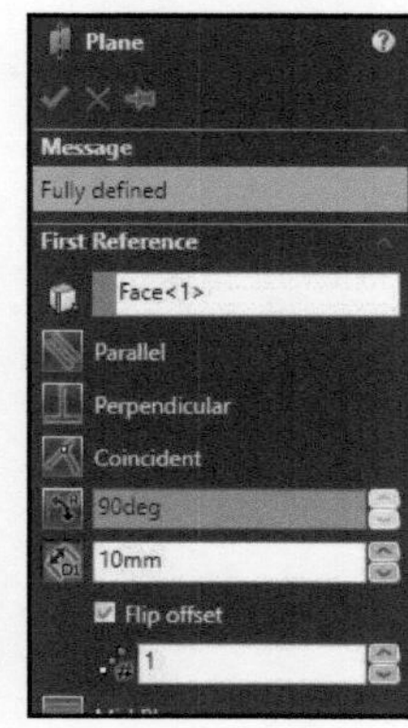

4.6.3.8 Data backup

Save as New / Enter a name of your choice.

Save as New

5

Dassault Systèmes
3DEXPERIENCE©
SOLIDWORKS Design
2026

Parts and Components

Create and Customize

Geometric Basic
Primitive Bodies

5 Geometric basics, Primitives bodies

5.1 Creating 3D solid primitive body

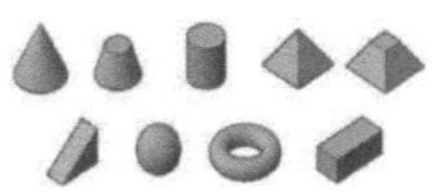

3D solid objects can start from simple primitives or from extruded, swept, revolved, or lofted profiles. You can combine these using Boolean operations, and you can also create various simple 3D shapes using basic solid commands.
You can also create 3D solids by performing operations such as extruding, revolving, or sweeping closed 2D objects. In the illustration, the same closed 2D polyline is drawn along a path, rotated about an axis, and extruded in a specified direction.
By combining 3D solids with Boolean operations such as union, subtraction, and intersection, you can create a composite solid.

5.1.1 Creating solids from 2D geometry

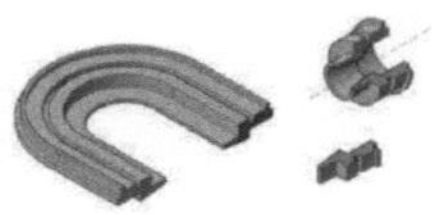

You can construct surfaces and 3D solids by extruding, sweeping, lofting, and revolving.

When you create an Extrude, revolving, sweeping, or lofting from curves, you can create both solids and surfaces.

Open curves always create surfaces, but closed curves can generate either solids or surfaces, depending on certain settings.

5.1.2 Feature-based solids

You can also create 3D solids from 2D geometry or other 3D objects. For example, 3D solids can also be based on extruding a 2D shape along a specified path in 3D space.

The following methods are available, an excerpt:

Sweep Boss:
Extend a 2D object along a path.

Extrude Boss:
Extend the shape of a 2D object vertically into 3D space.

Revolve Boss:
Rotate a 2D object around an axis.

Lofted:
Stretche the contours of a shape between one, or more open or closed objects.

Intersect:
Split a solid object into two separate 3D objects.

Extruded Surface:
Form surfaces into a solid:
Using the Reinforce command, you can create a solid element from a surface by specifying a wall thickness.

5.2 Geometric basics, Primitives bodies SOLIDWORKS 2026

5.2.1 Geometric basics, Primitives bodies SOLIDWORKS 2026, basics

SOLIDWORKS 2026 consists of several components called environments. These environments were specifically created for generating individual parts, sheet metal parts, assemblies, and detailed drawings.

In the SOLIDWORKS 2026 part environment, you can design a basic feature and then modify it with additional features such as features, cutouts, and holes to obtain a complete solid model.

In SOLIDWORKS 2026, you use the following basic workflow to model parts:

- Identify model requirements.
- Create a model concept based on the identified requirements.
- Develop a model based on the concepts.
- Analyze the model.
- Create a prototype.
- Construct the model.
- Edit the model if necessary.

5.2.2 Basics of construction

5.2.2.1 Sketches

Creating a model typically begins with a sketch. Features can then be created based on the sketch. A model usually contains at least one sketch and at least one feature. A sketch is a 2D profile or cross-section. To create a 2D sketch, you use a plane or a planar surface. In addition to 2D sketches, you can also create 3D sketches, which include a Z-axis in addition to the X and Y axes.

In many cases, you begin your sketch at the origin, which serves as an anchor for the sketch. Often, a centerline is sketched through the origin to establish the rotation. While a centerline isn't always necessary in a sketch, it does contribute to creating symmetry.

A centerline can also be used to apply a mirror relationship and to create equal and symmetrical relationships between sketch elements. Symmetry is an important tool for quickly creating axially symmetrical models.

Sketches can be fully defined, underdefined, or overdefined. In a fully defined sketch, all lines and curves in the sketch, as well as their positions, are described by dimensions, relations, or both.

Sketches do not need to be fully defined to be used for creating features. However, you should fully define sketches to maintain your design plan.

You can view the underdefined elements of a sketch to determine which dimensions or relations still need to be added for the sketch to be fully defined. Color coding indicates whether a sketch is underdefined.

5.2.2.2 Planes

Planes can be created in part or assembly documents. You can sketch on planes using sketching tools such as lines or rectangles and use the planes to create a section view of a model. In some models, the plane on which you sketch only affects how the model is displayed in the isometric view.

In other cases, models can be created more efficiently if you select the correct sketching plane right from the start. Choose a plane on which to sketch. The default planes are forward, top, and right. Planes can also be added and positioned as needed.

A reference plane is a flat surface commonly used for drawing 2D sketches in 3D space. Although the size of the reference plane is theoretically infinite, it is represented at a fixed size to simplify selection and visualization.

5.2.2.3 Dimensions

Product and manufacturing information consists of dimensions and labels added to the 3D model, which can be used in the inspection and manufacturing process.

In 3D modeling, dimensions are also an important tool for modifying the design. By editing dimension values, you can make changes to the model. You can lock and unlock dimensions to control how associated model surfaces behave when dimension values are edited.

You can also control the direction in which dimension changes are applied. This significantly simplifies the process of designing, testing, and updating.

The checkboxes next to the dimension elements listed in the FeatureManager toggle the individual elements on and off. Each group of dimensions and annotations also has a context menu.

5.2.2.4 Basics of construction, geometric relationships

Geometric relationships define the orientation of one element relative to another element or a reference plane.

Geometric relationships control how a sketch changes when it is edited. The geometric relationships are placed and displayed as you draw.

Once you have completed the sketch, you can assign geometric relationships using the various relationship commands and the relationship wizard.

Project V

Geometric basics, primitive bodies
Basic primitiv body “cuboid”

Page 128 to 136

- Geometric basic primitive body “Cuboid”
  Sketch function “Center Rectangle”, using “Extrude”
- Geometric basic primitive body “Cuboid”
  Sketch function “Corner Rectangle” using “Extrude”
- Geometric basic primitive body “Cuboid”
  “Line” sketch construction with dimension entries, using “Extrude”

5.3 Basic geometric primitive body "Cuboid"

5.3.1 Basic geometric primitiv body "Cuboid", geometric description

A three-dimensional solid with six pairs of parallel faces is called a parallelepiped, regardless of perpendicularity. Thus, every cuboid is a right-angled parallelepiped.

A parallelepiped is a geometric solid bounded by six pairs of congruent parallelograms lying in parallel planes.

A cuboid is a solid with six rectangular faces, all of whose angles are right angles, eight right-angled corners, and twelve edges, four of which are equal lengths and parallel to each other.

In geometry, Extrude refers to the dimensional increase of an element by parallel displacement in space.

By extruding a face, you obtain a solid with the cross-section of the face; by extruding a polygon, you create a prism.

5.3.2 Geometric basic primitive body "Cuboid" Sketch function "Center Rectangle", using "Extrude"

5.3.2.1 Sketch function "Center Rectangle"

5.3.2.2 Opening your own template file

- Start **SOLIDWORKS Design 2026** by double-clicking the desktop icon. Alternatively, you can start it using the Windows Start icon in the lower left corner of the screen.

New

Engelke2026.
PRTDOT

- Menu Bar **New** (1) /  /  click **Engelke2026.PRTDOT / OK**

5.3.2.3 The basic sketch construction

Flyout tool **Rectangle** (Sketch tab)

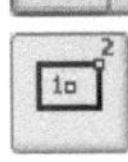

Center
Rectangle

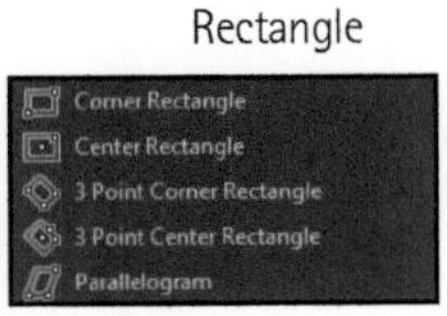

Center Rectangle
Select the **Top Plane** (1).
Click the intersection of the planes in the graphics area to define the center point (2).
Drag the cursor to define the rectangle's outer contour (3).
Click the dimensions to be approximately **100** mm long and **70** mm wide (4).

Close dialog
box

Close dialog box.

Finish sketch

Finish sketch
Click on the desktop icon in the upper right corner (5, 6, 7).

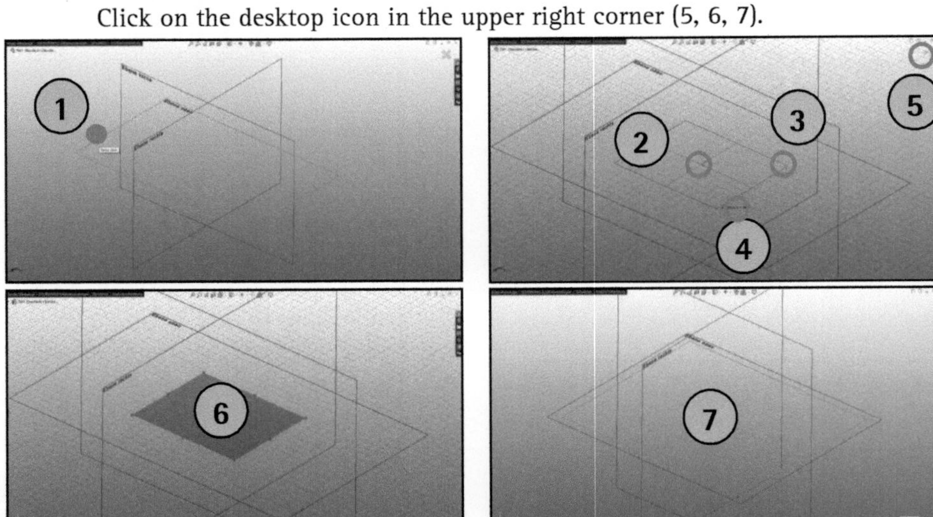

5.3.2.4 Creating an "Extrude" feature

Extrude (**Features** tab)
Select the constructed rectangle as the base sketch (8).
The **Extrude** PropertyManager appears (9).
A preview is displayed with the default depth of **10** mm (10).

Close dialog box (11).

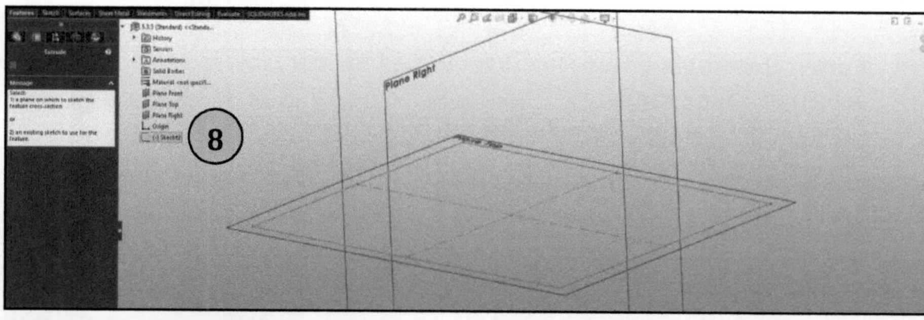

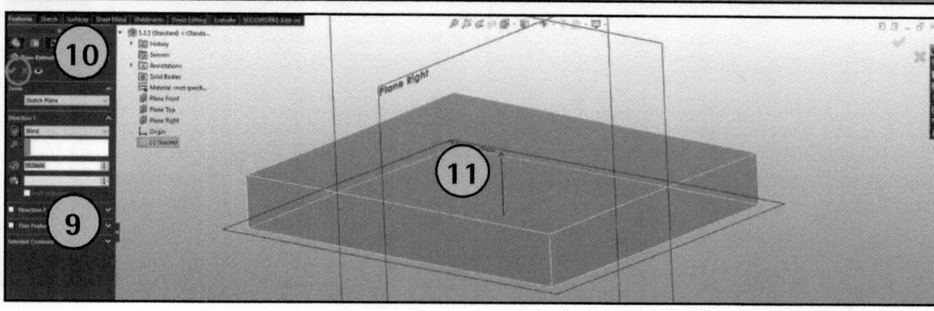

Extrude

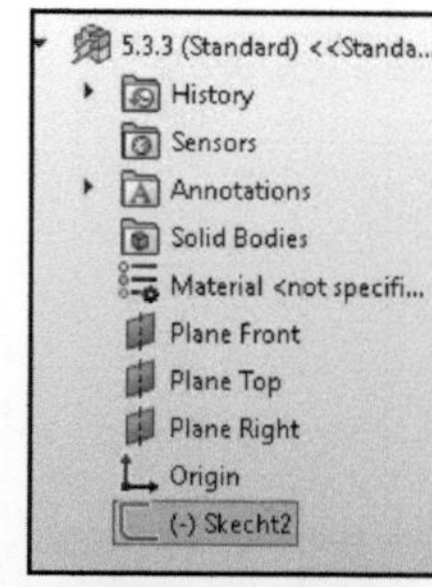

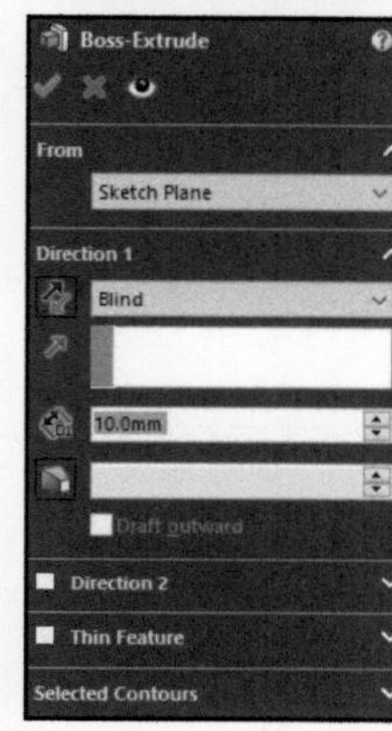

Close dialog box

5.3.2.5 Data backup

Save as New / Enter a name of your choice.

Save as New

Save as New opens the SOLIDWORKS dialog box so you can save the file to your local drive.

The **Save as New** dialog box appears (11).
Enter a file name of your choice and click **Save**.
The extension **.sldprt** is added to the file name.
The file is saved in the current directory.
The directory can be changed using the Windows Browse button.

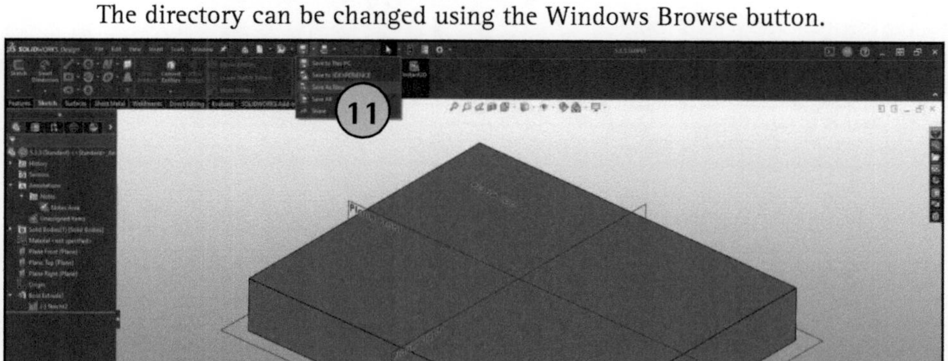

New

Engelke2026.
PRTDOT

Corner
Rectangle

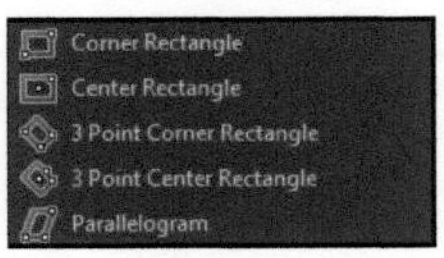

5.3.3 Geometric basic primitive body "Cuboid" Sketch function "Corner Rectangle", using "Extrude"

5.3.3.1 Opening your own template file

- Menu Bar **New** /  /  click **Engelke2026.PRTDOT** / **OK**

5.3.3.2 Cuboid using "Corner Rectangle", sketch construction

Corner Rectangle (Flyout tool **Rectangle** / **Sketch** tab)
Select the **Plane Right** (1).
Click on the intersection point for the first corner (2).
Click on the second corner (3), dimensions approximately **70** mm x **50** mm.

Close dialog box (4)

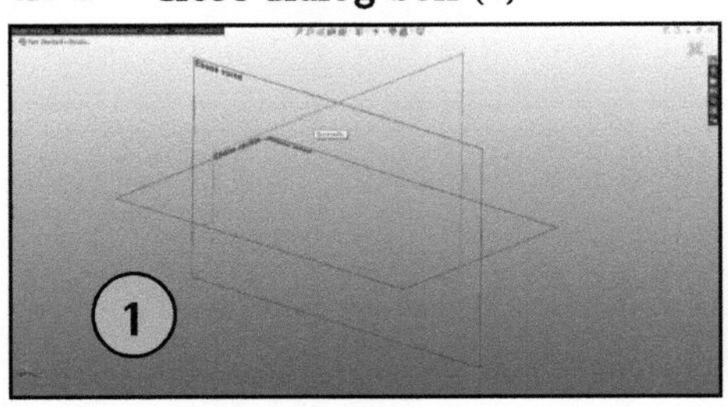

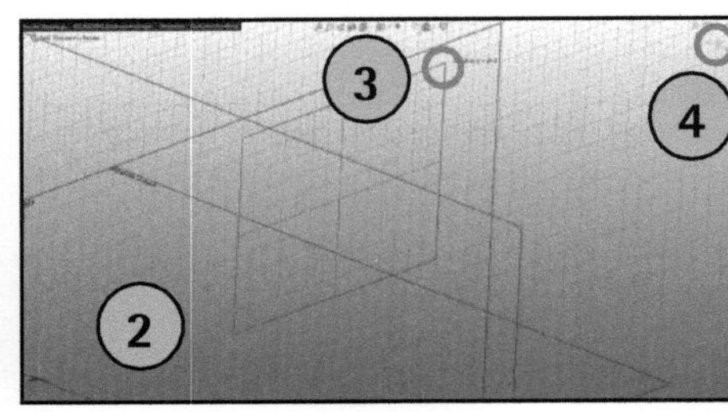

Smart
Dimension

Close dialog
box

5.3.3.3 Sketch dimensioning, horizontal

Smart Dimension (**Sketch** tab)
Select the bottom rectangle line (5).
Move the cursor to the location where you want to place the dimension.
Click the point to add the dimension (6).
Enter **70** in the modify field (7), and the length of the rectangle will increase to this value.

Close dialog box.

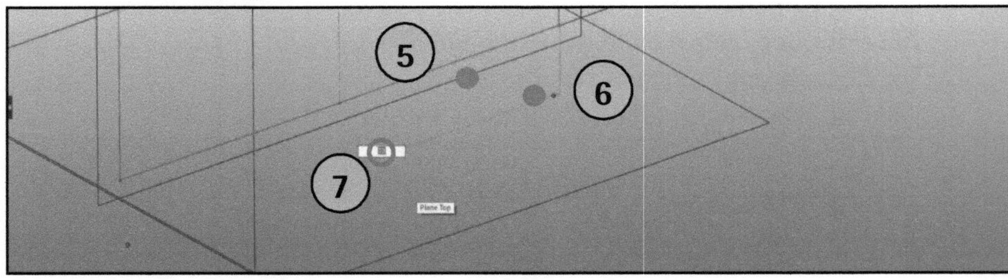

5.3.3.4 Sketch dimensioning, vertical

Smart Dimension (**Sketch** tab)
Select the side rectangle line (5).
Move the cursor to the location where you want to place the dimension.
Click the point to add the dimension (6).
Enter **50** in the modify field (7), and the length of the rectangle will increase to this value.

Close dialog box / Finish sketch

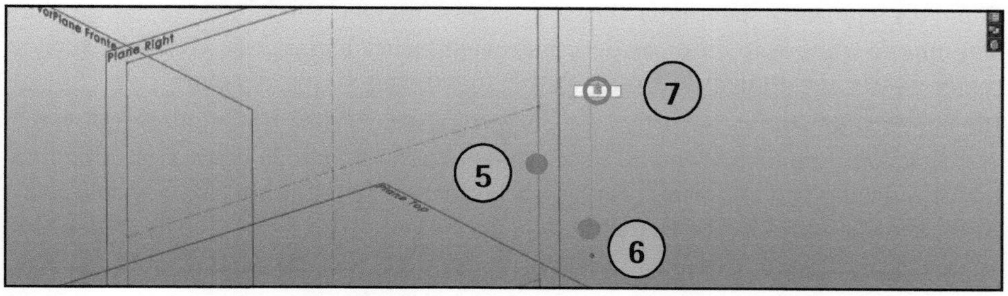

Smart Dimension

Close dialog box

Finish sketch

5.3.3.5 Create "Extrude" feature with depth change

Extrude (**Features** tab)
Select the constructed rectangle as the base sketch (8).
A preview is displayed with the default depth of **10** mm.
Click the drag arrow in the center of the rectangle (9).
Drag to **26** mm (9).

Close dialog box.

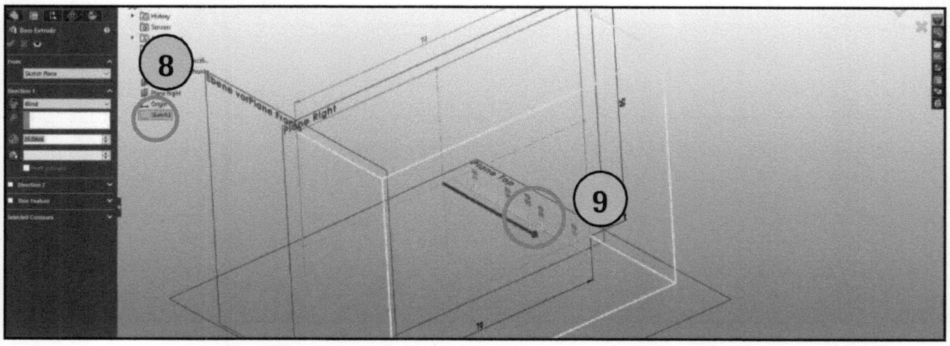

Extrude

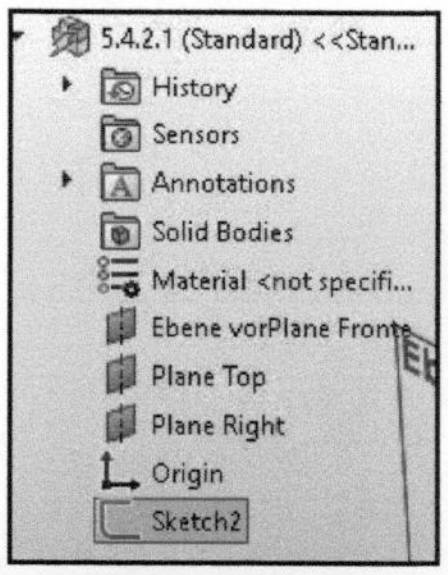

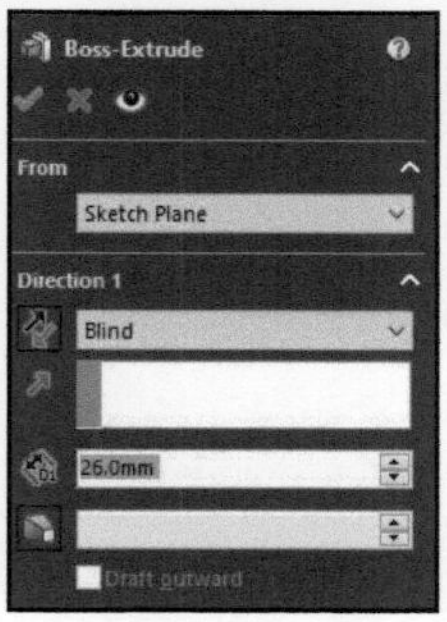

5.3.3.6 Data backup

Save as New / Enter a name of your choice.

Save as New

5.3.4 Geometric basic primitive body "Cuboid" "Line" sketch construction with dimension entries

5.3.4.1 Opening your own template file

New

Engelke2026.
PRTDOT

- Menu Bar **New** /  /  click **Engelke2026.PRTDOT / OK**

5.3.4.2 "Cuboid" construction using a line sketch Outline basics for guidelines and relationships

Guidelines work in conjunction with cursor symbols, sketch snaps, and relationships to graphically show how sketch elements interact. Guidelines are dotted lines that appear while sketching. As the cursor approaches highlighted elements, such as center points, the guidelines move relative to existing sketch elements.

The cursor indicator shows when the cursor is over a geometric relationship, which tool is active (line or circle), and dimensions (angle and radius of an arc). When the cursor indicates a relationship, such as a horizontal relationship, the relationship is automatically added to the element.

In addition to sketch snapping, you can display symbols for relationships between sketch entities. While you sketch, the entities display sketch snapping symbols; once you click to indicate that a sketch entity is complete, the relationships are displayed.

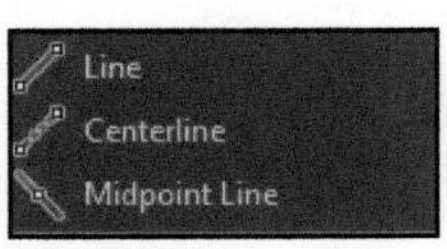

Line

5.3.4.3 The basic sketch construction

Line (**Sketch** tab)

Select the **Top Plane** (1)

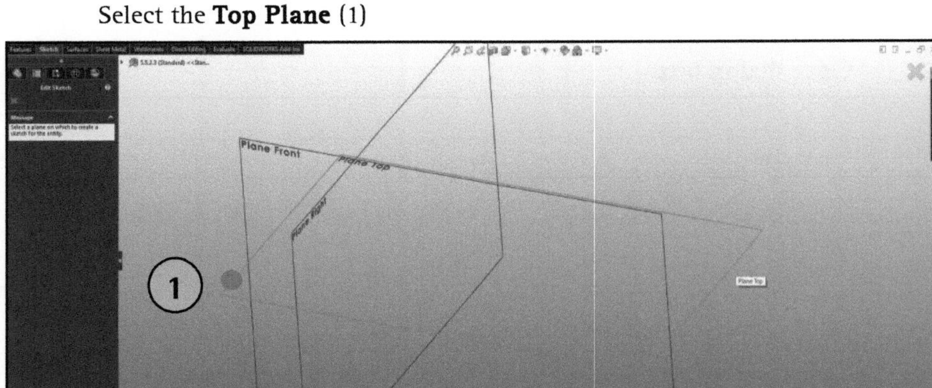

The cursor view changes.
In the Insert **Line** PropertyManager, select the **As Sketched** option.

Move the cursor over the **Origin point**.

The cursor changes, indicating a coincident relationship between the line's starting point and the origin.
Click to place the line at the origin (2).
Click the horizontal position, length approx. **75** mm, vector **0°** (3).
Select the endpoint of the line.
Click the vertical position, length approx. **50** mm, vector **90°** (4)
(The parallel position is represented by a dotted line).
Click the horizontal position, length approx. **75** mm, vector **180°** (5)
(Parallel position is represented by a dotted line).
Click the vertical position, length approx. **50** mm, vector **270°** (6)
(Parallel position is represented by a dotted line).
The line end is indicated with a snap symbol and the line is closed by double-clicking at the last point,
or by selecting **End chain** from the context menu (7)

Cursor for Line

Symbol for Origin

Cursor with Relationship

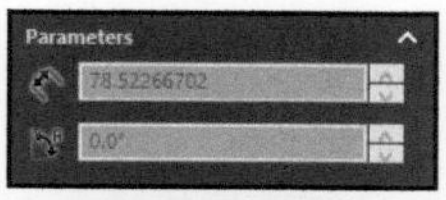

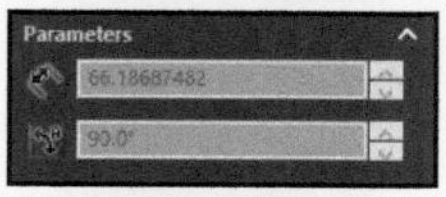

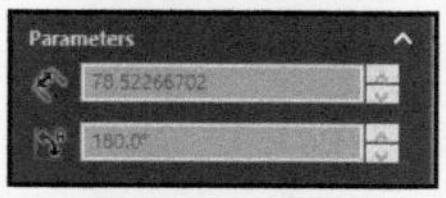

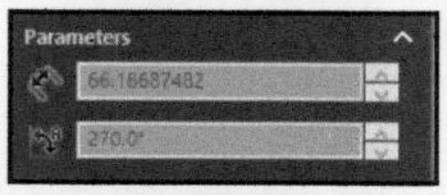

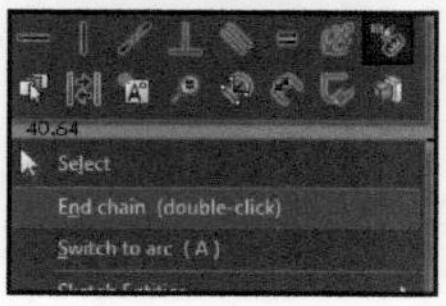

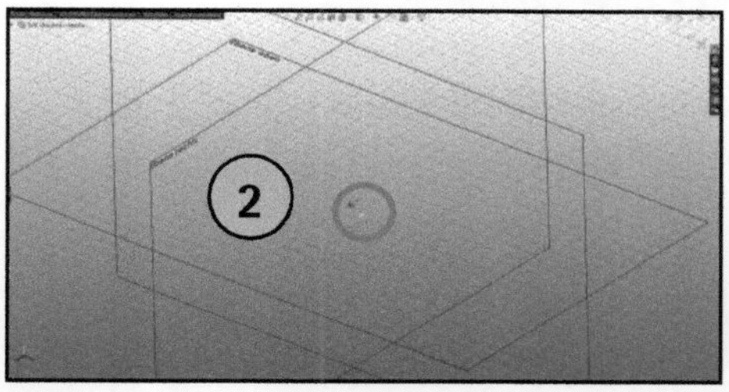

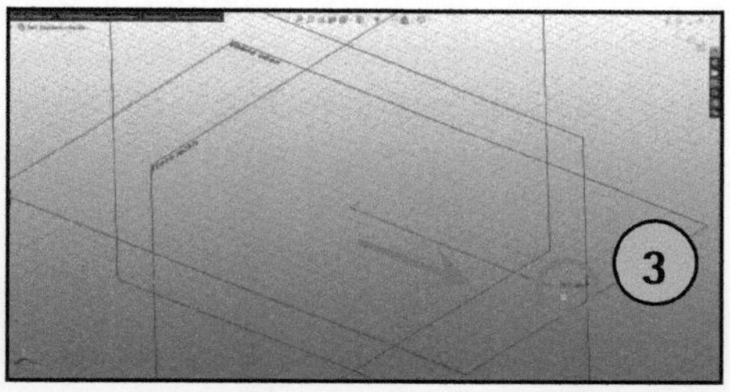

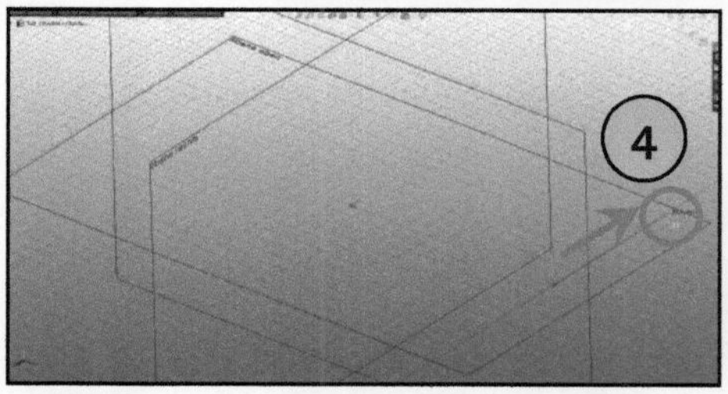

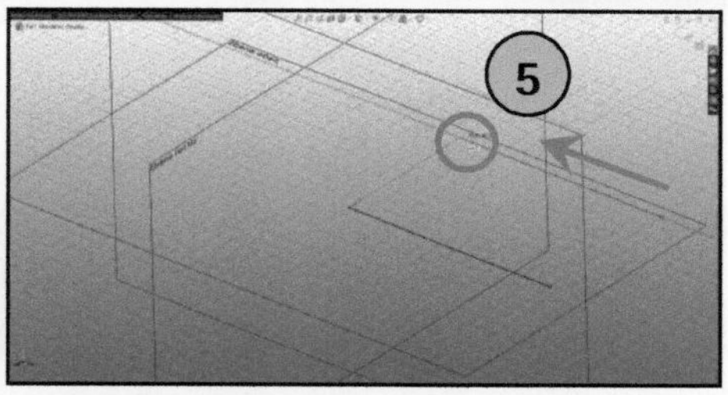

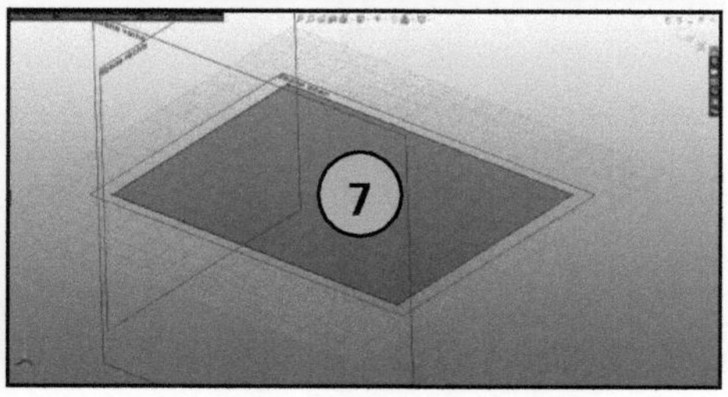

Smart Dimension

Close dialog box

Finish sketch

5.3.4.4 Sketch dimensioning, horizontal and vertical

Smart Dimension (**Sketch** tab)
Select the desired rectangle edge and drag the dimension to the position.
Change the dimension from approx. **70** mm to **80** mm (8)
Change the dimension from approx. **50** mm to **60** mm (9)
Close dialog box / Finish sketch.

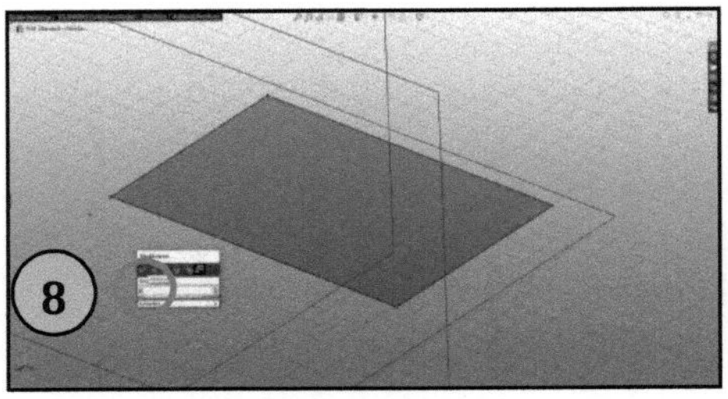

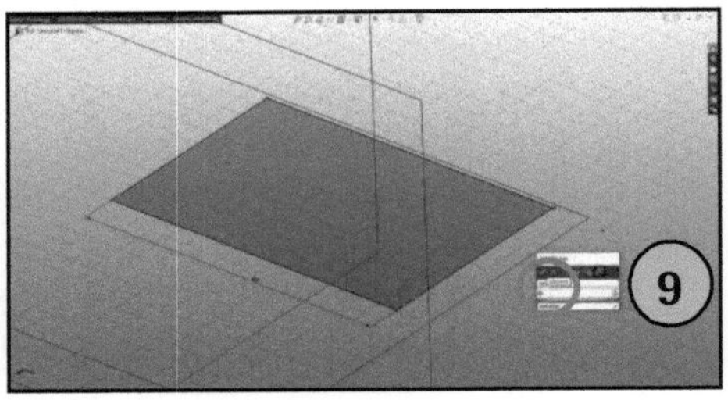

5.3.4.5 Create "Extrude" feature, change length

Extrude

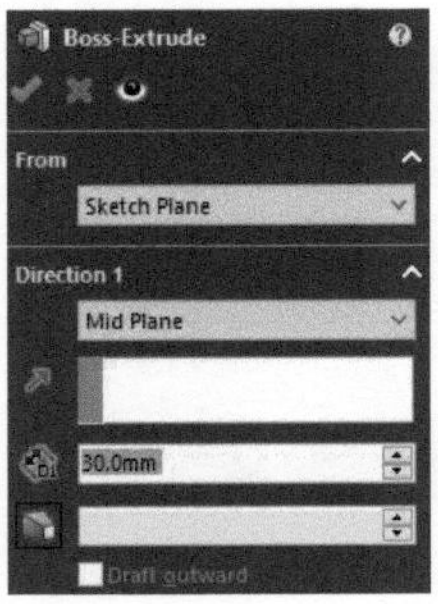

Close dialog box

Extrude (**Features** tab)
Select the constructed rectangle as the base sketch.
A preview is displayed with the default depth of **10** mm.
Set the end conditions for linear extrusions to **Mid Plane** (10).
Click the drag arrow in the center of the rectangle.
Drag to **30** mm (11).
Close dialog box.

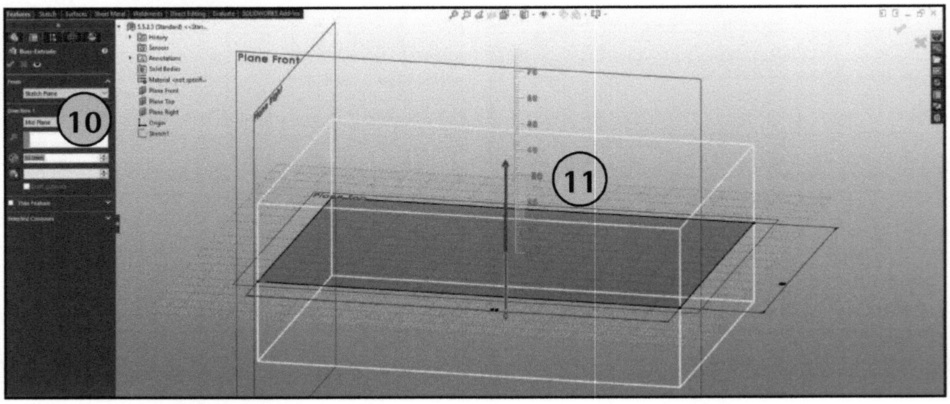

Save as New

5.3.4.6 Data backup

Save as New / Enter a name of your choice.

Project VI

Geometric basics, primitive body

Page 139 to 170

- Geometric basic primitive body “Cube”
  Sketch function “Center Rectangle”, using “Extrude”
- Geometric basic primitive body “Cylinder”
  Basic shape body circular areae, using “Extrude”
  Rotation of a standing rectangular area, using “Revolve”
- Geometric basic primitive body ”Sphere”
  Rotation of a halved circular area, using “Revolve”
- Geometric basic primitive body “Spherical cap“
  Rotation of a quarter circles, using “Revolve”
- Geometric basic primitive body
  “Cone“and “Truncated Cone“
  Rotation of a triangular area made of lines, using “Revolve”
  “Truncated Cone“ using “Extrude”
- Geometric basic primitive body
  “Pyramid“ and “Truncated Pyramid“
  “Pyramid“ using “Extrude” and “Draft” feature
  “Truncated Pyramid“using “Extrude” feature option “Draft”
- Geometric basic primitive body “Rotational ellipsoid”
  Rotation of half an elliptical surface, using “Revolve”
- Geometric basic primitive body “Torus”
  Rotation of a circular area at a distance from the central axis,
  using “Revolve"

5.4 Geometric basic primitive body "Cube"

5.4.1 Geometric basic primitive body "Cube", geometric description

The cube (from Latin cubus, cube) is one of the five Platonic solids, more precisely a three-dimensional polyhedron (polyhedron) with six congruent squares as boundary faces, twelve equal edges, and eight vertices where three boundary faces meet.

The cube is a special three-dimensional parallelepiped, a special equilateral cuboid, and a special right square prism. The size of a cube is determined by the edge length. Because of its high symmetry, all vertices, edges, and sides are identical, the cube is a regular polytope and has point symmetrical points about its center.

5.4.2 Geometric basic primitive body "Cube" Sketch function "Center Rectangle", using "Extrude"

5.4.2.1 Opening your own template file

New

Engelke2026.
PRTDOT

- Menu Bar **New** /  /  click **Engelke2026.PRTDOT** / **OK**

5.4.2.2 Creating the basic sketch

Center
Rectangle

Close dialog
box

Center Rectangle (Flyout tool **Rectangle** / **Sketch** tab)
Select the plane **Top** (1).
Click the intersection point for the first corner (2).
Click the second corner (3).
Dimensions approx. **100** mm x **100** mm.
Close dialog box.

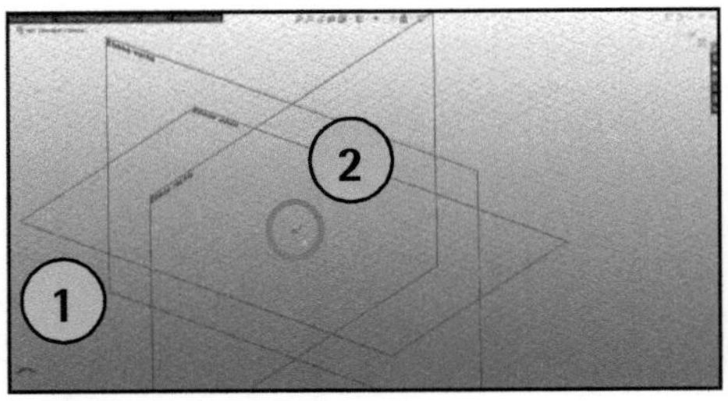

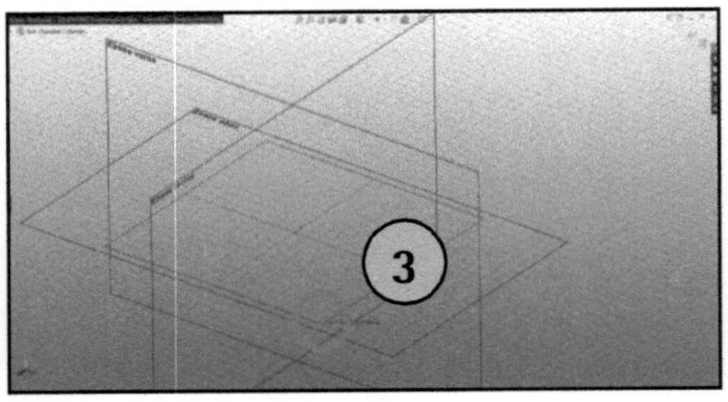

Smart
Dimension

Smart Dimension (**Sketch** tab)
Select the right rectangle line.
Click the point to add the dimension.
Enter **100** in the modify field (4).

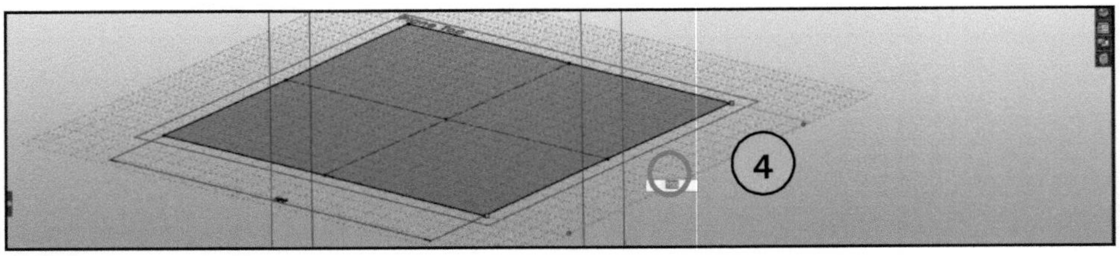

Smart
Dimension

Close dialog
box

Finish sketch

Smart Dimension (**Sketch** tab)
Proceed accordingly with the rectangle length, length **100** (5).
Close dialog box / Finish sketch

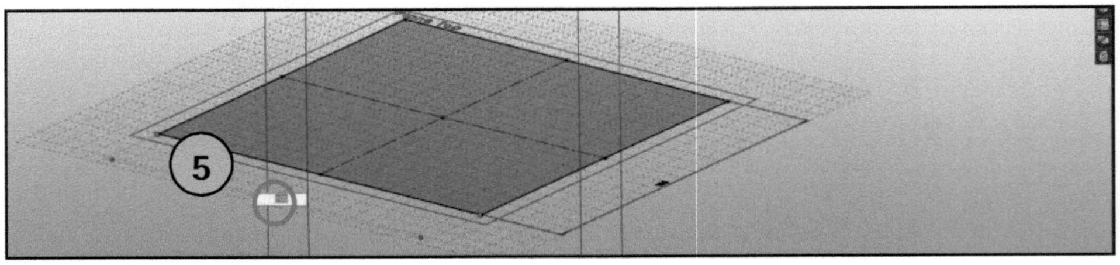

5.4.2.3 Creating an "Extrude" feature

Extrude (**Features** tab)
Select the constructed rectangle as the base sketch (6, 7).
A preview is displayed with the default depth of **10** mm.
Click the drag arrow in the center of the rectangle.
Drag to **100** mm (8).
Close dialog box.

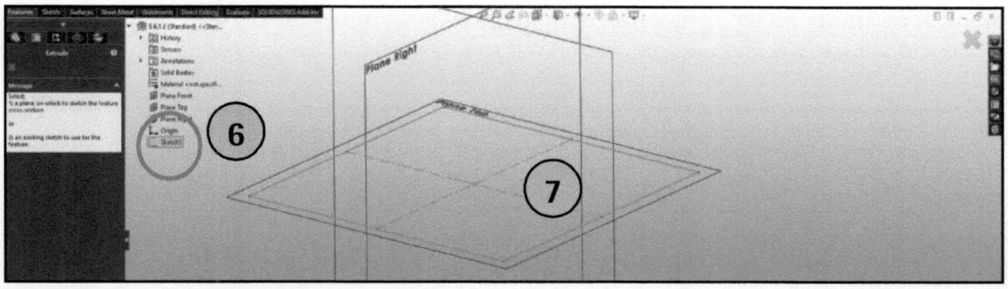

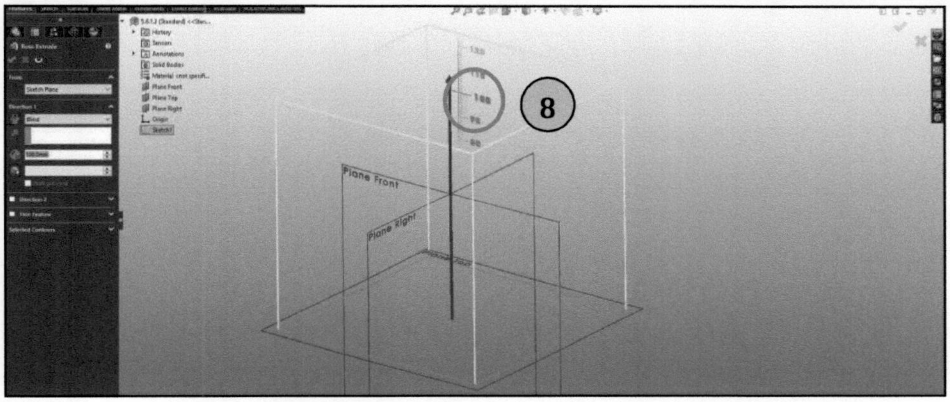

Extrude

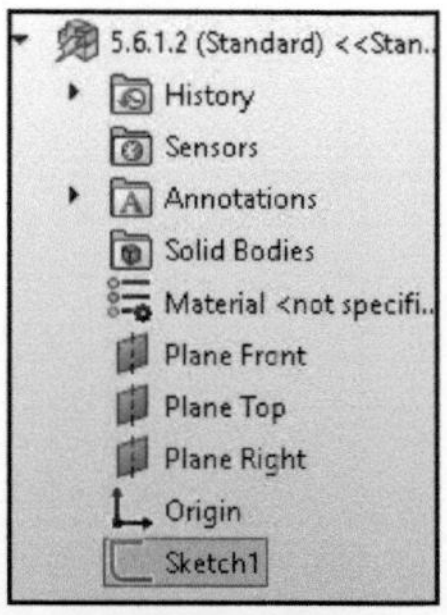

Close dialog box

5.4.2.4 Data backup

Save as New / Enter a name of your choice.

Save as New

5.5 Geometric basic primitive body "Cylinder"

5.5.1 Geometric basic primitive body "Cylinder", geometric description

A finite cylinder is, according to the general definition, bounded by two parallel, flat surfaces, a base and a top surface, and a peripheral or cylindrical surface formed by parallel lines. If the lines are perpendicular to the base and top surfaces, it is called a right cylinder. The height of the cylinder is given by the distance between the two planes in which the base and top surfaces lie. When a cylinder is mentioned in geometry, it is often a right circular cylinder.

5.5.2 Basic body "cylinder" using circular area Sketch creation within volume generation

5.5.2.1 Opening your own template file

- Menu Bar **New** / / click **Engelke2026.PRTDOT / OK**

New

Engelke2026. PRTDOT

5.5.2.2 Creating the basic sketch

Extrude (**Features** tab)
Select the Plane **Right** (1),
the plane is displayed as a flat surface.

Extrude

Circle (**Sketch** tab)

Circle

Move the cursor over the **Origin point**.
Click to position the circle's center at the origin.
As you move the mouse, a preview of the circle will appear, where the circle follows the pointer.
Drag the preview to approximately **100** mm in size (2).
Click to complete the circle.
Close dialog box.

Close dialog box

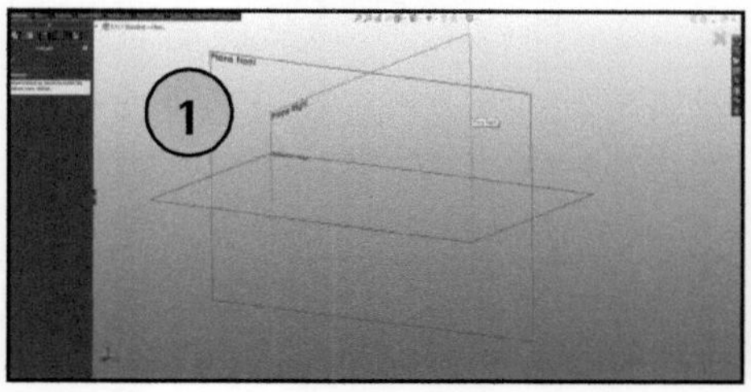

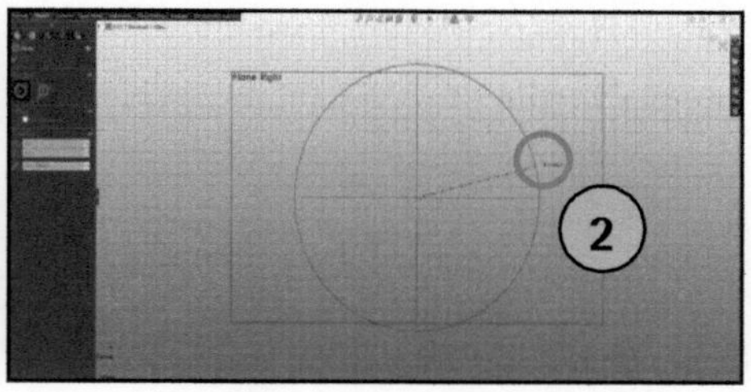

Smart Dimension (**Sketch** tab)
Select the circle outline and drag the dimension to the position.
Change the dimension entry to **100** mm (3).

Smart Dimension

Finish sketch

Finish sketch

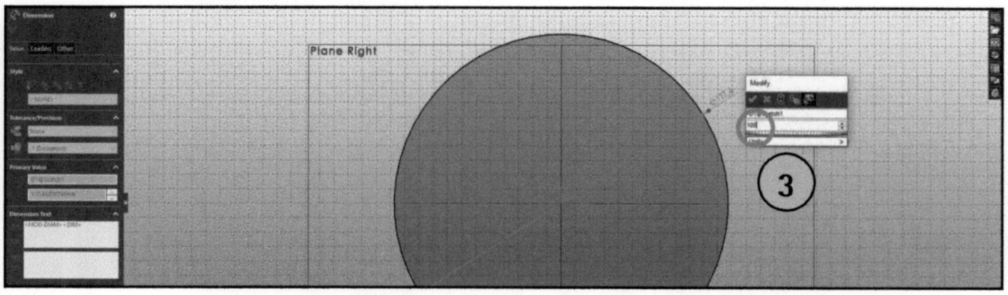

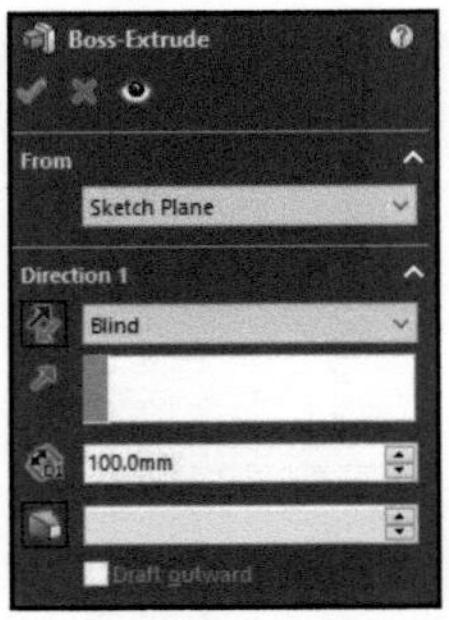

Close dialog box

5.5.2.3 Volume Generation

The graphics display switches to a perspective view.

- A preview is displayed with the default depth of **10** mm (4).
- Set the end conditions for linear extrusions to Center.
- Click the drag arrow in the center of the cylinder.
- Drag to **100** mm (5, 6).
- **Close dialog box**.

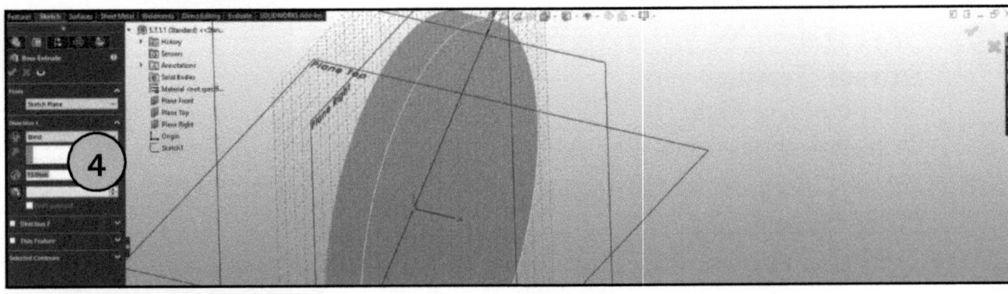

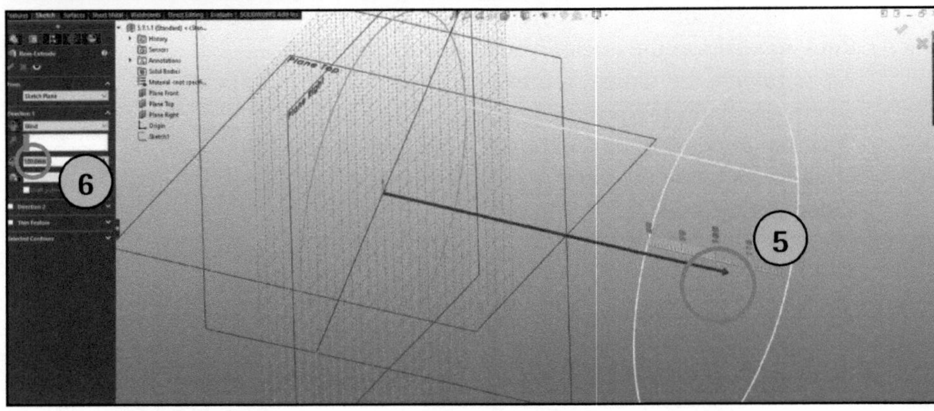

Save as New

5.5.2.4 Data backup

Save as New / Enter a name of your choice.

5.5.3 Geometric basic primitive body "Cylinder" Rotation over a stationary rectangular area Sketch creation within volume generation

5.5.3.1 Opening your own template file

- Menu Bar **New** /  /  click **Engelke2026.PRTDOT / OK**

5.5.3.2 Creating the basic sketch

Revolved (**Features** tab)
Select the plane **Front** (1).
The plane is displayed as a flat surface.

Center Rectangle (Flyout tool **Rectangle / Sketch** tab)
Click on the intersection point for the first corner (2).
Click on the second corner, dimensions approx. **70** mm x **50** mm.

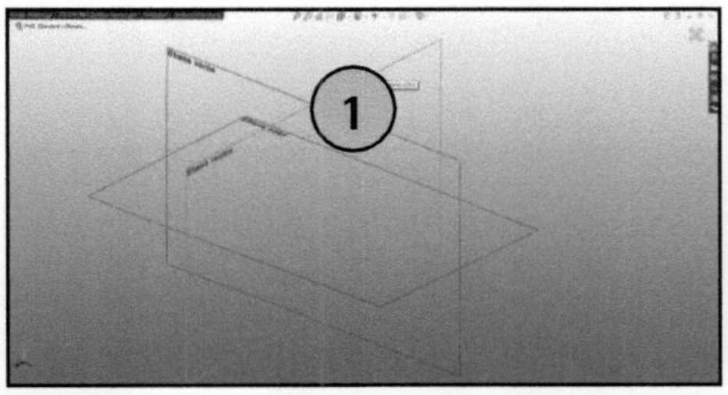

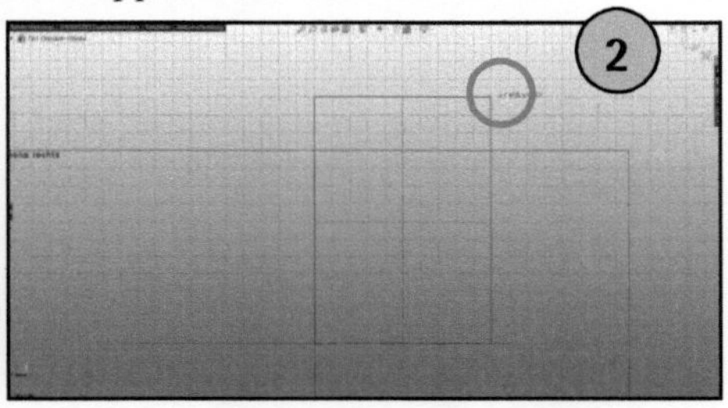

Smart Dimension (**Sketch** tab)
Select the desired rectangle edge and drag the corresponding dimension to the position.
Change the dimension to **70** mm (3).
Change the dimension to **50** mm (4).
Close dialog box.

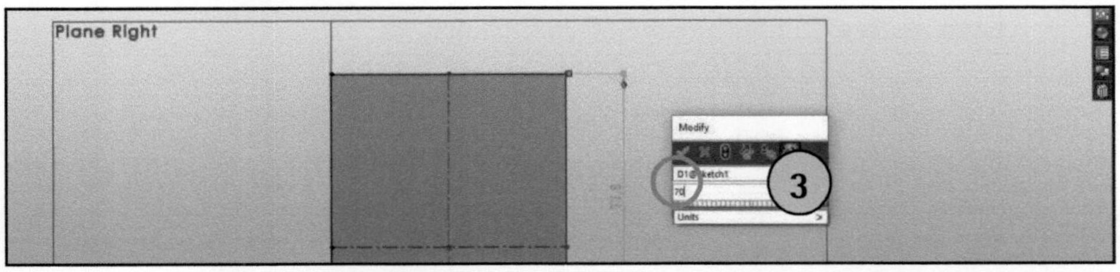

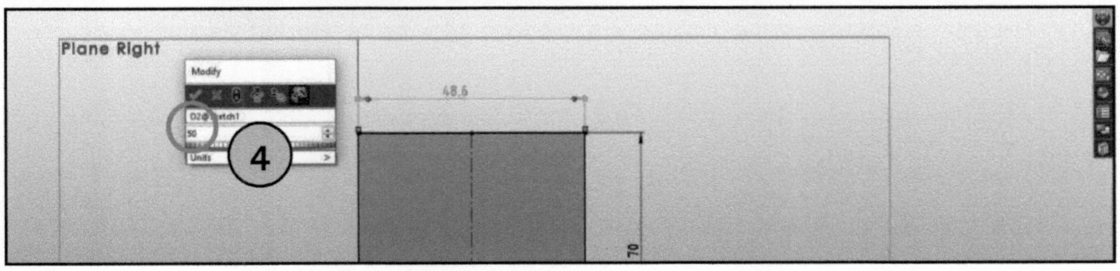

New

Engelke2026.
PRTDOT

Revolved

Center
Rectangle

Smart
Dimension

Close dialog
box

5.5.3.3 Revolve volume creation

Close dialog box

The graphics display switches to a **Perspective view**.

- Select the rectangular sketch area (5).
- Select the vertical line as the axis of rotation (6).
- A preview with **360°** rotation is displayed (7, 8).
- **Close dialog box**.

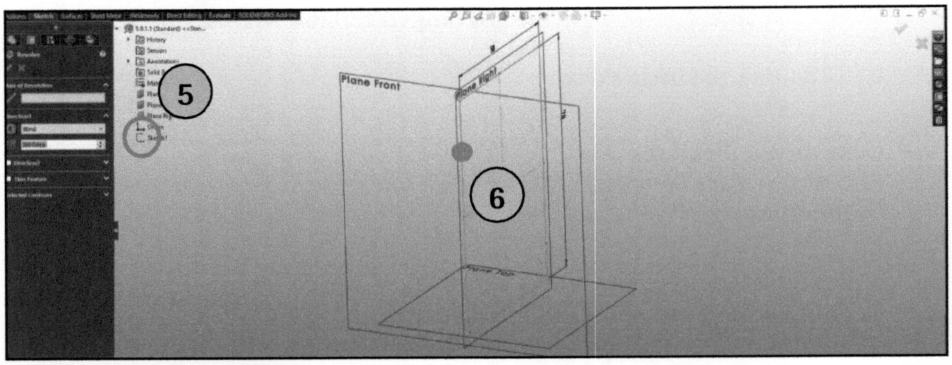

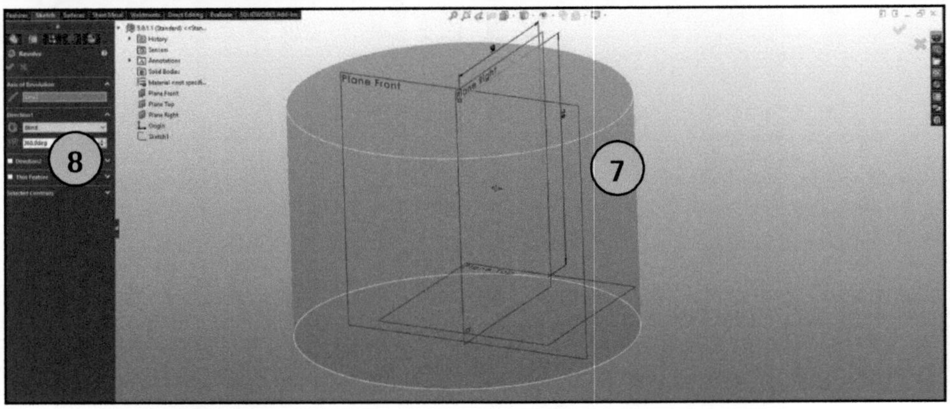

5.5.3.4 Data backup

Save as New

Save as New / Enter a name of your choice.

5.6 Geometric basic primitive body "Sphere" and "Spherical Cap"

5.6.1 Geometric basic primitive body "Sphere", geometric description

The spherical surface is the surface created by the rotation of a circle around a diameter, also called a surface of revolution. The sphere has the smallest surface area of all bodies with a given volume. Of all bodies with a given surface area, it encloses the largest volume.

The sphere has infinitely many planes of symmetry, namely the planes through the sphere's center. Furthermore, the sphere is rotationally symmetric with respect to every axis through the center and every angle of rotation, and point-symmetric with respect to its center.

Both a spherical surface and a spherical body are often referred to simply as a sphere; the union of a spherical surface and its interior is called a spherical body or solid sphere.

5.6.2 Geometric basic primitive body "Hemisphere" and "Spherical Cap", geometric description

A spherical segment or spherical section is a part of a spherical body formed by its intersection with a plane. A spherical segment has the shape of a dome and a circular disk as its base.

A hemisphere is a special case of a spherical segment in which the intersection plane contains the sphere's center. The curved part of the surface of a spherical segment is called the spherical cap, also called the spherical calotte or spherical dome.

5.6.3 Geometric basic primitive body "Sphere", using a rotation of a halved circular area

New

Engelke2026.
PRTDOT

5.6.3.1 Opening your own template file

- Menu Bar **New** /  /  click **Engelke2026.PRTDOT** / **OK**

5.6.3.2 Creating the basic sketch

Circle

Close dialog box

Smart Dimension

Circle (**Sketch** tab)
Select the plane **Top**.
Click to position the circle's center at the origin point.
Drag and click to define the radius, approx. **100** mm (1).
Close dialog box.

Smart Dimension (**Sketch** tab)
Select the line and drag the dimension to the position.
Change the dimension entry to **100** mm (2)

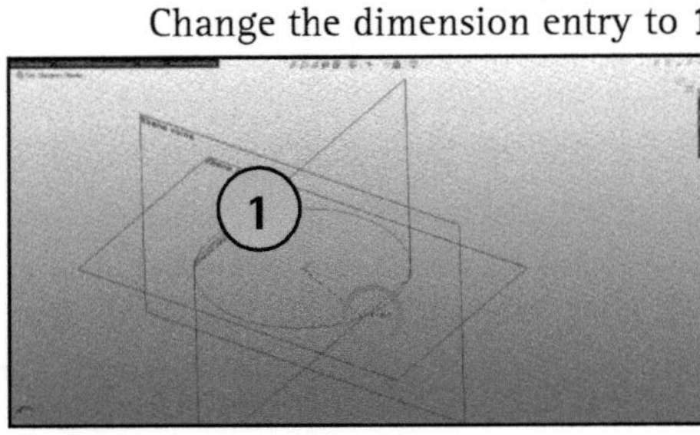

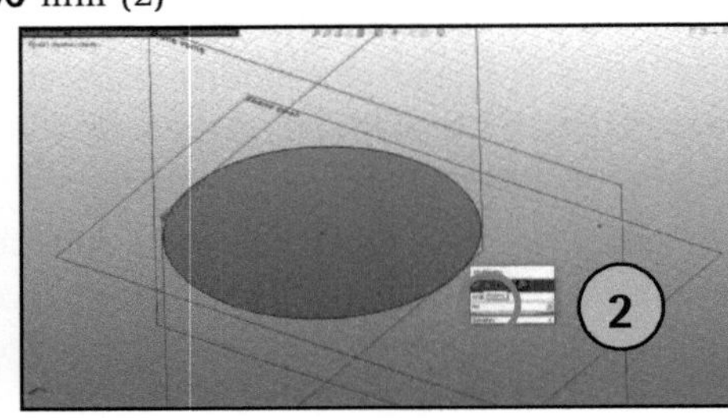

Line

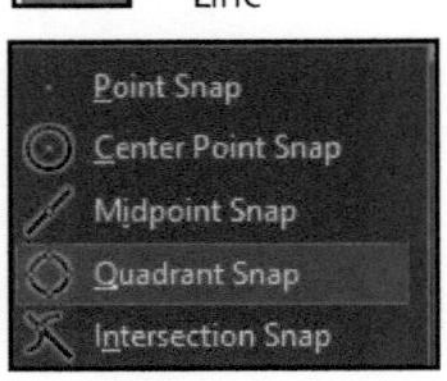

Close dialog box

Line (**Sketch** tab)
Click to place the line at the front quick snap **Quadrant point** (3).
Click to place the line at the back quick snap **Quadrant point** (4).
Double-clicking at the last point,
or by selecting **End chain** from the context menu.

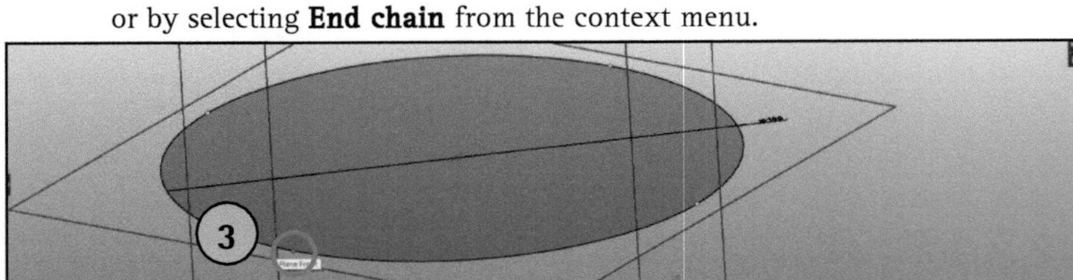

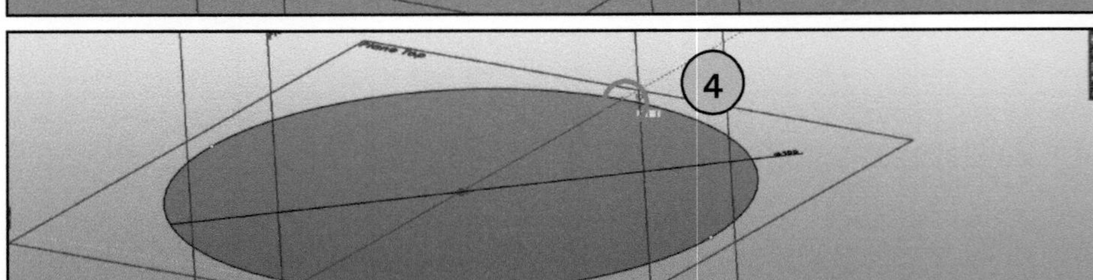

5.6.3.3 Creating the halved circular area

Trim Entities (**Sketch** tab)

Option **Trim to closest** (5)
Select the highlighted half of the circle (6, 7).
Close dialog box / Finish sketch

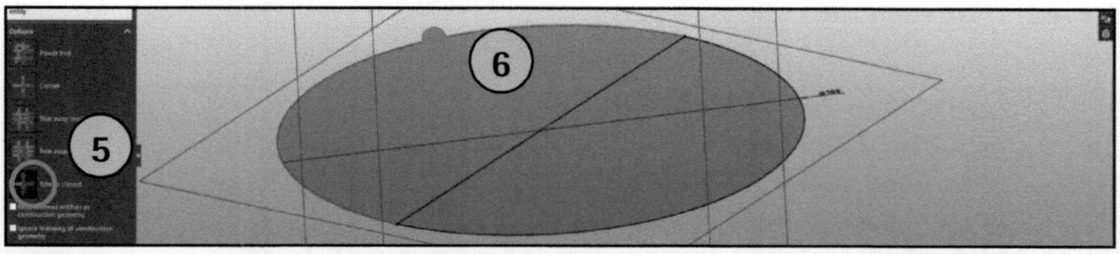

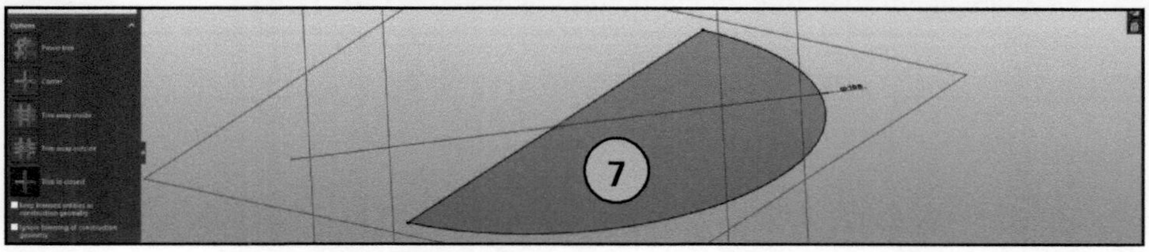

Trim Entities

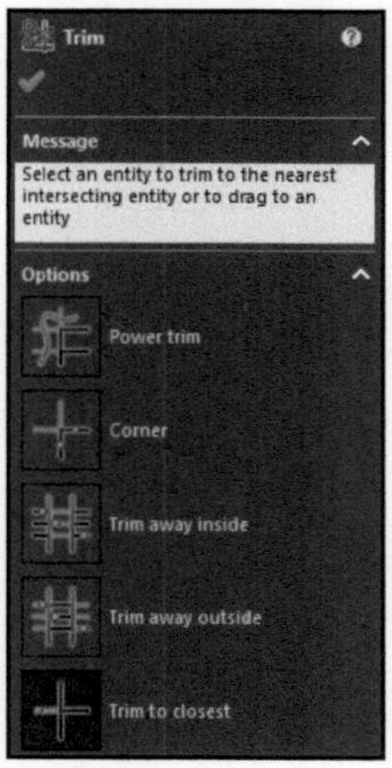

Close dialog box

Finish sketch

5.6.3.4 Revolved volume creation

Revolved (**Features** tab)
Select the circular sketch area (8).
Click the horizontal line as the axis of rotation (9, 10).
Close dialog box.

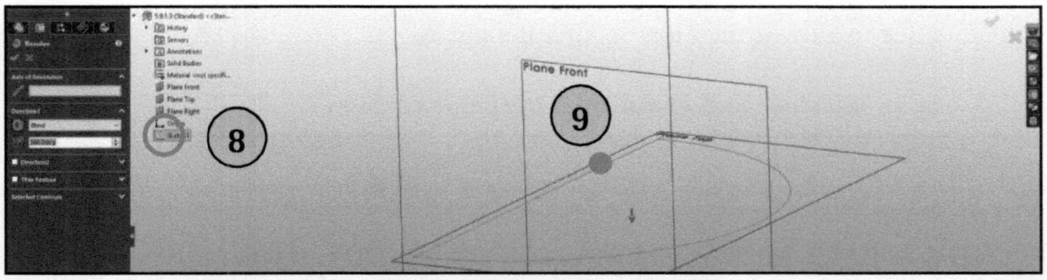

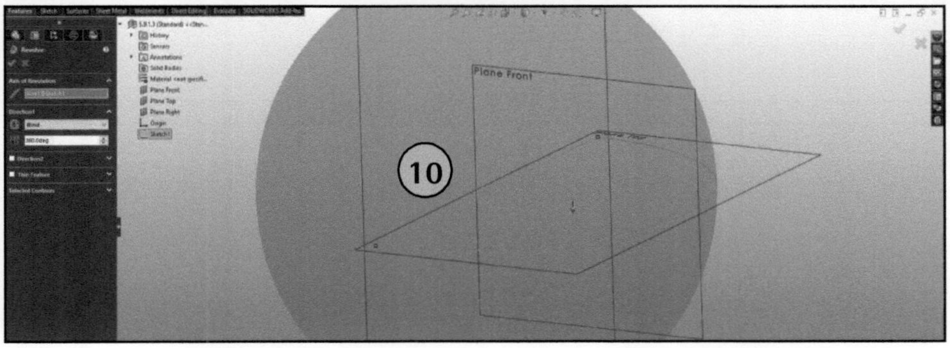

Revolved

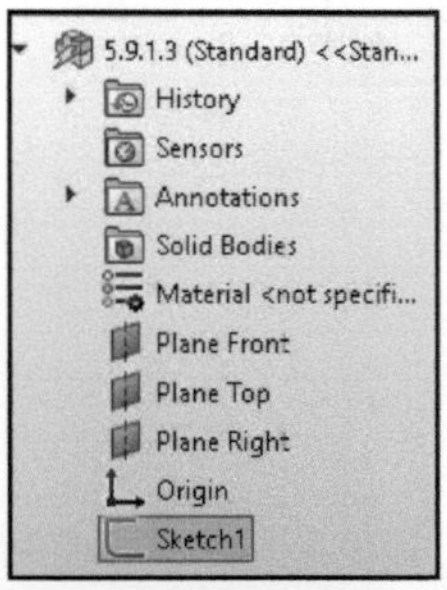

5.6.3.5 Data backup

Save as New / Enter a name of your choice.

Save as New

5.6.4 "Spherical Cap" using rotation of a circular segment area, sketch creation

New

Engelke2026.
PRTDOT

Centerpoint
Arc

5.6.4.1 Opening your own template file

- Menu Bar **New** /  /  click **Engelke2026.PRTDOT** / **OK**

5.6.4.2 Creating the basic sketch

Centerpoint Arc (**Sketch** tab)
Select the **Top Plane**.
Click on the center point of the circular arc (1).
Click to place a starting point (2).
Click again to define an endpoint, angle value **180°** (3, 4).

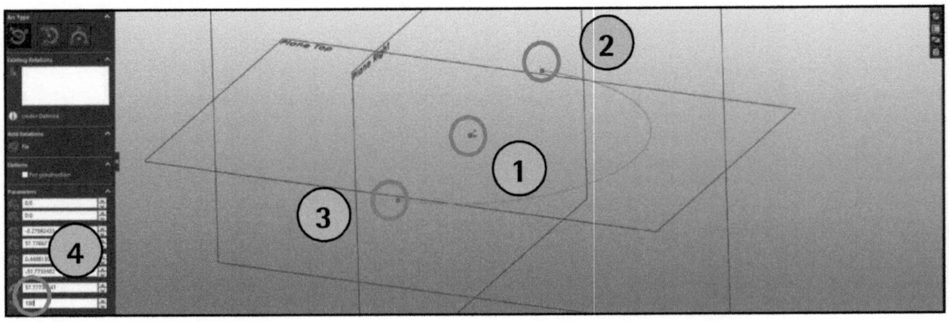

Line

Line (**Sketch** tab)
Click to place the **Line** at the line point (5).
Click to extend the **Line** beyond the arc (6).
Double-clicking at the last point,
or by selecting **End chain** from the context menu.

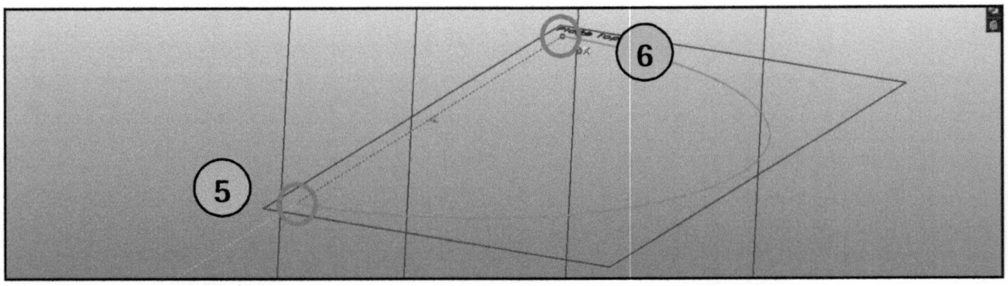

Line (**Sketch** tab)
Click to place the **Line** at the line point (7).
Click to extend the **Line** beyond the arc (8).
Double-clicking at the last point,
or by selecting **End chain** from the context menu.

Line

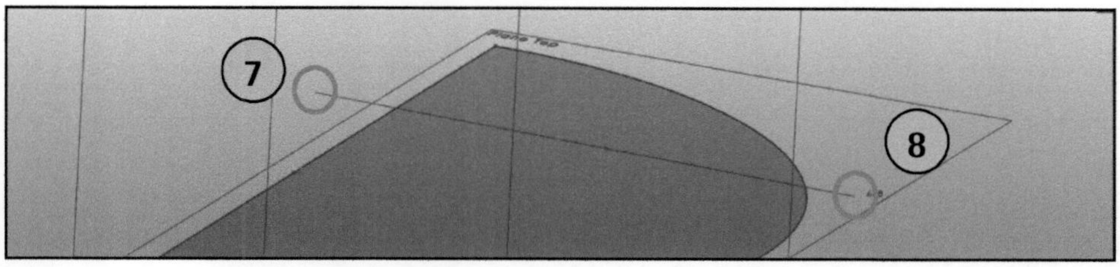

5.6.4.3 Creating the circular area

Trim Entities (Registerkarte **Skizze**)

Option **Trim to closest**.
Select the highlighted half of the circular arc (9, 10).

Trim Entities

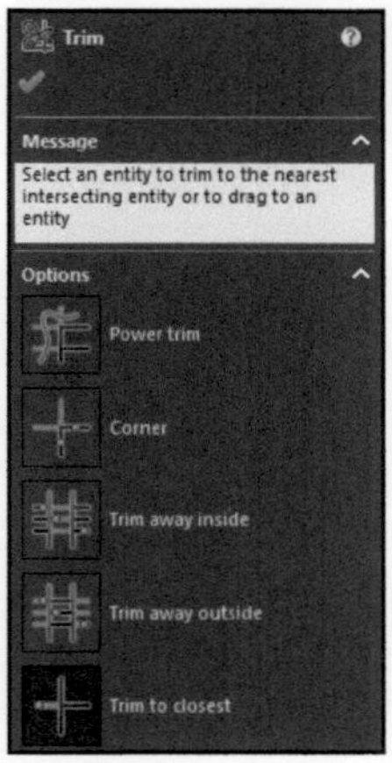

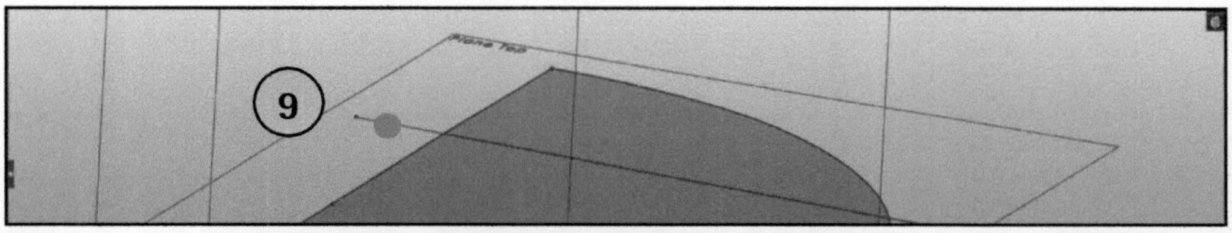

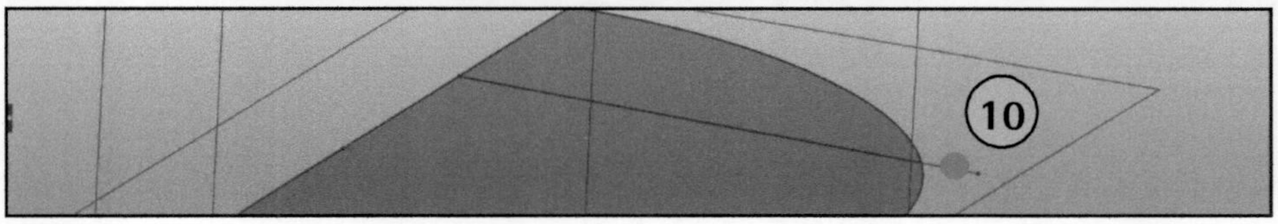

Trim Entities (Registerkarte **Skizze**)

Option **Trim to closest**.
Select the highlighted half of the circular arc and the line (11, 12).
Close dialog box / Finish sketch

Trim Entities

Close dialog box

Finish sketch

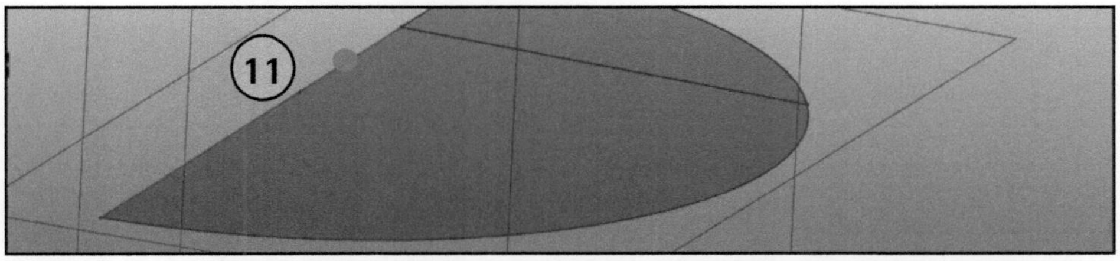

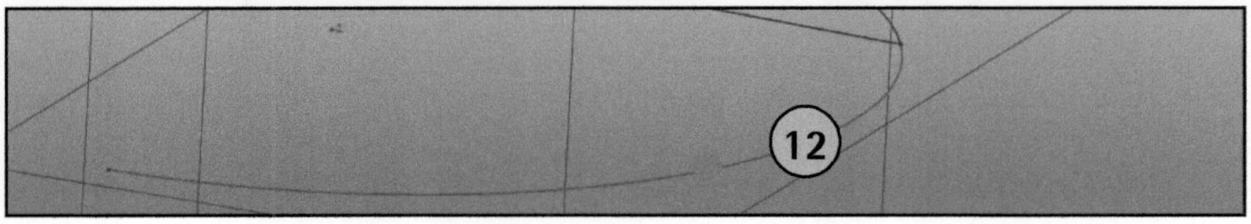

5.6.4.4 Revolved volume creation

Revolved

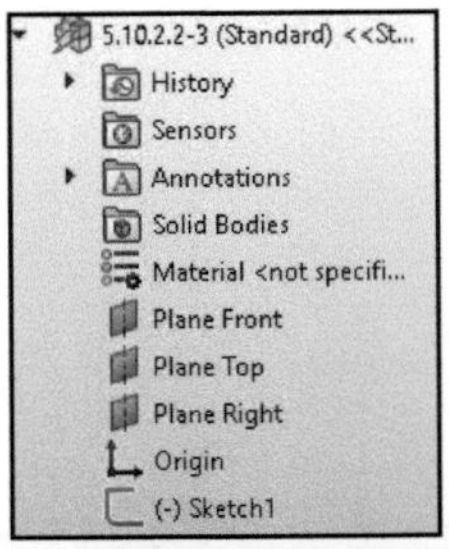

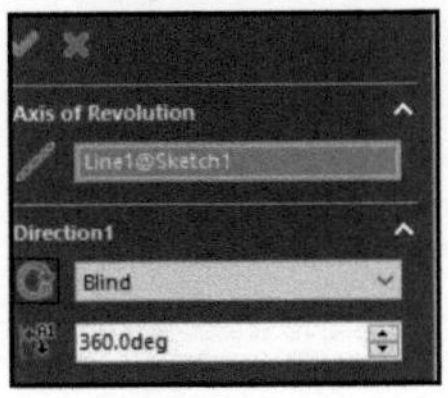

Revolved (Features tab)
Click the cleaned-up sketch (13).
Click the vertical line as the axis of rotation (14).
Close dialog box (15)

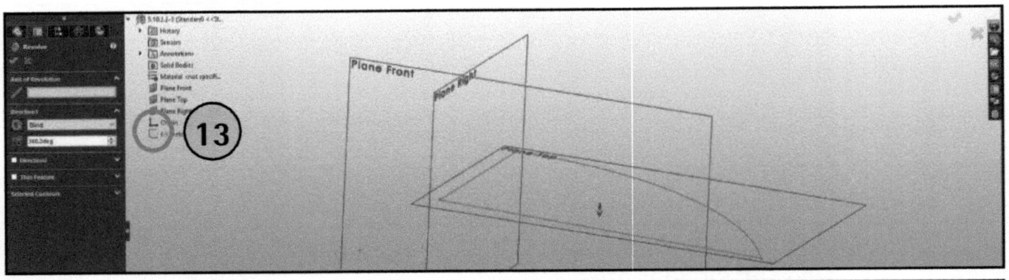

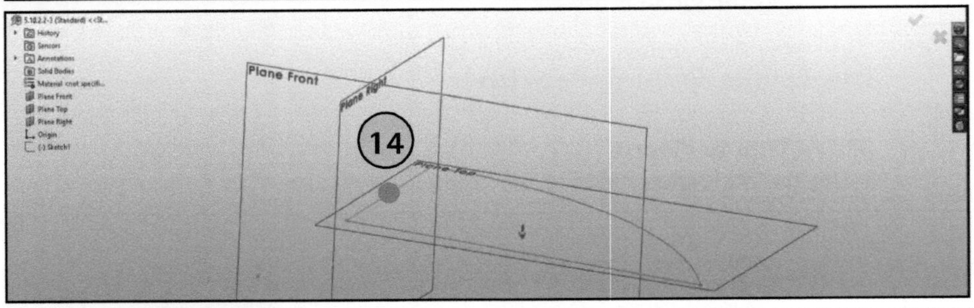

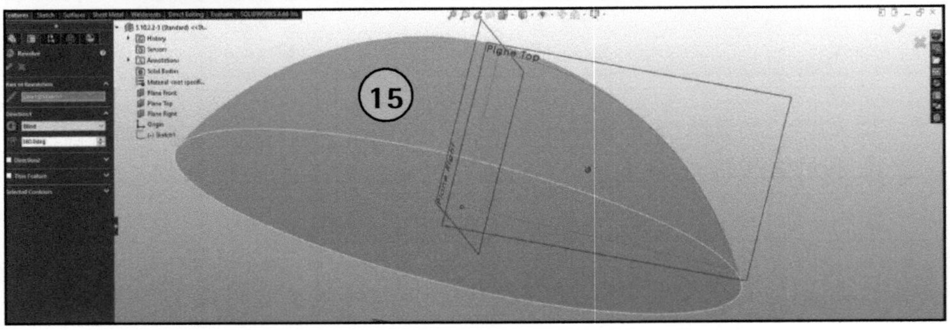

5.6.4.5 Data backup

Save as New

Save as New / Enter a name of your choice.

5.7 Geometric basic primitive body "Cone" and "Truncated Cone"

5.7.1 Geometric basic primitive body "Cone", geometric description

A cone is a geometric solid formed by connecting all points of a bounded, circular surface lying in a plane with a straight line to a vertex outside the plane. The surface is called the base, its boundary line is called the directrix, and the point is called the apex or vertex of the cone.

The distance between the apex and the base is the height of the cone. The lines connecting the apex to the directrix are called generatrix lines, and their union forms the cone's surface.

When a cone is mentioned in geometry, the special case of a right circular cone is often meant. Especially in engineering, the word cone (from Latin conus) is also used for a cone of revolution.

5.7.2 Geometric basic primitive body "Truncated Cone", geometric description

In geometry, a truncated cone is the name given to a special solid of revolution. A truncated cone is created by cutting a smaller cone from a right circular cone parallel to its base. This smaller cone is called the complementary cone of the truncated cone.

The height of a truncated cone is the distance between its base and its top.

New

Engelke2026.
PRTDOT

Line

5.7.3 Geometric basic primitive body "Cone", using rotation of a triangular area made of lines

5.7.3.1 Opening your own template file

- Menu Bar **New** /  /  click **Engelke2026.PRTDOT** / **OK**

5.7.3.2 Creating the basic sketch

Line (**Sketch** tab)
Select the **Right Plane** (1).
Click to place the line at the **Origin point** (2).
Click for the horizontal position, length approx. **80** mm, vector **90°** (3).
Click for the vertical position, length approx. **100** mm (4).
(The parallel position is indicated by a dotted line).
Click the vertical position, length approx. **60** mm, vector **180°** (5).
(Parallel position is indicated by a dotted line).
The line end is indicated by a snap symbol (5).

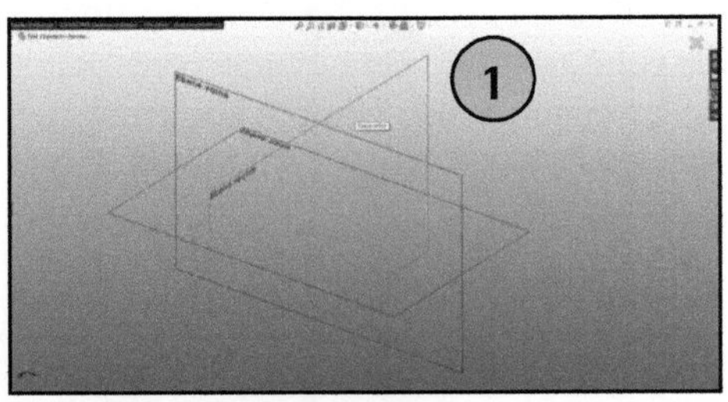

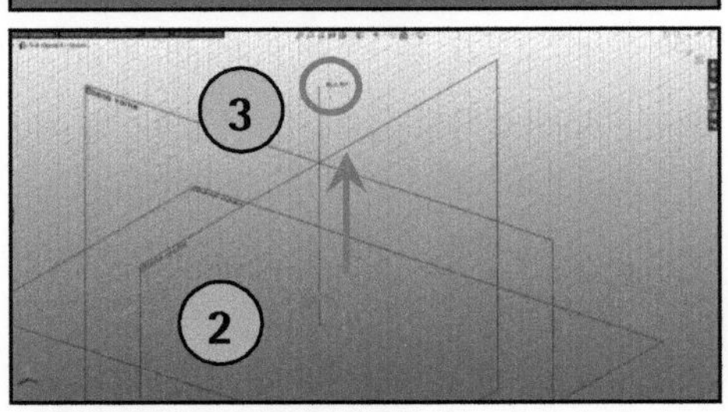

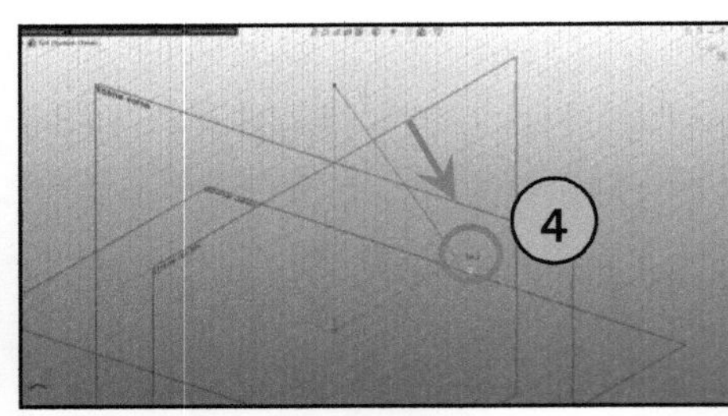

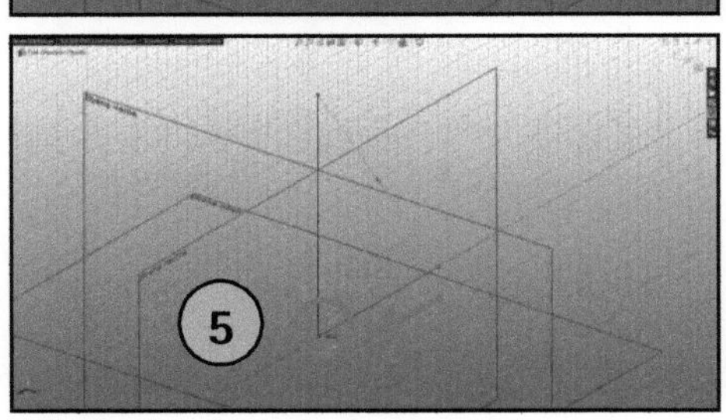

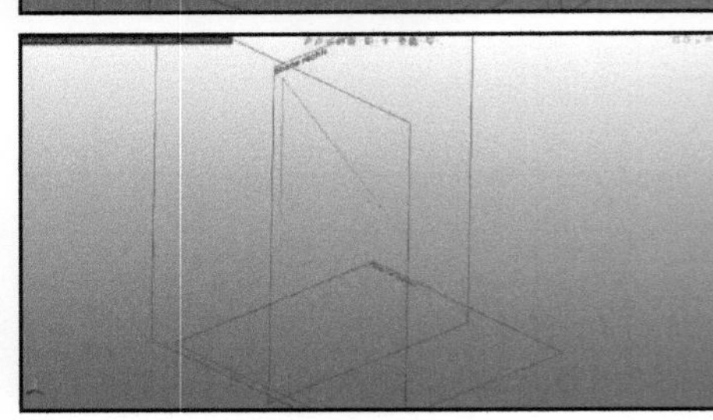

Smart Dimension (**Sketch** tab)
Select the desired rectangle edge and drag the dimension to the position.
Change the dimension to **80** mm (6).
Change the dimension to **60** mm (7).
Close dialog box / Finish sketch.

Smart Dimension

Close dialog box

Finish sketch

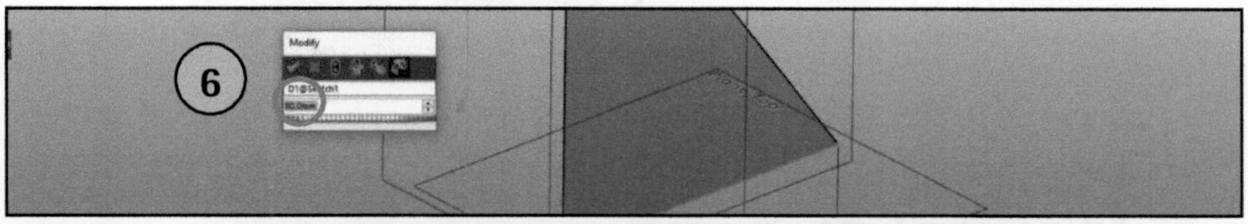

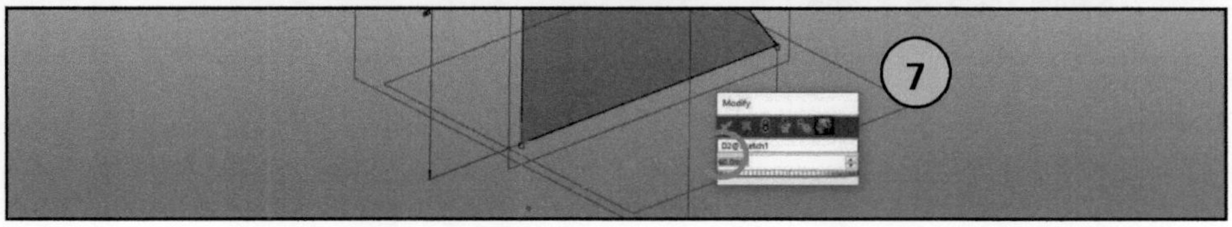

5.7.3.3 Revolved volume creation

Revolved (**Features** tab)
Click the created sketch as the outer contour (8).
Click the vertical line as the axis of rotation (9).
Close dialog box (10).

Revolved

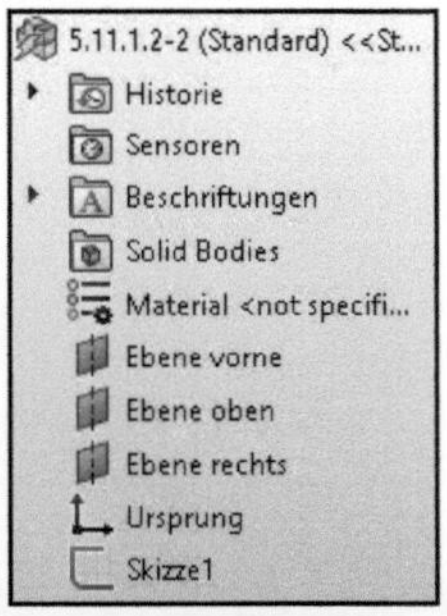

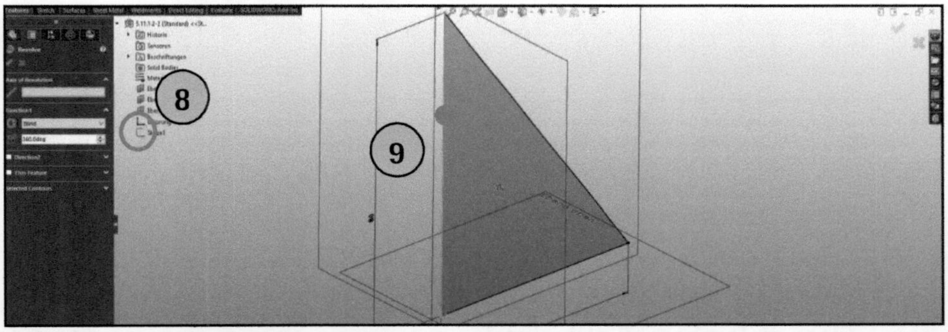

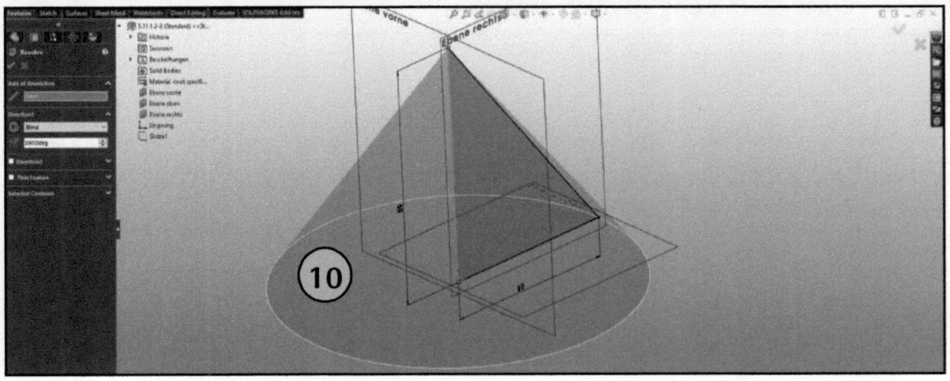

5.7.3.4 Data backup

Save as New / Enter a name of your choice.

Save as New

5.7.4 Geometric basic primitive body "Truncated Cone" using feature "Extrude" and "Draft"

5.7.4.1 Opening your own template file

New

Engelke2026. PRTDOT

- Menu Bar **New** / / click **Engelke2026.PRTDOT / OK**

5.7.4.2 Creating the basic sketch

Extrude

Extrude (**Features** tab)
Select the **Top Plane,**
the plane will be displayed as a planar surface.

Circle

Circle (**Sketch** tab)
Click to position the circle's center at the **Origin point.**
Drag the circle to a size of approximately **100** mm (1).

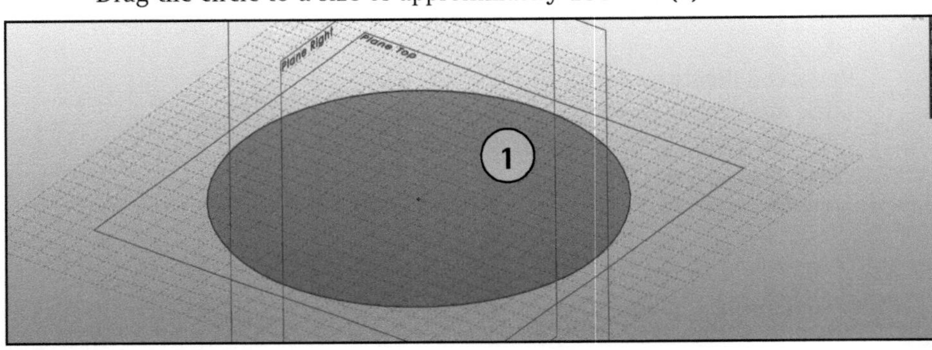

Smart Dimension

Close dialog box

Finish sketch

Smart Dimension (**Sketch** tab)
Select the circle outline and drag the dimension to the position.
Change the dimension to **100** mm (2).
Close dialog box / Finish sketch.

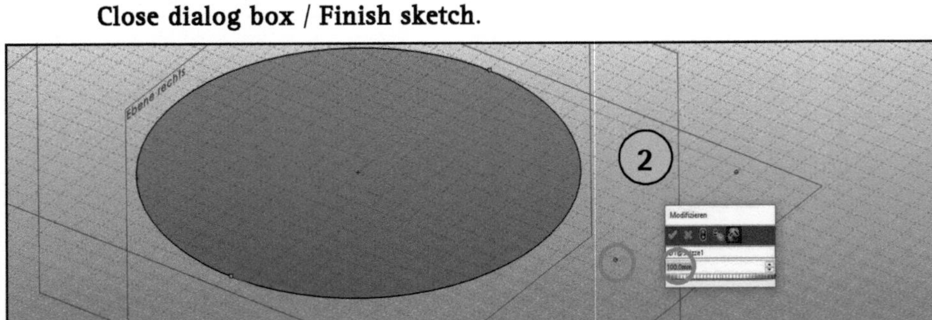

5.7.4.3 Draft volume generation

The graphics display switches to a **Perspective view**.

- A preview is displayed with the default depth of **10** mm (3).
- Switch the **Draft** option to **On** (4).
- Set the Draft value to **30°** (4).
- Drag the scale to **50** mm (5).
- **Close dialog box** (6).

Draft / On

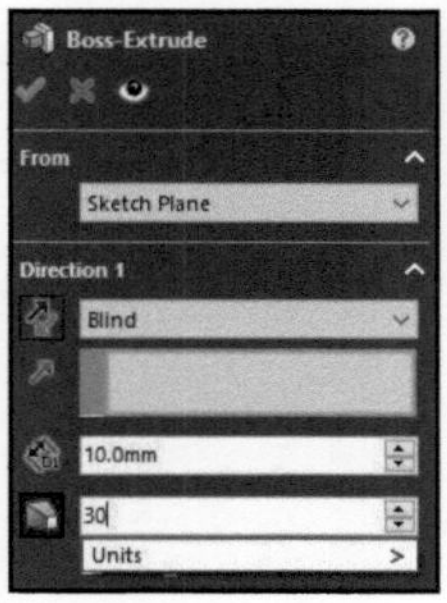

Close dialog box

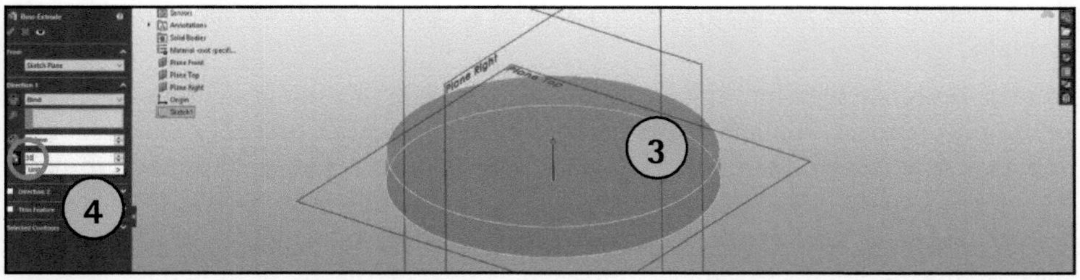

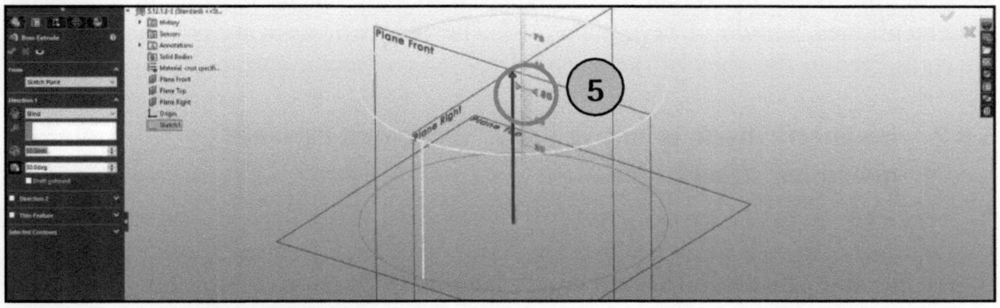

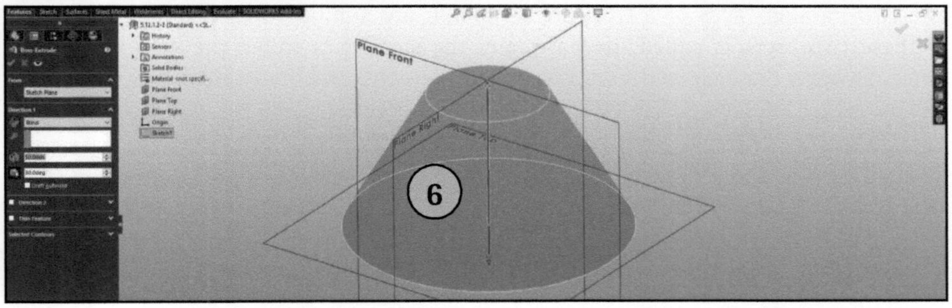

5.7.4.4 Data backup

Save as New / Enter a name of your choice.

Save as New

5.8 Geometric basic primitive body "Pyramid" and "Truncated Pyramid"

5.8.1 Geometric basic primitive body "Pyramid", geometric description

The pyramid is a geometric solid, more precisely a polyhedron, whose base is a polygon and whose sides are triangles that are adjacent to the polygon on one side and meet at a point, the so-called apex of the pyramid, on the other. The polygon is also called the base of the pyramid. The triangles together form the surface of the pyramid.

From a designated point, the apex of the pyramid, a bundle of rays emanates, whose rays intersect a plane at the vertices of the pyramid's base. For example, with four rays of a certain inclination in space, one obtains a square base, thus forming the square pyramid. One can also begin the construction with any base of a polygon in the plane and choose a point outside this plane, which then becomes the apex of the pyramid. By connecting each vertex of the base with the apex, the aforementioned bundle of rays is created. The points of each individual base edge are connected to the apex of the pyramid via the triangular surface.

5.8.2 Geometric basic primitive body "Truncated Pyramid", geometric description

A truncated pyramid is a geometric term that describes a special type of polyhedron. A truncated pyramid is created by cutting a smaller, similar pyramid (a complementary pyramid) from a pyramid parallel to its base.

The two parallel faces of a truncated pyramid are similar to each other. The larger of these two faces is called the base, and the smaller is called the vertex. The distance between the base and vertex is called the height of the truncated pyramid.

5.8.3 Geometric basic primitive body "Pyramid" using "Extrude" and "Draft" feature

5.8.3.1 Opening your own template file

- Menu Bar **New** /  /  click **Engelke2026.PRTDOT / OK**

New

Engelke2026.
PRTDOT

5.8.3.2 Creating the basic sketch

Corner Rectangle (Flyout tool **Rectangle / Sketch** tab)
Select the **Top Plane** (1).
Click the intersection point for the first corner (2).
Click the second corner, approx. **100** mm x **100** mm (3).
Close dialog box.

Corner
Rectangle

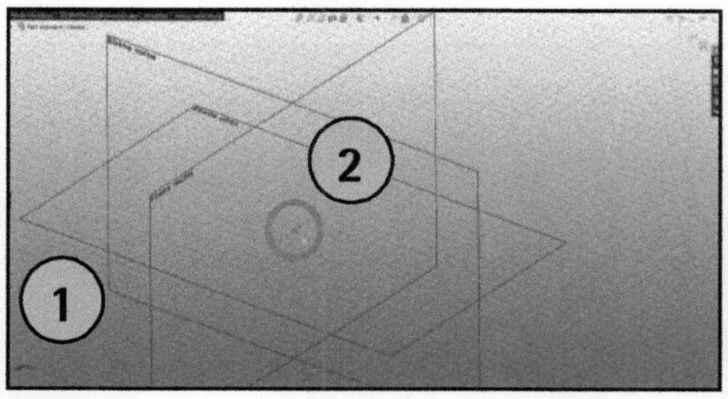

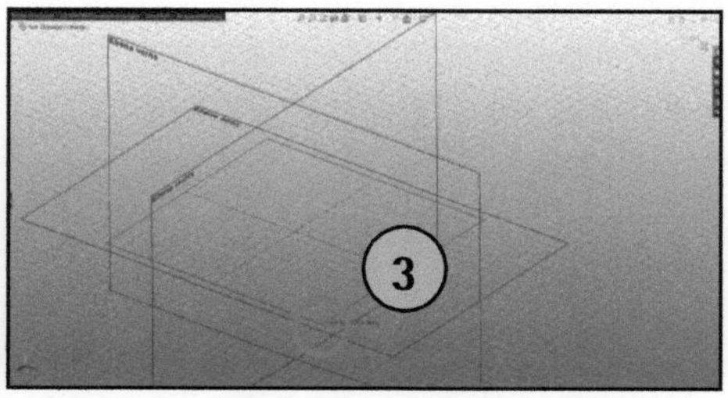

Smart Dimension (**Sketch** tab)
Select the right rectangle line.
Click the point to add the dimension.
Enter **100** in the Modify field (4).

Smart
Dimension

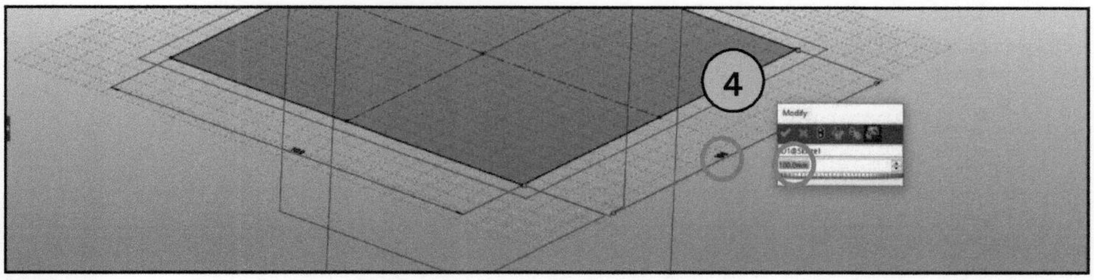

Smart Dimension (**Sketch** tab)
Select the right rectangle line.
Click the point to add the dimension.
Enter **100** in the Modify field (5).
Close dialog box / Finish sketch

Smart
Dimension

Close dialog
box

Finish sketch

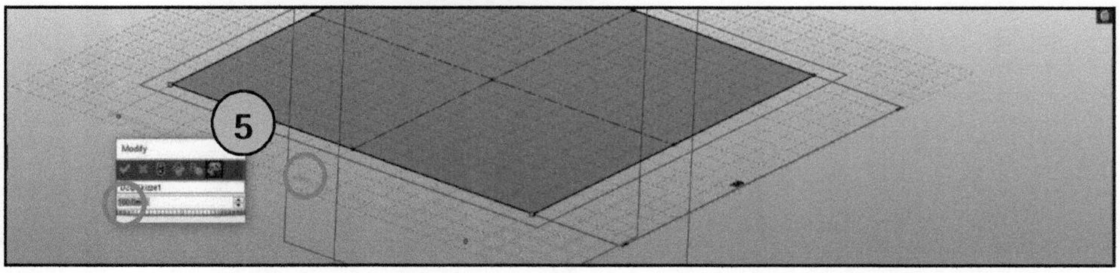

Extrude

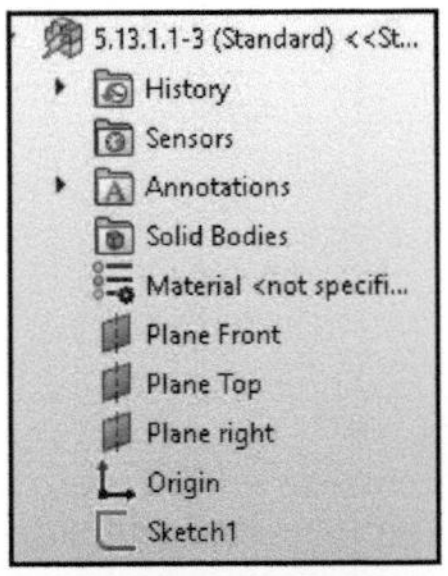

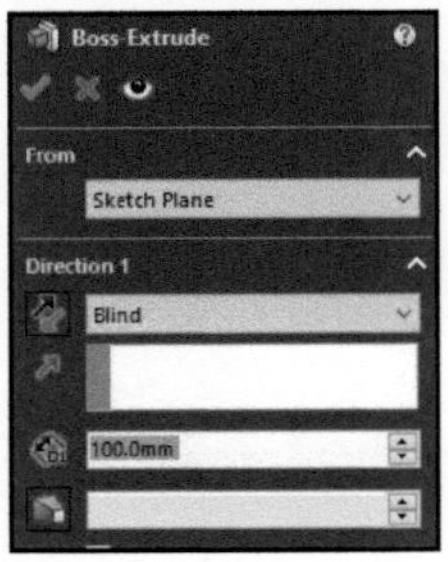

5.8.3.3 Extrude" and "Draft" volume creation

Extrude (Features tab)
Select the constructed rectangle as the base sketch.
A preview is displayed with the default depth of **10** mm (7).
Click the drag arrow in the center of the rectangle.
Drag to **100** mm (8).
Close dialog box.

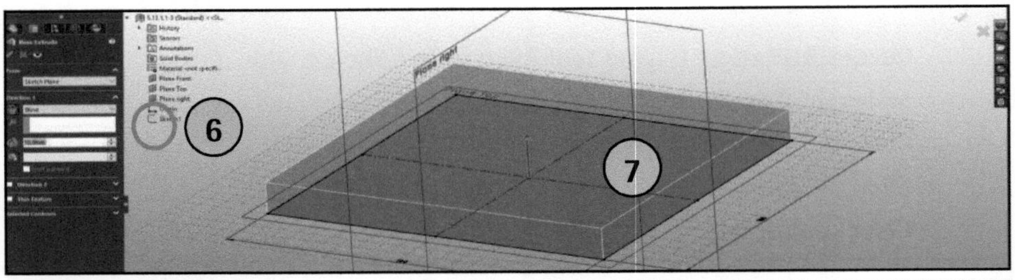

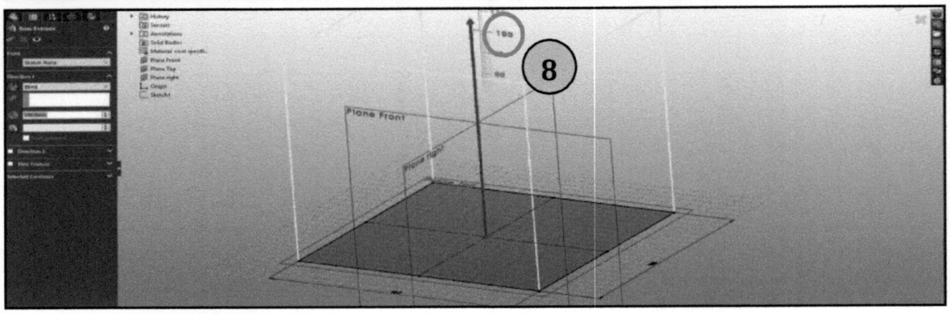

Draft

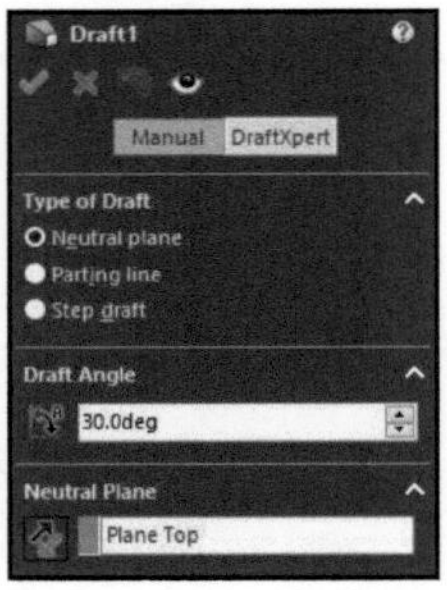

5.8.3.4 Create a "Pyramid" using "Draft"

Draft (Features tab)
In the **PropertyManager**, click **Manual** (9).
In the **PropertyManager**, under **Type of Draft**, select **Neutral plane** (10).
Enter **30°** under **Draft Angle** (10).
Select the bottom face as the neutral plane (11).

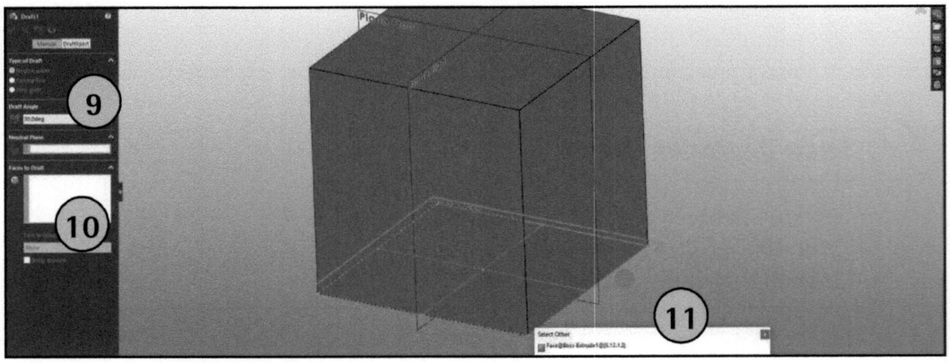

- Click to reverse direction if needed.
- Select all faces of the cube for the draft angle surfaces (12, 13).
  Activate **Show preview** (14).
  Close dialog box (15).

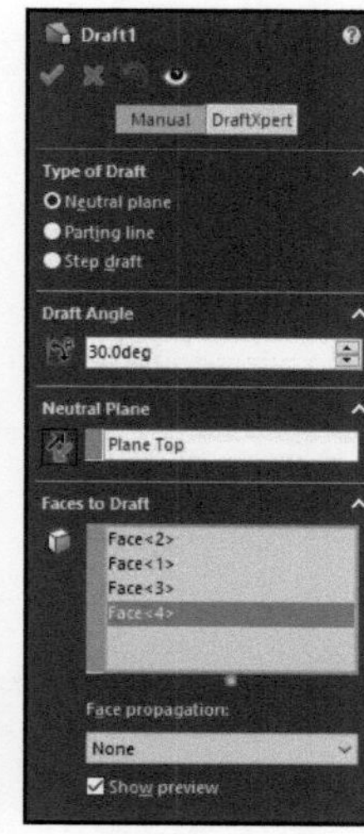

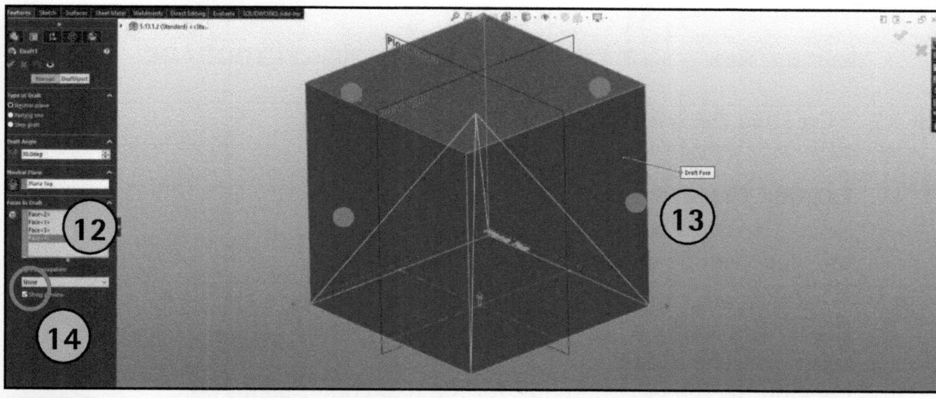

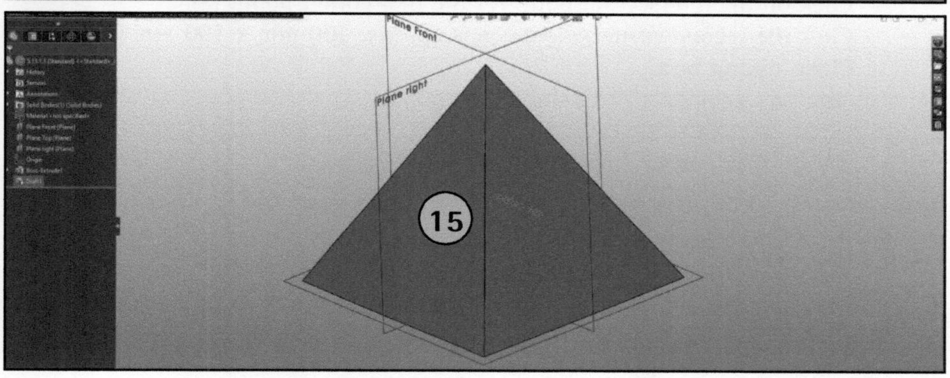

5.8.3.5 Data backup

Save as New / Enter a name of your choice.

Save as New

5.8.4 Geometric basic primitive body "Truncated Pyramid" using "Extrude" feature option "Draft"

New

Engelke2026. PRTDOT

5.8.4.1 Opening your own template file

- Menu Bar **New** / / click **Engelke2026.PRTDOT / OK**

5.8.4.2 Creating the basic sketch

Extrude

Extrude (Features tab)
Select the **Top Plane**,
the plane will be displayed as a planar surface.

Center Rectangle

Close dialog box

Center Rectangle (Flyout tool **Rectangle / Sketch** tab)
Select the **Top Plane.**
Click on the intersection point for the first corner point. (1).
Click the second corner, dimensions approx. **100** mm x **100** mm (2).
Close dialog box.

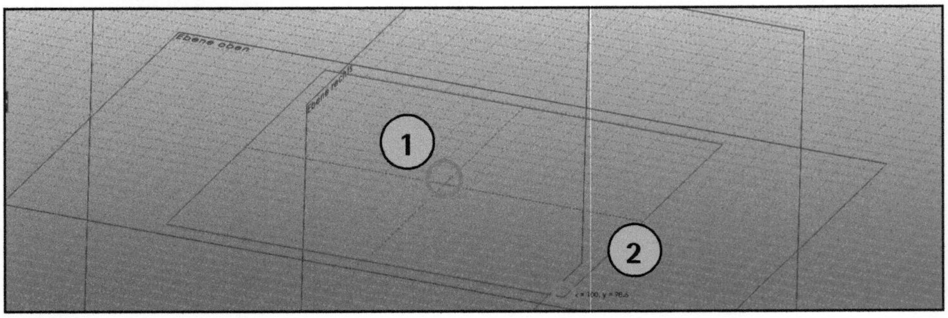

Smart Dimension

Smart Dimension (Sketch tab)

Select the desired rectangle outline and drag the dimensions to the desired position.

Change the dimension to **100** mm (3, 4).

Finish sketch

Finish sketch.

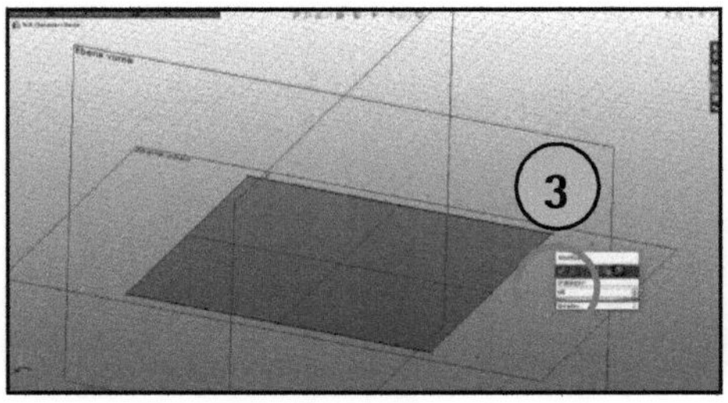

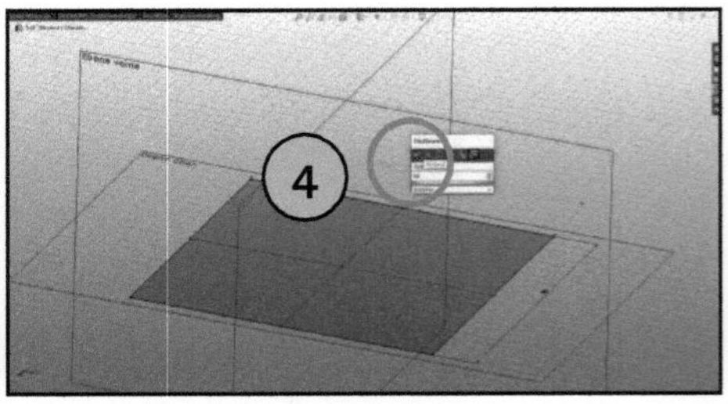

5.8.4.3 "Draft" volume generation

The graphics display switches to a **Perspective view**.

- A preview is displayed with the default depth of **10** mm (5, 6).
- Switch the **Draft** option to **On** (7).
- Set the **Draft** value to **30°** (7).
- Drag the scale to **50** mm (8).
- **Close dialog box** (9).

Draft / On

Close dialog box

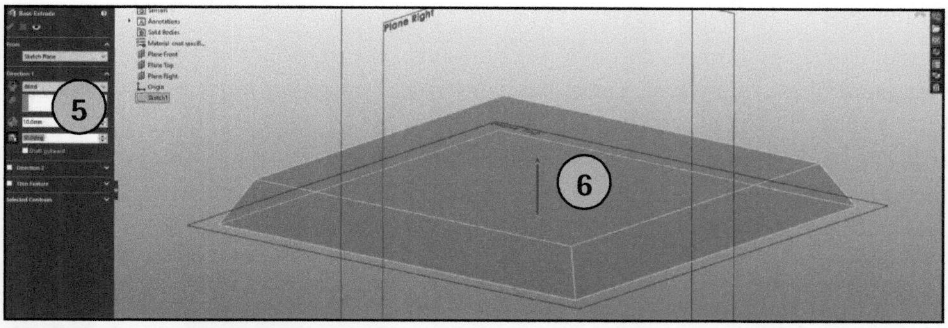

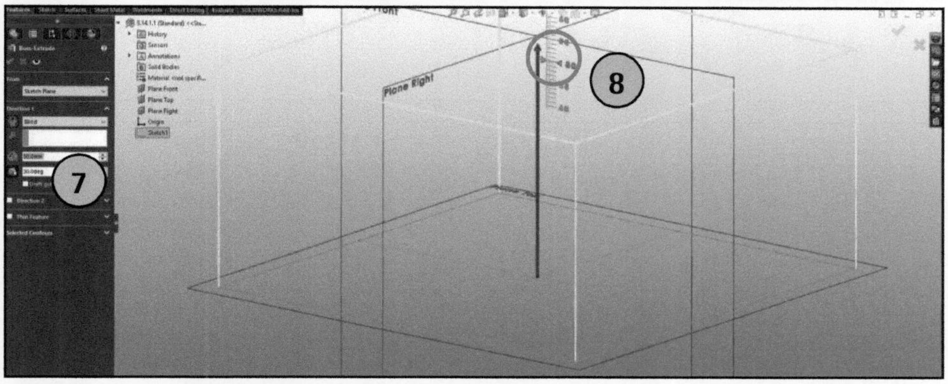

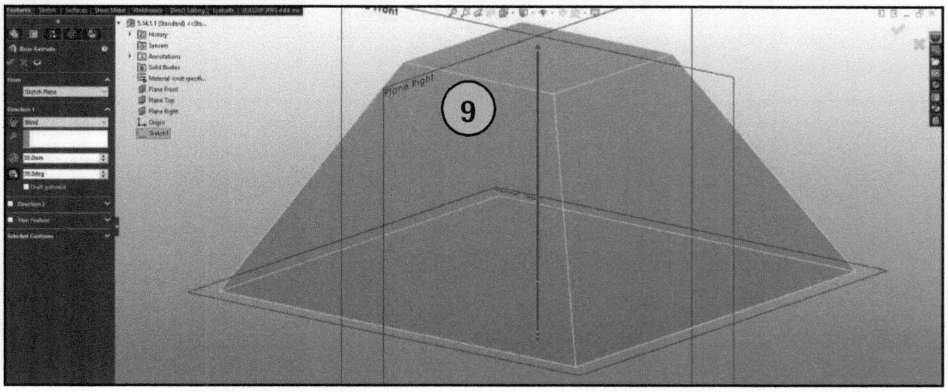

5.8.4.4 Data backup

Save as New / Enter a name of your choice.

Save as New

5.9 Geometric basic primitive body "Rotational ellipsoid"

5.9.1 Geometric basic primitive body "Rotational ellipsoid", geometric description

A spheroid, also known as an ellipsoid of revolution or rotational ellipsoid, is a quadric surface obtained by rotating an ellipse about one of its principal axes; in other words, an ellipsoid with two equal semi-diameters. A spheroid has circular symmetry.

If the ellipse is rotated about ist major axis, the result is a prolate spheroid, elongated like a rugby ball. The American football is similar but has a pointier end than a spheroid could.

If the ellipse is rotated about ist minor axis, the result is an oblate spheroid, flattened like a lentil. If the generating ellipse is a circle, the result is a sphere.

5.9.2 Geometric basic primitive body "Rotational ellipsoid" Rotation of half an elliptical surface

5.9.2.1 Opening your own template file

New

Engelke2026.
PRTDOT

- Menu Bar **New** /  /  click **Engelke2026.PRTDOT** / **OK**

5.9.2.2 Creating the basic sketch

Ellipse

Ellipse (**Sketch** tab)
Select the **Top Plane**.
Click to place the center point of the **Ellipse** (1).
Drag and click to define an axis of the **Ellipse**, approx. **100** mm (2).
Drag and click to define the second axis.
Dimension approximately **50** mm (3).
Then click to complete the **Ellipse**.
Close dialog box.

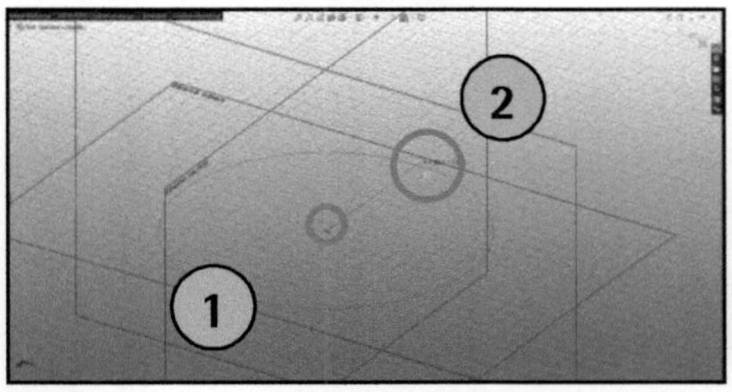

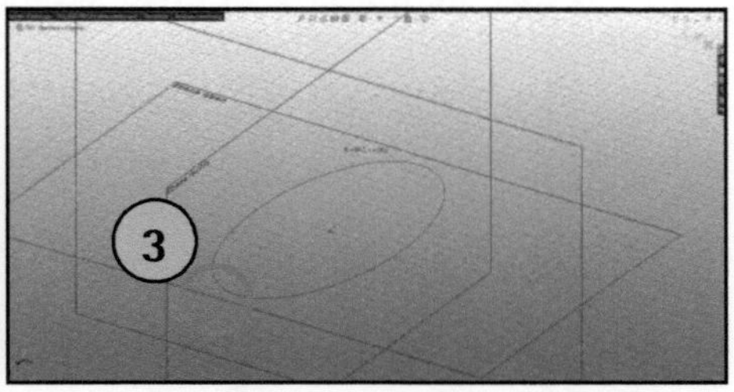

Smart
Dimension

Close dialog
box

Smart Dimension (**Sketch** tab)
Select the desired ellipse lengths and drag the dimensions to the desired position.
Change the dimension values to **100** mm (4) and **50** mm (5).
Close dialog box.

Line

Line (**Sketch** tab)
Click to place the line at the front point of the **Ellipse** (6).
Click to place the line at the back point of the **Ellipse** (7).

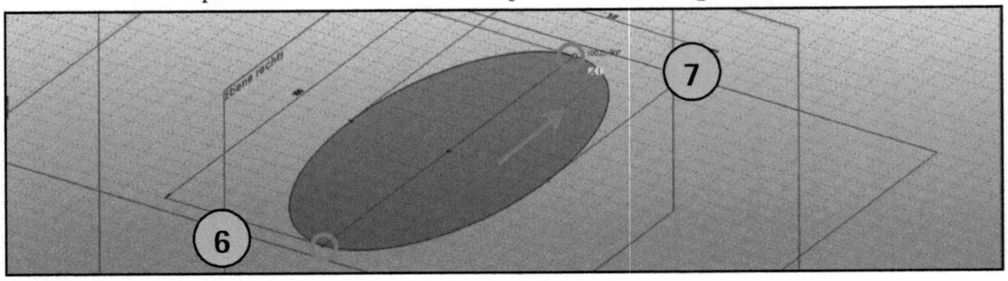

Trim Entities

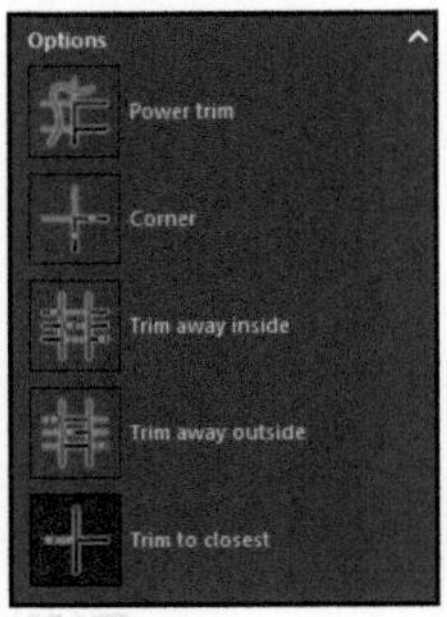

Close dialog box

Finish sketch

Trim Entities (**Sketch** tab)

Option **Trim to closest.**
Select the highlighted half of the circular arc (8).
Close dialog box / Finish sketch

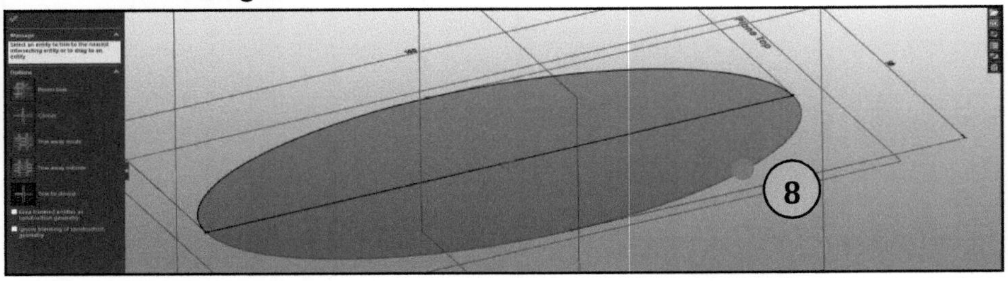

5.9.2.3 Revolved volume creation

Revolved

Close dialog box

Revolved (**Features** tab)
Click the created sketch as the outer contour (9).
Click the constructed line as the axis of rotation (10).
Close dialog box.

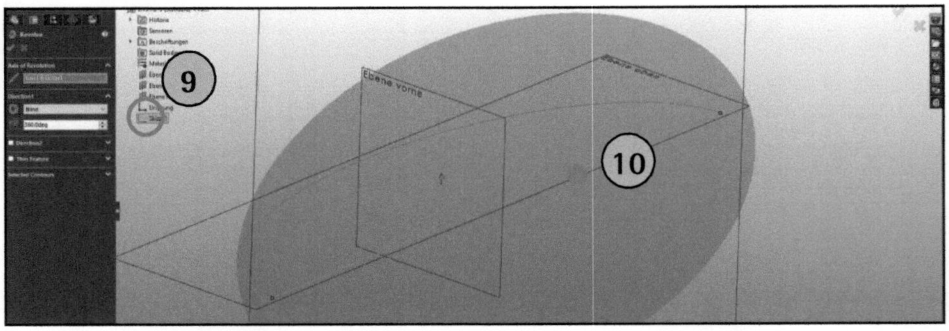

5.9.2.4 Data backup

Save as New

Save as New / Enter a name of your choice.

5.10 Geometric basic primitive body "Torus"

5.10.1 Geometric basic primitive body "Torus", geometric description

In geometry, a torus is a surface of revolution generated by revolving a circle in three-dimensional space one full revolution about an axis that is coplanar with the circle.

The main types of toruses include ring toruses, horn toruses, and spindle toruses. A ring torus is sometimes colloquially referred to as a donut or doughnut.

If the axis of revolution does not touch the circle, the surface has a ring shape and is called a torus of revolution, also known as a ring torus.

5.10.2 Geometric basic primitive body "Torus" Rotation of a circular area around a central axis

5.10.2.1 Opening your own template file

New

Engelke2026.
PRTDOT

- Menu Bar **New** / / click **Engelke2026.PRTDOT / OK**

5.10.2.2 Erstellung der Basisskizze

Line

Close dialog
box

Line (**Sketch** tab)
Select the Right Plane.
Click to place the line at the **Origin point** (1).
Click for the vertical position approx. **25** mm (2).
Click to place the line at the midpoint (3).
Click for the horizontal position, approx. **30** mm (4).
Close dialog box.

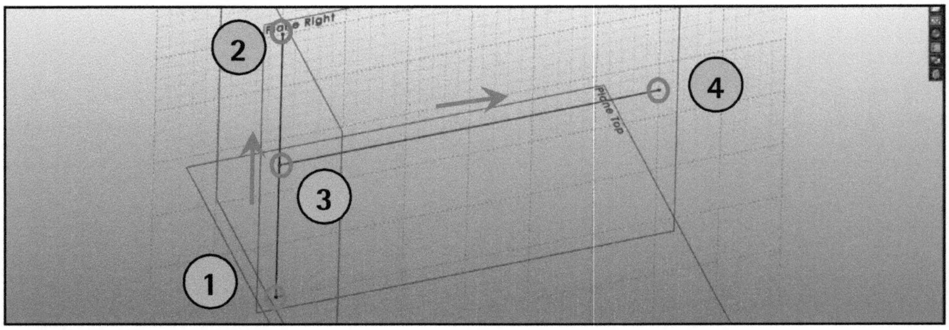

Circle

Close dialog
box

Circle (**Sketch** tab)
Click to place the circle at the endpoint of the line (5).
Drag the circle radius to **10** mm (6).
Close dialog box.

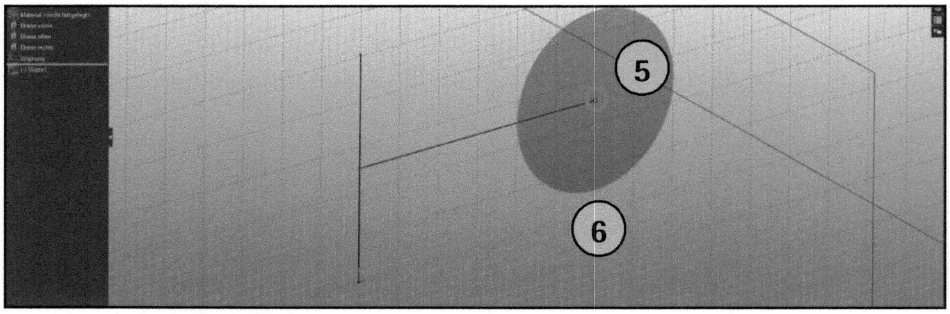

Smart Dimension (**Sketch** tab)
Select the relevant lines and drag the dimensions to their positions.
Change the dimension value to the respective value (7, 8, 9).
Close dialog box / Finish sketch

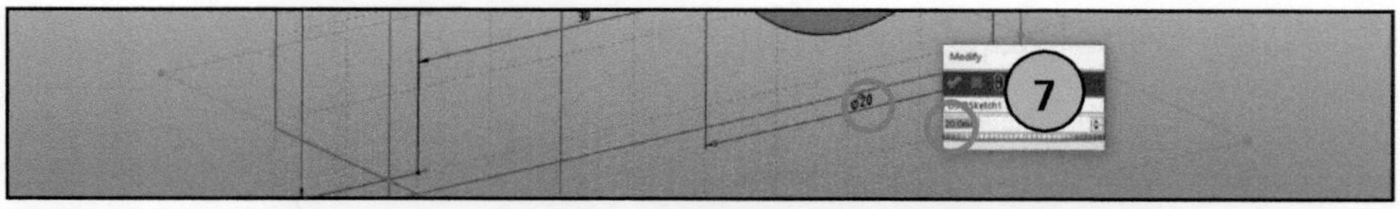

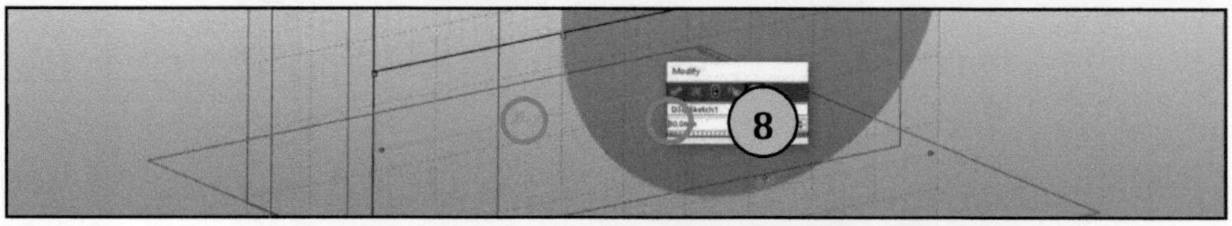

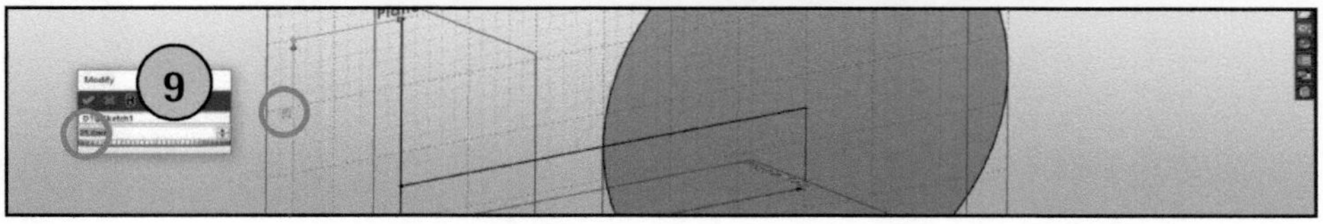

Smart Dimension

Close dialog box

Finish sketch

5.10.2.3 Revolved volume creation

Revolved (**Features** tab)
Click the created circular area as the outer contour (7, 8).
Click the constructed line as the axis of rotation (9, 10).
Close dialog box (9)

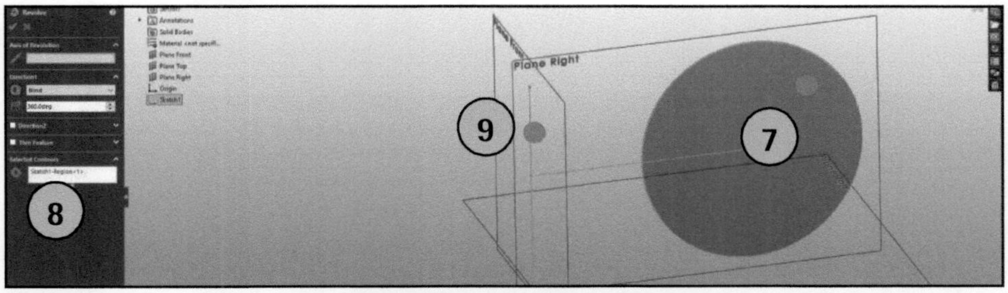

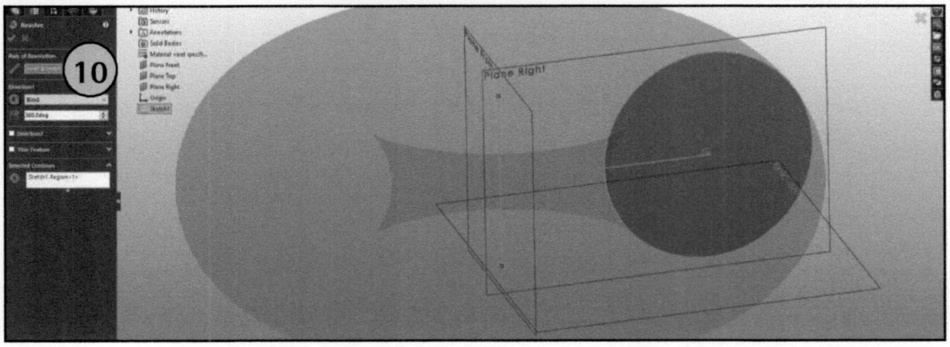

Revolved

Close dialog box

5.10.2.4 Data backup

Save as New / Enter a name of your choice.

Save as New

6

Dassault Systèmes
3DEXPERIENCE©
SOLIDWORKS Design
2026

Parts and Components

Create and Customize

Powerful commands
Optimized constructions

6 Powerful commands, optimized constructions

6.1 Powerful commands, optimized constructions, basics

SOLIDWORKS provides the functionality for designing individual parts. The necessary tools are included for everything from simple mechanical components to extremely complex castings, including all ribs, fillets, and drafts.

Simple form elements such as extrusions or rotations usually form the basis of a component, from which the finished model is created step by step.

For cast parts, special functions are available, ranging from thin-wall and ribs to highly specialized functions such as stiffening meshes or ventilation grilles. This is just a small sample of the possibilities offered by SOLIDWORKS technology.

Powerful curve and surface functions offer solutions for all spatial situations where only complex calculations would otherwise yield results. Control curves and cross-sections control and adjust the geometry.

All elements are fully parametric, robustly controllable, and thus suitable for automation. This applies to freeform surfaces as well as to construction elements that form construction geometry.

When designing a part, you create sketches, create three-dimensional elements using feature tools, and then combine these elements to create parts.

The shape of the sketch is controlled by constraints (which are automatically applied by default during sketching), and the size of the sketch is controlled by dimensions. You can leave some parts of the sketch geometry undimensioned if you want to resize it later.

Most features are created from sketched shapes (profiles), but some are well-defined mechanical operations that do not require sketches, such as chamfers, fillets, wall thicknesses, and face drafts. Sketched features can be joined to another feature using union, subtraction, or intersection operations.

To create complex parts, features are combined. Features are positioned using geometric constraints and dimensions.

By leaving some curves on entities undimensed, you can make the entity adaptive so that it can change its size if you specify the entity as constrained by fixed geometry in an assembly.

A feature of a part is generally created by adding or removing material from or to the part's base shape. This includes holes, cutouts, and protrusions.

In this chapter, you will learn the basics of modeling and modifying parts using Solid Edge Synchronous technology. The features and procedures are explained using several part function examples.

6.2 Technical principles for basic constructions, drilling

6.2.1 Drilling, technical basics

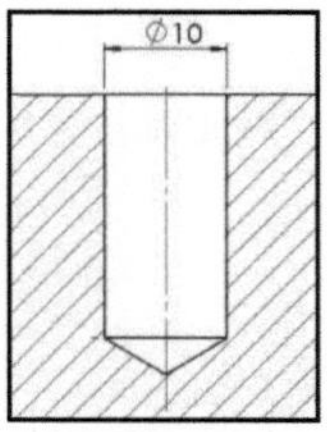

A bore, also known as a through-hole, is the technical term for a recess or opening created by a rotating tool. Different types are distinguished according to their technical use:

6.2.1.1 Simple Hole

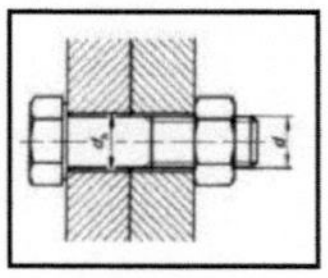

According to DIN EN 20273, through holes are referred to as through holes and blind holes; this standard also regulates the dimensions and accuracy of the drill diameters.

6.2.1.2 Threaded Hole

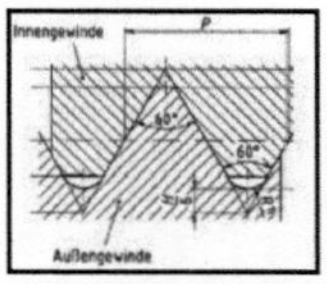

Threaded holes are designed as through holes and blind holes, with threads according to DIN 13. The drill diameter for the core holes is selected according to DIN 336.

6.2.1.3 Countersink DIN 974-1, for cylinder head screws

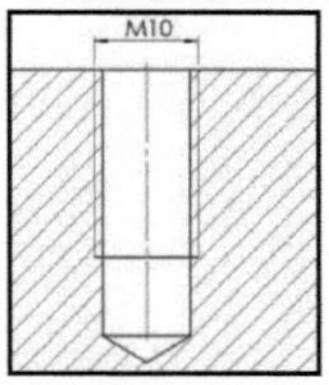

The standard for screw countersinks according to DIN 974-1 regulates the dimensions and accuracy for the stepped, round drill diameters for the assembly of a cylinder head screw according to DIN EN ISO 1207, 1580, 4762 and DIN 6912.

6.2.1.4 Countersink DIN 974-2, for hexagon head screws

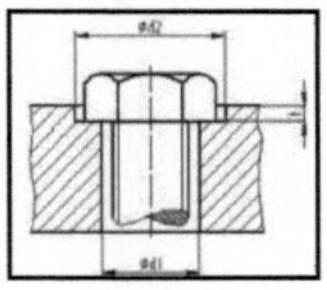

The standard for screw countersinks according to DIN 974-2 regulates the dimensions and accuracy for the stepped, round drill diameters for the assembly of a hexagon screw according to DIN EN ISO 4014 and 4017.

6.2.1.5 Countersink DIN 74 and DIN EN ISO 15065, for countersunk screws

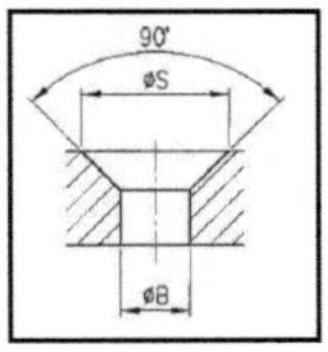

The standard for screw countersinks according to DIN 74 and DIN EN ISO 15065 regulates the dimensions and accuracy for the conical 90° countersink and the transition to the round drill diameter for the installation of a countersunk screw according to DIN EN ISO 2009, 2010, 7046, 7047 and 10642.

6.2.2 Holes as a SOLIDWORKS function

Hole Wizard

You can use the SOLIDWORKS Hole Wizard command to create simple holes, tapped holes, tapered holes, stepped holes, and countersunk holes. You can only specify one hole type per hole feature. To create a different hole type, you must create another hole feature.

6.2.2.1 SOLIDWORKS „Hole Wizard" feature, hole types

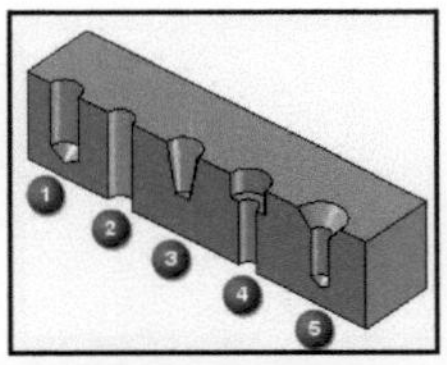

Use the **Type** option on the **Hole Options** dialog box to define the type of hole you want. You can construct several types of holes:
Simple hole (1), **tapped hole** (2), **tapered hole** (3), **counterbore hole** (4), **countersink hole** (5).

6.2.2.2 SOLIDWORKS „Hole Wizard" feature, "End condition"

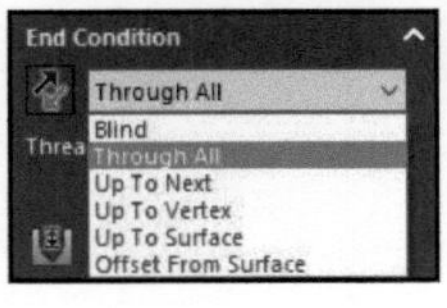

You can use different drilling depths when designing holes:
Blind, Through All, Up To Next, Up To Vertex, Up TO Surface,
and **Offset from Surface**.
The available drilling depths depend on the type of hole being created.

6.2.2.3 The "Hole Wizard", basics

Hole Wizard

The Hole Wizard allows you to create various types of custom holes. Depending on the selected hole type, the functions, available options, and graphical preview are displayed. After selecting a hole type, you must define the corresponding fasteners. The fastener dynamically updates the relevant parameters.

Use the PropertyManager to define the hole type parameters and position the holes. In addition to the dynamic graphical preview based on the end condition and depth, the graphics in the PropertyManager display specific details for the selected hole type.

When you create a hole using the Hole Wizard, the hole type and hole size are displayed in the FeatureManager.

The options available under Hole Specification depend on the hole type. Use the images and descriptive text in the PropertyManager to set the options.
You can create the following types of drilling assistants:

Counterbore	Cylinder screws DIN EN ISO 1207, DIN EN ISO 1580, DIN EN ISO 4762, DIN 6912.
Countersink	Countersunk screws DIN EN ISO 10642. Countersunk screws DIN EN ISO 2009, 2010
Hole	
Straight Tap	
Tapered Tap	
Legacy Hole	Holes created before the SOLIDWORKS 2000 release
Counterbore Slot	Hex screws DIN EN ISO 4017, DIN EN ISO 4014
Countersink Slot	
Slot	Keyway slots according to forms and dimensions DIN 6885

6.2.2.4 Threaded Holes

If you set the Type option to Threaded Hole, you can choose whether to create a standard thread, a cylindrical pipe thread, or a tapered pipe thread. If you set the Type option to Stepped Hole or Countersunk Hole, you can choose whether to create a standard thread or a cylindrical pipe thread.
Bei Gewindebohrungen entspricht der Bohrdurchmesser im Volumenmodell dem in der Toolbox Hole Wizard aufgelisteten Kerndurchmesser oder der von Ihnen ausgewählten Gewindegröße.
For threaded holes, the drill diameter in the volume model corresponds to the core diameter listed in the **Toolbox Hole Wizard** or the thread size you have selected.
The default value for the Threaded Cylinder option is the Thread style. Using the Thread style, you can also use the Render tab of the Format View dialog box to specify whether threaded features in a shaded view are assigned a photorealistic texture.

6.2.2.5 End Condition

The **End Condition** options vary depending on the hole type.

	**Blind Hole Depth** (Blind only).	Set the hole depth. For tap holes, you can set the thread depth and type.
	**Depth to Shoulder**	Applies to Blind, Up to Vertex, Up to Surface, or Offset to Surface.
	**Depth to Tip**	Applies to Blind, Up to Vertex, Up to Surface, or Offset to Surface.

6.2.2.6 "Hole Wizard" edit feature for holes

When you select a hole, a dialog box for definition editing appears so that you can change the hole values. If you want to change the hole type, you can click the **Edit Feature** button to open the **Hole Wizard PropertyManager**. To change the hole value, click the entry in the **PropertyManager**, enter new values, and close the **PropertyManager**. The hole will be changed to the new value.

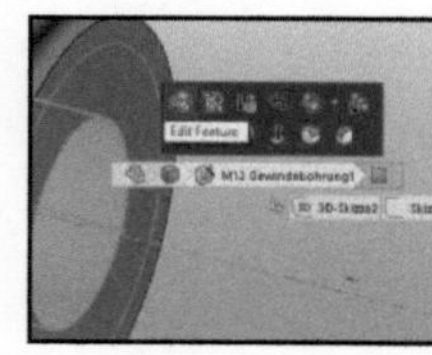

6.2.2.7 "Advanced Hole" tool

The **Advanced Hole** tool lets you define advanced holes in top and bottom surfaces. Hole feature flyouts assist you in this process.

Advanced Hole

6.2.2.8 The thread as a "cosmetic thread"

Thread representations describe the attributes of a particular hole, so you don't have to add actual threads to a model. A thread representation shows the inside diameter of a thread on a fitting or the outside diameter of a thread on a hole and may include a hole description in drawings.

Cosmetic Thread

6.2.2.9 The "Stud Wizard"

You can use the **Stud Wizard** to create threaded stud features with external threads. You define the threaded stud feature parameters and then position the threaded studs on the model. You can also apply thread parameters to existing cylindrical shafts. You can create helical threads on cylindrical edges or faces using profile sketches and save custom thread profiles as library features. The two methods for creating a thread feature are thread cutting and thread extrusion. The thread can be right-handed or left-handed. You can design a thread with multiple starts and align the thread trim to a start face or an end face.

Stud Wizard

6.2.2.10 The physical thread with the function "Thread"

Thread

You can create helical threads on cylindrical edges or faces using profile sketches and save custom thread profiles as library features. The two methods for creating a thread feature are thread cutting and thread extrusion. The thread can be right-handed or left-handed. You can design a thread with multiple starts and align the thread trim to a start face or an end face.

6.2.2.11 Keyway slot according to DIN 6885-1

A key is a machine element used in mechanical engineering to create a shaft-hub connection. The corresponding hub has a continuous, machined keyway and is axially slid over the keyway for assembly. The standard also specifies that a fit according to the standard shaft tolerance system as defined in DIN 7155 is used to tolerance the keyway width.

Project VII

Powerful commands
Optimized constructions

Page 178 to 200

- Basic constructions of the shaft element
  Closed surface of rotation using "Lines"
  Element editing command "Revolve"
  Measure allocation using "SmartDimension"
- Basic constructions of the shaft element
  Element editing command "Hole"
  Element editing command "Cosmetic Thread"
  Element editing command "Chamfer"
  Element editing command "Fillet"
  Element editing command "Hole Wizard Keyway slot"
- Basic construction "Drill Plate"
  "Cuboid" using a sketch construction
  Basic sketch, horizontal and vertical parallel lines
  Basic sketch with function "Rectangle over center"
  Create holes using the "Hole Wizard"
  Dowels hole, threaded holes, countersink holes and counterbore

6.3 Basic constructions of the shaft element

6.3.1 Shaft element using a line construction

6.3.1.1 The basic geometry

- Main cylinder **Ø40** mm, length **40** mm.
- Attached cylinder, **Ø20** mm, length **20** mm.

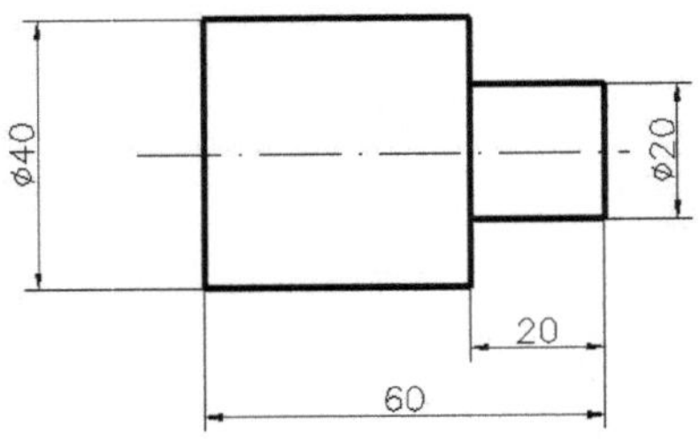

6.3.1.2 Opening your own template file

New

Engelke2026. PRTDOT

- Menu Bar **New** /  /  click **Engelke2026.PRTDOT / OK**

6.3.1.3 A closed surface of rotation using lines with vector data

Sketch

Line

Line starting point

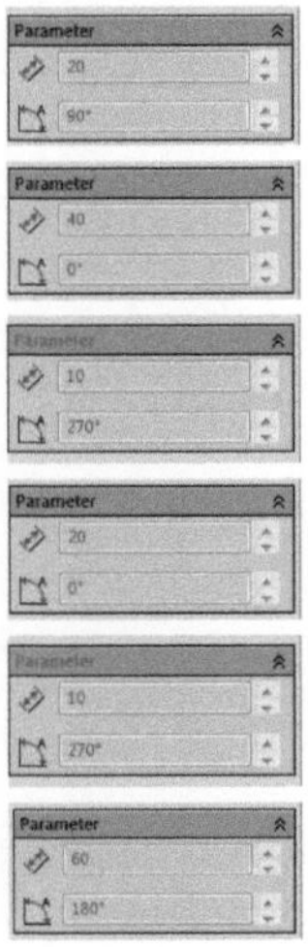

Line (**Sketch** tab)
Select the **Right** plane.
In the **PropertyManager**, select **Insert Line** and choose **As Sketched**.

The cursor changes, indicating a coincident relationship between the line's starting point and the origin.

- Click to place the line at the origin point.
- Click the vertical position, length **20** mm, vector **90°** (1).
- Click the horizontal position, length **40** mm, vector **0°** (2).
- Click the vertical position, length **10** mm, vector **270°** (3).
- Click the horizontal position, length **20** mm, vector **0°** (4).
- Click the vertical position, length **10** mm, vector **270°** (5).
- Click the horizontal position, length **60** mm, vector **180°** (6).
- The process is completed by double-clicking on the last point.

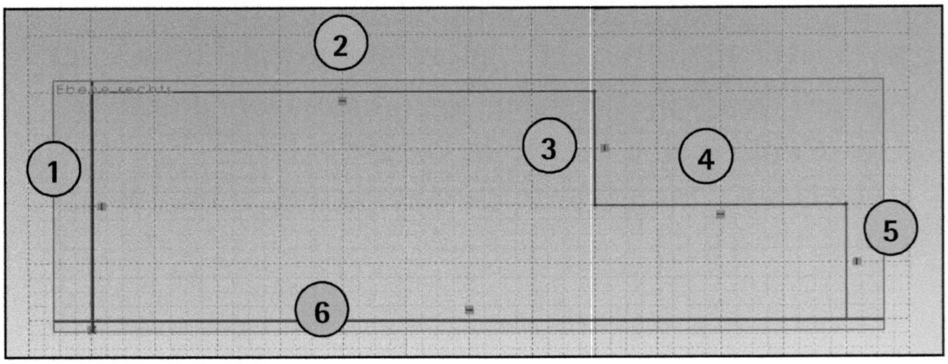

Close dialog box

Finish sketch

 **Close dialog box** /  **Finish sketch**

6.3.1.4 Revolved volume creation

Revolved (Features tab)
Click the area **Sketch1**, using **Select Contours** (7, 8).
Click the horizontal line to set it as the axis of rotation (9).

Close dialog box.

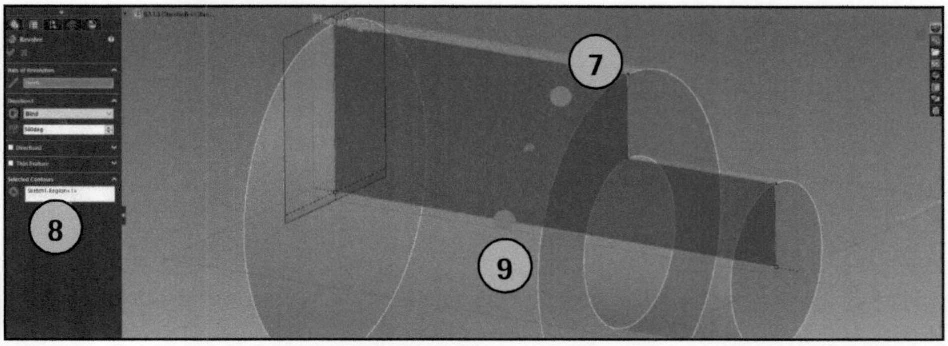

Revolved

Close dialog box

6.3.1.5 Material assignment, default settings

- For the **work planes** (10) and the **sketch** (11), set the **Hide** option in the **FeatureManager**.

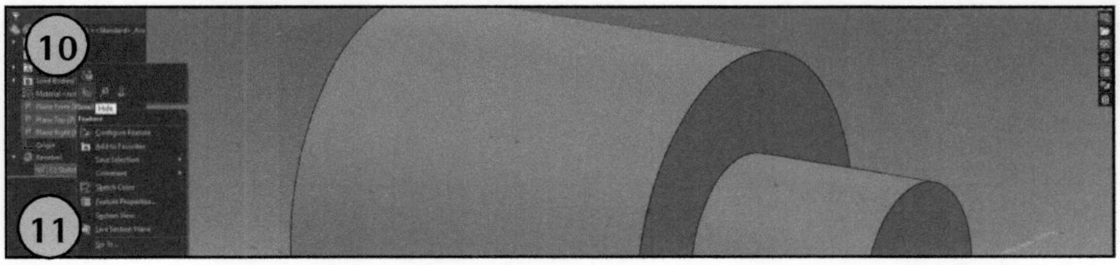

6.3.1.6 Reassigning component material

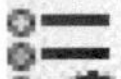

Edit Material (FeatureManager)
Right-click on **Material** to display the context menu for **Edit Material**.
Select **SOLIDWORKS-DIN Materials / DIN Copper Alloys 2.0367 CU ZN 40** (12, 13).
Click **Apply** and then **Close**.

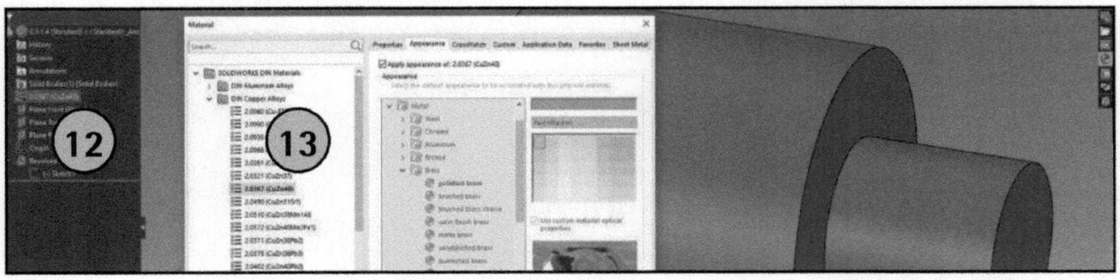

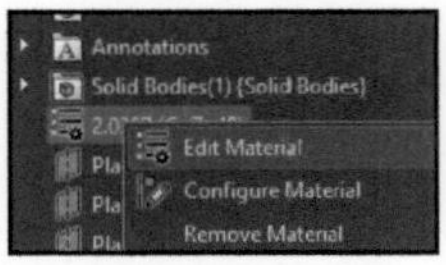

Edit Material

6.3.1.7 Data backup

Save as New / Enter a name of your choice.

Save as New

6.3.2 Basic constructions of the shaft element with a line construction using "SmartDimension"

6.3.2.1 Opening your own template file

New

Engelke2026.
PRTDOT

Sketch

Linie

- Menu Bar **New** /  /  click **Engelke2026.PRTDOT** / **OK**

6.3.2.2 A closed surface of Rotation using command "Line"

Sketch the line shown, disregarding line length, and ensure a precise finish at the origin point.

Line (**Sketch** tab)
Select the **Right** plane.
Draw the line shown without specifying any dimensions.
Finish by double-clicking at the last point (1).

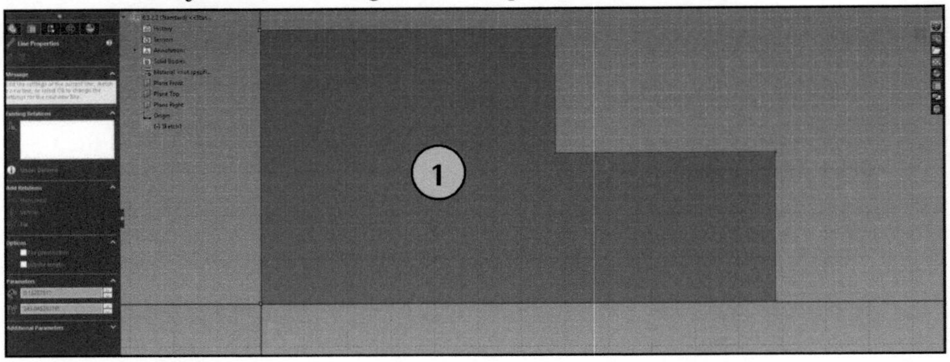

6.3.2.3 "SmartDimension" with resizing

The dimensions assigned using **SmartDimension** with resizing generate an automatic geometry change.

Smart
Dimension

Smart Dimension (**Sketch** tab)
Enter the dimensions shown and change the values to:
Ø40 mm (2), **40** mm (3), **20** mm (4), **60** mm (Drivin) (5), **Ø20** mm (6).

Close dialog
box

Finish sketch

 **Close dialog box** /  **Finish sketch**

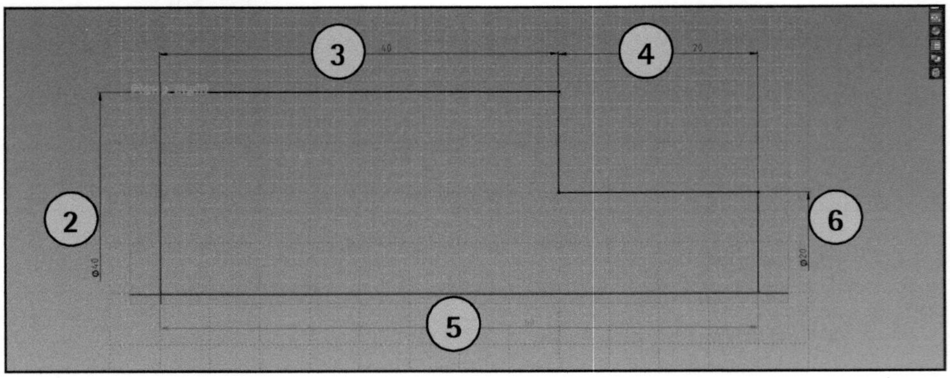

6.3.2.4 Revolved volume creation

Revolved (**Features** tab)
Click the area **Sketch1**, using **Select Contours** (7, 8).
Click the horizontal line to set it as the axis of rotation (9).

Close dialog box.

Revolved

Close dialog box

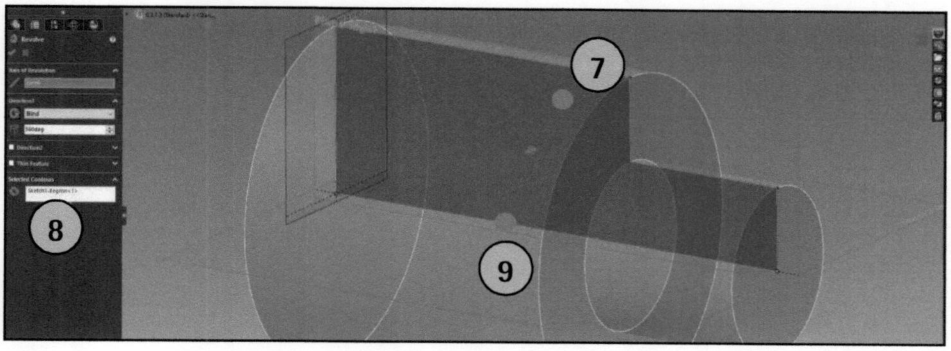

6.3.2.5 Material assignment, default settings

- For the **work planes** (10) and the **sketch** (11), set the **Hide** option in the **FeatureManager**.

6.3.2.6 Reassigning component material

Edit Material (**FeatureManager**)
Right-click on **Material** to display the context menu for **Edit Material**.
Select **SOLIDWORKS-DIN Materials / DIN Copper Alloys 2.0060 CU-ETP** (12, 13).
Click **Apply** and then **Close**.

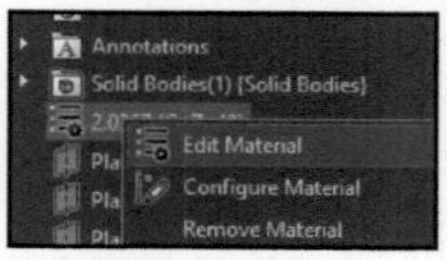

Edit Material

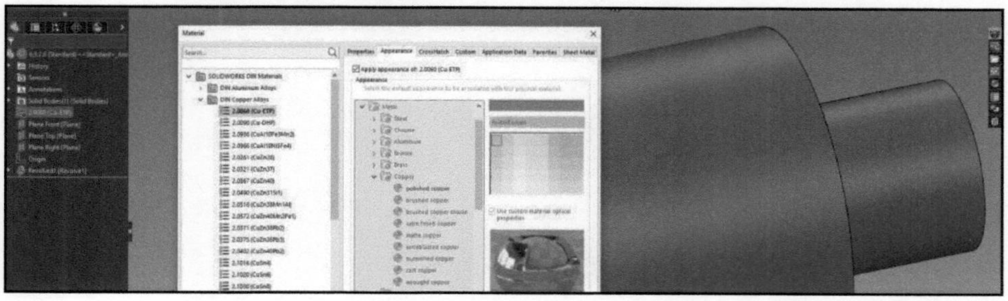

6.3.2.7 Data backup

Save as New / Enter a name of your choice.

Save as New

6.4 Basic constructions of the shaft element "Holes and Threading"

6.4.1 Drilling the through hole

6.4.1.1 Open the working file

Open

Open (Menu bar) / Component from the book-DVD / **OK** (1)

6.4.1.2 The "Through hole" using the "Hole Wizard"

Hole Wizard

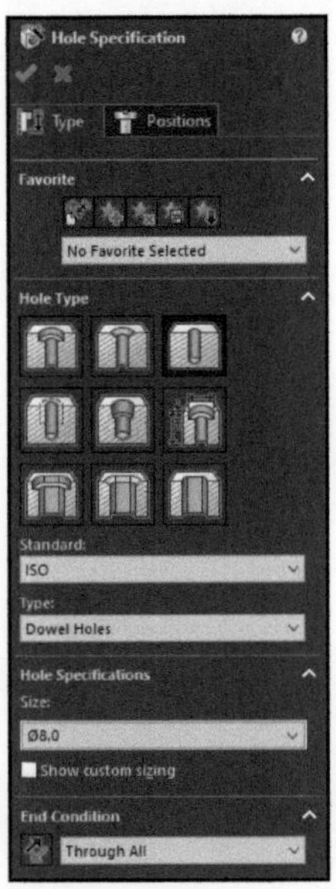

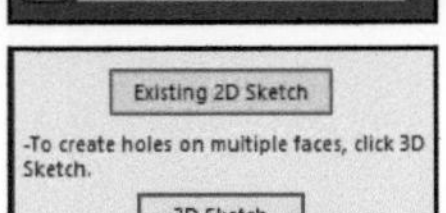

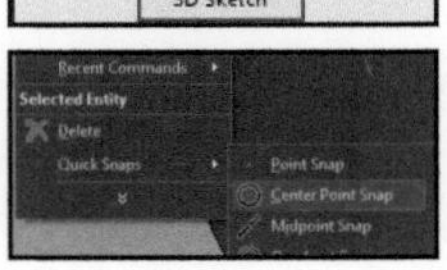

Hole Wizard (**Features** tab)
Click the **Type** tab.
Drill Type: **Hole**, Standard: **ISO**
Drill Size: **8** mm, End Condition: **Through All** (2).
Select the **Positions / 3D Sketch** tab (3).

Quick Snaps (**Sketch** tab) / **Center Point Snap** (4)
Select the cylinder center point (5).
Close dialog box (6, 7).

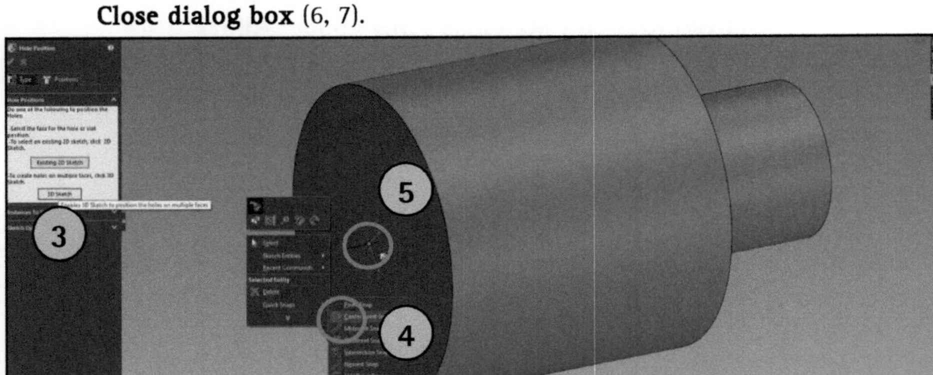

6.4.2 The "Threaded base hole", using the "Hole Wizard"

Hole Wizard

6.4.2.1 The "Threaded base hole", the creation

Hole Wizard (Features tab)
Click the **Type** tab.
Drill Type: **Bottoming Tapped Hole**, Standard: **ISO**
End Condition **Blind**, Size **M12**,
Base hole depth **30** mm, thread depth **24** mm (1).
Near side countersink, countersink Ø**15** mm, countersink angle **90°** (2).
Select the **Positions / 3D Sketch** tab.

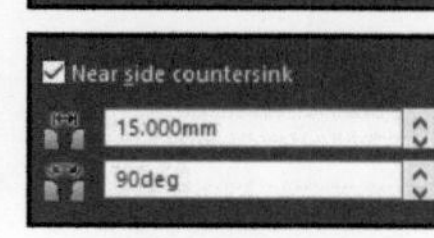

Quick Snaps (Sketch tab) / **Center Point Snap**
Select the cylinder center point (3).
Close dialog box.

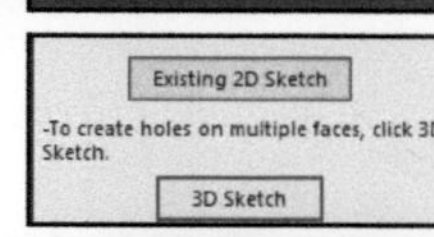

6.4.2.2 Adjusting the thread representation

- Enable **Annotations (FeatureManager)**
- Select **Details (Context menu)** (4)
- Set the option **Annotations/Properties/Shaded cosmetic threads** (5, 6).

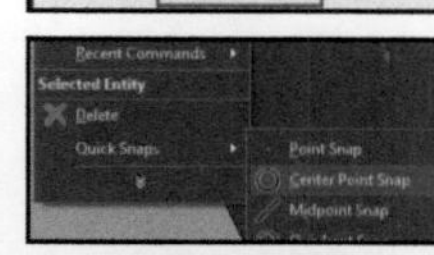

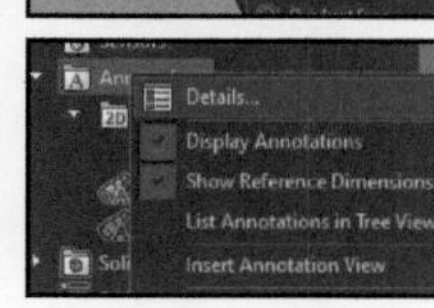

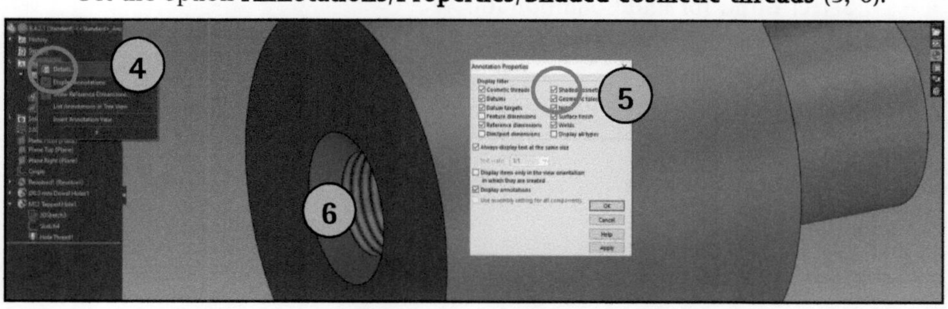

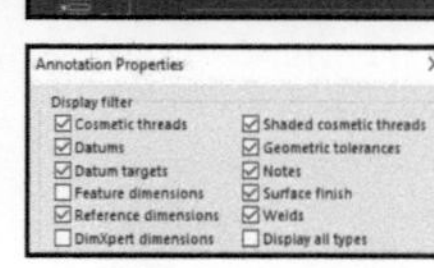

6.4.2.3 Data backup

Save as New / Enter a name of your choice.

Save as New

6.4.3 Basic constructions of the shaft element, external thread

6.4.3.1 External thread using "Stud Wizard", position change

View Selektor

View Selektor (Heads-up View Toolbar)

Select the cube face shown to display an ISO view of the small shaft end (1, 2, 3).

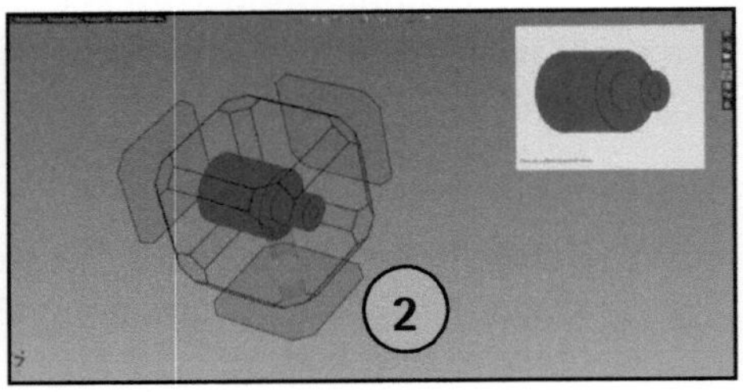

6.4.3.2 External thread using "Stud Wizard", the creation

You can use the **Stud Wizard** to create external threaded stud features. You define the stud parameters then position the studs on the model. You can also apply thread parameters to existing cylindrical shafts.

Stud Wizard

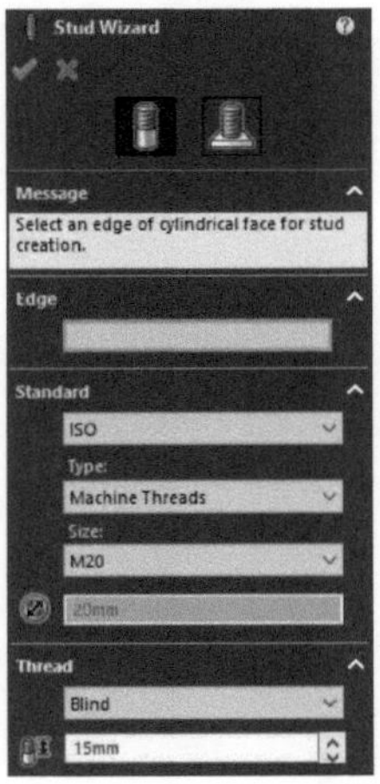

Stud Wizard (**Features** tab)

Select an edge of a cylindrical face to create the stud (4).

Standard: **ISO**, Size **M20** (5).

Select **Blind** for End Condition (6).

Thread length along the stud from the starting edge **15** mm (6).

Close dialog box (7).

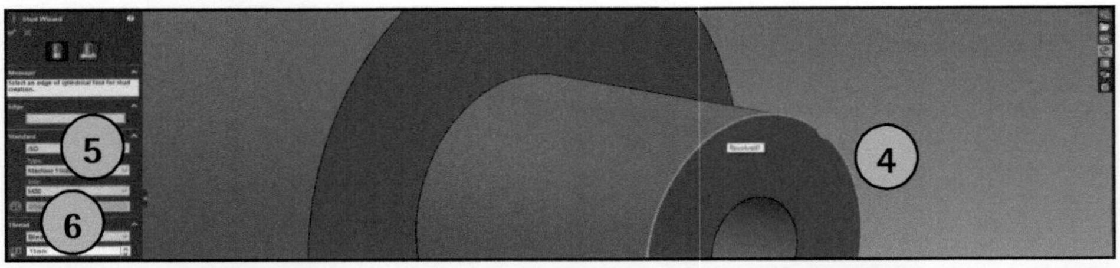

6.4.4 Basic constructions of the shaft element, "Chamfers" and "Fillets"

6.4.4.1 Edge breaking using "Chamfer", the creation

The chamfer tool creates a bevel on selected edges, faces, or at a corner point.

Chamfer

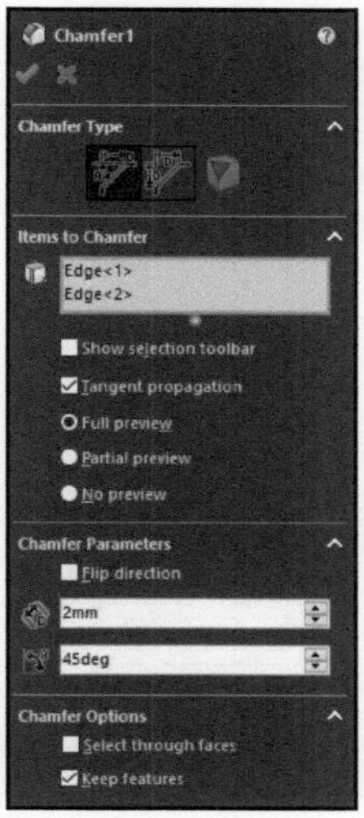

Chamfer (**Features** tab)
Select the **Angle/Distance** option (1).
Distance: **2** mm, Angle: **45°** (2).
Select **Keep feature** (3).
Enable **Full preview** (4).
Click the edges for the chamfer (5, 6).
Return the other settings to their default values.
Close dialog box.

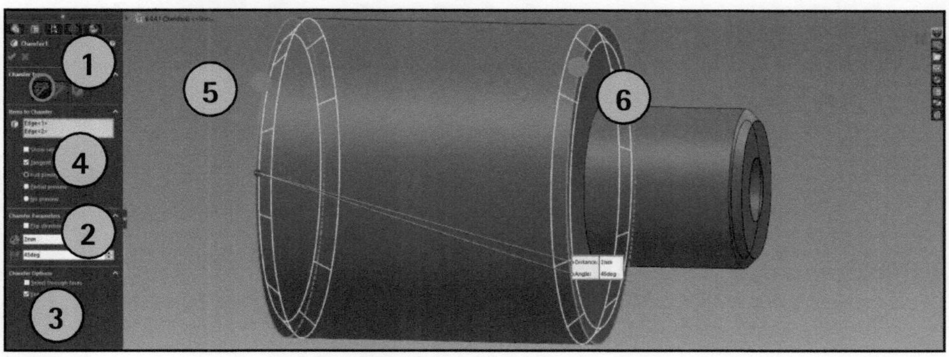

6.4.4.2 Edge breaking using "Fillet", the creation

Fillet

Constant Size Fillets

Fillet (**Features** tab)
Fillet parameters: Radius **2** mm (7), Type: **Constant Size Fillets** (8).
Select **Full Preview** (9).
For the other settings, accept the default values.
Click on the cylinder edge (10), the radius description will be displayed.
Close dialog box.

6.4.4.3 Data backup

Save as New

Save as New / Enter a name of your choice.

Section View

6.4.5 "Section View" for design control

Section View (Heads-up View Toolbar)
Click on **Plane Top** (1)
Show Section cap (2).

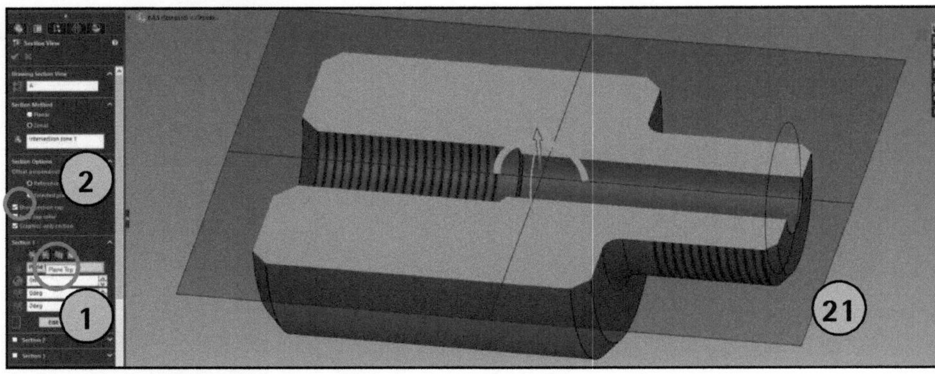

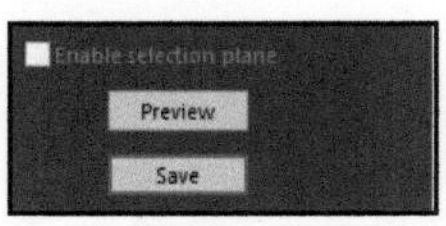

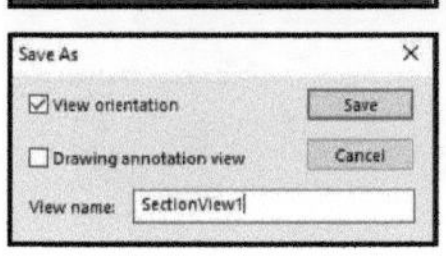

- **Save** (PropertyManager) (3).
  Save as the **View orientation**, give this view a name (4).

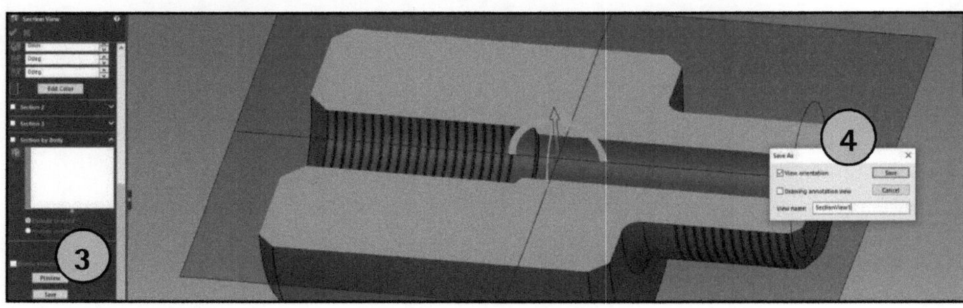

6.4.5.1 Data backup

Save as New

Save as New / Enter a name of your choice.

6.4.6 Basic constructions of the shaft element, Keyway slot, the creation

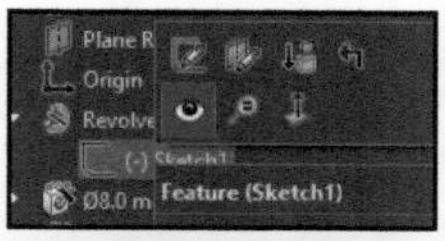

6.4.6.1 Create tangential working plane for the basic sketch of the keyway

- Switch the component sketch to **Show**.

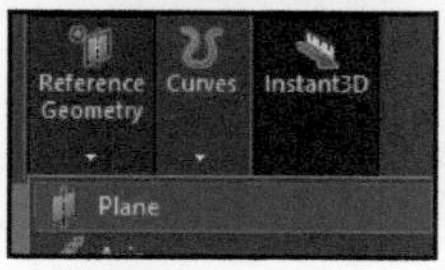

Plane (Reference Geometry toolbar)
Select the upper cylinder face (1).
Select the sketch point shown (2).
Click **Tangent** in the **FeatureManager** (3).
Close dialog box.

Tangent

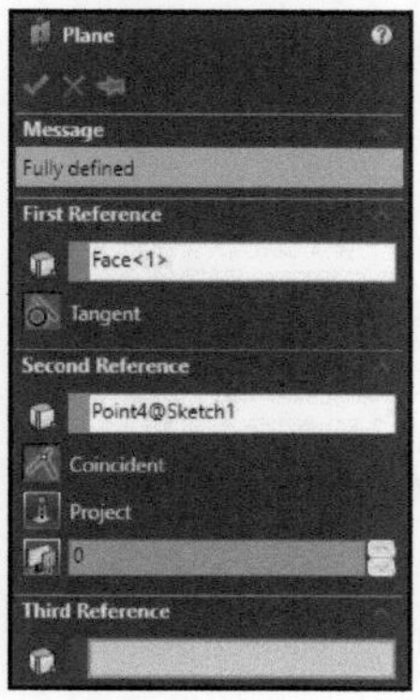

6.4.6.2 Creating the basic sketch

Click the **Sketch** icon (**Sketch** tab)

Sketch

Normal To (Heads-up View Toolbar)

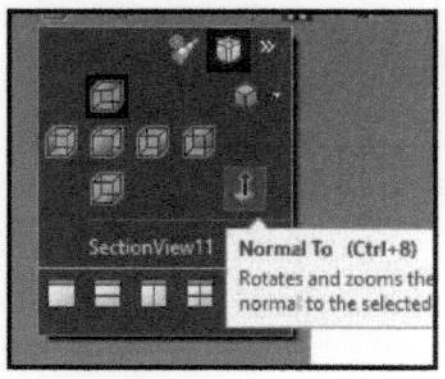

Normal To

Line (**Sketch** tab)
Select the new **Sketch1** (4).
Create the line construction shown to define the center point for the keyway (5, 6).
Close dialog box / Finish sketch

Line

Close dialog box

Finish sketch

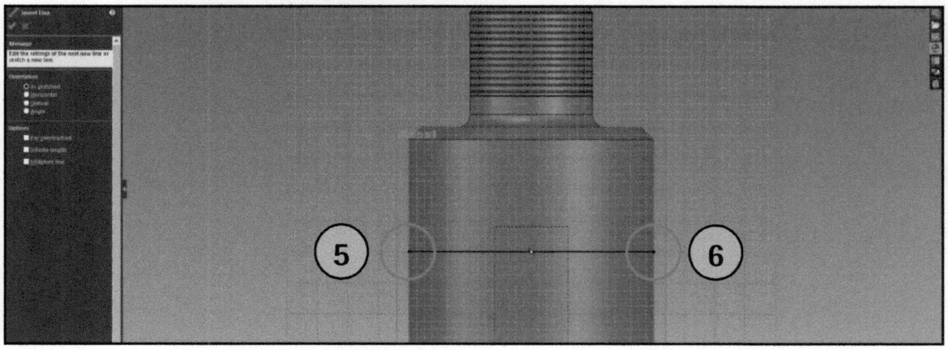

Hole Wizard

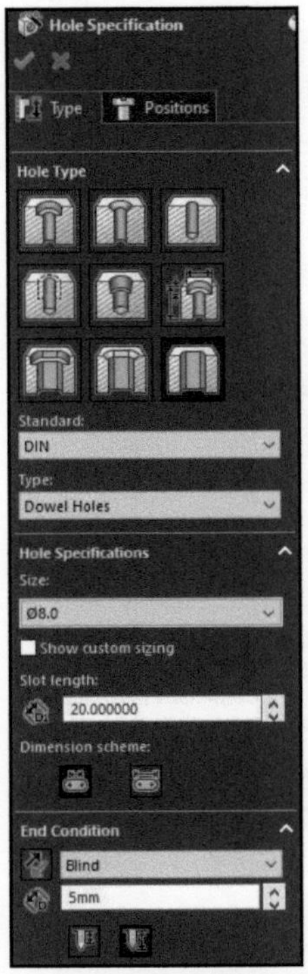

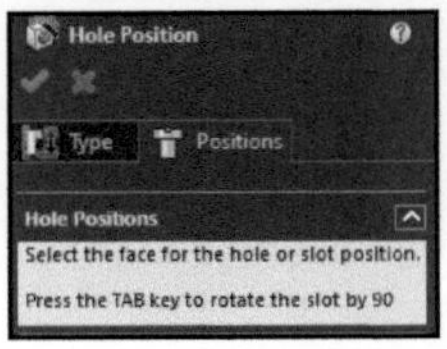

6.4.6.3 Keyway slot, the creation

Hole Wizard (Features tab)
Type options: **DIN**, **Blind 5** mm, Drill type: **Slot**.
Size **Ø8** mm, Slot length **20** mm (1).
Show custom sizing, no drill bit **180°**
Select the **Positions / 3D Sketch** tab (2).
Click the visible **Plane** (3).
Select the center point shown for the slot (4).
Possible change of position of the keyway slot using the **Tab** key.
Close dialog box (5).

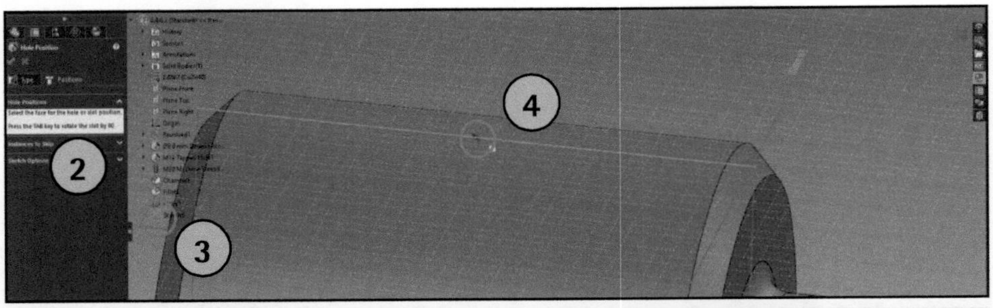

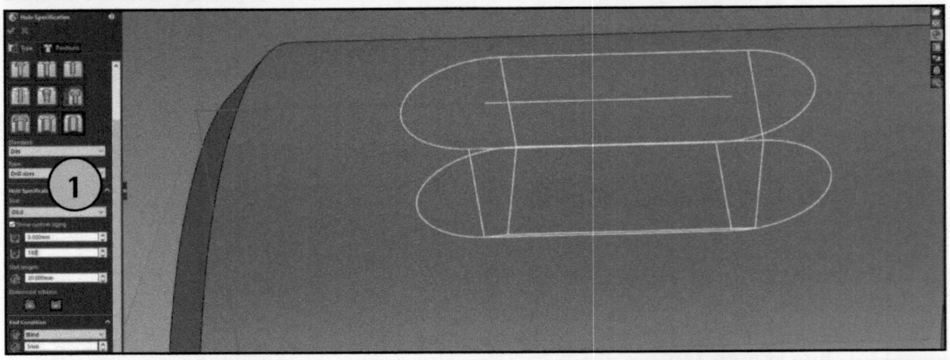

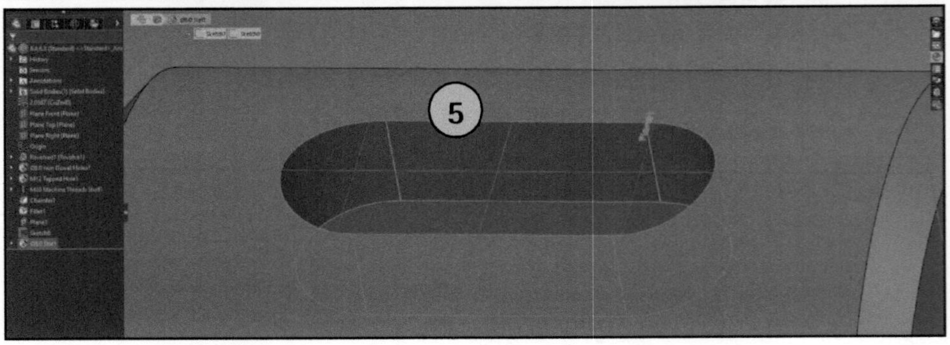

Save as New

6.4.6.4 Data backup

Save as New / Enter a name of your choice.

6.5 Creating a drill plate

6.5.1 Creating a drill plate, basics

- Opening your own template file.
- Create a rectangular sketch with dimensioned dimensions.
- Round off the four edges of the rectangle.
- Reposition the base sketch relative to the origin axes.
- Activate the origin planes, create reference edges, and project the geometry.
- Extrude the base surface.
- Construct the center axis for the holes to be drilled.
- Drill the four countersunk holes for socket head cap screws.
- Drill the four threaded through holes.
- Drill the center hole for the drill plate.
- Drill the four countersunk through holes.
- Assign materials.

6.5.2 The basic geometry, drawing representation

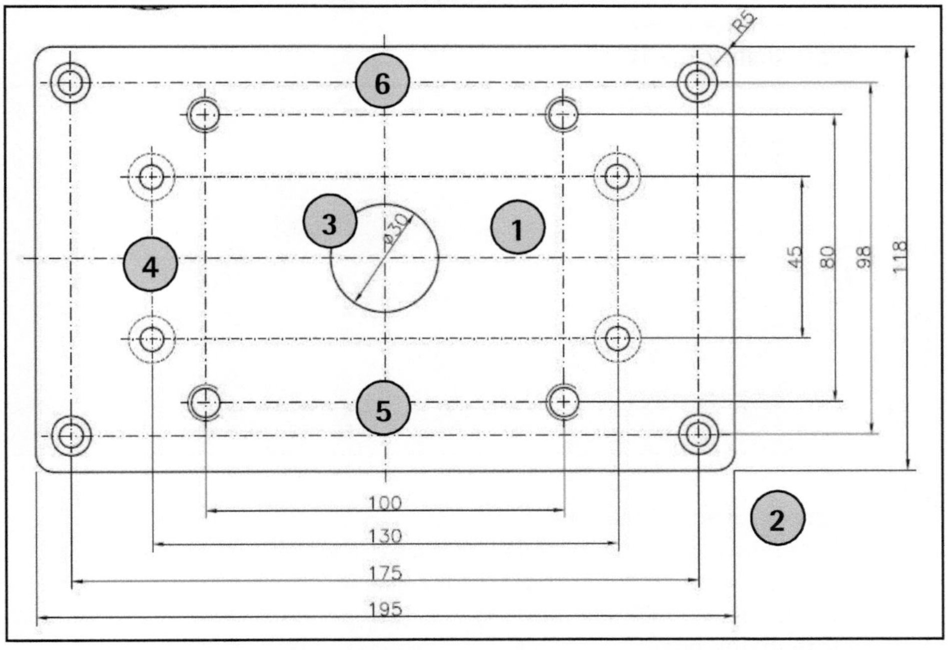

- Base plate, 25 x 200 x 120 mm, sketch dimensions corrected (1).
- Outer edges rounded with R=10 mm, sketch dimensions corrected (2).
- Center bore DIN EN 20273, Ø30 mm (3).
- Axis combination 1, spacing 80 mm to 100 mm for through-hole thread M10 x 1.5 (5).
- Axis combination 2, spacing 45 mm to 130 mm, countersunk hole DIN 74 for countersunk screw M10, DIN EN ISO 10642 (4).
- Axis combination 3, spacing 175 mm to 98 mm, countersunk hole DIN 974-1 for socket head cap screw DIN ISO 4762 (6).

6.5.3 Creating a drill plate, the basic body

6.5.3.1 Opening your own template file

New

Engelke2026.
PRTDOT

- Menu Bar **New** / / click **Engelke2026.PRTDOT / OK**

6.5.3.2 The basic sketch construction

Center
Rectangle

Center Rectangle (Flyout tool **Rectangle / Sketch** tab)
Select the **Front Plane.**
To find the center point, click the intersection of the layers.
Drag the rectangle's outer contour with the cursor.

Smart
Dimension

Smart Dimension (Sketch tab)
Select the rectangle outlines.

Sketch Fillet

Sketch Fillet (Symbolleiste **Skizzieren)**
Round off the line system with a 10 mm radius.
Add the dimensions.
Close dialog box (7).

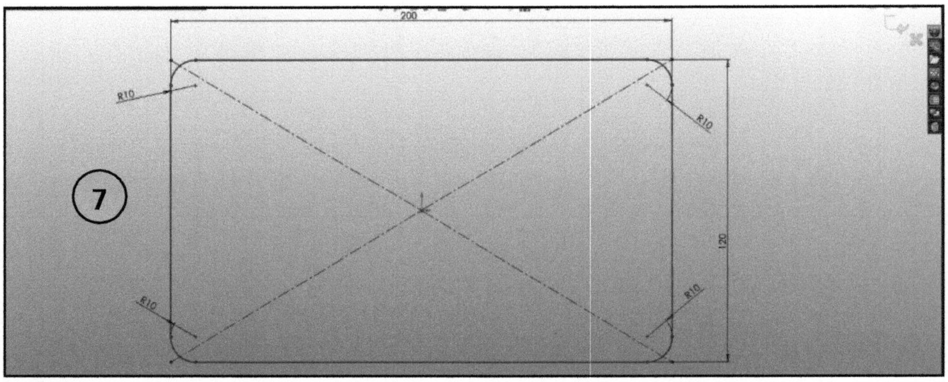

Extrude

Extrude (Features tab)
Choose the constructed rectangle as the basic sketch.
Click on the arrow in the middle of the cuboid.
Drag the scale to **25** mm (8).
Close dialog box.

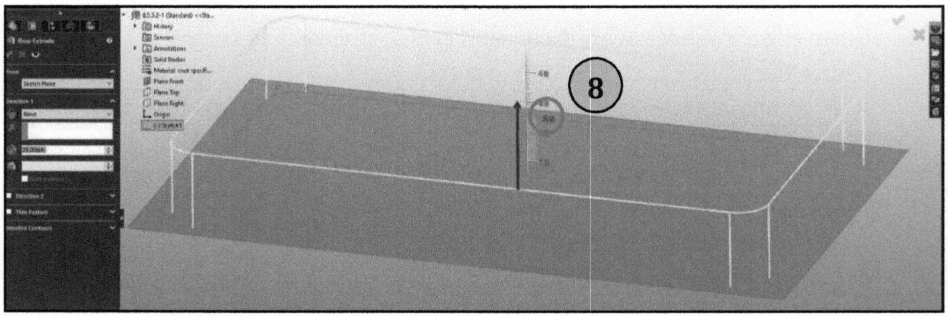

6.5.4 The basic sketch for the drilling, version 1

6.5.4.1 Basic sketch, center axes

Sketch (**Sketch** tab)
Create a new sketch.

Sketch

Normal To (Heads-up View Toolbar)

Normal To

Line (**Sketch** tab)
Add the center lines shown, option **For construction** (9, 10).

Line

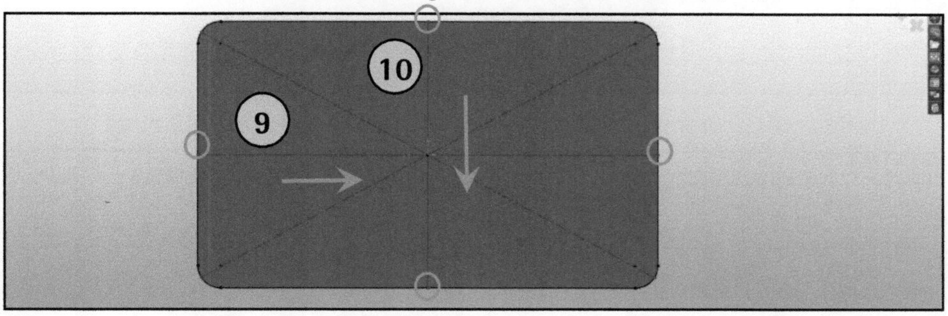

6.5.4.2 Basic sketch, vertical, parallel lines

Offset Entities (**Sketch** tab)
Select options: **Add dimensions**, **bi-directional**, distance **50** mm (11).
Select the vertical center axis (11).
The parallel lines will be created automatically (12).
Close dialog box.

Offset Entities

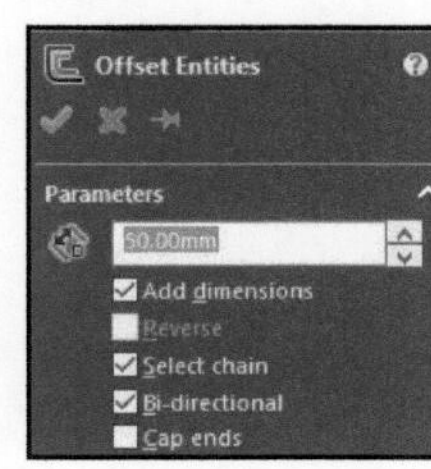

Close dialog box

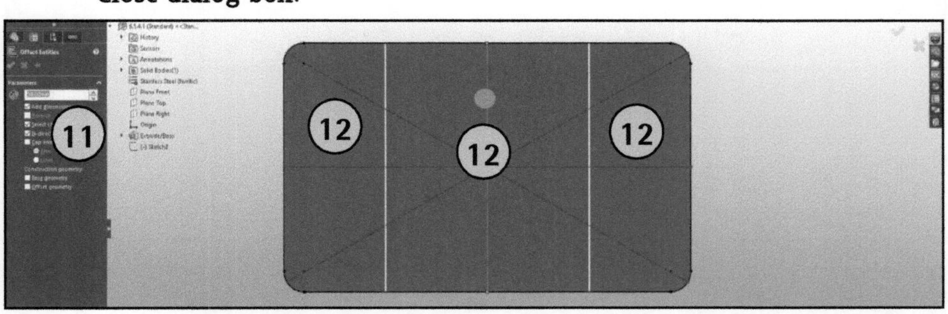

- Proceed accordingly with the dimensions **65** mm (13) and **87.50** mm (14).

Offset Entities

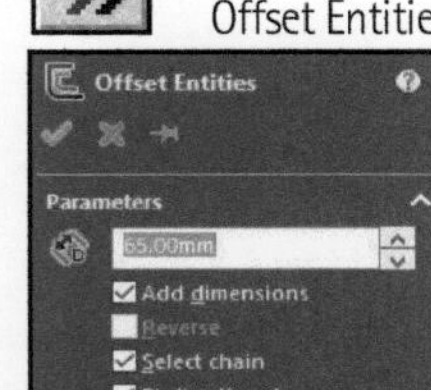

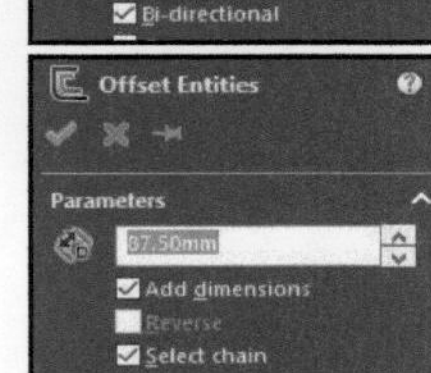

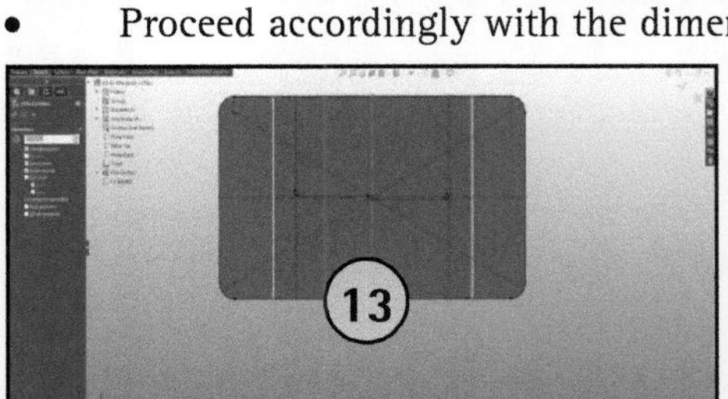

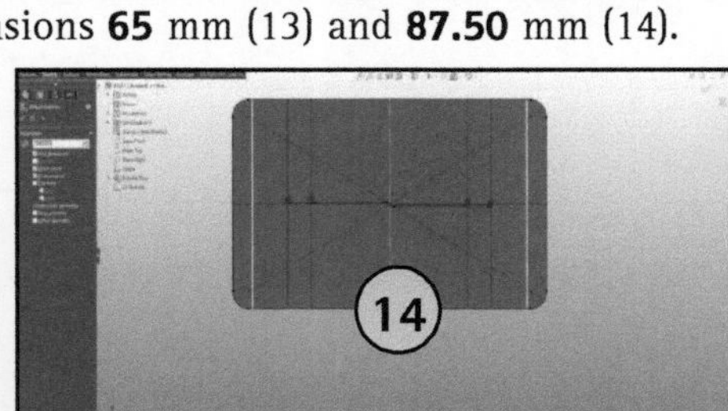

6.5.4.3 Basic sketch, horizontal, parallel lines

Offset Entities

Offset Entities (**Sketch** tab)
Select options: **Add dimensions, bi-directional**, distance **22.50** mm (15).
Select the horizontal central axis (16).
The parallel lines will be created automatically (17).
Close dialog box.

Close dialog box

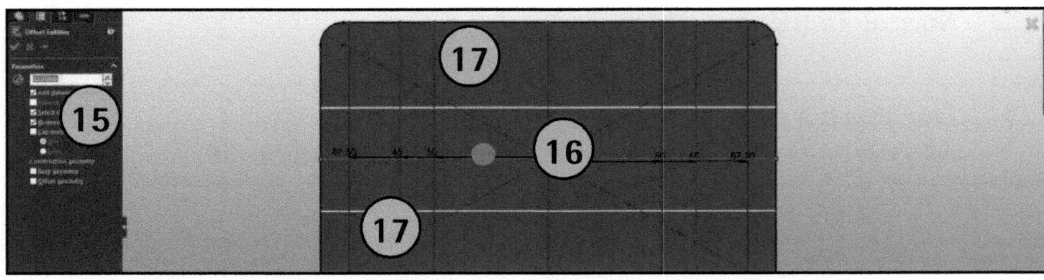

- Proceed accordingly with the dimensions **40** mm (13) and **49** mm (14).

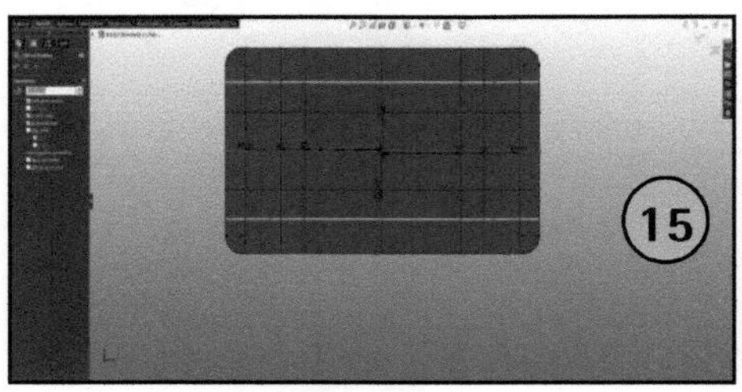

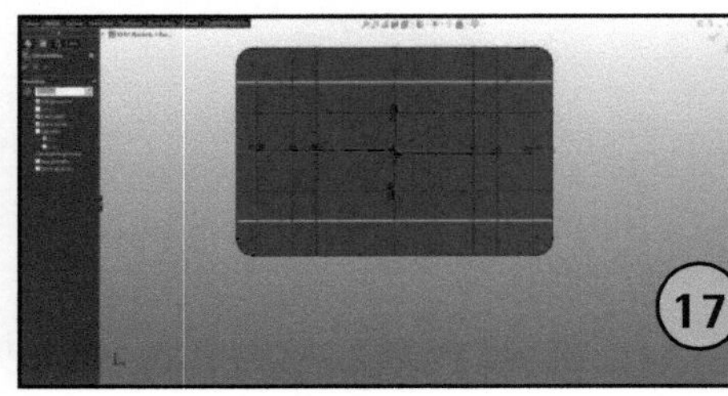

Close dialog box

Finish sketch

- **Close dialog box / Finish sketch**

6.5.4.4 Overview of sketch construction for parallel lines

- Drag the dimensions into a clear and organized position (18).

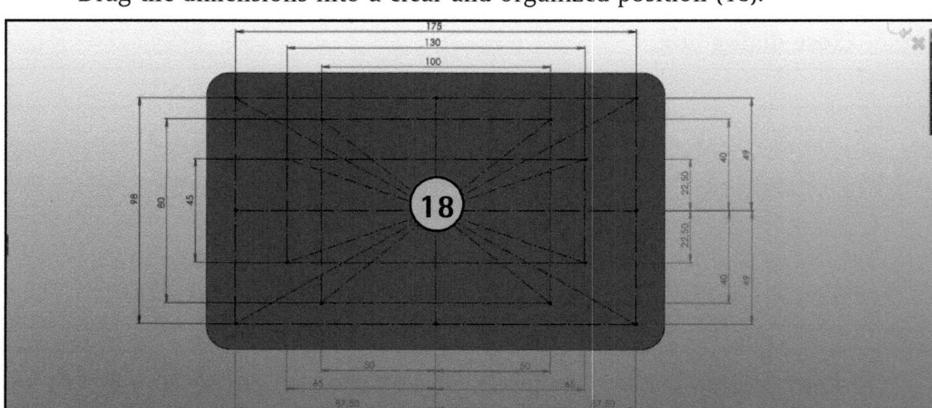

6.5.4.5 Data backup

Save as New

Save as New / Enter a name of your choice.

6.5.5 Basic sketch with function "Rectangle over center", version 2

Another way to create the basic sketch is to create the required intersection points using rectangles with the center point option.

6.5.5.1 Open the working file

Open (Menu bar) / Component from the book-DVD / **OK** (1).

6.5.5.2 Basic sketch with function "Rectangle over center"

Sketch (**Sketch** tab)
Create a new sketch.

Normal To (Heads-up View Toolbar)

Center Rectangle (Flyout tool **Rectangle** / **Sketch** tab)
Click on the intersection of the planes in the graphics area to define the center point (2).
Then drag the rectangle to approx. **100 x 80** mm (3).

Smart Dimension (**Sketch** tab)
Select the rectangle contour (4, 5).

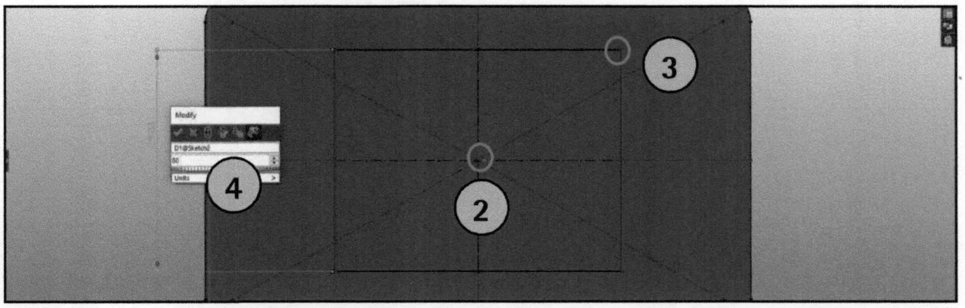

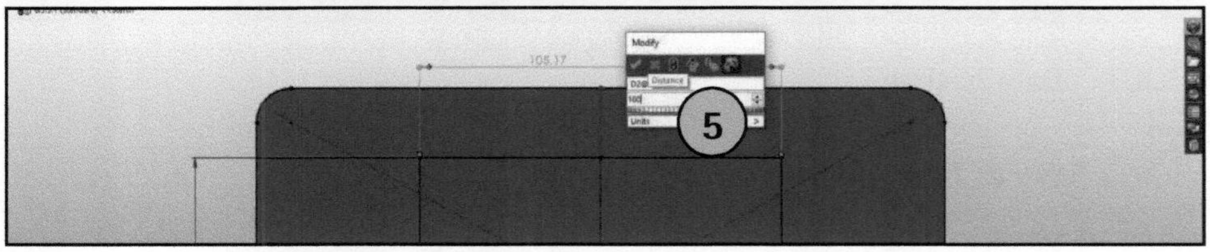

- **Close dialog box.**

Open

Sketch

Normal To

Center Rectangle

Close dialog box

Smart Dimension

- Proceed accordingly with the dimensions **130** x **45** mm (6, 7) and **175** x **98** mm (8, 9).

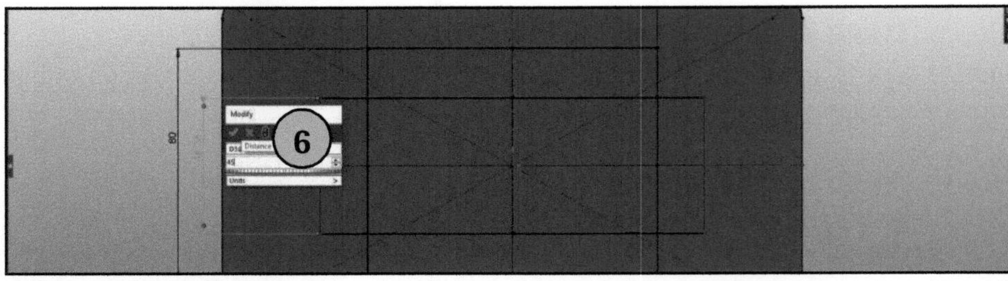

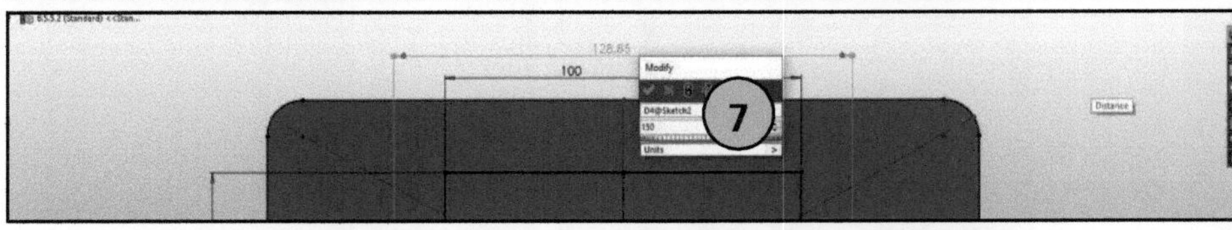

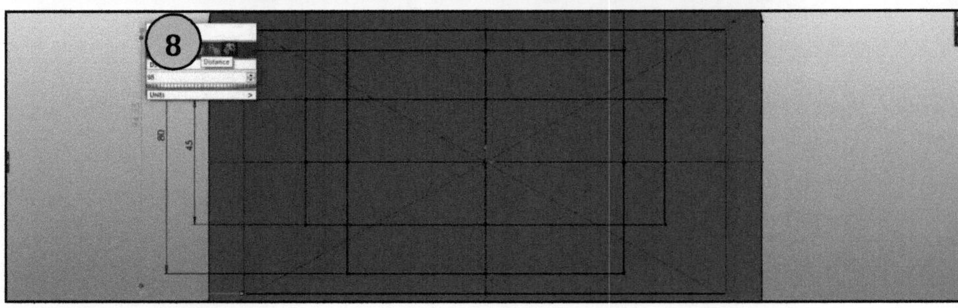

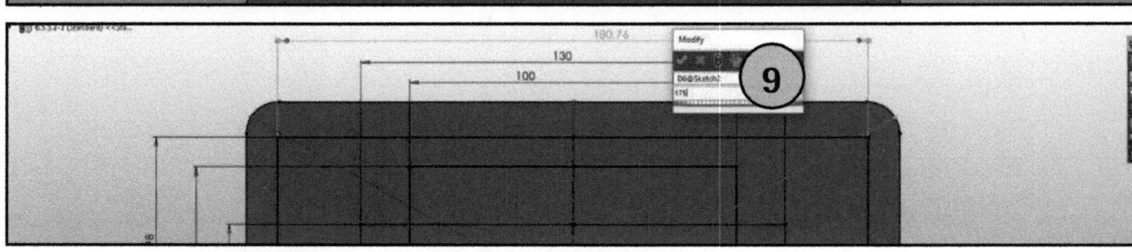

Close dialog box

Finish sketch

- **Close dialog box / Finish sketch** (10)

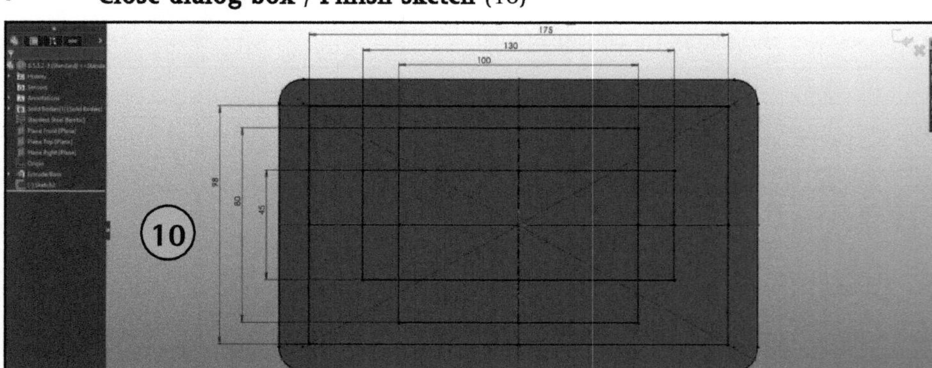

6.5.5.3 Data backup

Save as New

Save as New / Enter a name of your choice.

6.5.6 The "Dowel hole" in the center of the component

6.5.6.1 The Dowels hole

Hole Wizard

Dowels hole

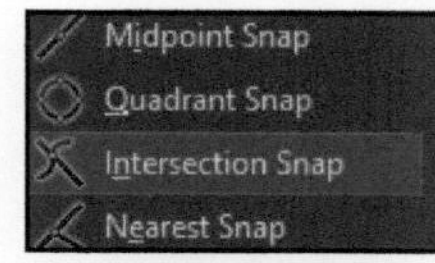

Hole Wizard (Features tab)
Click the **Type** tab.
Drill Type: **Hole**, Standard: **DIN** (1).
Bore diameter **Ø30** mm, depth: **Through all** (2).
Select the **Positions / 3D Sketch** tab.
Quick Snaps (Sketch tab) / **Intersection Snap** (3).
Select the **intersection** point (4).
Close dialog box (5).

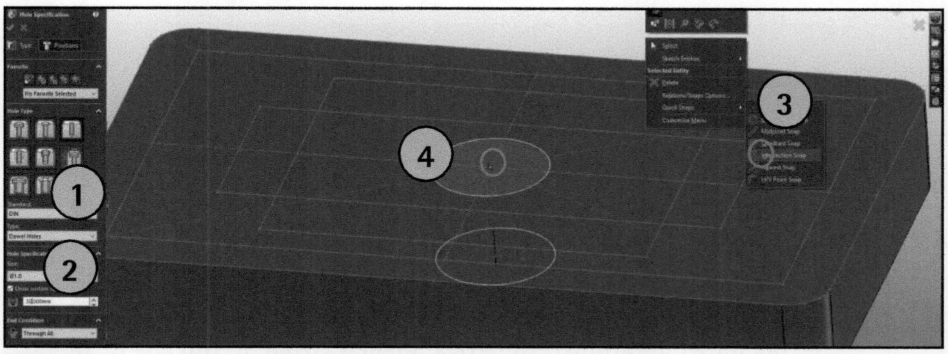

Close dialog box

6.5.6.2 Data backup

Save as New / Enter a name of your choice.

Save as New

6.5.7 Four M10 threaded holes, axle element 1

Hole Wizard

Hole Wizard (**Features** tab)
Click the **Type** tab.
DIN, **threaded hole**, **M10**, depth: **Through all** (1).
Select the **Positions** / **3D Sketch** tab.
Select the four center points for the threaded hole(2).
Close dialog box.

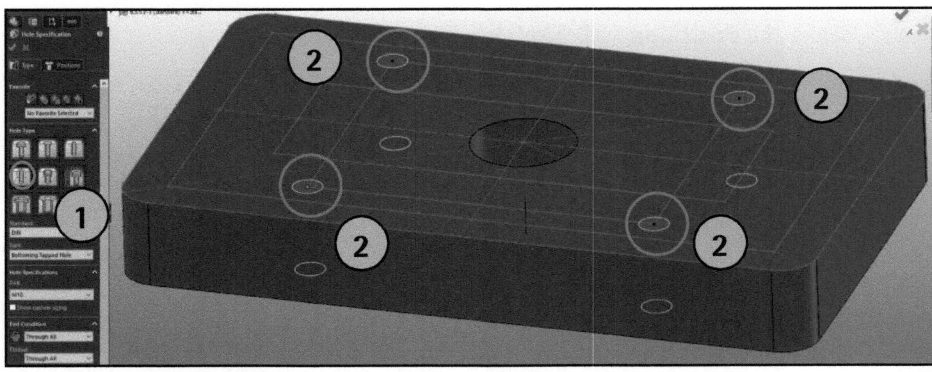

6.5.7.1 Adjusting the thread representation

- Enable **Annotations** (**FeatureManager**)
- Select **Details** (**Context menu**) (4)
- Set the option **Annotations/Properties/Shaded cosmetic threads** (5, 6).

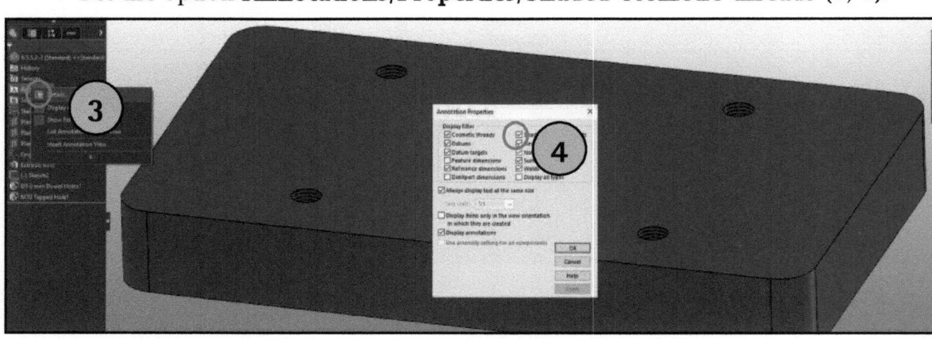

6.5.7.2 Data backup

Save as New

Save as New / Enter a name of your choice.

6.5.8 Four countersunk holes DIN 74, axle element 2, reverse side

6.5.8.1 Edit sketch plane, reverse side

In the **FeatureManager,** right-click a sketch.
Click **Edit Sketch Plane**.
Select the front face as the plane (1).
Click the back face; the sketch will be placed on the face (2, 3).

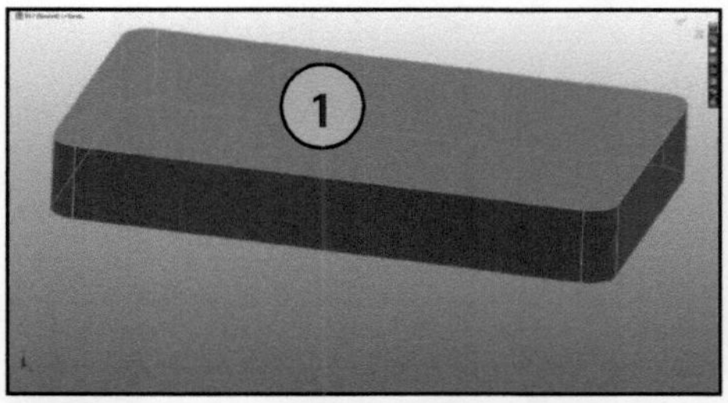

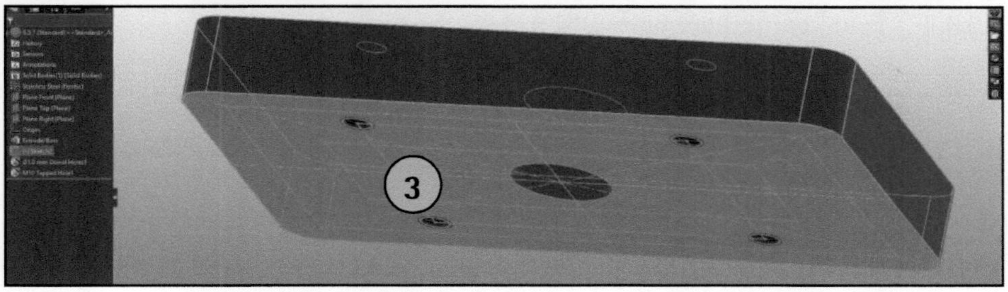

6.5.8.2 Four countersunk holes DIN 74, the ceation

Hole Wizard

Hole Wizard (**Features** tab)
Click the **Type** tab.
DIN, Countersunk head screw EN ISO 10642, M10,
Size: **M10**, depth: **Through all** (4).
Select the **Positions** / **3D Sketch** tab.
Select the four center points for the **Countersunk** hole (5).
Close dialog box.

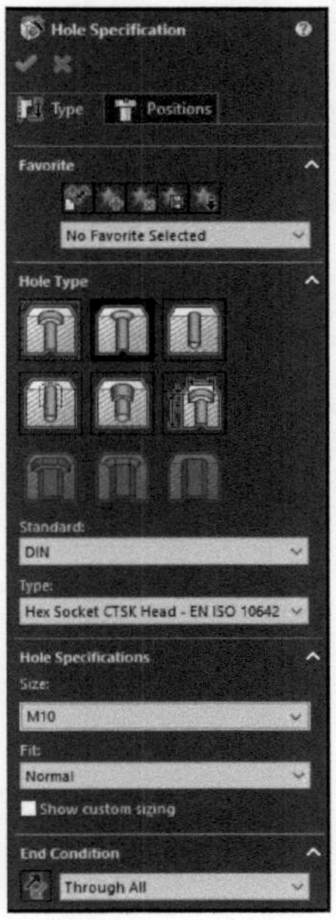

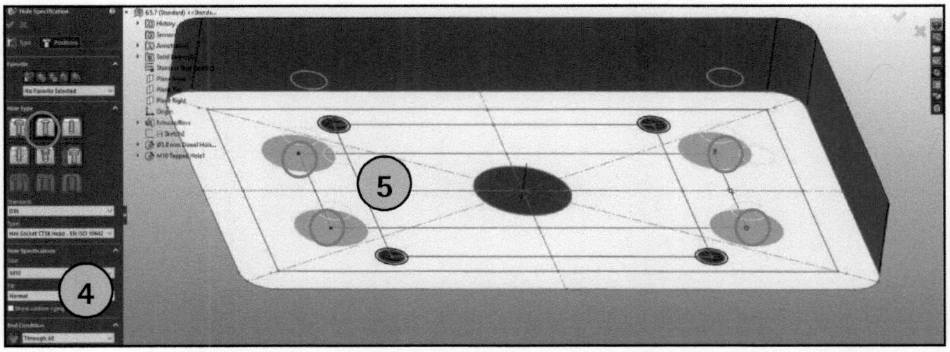

Close dialog box

6.5.8.3 Data backup

Save as New / Enter a name of your choice.

Save as New

6.5.9 Four countersunk holes DIN 974-1, axle element 3

6.5.9.1 Edit sketch plane, reverse side

In the **FeatureManager,** right-click a sketch.
Click **Edit Sketch Plane**.
Select the back face as the plane.
Click the; front face the sketch will be placed on the face (1).

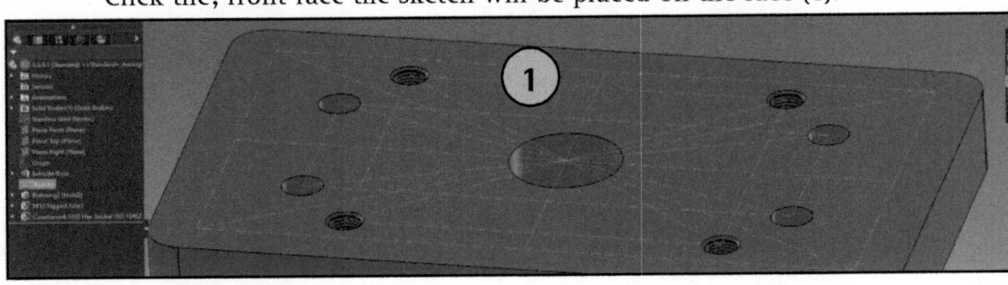

6.5.9.2 Four counterbore holes DIN 974-1, the ceation

Hole Wizard

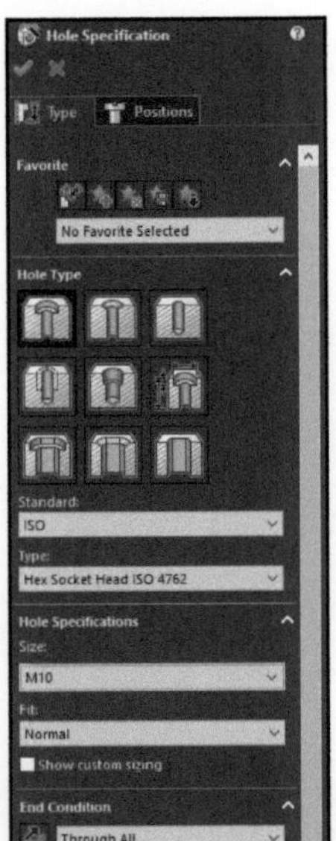

Close dialog box

Hole Wizard (**Features** tab)
Click the **Type** tab.
DIN, **Head socket screw ISO 4762**, **M10**,
Size: **M10**, depth: **Through all** (2).
Select the **Positions / 3D Sketch** tab.
Select the four center points for the **Counterbore** hole (3).
Close dialog box.

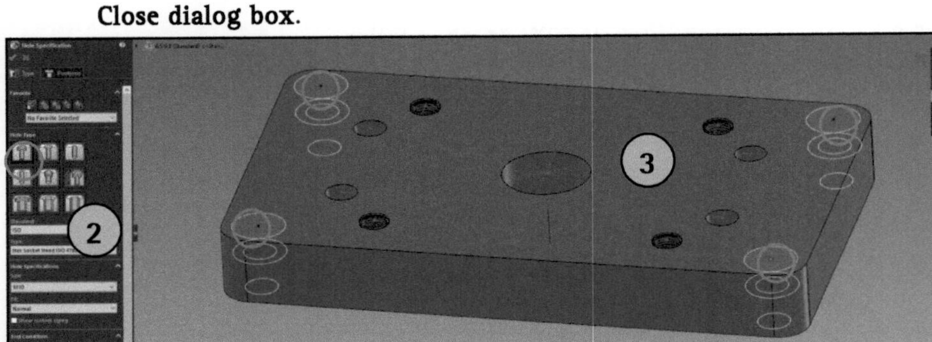

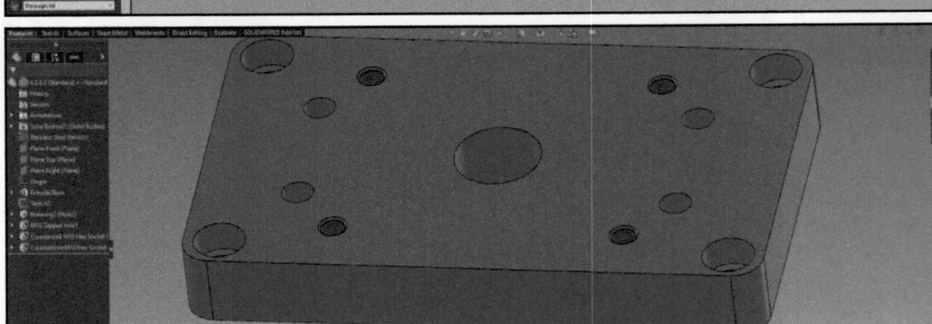

6.5.9.3 Data backup

Save as New

Save as New / Enter a name of your choice.

6.5.10 Assigning component material

6.5.10.1 Material assignment, default settings

- For the **work planes** and the **sketch**, set the **Hide** option in the **FeatureManager**.

6.5.10.2 Assigning component material, the creation

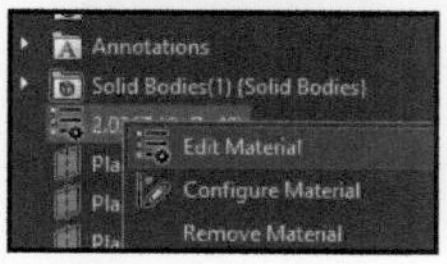

Edit Material (FeatureManager)
Right-click on **Material** to display the context menu for **Edit Material**.
Select **SOLIDWORKS-Materials / Steel / Chrome Stainless Steel**
Click **Apply** and then **Close**.

Edit Material

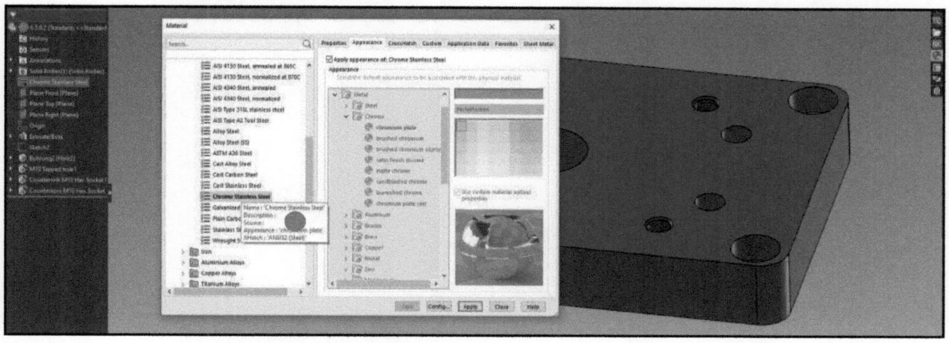

6.5.10.3 Data backup

Save as New / Enter a name of your choice.

Save as New

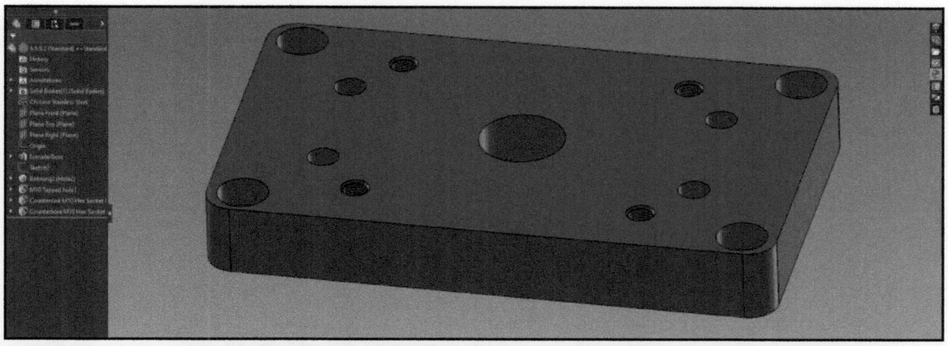

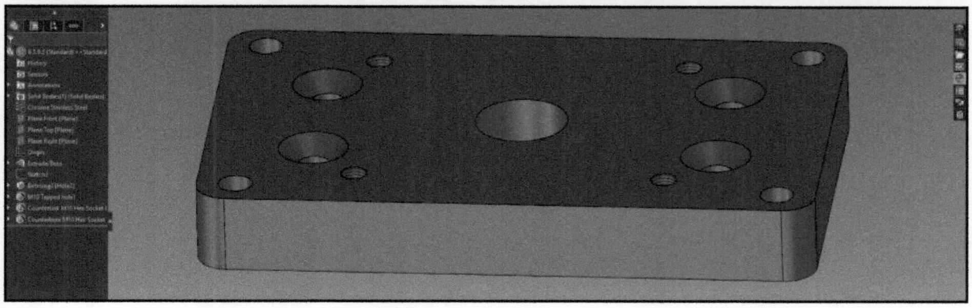

Project VIII

Powerful commands
Optimized constructions
Form element features

Page 206 to 230

- Basic construction “Cuboid with top”
  Form element feature “Draft”, “Shell”, “Fillet”
- Basic construction “Drill plate”
  Form element feature “Hole Wizard”, “Linear Pattern”
- Basic construction “Flange ring with mounting holes”
  Form element feature “Hole Wizard”, “Circular Pattern”
- Basic construction “Cuboid with top”
  Form element feature “Rib”, “Mirror”, “Cicular Pattern”
- Basic construction “Compression spring”
  Form element feature “Helix/Spiral”, “Swept Boss”
- Basic construction “Trapezoidal thread”
  Form element feature “Helix/Spiral”, “Cut/Sweep”
- Basic construction “Physical Thread Profile
  Simple hole with physical thread profile
  Physical thread, using outer diameter
  External thread with physical thread profile

6.6 Powerful commands, optimized constructions, Form element features

6.6.1 List of form element functions, basics

The following feature functions are intended for specific tasks in design engineering. The input process is prescribed in SOLIDWORKS and must be followed.
Before using these functions within the design of a component, they should be performed at least once; it also makes sense to save the component created up to that point before using these functions.
You will find that it makes sense to work through the learning units and learning objective checks, because the following tasks place a higher demand on the user.
Here is a list of the form element functions described in this chapter:

6.6.1.1 Form element function "Fillet"

Fillet

The **Fillet** tool creates a rounded internal or external surface on the part. You can round all edges of a surface, selected sets of surfaces, selected edges, or edge groups.

- Add larger fillets before smaller ones. If multiple fillets meet at a vertex, create the larger fillets first.
- Save cosmetic fillets for last. Try adding them only after the majority of the geometry is complete. Adding fillets earlier will increase the time it takes to rebuild the model for the part.
- To speed up the rebuild of a part, you should perform a single fillet operation on multiple edges with the same radius. However, if you change the radius of this fillet, all fillets created with the same operation will change.

6.6.1.2 Form element function "Chamfer"

Chamfer

The **Chamfer** tool creates a bevel on selected edges, faces, or vertices. The chamfer feature offers various edge-editing options.

- Angle distance, distance-distance, vertex, offset area and area to area.
- To speed up the rebuild of a part, you should perform a single chamfer operation on multiple edges with the same chamfer contour.

6.6.1.3 Form element function "Draft"

Draft

The **Draft** tool tapers surfaces using a specific angle to selected model surfaces.

- You can add a draft angle to an existing part or create the draft angle while extruding a feature. You can apply a draft angle to solid models or surface models.
- You can also apply a draft angle as part of a base, cap, or cut that has been extruded linearly.
- In most cases, you should add the draft features before the fillets.

6.6.1.4 Form element function "Shell"

Shell

The **Shell** tool allows you to hollow out a part, leaving the selected surfaces open and thin walls on the remaining surfaces.
If you do not select a surface on the model, you can hollow out a solid body part, creating a closed, hollow model.
You can also build a model using different wall thicknesses.

- Rounding should be applied before you move a part.
- The wall feature displays error messages and includes tools to help you determine why the wall feature caused an error.

6.6.1.5 Form element function "Linear Pattern"

Linear Pattern

Linear patterns allow you to create multiple referenced copies of one or more features, which you can arrange at equal intervals along one or two linear paths.

6.6.1.6 Form element function "Circular Pattern"

Circular Pattern

Use circular patterns to create multiple referenced copies of one or more features that you can arrange at equal intervals around an axis.

6.6.1.7 Form element function "Rib"

Rib

The rib is a special type of linearly extruded feature created from open or closed sketched contours. This feature adds material of a specific thickness and direction between the contour and an existing part.
You can create a rib by using one or more sketches, creating a draft angle, or selecting a reference contour for a draft angle.

6.6.1.8 Form element function Helix / Spiral

Helix / Spiral

The helix, also called screw, spiral, cylindrical spiral or helical, is a curve that winds around the surface of a cylinder with a constant slope.
In engineering, a helix (spiral) is an often self-supporting helical wire component; a typical helix is the helical spring, which accommodates the spring forces of a long spring in a small space.
You can create a helical or spiral curve in a part. The curve can be used as a path or guide curve for a blow-out feature or as a guide curve for a blow-out feature.

6.6.1.9 Form element function "Thread"

Thread

Using the options in the Thread tool, you can create spiral threads on cylindrical bodies. You must proceed carefully, as the interaction of these options can sometimes cause subtle errors.

Do not make any changes to profiles that will cause the thread to no longer fit the underlying shape.

You might have a profile with a cut-out thread that works well for shafts but isn't suitable for bores. For a bore, you often need to switch to a linear extrusion.

Or you have a working profile, but the offset is so large that contact with the underlying wave is lost.

6.6.1.10 Form element function "SOLIDWORKS Toolbox"

Toolbox

Power Transmission

Spur Gear

Internal Spur Gear

Straight Bevel

The SOLIDWORKS® Toolbox contains a library of standard parts that is fully integrated into SOLIDWORKS. Toolbox users select a standard and part type, and then drag a Toolbox component into an assembly. As a Toolbox Administrator, you can place the Toolbox components in a central location on your network and streamline the Toolbox so that only parts that meet your company's manufacturing standards are included. The Toolbox library contains main part files for supported standards and a database with component size and configuration data. Toolbox drives are representations for machine design purposes. These are not true involute gears suitable for production. The standard toolbox includes more than 2000 component types of various sizes for 12 standards, as well as other industry-specific content totaling several million components.

- The fasteners provided with Toolbox are approximate representations without precise thread details, making them unsuitable for certain analyses such as stress analyses.
- Toolbox drives are representations for machine design purposes. They are not true involute gears that can be used in production.

6.6.1.11 Form element function "Loft"

Lofted Boss/Base

The Loft function creates a feature by generating transitions between profiles. A feature can be a base, a top, a cut, or a surface. A feature can be created using two or more profiles.

Only the first, the last, or both profiles can be points. All sketch elements, including guide curves and profiles, can be contained in a single 3D sketch.

When shaping a body as a solid, the first and last profiles must be model surfaces, planar profiles, surfaces or faces created by dividing lines.

To generate the discharge geometry, the software creates a series of intermediate sections by replicating a profile at various positions along the path. These intermediate sections are then merged.

6.6.1.12 Form element function "Sweep"

Swept Boss/Base

Sweep creates a base, boss, cut, or surface by moving a profile (section) along a path. A sweep can be simple or complex.

To generate the sweep geometry, the software creates a series of intermediate sections made by replicating a profile at various positions along the path. The intermediate sections are then blended together. Additional parameters can be included in the sweep feature such as guide curves, profile orientation options, and twist to create a wide variety of shapes.

6.6.1.13 Form element function curved construction "Dome"

You can create multiple dome features on the same model simultaneously. You can apply domes to surfaces whose center of gravity lies outside the surface. This allows you to apply domes to irregularly shaped contours.

Dome

6.6.1.14 Form element function curved construction "Freeform"

The Freeform feature modifies the surfaces of solid or three-dimensional objects. Only one surface can be modified at a time, and a surface can have any number of sides.

Freeform

Deformations can be controlled directly and interactively by creating control curves and points, and then dragging and pushing the control points to modify the surface.

Use the triad to constrain the deformation or demolding direction. The freeform feature offers a more direct influence compared to deformation features. It is particularly suitable for consumer product designers creating curvilinear designs.

6.6.1.15 Form element function curved construction "Deform"

Using the Deform feature, you can change the shape of complex surface and solid models, both locally and globally, without having to consider the sketches or feature constraints used to create the models.

Deform

Deformation offers a simple method to modify virtually any model, whether organic or mechanical.

Furthermore, deformation is extremely helpful in creating design concepts or making geometric changes to complex models, which would otherwise take too long using conventional methods for editing sketches, features and profiles.

6.6.1.16 Form element function curved construction "Flex"

Flex features allow complex models to be deformed in an intuitive way.

Flex

Flex features are suitable for modifying complex models using intuitive tools that deliver predictable results.

Bend one or more bodies about the triad's red X-axis, the bend axis. Position the triad and trim planes to control the degree, location, and extent of bending.

Twist solids and surface bodies around the blue Z-axis of the triad. Position the triad and trim planes to control the degree, location, and extent of twisting.

Taper solids and surface bodies along the blue Z-axis of the triad. Position the triad and trim planes to control the degree, location, and extent of tapering.

Stretch solids and surface bodies along the blue Z-axis of the triad. Specify a distance or drag the edge of a trim plane with the left mouse button.

6.7 Basic construction "Cuboid with top" Form element feature "Draft", "Shell", "Fillet"

6.7.1 The basic geometry, specifications

- Open the basic geometry from the book DVD.
- **10°** draft for cylinders and cuboids.
- Wall thickness **5** mm.
- Fillet radius **2** mm.

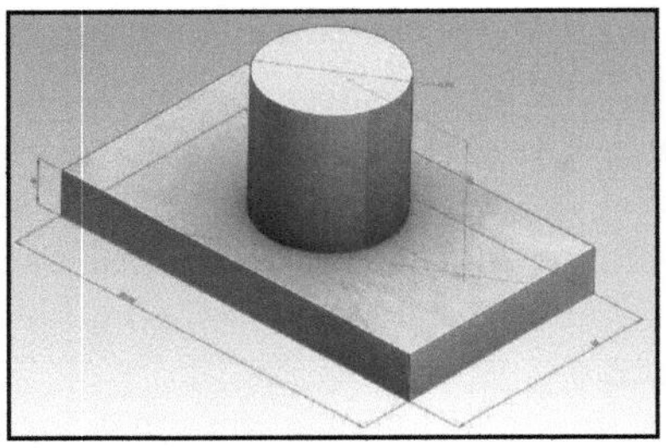

6.7.2 Conical adaptations

6.7.2.1 Open the working file

Open

Open (Menu bar) / Component from the book-DVD / **OK**

6.7.2.2 Draft angle for the cylinder using "Manual Draft"

Draft

Draft (**Features** tab)
In the **PropertyManager**, click **Manual Draft** (1).

Draft Angle

Set the **draft angle** to **10°**.
Select a **Neutral plane**, cylinder top edge (2).
Select Faces to Draft, then the bottom edge of the cylinder (3).
The arrow indicated the direction point upwards (4).
Set otion **Show preview** (5, 6).
Close dialog box.

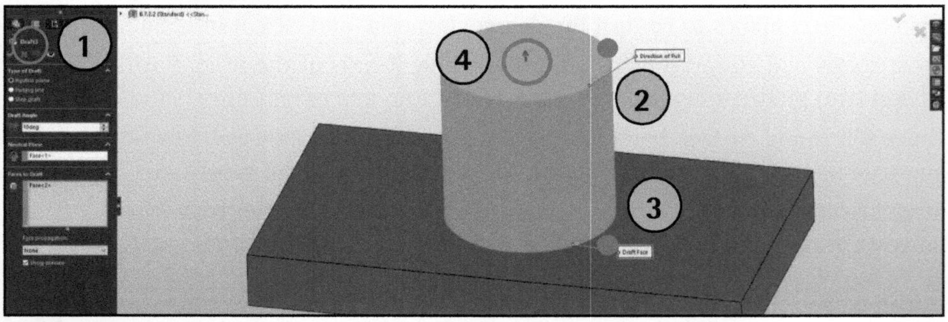

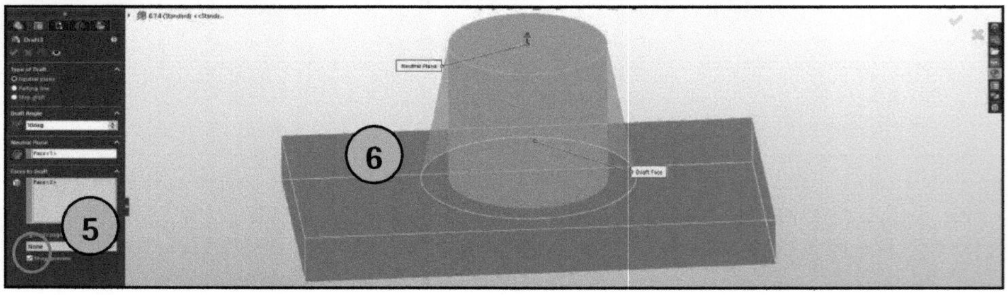

6.7.2.3 Draft angle for the base cuboid using "Manual Draft"

Draft (Features tab)
In the **PropertyManager**, click **Manual Draft**.
Set the **draft angle** to **30°** (7).
Select a **Neutral plane**, cylinder top edge (8).
The arrow indicating the demolding direction points upwards.
Select the four areas for draft angle (9).
Set otion **Show preview** (10).
Close dialog box.

Draft

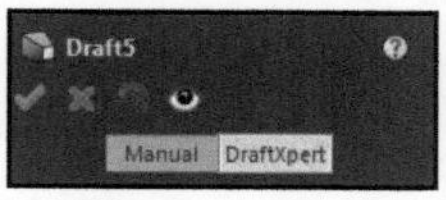

Draft Angle

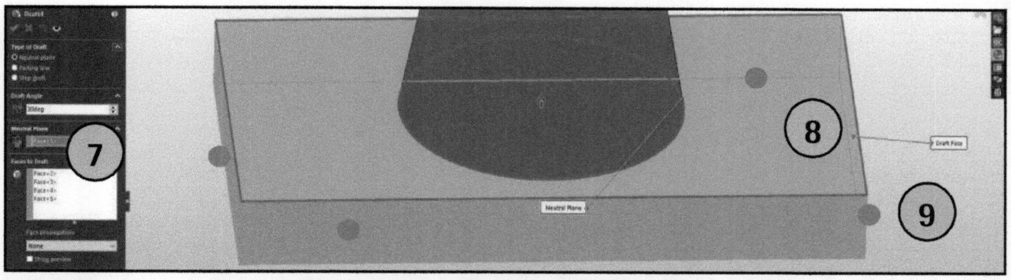

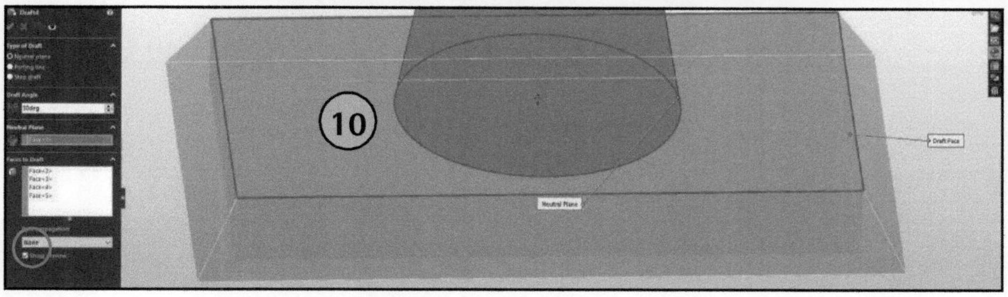

6.7.3 "Shell" Feature, the creation

Shell (Features tab)
Set the **Thickness** to **5** mm (11).
Option **Faces to Remove** (12).
Select the base and top surfaces in the graphics area (13, 14).
Set otion **Show preview.**
Close dialog box.

Shell

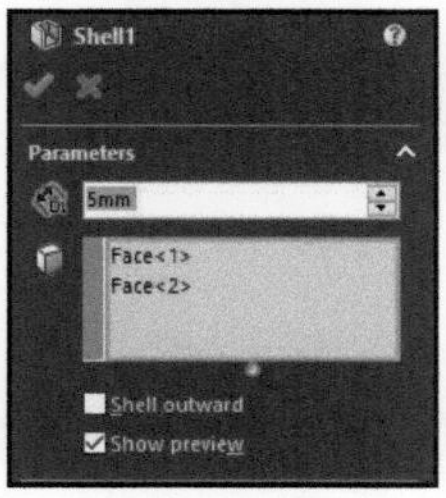

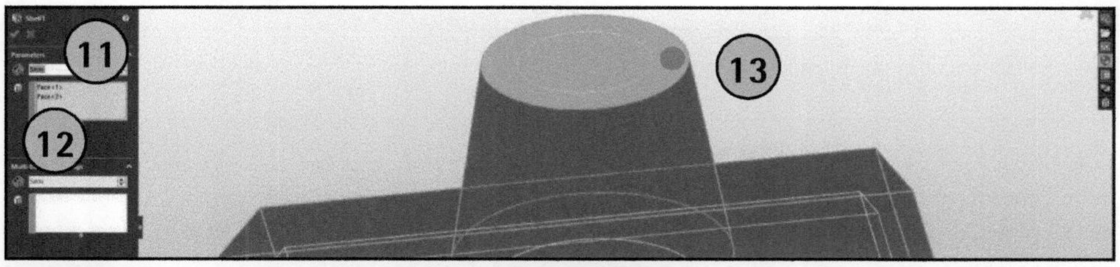

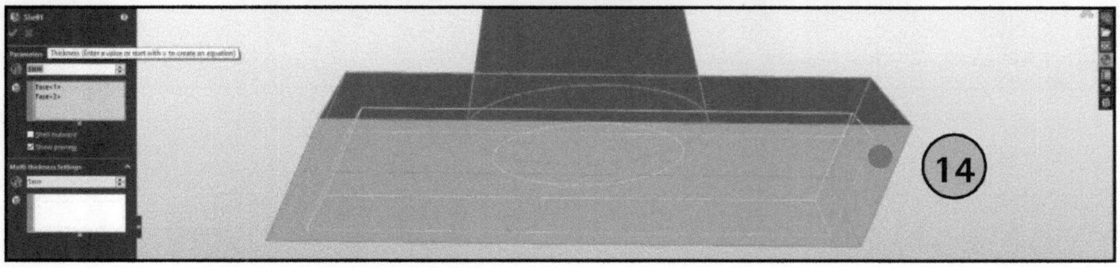

6.7.4 "Fillet" Feature, the creation

Fillet

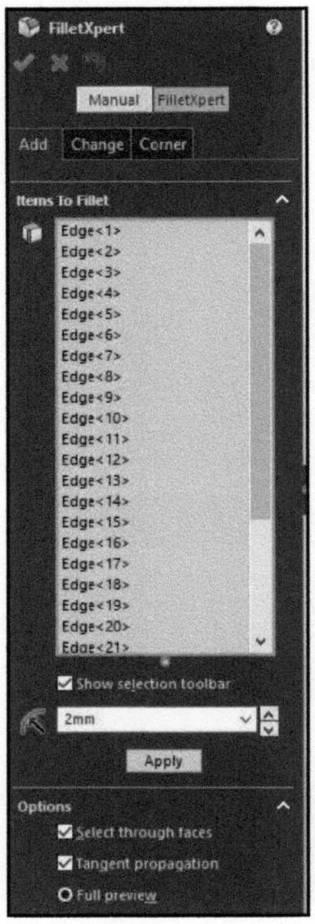

Fillet (Features tab)
In the **PropertyManager**, click **Manual Fillet.**
Set the radius to **2** mm.
Select the entire model with a frame to capture all surfaces (15).
Set otion **Show preview** (16).
Close dialog box.

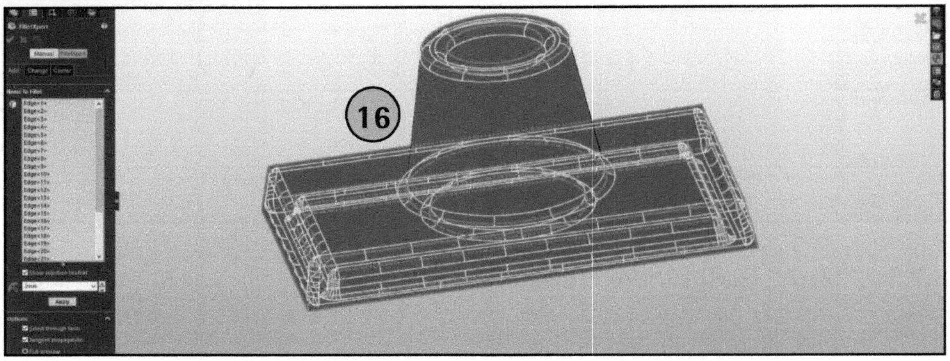

6.7.4.1 Data backup

Save as New

Save as New / Enter a name of your choice.

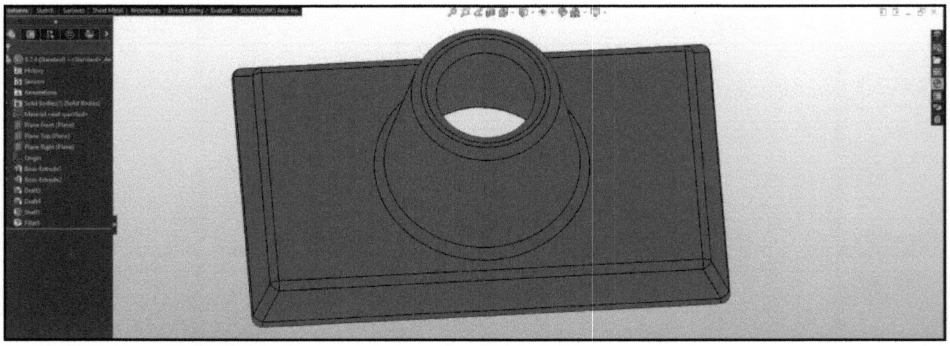

6.8 Basic construction "Drill plate"
Form element feature "Hole Wizard", "Linear Pattern"

6.8.1 The basic geometry, specifications

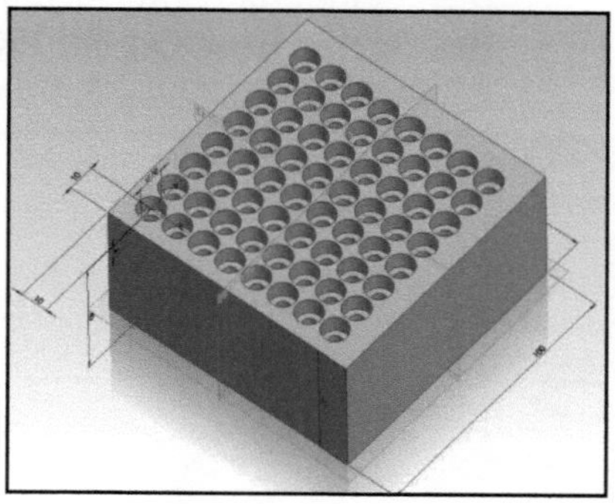

- Cuboid **100** x **100** mm, **40** mm thick on the **XZ** plane.
- Counterbore **Ø9** mm, **5.4** mm deep, through **Ø5.5** mm, **10** mm side distance.
- The sample data is:
  9 holes in the **X** direction
  8 x spacing x **10** mm
  9 holes in the **Y** direction
  8 x spacing y **10** mm.

6.8.2 Creating the basic body

6.8.2.1 Opening your own template file

- Menu Bar **New** /  /  click **Engelke2026.PRTDOT / OK**

New

Engelke2026.
PRTDOT

6.8.2.2 The "Cuboid" as a basic geometry, using feature "Extrude"

Extrude (**Features** tab)

Center Rectangle (Flyout tool **Rectangle** / **Sketch** tab)
Selection Top

Smart Dimension (**Sketch** tab)
Enter **100** mm for both length and width (1, 2).
Finish sketch
Click on the arrow in the middle of the cuboid.
Drag the scale to **40** mm (3).
Close dialog box.

Extrude

Center
Rectangle

Smart
Dimension

Close dialog
box

Finish Sketch

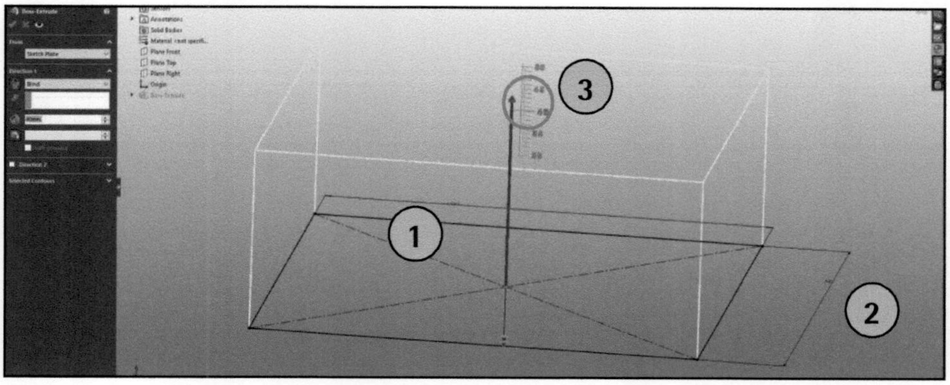

6.8.3 "Hole wizard" feature, type "Counterbore", the creation

Hole Wizard

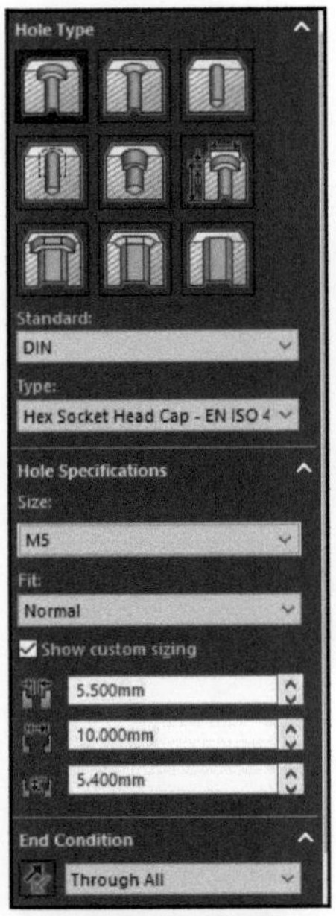

Smart Dimension

Hole Wizard (**Features** tab)
Click the **Type** tab.
DIN, **Counterbore**, **M5**, depth: **Through all** (4).
Hex Socket Head Cap EN ISO 4672
Countersink-Ø **10** mm, **5.4** mm deep, through hole Ø **5.5** mm (5).

- Then switch to the **Positions / Exiting 2D Sketch tab.**
- Simply place the cursor on the upper surface of the component approx. where the hole is to be drilled (6).
- Use the **Smart Dimension function** to dimension the point to the two component edges.
  Enter **10** mm for both length and width (7).
- Close dialog box (8).

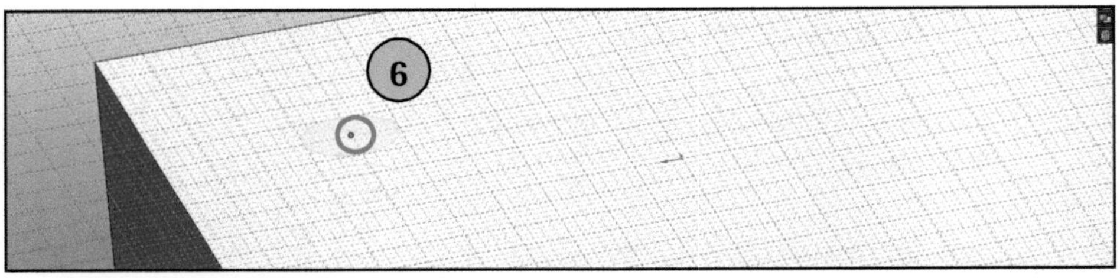

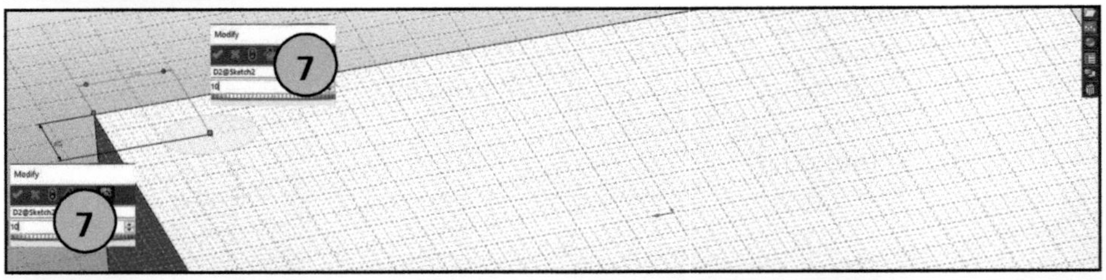

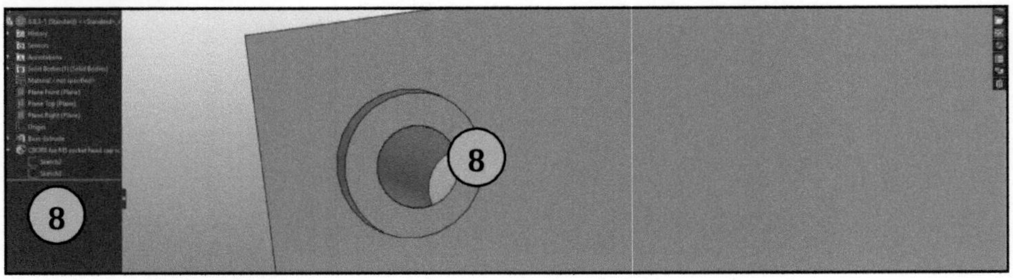

6.8.4 "Linear Pattern" feature, the creation

Lineares Muster

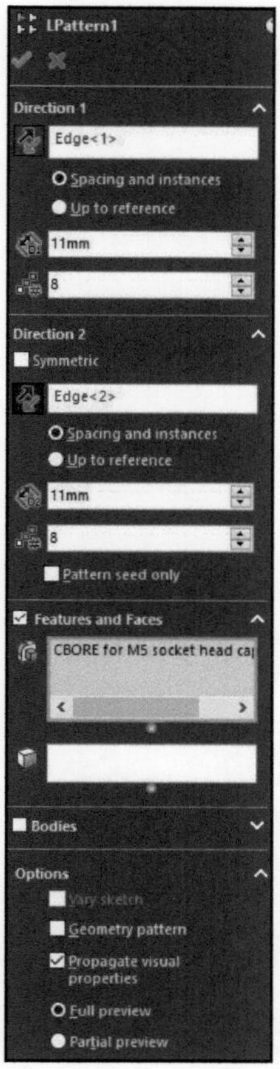

Linear Pattern (**Features** tab)
Direction 1
Click edge for **Direction 1** (8).
Distance
Distance Direction 1: **11** mm.
Number of Instances direction 1: **8** Stück.

Direction 2
Click edge for **Direction 2** (9).
Distance
Distance Direction 2: **11** mm.
Number of Instances direction 2: **8** Stück.

- Select the counterbore as a sample feature (10).

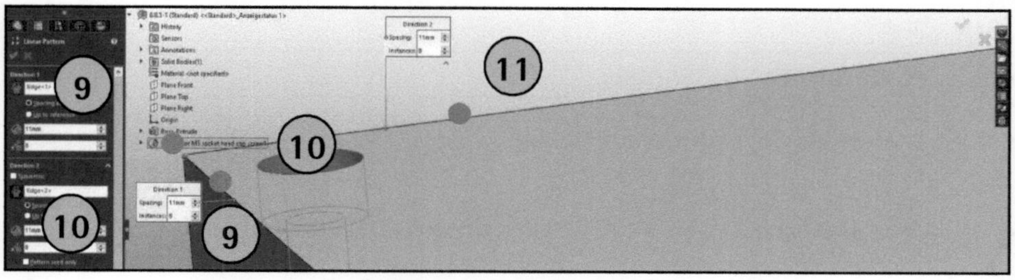

- Set the display option to **Full Preview** (12, 13).
- **Close dialog box.**

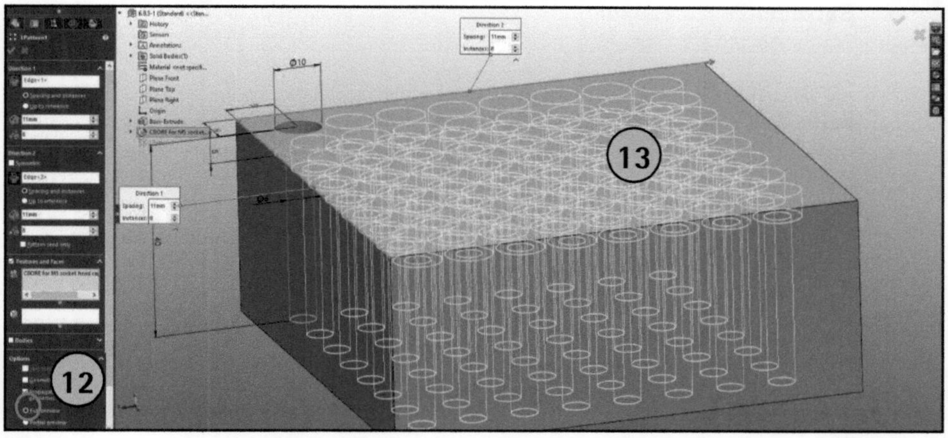

6.8.4.1 Data backup

Save as New / Enter a name of your choice.

Save as New

6.9 Basic construction "Flange ring with mounting holes" Form element feature "Hole Wizard", "Circular Pattern"

6.9.1 The basic geometry, specifications

- Ring outer diameter **100** mm, inner diameter **50** mm, **30** mm thick, create on the top plane.
- Counterbore **Ø11** mm, **5** mm deep, through **Ø8** mm, on a bolt circle **Ø66** mm.
- **12** holes distributed across the bolt circle.

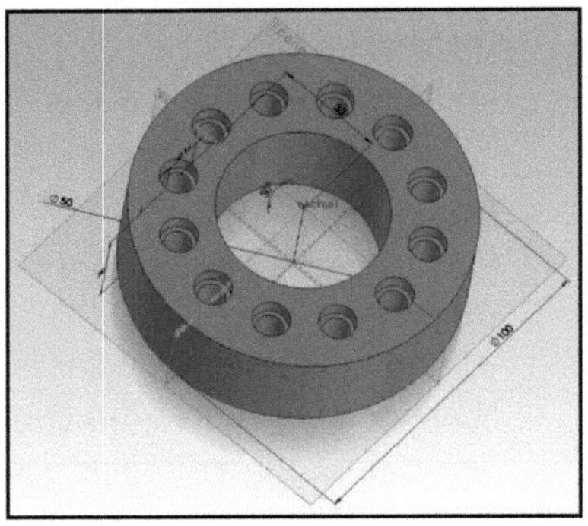

6.9.2 Creating the basic body

6.9.2.1 Opening your own template file

New

- Menu Bar **New** / / click **Engelke2026.PRTDOT / OK**

6.9.2.2 The ring cylinder as the basic geometry

Engelke2026.
PRTDOT

Extrude

Circle

Smart
Dimension

Close dialog
box

Finish sketch

Extrude (**Features** tab)

Circle (**Sketch** tab)
Selection Top, outer circle and inner circle.

Smart Dimension (**Sketch** tab)
Enter the outer diameter of **100** mm and the inner diameter of **50** mm (1, 2).
Close dialog box / Finish sketch
Click on the arrow in the middle of the cuboid.
Drag the scale to **30** mm (3).
Close dialog box.

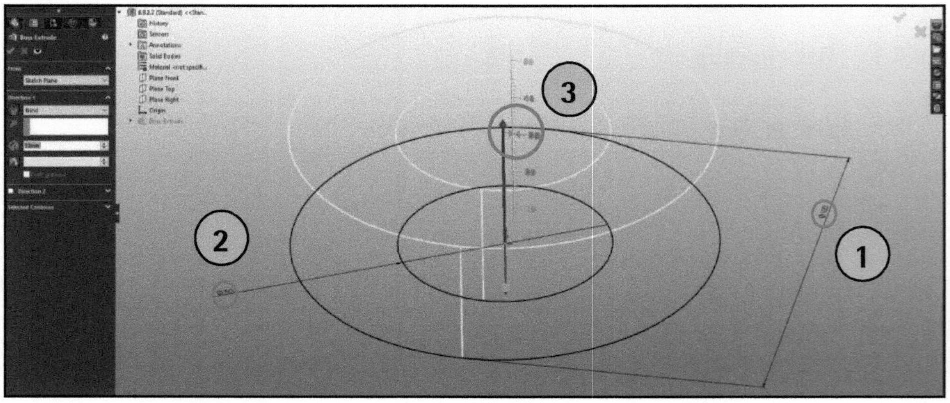

6.9.3 "Hole wizard" feature, type "Counterbore", the creation

Hole Wizard (**Features** tab)
Click the **Type** tab.
DIN, **Counterbore**, **M8**, depth: **Through all** (4).
Hex Socket Head Cap EN ISO 4672
Countersink-Ø **15** mm, **8.6** mm deep, through hole Ø **9** mm (5).

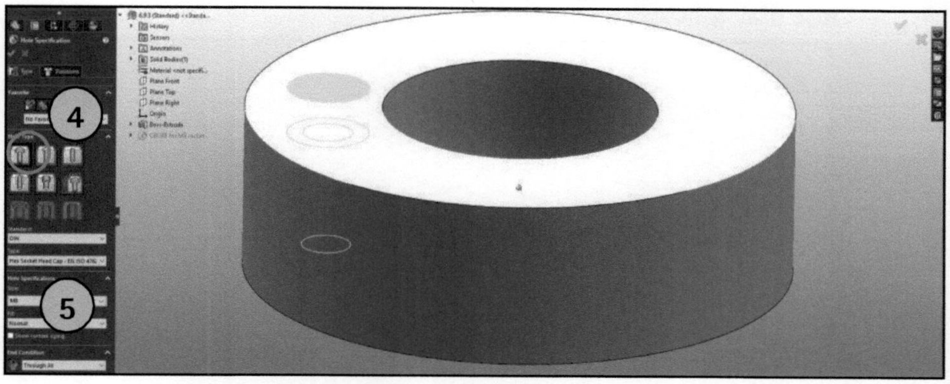

- Then switch to the **Positions / 3D Sketch**.
- Simply place the cursor on the upper surface of the component approx. where the hole is to be drilled (6).

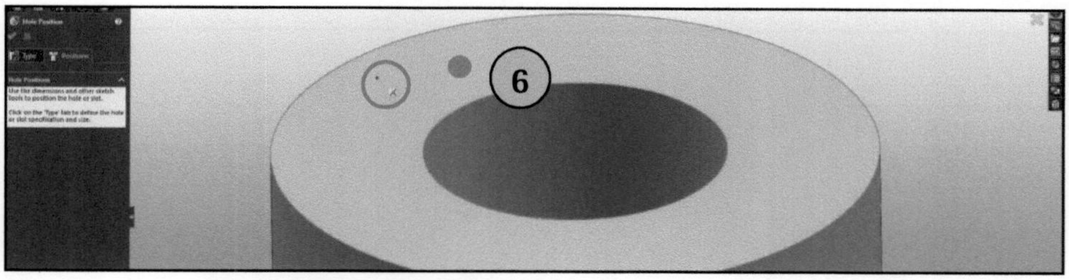

- Use the **Smart Dimension function**, click the inner hole (7), click the upper ring (8), enter the spacing diameter of **36** mm (9).
- **Close dialog box**.

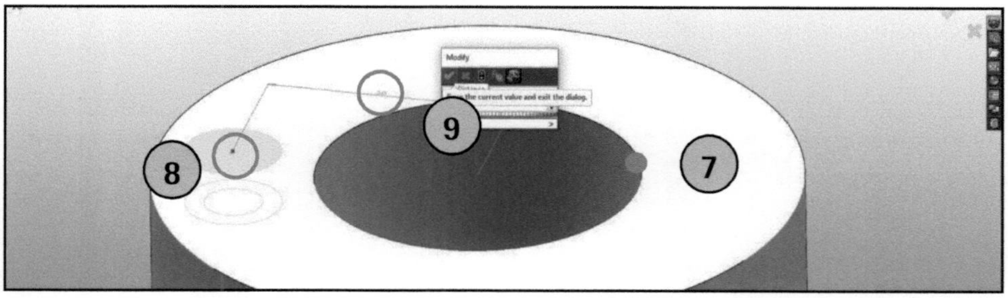

Hole Wizard

Smart Dimension

Circular Pattern

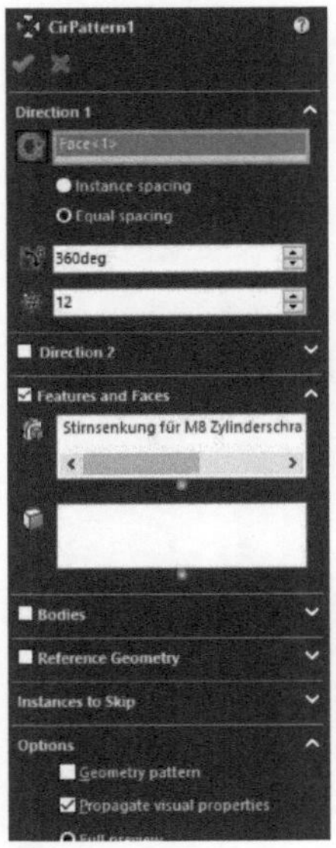

Save as New

6.9.4 "Circular Pattern" feature, the creation

Circular Pattern (**Features** tab)
Pattern-Axis, select the outer cylinder (10).
Number of instances: **12**, total angle **360°** (11)

Select the counterbore as a sample feature (12).
Set the display option to **Full Preview** (13).
Close dialog box.

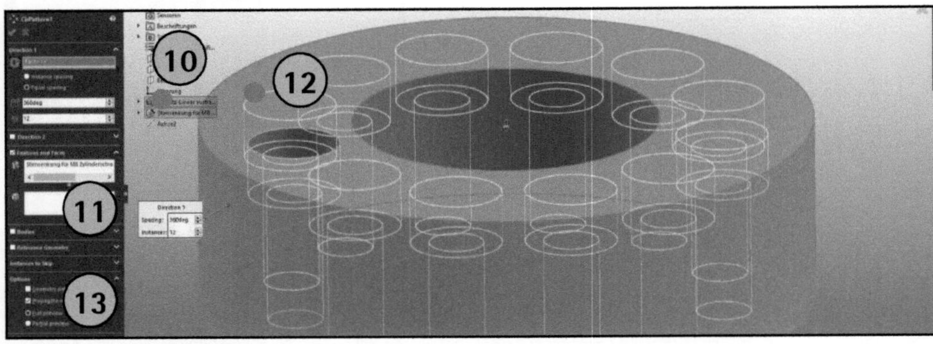

6.9.4.1 Data backup

Save as New / Enter a name of your choice.

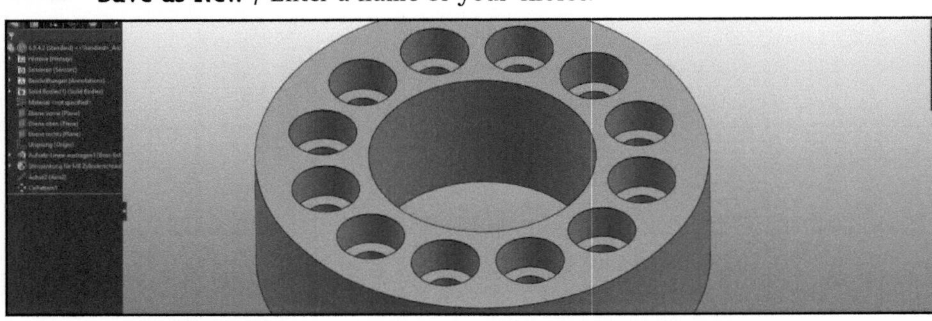

6.10 Basic construction "Cuboid with top" Form element feature "Rib", "Mirror", "Circular Pattern"

6.10.1 The basic geometry, specifications

- A rib **5** mm wide across the center and **5** mm high was added as reinforcement.
- The mirror function will create an opposite rib.
- The **circle pattern** function creates **6** ribs from this.

6.10.2 Basic body processing

6.10.2.1 Open the working file

Open (Menu bar) / Component from the book-DVD / **OK**

Open

6.10.2.2 Create a central plane between planar surfaces

Plane (Reference Geometry toolbar)
Select the front surface for the first reference (1).
Select option **Mid Plane** (2).
Select the rear surface for the second reference (3).
Close dialog box.

Plane

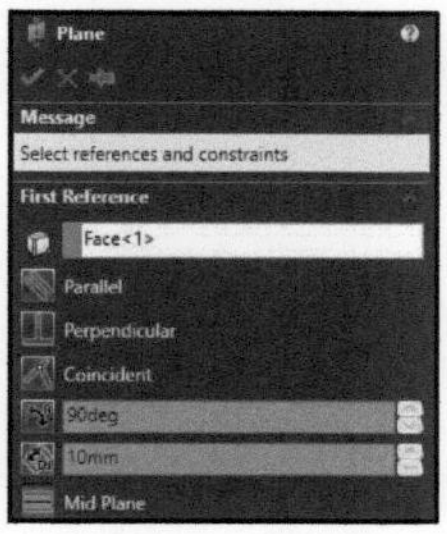

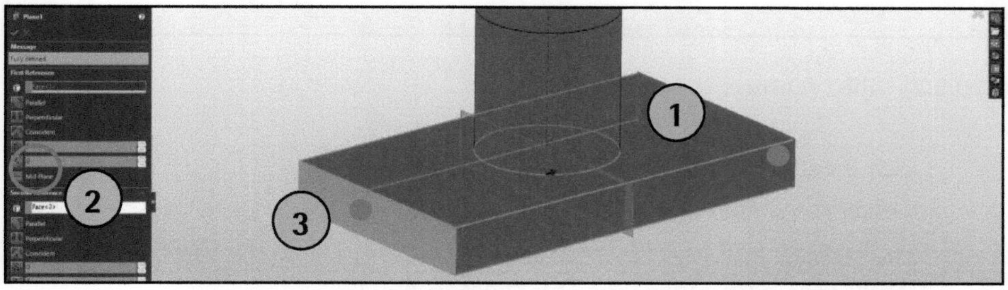

- Proceed with the assignment of the other central plane between planar surfaces accordingly.

Plane

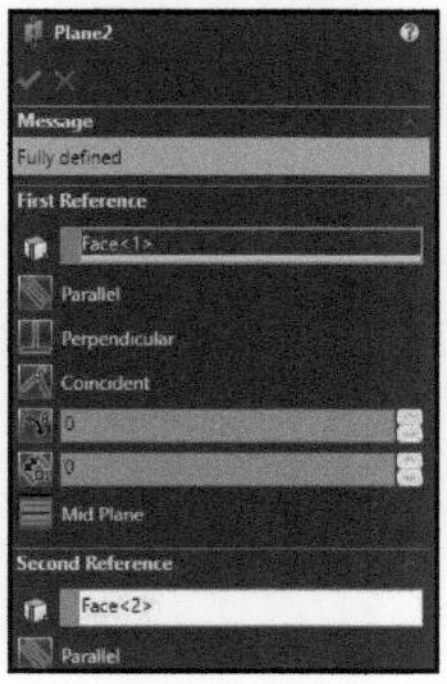

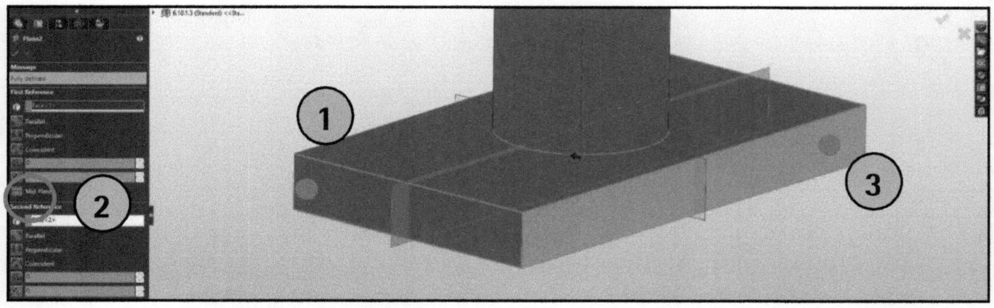

6.10.2.3 Data backup

Save as New / Enter a name of your choice.

Save as New

Sketch

Normal To

Line

Smart Dimension

Close dialog box

Finish sketch

6.10.3 "Rib" feature, one rib, the creation

6.10.3.1 The basic sketch construction

Sketch (**Sketch** tab)
Create a new sketch.

Normal To (Heads-up View Toolbar)
Select the middle plane (1).

Line (**Sketch** tab)
Create a line between the vertical cylinder edge (2) and the horizontal cuboid edge (3) (snap point).

Smart Dimension (**Sketch** tab)
Apply the measurement **5** mm (4).
Close dialog box / Finish sketch

Verstärkungsrippe

Beide Seiten

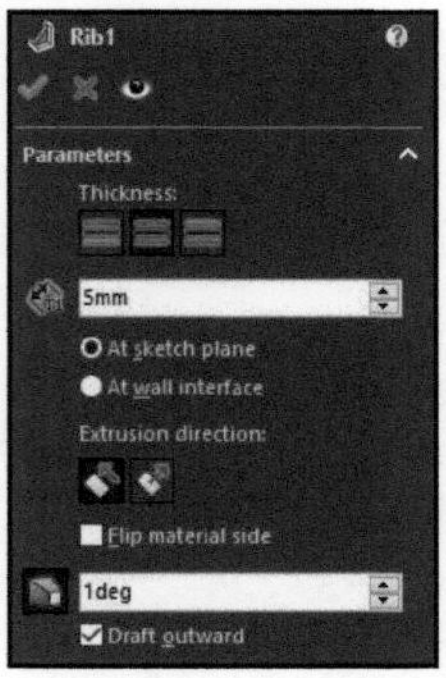

6.10.3.2 "Rib" feature, the basic rib

Rib (**Features** tab)

Select the sketch line as the contour (5).

Thickness both Sides (6) / **Thickness**: **5** mm (7)
Close dialog box.

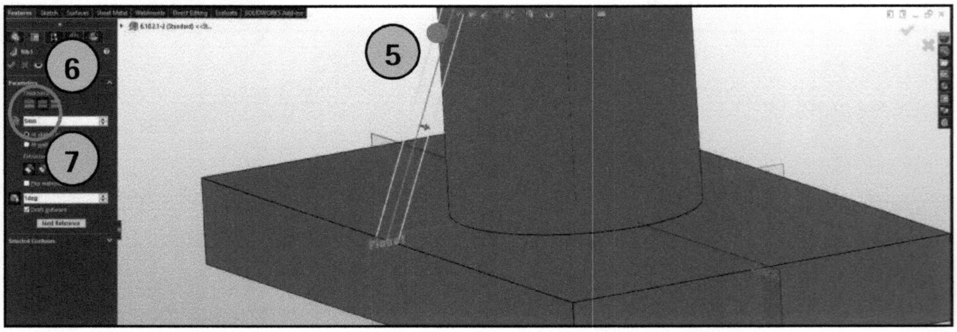

6.10.4 "Rib" feature, mirrored rib construction, the creation

Mirror (Features tab)
Select the **Rib** in the **temporary FeatureManager** (1).
Select the **Mid Plane** (2).
Set the display option to **Full Preview** (3, 4).
Close dialog box.

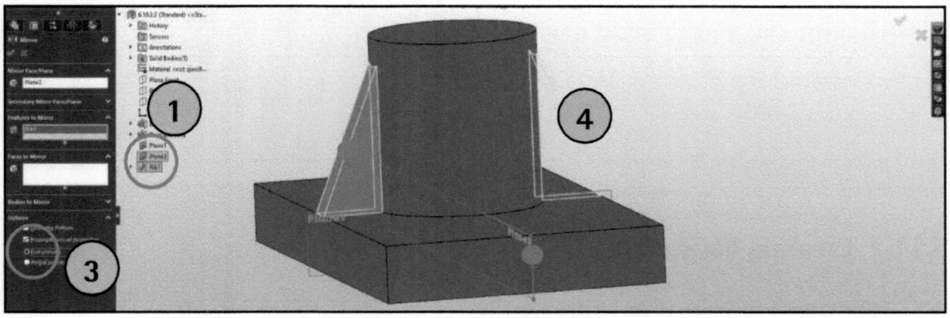

Spiegeln

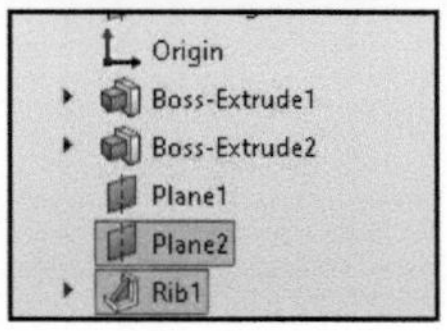

6.10.5 "Rib" feature, multiple ribs over "Circular pattern", the creation

Circular Pattern (Features tab)
Pattern-Axis, select the outer cylinder (5).
Number of instances: **3**, total angle **360°** (6)
Select the **Rib** and **Mirror** in the **temporary FeatureManager** (7).
Set the display option to **Full Preview**.
Close dialog box.

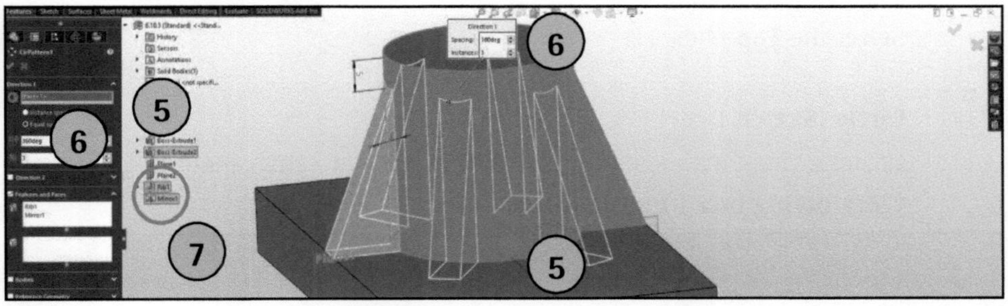

Circular Pattern

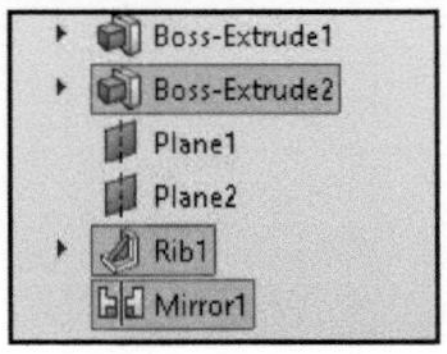

6.10.5.1 Data backup

Save as New / Enter a name of your choice.

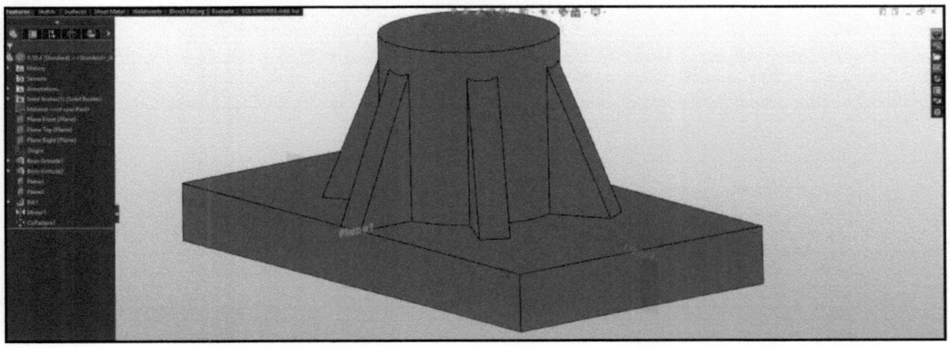

Save as New

6.11 Basic construction "Compression spring" Form element feature "Helix/Spiral", "Swept Boss"

6.11.1 The basic geometry, specifications

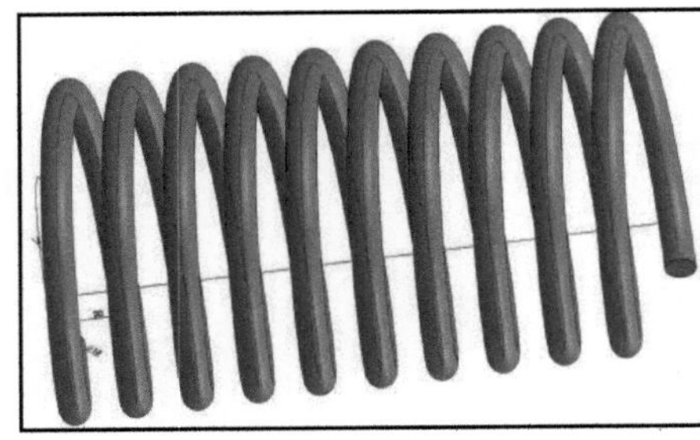

- Base circle **Ø100** mm.

- Helix with:
- **10** turns and a pitch of **20** mm.

6.11.2 Creating basic body

6.11.2.1 Opening your own template file

- Menu Bar **New** /  /  click **Engelke2026.PRTDOT / OK**

New

Engelke2026.
PRTDOT

Sketch

Circle

6.11.3 The "Helix/Spiral" feature

6.11.3.1 The basic sketch construction

Sketch (**Sketch** tab)
Create a new sketch.
Select the **Top** plane (1).

Circle (**Sketch** tab)
Create a circle with a diameter of **100** mm at the center point (2, 3).
Close dialog box / Finish sketch

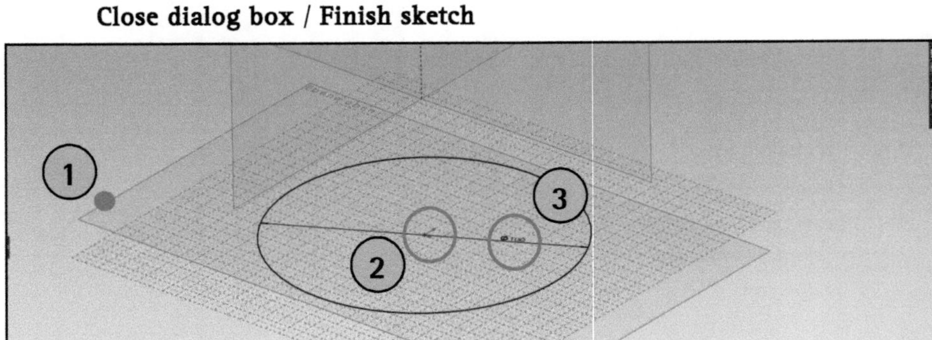

6.11.3.2 The Helix/Spiral feature, the creation

Helix/Spiral (**Insert** command tab / **Curve**-Flyout)
Select the sketch in the **temporary FeatureManager** (4).
Defined By: **Pitch and Revolution** (5).
Parameters (6):
Constant pitch, Pitch: **20 mm**
Revolution: **10**, Start Angle **270°**, **Clockwise**.
Close dialog box (7).

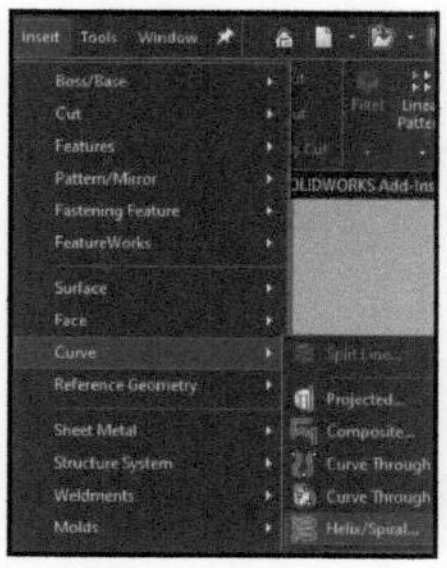

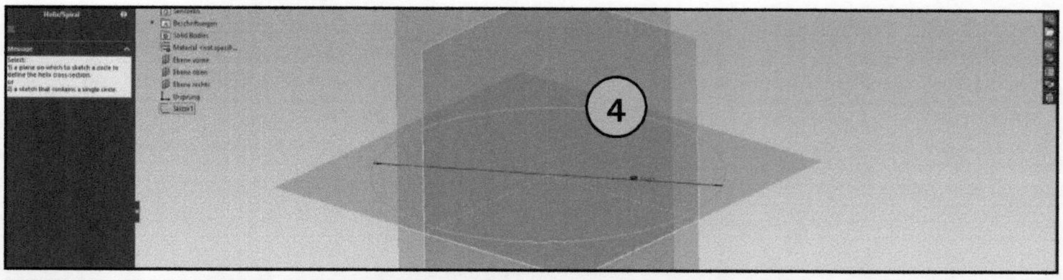

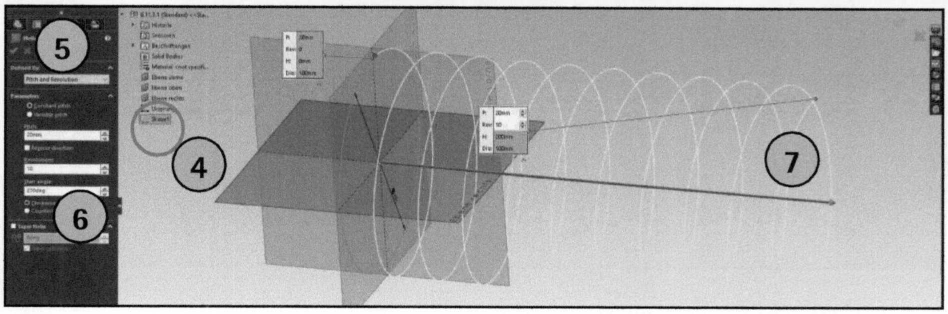

Helix / Spiral

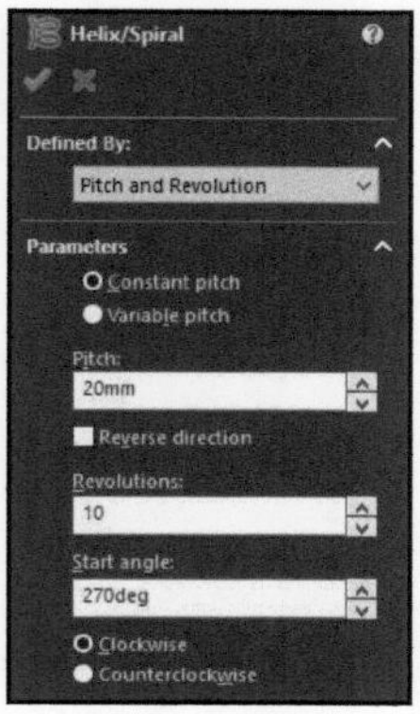

6.11.4 The Compression spring, a "Swept/Boss" feature

6.11.4.1 The profil sketch construction

Sketch (**Sketch** tab)
Create a new sketch / select the **Front** plane (8).

Normal To (Heads-up View Toolbar)

Circle (**Sketch** tab)
Create a circle with a diameter of **10** mm (10) at the endpoint (9) of the helix.
Finish sketch (8)

Sketch

Normal To

Circle

Finish sketch

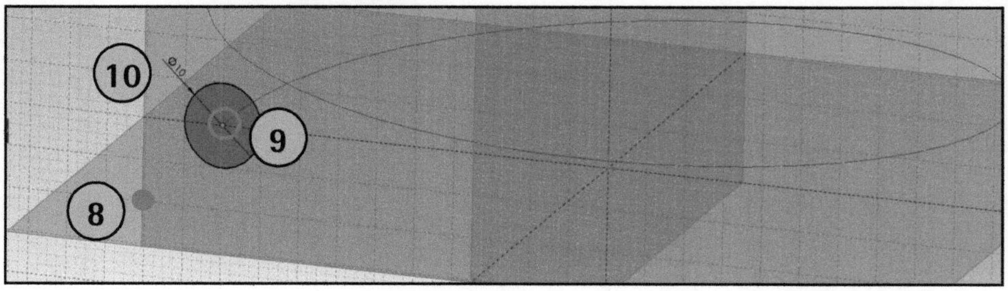

Swept Boss

6.11.4.2 The Compression spring, a "Swept/Boss" feature, the creation

Swept Boss (**Features** tab)
Select the **Sweept profile** (9).
Select the **Sweept path** (10).
Close dialog box (11)

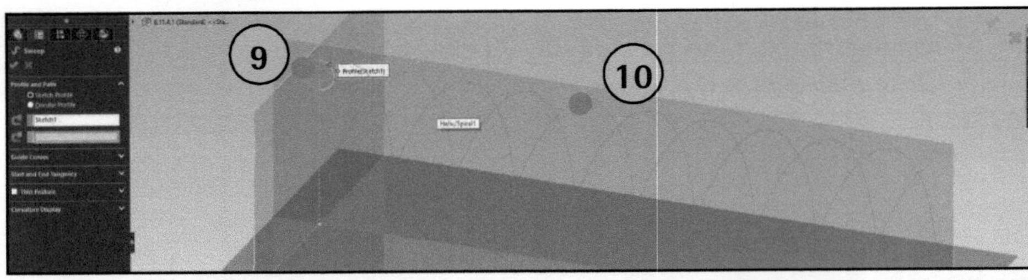

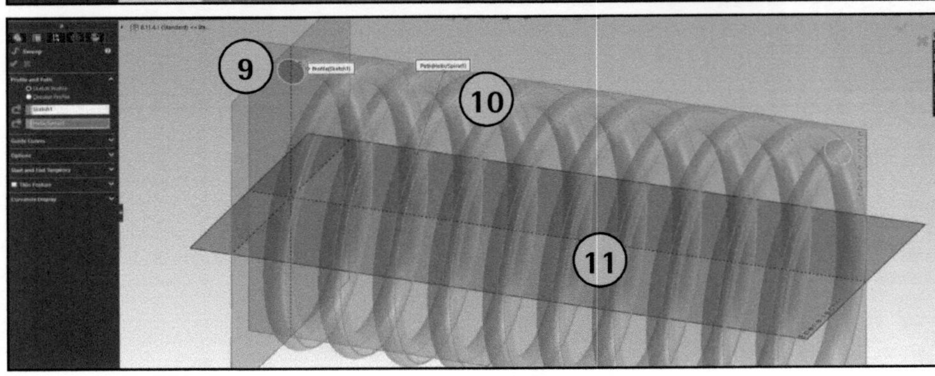

6.11.4.3 Assigning component material

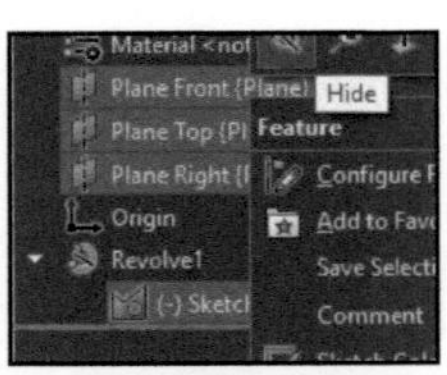

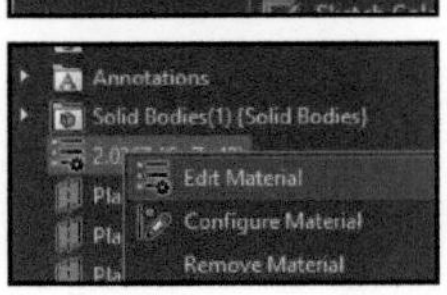

Edit Material

- For the **work planes** and the **sketch**, set the **Hide** option in the **FeatureManager**.

Edit Material (FeatureManager)
Right-click on **Material** to display the context menu for **Edit Material**.
Select SOLIDWORKS-DIN-Material / DIN Steel / Unalloyed 1.8159 (51CrV4) (12, 13).
Click **Apply** and then **Close**.

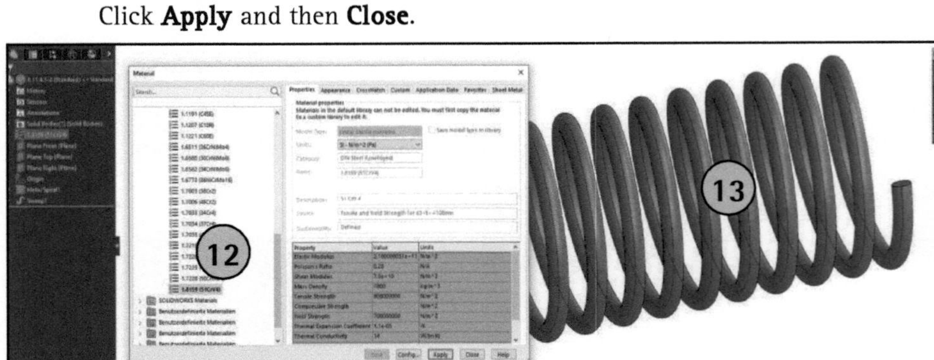

6.11.4.4 Data backup

Save as New

Save as New / Enter a name of your choice.

6.12 Basic construction "Trapezoidal thread" Form element feature "Helix/Spiral", "Cut/Sweep"

6.12.1 The basic geometry, specifications

- Base circle **Ø52** mm, **Front** plane.
- Cylinder length **200** mm
  Mid plane.
- Trapezoidal sketch profile DIN **103**:
  Nominal Ø: **52** mm
  Core Ø: **43** mm
  Flank Ø: **48** mm
  Pitch: **16** mm
  Flank angle: **30°**
  Number of turns: **20**
  Shaft end **chamfer** with **45°**,
  Ø36 mm.

6.12.2 Creating basic body

6.12.2.1 Opening your own template file

New

Engelke2026.
PRTDOT

- Menu Bar **New** /  /  click **Engelke2026.PRTDOT / OK**

6.12.2.2 Creating basic cylinder

Extrude

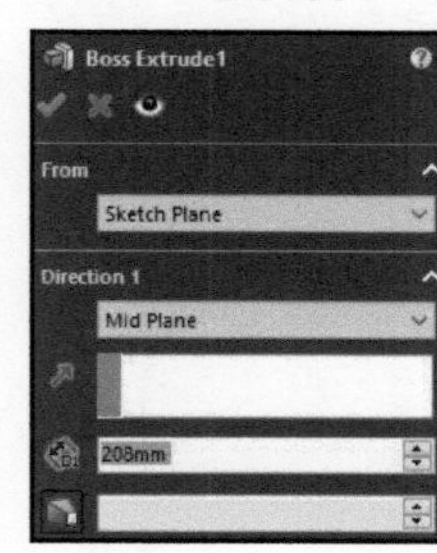

Circle

Extrude (**Features** tab)

Select the **Front** plane.

Circle (**Sketch** tab)

Create a circle with a diameter of **52** mm at the center point (1).

Close dialog box / Finish sketch.

Linear discharges on **Mid Plane**, pull length **208** mm (2).

Close dialog box.

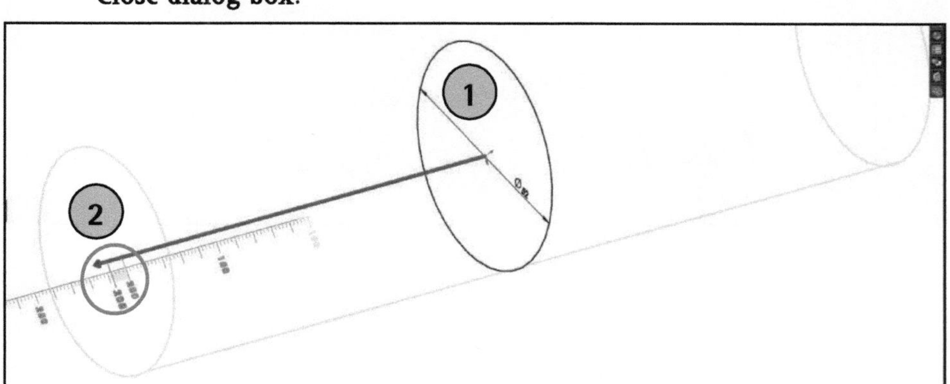

6.12.3 Basic body processing, the "Helix/Spiral" feature

Sketch

Sketch (**Sketch** tab)
Create a new sketch.
Select the end face of the cylinder (3).

Circle

Circle (**Sketch** tab)
Create a circle with a diameter of **52** mm (4).
Close dialog box.

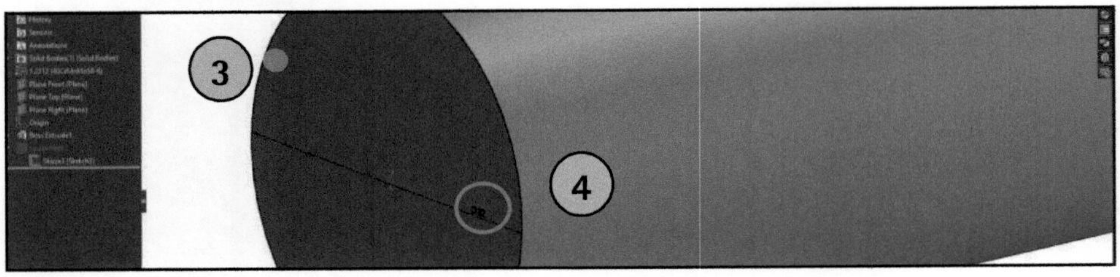

Helix / Spiral

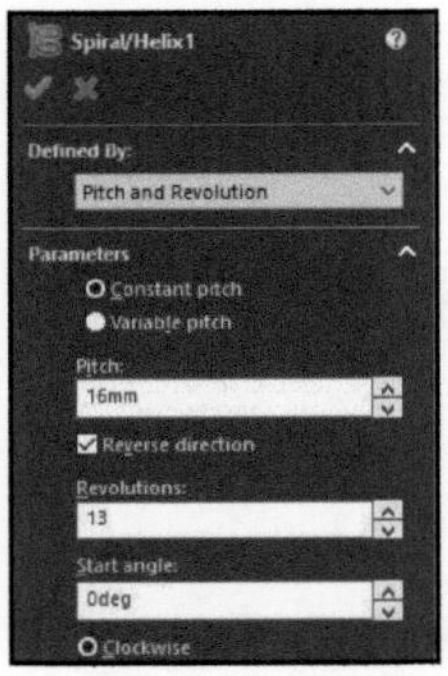

Helix/Spiral (**Insert** command tab / **Curve**-Flyout)
The helix is defined by: **Pitch and Revolution** (5).
Parameters (6):
Constant pitch, Pitch: **16** mm
Revolution: **13**, Start Angle **0°**, **Clockwise**.
Close dialog box (7).

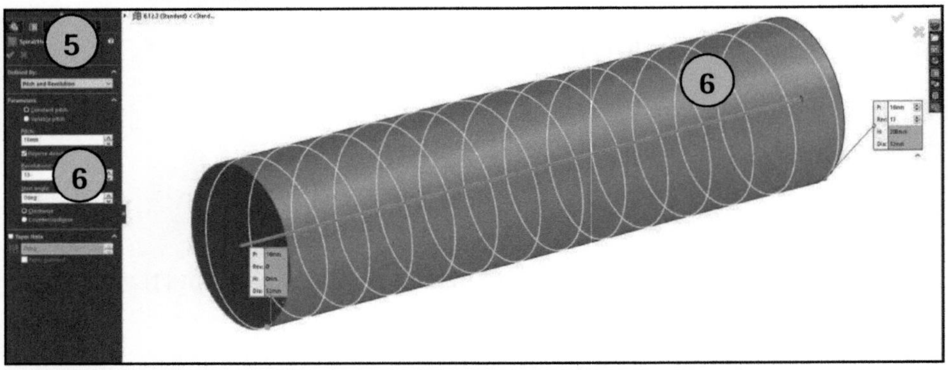

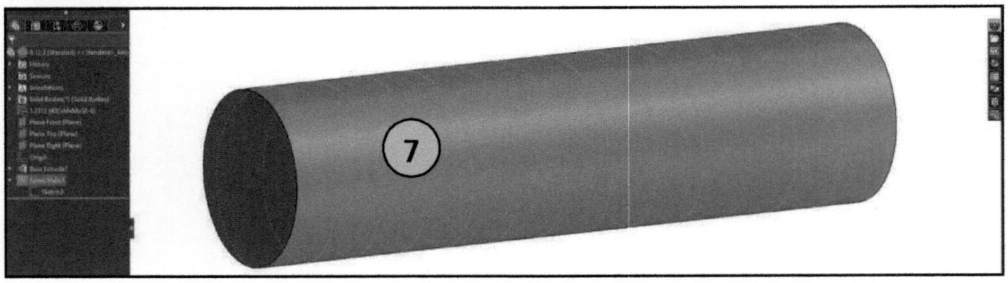

6.12.4 The "Trapezoidal thread", the creation

6.12.4.1 Basic body processing, the revolve sketch

Sketch (Sketch tab)
Create a new sketch.
Select the **Top** plane.

Add Relation (Sketch tab)
The line (8) must be **Collinear** to the cylinder edges (9).
Click to add this relationship to these lines.

Move Entities / Move (Sketch bar)
Select the entire sketch with a frame to capture all surfaces (10).
Move the sketch lines to the end edge of the cylinder (11, 12).

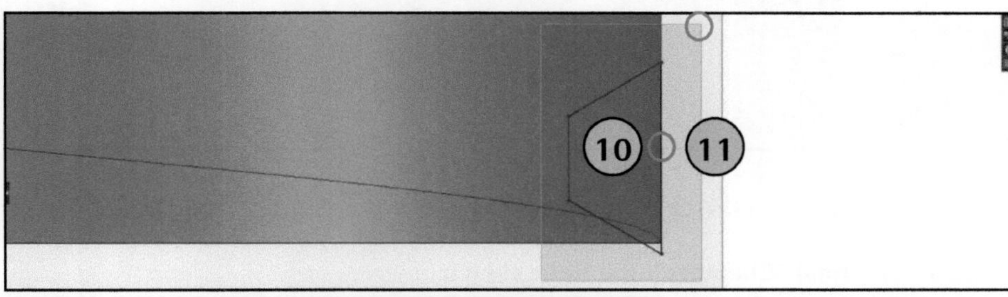

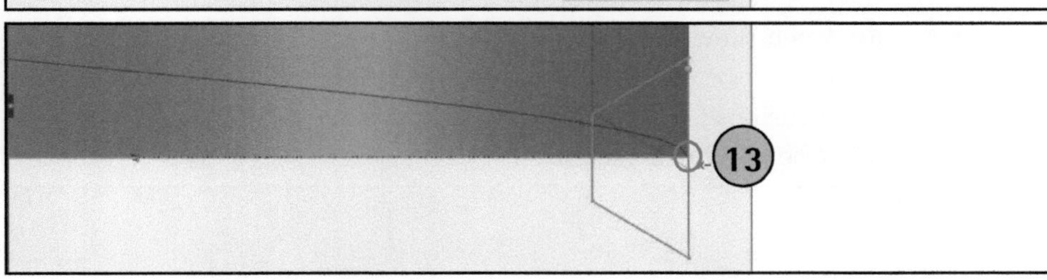

- Enter the dimensions (14).

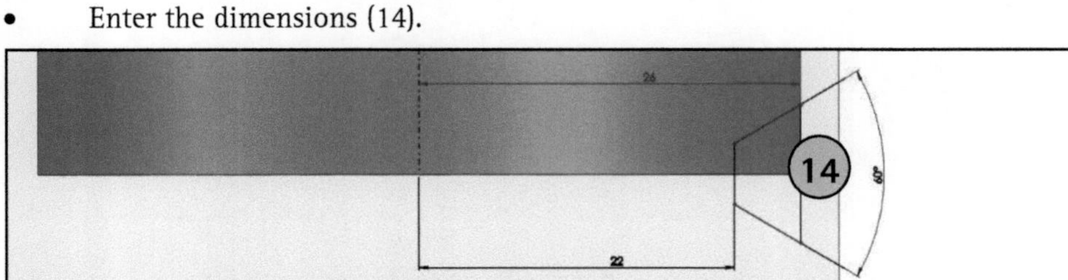

- **Close dialog box / Finish sketch**

Sketch

Line

Add Relation

Collinear

Move Entities

6.12.4.2 The "Trapezoidal thread" using the feature "Cut Sweep"

Cut Sweep

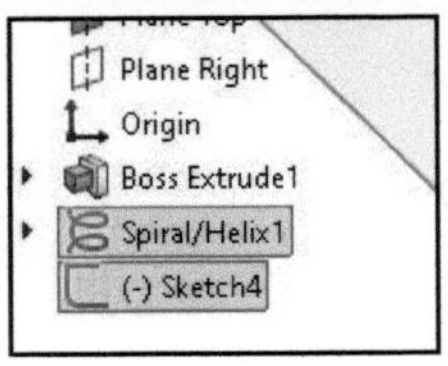

Cut Sweept (**Features** tab)
Select the **Profile** (14).
Choose the **Path** (15).
Close dialog box (16).

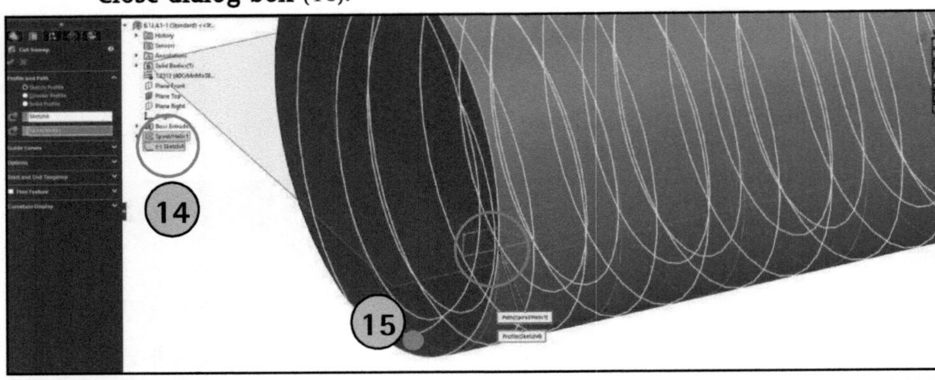

6.12.5 The final "Chamfer", the creation

6.12.5.1 The final "Chamber", the basic sketch

Line

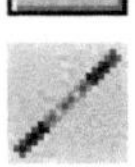

Kollinear

- Create the sketch shown on the Top plane.
- The edge line must be collinear to the cylinder edge.
- Enter the dimensions (17).
- **Close dialog box / Finish sketch.**

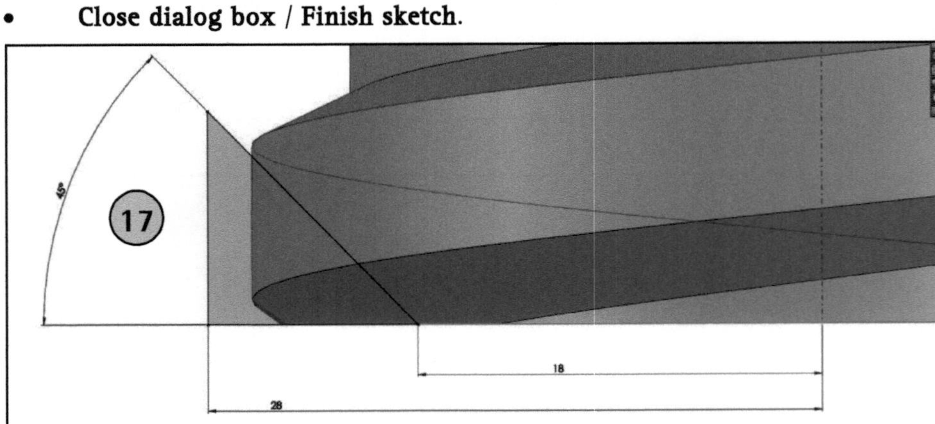

6.12.5.2 The final "Chamfer", using the feature "Cut Revolve"

Cut Revolve (Features tab)
Select the created sketch from the **Temporary FeatureManager** (18).
Select the displayed axis for rotation (19).
Close dialog box (20).

Cut Revolve

6.12.6 Assigning component material

Edit Material (FeatureManager)
Right-click on **Material** to display the context menu for **Edit Material**.
Select **SOLIDWORKS-DIN-Material/DIN Steel 1.2312 (40CrMnMoS8)** (21, 22).
Click **Apply** and then **Close**.

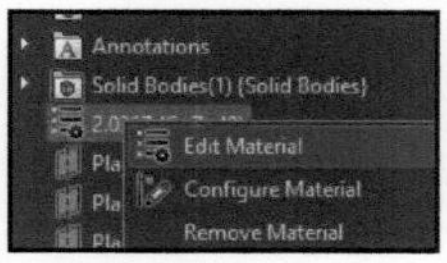

Edit Material

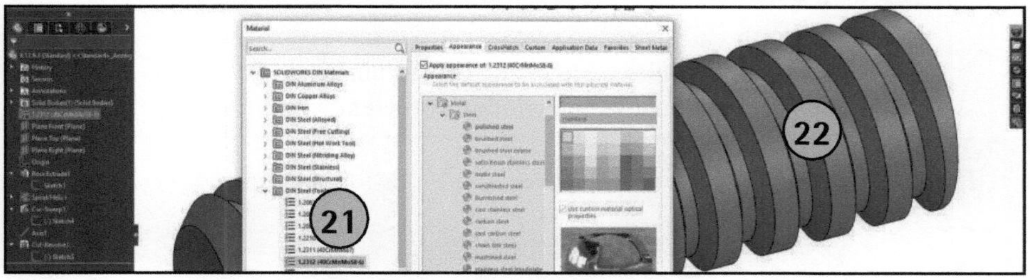

6.12.6.1 Data backup

Save as New / Enter a name of your choice.

Save as New

6.13 Basic construction "Physical Thread Profile" Form element feature "Thread"

6.13.1 Simple hole with physical thread profile, specification

The **Thread** feature allows you to insert a physical thread profile M36x4 into a simple hole.

Thread values for internal threads ISO **261**:

Outer-Ø **M36**, core-Ø **31.67** mm, pitch **4** mm

6.13.2 Form element feature "Thread" using core diameter

6.13.2.1 Open the working file

Open

Open (Menu bar) / Component from the book-DVD / **OK**.

6.13.2.2 Change the specified bore diameter to the core diameter

Smart Dimension

- Activate the **Sketch** entry under **Extruded Cut** (1).
- Select **Edit Sketch** in the **PropertyManager**.
- Change the bore-Ø to **31.67** mm using **SmartDimension** (2).
- **Close dialog box / Finish sketch**

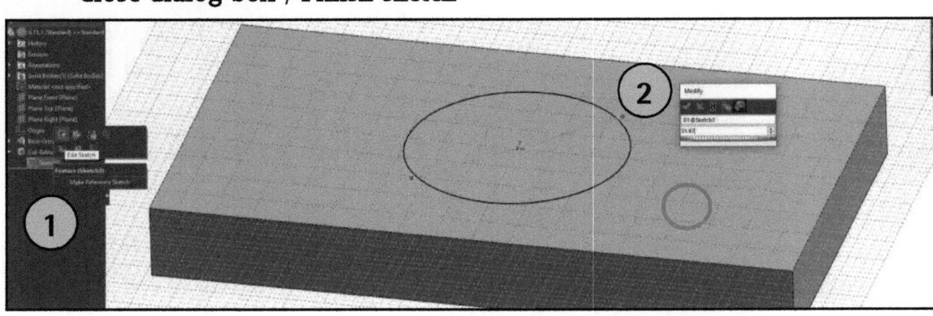

6.13.2.3 Form element feature "Thread", the creation

Thread

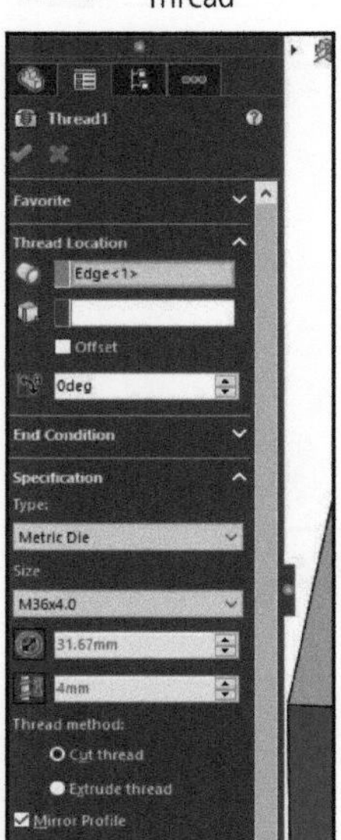

Thread (**Features** tab / **Hole wizard**)

Select metric thread size **M36x4** (3).

Select the upper cylinder edge as the thread position (4).

Select the bottom edge of the cylinder as the end condition (5).

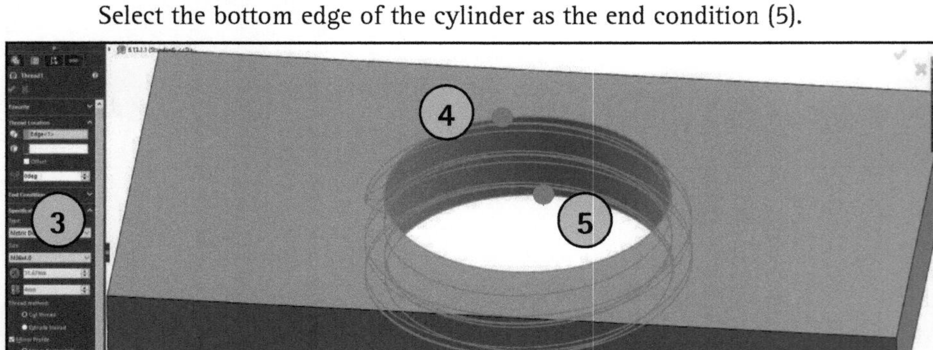

- **Mirror Profile, Mirror horizontally** (6).
- Option **Cut Thread, Red** preview (7).
- Option **Trim with start face** und **Trim with end face** (8).
- **Close dialog box** (9).

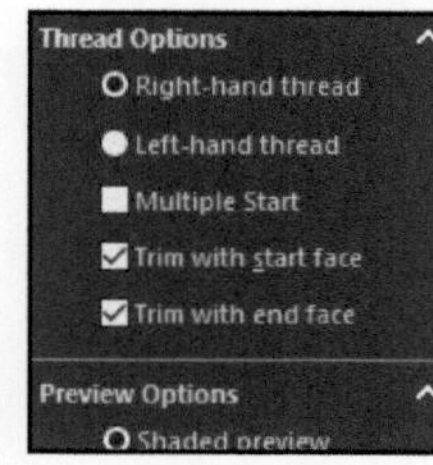

6.13.2.4 Data backup

Save as New / Enter a name of your choice.

Save as New

6.13.3 Form element feature "Thread" with physical thread, using outer diameter

6.13.3.1 Open the working file

Open

Open (Menu bar) / Component from the book-DVD / **OK**.

6.13.3.2 Change the specified bore diameter to the core diameter

Smart Dimension

- Activate the **Sketch** entry under **Extruded Cut**.
- Select **Edit Sketch** in the **PropertyManager**.
- Change the bore-Ø to **36** mm using **SmartDimension** (1).
- **Close dialog box / Finish sketch**

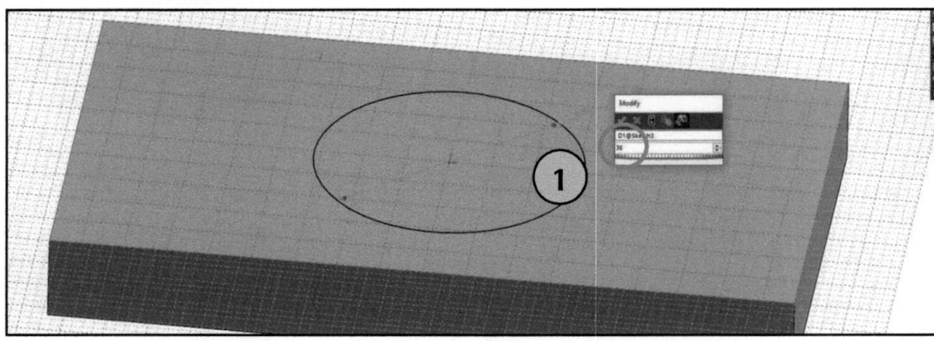

6.13.3.3 Form element feature "Thread", the creation

Thread

Thread (**Features** tab / **Hole wizard**)
Select metric thread size **M36x4** (2).
Select the upper cylinder edge as the thread position (3).
Select the bottom edge of the cylinder as the end condition (4).
Option **Extruded thread, Green** preview (5).
Option **Trim with start face** und **Trim with end face** (6).
Close dialog box.

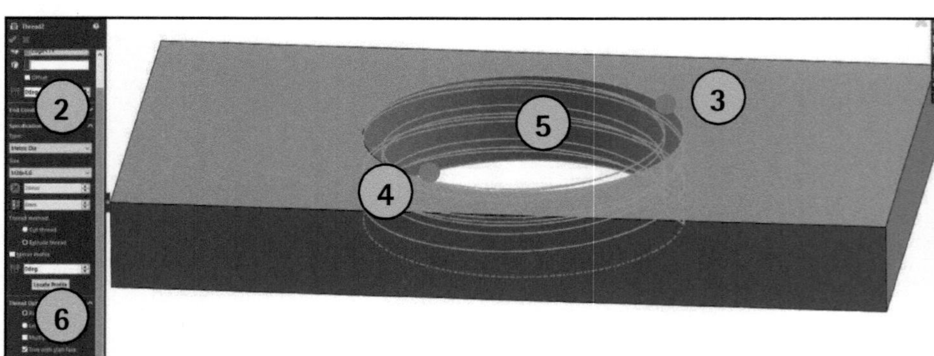

6.13.3.4 Data backup

Save as New

Save as New / Enter a name of your choice.

6.13.4 External thread with physical thread profile, specification

The **Thread** feature allows you to insert a physical thread profile **M30x3,5** using outer diameter.

Thread values for external threads ISO **261**:

Outer-Ø **M30**, pitch **3,5** mm

6.13.5 Form element feature "Stud Wizard" using outer diameter

6.13.5.1 Open the working file

Open (Menu bar) / Component from the book-DVD / **OK**.

Open

6.13.5.2 External thread using "Stud Wizard", the creation

Stud Wizard (**Features** tab)
Select an edge of a cylindrical face to create the stud (1).
Standard: **ISO**, Size **M30** (2).
Select **Up to Next** for End Condition (3).
Set the **UnderCut** option; the values will be applied (4).
Set the Annotations Propertie to **Shaded cosmetic threads** (5).
Close dialog box (6).

Stud Wizard

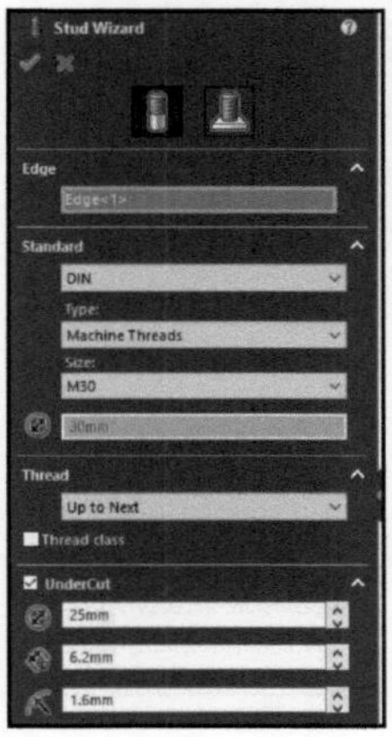

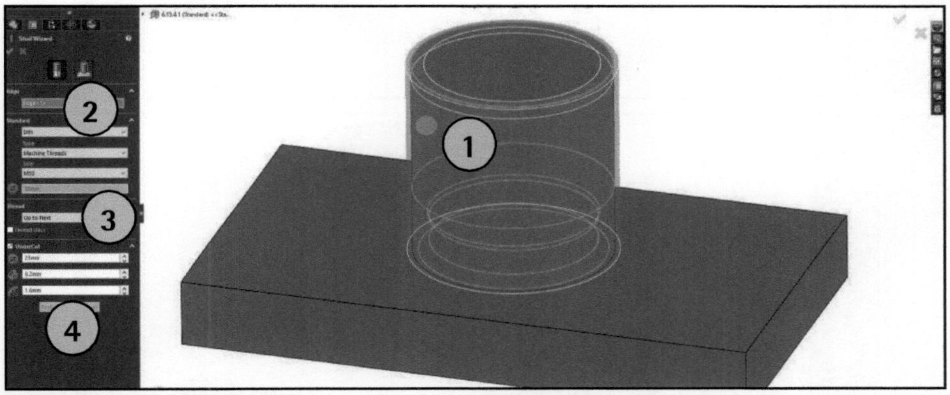

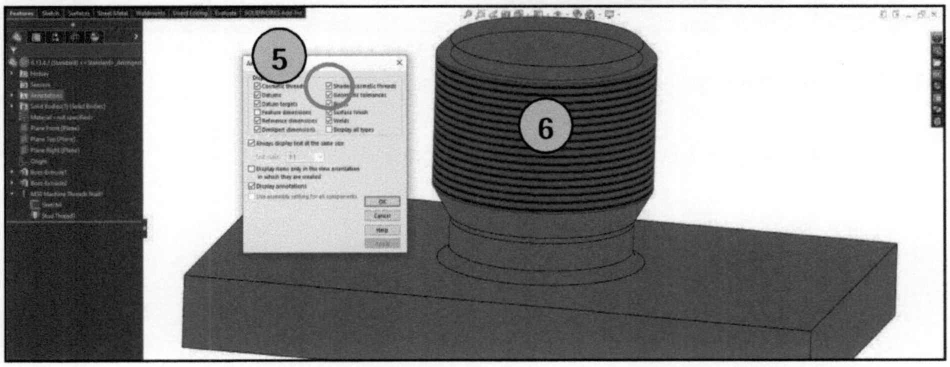

6.13.5.3 Data backup

Save as New / Enter a name of your choice.

Save as New

Thread

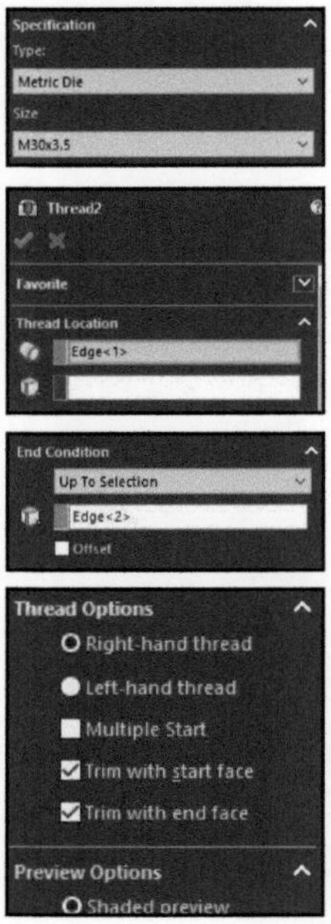

6.13.5.4 Form element feature "Thread", the creation

Thread (Features tab / **Hole wizard)**

Select metric thread size **M30x3.5** (7).

Thread Location:

Select the upper cylinder edge as the thread position (8).

End Condition:

Option Up to Selection, select the bottom edge of the cylinder as the end condition (9).

Option **Cut Thread, Red** preview (10).

Option **Trim with start face** und **Trim with end face** (11).

Close dialog box (12).

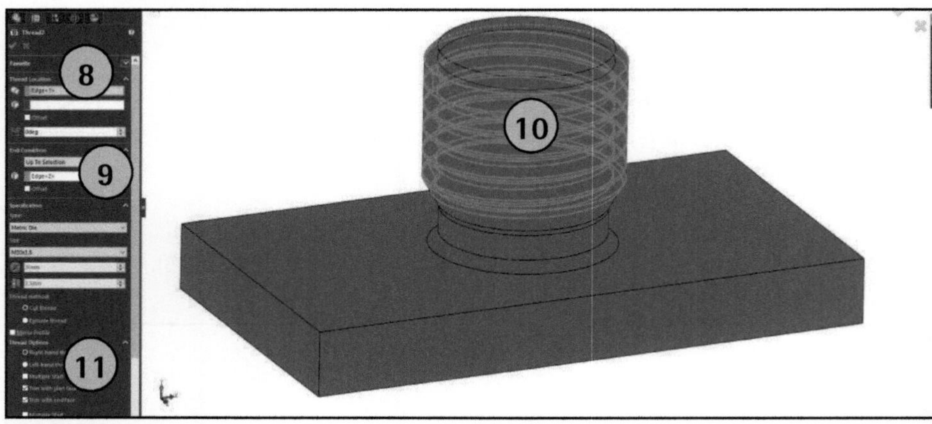

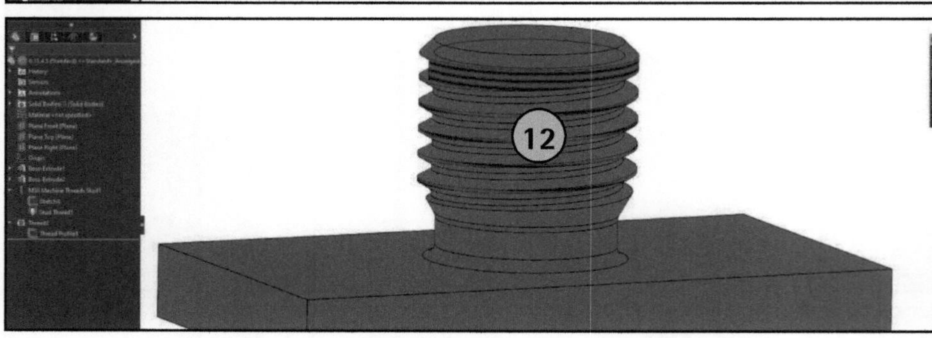

6.13.5.5 Data backup

Save as New

Save as New / Enter a name of your choice.

Project IX

Powerful commands
Optimized constructions
SOLIDWORKS Toolbox

Page 233 to 249

- Basic construction “Gear Shaft”
  Creation using the SOLIDWORKS toolbox
- Basic construction
  “Internally toothed Spur Gear”
  Creation using the SOLIDWORKS toolbox
- Basic construction “Bevel Gear”
  Creation using the SOLIDWORKS toolbox

6.14 Basic construction "Gear Shaft" creation using the SOLIDWORKS toolbox

6.14.1 Basic construction "Gear Shaft", specification

- Straight spur gear from the toolbox with the following specifications:
- Module 3, 23 teeth, tooth width 25 mm, hub type A
- Assign material
- Countersink and through hole
- Add shaft shoulders
- Set keyway
- Chamfer edge
- Omit undercuts, the mounting hole at the shaft end, and the retaining ring recesses.

6.14.1.1 The design sketch for component production

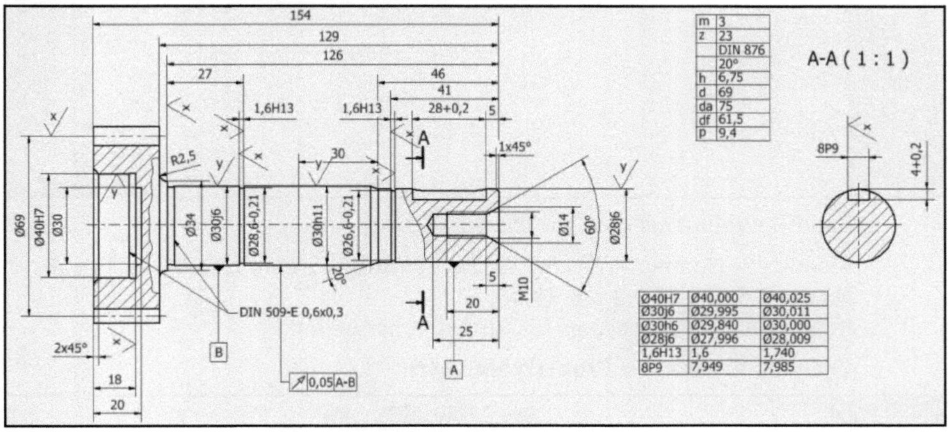

6.14.1.2 Basic construction "Gear Shaft", component representations

New

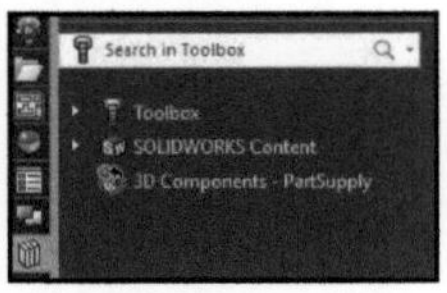

Design Library

Toolbox

DIN

Power Trans-
mission

Gears

Spur Gear

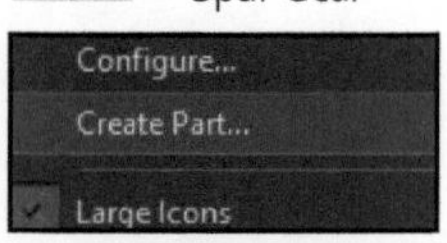

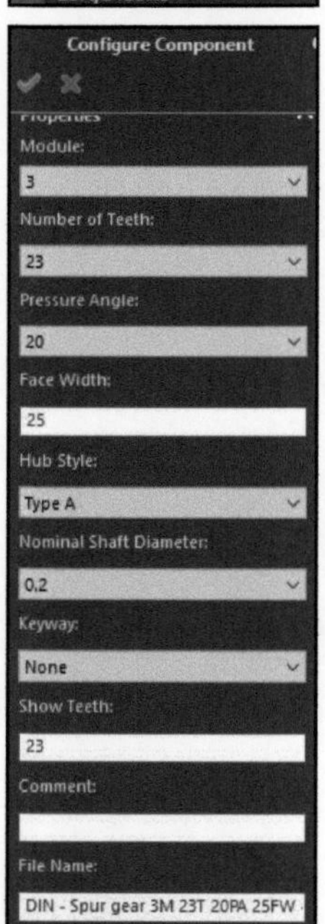

Save as New

6.14.2 Gear creation using the SOLIDWORKS toolbox

6.14.2.1 Opening your own template file

- Menu Bar **New** / / click **Engelke2026.PRTDOT** / **OK**

6.14.2.2 Gear creation

Design Library / **Toolbox** / **DIN** (DIN)
Power Tansmission / **Gear** / **Spur Gear** (1)
Select: **Create Part** (2)

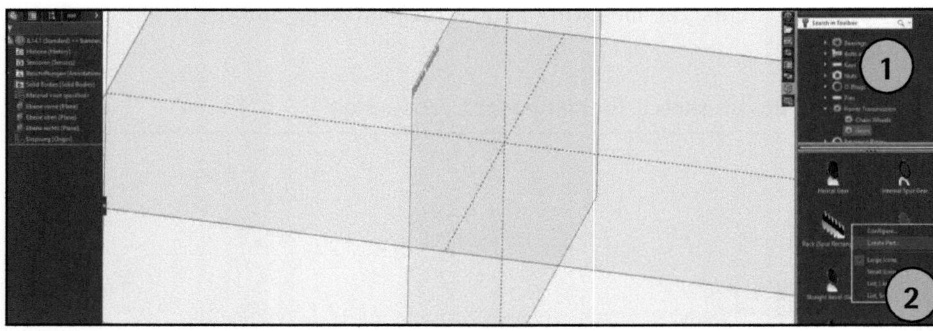

- Enter the following data for the gear definition:
  Module: **3**, Number of Teeth: **23**, Face Width: **25** mm, Hub Style: **Typ A**
  Nominal Shaft-Ø: **0.2** mm (3, 4).
  (It will be used as a center for further construction.)
  Click **OK** to close the **PropertyManager**.

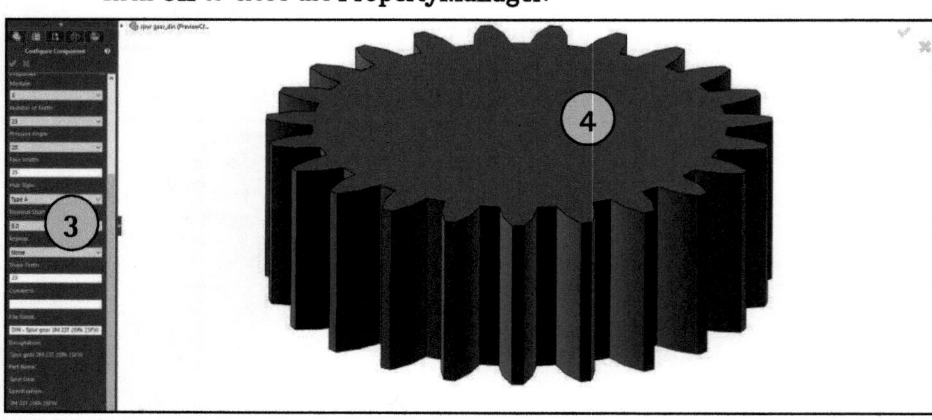

- **Save** the gear created in the background in your own project folder, once with the **Toolbox name** and once with your own name.

6.14.2.3 Assigning component material

Edit Material (FeatureManager)

Right-click on **Material** to display the context menu for **Edit Material**. Select **SOLIDWORKS-DIN-Material / DIN Steel 1.7225 (42CroMo4)** (5).

Click **Apply** and then **Close** (6).

Edit Material

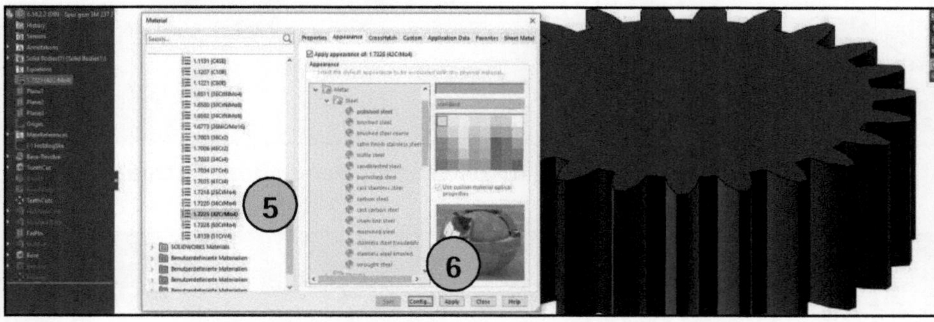

6.14.3 Basic construction "Gear Shaft", editing of the basic geometry

6.14.3.1 Insert cylindrical countersink

Hole Wizard (Features tab)

Hole Wizard

Drill a cylindrical countersink **Ø40** mm, **18** mm deep, through hole **Ø30** mm **20** mm deep at the central point (7, 8).

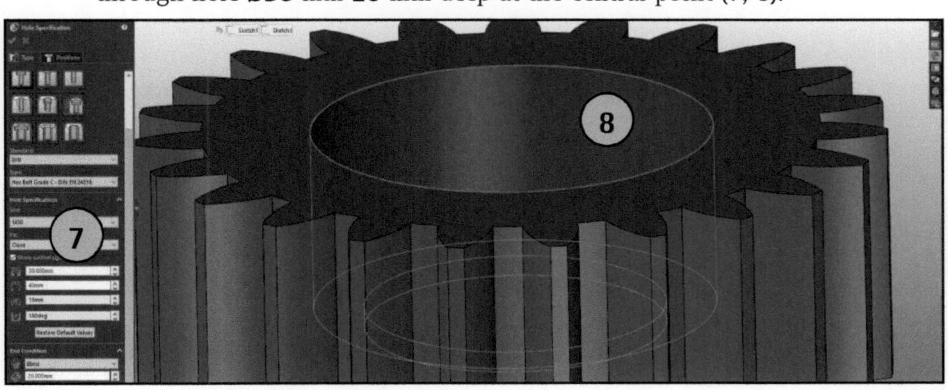

6.14.3.2 Creating drive shaft attachments

- Create a cylinder from a circular sketch using feature **Boss-Extrude** height **3** mm **Ø34** mm (9, 10).

Sketch

Boss-Extrude

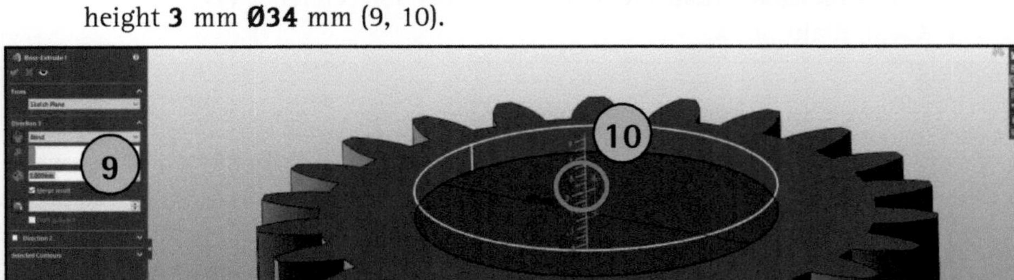

Sketch

Boss-Extrude

- Create a cylinder from a circular sketch using feature **Boss-Extrude** length **80** mm **Ø30** mm (11, 12).

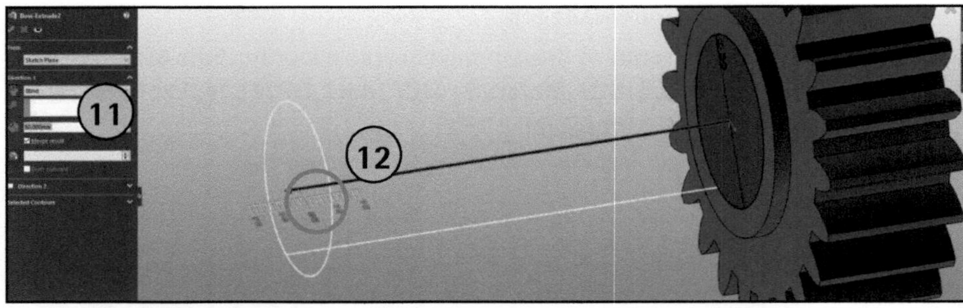

Sketch

Boss-Extrude

- Create a cylinder from a circular sketch using feature **Boss-Extrude** length **46** mm **Ø28** mm (13, 14).

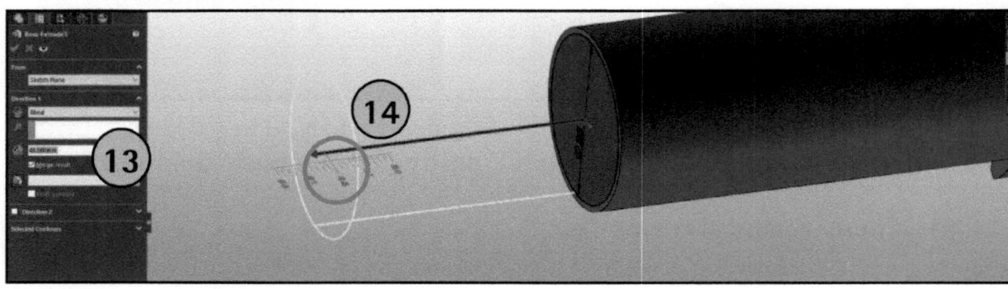

6.14.4 Basic constructions of the shaft element, Keyway slot, the creation

6.14.4.1 Construction point for the working plane

Sketch

- Create a point on the shaft quadrant using Quick Snap **Quadrant Snap** (15).

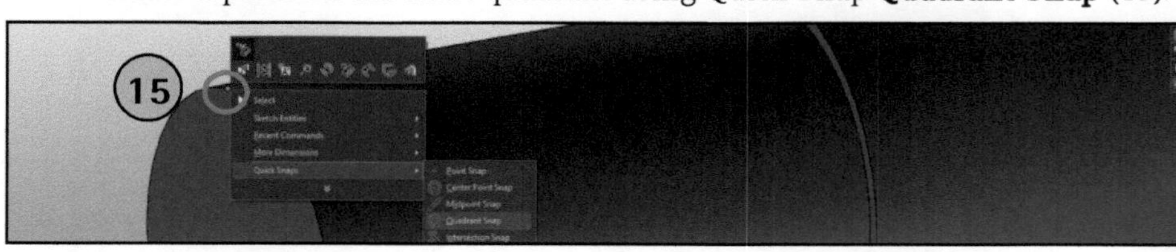

6.14.4.2 Create tangential working plane for the basic sketch of the keyway

Plane

Plane (Reference Geometry toolbar)
Select the **Plane1** plane as the first reference (16).
Select the **shaft quadrant point** as the second reference (17).
Close dialog box.

6.14.4.3 Basic sketch for the keyway slot

- Create the sketch shown on the newly created plane (18).

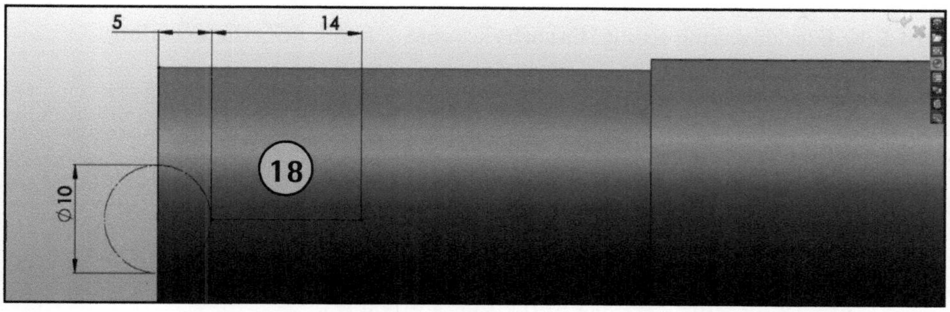

Sketch

Normal To

Line

Circle

6.14.4.4 Keyway slot, the creation

Hole Wizard (**Features** tab)
Type options: **DIN**, **Blind 4** mm, Drill type: **Slot**.
Size **Ø8** mm, Slot length **28** mm.
Show custom sizing, no drill bit **180°** (19).
Select the **Positions / 3D Sketch** tab.
Click the visible plane.
Select the center point shown for the slot (20).
Possible change of position of the keyway slot using the **Tab** key.
Close dialog box (21).

Hole Wizard

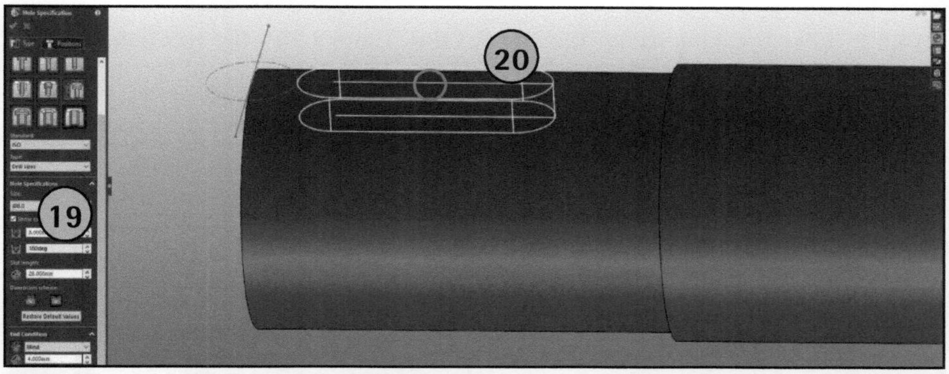

6.14.5 Basic constructions of the shaft element Edge breaking using "Chamfer", the creation

6.14.5.1 Edge breaking using "Chamfer", value 2 mm x 45°, the creation

Camfer

Chamfer (**Features** tab)
Select the **Angle/Distance** option.
Distance: **2** mm, Angle: **45°** (22).
Select **Keep feature** (23).
Enable **Full preview** (23).
Click the edges for the chamfer (24).
Return the other settings to their default values.
Close dialog box.

6.14.5.2 Edge breaking using "Chamfer", value 1 mm x 20°, the creation

Camfer

Chamfer (**Features** tab)
Select the **Angle/Distance** option.
Distance: **1** mm, Angle: **20°** (25).
Select **Keep feature** (26).
Enable **Full preview** (26).
Click the edges for the chamfer (27).
Return the other settings to their default values.
Close dialog box.

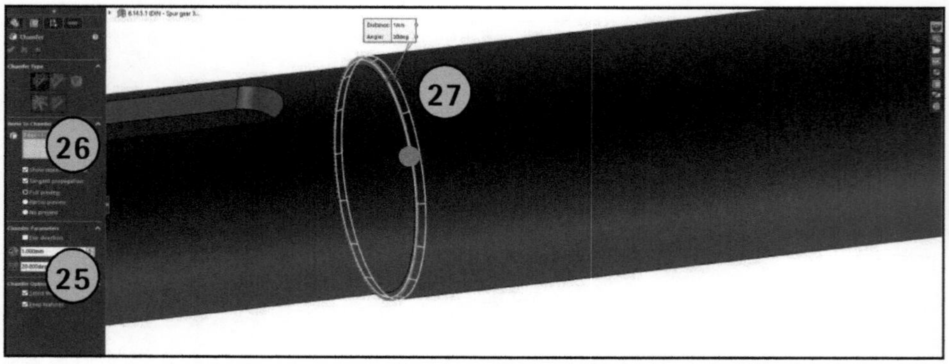

6.14.5.3 Data backup

Save as New

Save as New / Enter a name of your choice.

6.15 Basic construction "Internally toothed Spur Gear" Creation using the SOLIDWORKS toolbox

6.15.1 The design sketch for component production

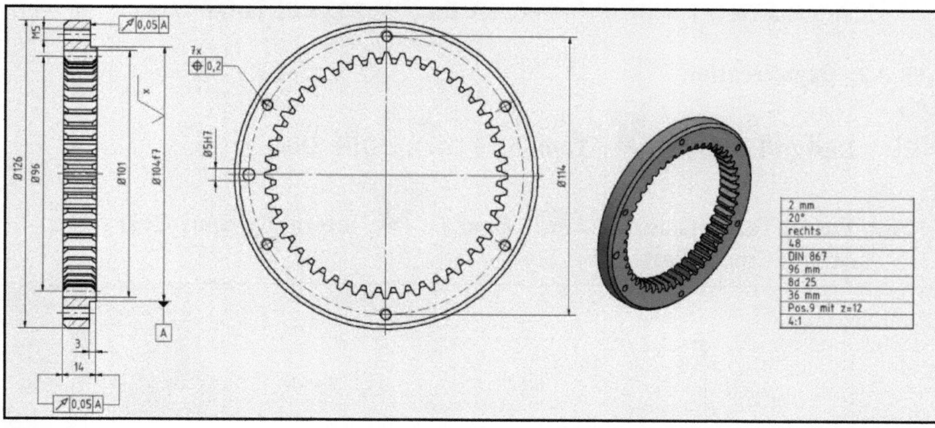

6.15.2 Basic construction "Internally toothed Spur Gear", component representations

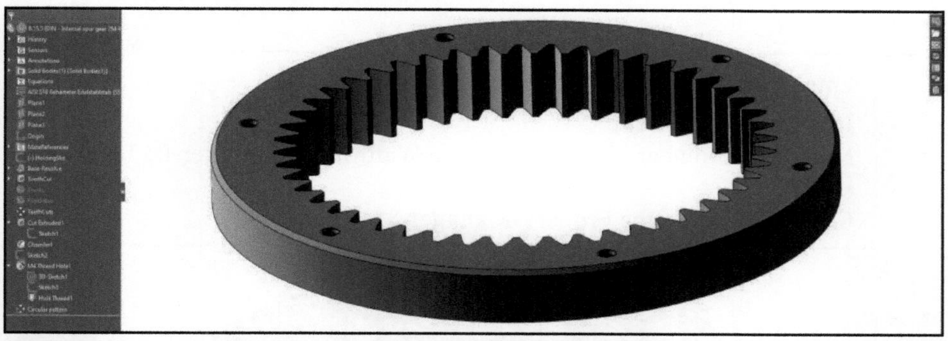

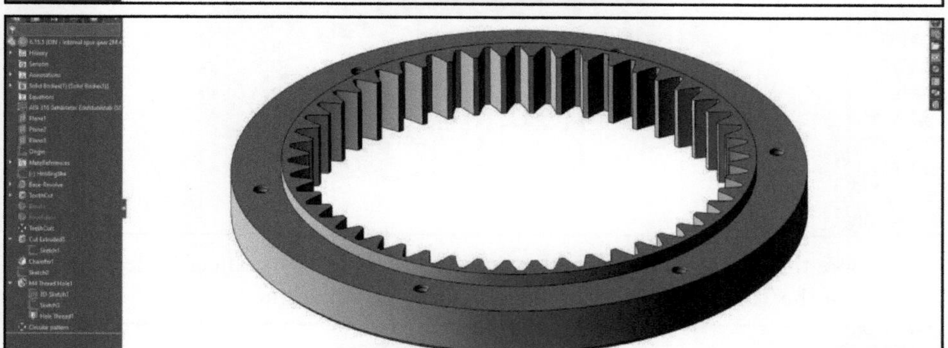

6.15.3 Gear creation using the SOLIDWORKS toolbox

6.15.3.1 Opening your own template file for assemblies

New

- Menu Bar **New** / / click **Engelke2026.PRTDOT** / **OK**

6.15.3.2 Gear creation

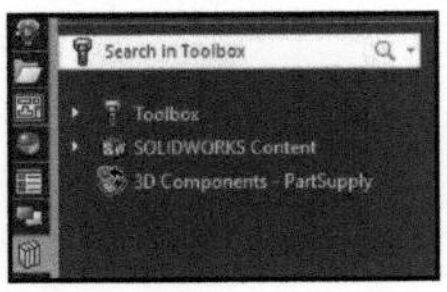

Design Library

Toolbox

DIN

Power Trans-mission

Gears

Internally toothed Spur Gear

Design Library / **Toolbox** / **DIN** (DIN)

Power Tansmission / **Gear** / **Internally Spur Gear** (1)

Select: **Create Part**

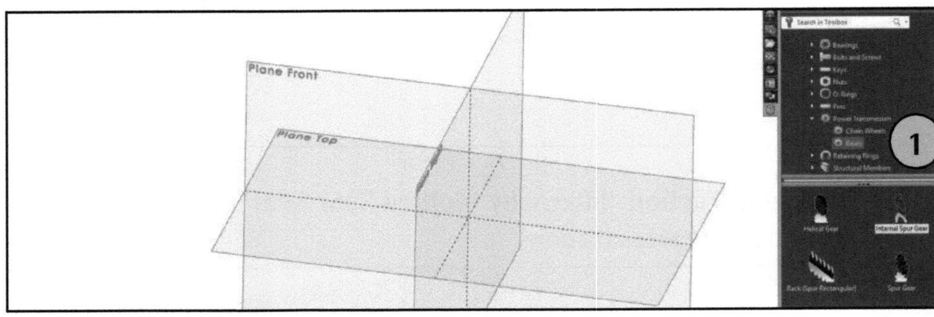

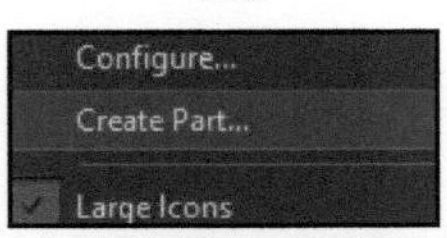

- Enter the following data for the gear definition:

  Internally Spur Gear

  Module: **2**, Number of Teeth: **48**, Face Width: **14** mm, Outer-Ø: **126** mm (2, 3).

  Click **OK** to close the **PropertyManager**.

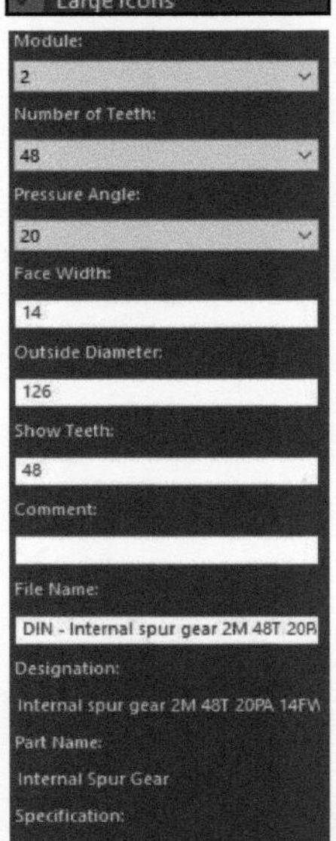

- **Save** the gear created in the background in your own project folder, once with the **Toolbox name** and once with your own name.

Save as New

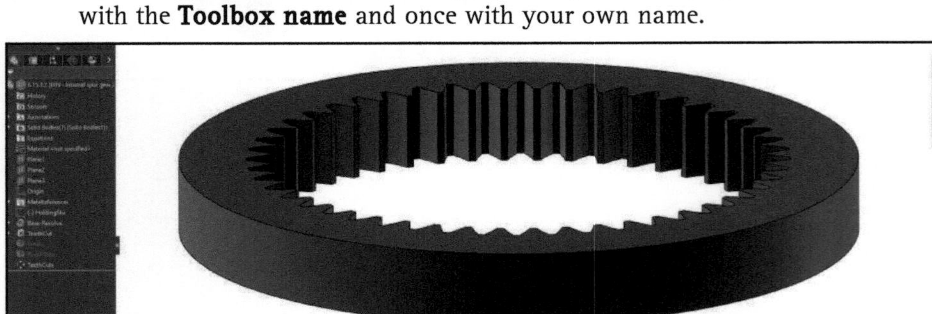

6.15.3.3 Assigning component material

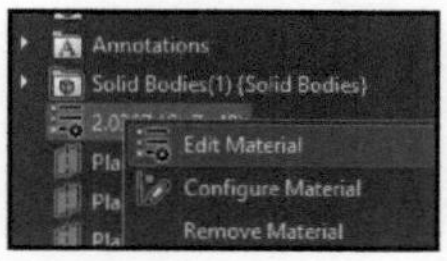

Edit Material

Edit Material (FeatureManager)

Right-click on **Material** to display the context menu for **Edit Material**. Select **SOLIDWORKS-DIN-Material / DIN Steel 1.7225 (42CroMo4)** (4). Click **Apply** and then **Close** (5).

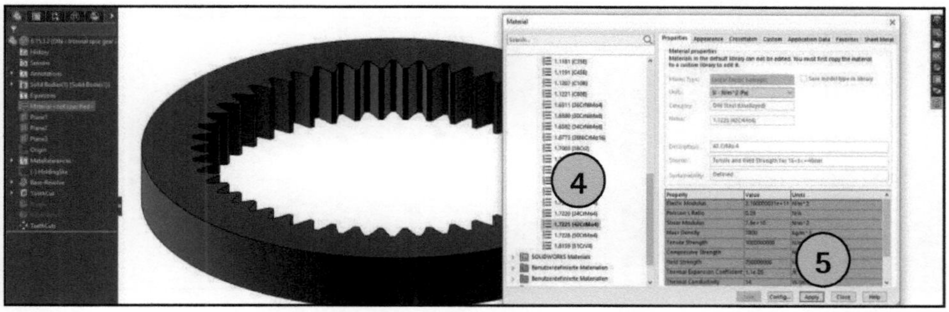

6.15.4 Basic construction "Internally toothed Spur Gear" the outer contour editing

6.15.4.1 Create cut rotation

Sketch

- To create a gear cut rotation, create a sketch construction on the upper gear plane outer-Ø: **126** mm, inner-Ø: **104** mm (2).

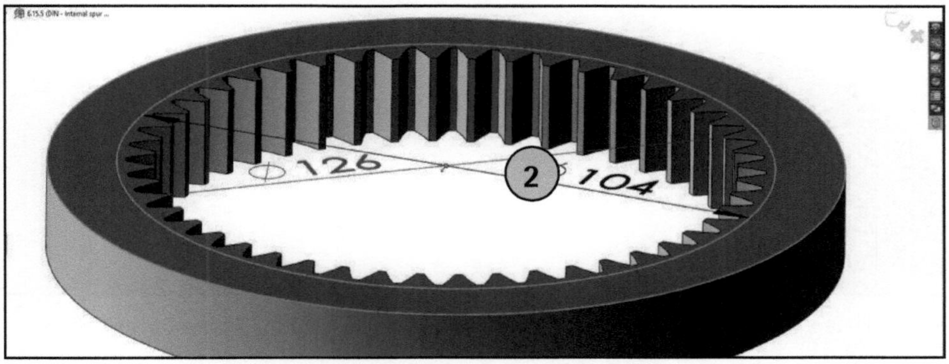

Extruded Cut

- Select the created sketch and use **Extruded Cut** to create the recess, depth **3** mm (3, 4).

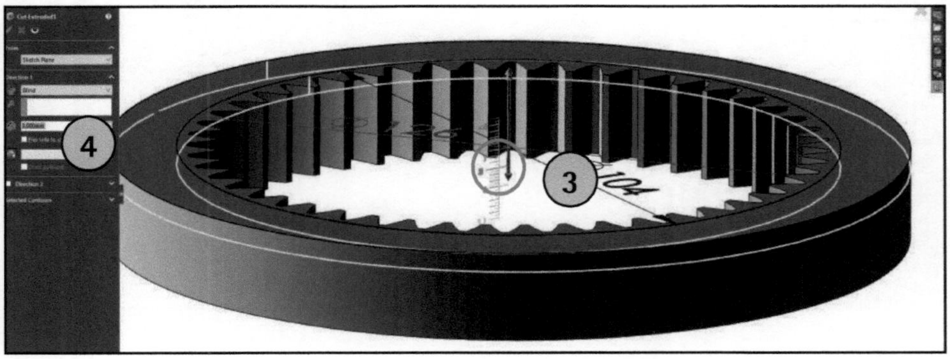

Chamfer

6.15.4.2 Edge breaking using "Chamfer", value 1 mm x 45°, the creation

Chamfer (**Features** tab)
Select the **Angle/Distance** option, distance: **1** mm, Angle: **45°**.
Select **Keep feature**, enable **Full preview** (4).
Click the edges for the chamfer (5).
Close dialog box.

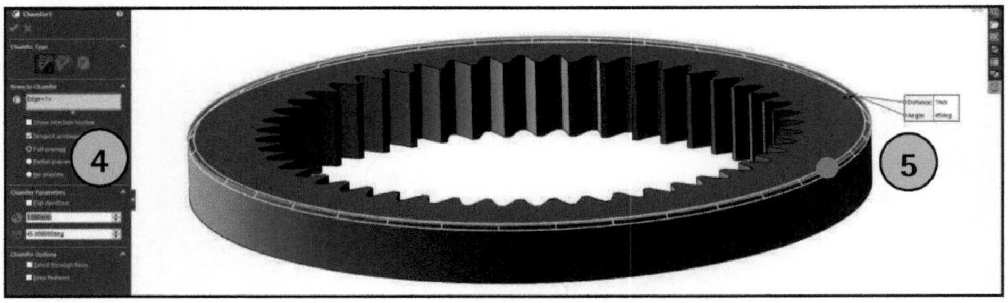

6.15.5 Creating mounting holes

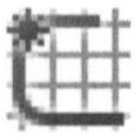

Sketch

6.15.5.1 Creating M4 threaded hole

- Using a new **Sketch**, create a circle of holes with a diameter of **114** mm on the inner ring (6).
- Place a **Point** at the intersection of the axes (7).

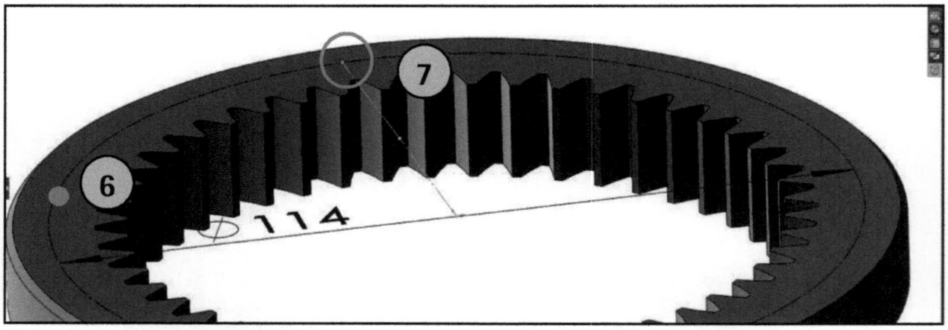

Hole Wizard

- Using the **Hole Wizard**, create an **M4** threaded hole (8) at the point shown (9).

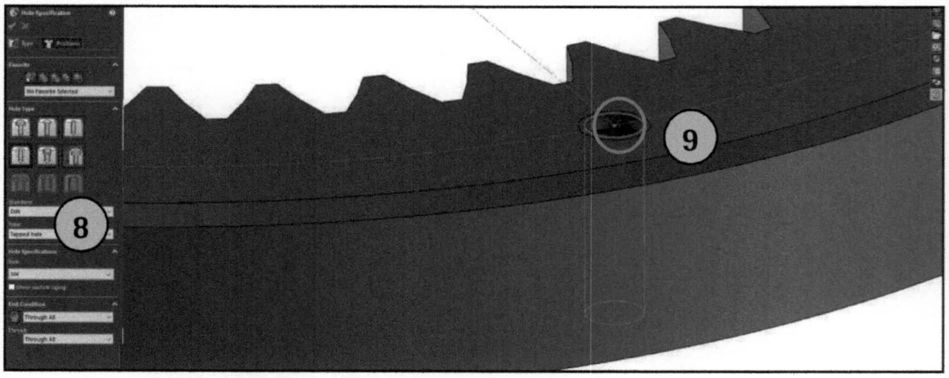

6.15.5.2 Threaded hole M4, creating "Circular Pattern" feature

Circular Pattern

Circular Pattern (**Features** tab)
Pattern-Axis, select the outer cylinder (10).
Number of instances: **6**, total angle **360°** (11)
Select the counterbore as a sample feature (12).
Set the display option to **Full Preview** (13).
Close dialog box.

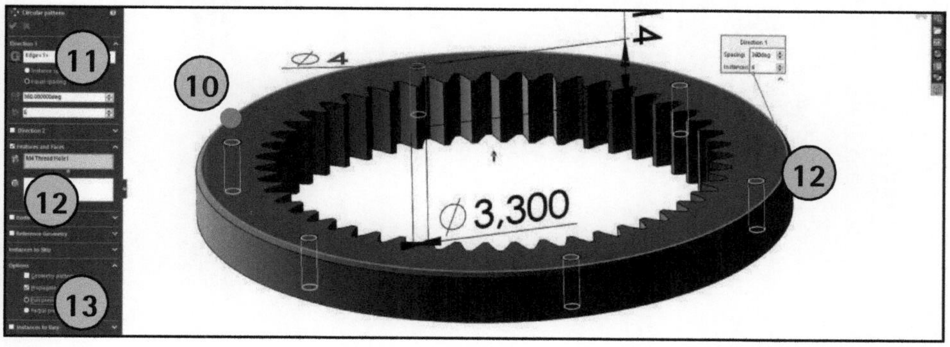

6.15.5.3 Data backup

Save as New

Save as New / Enter a name of your choice.

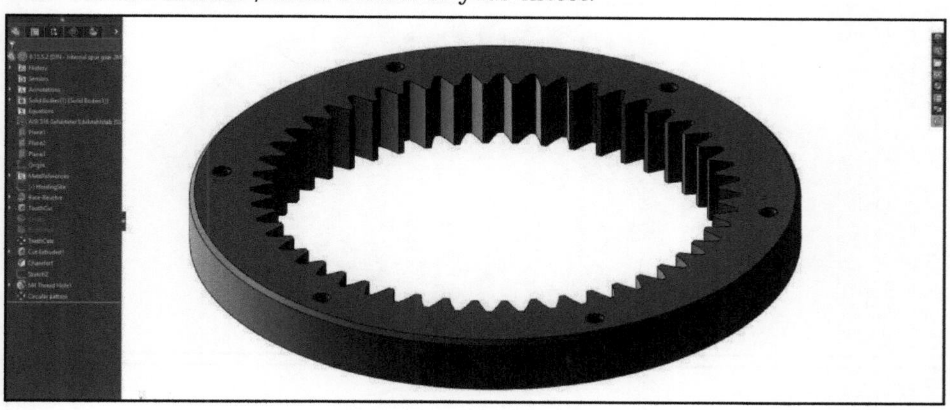

6.16 Basic construction "Bevel Gear" Creation using the SOLIDWORKS toolbox

6.16.1 The design sketch for component production

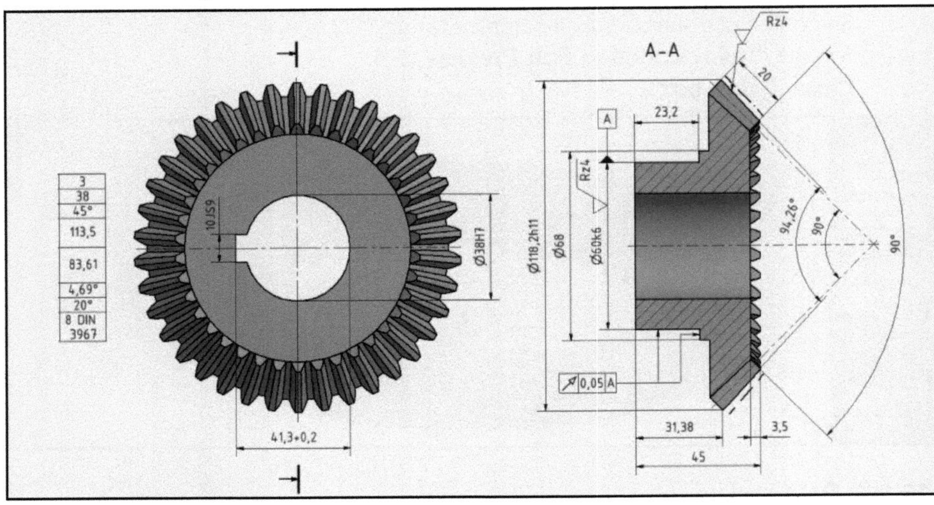

6.16.2 Basic construction "Bevel Gear", component representations

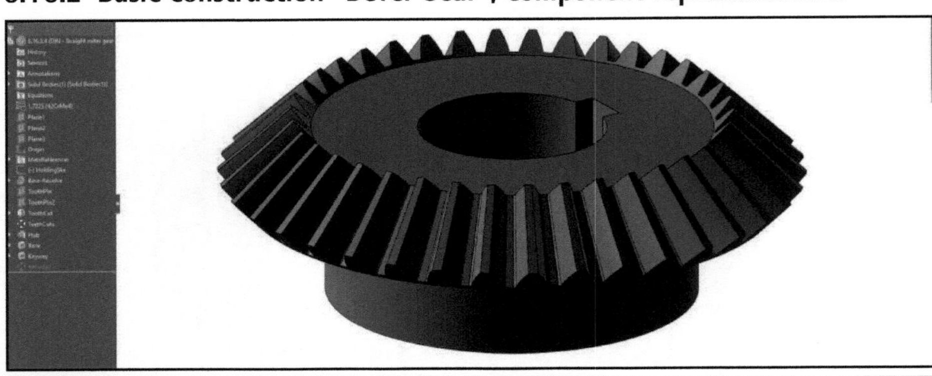

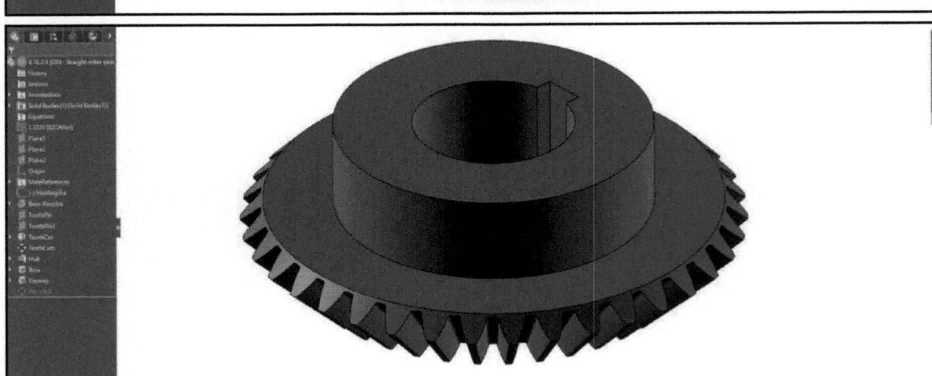

6.16.3 Gear creation using the SOLIDWORKS toolbox

6.16.3.1 Opening your own template file

- Menu Bar **New** / / click **Engelke2026.PRTDOT / OK**

New

6.16.3.2 Gear creation

Design Library / **Toolbox** / **DIN** (DIN)

Power Tansmission / **Gear** / **Bevel Gear**
Select: **Create Part**

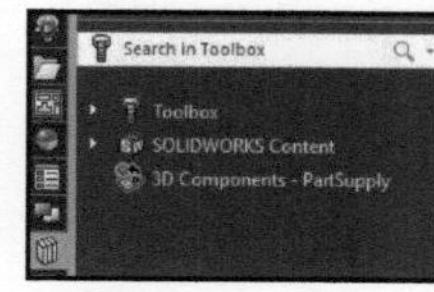

Design Library

Toolbox

DIN

Power Trans-mission

Gears

Bevel gear

6.16.3.3 The "Bevel gear", the creation

- Enter the following data for the gear definition:

  Bevel Gear
  Module: **3**, Number of Teeth: **38**, Face Width: **20** mm,
  Center Distance: **80** mm, Keyed Hub: Rectangular, Shaft Diameter: **38** mm
  (2, 3), click **OK** to close the **PropertyManager**.

- **Save** the gear created in the background in your own project folder, once with the **Toolbox name** and once with your own name.

Save as New

6.16.3.4 Assigning component material

Edit Material (FeatureManager)
Right-click on **Material** to display the context menu for **Edit Material**.
Select **SOLIDWORKS-DIN-Material / DIN Steel 1.7225 (42CroMo4)** (3).
Click **Apply** and then **Close** (5).

Edit Material

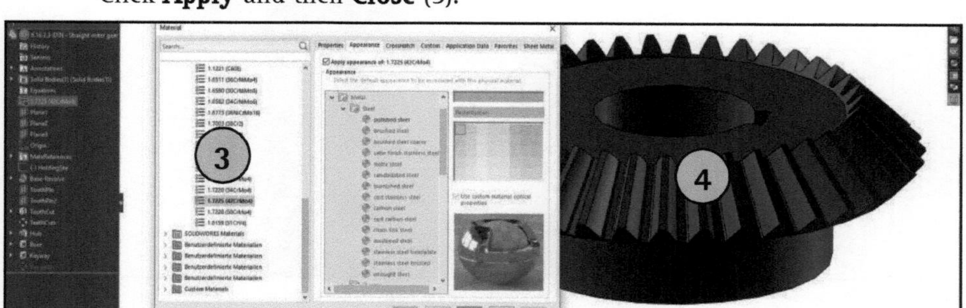

6.16.4 Basic construction "Bevel Gear", the outer contour editing

6.16.4.1 Outer contour editing, length change

Instant 3D

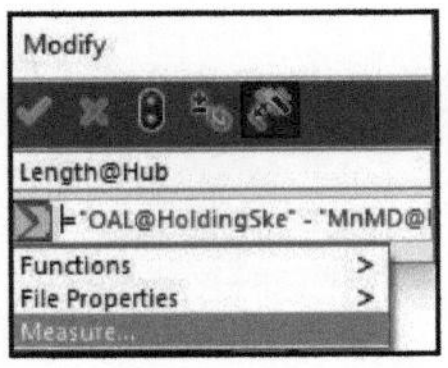

Click **Instant3D** (Features toolbar)
Select the upper gear face (5).
Double-click the height measurement (6).
Activate the **Measure** entry (7).
Delete the contents of the entire entry row (8).

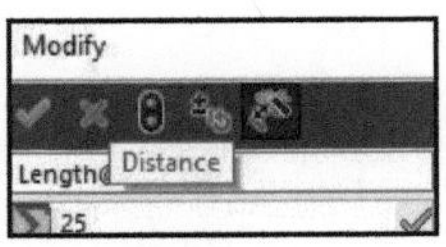

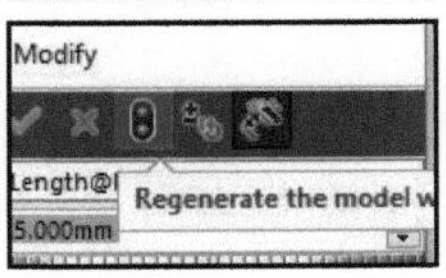

- Enter the new dimension 25 mm (9).
- Renegate the model with the current value (10).
- **Close dialog box**.

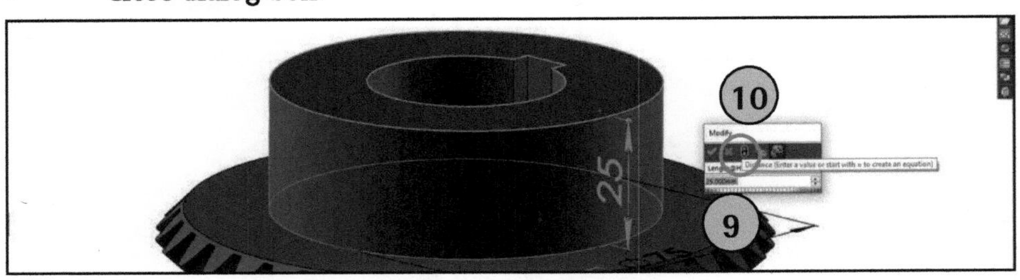

6.16.4.2 Outer contour editing, diameter change of the attachment cylinder

Offset Entities

Offset Entities (**Sketch** tab)
Select options: **Add dimensions**, distance **23.2** mm und **4** mm.
Select the lines of the outer contour.
The lines will be created automatically.

Trim Entities

Trim Entities (**Sketch** tab)
Select the interfering lines.
Close dialog box / Finish sketch (11).

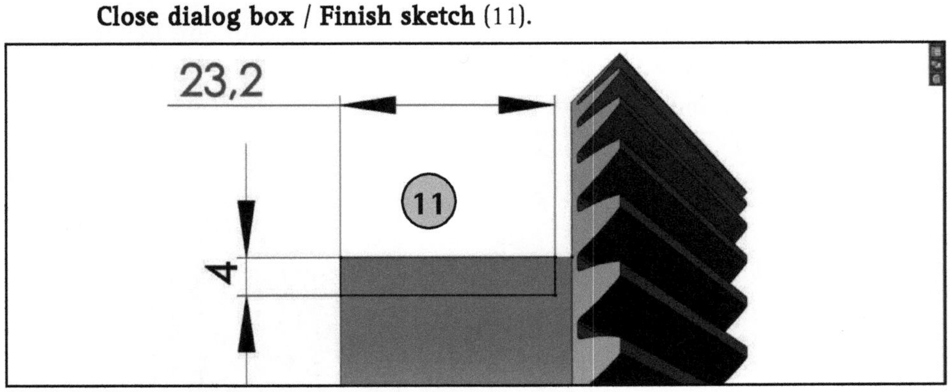

Cut Revolve (Features tab)
Activate the display of axes (12).
Select the created sketch from the **Temporary FeatureManager.**
Select the displayed axis for rotation (13).
Close dialog box (14).

Cut Revolve

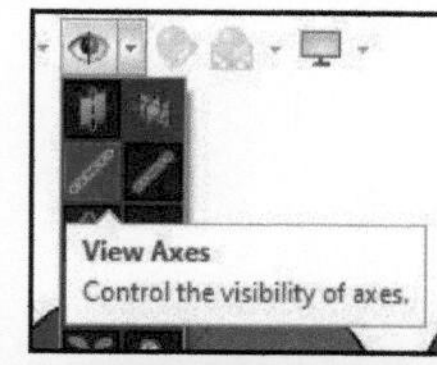

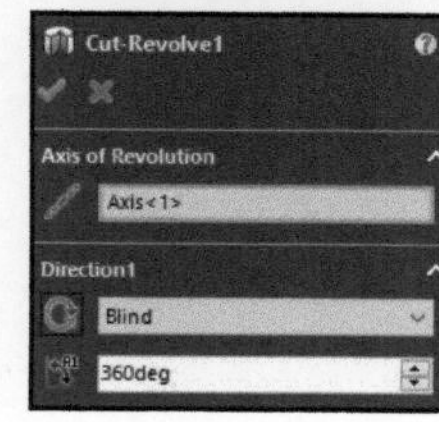

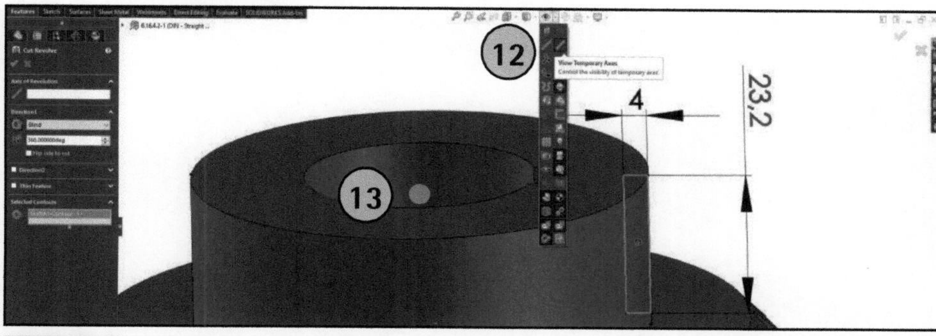

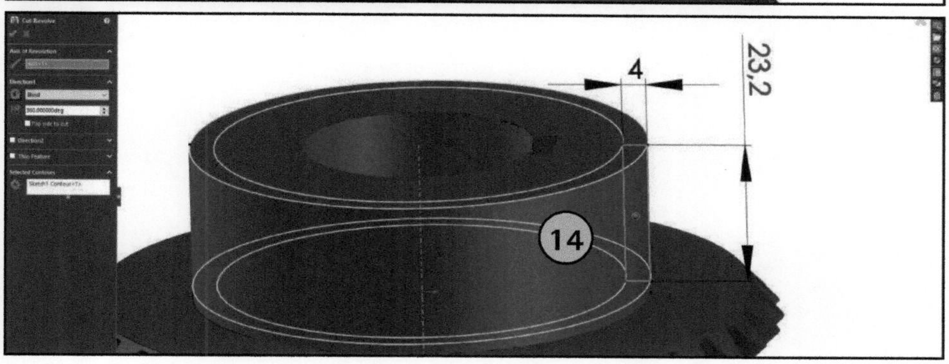

6.16.4.3 Data backup

Save as New / Enter a name of your choice.

Save as New

Project X

Powerful commands
Optimized constructions
Transition bodies
Page 250 to 272

- Basic construction
  "Cone element with draft angle"
  Form element feature "Chamfer", "Draft", "Shell"
- Basic construction
  "Rectangular cone element"
  Form element feature "Planes", Lofted-Boss", "Shell"
- Basic construction "Round to Square"
  Form element feature "Planes", Lofted-Boss", "Shell"
- Basic construction "3D Piping"
  Form element feature "Planes, "3D Sketch", Lofted-Boss"
- Basic construction "Pipe Bend"
  Form element feature "3D Sketch","Lofted-Boss"
- Basic construction "Hollow body"
  Form element feature "Curve Through XYZ Points"

6.17 Basic construction "Cone element with draft angle" Form element feature "Chamfer", "Draft", "Shell"

6.17.1 The basic geometry, specifications

- Chamfer the vertical edges by **20** mm at a **45°** angle.
- Add a **20°** upward draft angle.
- Create a hollow body with a wall thickness of **5** mm.

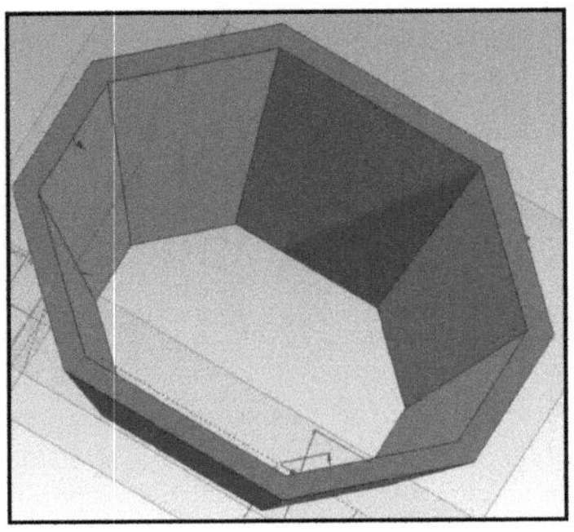

6.17.2 Open the working file and make adjustments

6.17.2.1 Open the working file

 Open

Open (Menu bar) (1) / Component from the book-DVD / **OK**)

6.17.2.2 Edge breaking of the base body, the creation

 Chamfer

Chamfer (**Features** tab)

Distance **20** mm, angle **45°** (2)

Select the shown edges of the cuboid (3).

Activate **Full preview** (4).

Close dialog box.

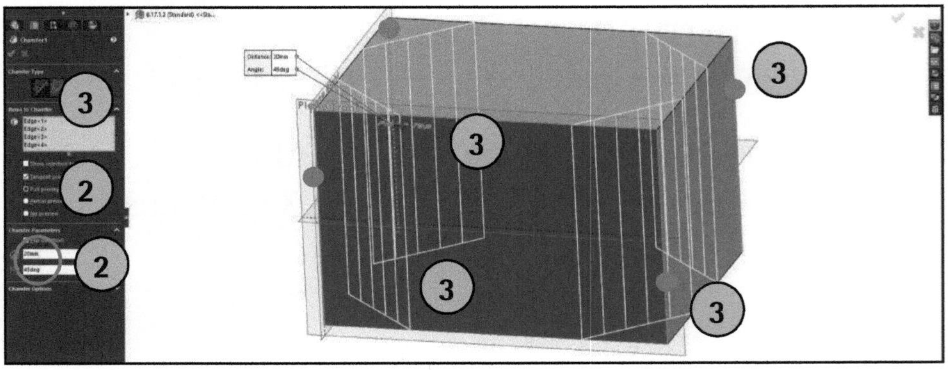

6.17.3 Draft angle for the basic body, the creation

Draft (**Features** tab)
In the **PropertyManager**, click **Manual**.
In the **PropertyManager**, under **Type of Draft**, select **Neutral plane** (4).
Enter **20°** under **Draft Angle** (5).
Select the bottom face as the neutral plane (6).

Select all faces of the cube for the draft angle surfaces. (7).
Activate **Show preview** (8).
Close dialog box (9).

Draft

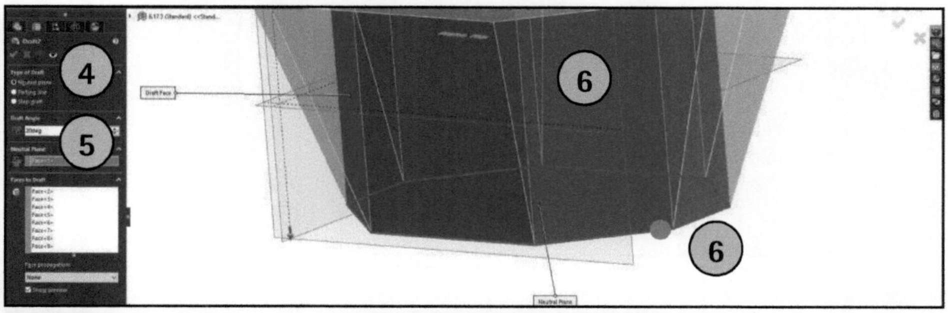

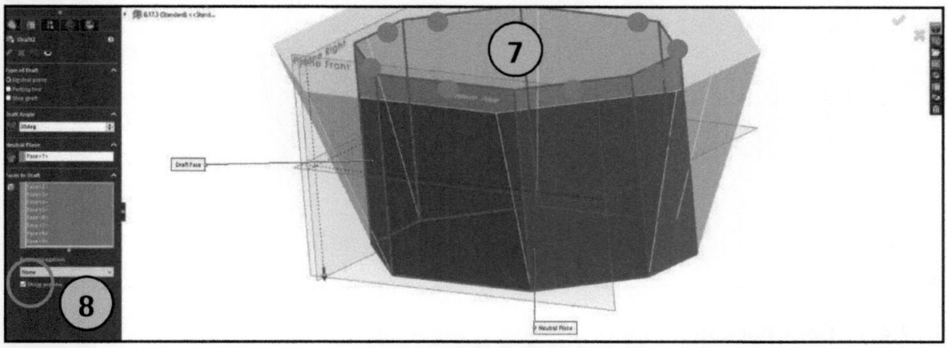

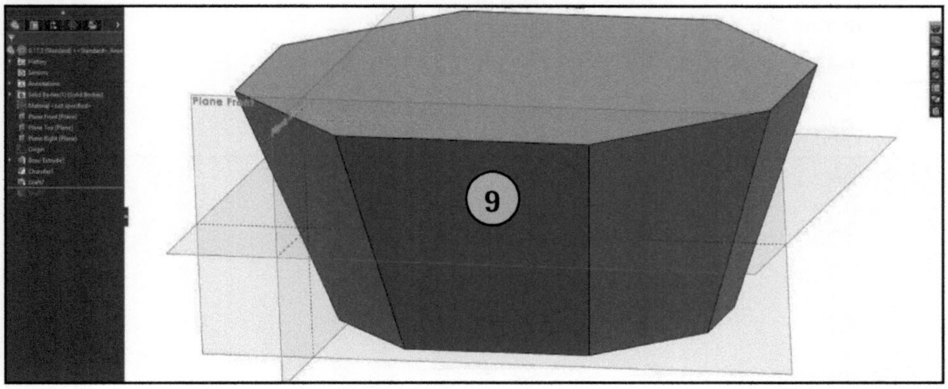

Shell

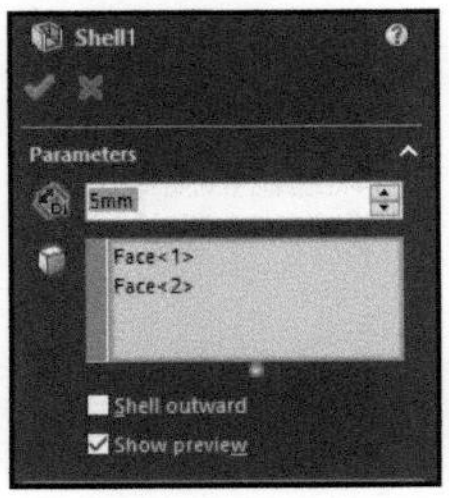

6.17.4 Creating a cone element, using "Shell"

Shell (**Features** tab)
Set the **Thickness** to **5** mm (10).
Option **Faces to Remove**.
Select the base and top surfaces in the graphics area (11, 12).
Set otion **Show preview** (13).
Close dialog box.

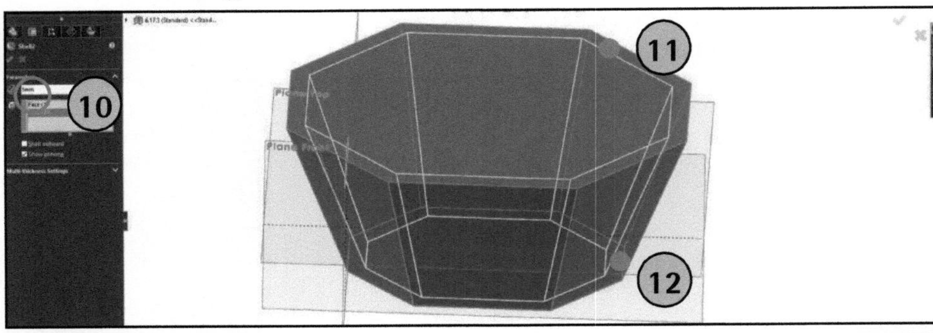

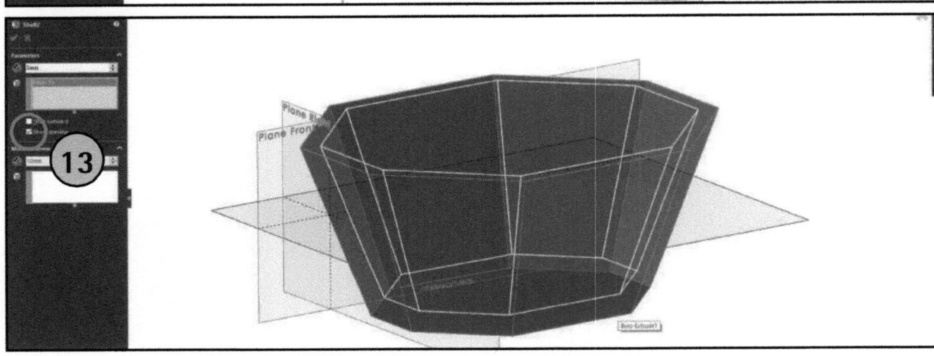

6.17.4.1 Data backup

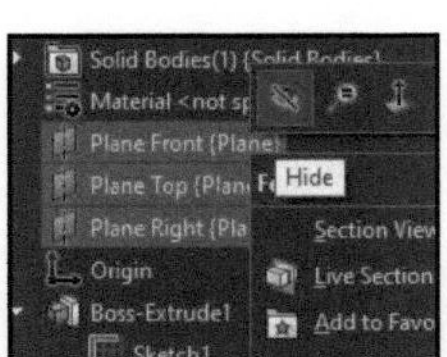

Save as New

- Disable the display for dimension entries.
- Disable the display for reference planes.

Save as New / Enter a name of your choice.

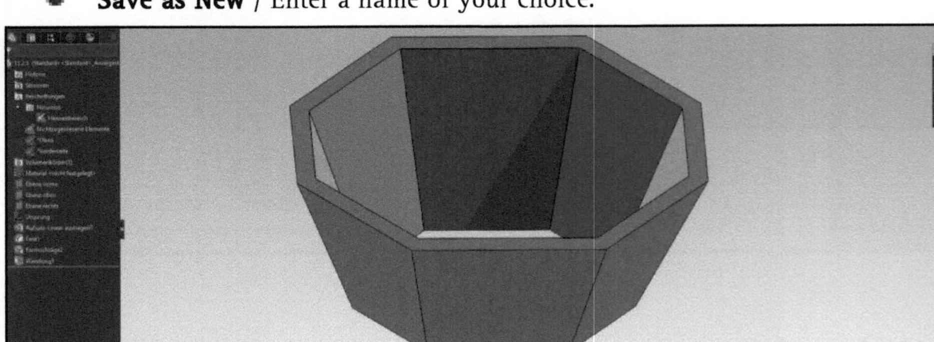

6.18 Basic construction "Rectangular cone element" Form element feature "Planes", Lofted-Boss", "Shell"

6.18.1 The basic geometry, specifications

- Create a rectangle above the center on the top plane, dimensions optional.
- Create a rectangle centered on another parallel plane, **80** mm away, offset by **90°**.
- Adding wall thickness to create a hollow body.

6.18.2 Creating the basic sketch

6.18.2.1 Opening your own template file

- Menu Bar **New** /  /  click **Engelke2026.PRTDOT / OK**

New

Engelke2026.
PRTDOT

6.18.2.2 Basic sketch, the creation

Sketch (**Sketch** tab)
Create a new sketch.

- On the work plane **Top**, construct a **Center rectangle** at the top, dimensions optional (1).

Sketch

Center
Rectangle

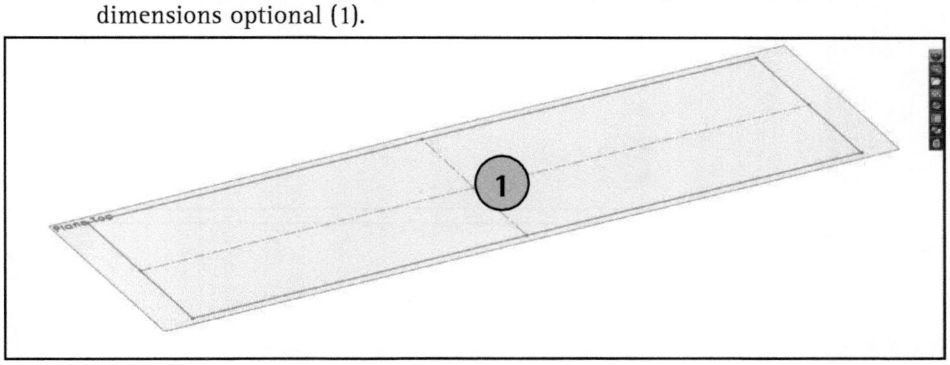

6.18.2.3 Additional work plane above

- Create an additional work plane above the base **Top Plane**, offset distance **80** mm (2, 3).

Plane

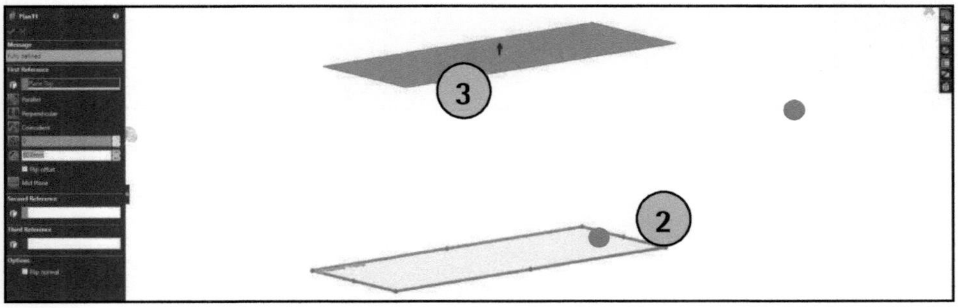

Center Rectangle

6.18.2.4 Final sketch, the creation

- On the new work plane 1, construct a **Center Rectangle**, offset by **90°**, dimensions optional.

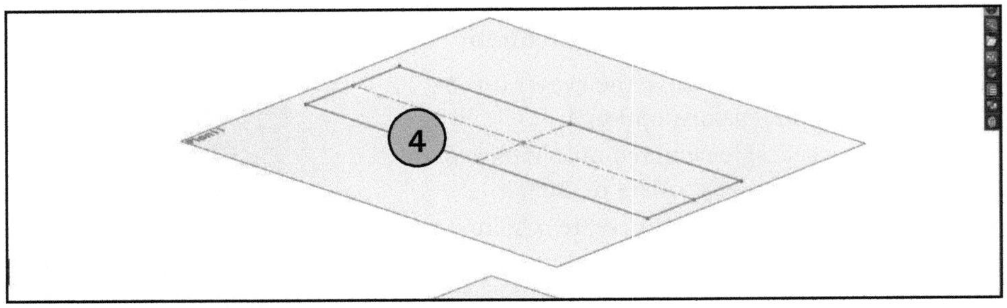

6.18.3 The transitional body

6.18.3.1 The transitional body, using "Lofted Boss", the creation

Lofted Boss

Lofted Boss (Registerkarte **Features**)
Select **Sketch1** and **Sketch2** in the **temporary FeatureManager** (5, 6).
The position of the corners should be accepted (7).
Close dialog box (8).

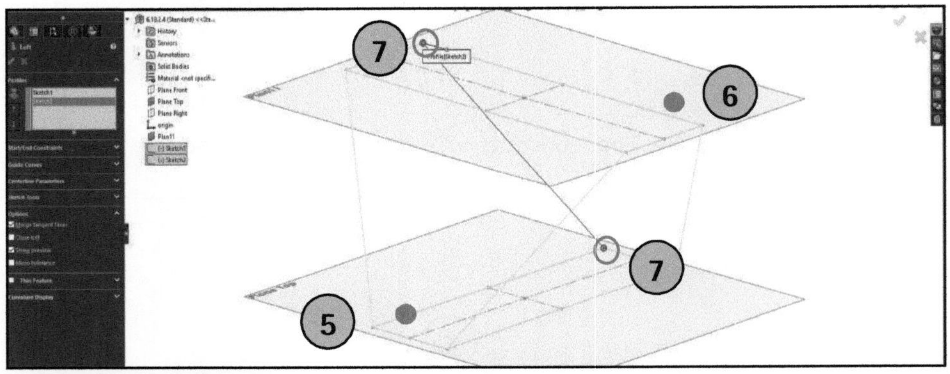

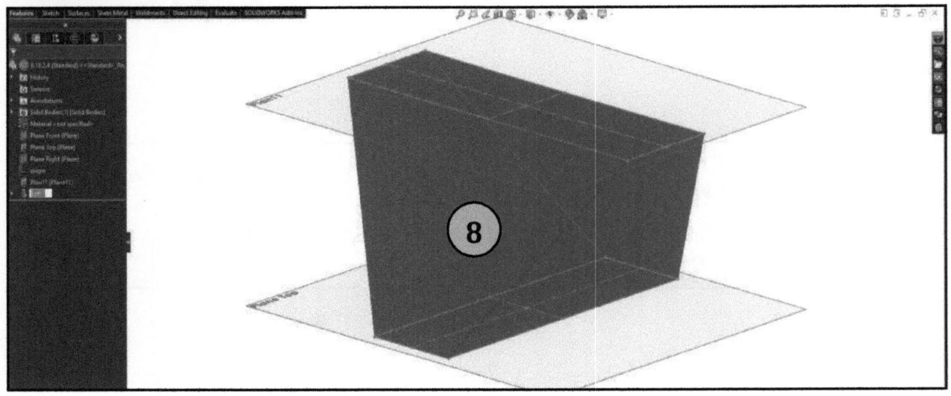

6.18.3.2 Creation of the hollow body, using "Shell"

- Disable the display for dimension entries.
- Disable the display for reference planes.

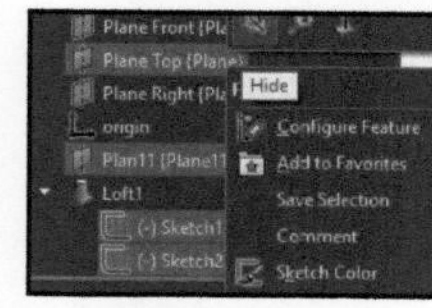

Shell (Features tab)
Set the **Thickness** to **2** mm (9).
Option **Faces to Remove**.
Select the base and top surfaces in the graphics area (10, 11).
Set otion **Show preview** (12).
Close dialog box.

Shell

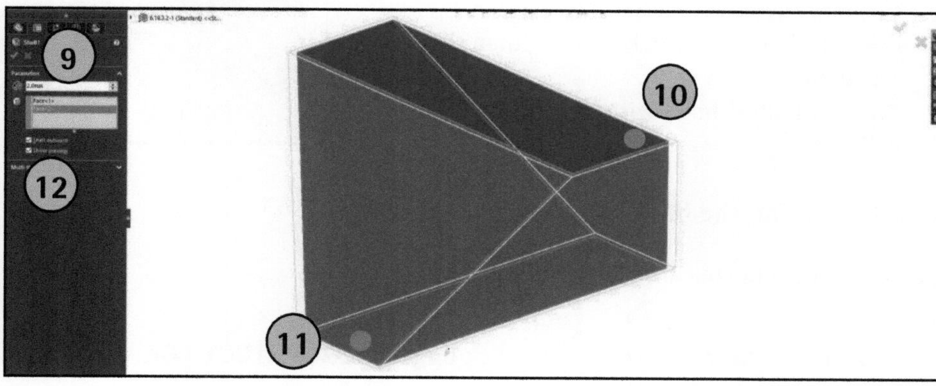

6.18.3.3 Data backup

Save as New / Enter a name of your choice.

Save as New

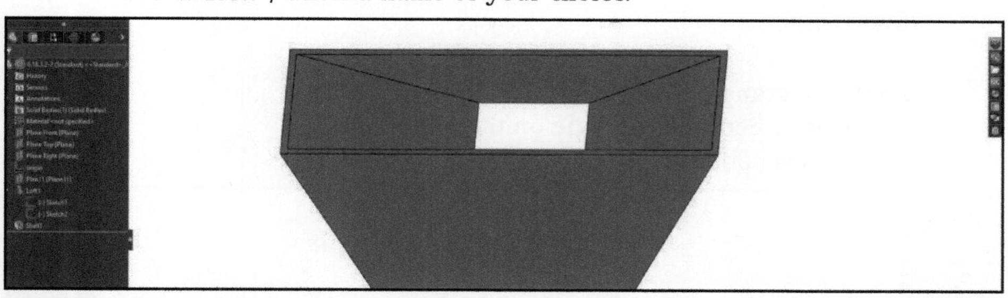

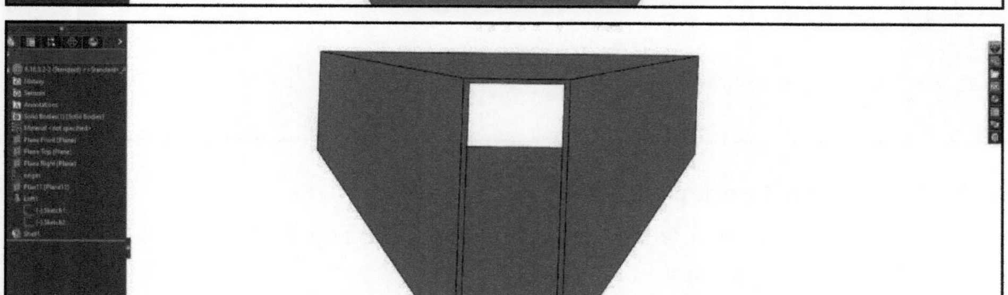

6.19 Basic construction "Round to Square" Form element feature "Planes", Lofted-Boss", "Shell"

6.19.1 The basic geometry, specifications

- Create a rectangle on the top plane dimensions optional.
- Create a circle on another upper parallel plane, dimensions optional, but larger than the rectangle.
- Create a circle on another lower parallel plane, dimensions optionally, but larger than the rectangle.
- Create a hollow body with a wall thickness of **5** mm.

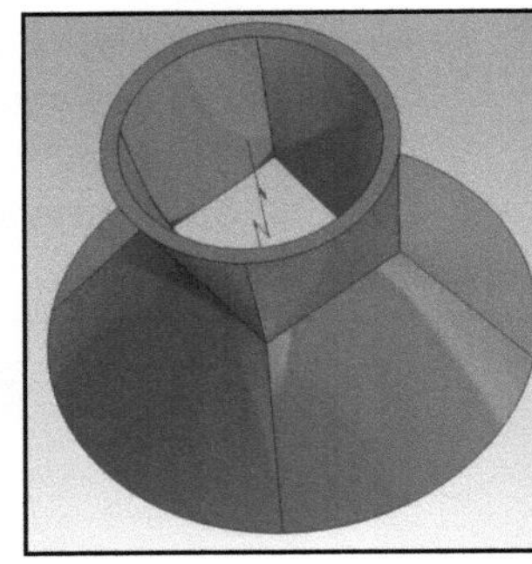

6.19.2 Creating the basic body

New

Engelke2026.
PRTDOT

6.19.2.1 Opening your own template file

- Menu Bar **New** /  /  click **Engelke2026.PRTDOT** / **OK**

Sketch

Center
Rectangle

6.19.2.2 Basic sketch, the creation

Sketch (**Sketch** tab)
Create a new sketch.

Center Rectangle (**Sketch** tab)
Construct a **Center Rectangle** on the **Top Plane**, dimensions optional (1).

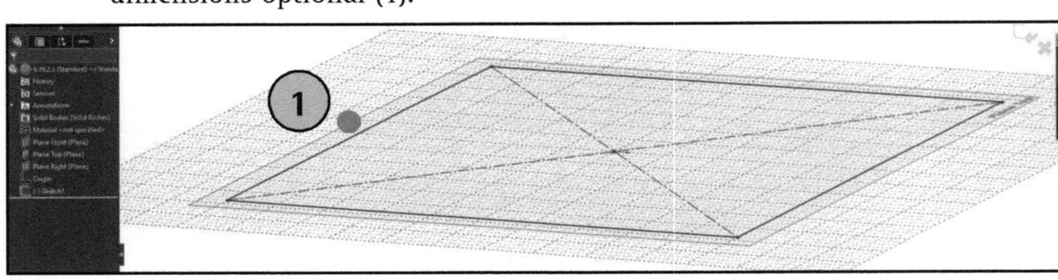

Plane

6.19.2.3 Additional work plane above

- Create an additional work plane above the base **Top Plane**, offset distance **60** mm (2, 3).

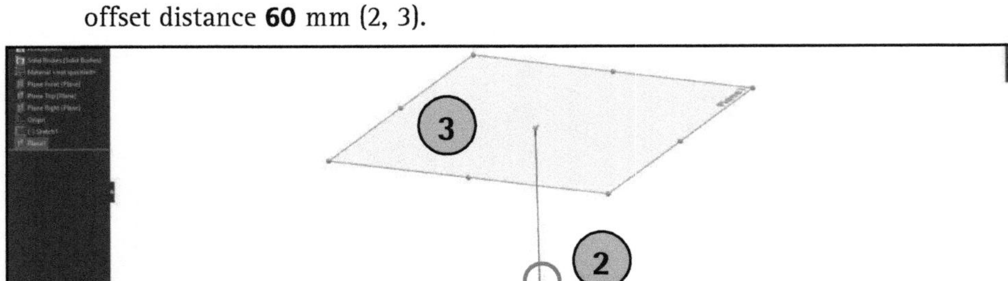

6.19.2.4 Additional sketch, "Circle" on the upper work "Plane1"

Circle

- On **Work Plane1**, construct a **Circle** on the central point, larger than the base rectangle (4, 5).

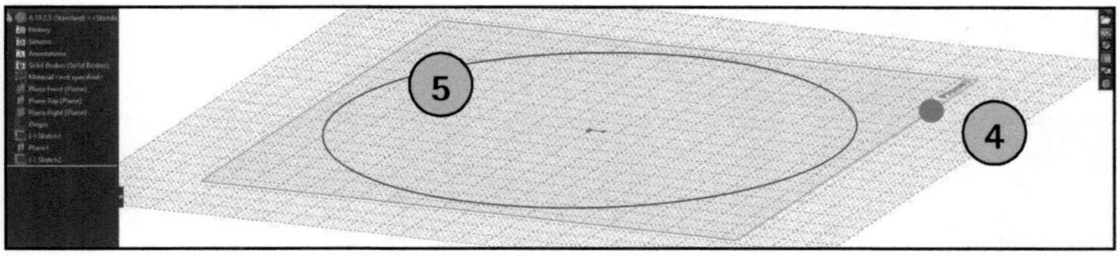

6.19.2.5 Additional work plane below

Plane

- Create an additional work plane below the base **Top Plane**, offset distance **60** mm (6, 7).

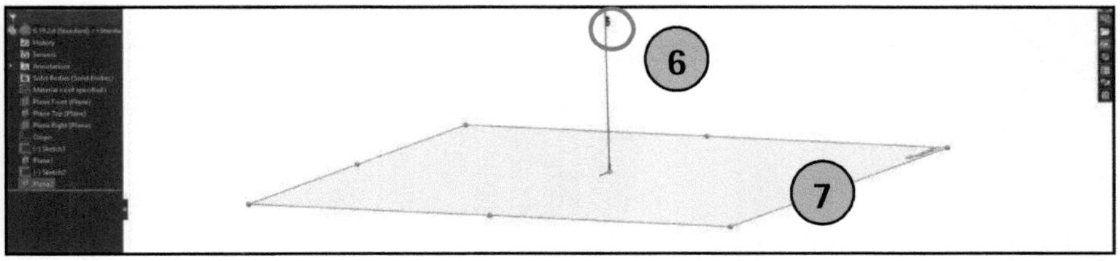

6.19.2.6 Additional sketch, "Circle" on the lower working "Plane2"

Circle

- On **Work Plane2**, construct a **Circle** on the central point, larger than the base rectangle (8, 9).

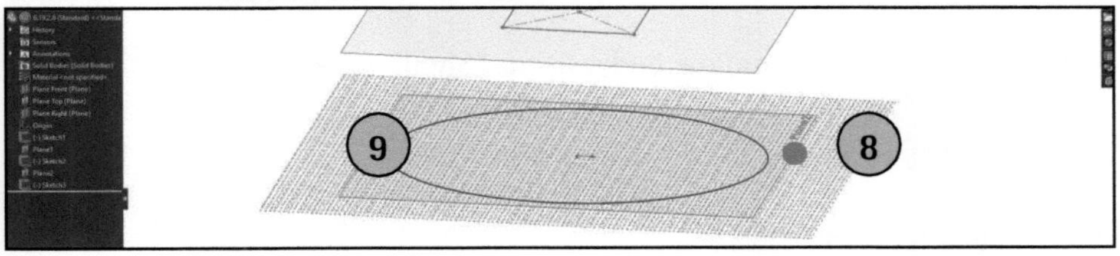

6.19.3 Basic construction "Round to Square", the creation

6.19.3.1 The upper basic body

Lofted Boss

Lofted Boss (**Features** tab)
Select **Sketch1** and **Sketch2** in the **temporary FeatureManager** (10).
The position of the corners should be accepted (11).
Close dialog box.

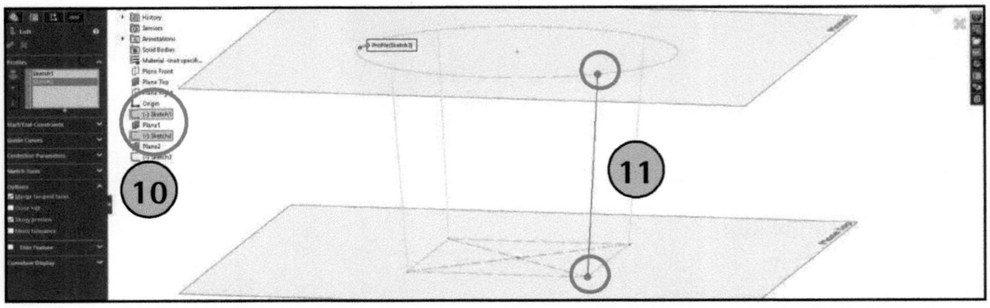

Lofted Boss

6.19.3.2 The lower basic body

Lofted Boss (Features tab)
Select **Sketch1** and **Sketch3** in the **temporary FeatureManager** (12).
The position of the corners should be accepted (13).
Close dialog box (14).

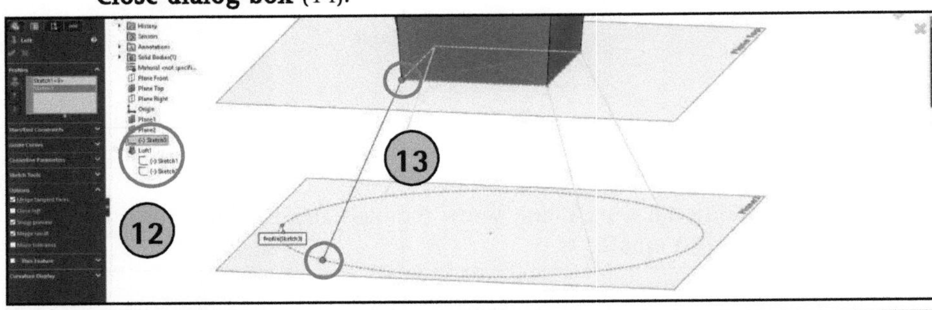

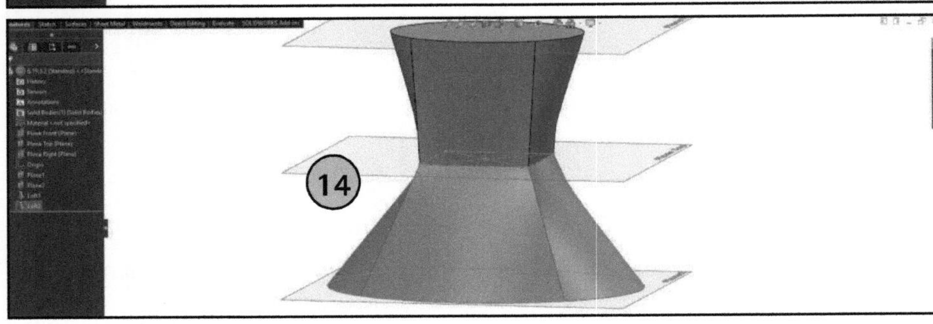

6.19.4 Creation of the hollow body, using "Shell"

- Disable the display for dimension entries.
- Disable the display for reference planes.

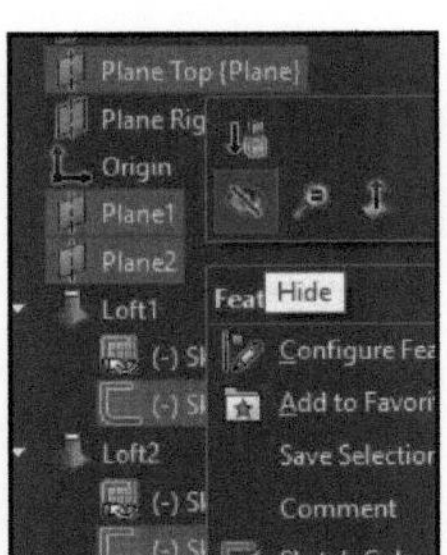

Shell

Shell (Features tab)
Set the **Thickness** to **0.5** mm (15).
Option **Faces to Remove.**
Select the base and top surfaces in the graphics area (16, 17).
Set otion **Show preview** (18).
Close dialog box.

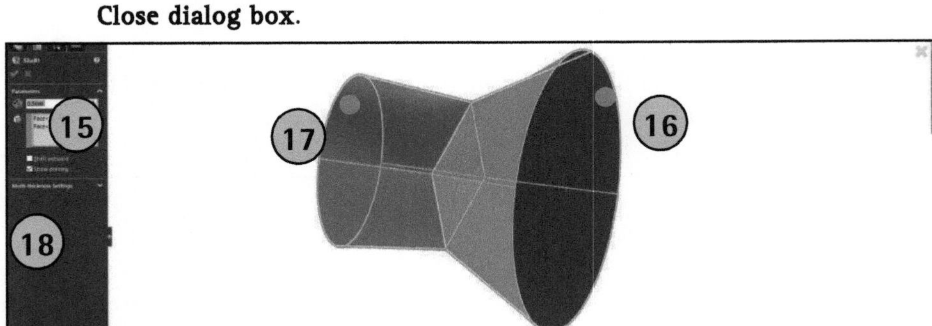

6.19.4.1 Data backup

Save as New

Save as New / Enter a name of your choice.

6.20 Basic construction "3D Piping"
Form element feature "Planes, "3D Sketch", Lofted-Boss"

6.20.1 The basic geometry, specifications

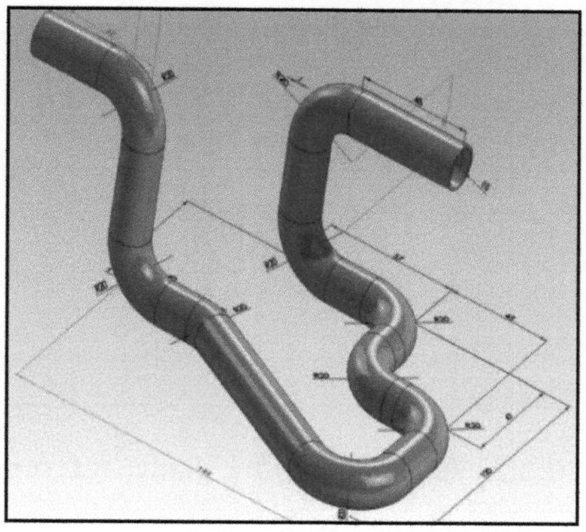

- Lines as an auxiliary construction for the 2D pipe profile path.
- Lines and rounded edges as auxiliary constructions for the pipe profile path as a **3D Sketch** overlay of the 2D sketch.
- Pipe cross-section Ø15 mm at the end of the pipe profile path.
- Edit circle and profile path with feature **Sweept-Boss** option **Thin 1** mm.

6.20.1.1 2D sketch cannot be converted to 3D sketch

Unfortunately, SOLIDWORKS 2026 still cannot convert a 2D sketch with the drawn elements into a 3D sketch, therefore the created 2D sketch is used as the design basis here.
(Info Unofficial German SolidWorks Help Page)
Therefore, create a line system according to the sketch shown, based on a 3D sketch, by overdrawing the open sketch at the snap points using the line command.

6.20.2 The 2D-basic sketch, the creation

6.20.2.1 Opening your own template file

- Menu Bar **New** /  /  click **Engelke2026.PRTDOT / OK**

6.20.2.2 The rectangular basic sketch

- Select the **Top** plane.
- Top view above **Normal To.**
- Create the sketch lines and add the dimensions (1).

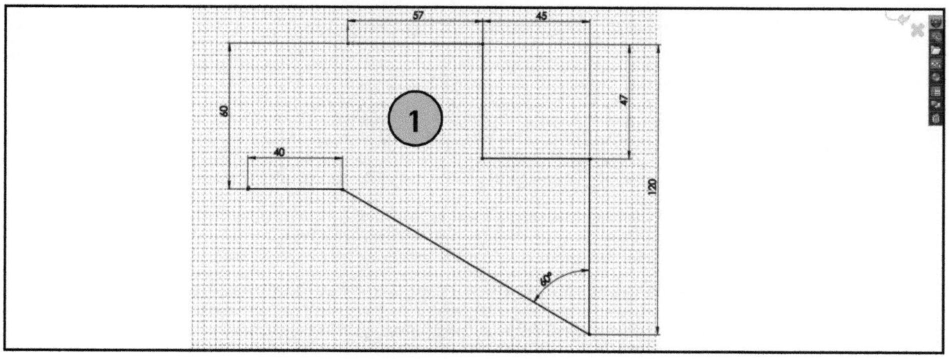

New

Engelke2026.
PRTDOT

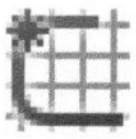
Sketch

Normal To

Line

Offset Entities

6.20.3 Additional work planes

6.20.3.1 Additional work plane, reference Plane "Right"

Plane

- Select the **Right Plane** (2).
- Select the endpoint of the displayed line end (3).

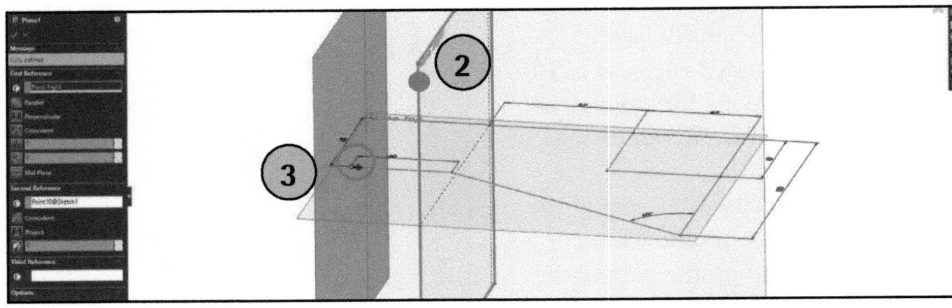

6.20.3.2 Additional work plane, reference Plane "Front"

Plane

- Select the **Front Plane** (4).
- Select the endpoint of the displayed line end (5).

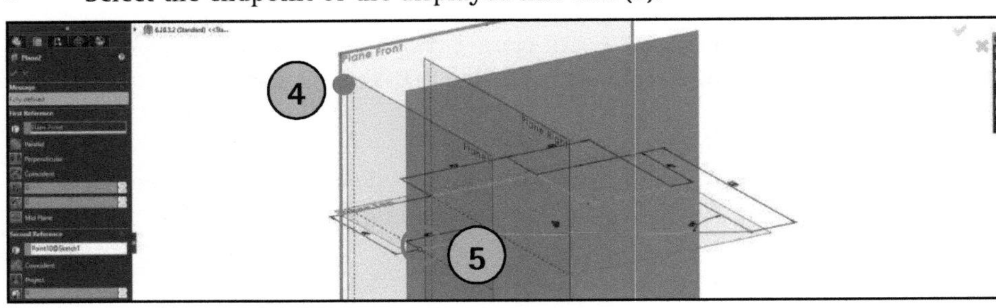

6.20.4 "3D Sketch" for the pipeline path, the creation

6.20.4.1 The basic sketch for the lower pipeline

3D Sketch

Line

3D Sketch (**Sketch** tab)
Double-click the **Top** plane.
Use the line function to draw a line along the snap points (6, 7).

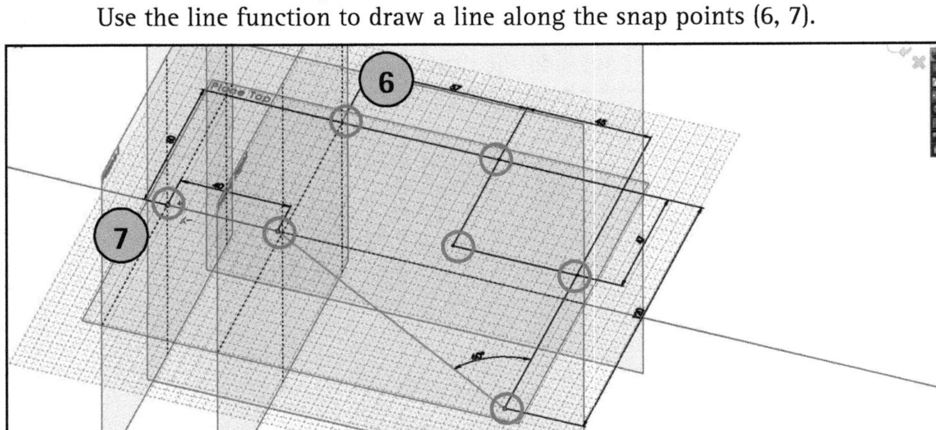

6.20.4.2 The basic sketch, line extensions on "Plane2"

Line

- At endpoint (8) on the new **Work Plane 2**, create the two lines shown (9, 10).

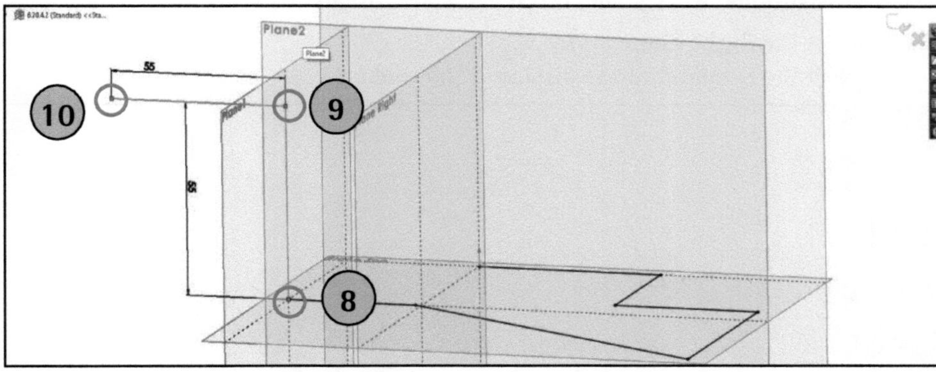

6.20.4.3 The basic sketch, line extensions on "Front Plane"

Line

- At endpoint (11) on the new **Work Plane 2**, create the two lines shown (12, 13).

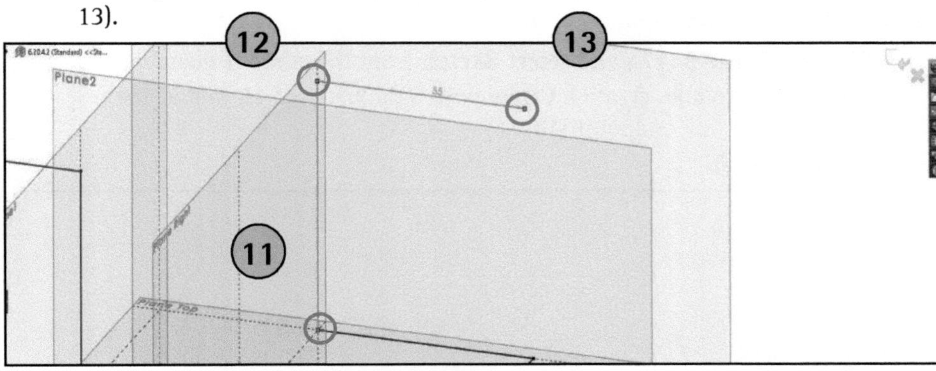

6.20.4.4 The basic sketch, "Sketch Fillet"

Sketch Fillet

- Round off the line system according to the sketch shown with a radius of **20** mm (14).
- **Finish 3D-sketch.**

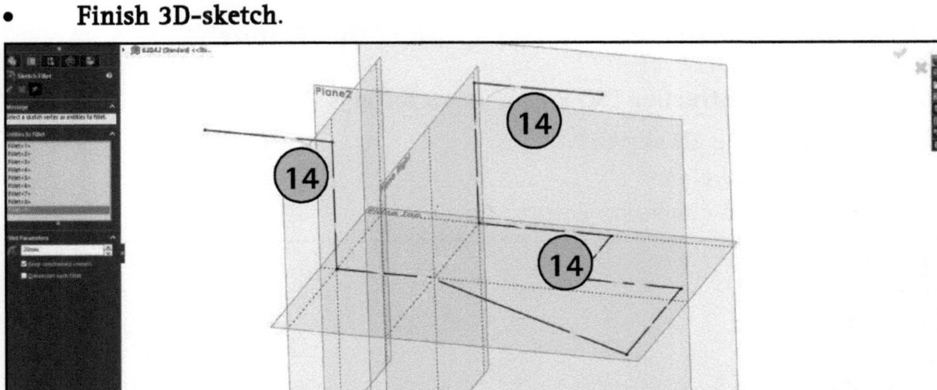

6.20.5 The cross-sectional area for the pipe body

6.20.5.1 Additional work plane, reference Plane "Right"

Plane

- Select the **Right Plane** (15).
- Select the endpoint of the displayed line end (16).

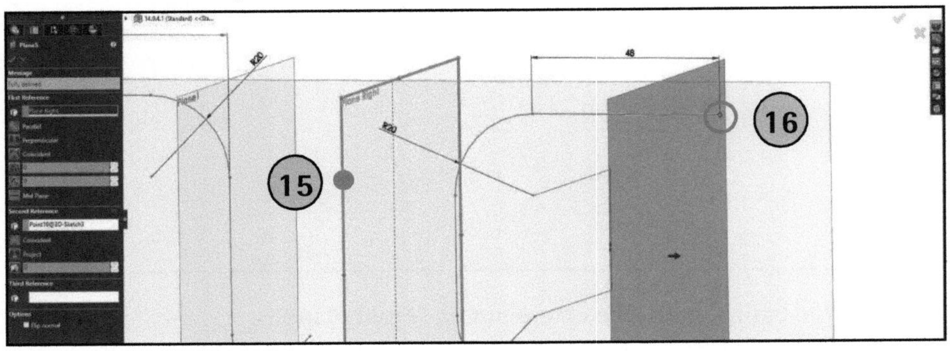

6.20.5.2 The cross-sectional area, the creation

Sketch

Circle

- Click on **Plane 5** (17), and select **Sketch** from the context menu.
- On the work plane, create a **Circle** with a diameter of **15** mm at the construction line endpoint (18).
- **Finish Sketch**.

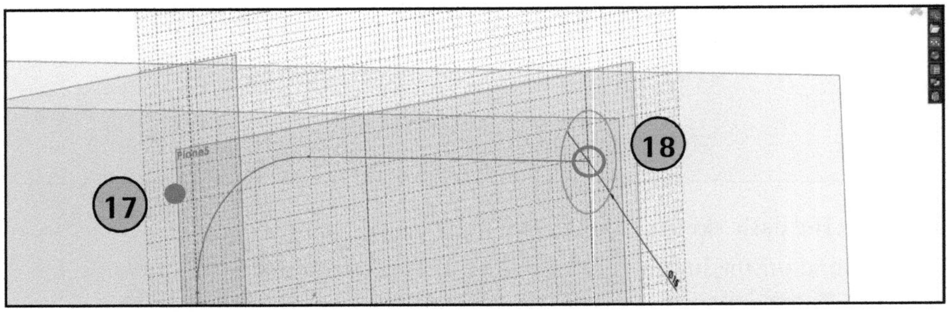

6.20.6 Basic construction "3D Piping" with "Thin feature"

6.20.6.1 Basic construction "3D Piping", view settings

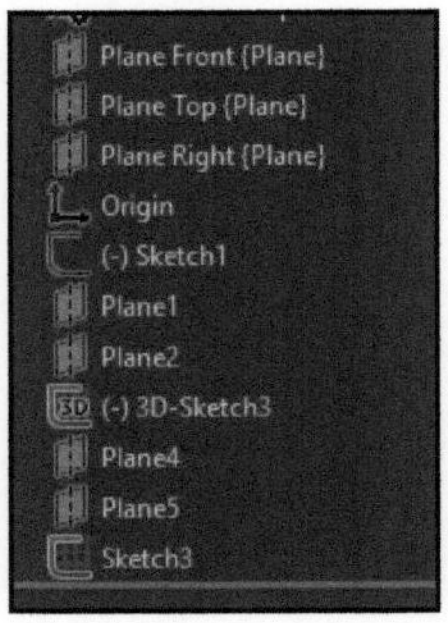

- Deactivate the **2D sketch1**.
- Deactivate all planes.
- Deactivate all dimension entries (19).

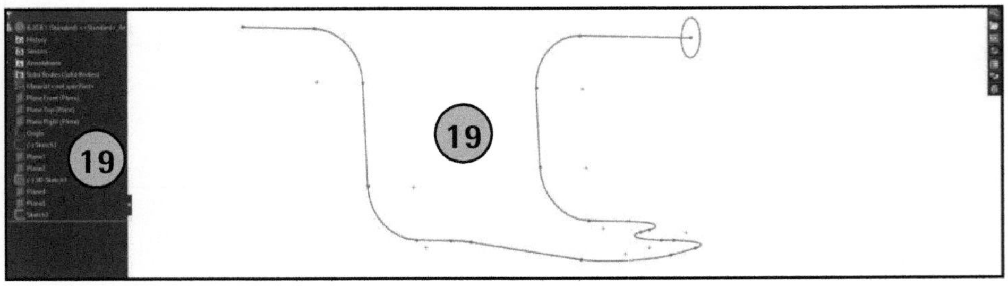

6.20.6.2 Basic construction "3D Piping" with "Thin feature", the creation

Sweep-Boss (**Features** tab)
Select the circular area as the **Profile** (20).
Select the 3D sketch curve as the **Path** (21).
Activate the option **Thin feature**, wall thickness **1** mm, **one direction** (22).
Close dialog box

Sweept-Boss

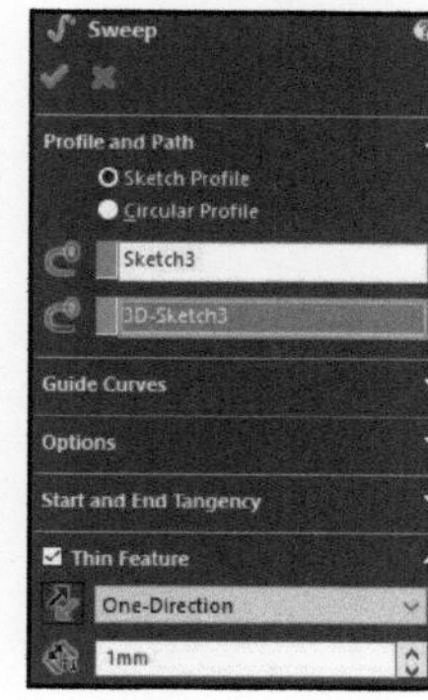

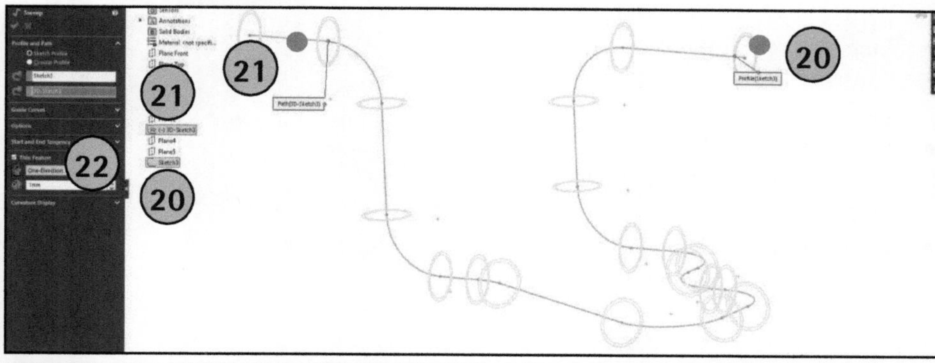

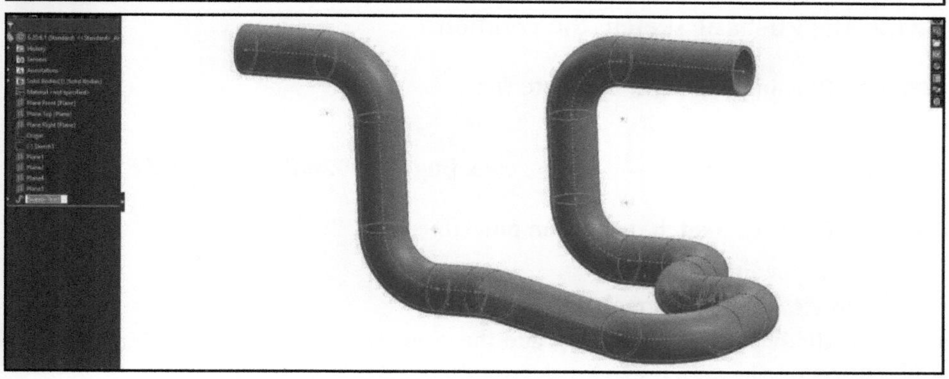

6.20.6.3 Data backup

Save as New / Enter a name of your choice.

Save as New

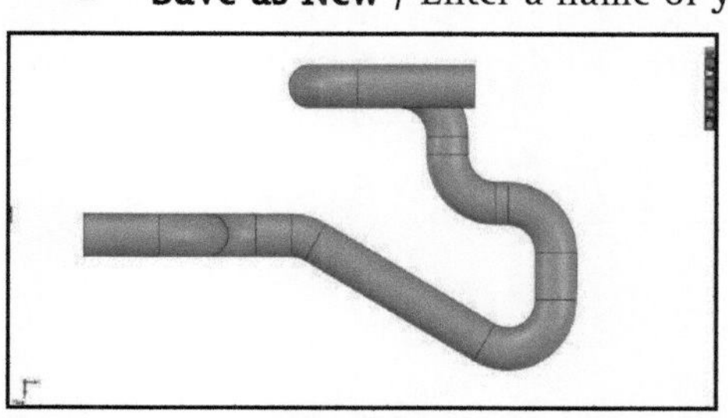

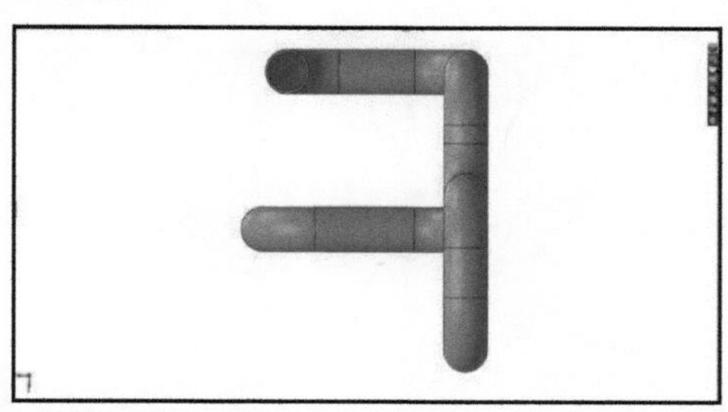

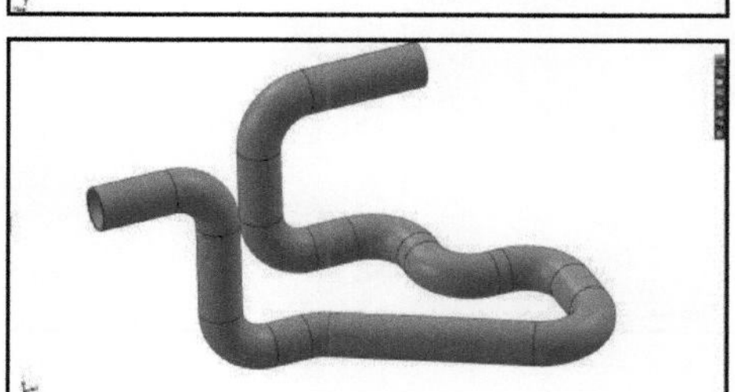

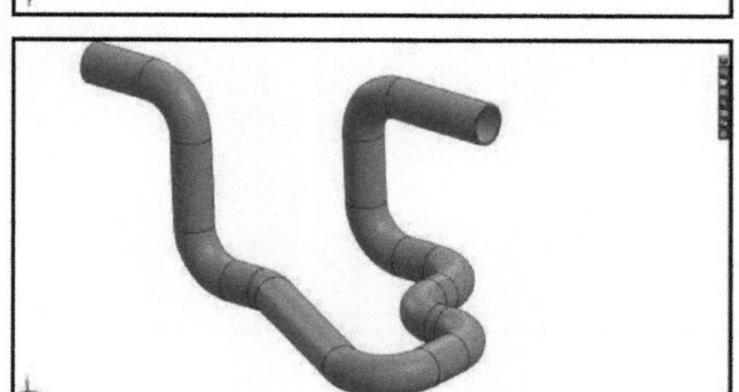

6.21 Basic construction "Pipe Bend" Form element feature "Planes", "3D Sketch","Lofted-Boss"

6.21.1 The basic geometry, specifications

- Line and rounding as an auxiliary construction for the inner profile path.
- Line and rounding as an auxiliary construction for the outer profile path.
- Circles and profile paths become an arc element with the Lofted-Boss feature.
- Create a pipe element with a wall thickness of 5 mm using the Thin feature.

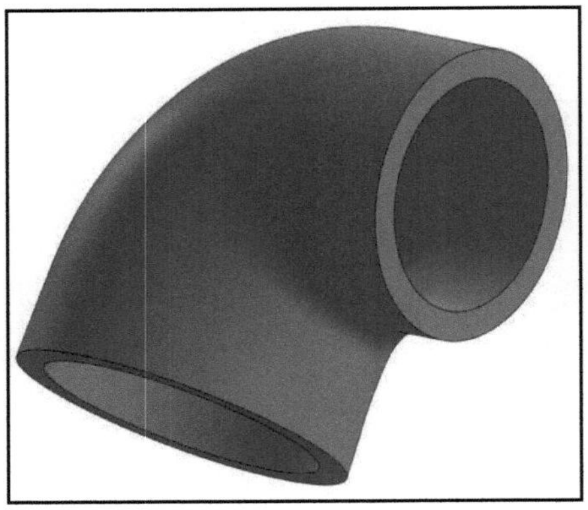

6.21.2 The 2D-basic sketch, the creation

New

Engelke2026.
PRTDOT

6.21.2.1 Opening your own template file

- Menu Bar **New** /  /  click **Engelke2026.PRTDOT / OK**

6.21.2.2 The basic sketch, transition guidelines

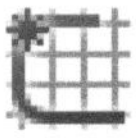
Sketch

Normal To

Line

Offset Entities

Sketch Fillet

Trim Entities

- Select the **Front** plane.
- Top view above **Normal To**.
- Create the sketch lines (1, 2), add the dimensions (3).
- Clean up the sketch using the **Trim** feature.
- **Finish Sketch**.

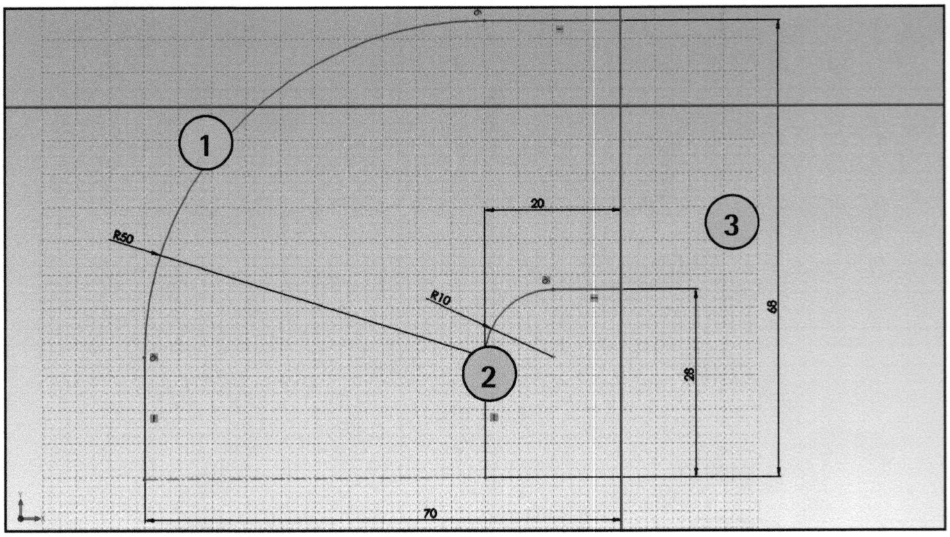

6.21.3 "3D Sketch" for the "Pipe Bend path", the creation

6.21.3.1 Additional work plane, reference Plane "Top"

- Select the **Front Plane** (4).
- Select the endpoint of the displayed line end (5).

Plane

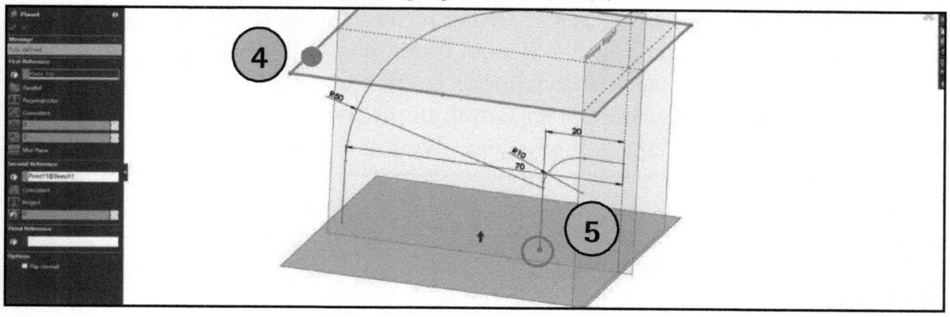

6.21.3.2 The basic sketch for the end circles, using "3D Sketch"

3D Sketch (**Sketch** tab)
Double-click the **Right Plane** (6).

3D Sketch

Perimeter Circle (**Sketch** tab)
Click the top point of the sketch (7).
Click the bottom point of the sketch (8).

Perimeter Circle

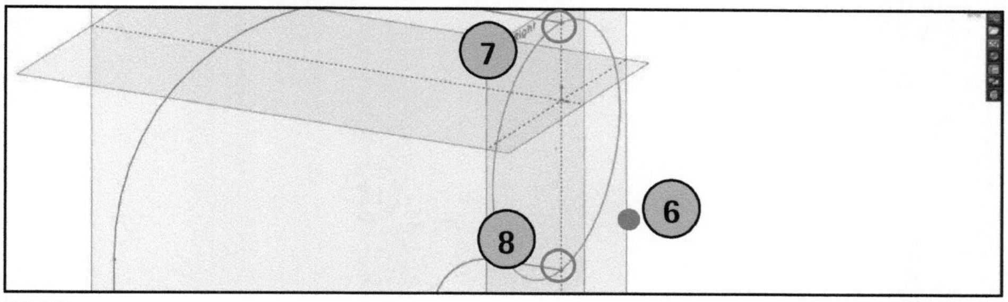

3D Sketch (**Sketch** tab)
Double-click the **Work Plane 4** (9).

3D Sketch

Perimeter Circle (**Sketch** tab)
Click the front point of the sketch (10).
Click the back point of the sketch (11).

Perimeter Circle

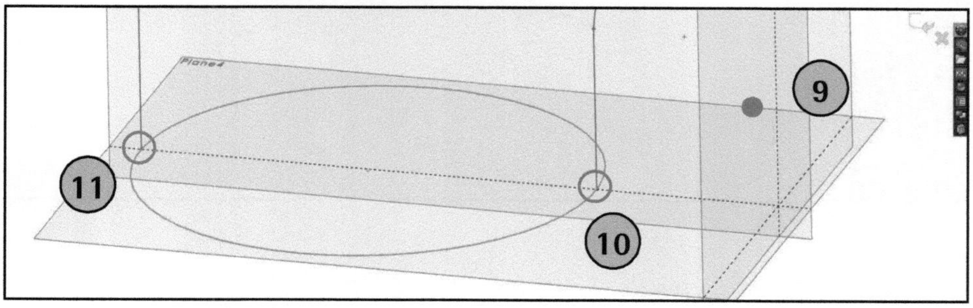

- **Finish 3D-sketch**.

6.21.4 The "Pipe Bend" creation, using feature "Lofted-Boss"

Lofted-Boss

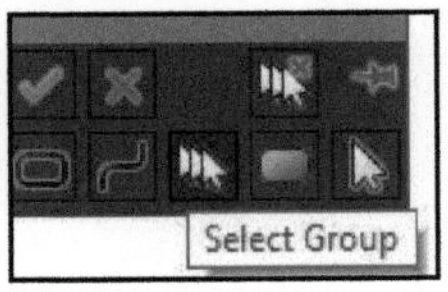

Lofted-Boss (Features tab)
Wählen Sie die beiden **Kreise** nacheinander (12).
Click the large sketch curve as **Guide Curves** (13).
Select the object using **Select Group** in the Symbol flyout box (14).
Accept the line path in the Symbol flyout box (14).
Select the small sketch curve line as Guide Curves (15),
Select the object using **Select Group** in the Symbol flyout box (14).
Accept the line path in the Symbol flyout box (14).

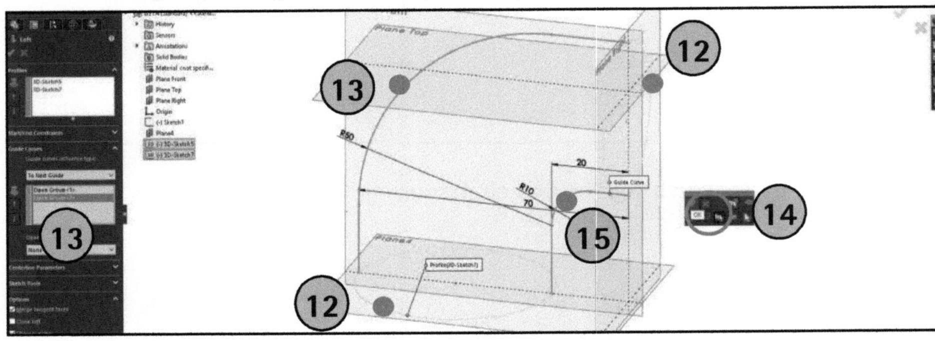

- Activate the option **Thin feature**, wall thickness **5** mm, **one direction** (16).
  Close dialog box (17).

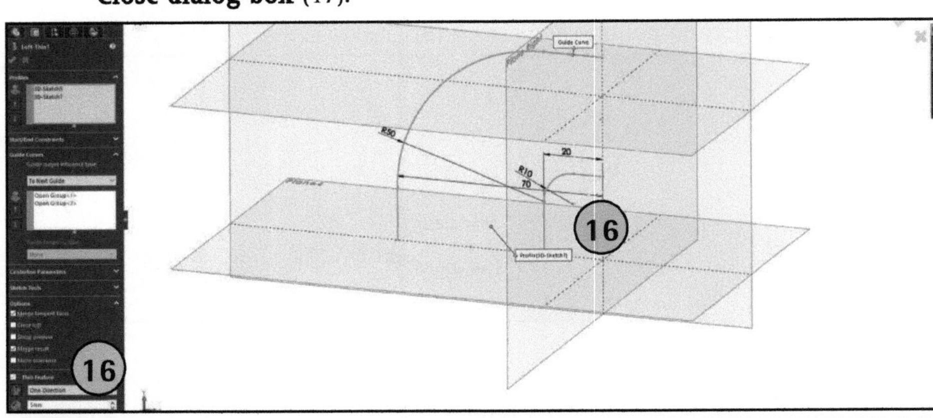

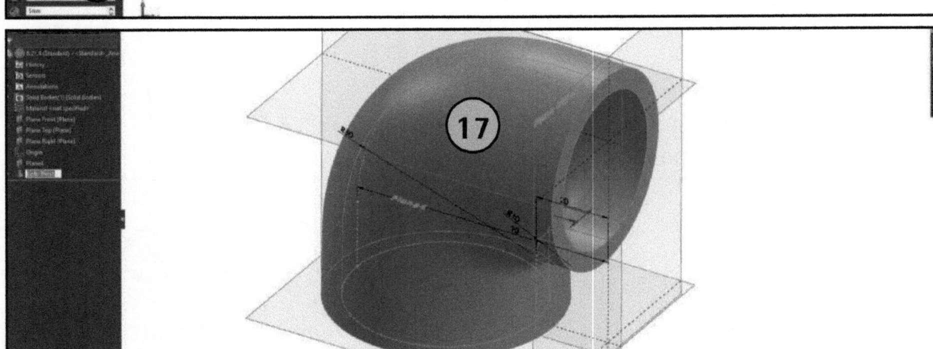

6.21.4.1 Data backup

- Deactivate the 2D sketches.
- Deactivate all planes.
- Deactivate all dimension entries.

Save as New / Enter a name of your choice.

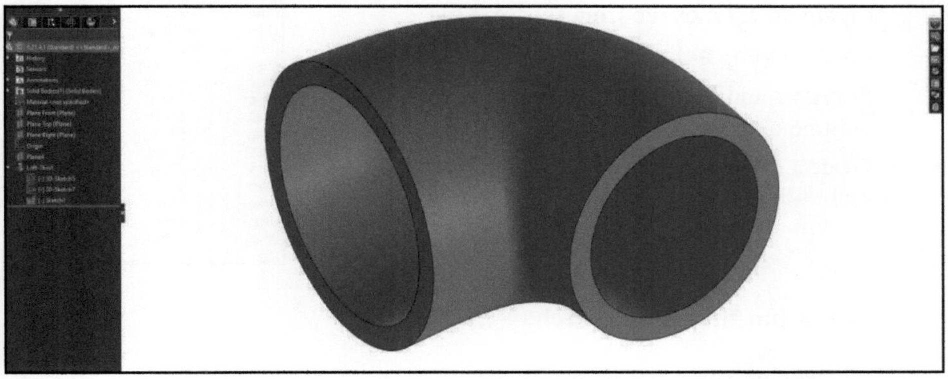

Save as New

6.22 Basic construction "Hollow body" Form element feature "Curve through XYZ Points"

6.22.1 The basic geometry, specifications

- Create a **Text** file with the content shown here.
- Create an **XYZ curve** from this text file.
- Create a vertical lineas the axis of rotation.
- **Polygon** and **Profile path** becomes a sweeping volume object with the **Sweept Boss** feature.
- Create a hollow element with the **Shell** feature and a wall thickness of **1** mm.

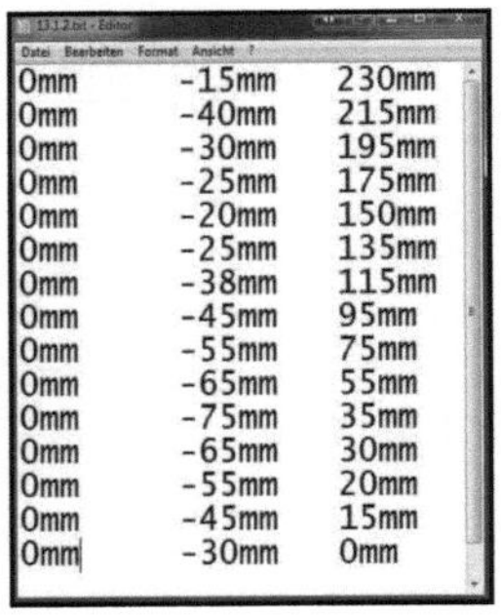

0mm	-15mm	230mm
0mm	-40mm	215mm
0mm	-30mm	195mm
0mm	-25mm	175mm
0mm	-20mm	150mm
0mm	-25mm	135mm
0mm	-38mm	115mm
0mm	-45mm	95mm
0mm	-55mm	75mm
0mm	-65mm	55mm
0mm	-75mm	35mm
0mm	-65mm	30mm
0mm	-55mm	20mm
0mm	-45mm	15mm
0mm	-30mm	0mm

6.22.2 Creating the curve sketch

6.22.2.1 Opening your own template file

New

- Menu Bar **New** / / click **Engelke2026.PRTDOT / OK**

Engelke2026. PRTDOT

6.22.2.2 The text file for the XYZ points

Using a text editor or spreadsheet application, create a file containing coordinate values for curve points. The file format must be a three-column list, delimited by tabs or space containing only X, Y, and Z coordinates.
Do not add column headings such as X, Y, or Z, or any other additional data. Click Browse and navigate to the curve file you want to open.
You can open .sldcrv files or .txt files, which use the same format as .sldcrv files.
You can create 3D curves in Microsoft Excel, save them as a .txt file, and later open them in SOLIDWORKS.

6.22.2.3 Curve line as "Curve through XYZ Points" from a text list

Curve Through XYZ Points

Curve Through XYZ Points (Features tab / **Curves)** / **Browse** (1)
Open the text file from the book DVD (2).
Click **Save** (3).
Close dialog box.

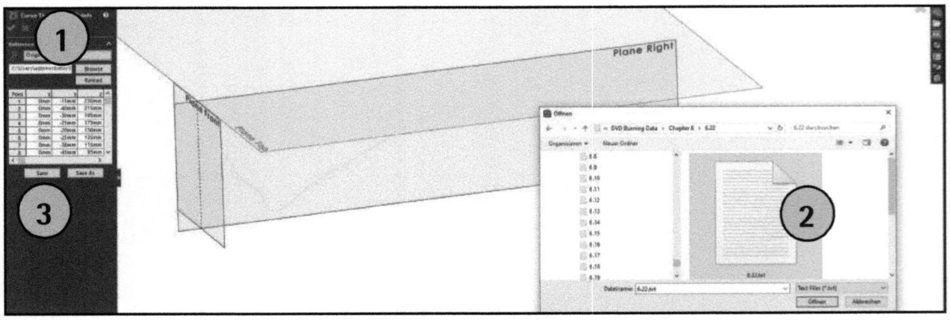

6.22.3 The basic sketch, the creation

6.22.3.1 The hollow body axis, as an alignment element of the base surface

Reference Geometry (**Features** tab)

Axis / Two Planes (4)
Select the planes (5, 6).
Close dialog box (7).

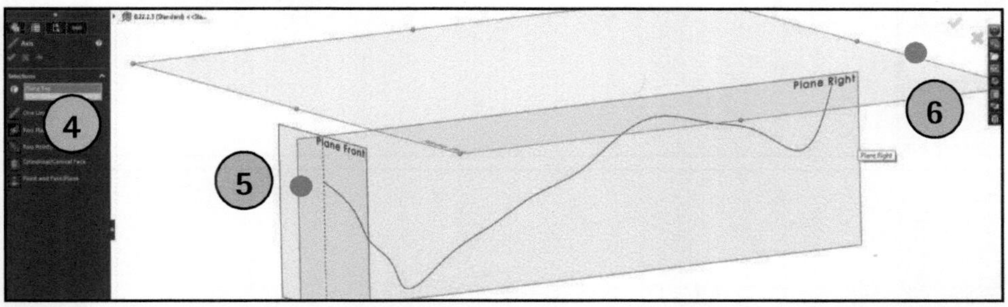

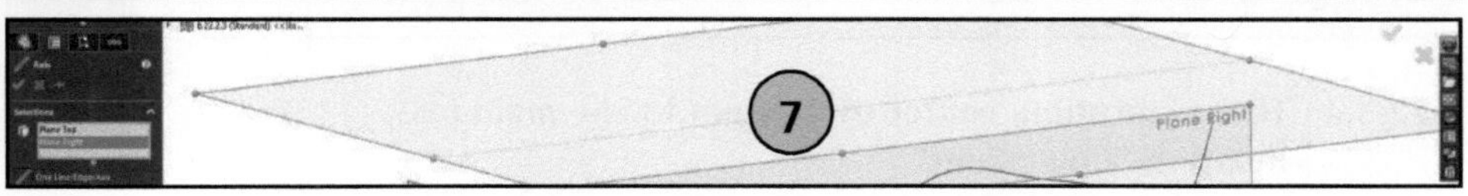

Reference-
Geometry

Axis

6.22.3.2 The hollow body base, using sketch feature "Polygon"

Sketch (**Sketch** tab)
Create a new sketch.
Select plane **Front**.

Polygon (**Sketch** tab)
Draw a polygon with **6** sides (8).
The center point of the polygon is the **Origin Point** (9).
Draw out size freely approx. **Ø40** mm.

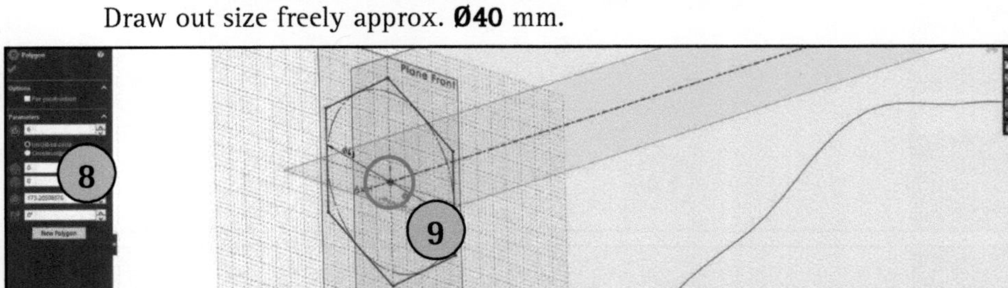

Sketch

Polygon

6.22.3.3 The orientation, "Polygon to Curve", relation "Pierce"

The **Pierce relation** connects a sketch point and an axis, edge, line, or spline.

The sketch point coincides where the axis, edge, or curve intersects the sketch plane.

The **Pierce relation** is used for sweeps with guide curves.

Add Relations

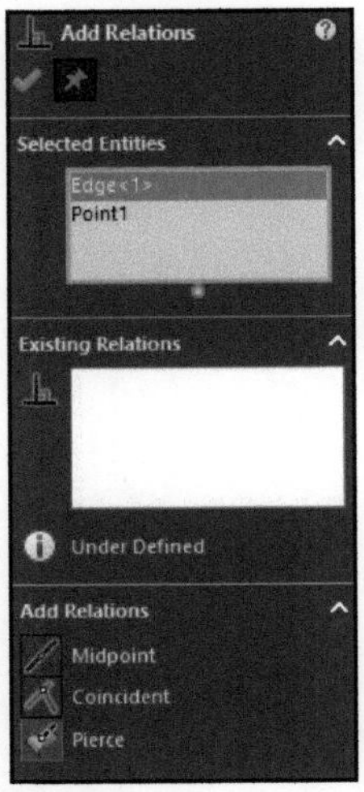

Add Relations (**Sketch** tab)
Select the vertex of the hexagon (10).
Select the curve contour (11).

Relation **Pierce** (12)
The hexagonal surface shifts to the selected curve endpoint (13).

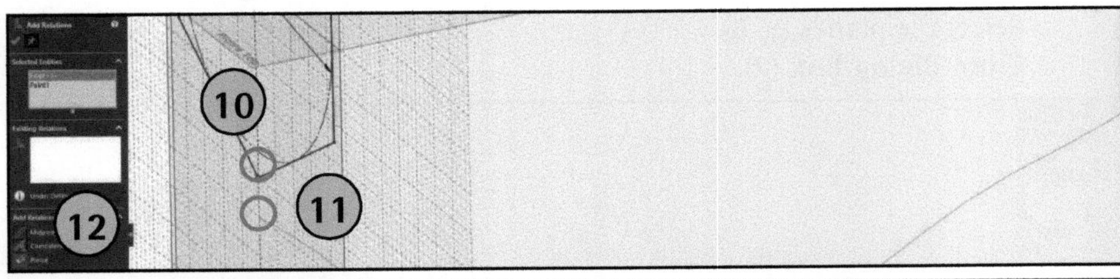

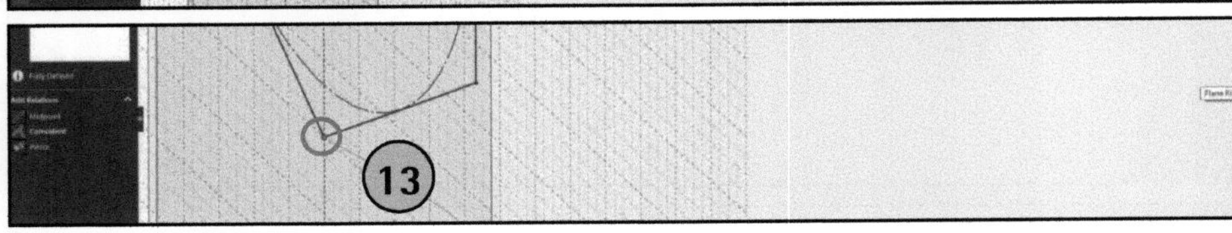

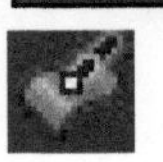

Relation Pierce

Add Relations

6.22.3.4 The orientation, center of polygon to the main axis, Relation "Coincident"

Add Relations (**Sketch** tab)

Select the center point of the hexagonal face (14).

Select the endpoint of the main axis (15).

Relation Coincident

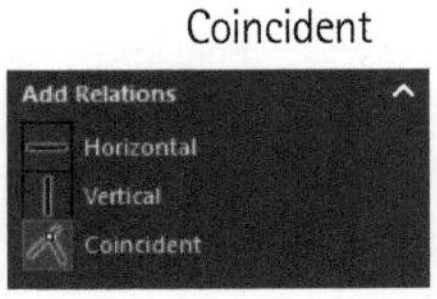

Relation **Coincident**

The hexagonal surface shifts to the selected axis endpoint (16).
Finish sketch

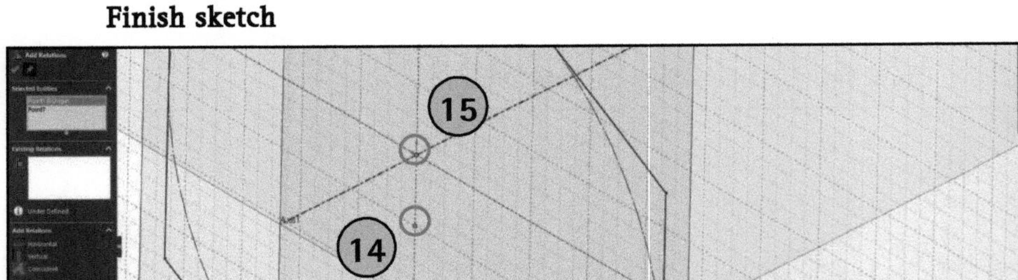

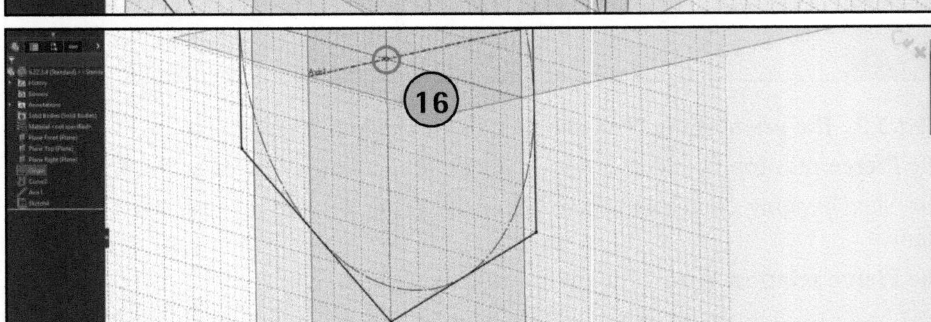

6.22.4 Creating a hollow body, using "Shell"

6.22.4.1 Axis of rotation as a line sketch

For the **Sweept Boss** feature, the planned axis cannot be used as a rotation element therefore a line must be drawn as the axis of rotation.

Sketch (**Sketch** tab)
Create a new sketch / select plane **Right**.

Sketch

Line (**Sketch** tab)
Draw a line from the origin point, length **260** mm, **180°** (17, 18)
Finish sketch

Line

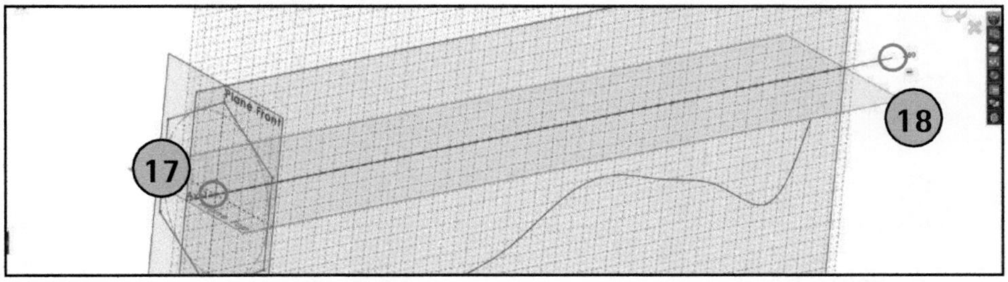

6.22.4.2 The hollow body, the creation

Sweept-Boss (**Features** tab)
Select the circular area as the **Profile** (20).
Select the 3D sketch curve as the **Path** (21).
Select the **sketch centerline** (22).
Close dialog box (23).

Sweept-Boss

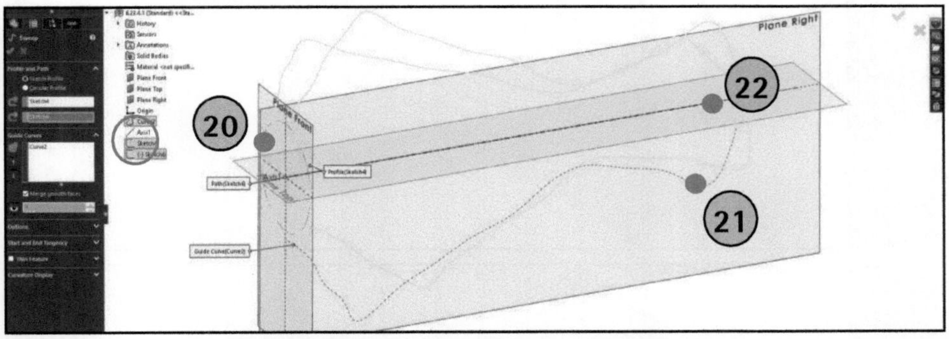

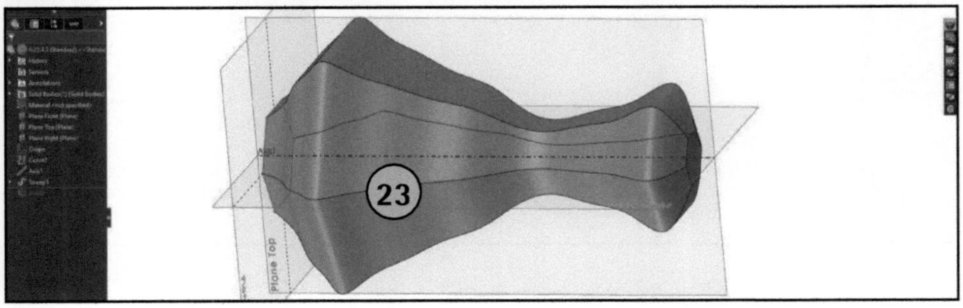

6.22.4.3 Creation of the hollow body, using "Shell"

Shell

Shell (**Features** tab)
Set the **Thickness** to **1** mm (24).
Option **Faces to Remove**.
Select the top surface in the graphics area (25).
Set otion **Show preview** (26).
Close dialog box.

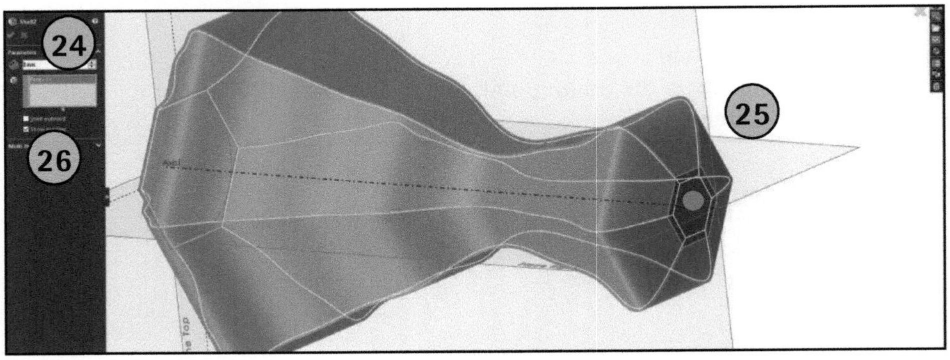

6.22.4.4 Data backup

- Deactivate the 2D sketches.
- Deactivate all planes.
- Deactivate all dimension entries.

Save as New

Save as New / Enter a name of your choice.

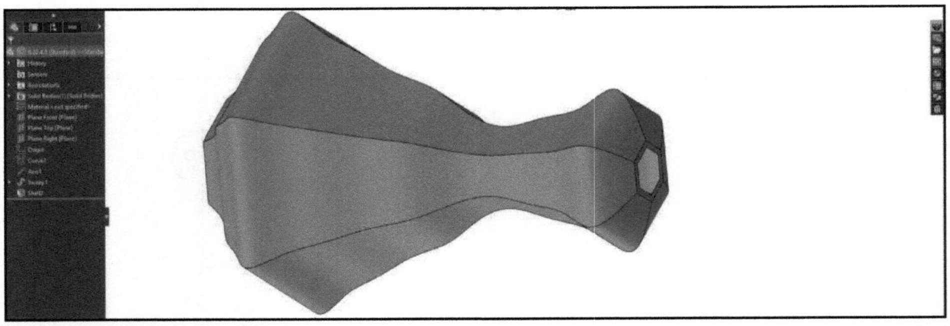

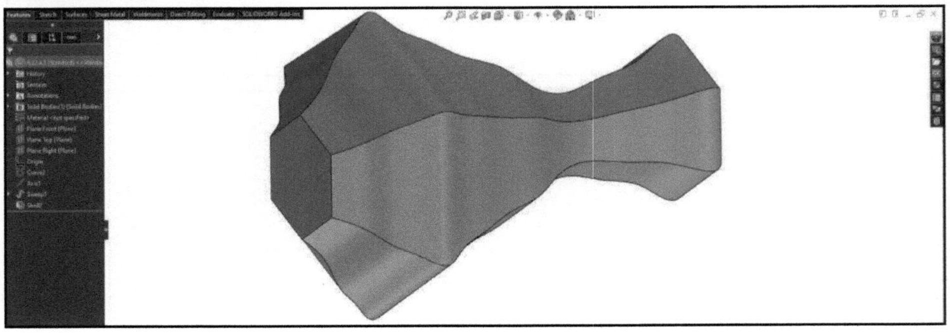

Project X

Powerful commands
Optimized constructions
Surface modeling
Page 275 to 290

- Surface modeling „Rectangular funnel element“
  Form element feature ”Lofted Surface ”, “Thicken”
- Surface modeling ”Boundary Surface“
  Different profile surfaces, corner-determined
- Surface modeling ”Molded surfaces”
  Differentiate curve surface over trim surface
- Surface modeling ”Freeform Editing”
  Form element feature “Surface Extrude”, “Freeform”
- Surface modeling ”Molded surfaces”
  “3D-Sketch”, basic profile curves

6.23 Surface modeling „Rectangular funnel element" Form element feature "Lofted Surface ", "Thicken"

6.23.1 "Lofted Surface", the creation

6.23.1.1 Open the working file

Open (Menu bar) / Component from the book-DVD / **OK** (1)

Open

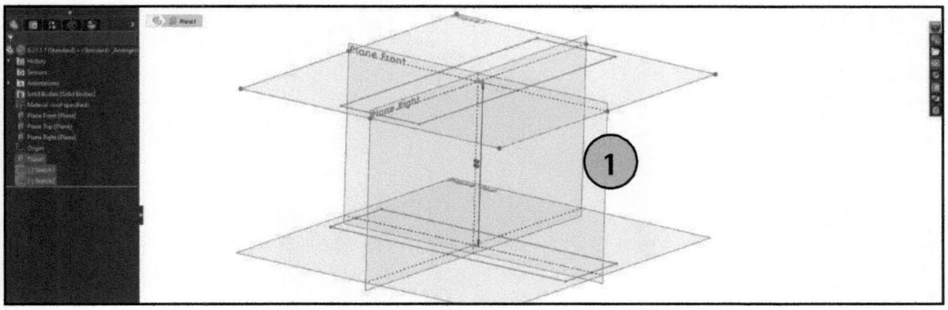

6.23.1.2 Basic profile curves for a "Lofted Surface", the creation

Lofted Surface (**Surface** tab)
Select the **first** curve profile using **Sketch1** (3).
Select the **second** curve profile using **Sketch2** (3).
Accept the **curve path** (4).
Close dialog box (5).

Lofted Surface

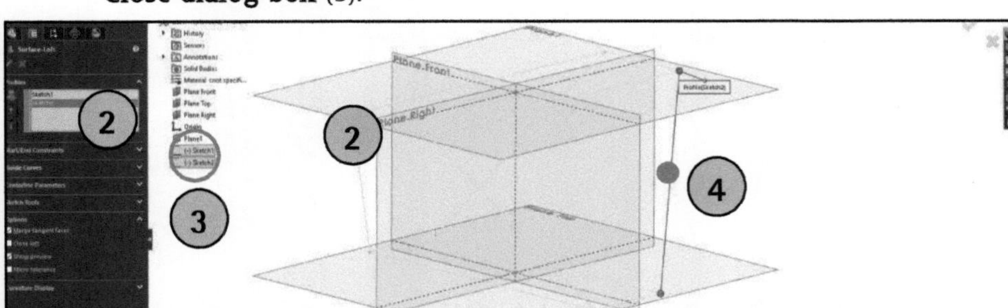

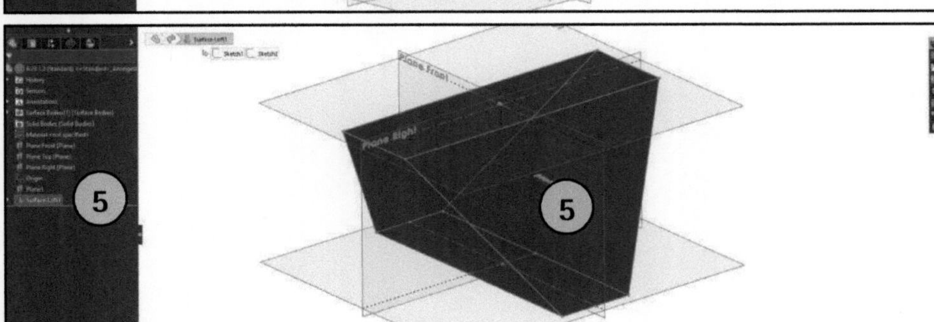

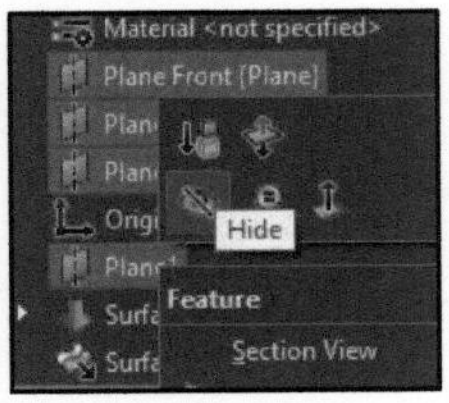

Thicken

6.23.2 Apply wall thickness, using the "Thicken" feature

- For the **work planes** set the **Hide** option in the **FeatureManager**.

Thicken (**Surface** tab)
Select the created surfaces (6).
Set the wall thickness to **1** mm (7).
Thicken side 2 (8).
Close dialog box (9).

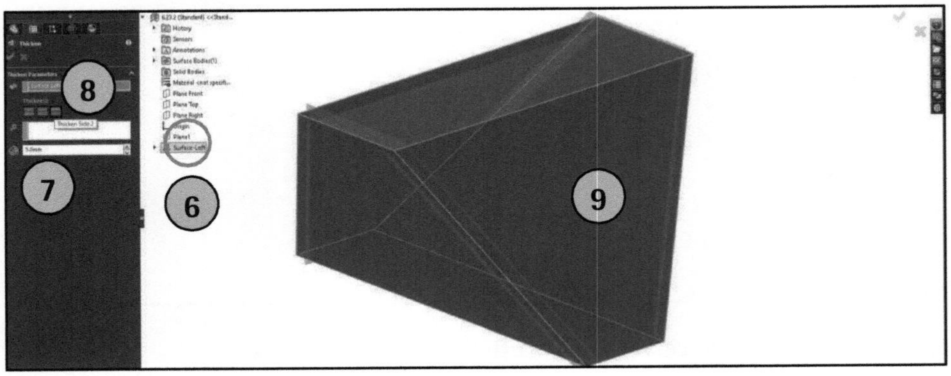

Save as New

6.23.2.1 Data backup

Save as New / Enter a name of your choice.

6.24 Surface modeling "Boundary Surface" Different profile surfaces, corner-determined

6.24.1 "Boundary Surface", the creation

6.24.1.1 Open the working file

Open (Menu bar) / Component from the book-DVD / **OK** (1)

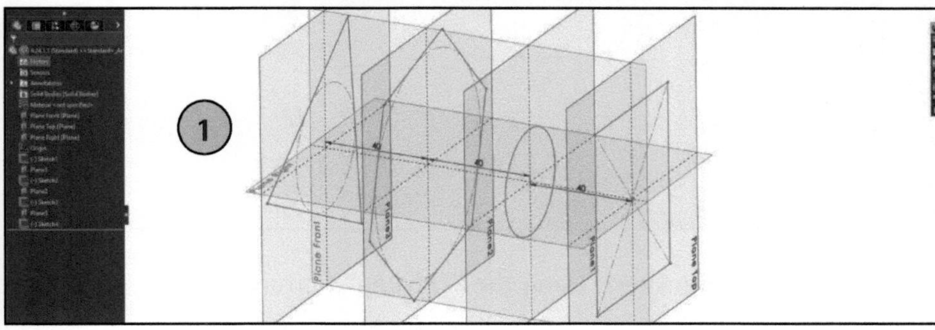

Open

6.24.1.2 Basic profile curves for a "Boundary Surface", the creation

Boundary Surface (**Surface** tab)
Select the **first** curve profile using **Sketch1** (2).
Select the **second** curve profile using **Sketch2** (3).
Select the **third** curve profile using **Sketch3** (4).
Select the **fourth** curve profile using **Sketch4** (5).
Show preview (6)
Correct the **curve path** at the indicated location (7).
Close dialog box.

Boundary Surface

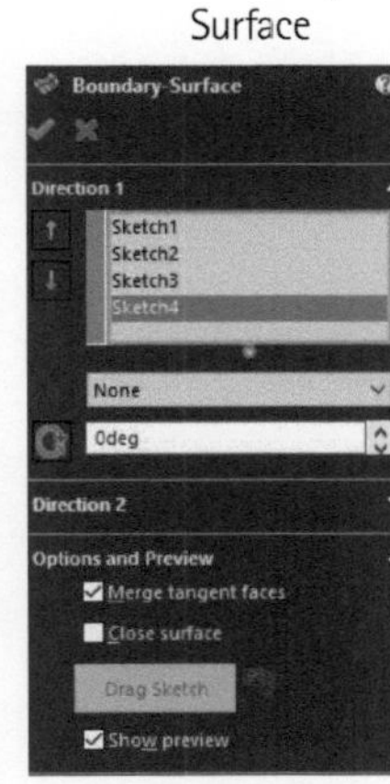

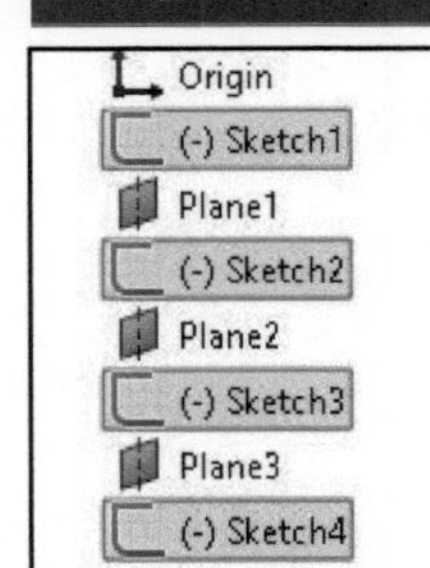

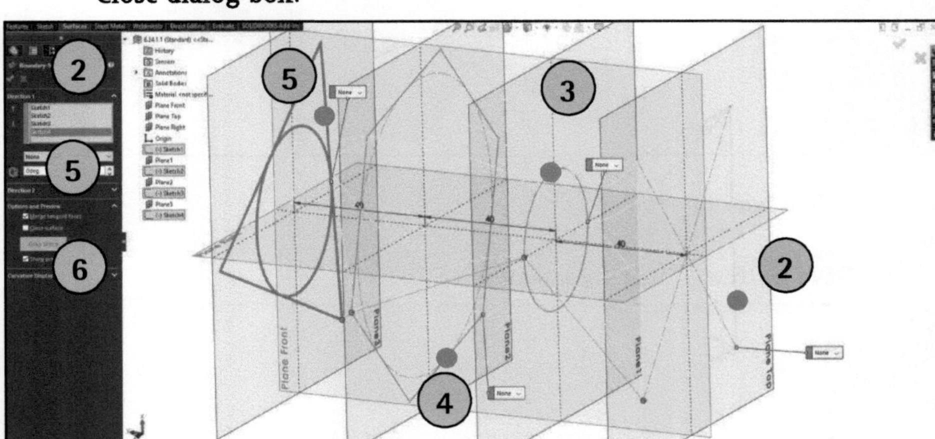

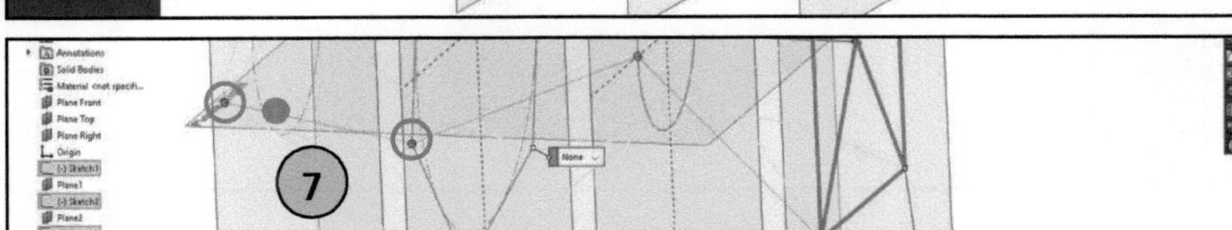

6.24.2 Closing the base area using "Planar surface"

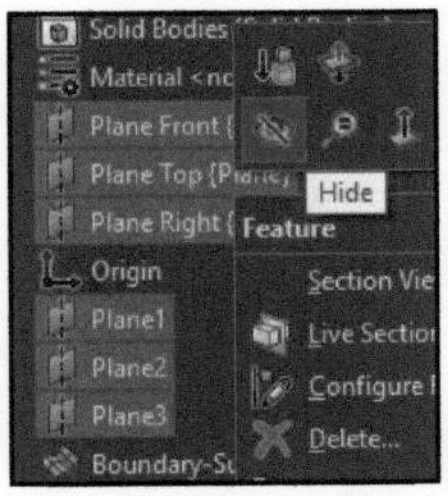

Planar Surface

- For the **work planes** set the **Hide** option in the **FeatureManager**.
- Rotate the component position.

Planar Surface (**Surface** tab)
Bounding Entities, select all four sides of the base area (8, 9).

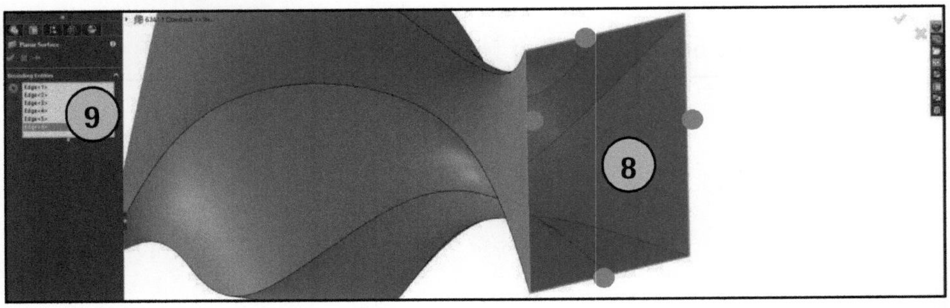

6.24.3 Apply wall thickness, using the "Thicken" feature

Thicken

Thicken (**Surface** tab)
Select the created surfaces (10).
Set the wall thickness to **1** mm (11).
Thicken side 2 (12).
Close dialog box (13).

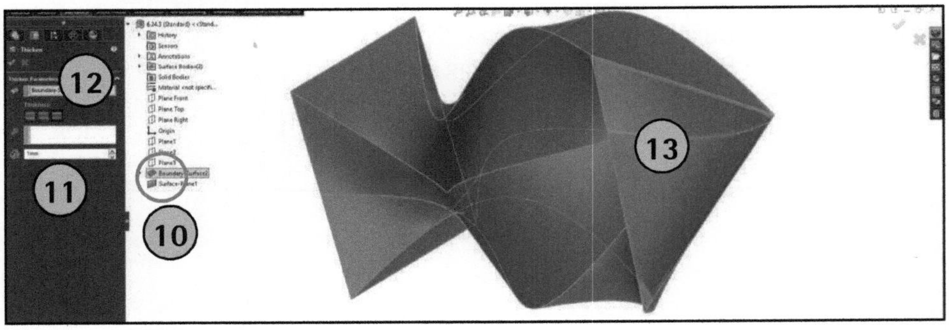

6.24.3.1 Data backup

Save as New

Save as New / Enter a name of your choice.

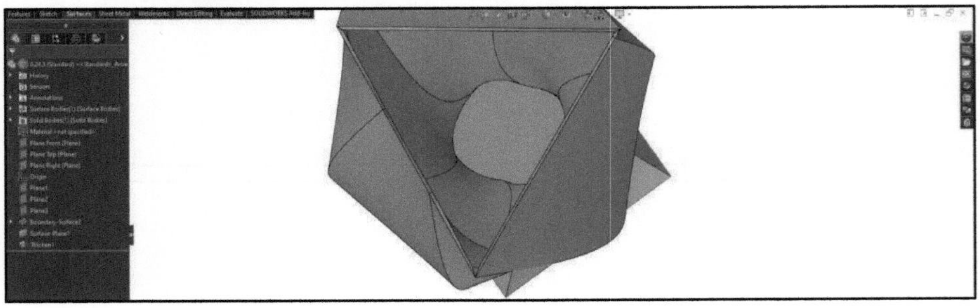

6.25 Surface modeling "Molded surfaces" Differentiate curve surface over trim surface

6.25.1 "Trim Surface", the creation

6.25.1.1 Open the working file

Open (Menu bar) (1) / Component from the book-DVD / **OK**

Open

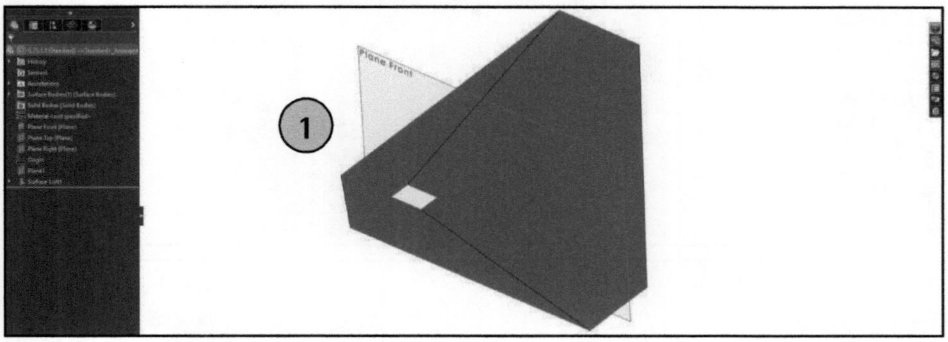

6.25.1.2 Create a basic sketch for "Trim Surface"

Spline

- On the **Front** plane (2), create a freely chosen **Curve** using the **Spline** function (3, 4).

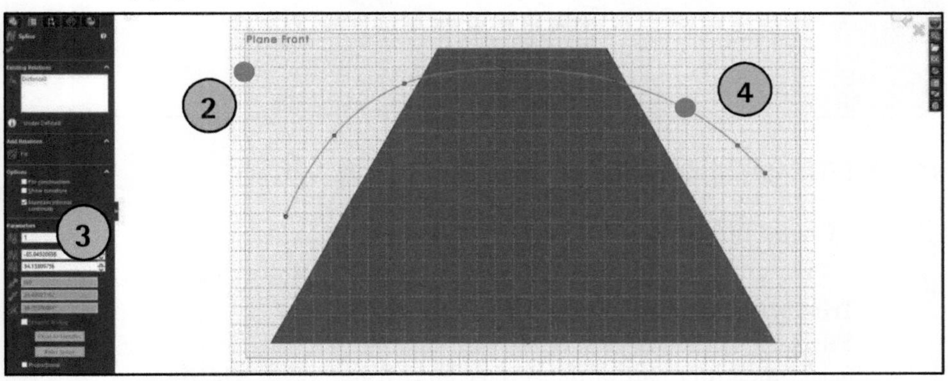

- Move the center point of the curve approx. **32** mm downwards (5, 6).

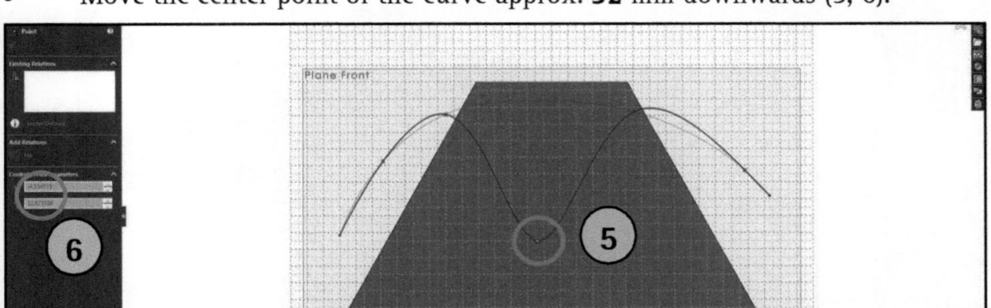

Surface Extrude

6.25.1.3 Create a "Trim Surface" using "Surface-Extrude"

Surface-Extrude (**Surface** tab)
Select the **Center** option (7).
Drag the selected curve to approx. **190** mm (8, 9).
Close dialog box (13).

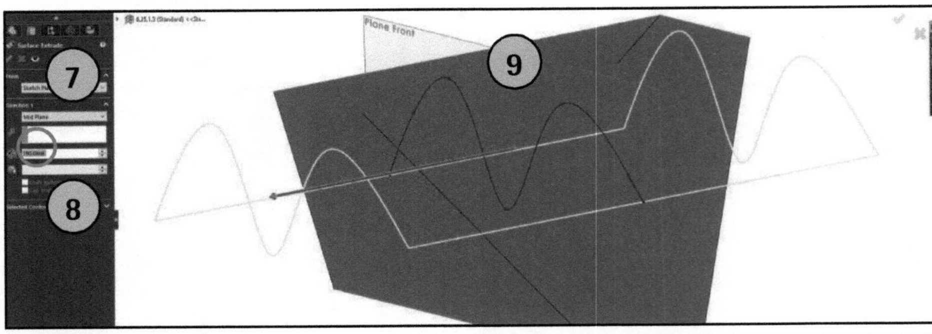

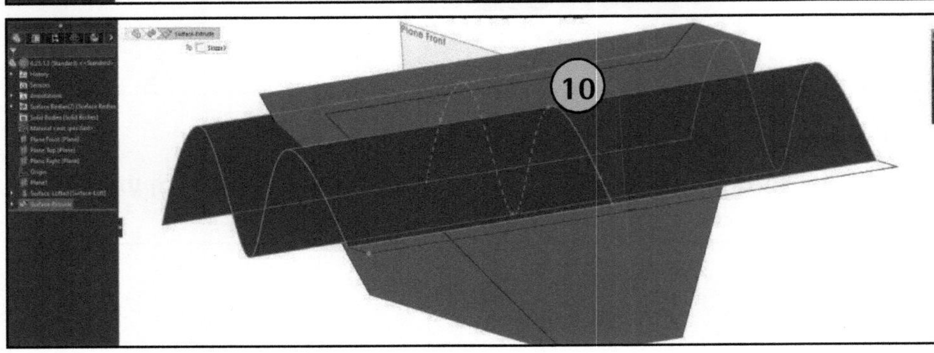

6.25.2 Differentiating surface bodies using "Trim Surface"

Trim Surface

6.25.2.1 Create the differentiating surface bodies

Trim Surface (**Surface** tab)
Select the trimming surface as the trimming tool (11).
Select the lower part of the surface body using **Keep Selection** (12).

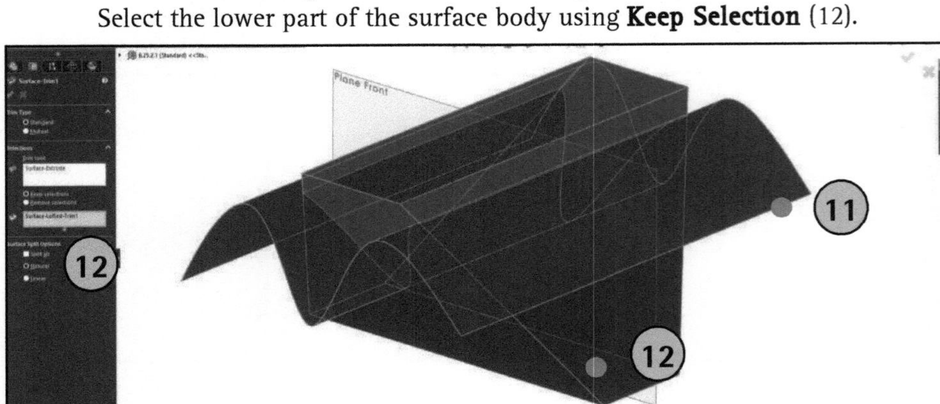

6.25.2.2 Disable "Trim Surface"

- Disable the feature **Surface Extrude** using **Hide** in the **FeatureManager** (13).

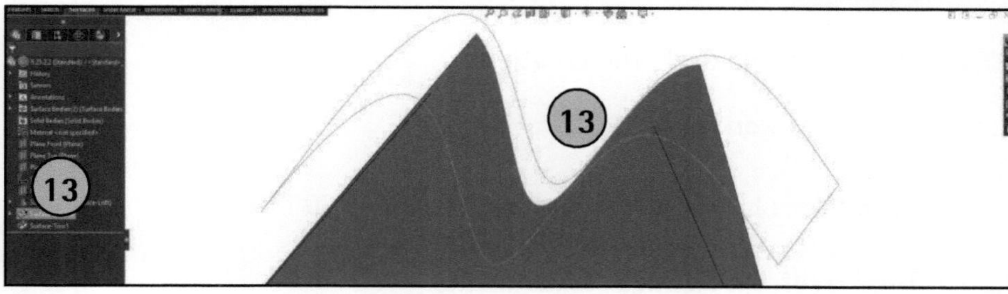

6.25.3 Apply wall thickness, using the "Thicken" feature

Thicken (**Surface** tab)
Select the created surfaces (10).
Set the wall thickness to **1** mm (11).
Thicken side 2 (12).
Close dialog box (13).

Thicken

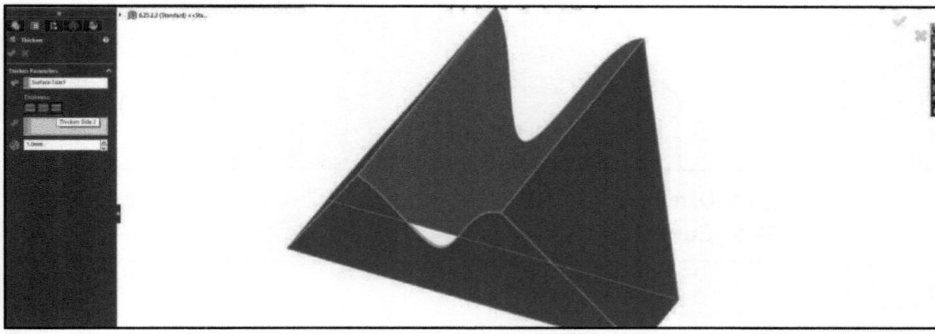

6.25.3.1 Data backup

Save as New / Enter a name of your choice.

Save as New

6.26 Surface modeling "Freeform Editing" Form element feature "Surface Extrude", "Freeform"

6.26.1 "Freeform Surface", the creation

6.26.1.1 Open the working file

Open

Open (Menu bar) / Component from the book-DVD / **OK**

6.26.2 The "Freeform Fittings" adjustments

6.26.2.1 The "Freeform", adjustment of the cover surface

Freeform

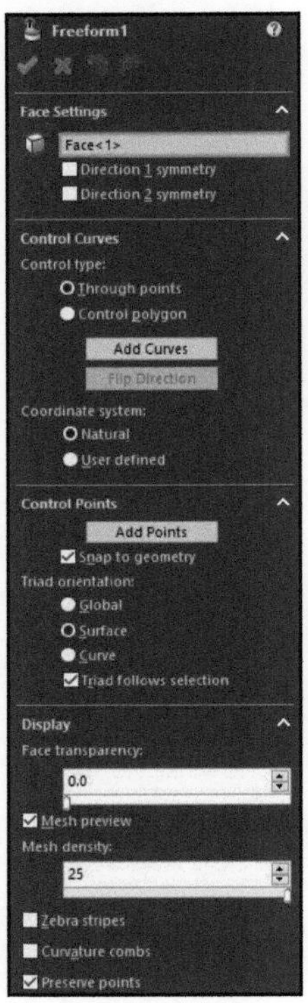

Freeform (**Surface** tab)
Option **Mesh density**: **25**
Select the top surface (2).
Option **Add Curves** (3, 4).

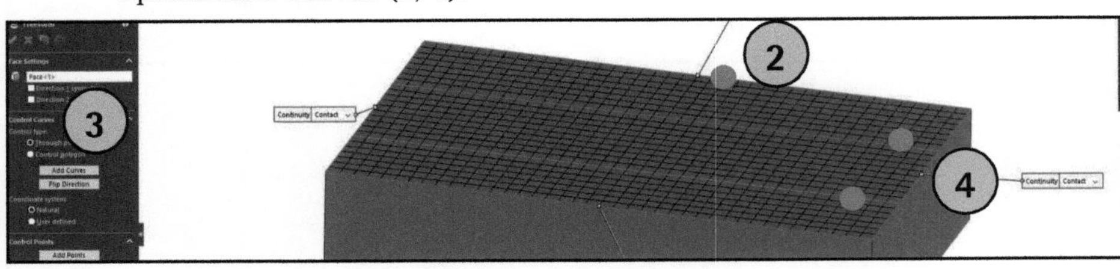

- Option **Flip Direction** (5).
- Option **Add Curves** (6, 7).

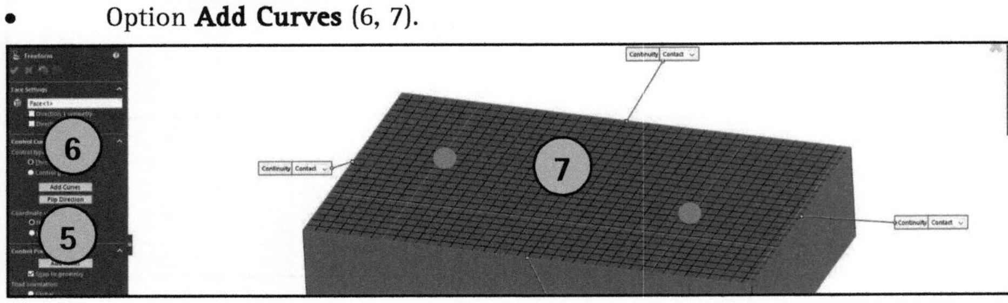

- Option **Add Points** (8)
- Click the displayed point (9).
- Deactivate the **Add Points** option by clicking (8).

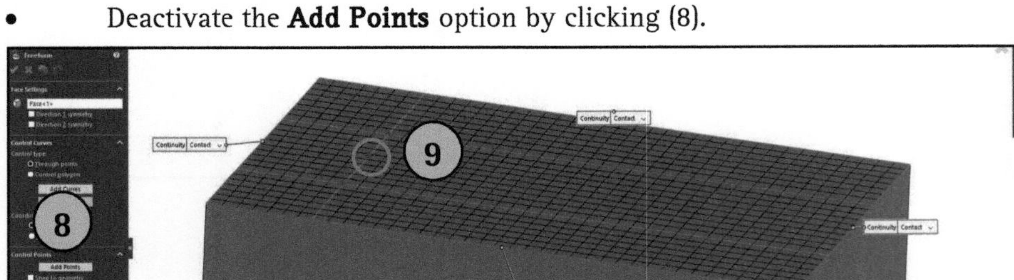

- Carefully pull the **Z-direction** upwards on the **Triad** (10).
- Approx. values: **X=23.6** mm, **Y=0 mm**, **Z=25.8** mm (11).

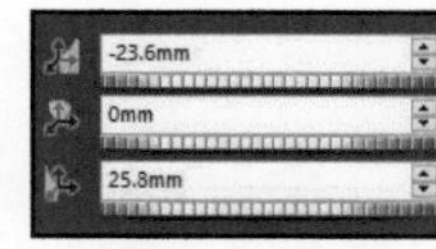

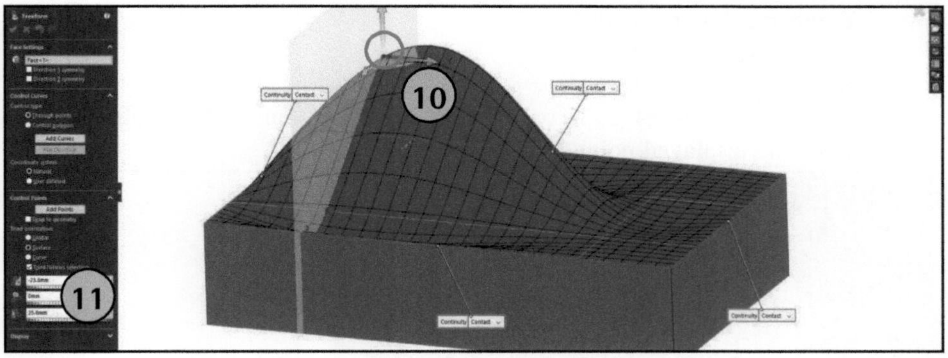

- Option **Add Points** (13)
- Click the displayed point (13).

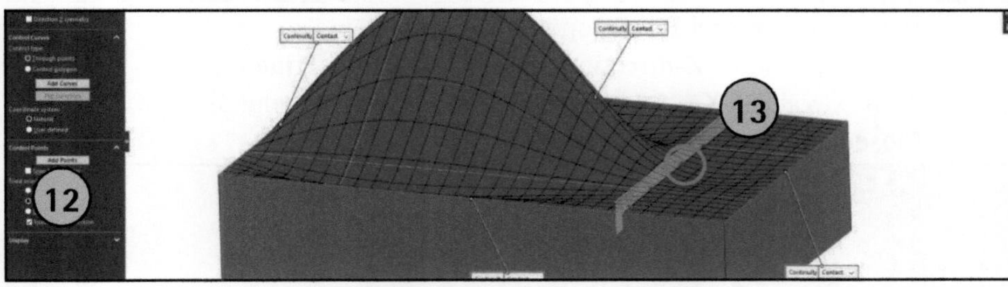

- Deactivate the **Add Points** option by clicking (13).
- Carefully pull the **Z-direction** downwards on the **Triad** (14).
- Approx. values: **X=-5.3** mm, **Y=3.1** mm, **Z=-13.6** mm (15).
- **Close dialog box** (16).

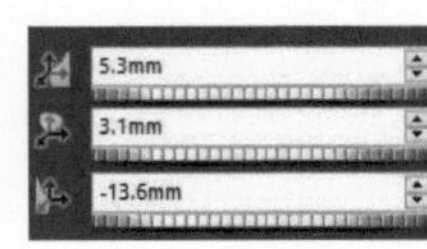

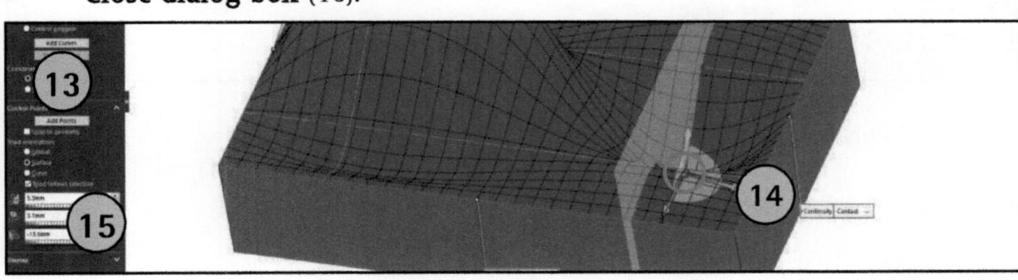

6.26.2.2 Data backup

Save as New / Enter a name of your choice.

Save as New

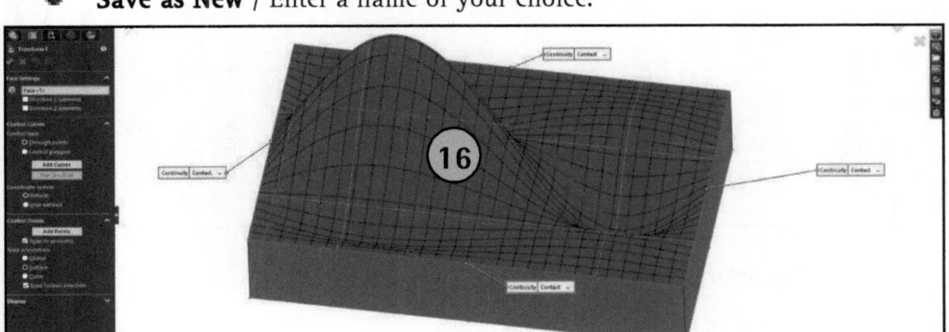

Freeform

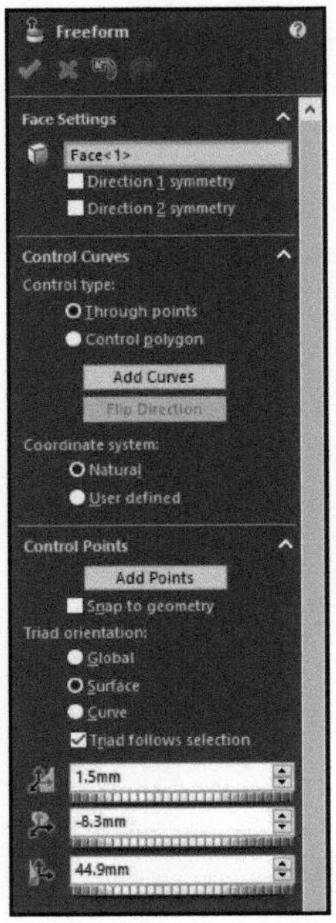

6.26.2.3 The "Freeform", adjustment of the front surface

Freeform (**Surface** tab)
Option **Mesh density**: **25**
Select the front surface (1)
Option **Add Curves** (2, 3), option **Flip Direction**, option **Add Points**
Click the displayed point (4).

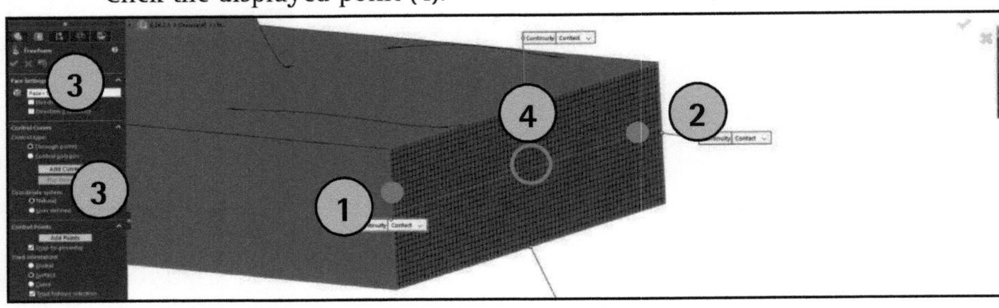

- Deactivate the **Add Points** option by clicking.
- Carefully pull the **Z-direction** downwards on the **Triad** (4).
- Approx. values: **X=-1.5** mm, **Y=-8.3** mm, **Z=-44.9** mm (5).
- **Close dialog box**.

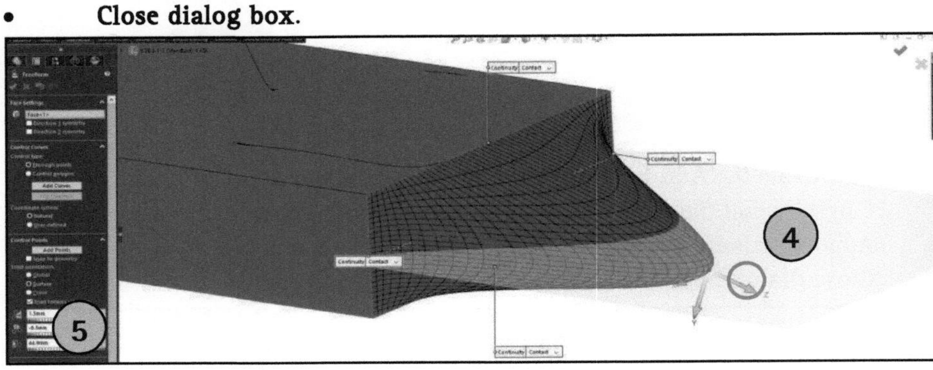

6.26.2.4 Apply wall thickness, using the "Thicken" feature

Thicken (**Surface** tab)
Select the created surfaces (6).
Set the wall thickness to **1** mm, **Thicken side 2** (7).
Close dialog box.

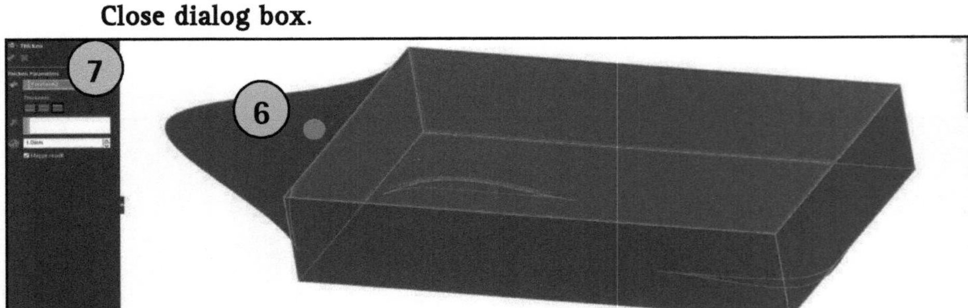

Save as New

6.26.2.5 Data backup

Save as New / Enter a name of your choice.

6.27 Surface modeling "Molded surfaces" "3D-Sketch", basic profile curves

6.27.1 "Molded surfaces", basics

- Create a plane for each profile of the shape.
- Sketch the section profiles on the planes. You can create all section and guide curve sketches in a single 3D sketch.
- Guide curves must intersect all base profile curves.

6.27.2 Creating sketches of the three basic profile curves

6.27.2.1 Opening your own template file

New

Engelke2026.
PRTDOT

- Menu Bar **New** /  /  click **Engelke2026.PRTDOT / OK**

6.27.2.2 Basic sketch, the creation

Sketch (**Sketch** tab)
Create a new sketch.

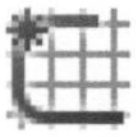
Sketch

6.27.2.3 Additional work plane above

Plane

- Create an additional work plane above the base **Right Plane**, offset distance **60** mm (1).

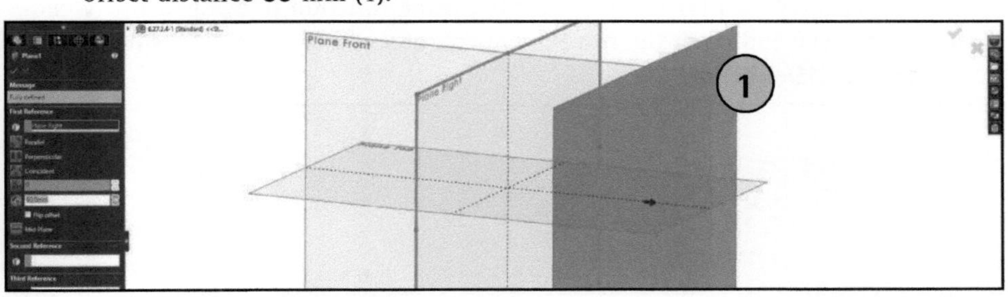

6.27.2.4 Additional work plane above

Plane

- Create an additional work plane above the base **Right Plane**, offset distance -**60** mm (2).

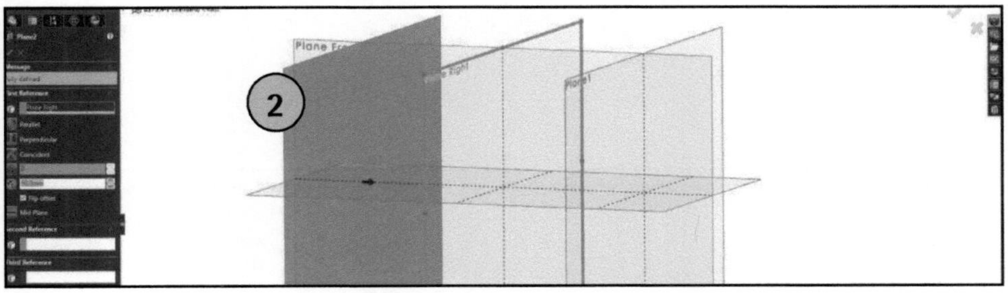

6.27.2.5 Creating the frame geometry

3D-Skizze neu

Center Rectangle

- Select a **Plane** in the **FeatureManager**.
- Click **3D Sketch** to remain in this function.
- On the selected work plane, construct:
  A **Center Rectangle** on the work plane, approx. **150** mm x **75** mm, at the work plane's center point.
  Set Line structure for construction (3, 4, 5).

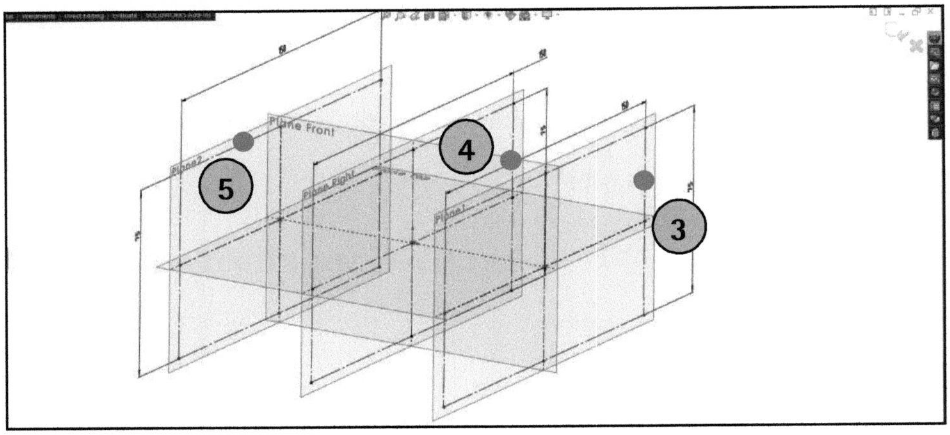

6.27.2.6 Creating the basic profile curves

Style Spline

Style Spline (Sketch toolbar)
On each **Work plane**, use the **Style Spline** function to create a freely chosen curve ending at the respective perpendicular rectangle lines (6, 7, 8).
Finish 3D-Sketch.

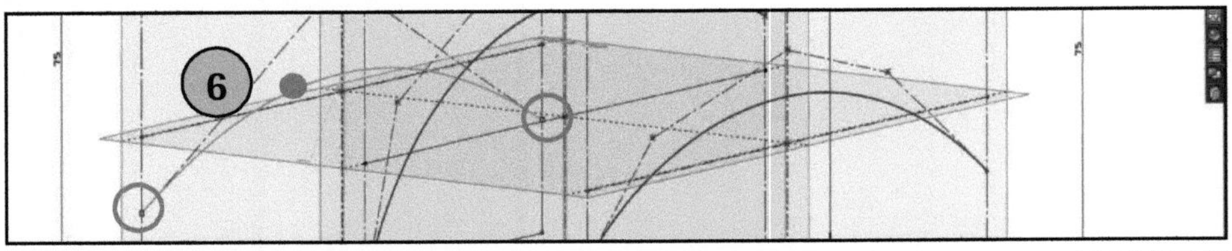

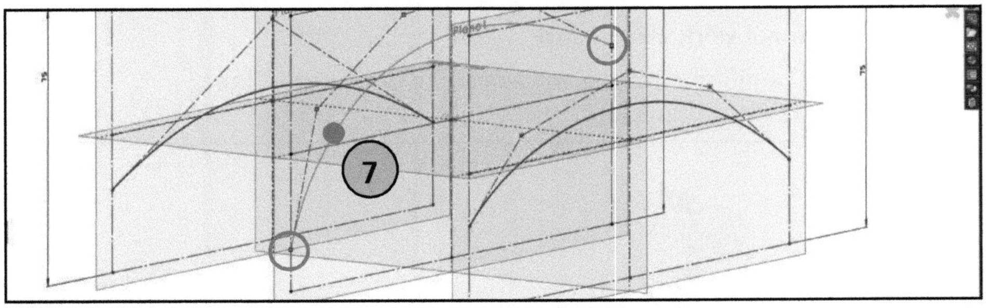

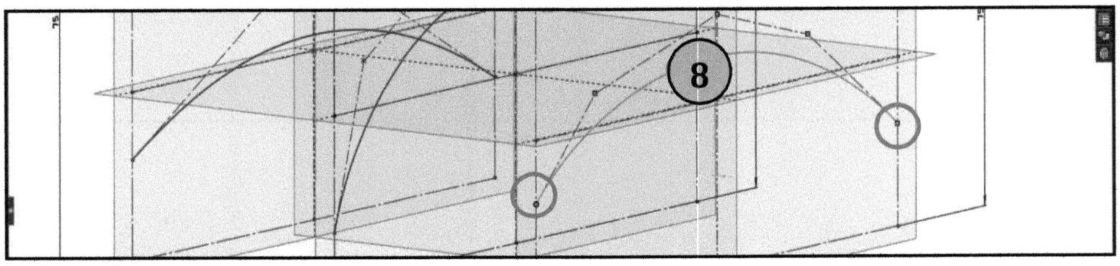

6.27.3 Generating basic profile curves for a surface shape

Lofted Surfaces

Lofted Surfaces (**Surface** tab)
Mesh density: **20**.
Select the **first** curve profile (9), accept the selection with **OK** (10).
Select the **second** curve profile (11), accept the selection with **OK** (12).
Select the **last** curve profile (13), accept the selection with **OK**.
Close dialog box (14).

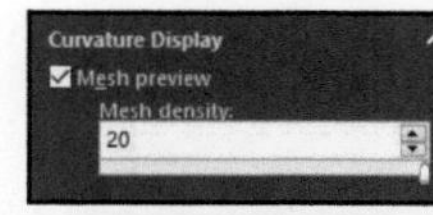

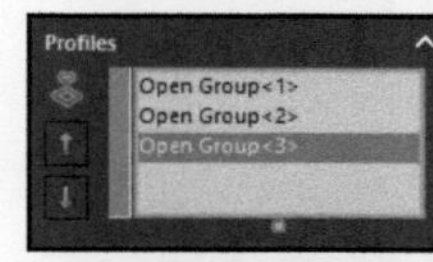

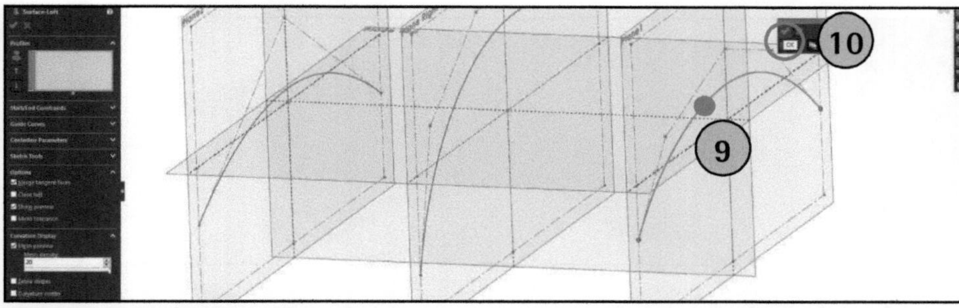

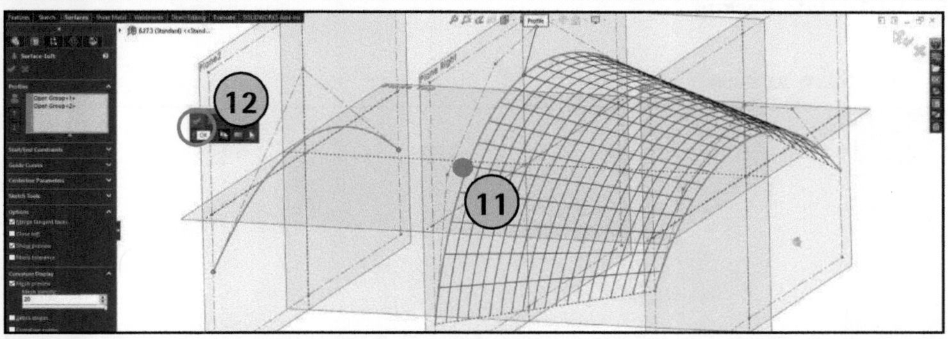

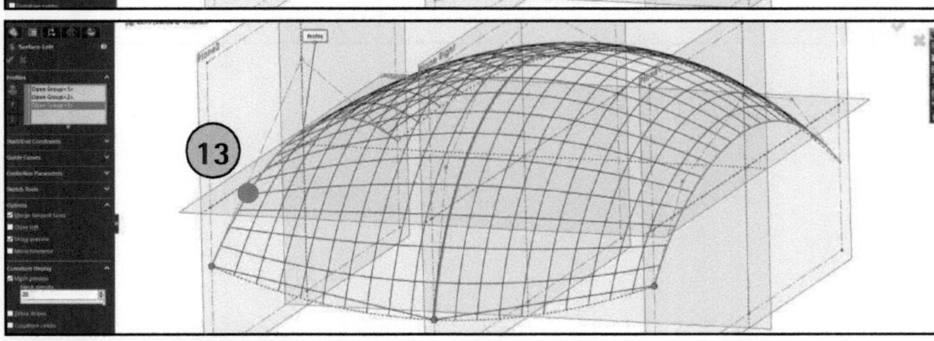

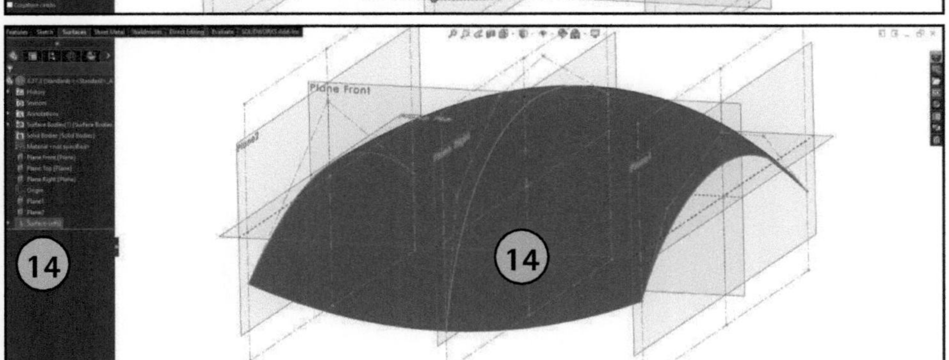

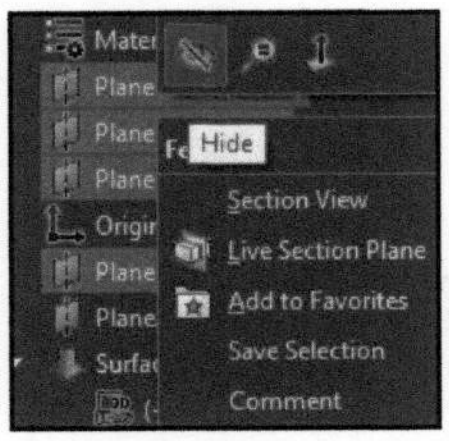

Thicken

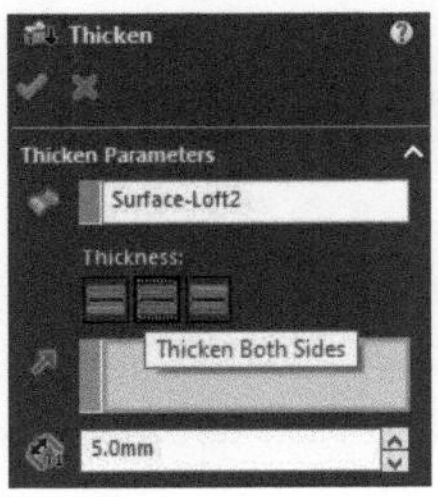

Save as New

6.27.4 Apply wall thickness, using the "Thicken" feature

- For the **Work planes** and **3D-Sketch** set the **Hide** option in the **FeatureManager**.

Thicken (**Surface** tab)
Select the created surfaces (6).
Set the wall thickness to **2** mm, **Thicken both sides 2** (7).
Close dialog box.

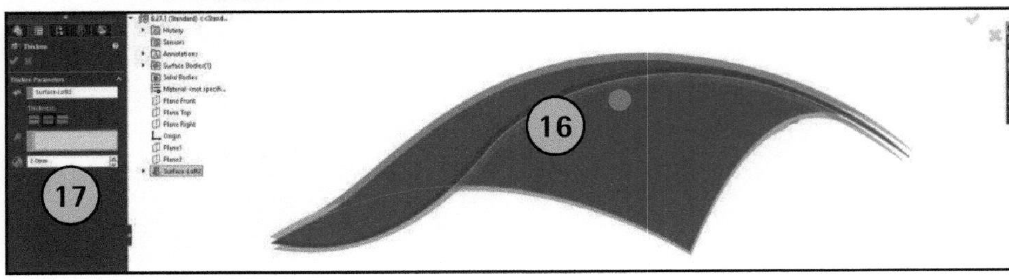

6.27.4.1 Data backup

Save as New / Enter a name of your choice.

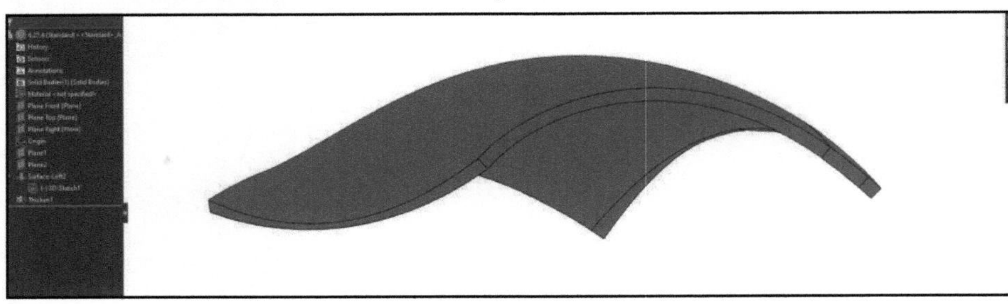

7

Dassault Systèmes
3DEXPERIENCE©
SOLIDWORKS Design
2026

Parts and Components

Create and Customize

Boolean form elements

7 Boolean form elements

7.1 Boolean form elements, basics

Constructive solid geometry is a technique for modeling solids used in 3D computer graphics and CAD programs, among other applications. Constructive Solid Geometry (CSG) allows a designer to create complex surfaces and solids by using Boolean operators to combine objects. Solids resulting from CSG often appear very complex, but in reality are nothing more than cleverly linked objects.

CSG is particularly common in CAD; approximately 60% of all mechanical components can be modeled with a CSG system that uses only cuboids and right circular cylinders. If more basic solids are permitted, 90% of all components in traditional mechanical engineering, primarily drilling, milling, and turning of components or their casting molds, can be naturally described using CSG.

7.1.1 Commands for "Boolean operations"

Solid bodies are commonly used in 3D modeling. You can perform the following operations with them:

- Combine multiple bodies into a single body.
- Remove sections from a body.
- Work with the intersection of bodies.
- Split a body.

You can use Boolean operation commands to create the required body from existing bodies. The Boolean operation commands are accessed once in the Part environment from the Home ribbon using the Add Body command, and again from the Surfacing ribbon using the Replace Face command.

The body type output from a Boolean operation matches that of the target body. When performing Boolean operations, Boolean features are displayed in PathFinder.

7.1.2 "Boolean operation" dynamic preview mode

After selecting a target body, the Boolean Operation command automatically enters preview mode. Preview mode:

- Shows only new faces created after the operation.
- Show the edges of the target body in a half the selection color.
- Shows tool bodies transparent with edges in the selection color.

7.1.3 "Boolean operations"

7.1.3.1 "Boolean Union", operation type "Add"

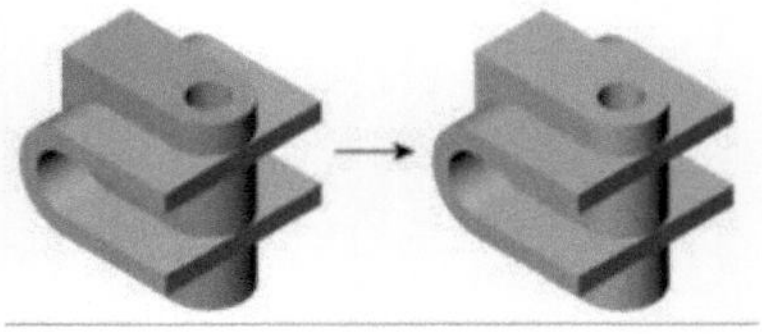

The Boolean union combines the selected bodies into a single body. All selected tool bodies are absorbed by the target body.

7.1.3.2 "Boolean Difference", operation type "Subtract"

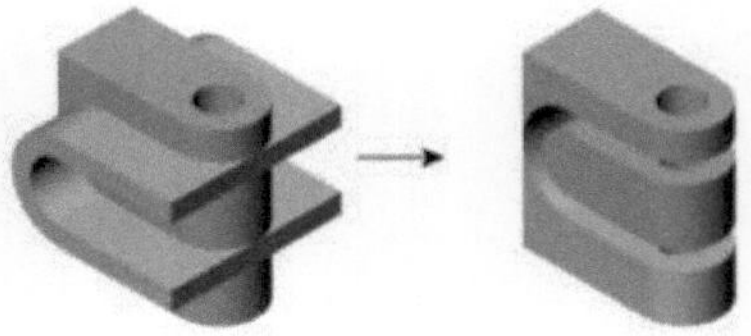

The Boolean union combines the selected bodies into a single body. All selected tool bodies are absorbed by the target body.

7.1.3.3 "Boolean Intersection", operation type "Combine"

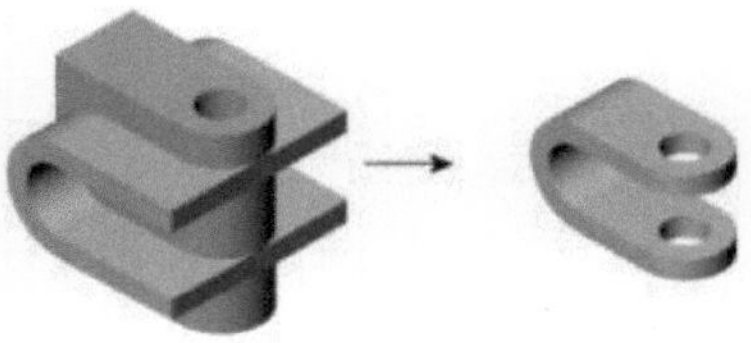

The Boolean intersection removes any volume that is not common to the selected bodies.

7.1.3.4 "Boolean Split"

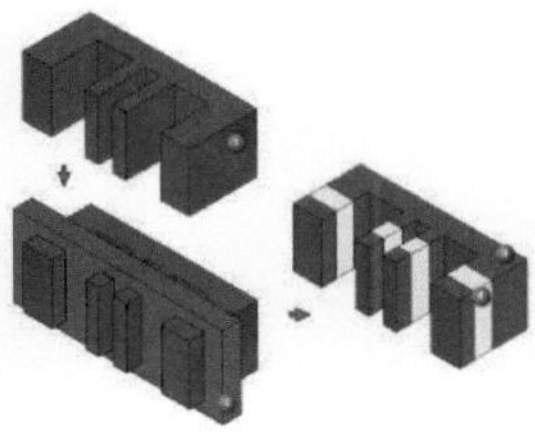

Boolean split uses a tool body to split a target body. The tool body can be a solid, a reference plane, or a surface. This can result in one or more additional bodies. If you use a reference plane or a surface to split a target body, two bodies are created.

Project XI

Boolean Basic Body

Create and Customize

Page 294 to 311

- Boolean Operations for Surfaces
  Base Areas using “Trim” feature
- “Boolean Difference”
  Operation type “Subtract”
  Rectangle-Circle-Difference using “Extrude” feature
- Boolean Operations for basic bodies
  Operation type “Add” and “Subtract”
  Converting “Features to Bodies
- Boolean Operation ”Combine Bodies“
  Operation type “Add”, “Subtract” and “Common”
- Boolean Operation ”Combine Bodies“
  Distance Shaft, using “Combine Bodies” feature
- Boolean Operation ”Combine Bodies“
  using “Split” feature
- Boolean Operation ”Multibody Part“
  Creating one part using “Combine Bodies” feature

7.2 Boolean Operations for Surfaces Base Areas using "Trim" feature

7.2.1 Creating the basic sketch

Neu

Engelke2026.
PRTDOT

7.2.1.1 Opening your own template file

- Menu Bar **New** / / click **Engelke2026.PRTDOT / OK**

Sketch

7.2.1.2 Boolean operations for surfaces, basic sketch

Sketch (**Sketch** tab)
Create a new sketch.
Select the **Top** plane (1).

Circle

Circle (**Sketch** tab)
Create a circle with a diameter of approx. **100** mm (2, 3).
Close dialog box
Proceed with the second circle in the same way.

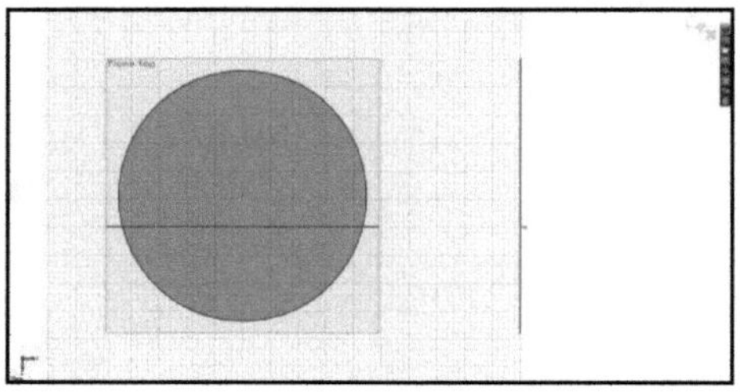

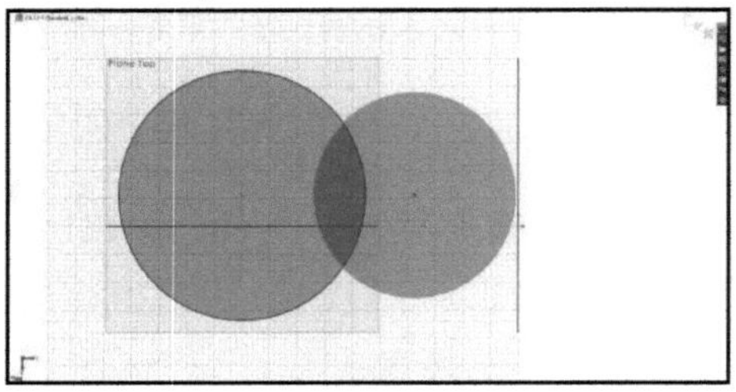

7.2.1.3 Resizing circular objects to the same size

Add Relation

Relation Equal

Add Relation (**Sketch** tab)
Select the two circles you created.
Activate relation **Equal**.
Close dialog box

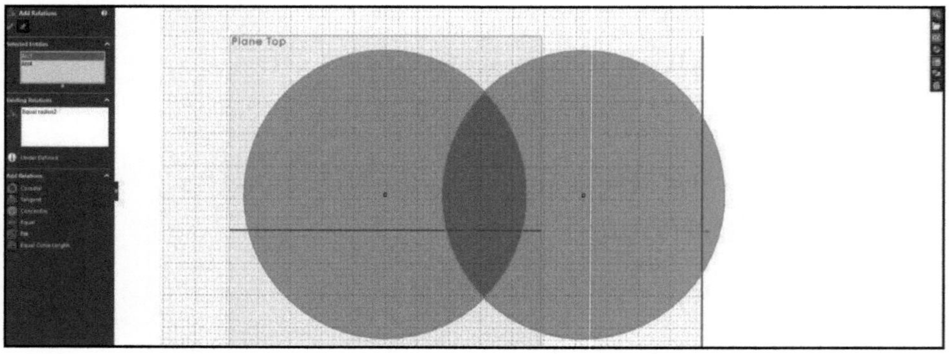

7.2.1.4 Data backup

Save as New

Save as New / Enter a name of your choice.

7.2.2 Boolean Operations for Surfaces Editing with Sketch functions

7.2.2.1 "Boolean Union", operation type "Add", using "Trim" function

Trim Entities (**Sketch** tab)
Select the highlighted circle segments (1, 2).
Close dialog box (3).

Trim Entities

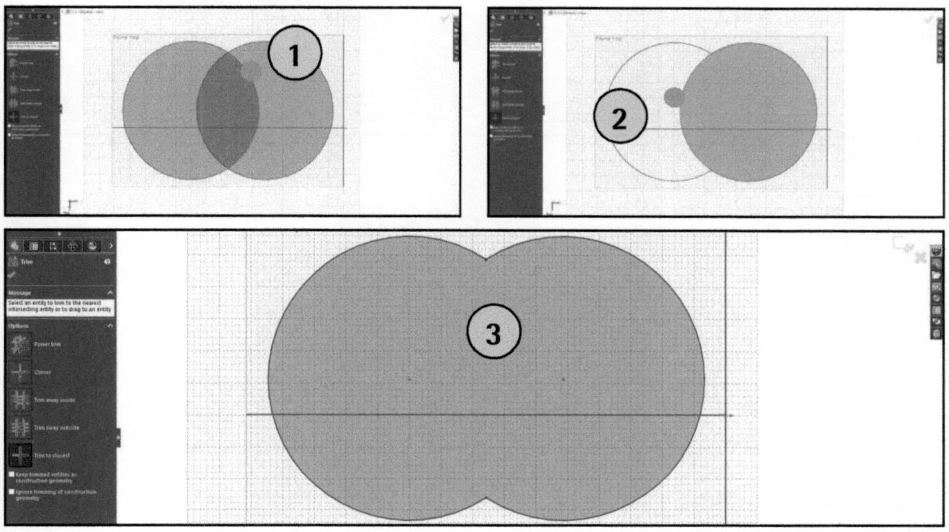

7.2.2.2 "Boolean Difference", operation type "Subtract", using "Trim" function

Trim Entities (**Sketch** tab)
Select the highlighted circle segments (4, 5).
Close dialog box (6).

Trim Entities

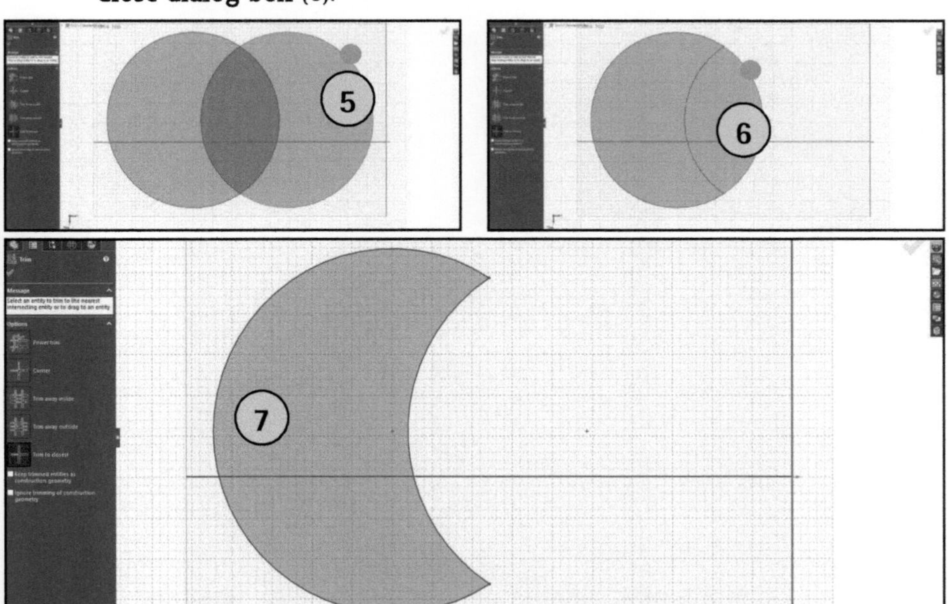

Trim Entities

7.2.2.3 "Boolean Intersection", operation type "Combine", using "Trim" function

Trim Entities (**Sketch** tab)
Select the highlighted circle segments (8, 9).
Close dialog box (10).

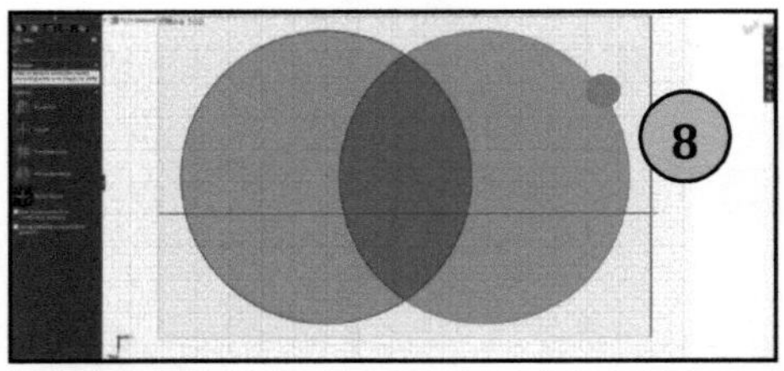

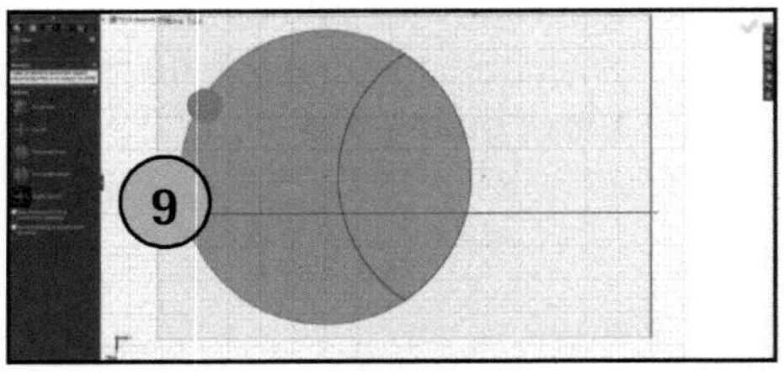

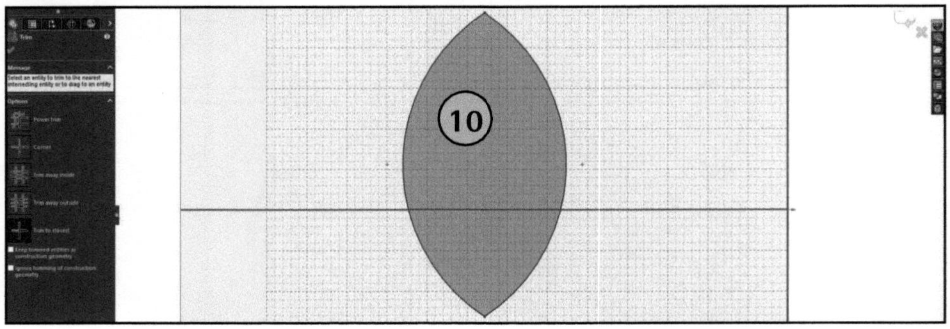

Save as New

7.2.2.4 Data backup

Save as New / Enter a name of your choice.

7.3 "Boolean Difference", operation type "Subtract", Rectangle-Circle-Difference using "Extrude" feature

7.3.1 Creating the base surface for differential extrusion

7.3.1.1 Opening your own template file

New

Engelke2026. PRTDOT

- Menu Bar **New** / / click **Engelke2026.PRTDOT / OK**

7.3.1.2 Base area using function "Center Rectangle"

Sketch

Center Rectangle

Circle

Sketch (**Sketch** tab), set a new sketch on the work plane **Top**.

Center Rectangle (**Sketch** tab)
Construct a **Center rectangle** at the plane center, dimensions optional (1).

Circle (**Sketch** tab)
Create a circle, dimensions optional (2).
Close dialog box / finish the sketch

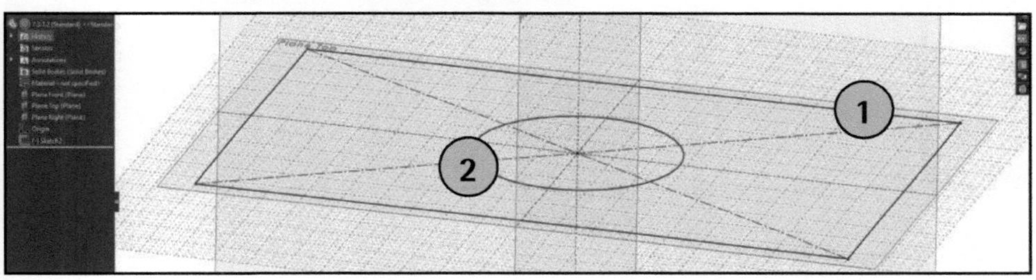

7.3.1.3 Creating volumes using the "Extrude" feature

Extrude

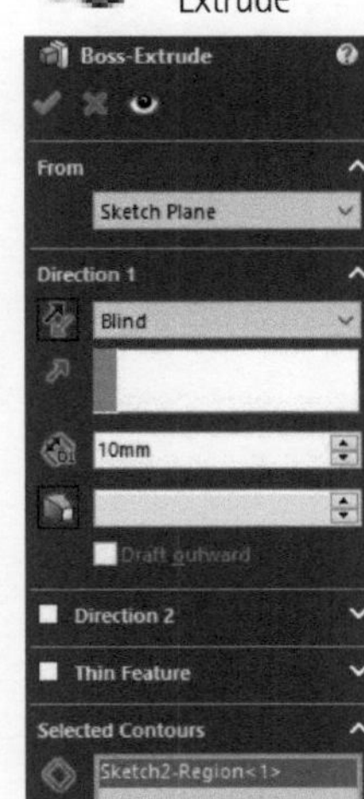

Extrude (**Features** tab)
Choose the constructed **sketch2-Region** (3).
Click on the arrow in the middle of the cuboid (4).
Drag the scale to **10** mm (5).
Close dialog box.

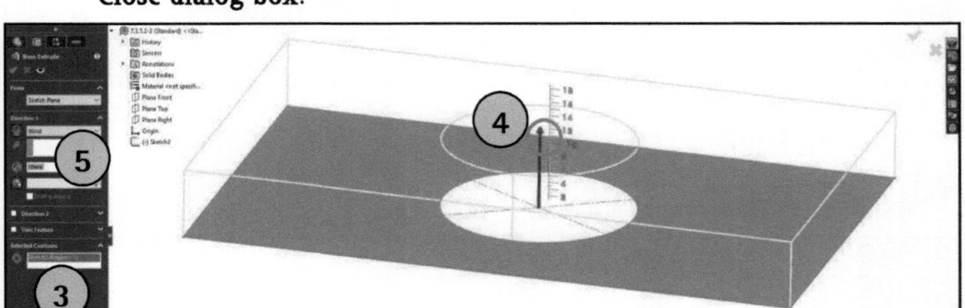

7.3.1.4 Data backup

Save as New / Enter a name of your choice.

Save as New

7.4 Boolean Operations for basic bodies Operation type "Add" and "Subtract" Converting "Features to Bodies"

7.4.1 Boolean Operations for basic bodies, Operation type "Add", using "Extruded-Boss"

7.4.1.1 Open the working file

Open

Open (Menu bar) / Component from the book-DVD / **OK**

7.4.1.2 Operation type "Add", using "Extruded-Boss", the creation

Extrude (Features tab)
Choose the constructed **Sketch2-Region1** and **Region2** as the basic sketch.
Click on the arrow in the middle of the cuboid, drag the arrow down.
Drag the scale to **10** mm (1) / **Close dialog box**.

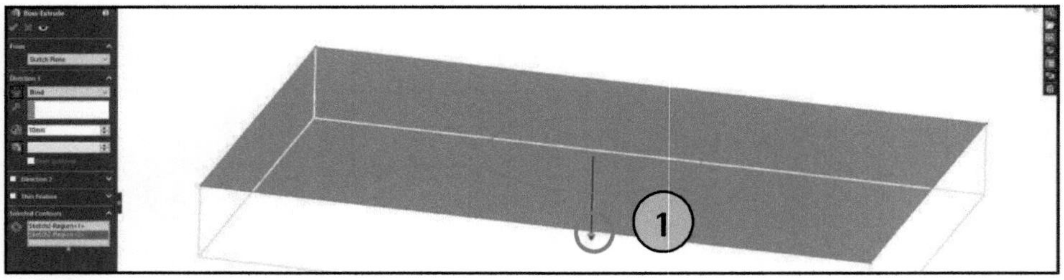

Extrude (Features tab)
Choose the constructed **Sketch2-Region1** as the basic sketch.
Click on the arrow in the middle of the cuboid, drag the arrow upwards.
Drag the scale to **25** mm (2) / **Close dialog box**.

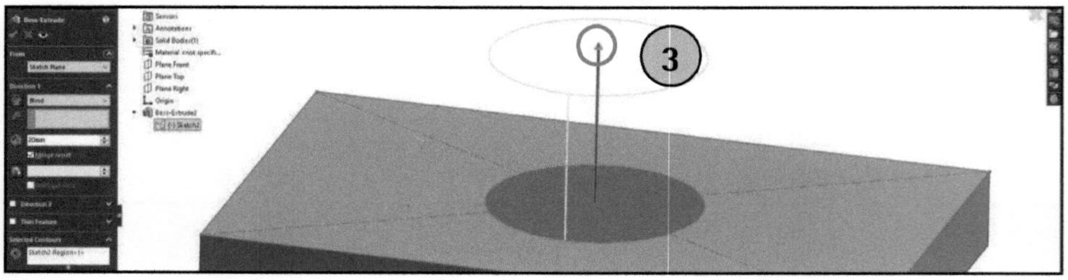

7.4.1.3 Data backup

Save as New

Save as New / Enter a name of your choice.

7.4.2 "Converting Features to Bodies"

For parts, you can convert features to bodies and surfaces while maintaining geometric references from other parts, assemblies, and drawings. This tool lets you remove unneeded feature history, while retaining the bodies and surfaces.
When you use this tool, you should create a back up of the original document because you cannot edit the original geometry after the conversion.

7.4.2.1 Converting "Features to Bodies", the creation

The converting **Features to Bodies** results in the merging of all feature operations into a component.

Converted Body (FeatureManager design tree)
Right click to the part.
Enter a new **File Name** and **File path**.
Close dialog box (5).

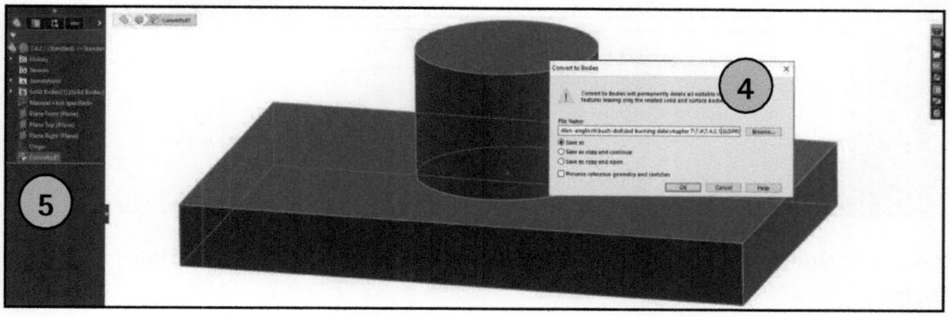

Converted Body

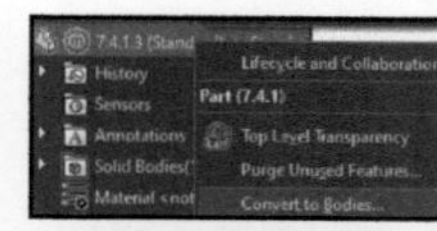

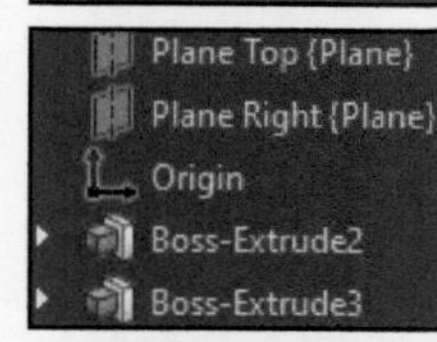

7.4.2.2 Data backup

Save as New / Enter a name of your choice.

Save as New

Open

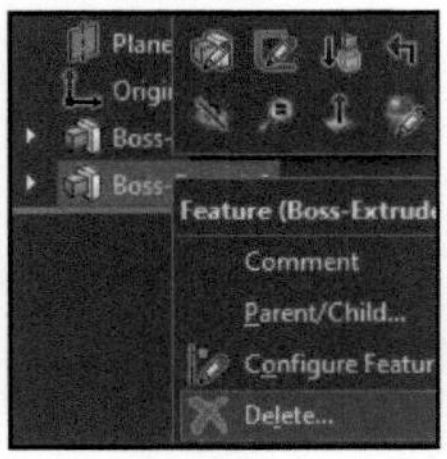

7.4.3 Boolean Operations for basic bodies Operation type "Subtract", using "Extruded Cut"

7.4.3.1 Open the working file

Open (Menu bar) / Component from the book-DVD / **OK**

7.4.3.2 Create basic component

- In the **FeatureManager**, delete the cylinder entry **Boss-Extrude3** (1, 2, 3).

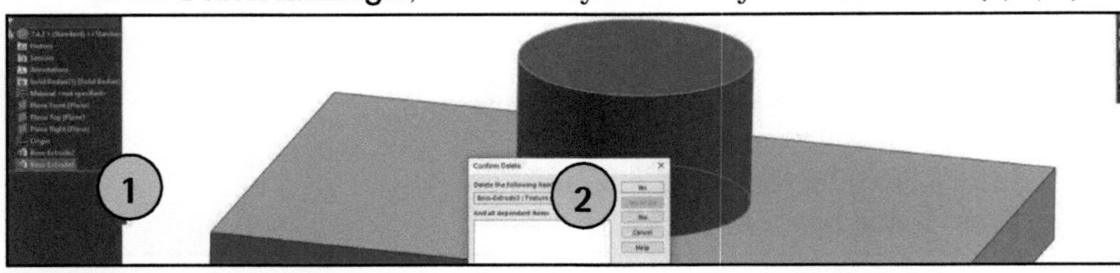

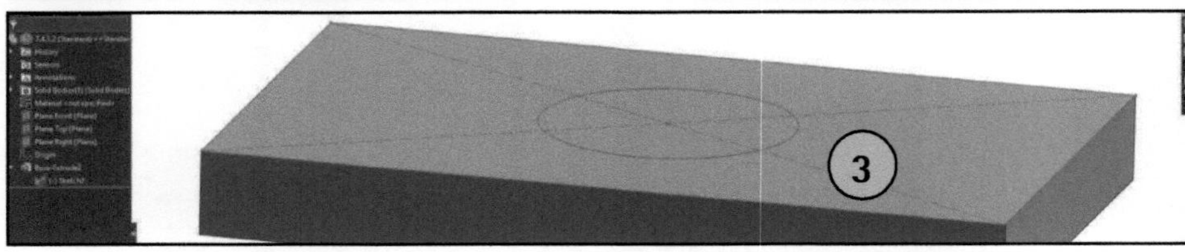

7.4.3.3 Operation type "Subtract", using "Extruded Cut", the creation

Extruded Cut

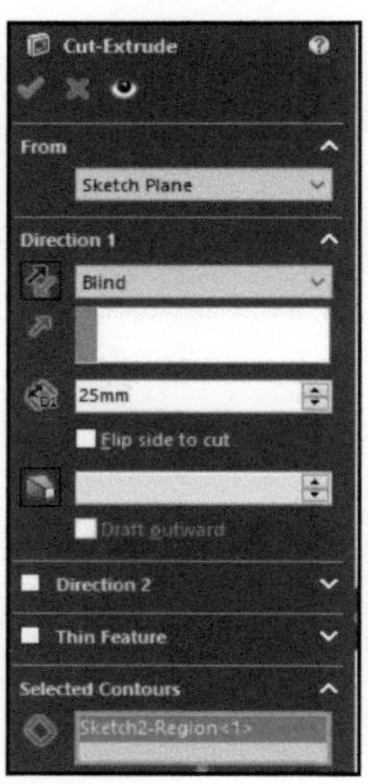

Extrude Cut (**Features** tab)
Choose the constructed **Sketch2-Region1** as the basic sketch (4).
Click on the arrow in the middle of the cuboid, drag the arrow down (5).
Drag the scale to **25** mm / **Close dialog box**.

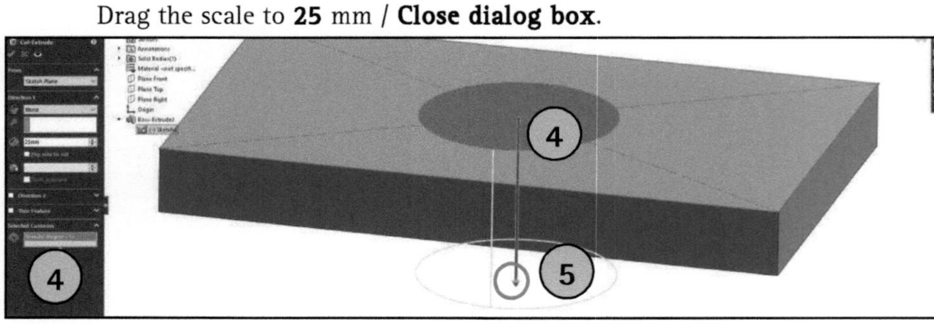

7.4.3.4 Data backup

Save as New

Save as New / Enter a name of your choice.

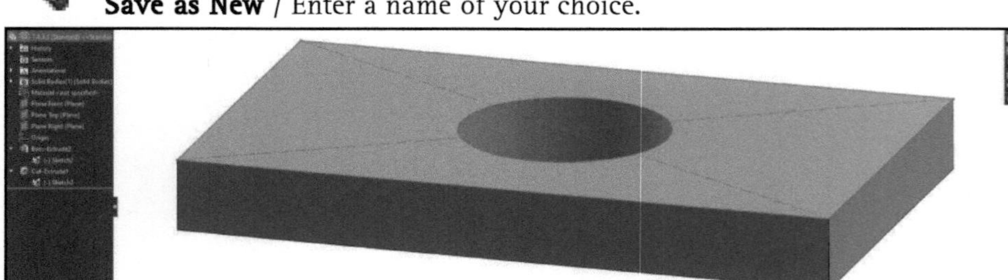

7.4.3.5 Converting "Features to Bodies", the creation

The converting **Features to Bodies** results in the merging of all feature operations into a component.

Converted Body (FeatureManager design tree)
Right click to the part.
Enter a new **File Name** and **File path** (6).
Set the option **Preserve reference geometry and sketches** (7), for further editing.
Close dialog box (8).

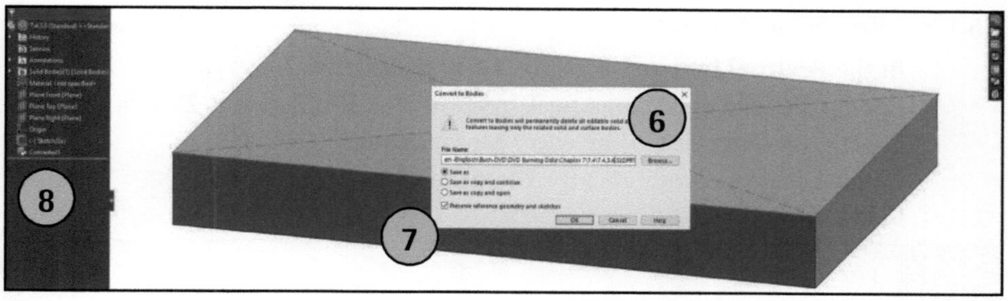

Converted Body

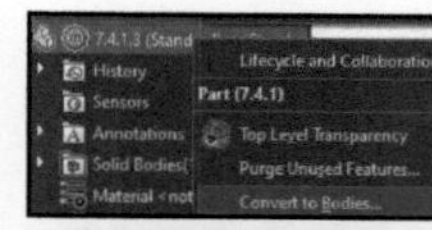

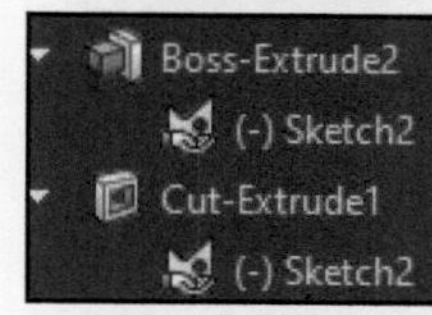

7.4.3.6 Data backup

Save as New / Enter a name of your choice.

Save as New

7.5 Boolean Operation "Combine Bodies" Operation type "Add", "Subtract" and "Common"

7.5.1 Boolean Operations "Combine Bodies" Cuboid and cylinder operation type "Add"

7.5.1.1 Adjusting the basic body, open the working file

Open

Open (Menu bar) / Component from the book-DVD / **OK**

7.5.1.2 Create basic component

- In the **FeatureManager**, activate the **Boss-Extrude3** entry.
- Change the end conditions for **Direction 1** to **Blind** height **25** mm (1)
- Disable for **Direction 1** the entry **Merge results** (2).
- Change the end conditions for **Direction 2** to **Through All** (3).
  Close dialog box.

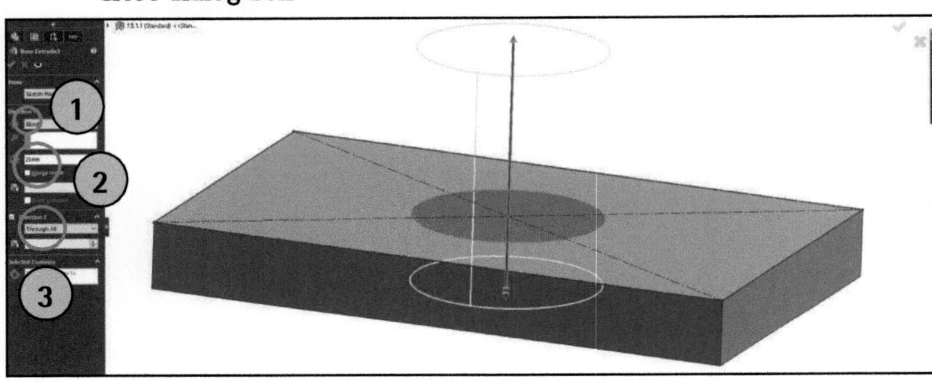

7.5.1.3 "Combine Bodies" "Add", basics

In a multibody part, you can combine multiple bodies to create a single body.

You can only combine bodies contained within one multibody part file. You cannot combine two separate parts. However, you can create a multibody part by using Insert Part to place one part into the other part file. Then you can use Combine on the multibody part.

Combine

Combine (Menu tab **Insert** / **Features**) (4)

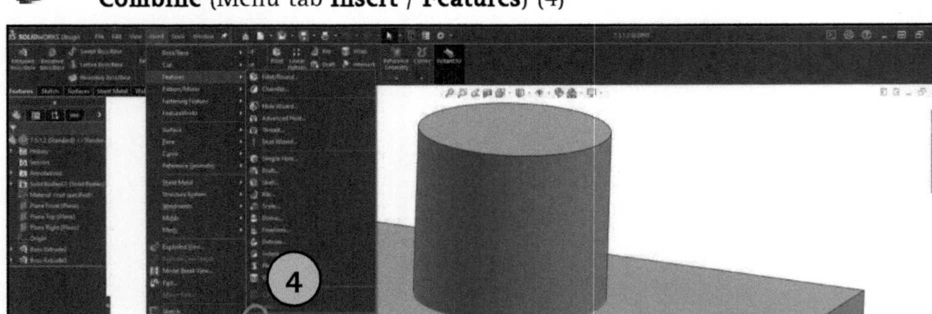

7.5.1.4 "Combine Bodies" "Add", the creation

- In the **PropertyManager**, under **Operation Type**, click **Add** (5).
- Select the **Cuboid** and the **Cylinder** (6, 7).
- To check, click **Show Preview** (7).
- **Close dialog box**

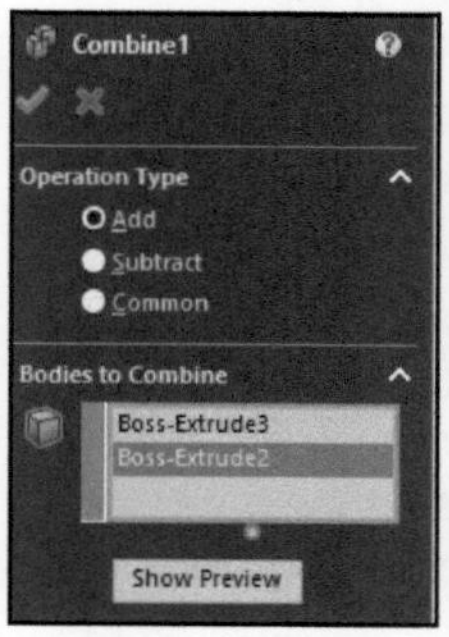

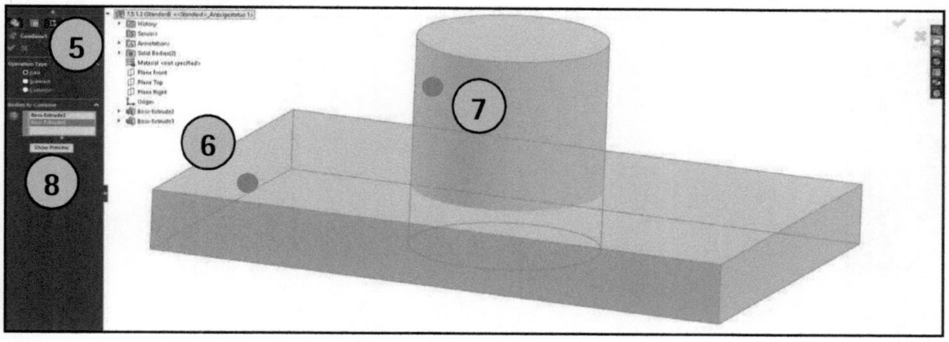

7.5.2 "Combine Bodies" "Subtract", the creation

- In the **PropertyManager**, under **Operation Type**, click **Subtract** (9).
- Select the Main Body: **Cuboid** (10).
- Select the Body to Subtract: **Cylinder** (11).
- To check, click **Show Preview** (12).
- **Close dialog box** (13).

Combine

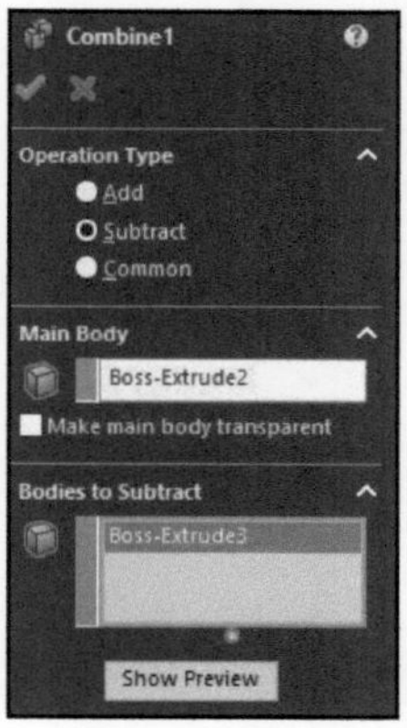

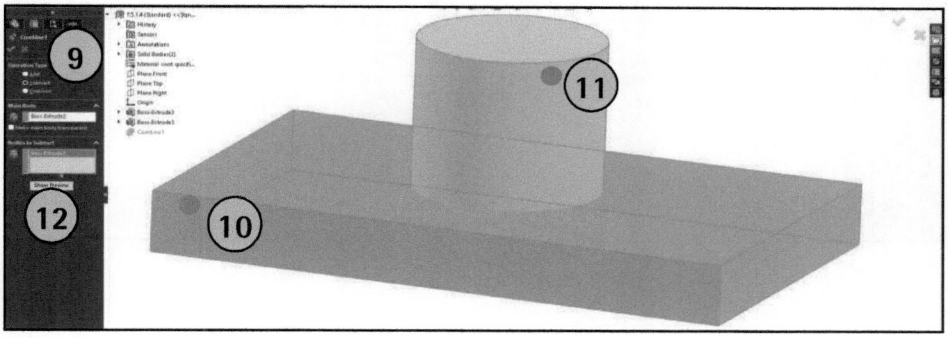

7.5.2.1 Data backup

Save as New / Enter a name of your choice.

Save as New

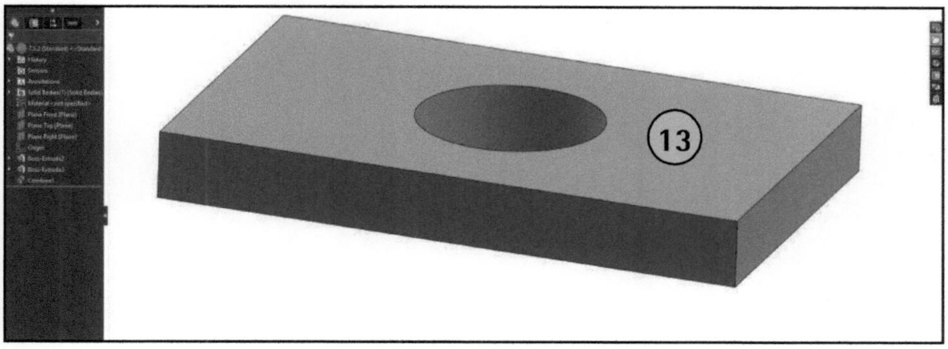

Combine

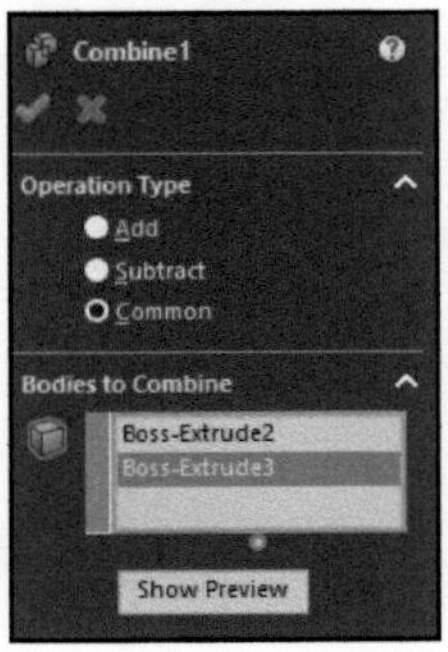

7.5.3 "Combine Bodies" "Common", the creation

- In the **PropertyManager**, under **Operation Type**, click **Add** (15).
- Select the **Cuboid** and the **Cylinder** (16, 17).
- To check, click **Show Preview** (18).
- **Close dialog box** (19).

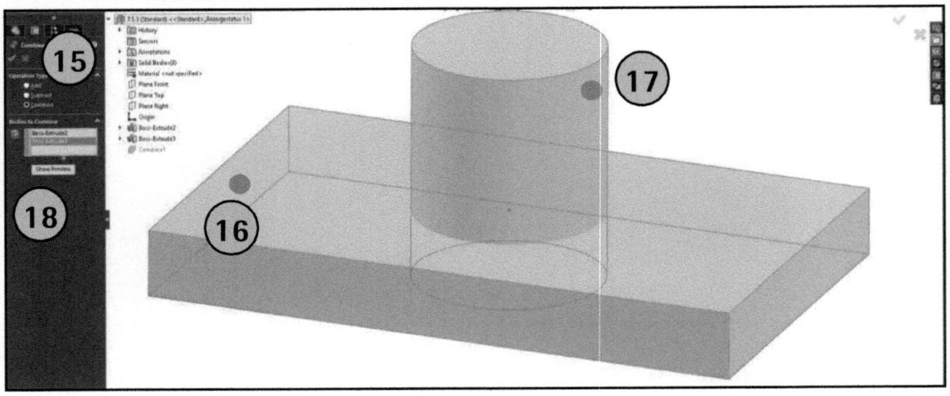

7.5.3.1 Data backup

Save as New

Save as New / Enter a name of your choice.

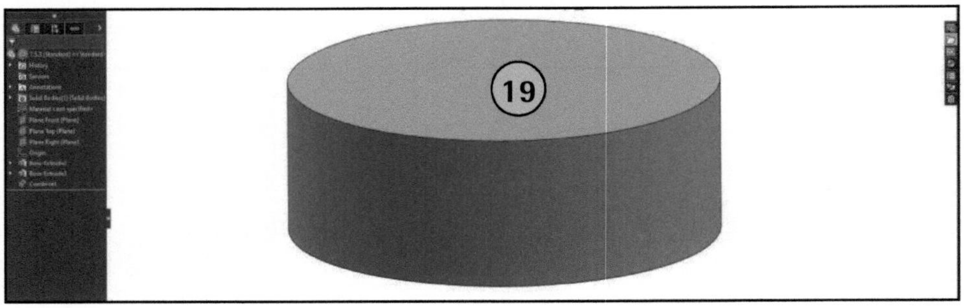

7.6 Boolean Operation "Combine Bodies" Distance Shaft, using "Combine Bodies" feature

7.6.1 Positioning basic sketches

7.6.1.1 Positioning the basic sketches, open the working file

Open (Menu bar) / Component from the book-DVD / **OK**

Open

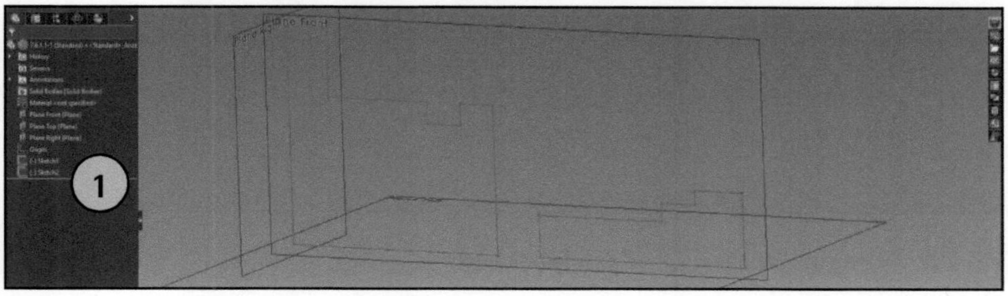

7.6.1.2 Positioning the basic body, moving the "Sketch2"

- Activate the **Sketch** entry under **Extruded Cut** (1).
- Select **Edit Sketch** in the **PropertyManager**.
- Activate **Move Entities** (**Sketch** tab)
- Select individual objects in **Sketch2** (2).
- Set the **From/To** and **Keep relations** parameters (2).
- Select the displayed starting point (3).
- Select the **Origin point** for repositioning (4).
- **Close dialog box / finish the sketch**

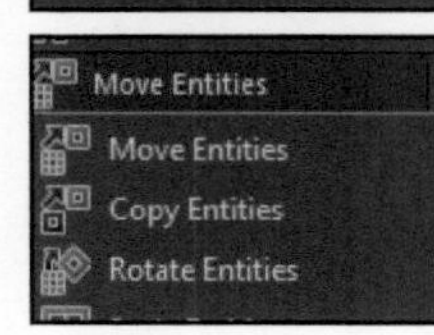

Move Entities

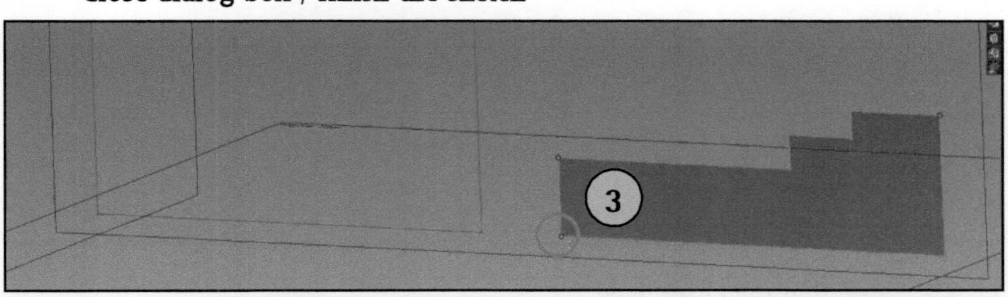

7.6.2 Distance Shaft, volume creation

7.6.2.1 Creating the inner body

Revolved

Revolved (**Features** tab)
Click the area **Sketch2**, using **Select Contours** (5).
Click the horizontal line to set it as the axis of rotation (6).
Close dialog box (7).

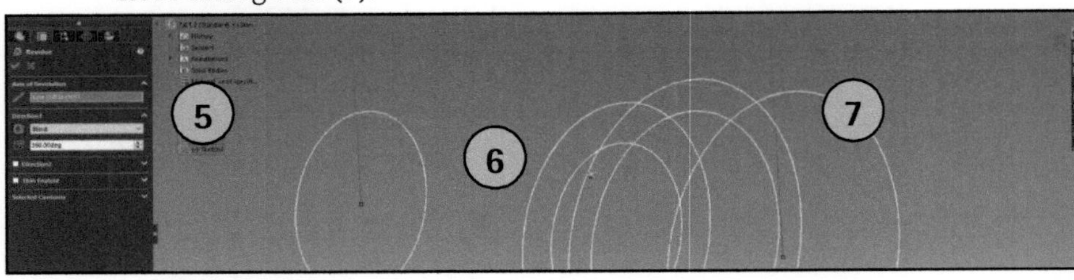

7.6.2.2 Length adjustment of the inner body

Instant 3D

Click **Instant3D** (Features toolbar)
Select the front face (8).
Click the pull arrow of the cylinder, drag to **5** mm (9).
Close dialog box.

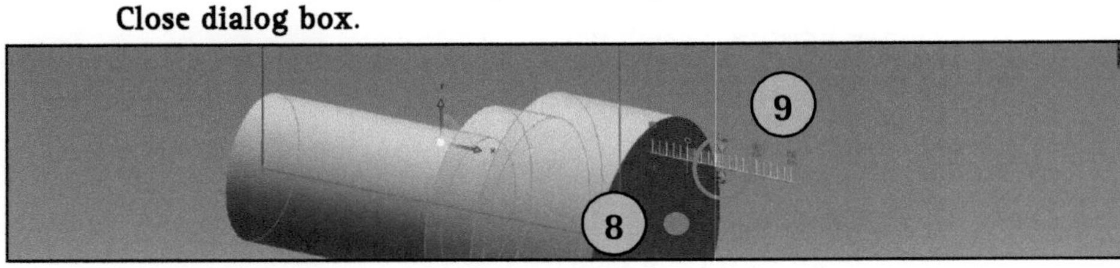

- Repeat the same process on the reverse side.

7.6.2.3 Creating the outer body

Revolved

Revolved (**Features** tab)
Click the area **Sketch1**, using **Select Contours** (10).
Click the horizontal line to set it as the axis of rotation (11).
Close dialog box (12).

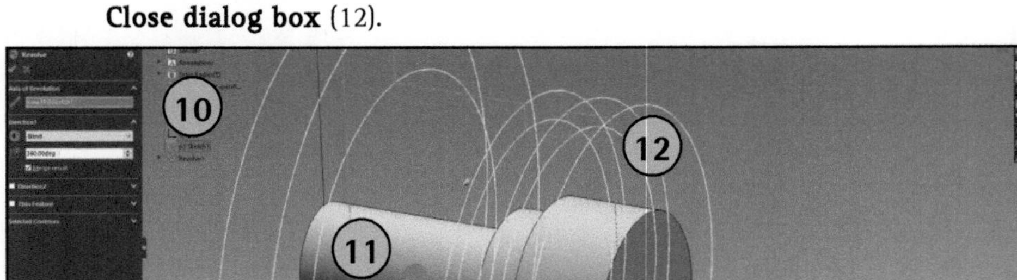

7.6.3 Boolean Operations "Combine Bodies" operation type "Subtract"

Combine (Menu tab **Insert / Features**) (4)

In the **PropertyManager**, under **Operation Type**, click **Subtract** (13).
Select the **Main Body**: Outer Cylinder (14).
Select the **Body to Subtract**: Inner Cylinder (15).
To check, click **Show Preview** (16).
Close dialog box.

Combine

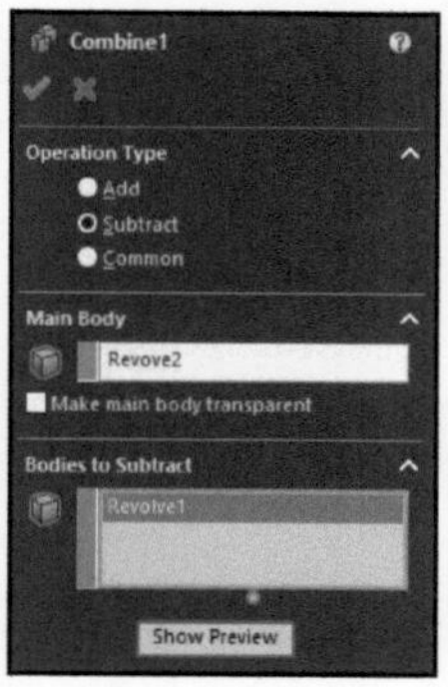

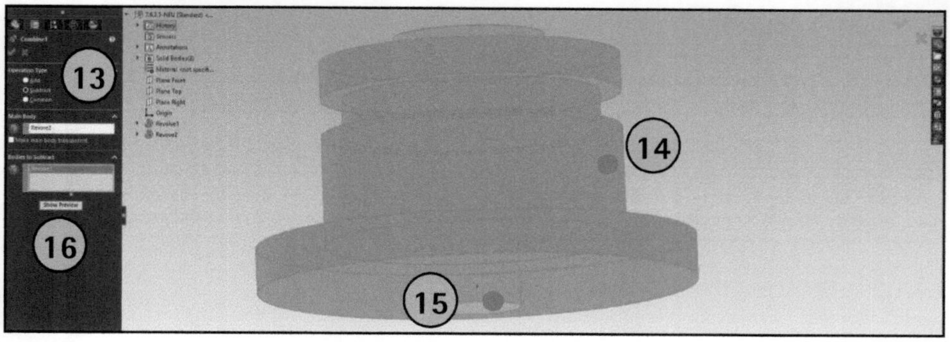

7.6.3.1 Data backup

Save as New / Enter a name of your choice.

Save as New

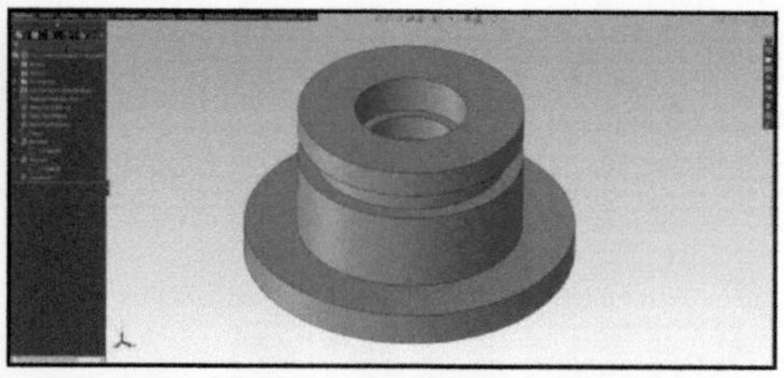

7.7 Boolean Operation "Combine Bodies" using "Split"

7.7.1 Boolean Operation "Combine Bodies" using feature "Split"

7.7.1.1 Open the working file

Open

Open (Menu bar) / Component from the book-DVD / **OK**

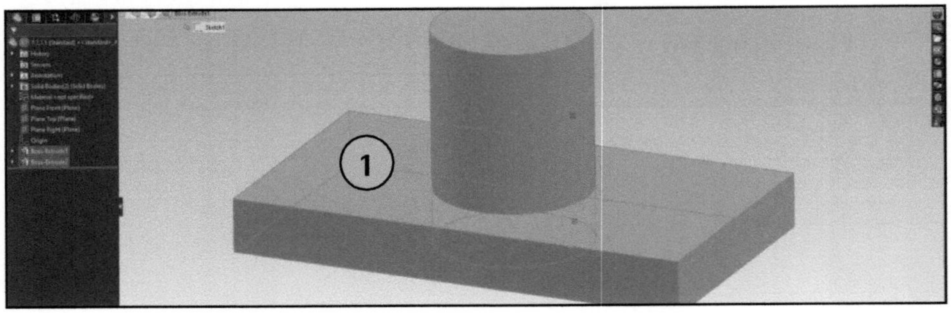

7.7.1.2 Splitting the Base Body

Split

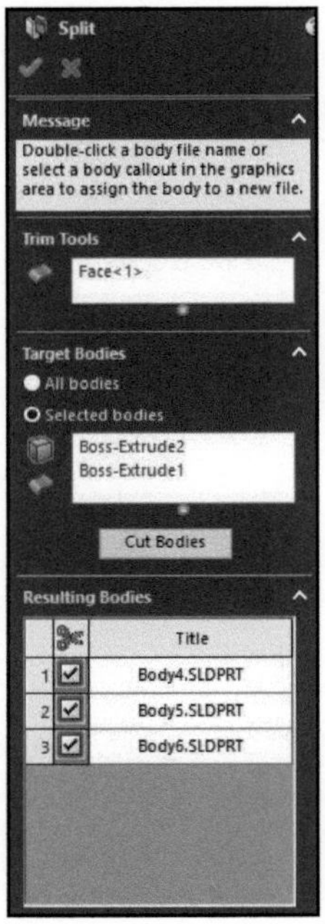

Split (Menu tab **Insert** / **Features**)
Select the base templates of your choice (1).
Select the upper face using the **Trim Tools** (2).

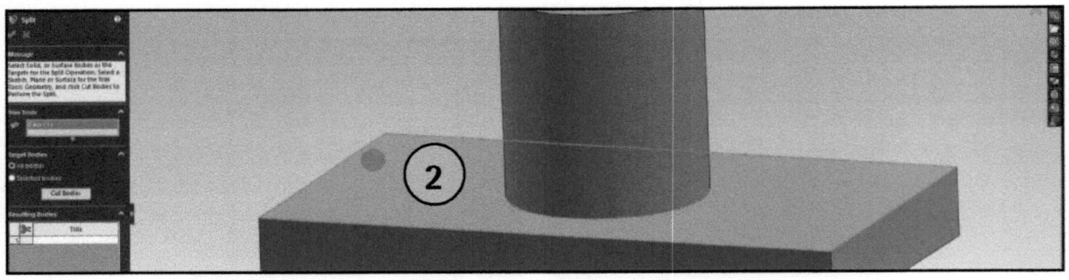

Activate option **Selected bodies** and **Cut Bodies** (3).

Select all the **Resulting Bodies** (4, 5).

Close dialog box.

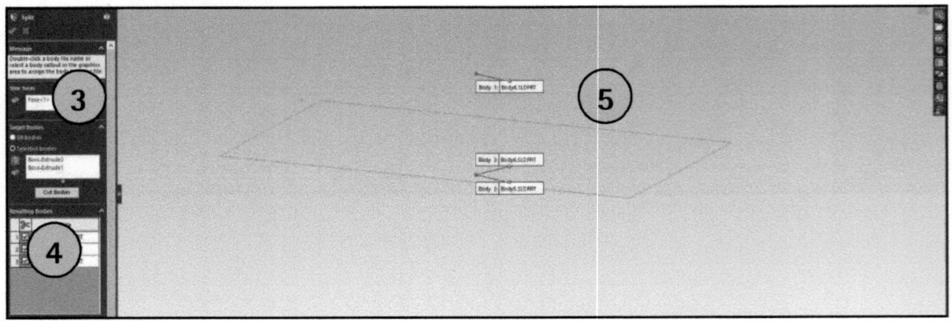

- The automatic data backup consists of three separate components.

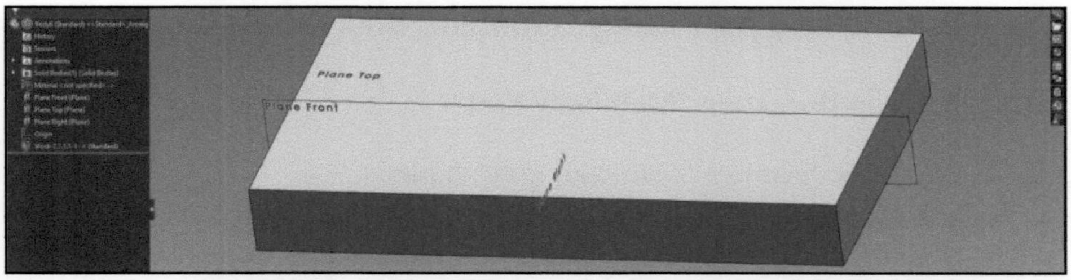

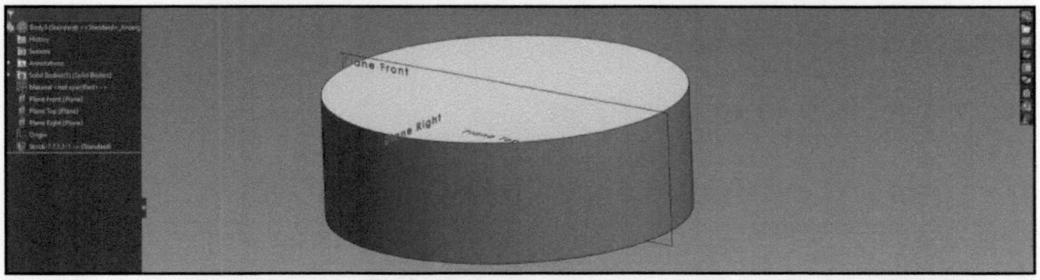

7.7.1.3 Data backup

Save as New / Enter a name of your choice.

Save as New

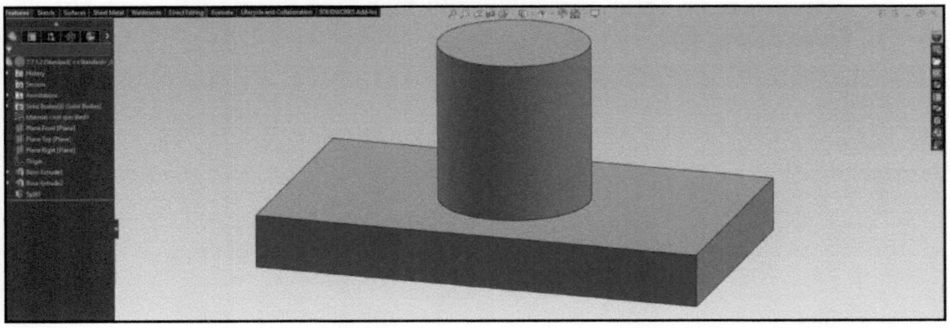

7.8 Boolean Operation "Multibody Part" Creating one part using "Combine Bodies" feature

7.8.1 Boolean Operation "Multibody Part"

7.8.1.1 Boolean Operation "Multibody Part", basics

The **Make Multibody Part** tool converts an entire assembly into a separate, single multibody part. The multibody part reflects all the assembly features that you create in the parent assembly. Features that you create on the multibody part will not be reflected in the parent assembly.

7.8.1.2 Open the working assembly file

Open

Open (Menu bar) / Component from the book-DVD / **OK** (1)

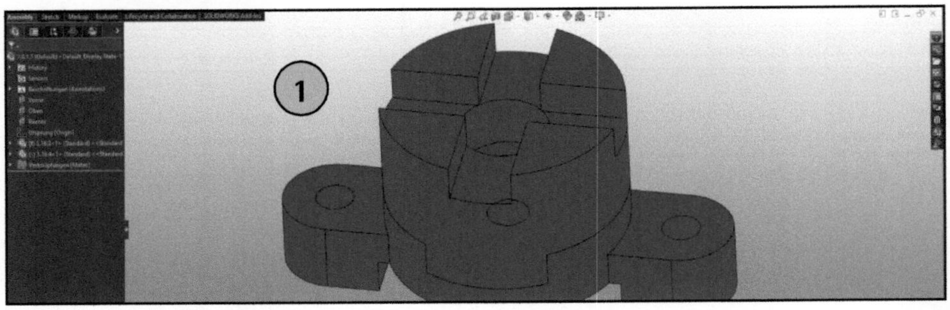

7.8.1.3 Boolean Operation "Multibody Part", the creation

Make Multibody Part

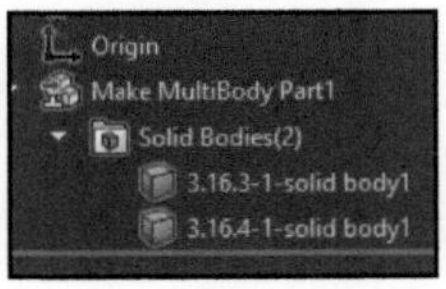

Make Multibody Part (Menu tab **Tools**)
Select the base templates of your choice.
Activate option **Solid bodies** (2) and **Break Link to original assembly** (3).
Close dialog box.

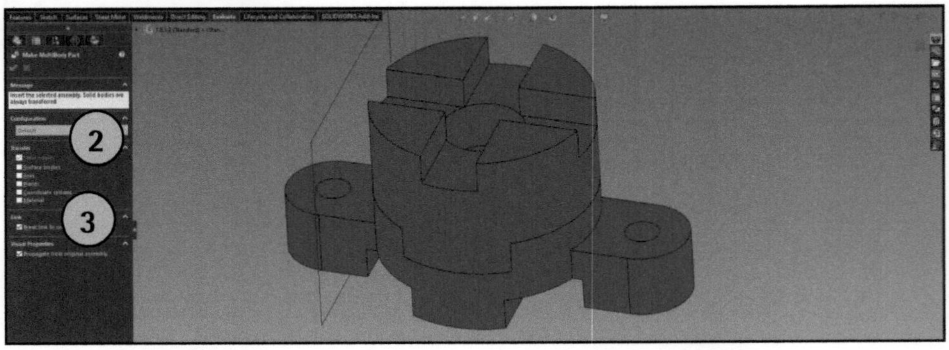

The assembly is converted into a part file using the **Make Multibody Part** feature.

7.8.1.4 Data backup

Save as New

Save as New / Enter a name of your choice.

7.8.2 Creating one part using "Combine Bodies" feature

Combine (Menu tab **Insert / Features**)
In the **PropertyManager**, under **Operation Type**, click **Add** (4).
Select the **solid body1** and **solid body2** (5, 6).
To check, click **Show Preview** (7).
Close dialog box

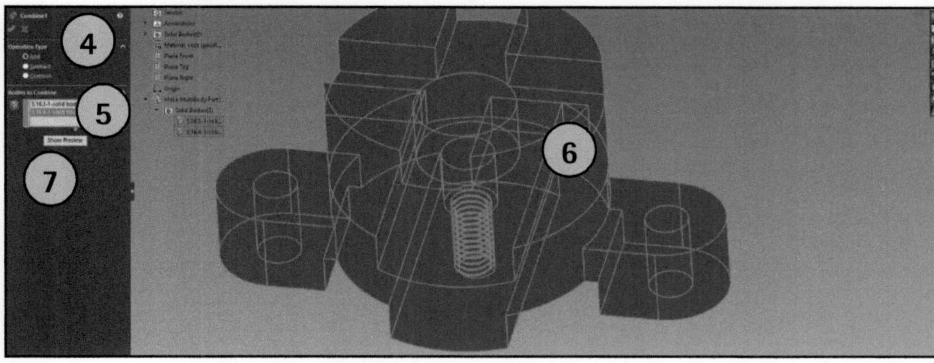

Combine

7.8.2.1 Data backup

Save as New / Enter a name of your choice.

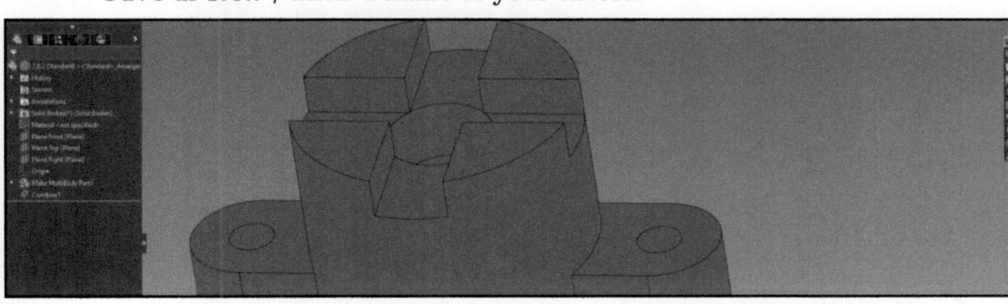

Save as New

8

Dassault Systèmes

3DEXPERIENCE©

SOLIDWORKS 2026

Parts and Components

Create and Customize

Model Changes

8 Model Changes

8.1 Model Changes, basics

The following feature functions are intended for specific tasks in design engineering. The input process is prescribed in SOLIDWORKS and must be followed.

Before using these functions within the design of a component, they should be performed at least once; it also makes sense to save the component created up to that point before using these functions.

8.1.1 Instant3D

Instant3D supports click and drag, enabling fast, intuitive edits with just a few mouse clicks.

With Instant3D, any user can edit their designs on screen in real time, enabling them to design like an expert. Instant3D offers new possibilities for design visualization while significantly reducing the number of steps required to complete design tasks.

When a design area is selected, new handles appear, allowing designs to be edited and created in real time. There are no dialog boxes or input fields.

The user simply selects areas to drag. These are then snapped to rulers on the screen to obtain precise values. Thanks to Instant3D, the user can truly focus their full attention on design and development and doesn't have to concentrate on operating the CAD system.

Here is a list of the form element functions that will be presented in this chapter:

8.1.1.1 Modifying sketches, geometry changes, an excerpt

Dimensional changes **Circle**, **Center Rectangle** and **Centerpoint Straight Slot**.

8.1.1.2 Modifying sketches, changing positions, an excerpt

Position changes for **Circles**, **Center Rectangle** and **Centerpoint Straight Slot**.

8.1.1.3 Modifying sketches, changes in position regarding relationship, an excerpt

Relationship **Merge**, **Horizontal**, **Parallel**, **Symmetric**, **Tangent** and **Collinear**.

8.1.1.4 Model Changes, example lists

- Modifying sketches changing positions, modifying sketches geometry changes, modifying sketches changes in position regarding relationship.
- Change cube model, change polygon model, change pyramid model, change Feature Hole Wizard, change Pattern Arrangement, changing edge breaking.
- Cube over geometry changes, hole changes in the component, changing the rotation angle, truncated cone to cone, truncated pyramid to pyramid, component adjustments using triad.
- Model changes using feature Flex, model changes using feature deform.

Project XII

Model Changes
Modifying Sketches

Page 316 to 322

- Modifying sketches, geometry changes
  Dimensional change for a sketch "Circle"
  Dimensional change of a sketch "Center Rectangle"
  Dimensional change for a sketch "Centerpoint Straight Slot"
- Modifying sketches, changing positions
  Position change for "Circles"
  Position change for a "Center Rectangle"
  Position change for a "Centerpoint Straight Slot"
- Modifying sketches,
  changes in position regarding relationship
  Change of position using the "Merge" relation
  Change of position using the "Horizontal" relation
  Change of position using the "Parallel" relation
  Change of position using the "Symmetric" relation
  Change of position using the "Tangent" relation
  Rectangle position change, alignment to center line,
  using the "Collinear" relation
  Rectangle position change, alignment to a guideline,
  using the "Parallel" relation

8.2 Modifying sketches, geometry changes

8.2.1 Dimensional change, a selection

8.2.1.1 Dimensional change for a sketch "Circle" using "SmartDimension"

Sketch

Circle

Smart Dimension

- Create a new sketch.
- Create a **Circle** (1).
- Enter the diameter measurement.
- Change the value for the measurement entry using the Modify box (2).

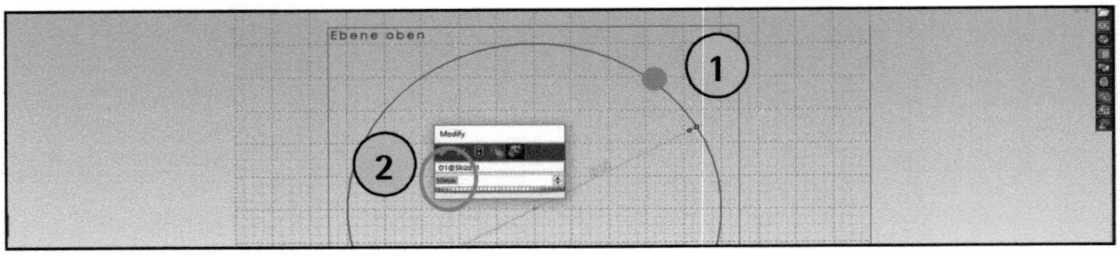

8.2.1.2 Dimensional change of a sketch "Center Rectangle" using SmartDimension

Center Rectangle

Smart Dimension

- Create a **Center rectangle** (3).
- Enter the dimensions for length and width.
- Change the values for the dimension entries using the Modify box (4, 5)

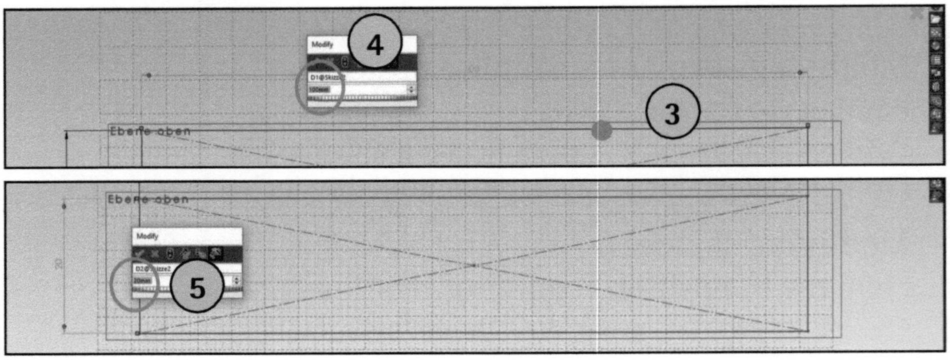

8.2.1.3 Dimensional change for a sketch "Centerpoint Straight Slot" using "SmartDimension"

Centerpoint Straight Slot

Smart Dimension

- Create a **Centerpoint Straight Slot** (6).
- Enter the length and width dimensions.
- Change the dimension values using the Modify box (4, 5).

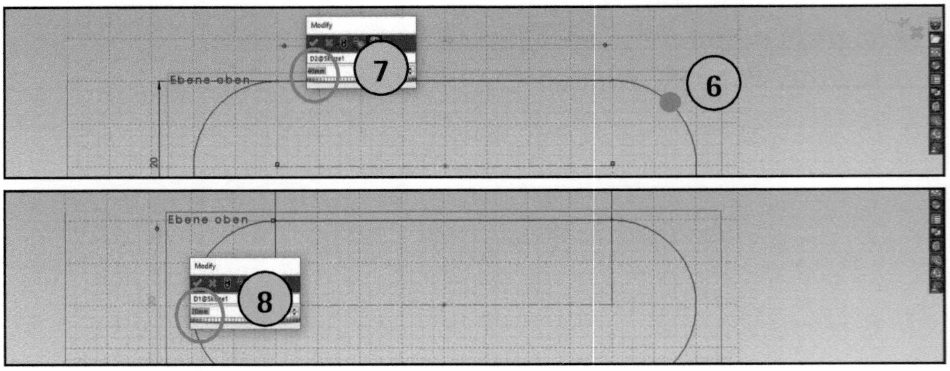

8.3 Modifying sketches, changing positions

8.3.1 Modifying sketches, changing positions, a selection

8.3.1.1 Position change for "Circles"

- Click on the central point, and then drag the **Circle** to a new position while holding down the mouse button (1, 2).

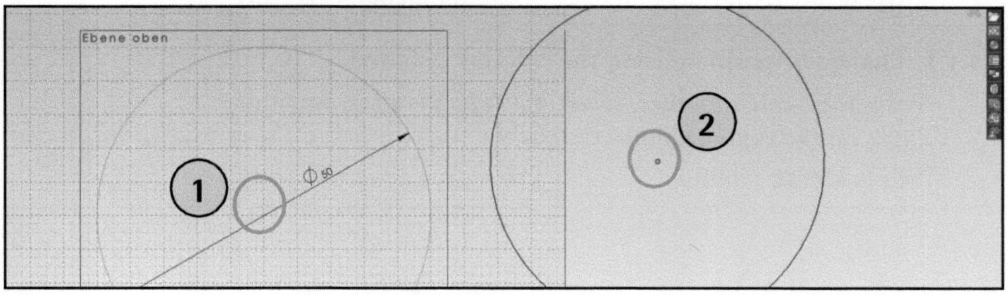

8.3.1.2 Position change for a "Center Rectangle"

- Click on the central point, and then drag the **Rectangle** to a new position while holding down the mouse button (3, 4).

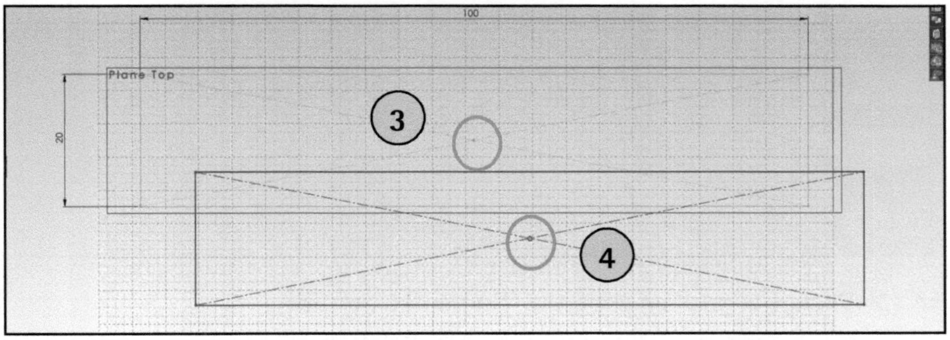

8.3.1.3 Position change for a "Centerpoint Straight Slot"

- Click on the central point, and then drag, while holding down the mouse button, the **Centerpoint Straight Slot** to a new position (5, 6).

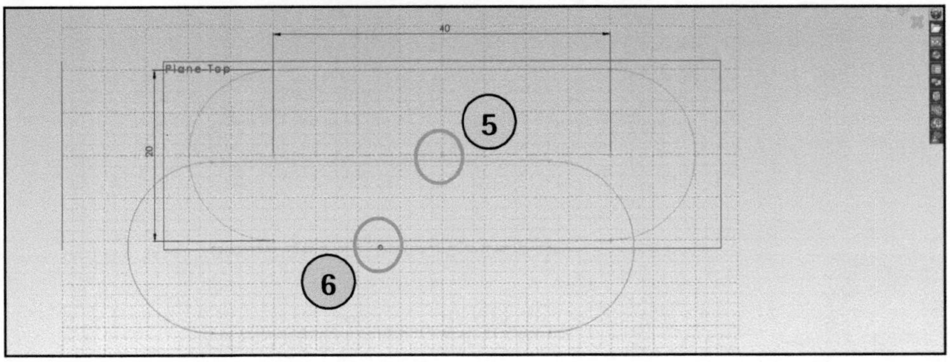

8.4 Modifying sketches, Changes in position regarding relationship

8.4.1 Changes in position regarding relationship, a selection open the working file

Open

Add Relation

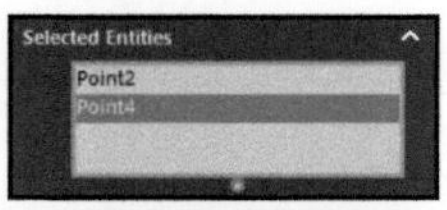

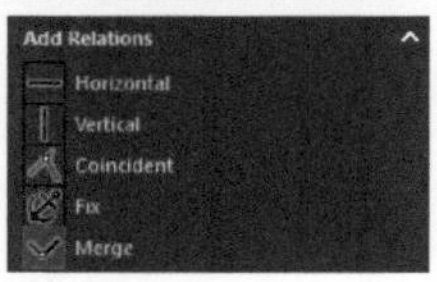

Relation Merge

Open (Menu bar) / Component from the book-DVD / **OK**.

8.4.1.1 Change of position using the "Merge" relation

- From the Sketch toolbar, select the **Add Relation** function.
- Click on the center points (1, 2, 3).
- Select **Merge** relation.

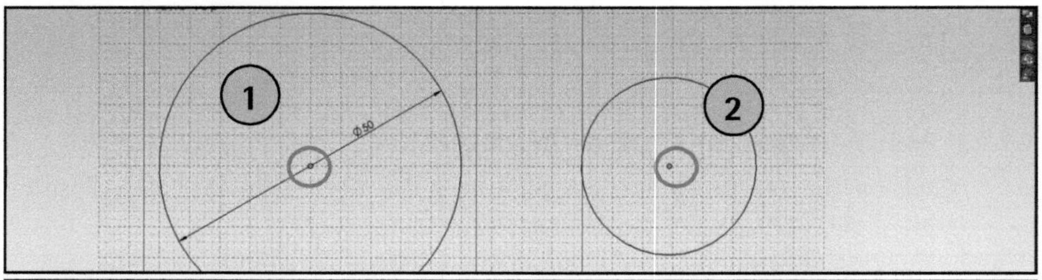

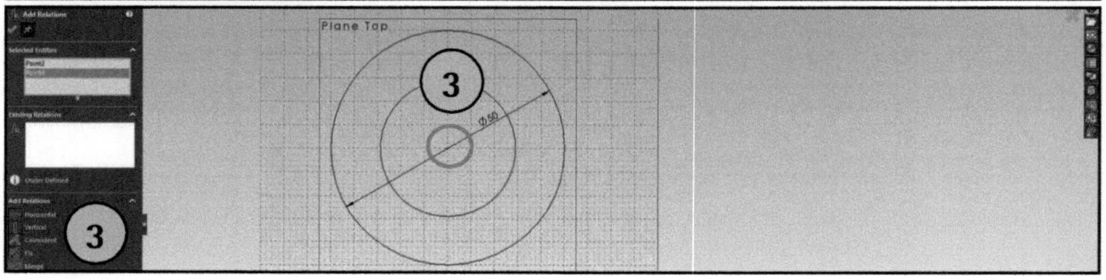

8.4.1.2 Change of position using the "Horizontal" relation

Add Relation

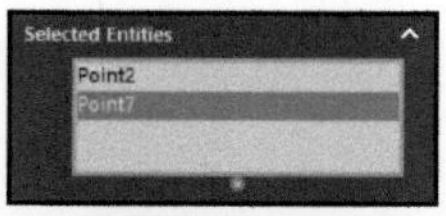

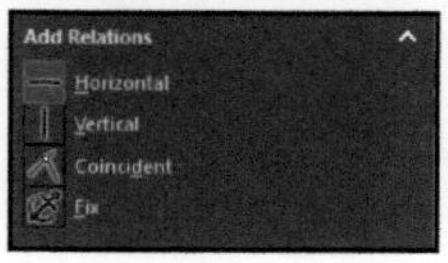

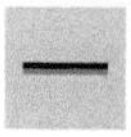
Relation Horizontal

- From the Sketch toolbar, select the **Add Relation** function.
- Click the center point (4).
- Click the horizontal line (5).
- Select **Horizontal** relation (6).

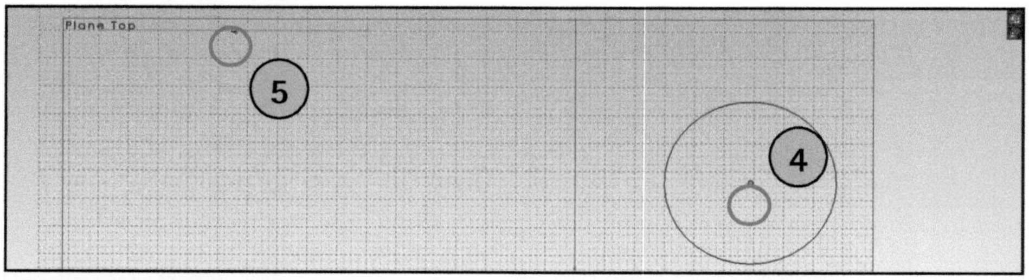

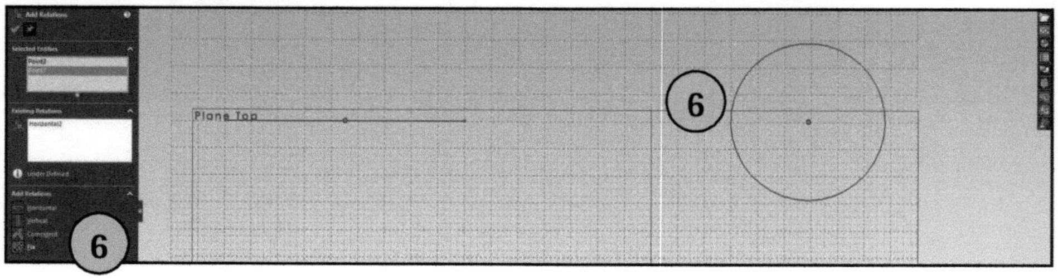

8.4.1.3 Change of position using the "Parallel" relation

- From the Sketch toolbar, select the **Add Relation** function.
  Click on the lines (7).
  Select **Parallel** relation (8).

Add Relation

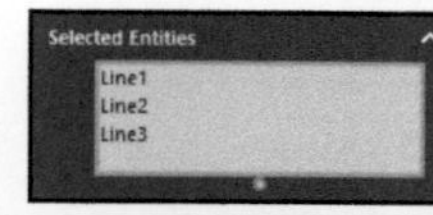

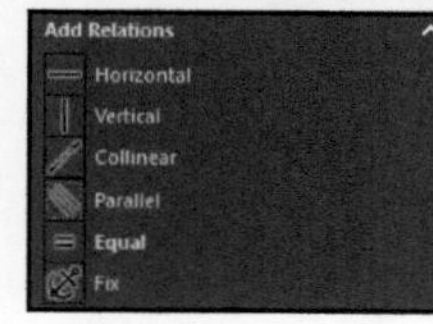

Relation Parallel

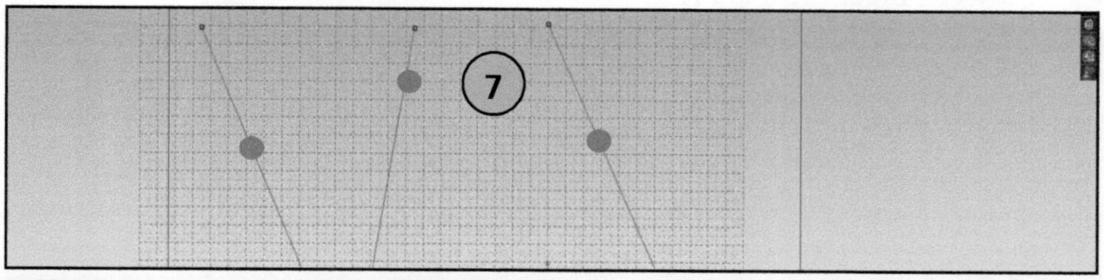

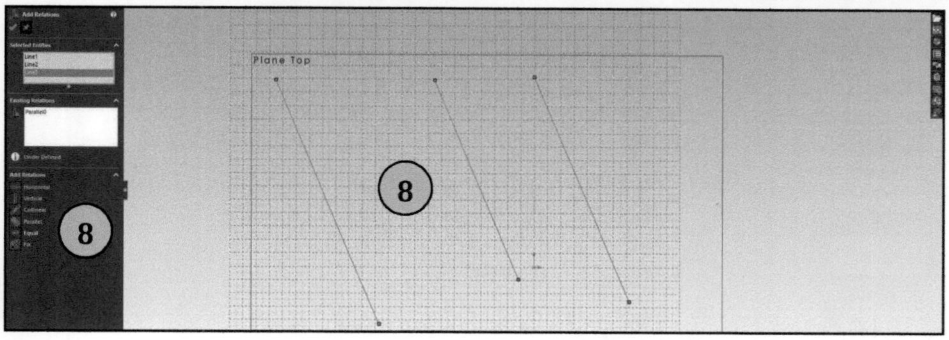

8.4.1.4 Change of position using the "Symmetric" relation

- Change the **Line properties** to **For Construction** (9).

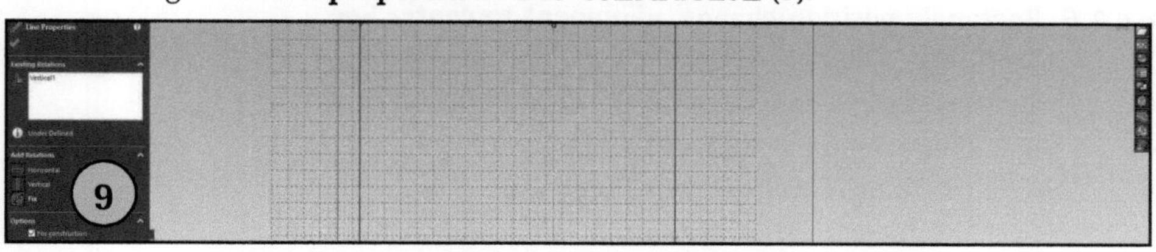

- From the Sketch toolbar, select the **Add Relation** function.
- Click on the lines (10).
- Select **Symmetric** relation (11).

Add Relation

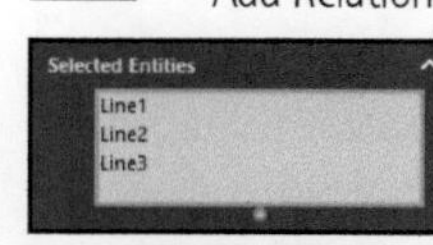

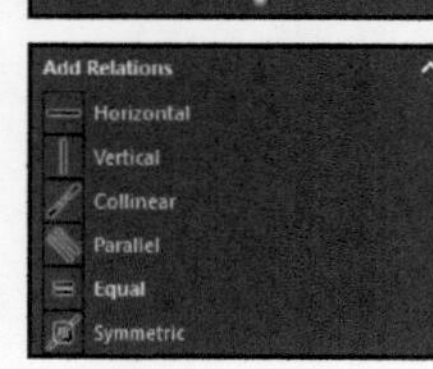

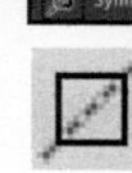

Relation Symmetric

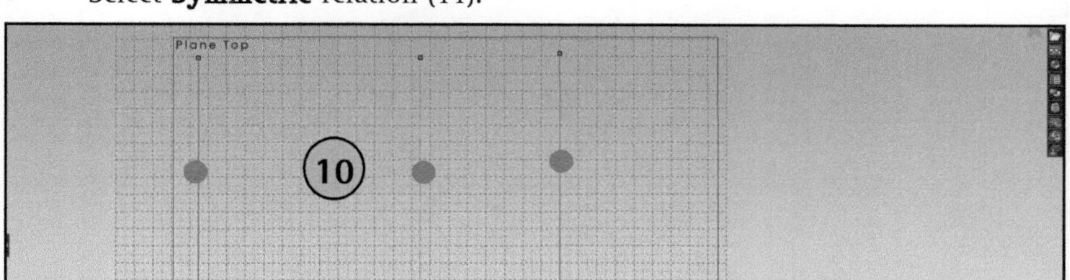

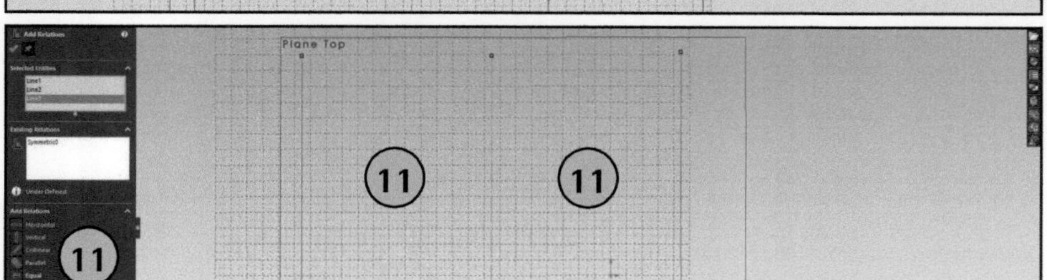

8.4.1.5 Change of position using the "Tangent" relation

Add Relation

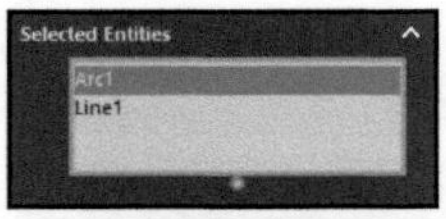

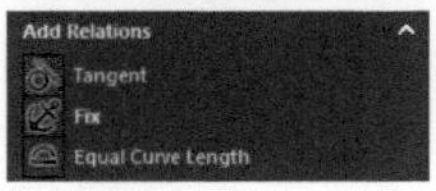

Relation Tangent

- From the Sketch toolbar, select the **Add Relation** function.
- Click on the Circle and the line (12, 13).
- Select **Tangent** relation (14).

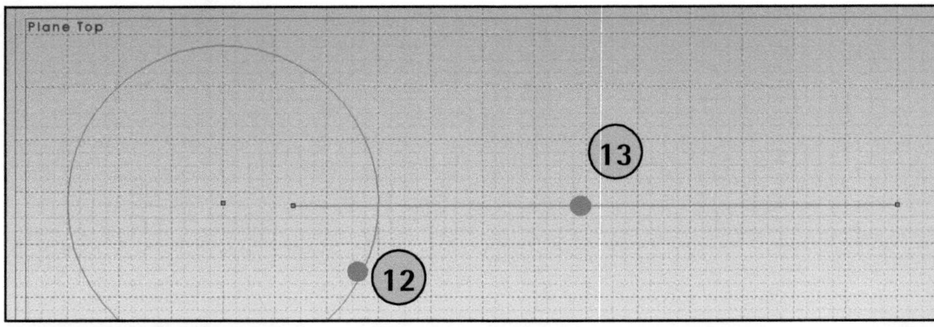

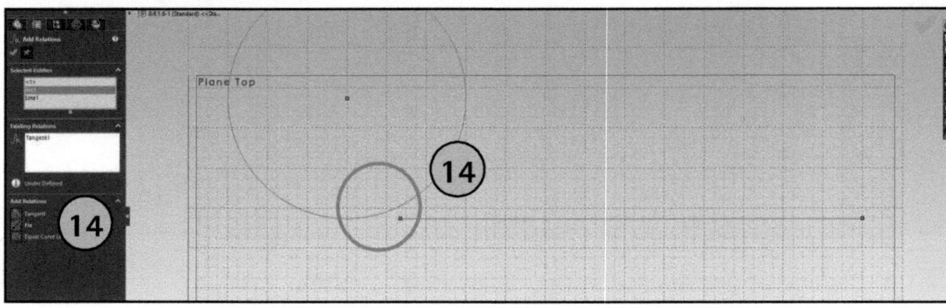

8.4.1.6 Rectangle position change, alignment to center line, using the "Collinear" relation

Add Relation

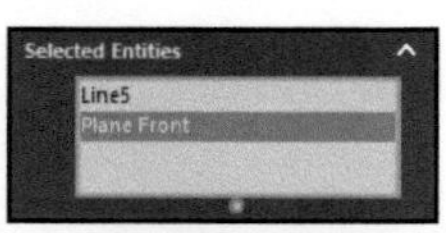

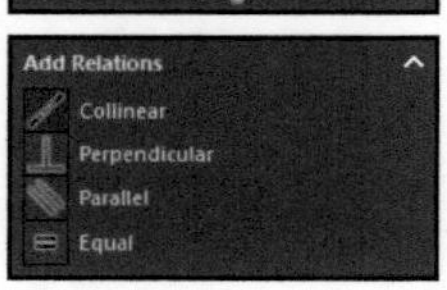

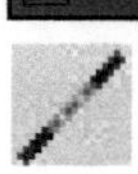

Relation Collinear

- From the Sketch toolbar, select the **Add Relation** function.
- Select the rectangle center line (15).
- Select the frame outline, **Front Plane** (16).
- Select **Collinear** relation (17).

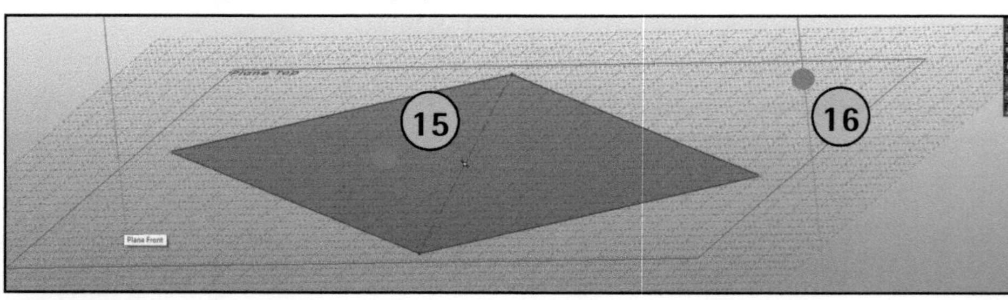

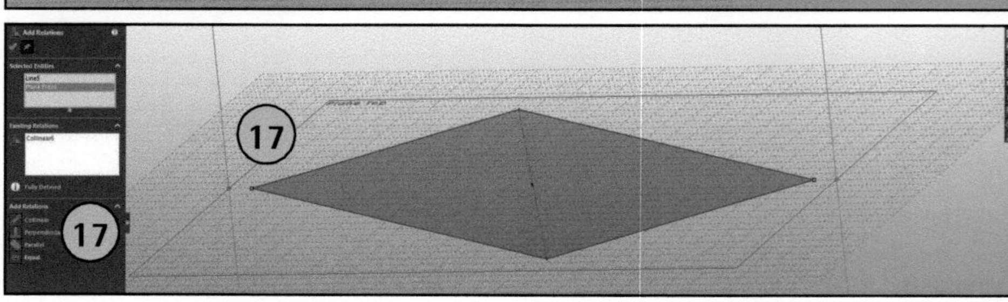

8.4.1.7 Rectangle position change, alignment to a guideline, using the "Parallel" relation

- From the Sketch toolbar, select the **Add Relation** function.
- Select the rectangle's outer contour (18).
- Select the drawn guideline (19).
- Select **Parallel** relation (20).

Add Relation

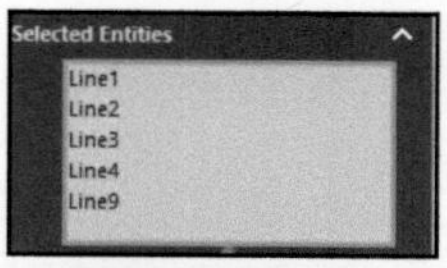

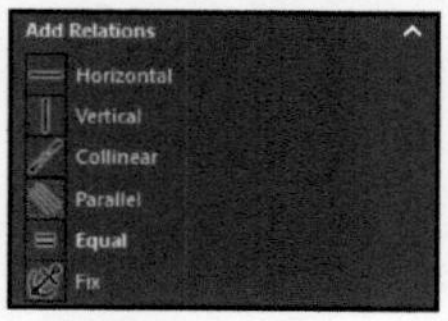

Relation Parallel

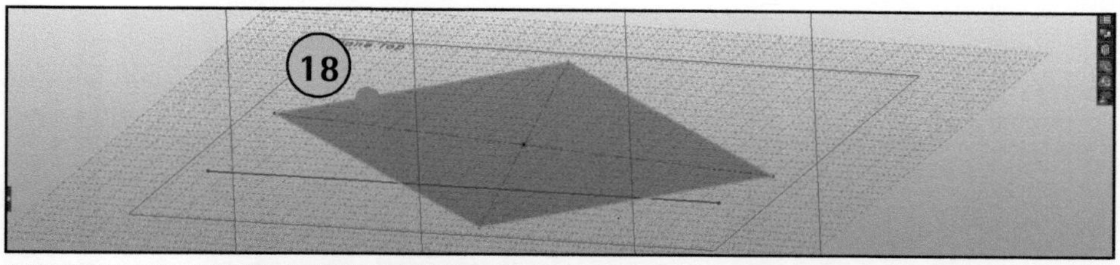

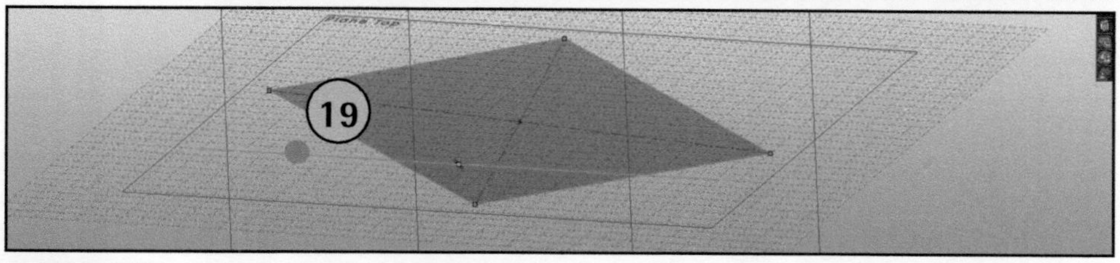

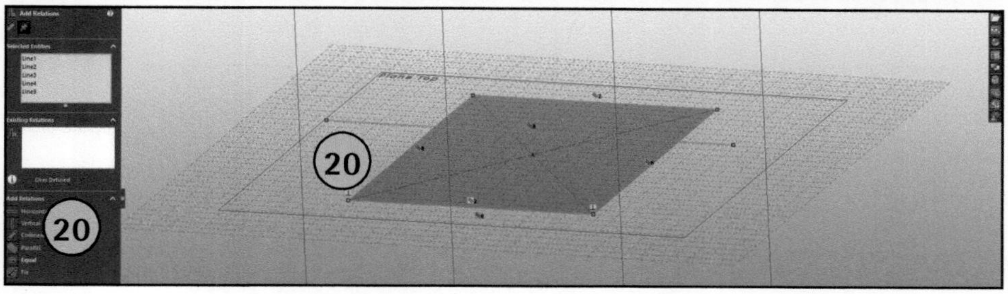

Project XIII

Model changes

Page 323 to 333

- Change cube model
  Changing the dimensions of the basic sketch
  Feature "Extrude-Boss" change dimension assignment
  Basic body "cube", change of position
- Change polygon model
  Feature "Extrude Boss", change polygon height
  Changing the polygon size using the base sketch
  Sketch geometry "Polygon", change number of corners
- Change pyramid model
  Modifying the basic body using the "Extrude" option "Draft"
- Change Feature "Hole Wizard"
  Change "Hole size"
  Change "Hole type"
- Change Pattern Arrangement
  Changing "Linear Pattern"
  Changing "Circular Pattern"
- Changing edge breaking
  Changing the edge breaking "Chamfer"
  Delete "Fillet"
  Feature "Thread Stud", set a "Undercut"

Open

Extrude

8.5 Model changes, modifying features

8.5.1 Cube over geometry changes, the creation

8.5.1.1 Open the working file

Open (Menu bar) / Component from the book-DVD / **OK**.

8.5.1.2 Changing the dimensions of the basic sketch

Extrude (**Features** tab)
In the **FeatureManager**, expand the **Extrude Boss** function.
Select **Edit Sketch** from the context toolbar.
Click on the **70** mm dimension and change it to **100** mm. (1, 2).
Click on the **50** mm dimension and change it to **100** mm. (3, 4).
Close dialog box.

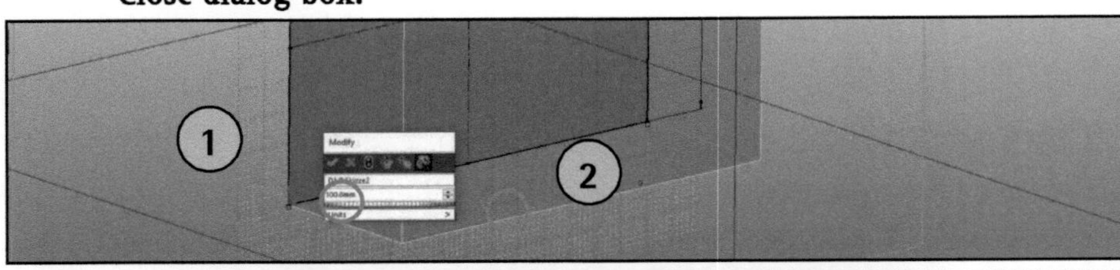

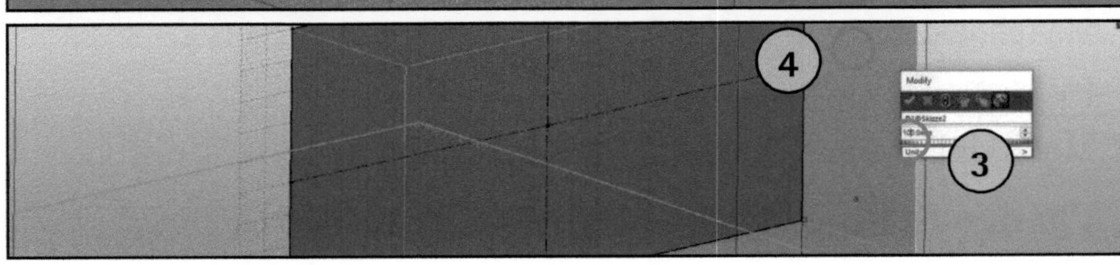

Extrude

8.5.1.3 Feature "Extrude-Boss" change dimension assignment

Extrude (**Features** tab)
In the **FeatureManager**, expand the **Extrude Boss** function.
Select **Edit Feature**.
Change the dimension entry in the **PropertyManager** to **100** mm (5).
Close dialog box.

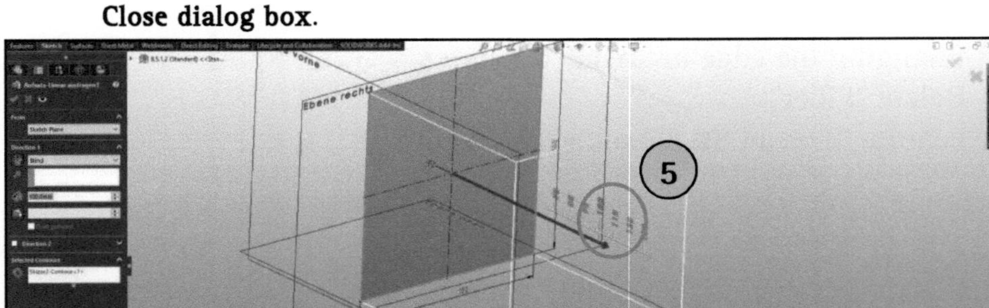

Save as New

8.5.1.4 Data backup

Save as New / Enter a name of your choice.

8.5.2 Basic body "cube", change of position

8.5.2.1 Open the working file

Open (Menu bar) / Component from the book-DVD / **OK**.

Open

8.5.2.2 The sketch position change

- In the **FeatureManager**, expand the **Extrude Boss** function.
- Select **Edit Sketch** from the context toolbar.

Add Relation
Select the new center line (1).
Select the frame outline: **Front Plane** (2).

Add Relation

Select **Collinear** relation (3).
Close dialog box (4).

Relation Collinear

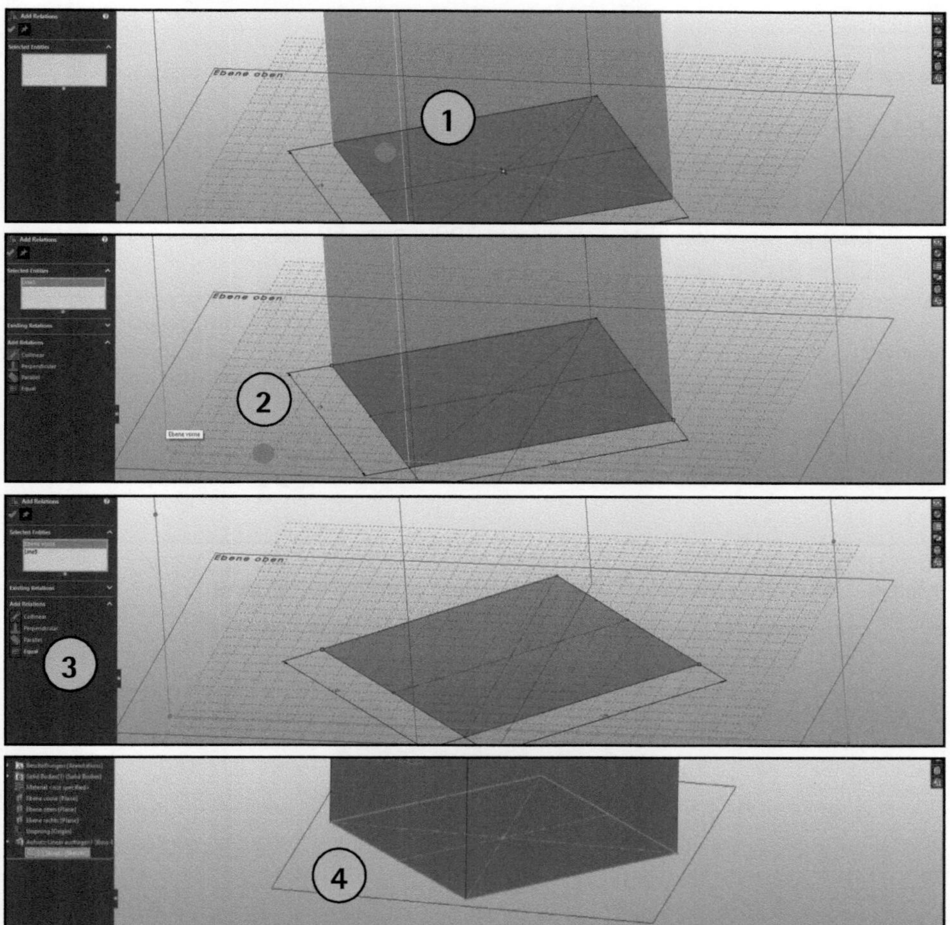

8.5.2.3 Data backup

Save as New / Enter a name of your choice.

Save as New

8.5.3 Changing the polygon prism

8.5.3.1 Open the working file

Open

Open (Menu bar) / Component from the book-DVD / **OK** (1).

8.5.3.2 Feature "Extrude Boss", change polygon height

Extrude

Extrude (**Features** tab)
In the **FeatureManager**, expand the **Extrude Boss** function.
Select **Edit Feature**.
Change the dimension entry in the **PropertyManager** to **40** mm (1, 2).
Close dialog box.

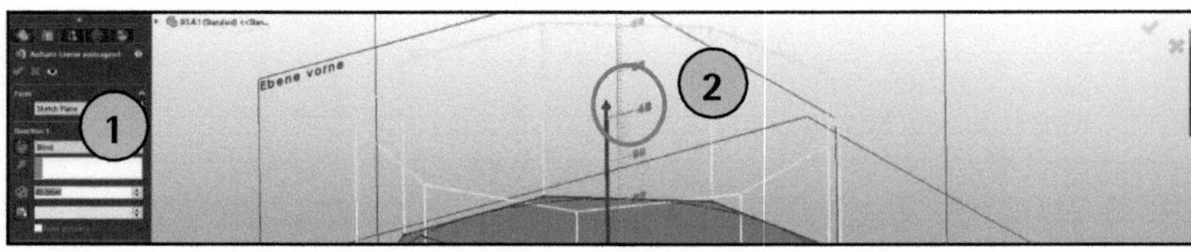

8.5.3.3 Changing the polygon size using the base sketch

- In the **FeatureManager**, expand the **Extrude Boss** function.
- Select **Edit Sketch** from the context toolbar.
- Change the radius dimension from **100** mm to **50** mm (3, 4).
- **Close dialog box**.

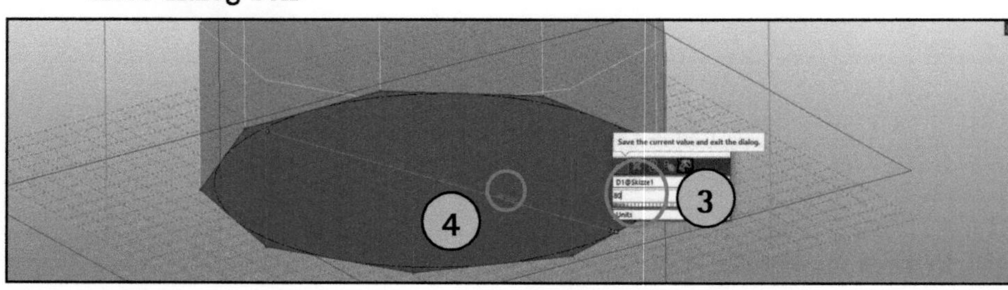

8.5.3.4 Sketch geometry "Polygon", change number of corners

Edit Sketch

- In the **FeatureManager**, expand the **Extrude Boss** function.
- Select **Edit Sketch** from the context toolbar.

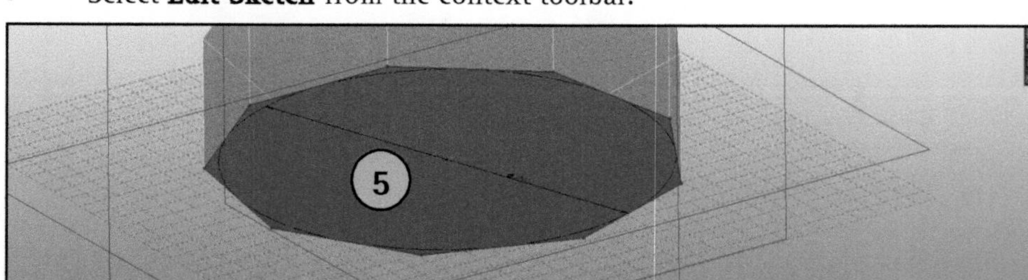

- Click on a polygon line (6).
- Right-click to open the **Context menu**.
- Select **Edit Polygon** (7).
- Change from **9** corners to **6** corners (8).
- **Close dialog box**.

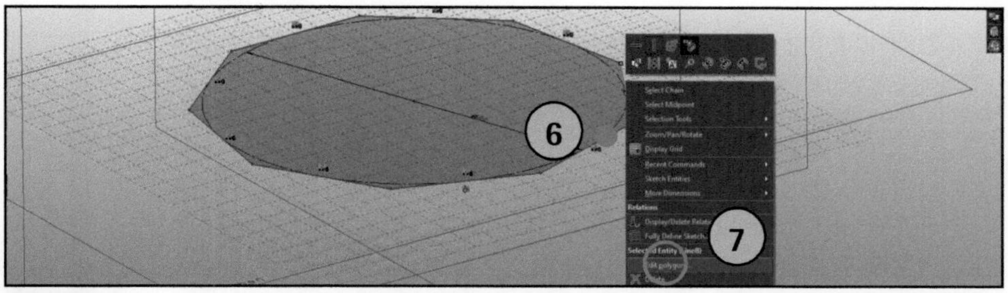

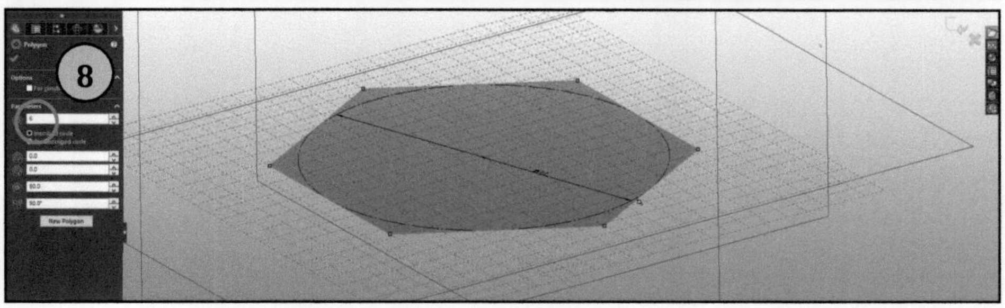

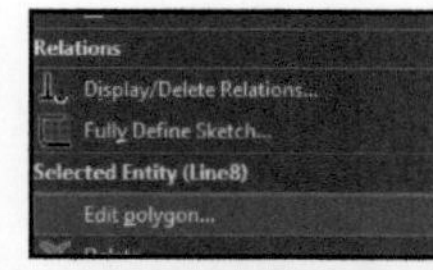

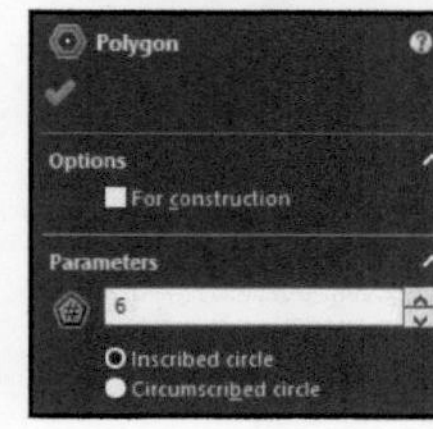

8.5.3.5 Data backup

Save as New / Enter a name of your choice.

Save as New

8.5.4 Draft angle adjustment by entering the angle value

8.5.4.1 Open the working file

Open

Open (Menu bar) / Component from the book-DVD / **OK**.

8.5.4.2 Modifying the basic body using the "Extrude" option "Draft"

Extrude

Draft

Extrude (**Features** tab)
In the **FeatureManager**, expand the **Extrude Boss** function.
Select **Edit Feature** and the **Draft** option (1).
Change the value from **15°** to **30°** (2, 3).
Close dialog box.

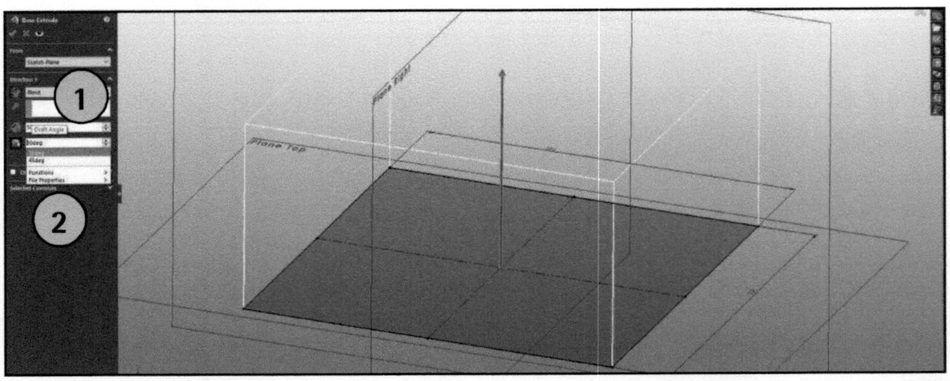

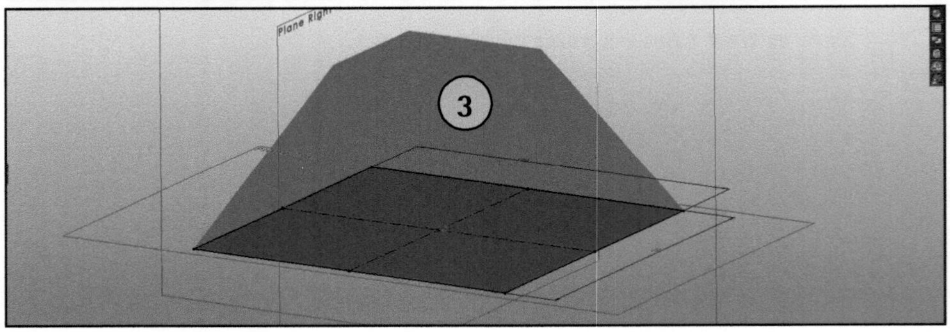

8.5.4.3 Data backup

Save as New

Save as New / Enter a name of your choice.

8.6 Feature "Hole Wizard" Change "Hole size" and "Hole type"

8.6.1 Feature "Hole Wizard" change "Hole size"

8.6.1.1 Open the working file

Open (Menu bar) / Component from the book-DVD / **OK**.

Open

8.6.1.2 Feature "Hole Wizard" Change hole size, the creation

Hole Wizard (**Features** tab)
In the **FeatureManager**, expand the **Hole Wizard** function.
Select **Edit Feature**.
Change the hole size to **M6** in the **PropertyManager** (1, 2, 3).
Close dialog box.

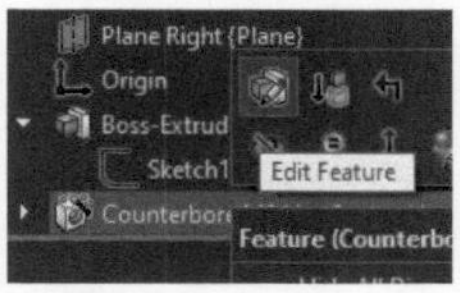

Hole Wizard

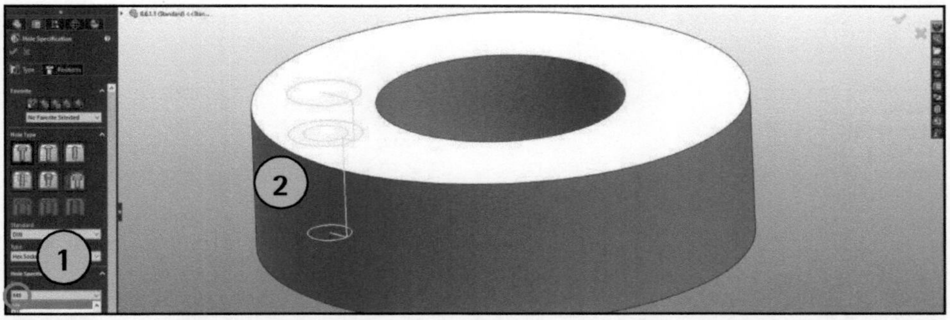

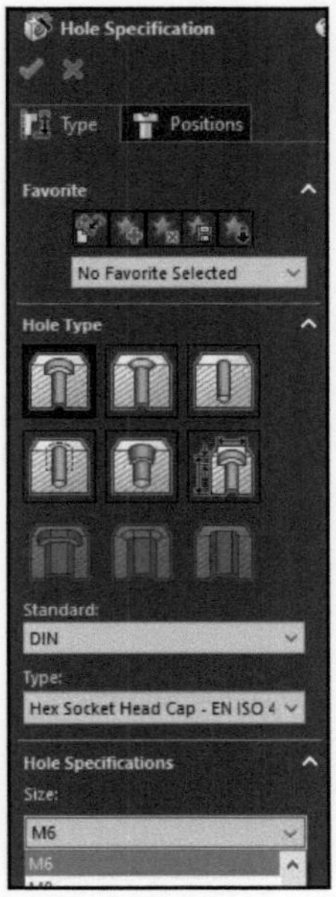

8.6.1.3 Data backup

Save as New / Enter a name of your choice.

Save as New

8.6.2 Feature "Hole Wizard", change „Hole type“

8.6.2.1 Open the working file

Open

Open (Menu bar) / Component from the book-DVD / **OK**.

8.6.2.1 Feature "Hole Wizard", change "Hole type", the creation

Hole Wizard

Hole Wizard (**Features** tab)
In the **FeatureManager**, expand the **Hole Wizard** function.
Select **Edit Feature**.
Change in the **PropertyManager**:
Hole type on **Tapped hole**, Size **M10**, **DIN** standard,
End Condition **Through All**, Thread **Through All** (1, 2, 3).
Cosmetric thread.
Close dialog box

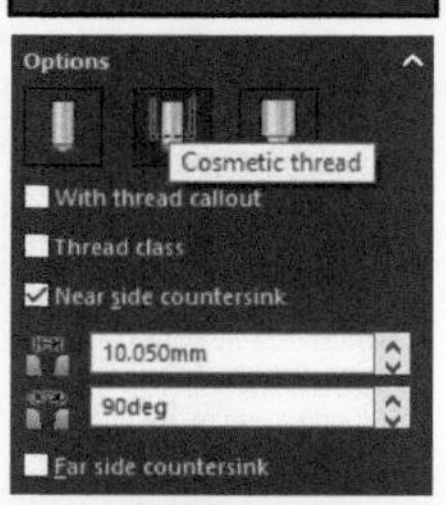

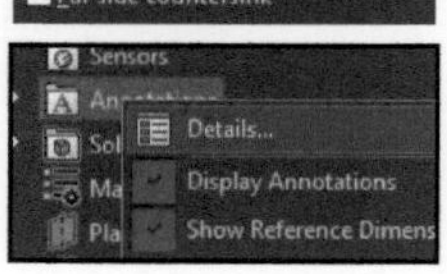

8.6.2.2 Assign display filter "Shaded cosmetic threads"

- Select **Annotations** (**Feature-Manager**)
- **Details** (**Context menu**)
- **Display Filter / Shaded cosmetic threads** (3, 4).

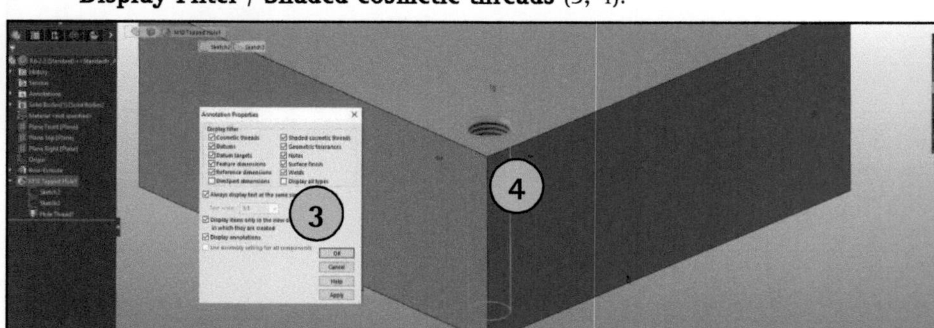

8.6.2.3 Data backup

Save as New

Save as New / Enter a name of your choice.

8.7 Pattern Arrangement
Changing "Linear Pattern" and "Circular Pattern"

8.7.1 Changing "Linear Pattern"

8.7.1.1 Open the working file

Open (Menu bar) / Component from the book-DVD / **OK**.

Open

8.7.1.2 Feature "Linear Pattern", pattern change

Linear Pattern (**Features** tab)
In the **FeatureManager**, expand the **Linear Pattern** function.
Select **Edit Feature / PropertyManager**
Change the number of holes in **Direction1** and **Direction2** to **6** (1).
Change the hole spacing in **Direction1** and **Direction2** to **16** mm (2).
Close dialog box (3).

Linear Pattern

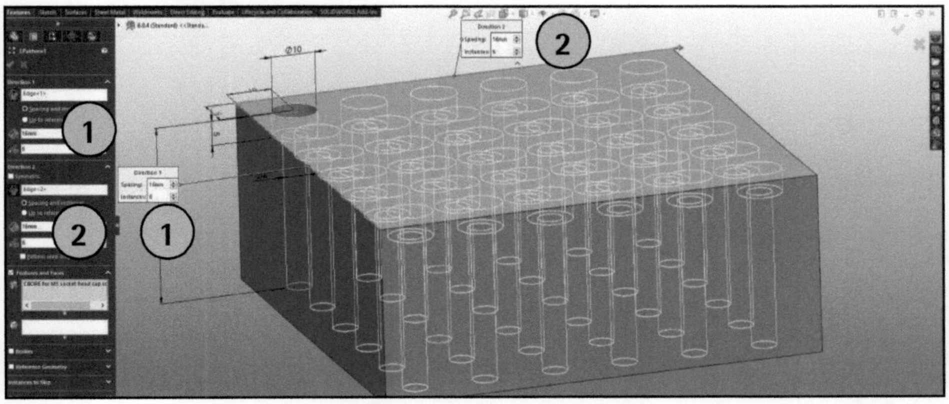

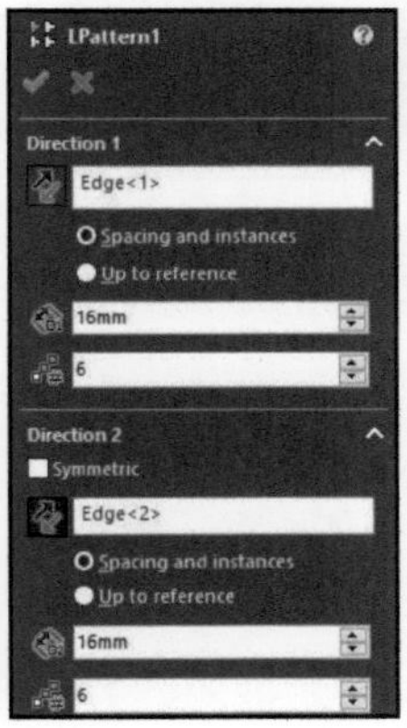

8.7.1.3 Data backup

Save as New / Enter a name of your choice.

Save as New

8.7.2 Changing "Circular Pattern"

8.7.2.1 Open the working file

Open

Open (Menu bar) / Component from the book-DVD / **OK**.

8.7.2.2 Feature "Circular Pattern", pattern change

Circular Pattern

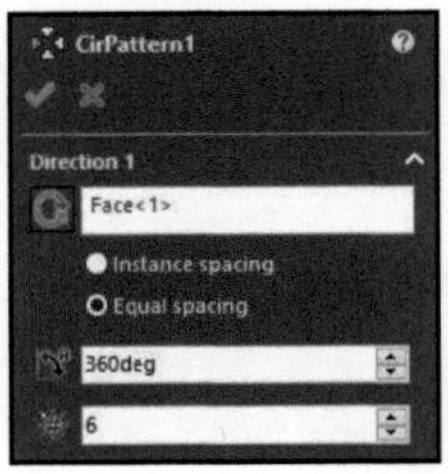

Circular Pattern (**Features** tab)
In the **FeatureManager**, expand the **Circular Pattern** function.
Select **Edit Feature**.
Change the number of holes to **6** in the PropertyManager (1, 2).
Close dialog box (3).

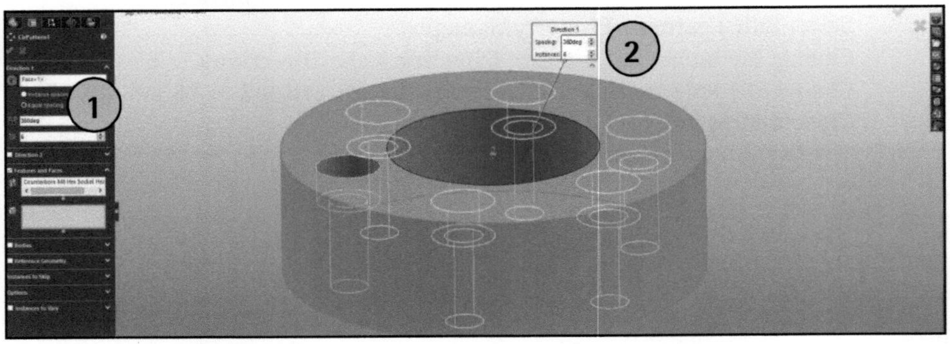

8.7.2.3 Data backup

Save as New

Save as New / Enter a name of your choice.

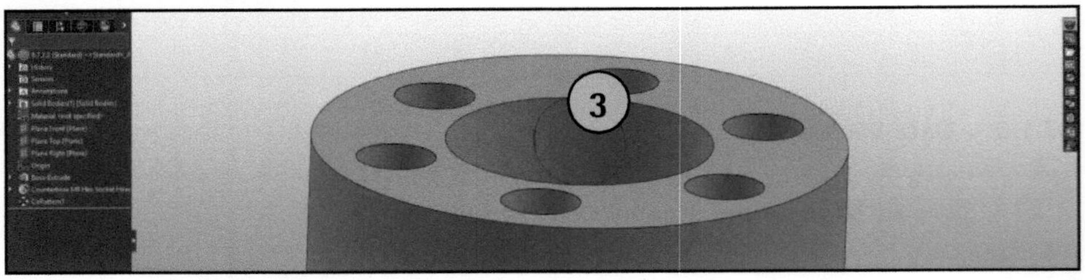

8.8 Changing edge breaking "Chamfer" and "Thread Stud"

8.8.1 Changing the edge breaking "Chamfer"

8.8.1.1 Open the working file

Open (Menu bar) / Component from the book-DVD / **OK**.

Open

8.8.1.2 Feature "Chamfer", change distance assignment

Chamfer (**Features** tab)
In the **FeatureManager**, expand the **Chamfer1** function.
Select **Edit Feature**.
Change the Chamfer Parameters, in the **PropertyManager**, to **3** mm. (1, 2).
Close dialog box

Chamfer

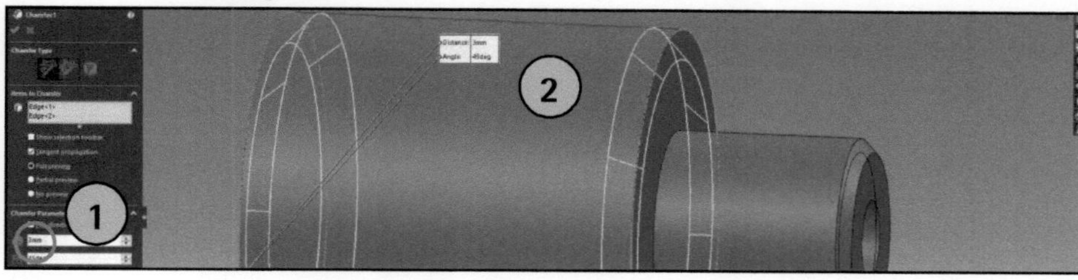

8.8.1.3 Feature "Thread Stud", set a "Undercut"

- Remove rounding at the thread base (3, 4).

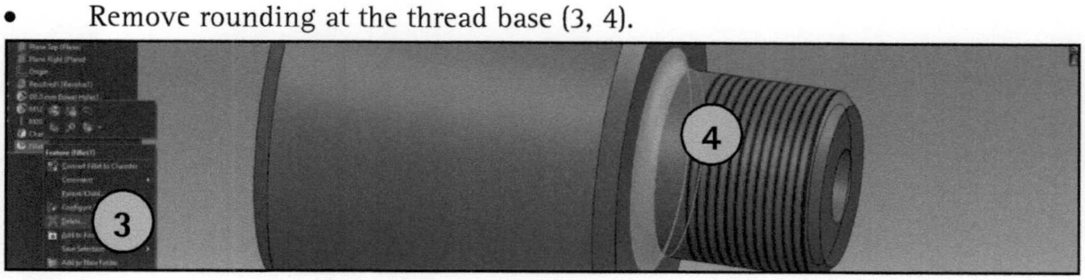

Stud Wizard (**Features** tab)
In the **FeatureManager**, expand the **Stud Wizard** function.
Select **Edit Feature**.
Activate the **Undercut** option and the predefined values (5, 6).

Stud Wizard

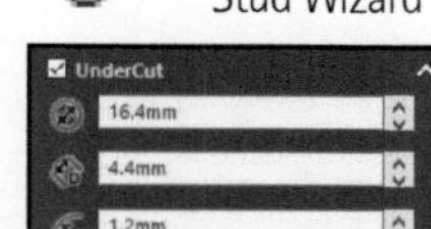

8.8.1.4 Data backup

Save as New / Enter a name of your choice.

Save as New

Project XIV

Model changes
Instant3D
Page 336 to 349

- Cube over geometry changes
  Cuboid height
  Cuboid surfaces
- Hole changes in the component
  Shifting the center point
  Shifting the center point using sketch
  Hole size
  Position of the hole
  Center point on corner point
  Copy hole in component
  Hole to front side of the cuboid
- Changing the rotation angle
- Truncated Cone to Cone
- Truncated Pyramid to Pyramid
- Component adjustments using “Triad”
  Adjusting the angle of the base body
  Adjusting the high of the base body
  Adjust the position of the cone attachment
  Adjusting the hollow body height

8.9 "Instant3D" model changes

Instant 3D

8.9.1 Dynamic Feature Editing

Instant3D lets you drag geometry and dimension handles to create and modify features. To create features, you must exit Sketch Edit mode; **Instant3D** is enabled by default.

You can dynamically edit features by dragging the elements of a sketch, with the option to open the sketch itself or not.

Elements cannot be moved or enlarged/reduced if they are constrained by dimensions or relations.

The feature is highlighted in the graphics area. The model is not put into insert mode. If more than one sketch is used to create the feature (for example, if the selected feature is a burr or extrusion), then all sketches used in the feature are highlighted.

If you are satisfied with the feature, click on an empty area of the document window, or press the Esc key to undo the editing steps.

Although the fillet feature was created separately from the linearly extruded cut, it moves with the extruded cut and changes its size with it due to parent and child relationships.

8.9.2 "Instant3D", Unit Adjustment

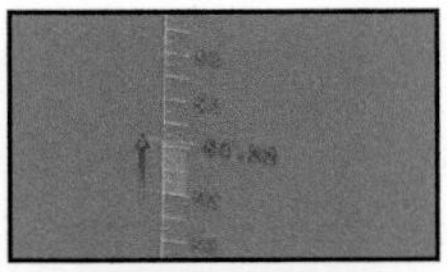

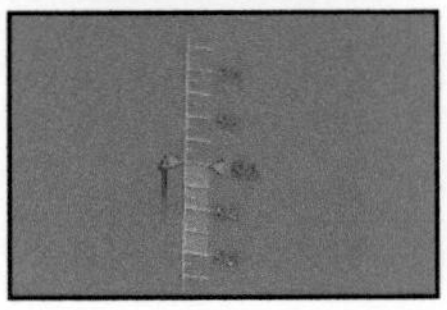

You can influence the assigned length change in the assigned units, number of decimal places, using the position of the mouse pointer.

In addition to the number line: Unreduced number of decimal places, correction by subsequently selecting the resulting measurement and correcting to the desired value.

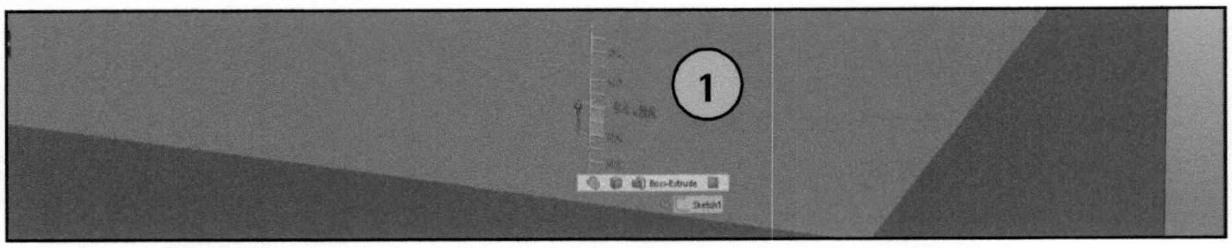

On the number line: A green double-arrow symbol appears, the measurement jumps according to the preset accuracy, here 1 mm (1, 2).

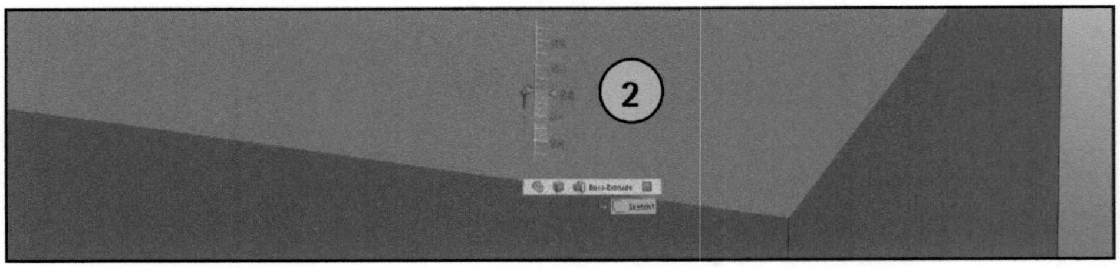

8.9.3 "Instant3D", Cube over geometry changes

8.9.3.1 Open the working file

Open (Menu bar) / Component from the book-DVD / **OK**.

Open

8.9.3.2 Adjusting the basic dimensions, assigning "Driven"

- In the **FeatureManager**, expand the **Extrude** function.
- Select **Edit Sketch** from the context toolbar.
- Activate the **Driven** assignment for the two dimensions **56** mm and **80** mm in the **Context menu** (1, 2, 3).

8.9.3.3 "Instant3D", changing the dimension of the cuboid height

Instant3D (Features toolbar)
Click on the top face of the cuboid.
Drag the length to **100** mm using the drag handle (4).
Finally, click on an empty area of the document window.

Instant3D

8.9.3.4 "Instant3D", changing the dimensions of the cuboid surfaces

Instant3D (Features toolbar)
Click on the surface of the cuboid.
Drag the length to **20** mm (80 mm + 20 mm) using the drag handle (5).
Finally, click on an empty area of the document window.

Instant 3D

Instant 3D

Instant3D (Features toolbar)
Click on the surface of the cuboid.
Drag the length to **44** mm (56 mm + 44 mm) using the drag handle (7).
Finally, click on an empty area of the document window.

8.9.3.5 Data backup

Save as New

Save as New / Enter a name of your choice.

8.9.4 Hole changes in the component

8.9.4.1 Open the working file

Open (Menu bar) / Component from the book-DVD / **OK**.

Open

8.9.4.2 Changing the position of the hole, shifting the center point

- Click the wall of the hole (1).
- Click **Delete** to delete all feature relationships. (2).
- Click the directional arrow **X** (3).

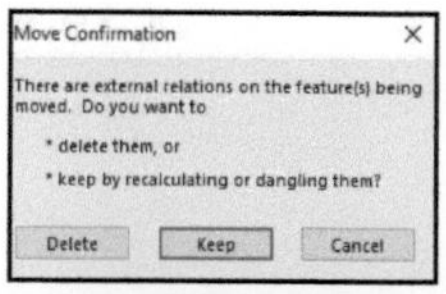

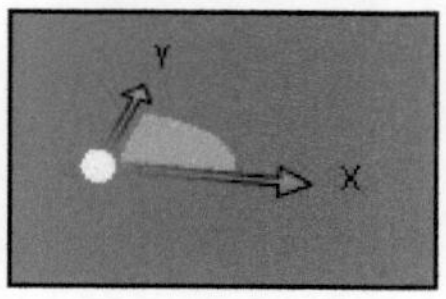

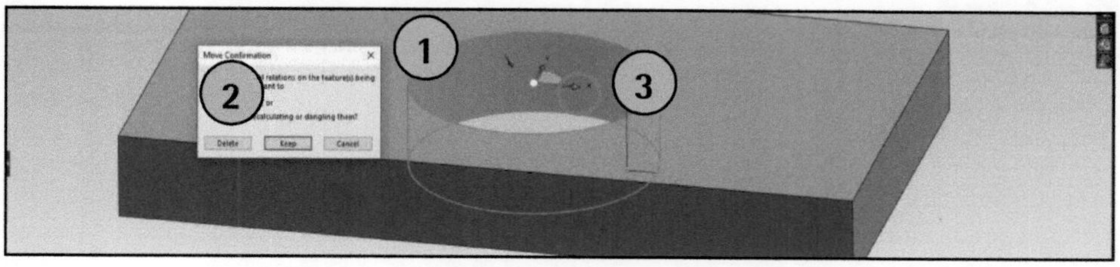

- Use this to drag the hole into the desired position (4).

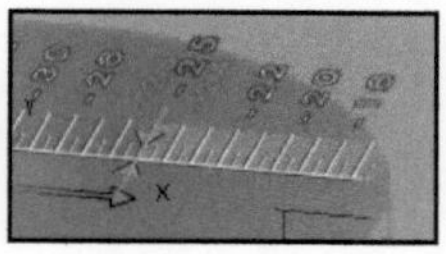

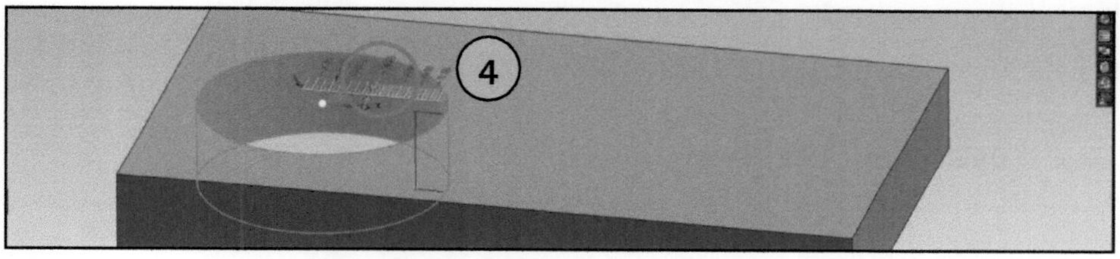

8.9.4.3 Changing the position of the hole, shifting the center point using sketch

- Activate the sketch below the **Cut-Extrude** function (5).
- Click the directional arrow **X** (6).

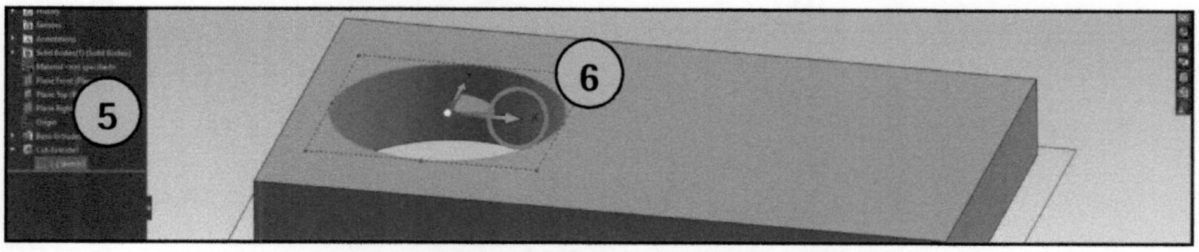

- Use this to pull the hole into the desired position (7, 8).

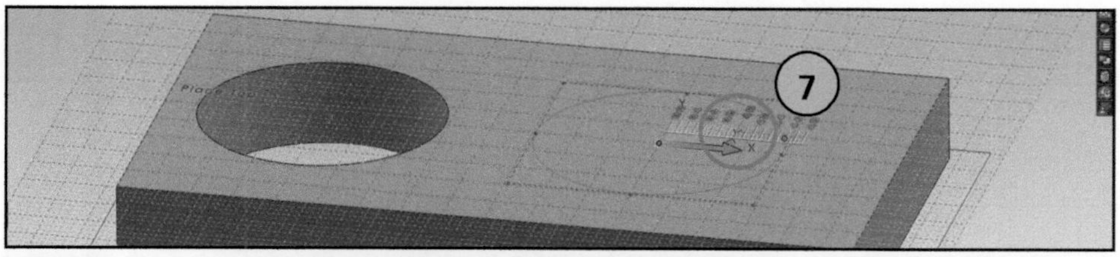

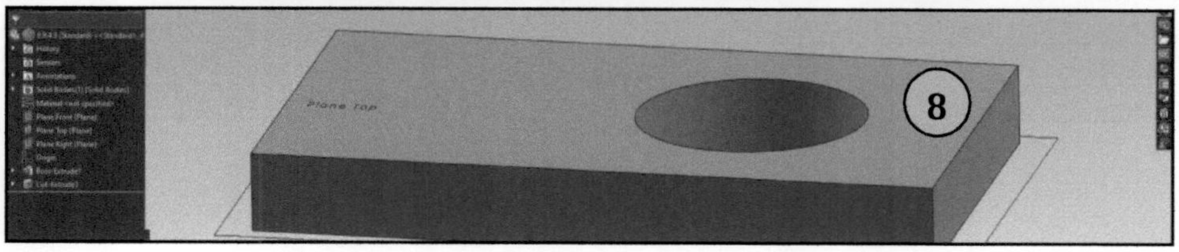

8.9.4.4 Changing the hole size using "Instant3D"

- Click the wall of the hole (9).
- Click the arrow shown to resize (10).
- Drag the size vector by **5** mm (11).

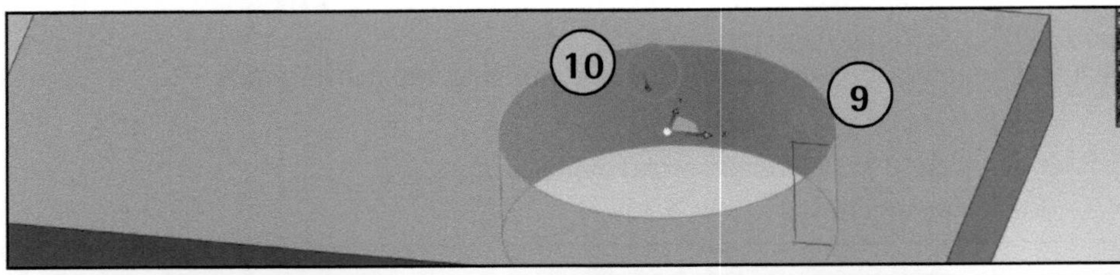

8.9.4.5 Changing the position of the hole, shifting the center point

Open

Open (Menu bar) / Component from the book-DVD / **OK**.

- Click the wall of the hole (12).
- Click the center of the hole (13).
- Drag the hole to the desired position (14, 15).

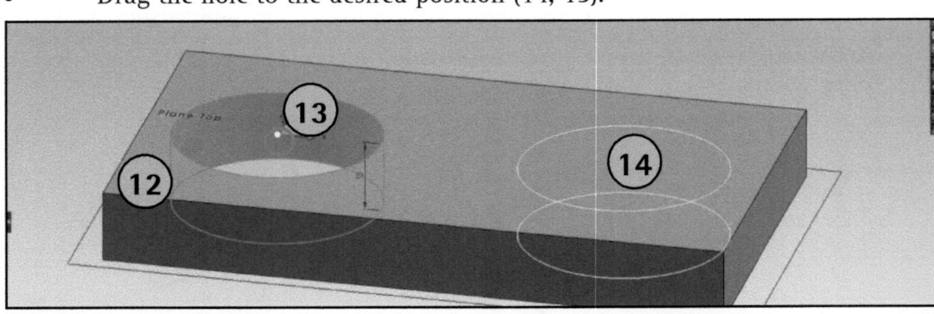

8.9.4.6 Change the position of the hole, center point on corner point

Open

Open (Menu bar) / Component from the book-DVD / **OK**.

- Activate the sketch below the **Hole** function.
- Select **Edit Sketch** from the context toolbar.
- Click the hole center point (16).
- Drag the hole center point to the corner point (17).
- **Close dialog box / Finish Sketch** (18)

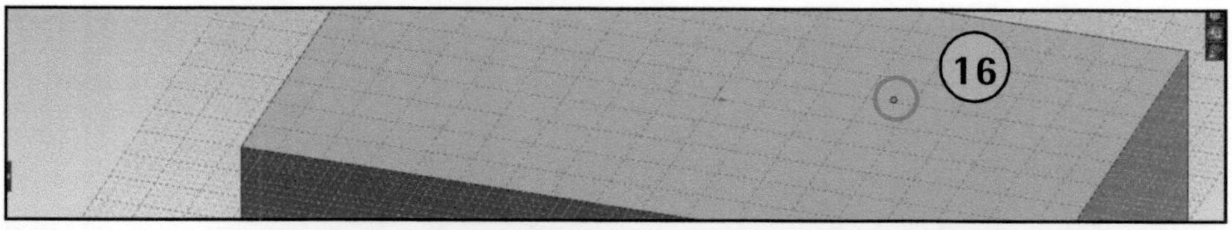

8.9.4.7 Copy hole in component

- Click the wall of the hole (19).
- Hold down the **Ctrl** key while dragging.
- Pull the hole to the other side of the cuboid (20).
- Release the **Ctrl** key to fix the copied hole (21).

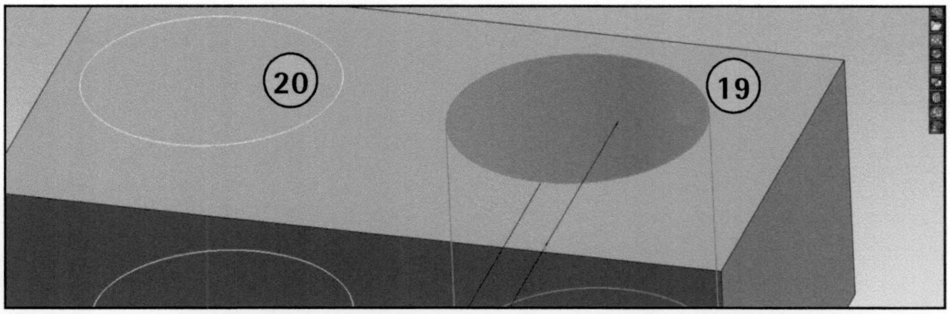

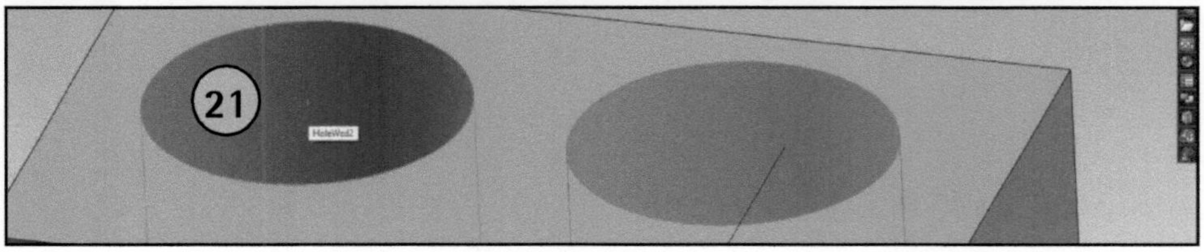

8.9.4.8 Copying the hole to front side of the cuboid

- Click the wall of the hole (22).
- Hold down the **Ctrl** key while dragging.
- Pull the hole to the front side of the cuboid (23).
- Release the **Ctrl** key to fix the copied hole (24).

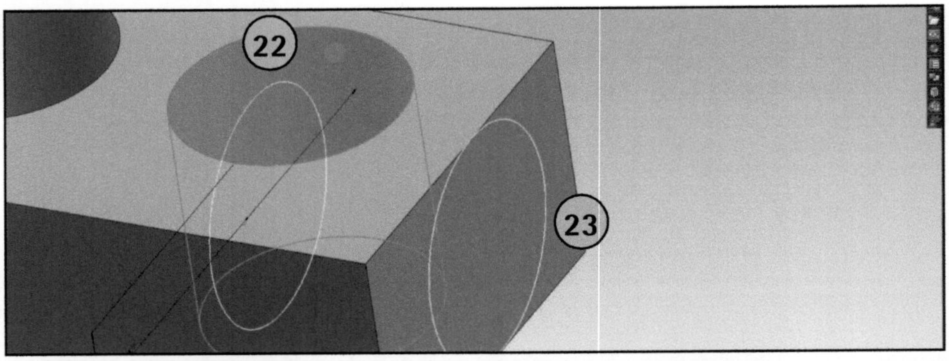

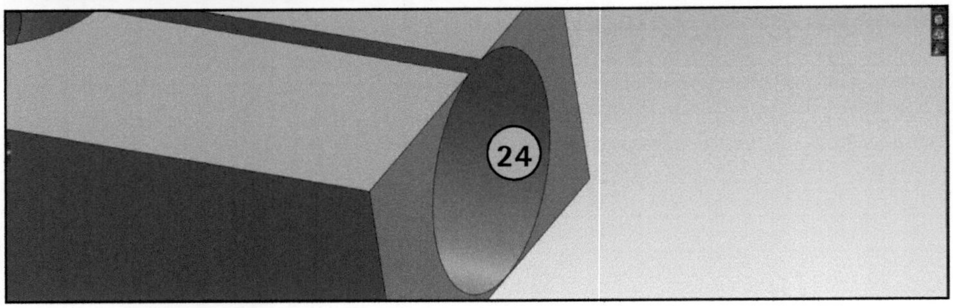

8.9.4.9 Data backup

Save as New

Save as New / Enter a name of your choice.

8.9.5 Changing the rotation angle using "Instant3D"

8.9.5.1 Open the working file

Open (Menu bar) / Component from the book-DVD / **OK**.

Open

8.9.5.2 Changing the rotation angle using "Edit Feature"

Revolved (**Features** tab)
In the **FeatureManager**, expand the **Revolved** function.
Select **Edit Feature**.
Enter the new degree value, for example **230°** (1, 2).
Close dialog box (3)

Revolved

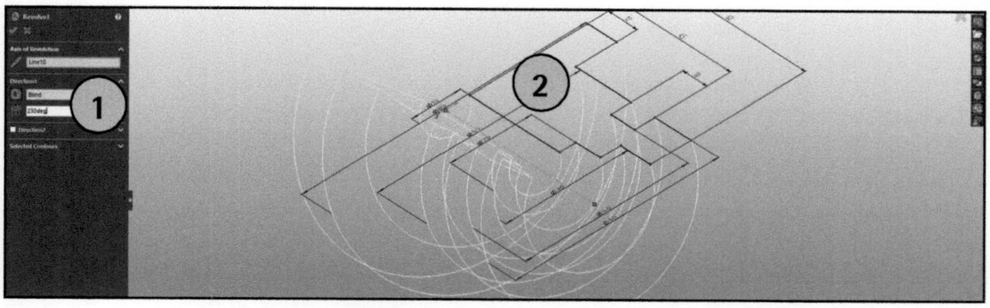

8.9.5.3 Changing the rotation angle using "Instant3D", the creation

- Click the left wall of the vector section (3).
- Now click the single arrow that appears (4).
- Hold down the left mouse button, drag to change the angle vector. The angle value is displayed as a number (5).

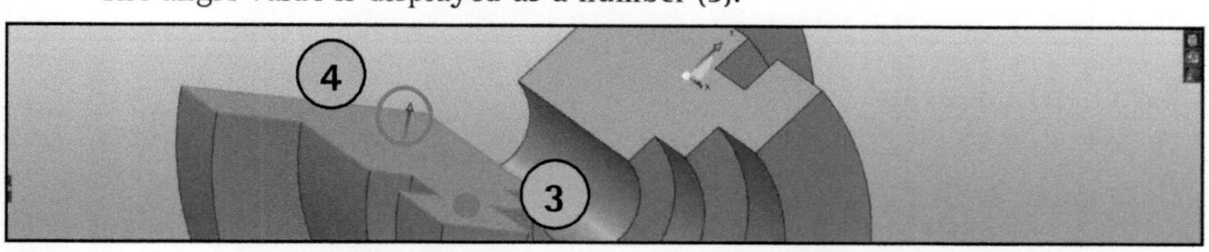

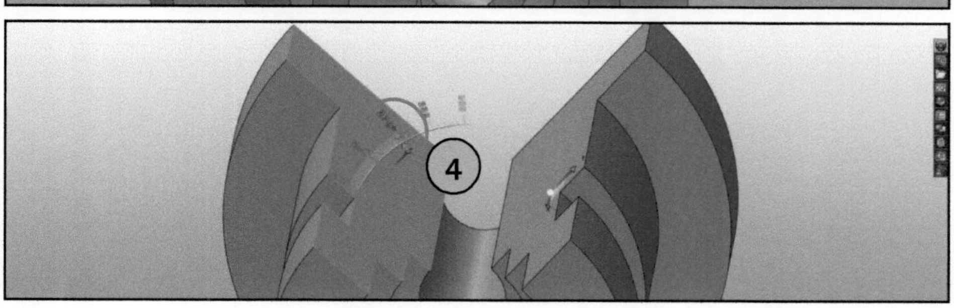

8.9.5.4 Data backup

Save as New / Enter a name of your choice.

Save as New

8.9.6 Geometry changes using "Instant3D", Truncated cone to cone

8.9.6.1 Open the working file

Open

Open (Menu bar) / Component from the book-DVD / **OK**.

8.9.6.2 Truncated cone to cone, adapting the base body

- Select the upper face of the truncated cone (1).
- Click the direction arrow (2).

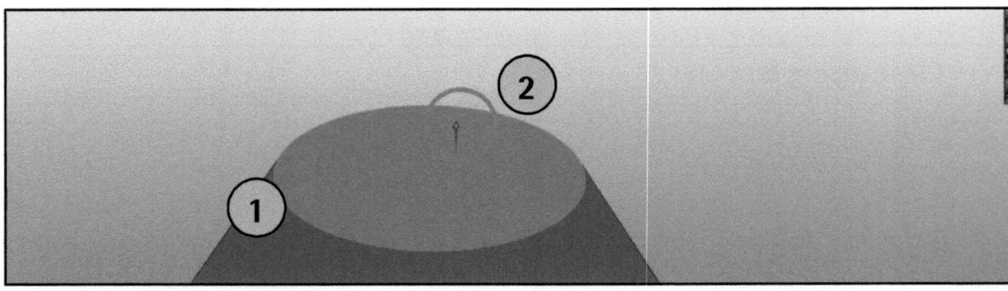

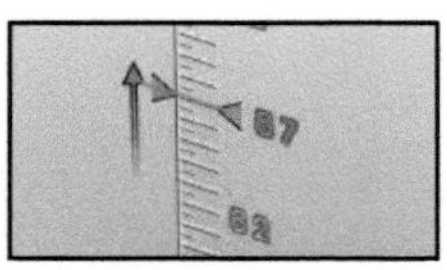

- Drag the surface upwards using the arrow until a basic body **Cone** is formed. (3, 4).

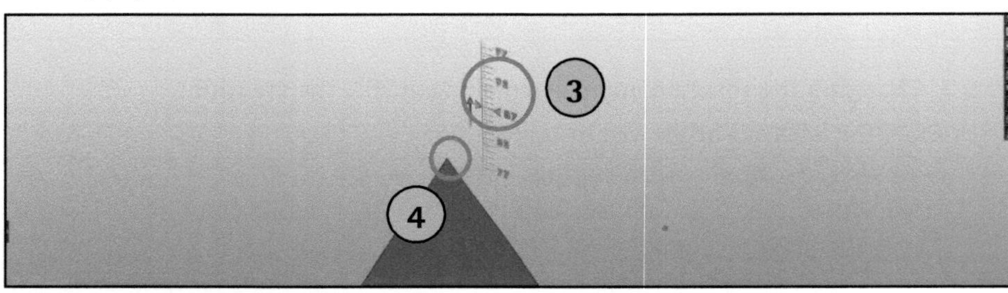

8.9.6.3 Data backup

Save as New

Save as New / Enter a name of your choice.

8.9.7 Geometry changes using "Instant3D", Truncated pyramid to pyramid

8.9.7.1 Open the working file

Open (Menu bar) / Component from the book-DVD / **OK**.

Open

8.9.7.2 Truncated pyramid to pyramid, adapting the base body

- Select the upper face of the truncated pyramid (1).
- Click the direction arrow (2).

- Drag the surface upwards using the arrow until a basic body **Pyramid** is formed (3, 4).

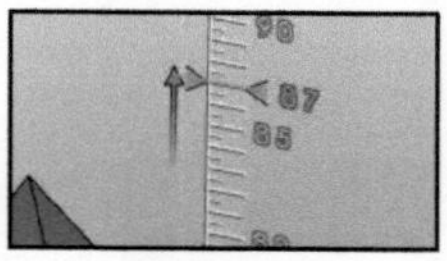

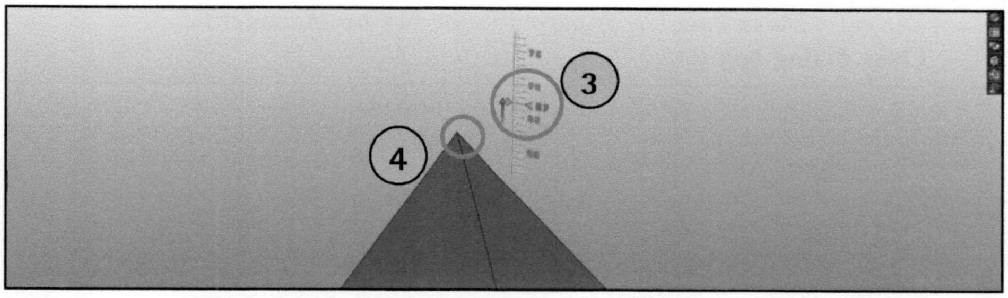

8.9.7.3 Data backup

Save as New / Enter a name of your choice.

Save as New

8.9.8 Component adjustments using "Triad"

8.9.8.1 Open the working file

Open

Open (Menu bar) / Component from the book-DVD / **OK**.

8.9.8.2 Adjusting the angle of the base body

Move Face
Rotate

Triad

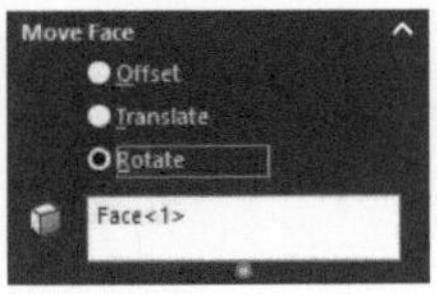

Move Face option **Rotate** (Features toolbar **Direct Editing**) (1)
Select the front basic body slope by clicking (2).
Activate the vector display using the triad's circular ring (3).

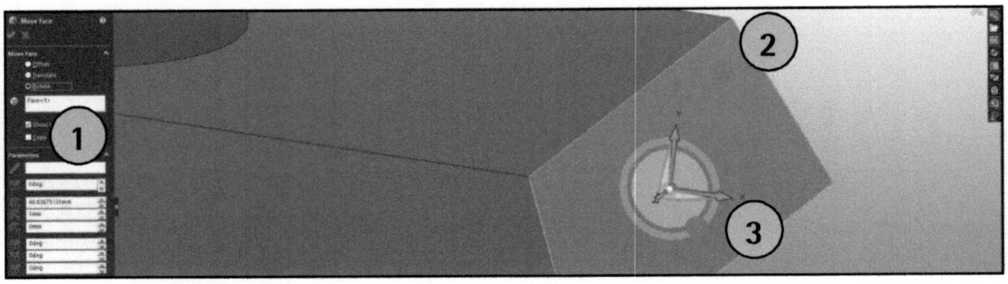

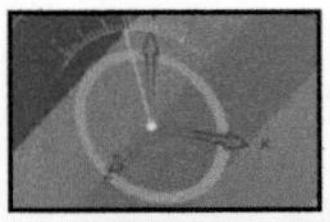

- Rotate the vector display arrow to the desired angle value (4).
  The entry **Move Face1** is displayed in the **FeatureManager** (5).
  Close dialog box (6).

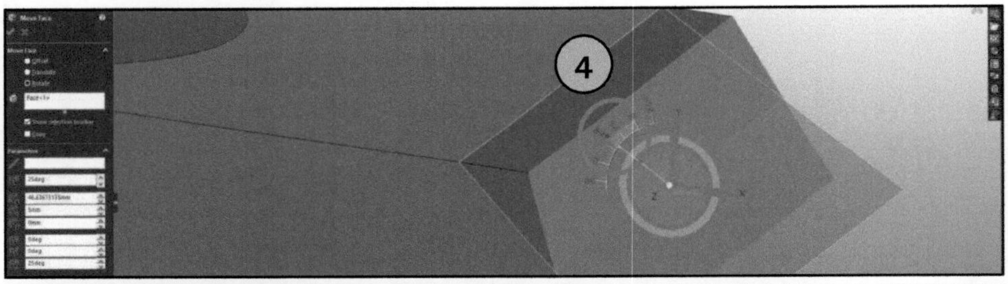

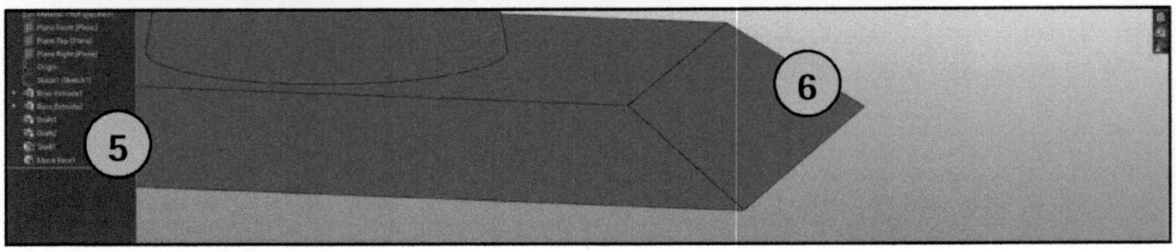

8.9.8.3 Data backup

Save as New

Save as New / Enter a name of your choice.

8.9.8.4 Adjusting the high of the base body

Move Face
Translate

Move Face option **Translate** (Features toolbar **Direct Editing**) (1)
Select the top cover area by clicking (2).
Activate the vertical arrow of the **Triad** (3).

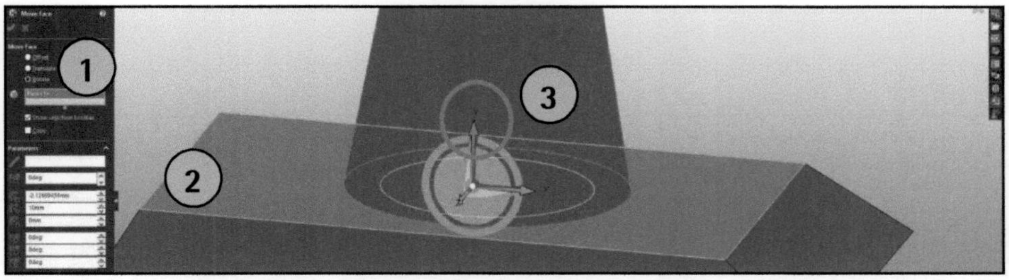

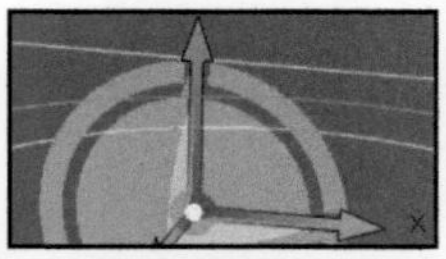

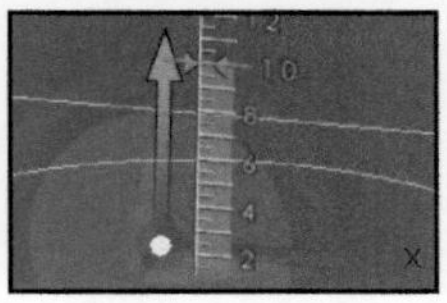

- Pull the top surface upwards by **10** mm using this vertical arrow (4).
  The entry **Move Face2** is displayed in the **FeatureManager** (5).
- **Close dialog box** (6).

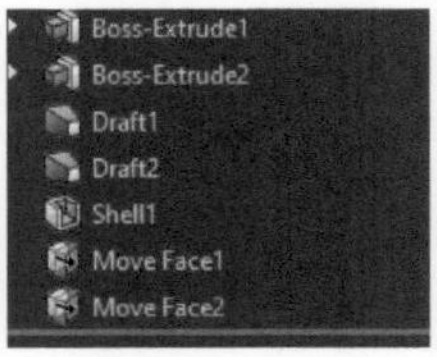

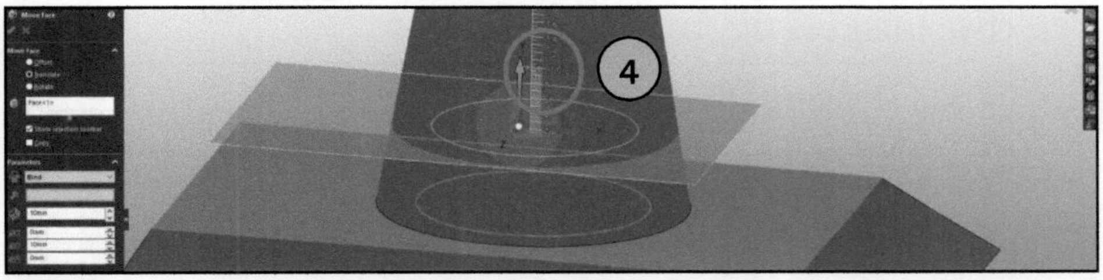

8.9.8.5 Data backup

Save as New

Save as New / Enter a name of your choice.

8.9.8.6 Adjust the position of the cone attachment

Move Face
Translate

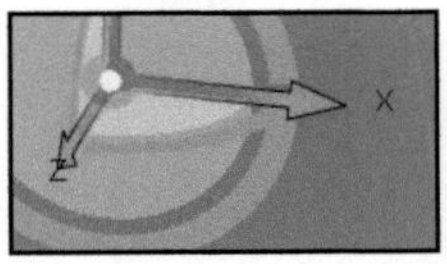

Move Face option **Translate** (Features toolbar **Direct Editing**) (1)
Select the two cone faces by clicking (2, 3).
Activate the horizontal arrow of the **Triad** (4).

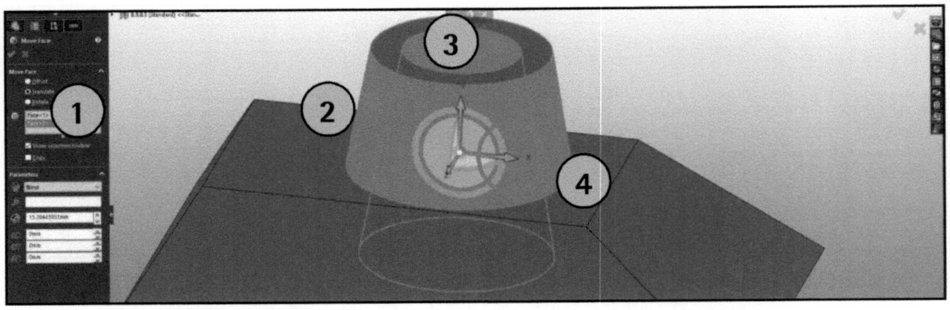

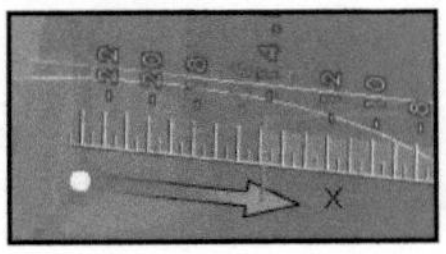

- Pull the cone surface back approx. **15** mm using this horizontal arrow (5). The entry **Move Face4** is displayed in the **FeatureManager** (6).
- **Close dialog box** (7).

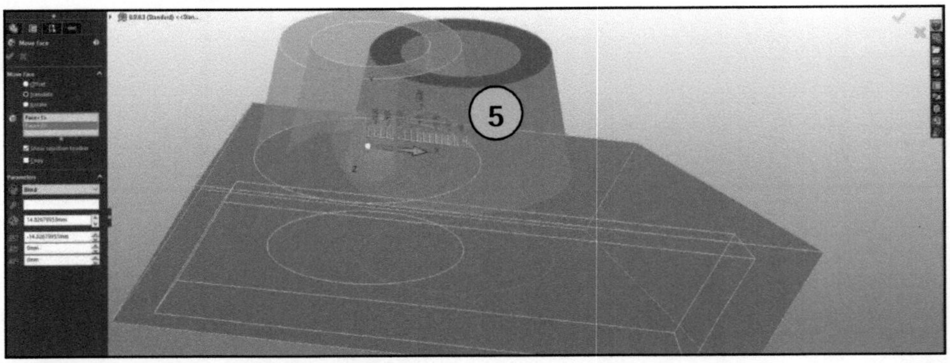

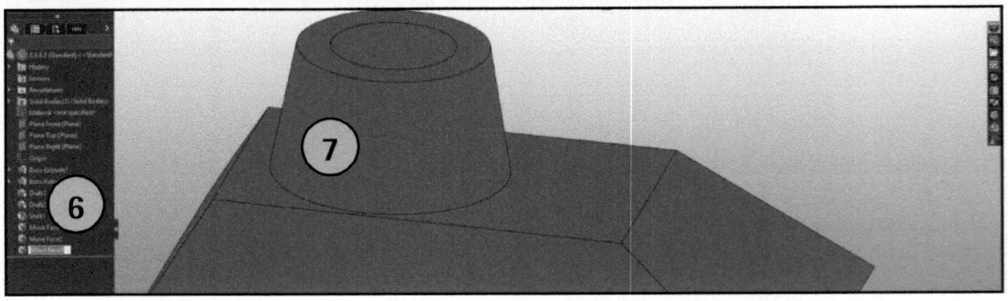

8.9.8.7 Data backup

Save as New

Save as New / Enter a name of your choice.

8.9.8.8 Adjusting the hollow body height

Move Face option **Translate** (Features toolbar **Direct Editing**) (1)

Move Face
Translate

- Select the inner wall, **Shell1**, by clicking (2).
- Pull the inner surface **4** mm downwards using this vertical arrow (3).
- The entry **Move Face5** is displayed in the **FeatureManager** (4).
- **Close dialog box** (5).

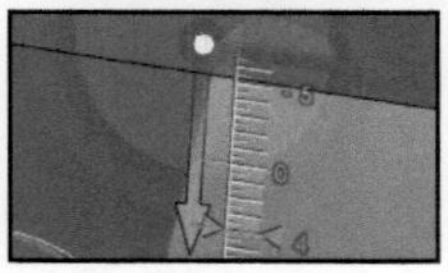

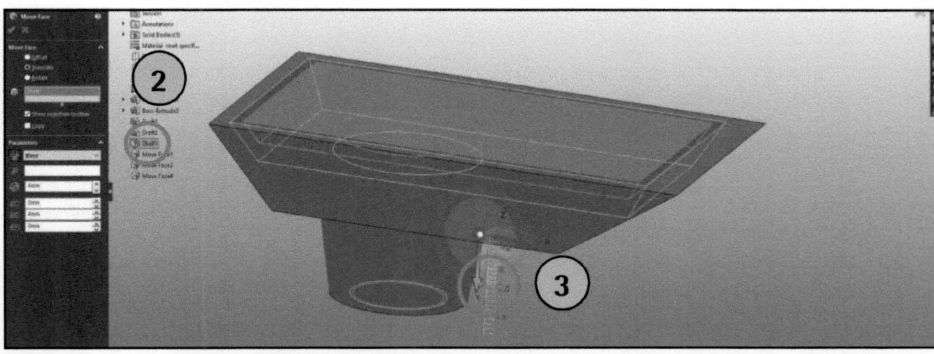

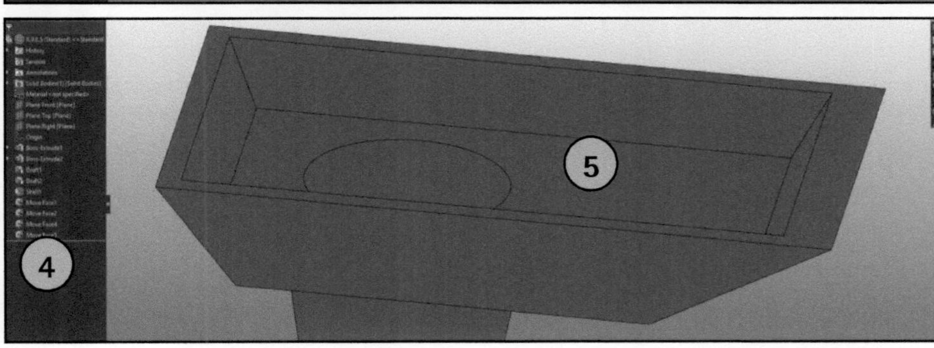

8.9.8.9 Data backup

Save as New / Enter a name of your choice.

Save as New

Project XV

Model Changes
Twist and Deformation

Page 353 to 361

- Model Changes using feature “Flex”
  - Option ”Bending”
  - Option ”Twisting”
  - Option ”Tapering”
- Model Changes using feature ”Deform”
  - Option “Point“
  - Option “Point“ and “Edge”
  - Option “Curve to Curve“

8.10 Deformation functions on a basic body, using feature „Flex"

8.10.1 Feature "Flex", basics

Flex features are suitable for modifying complex models using intuitive tools that deliver predictable results.

This also allows for the addition of draft angles and bulges to improve the appearance and physical properties of a finished part and to make it easier to remove the part from the mold.

Triad Symbol

The Flex features allow you to deform complex models intuitively. You can create four different types of bending:

Bending, Twisting, Tapering and Stretching.

8.10.1.1 Feature "Flex", option "Bending"

Flex, option Bending

This option bends one or more bodies around the red X-axis of the Triad (the bending axis). Position the triad and the trim planes to control the degree, position, and extent of the bend.

The neutral plane of the bend passes through the origin of the triad and corresponds to the XZ plane of the triad. The arc length between the trim planes along the neutral plane remains constant throughout the entire bend.

8.10.1.2 Feature "Flex", option "Twisting"

Flex, option, Twisting

This option rotates solid and surface bodies around the blue Z-axis of the triad. Position the triad and the trim planes to control the degree, position, and extent of the rotation.

8.10.1.3 Feature "Flex", option "Tapering"

Flex, option, tapering

This option tapers solid and surface bodies along the blue Z-axis of the triad. Position the triad and the trim planes to control the degree, position, and extent of the taper.

8.10.1.4 Feature "Flex", option "Stretching"

Flex, option, Stretching

This option stretches solid and surface bodies along the blue Z-axis of the triad. Specify a distance, or hold down the left mouse button and drag the edge of a trim plane.

Open

Bending

8.10.2 Model changes using feature "Flex", option "Bending"

8.10.2.1 Open the working file

Open (Menu bar) / Component from the book-DVD / **OK**.

8.10.2.2 Editing a component using the "Bending" option

Flex option **Bending** (Menu bar/ **Insert/Feature**)
Select the loaded component (1).
Select the **Bending** option (2).
Option **Angle 45°**, option **Hard edges**, base radius **60** mm (3).

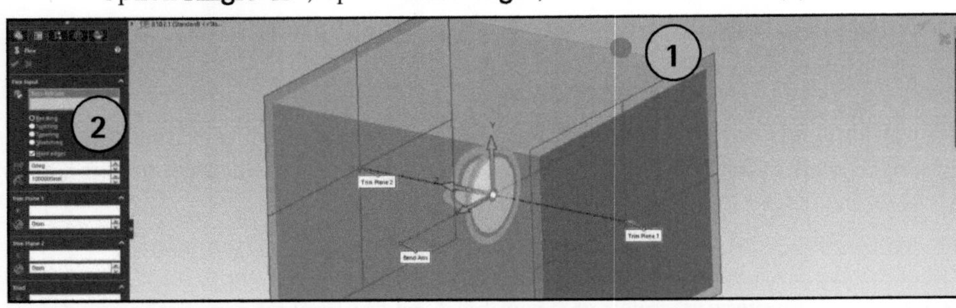

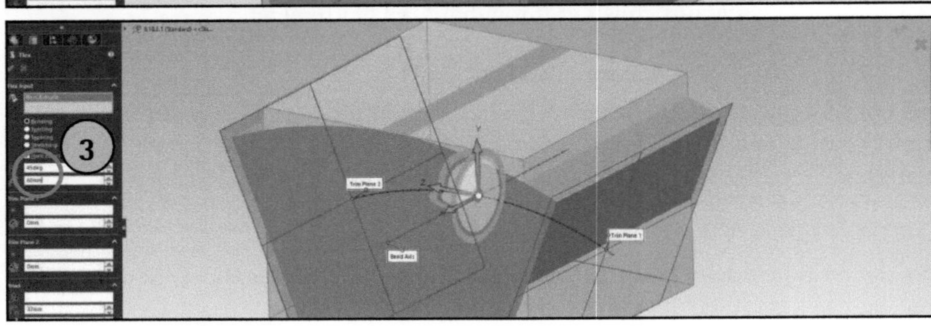

- Draw the **Y**-arrow of the **Triad**, as desired (4, 5).

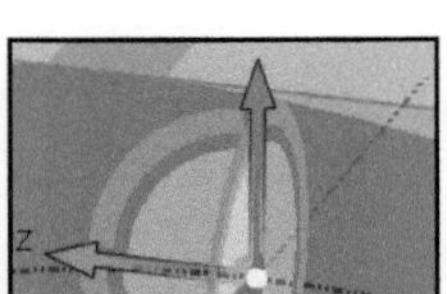

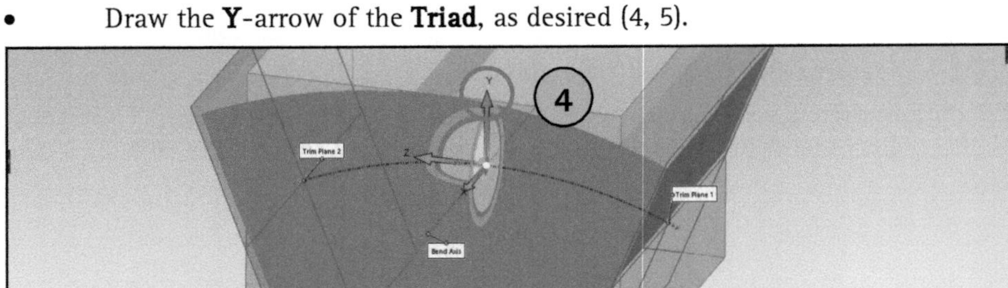

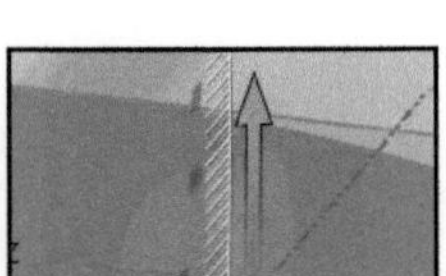

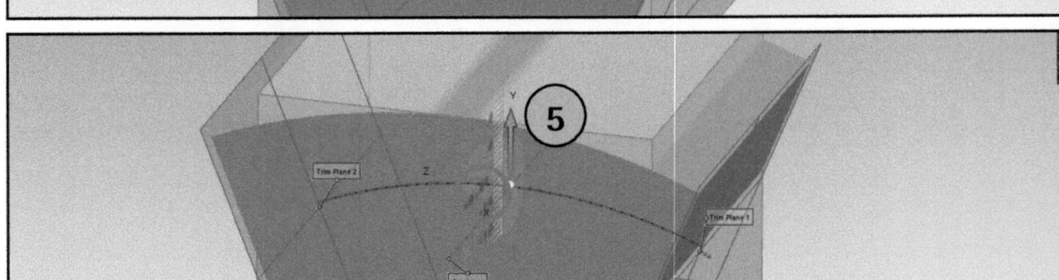

- Draw the **Z**-arrow of the **Triad**, as desired (6, 7).

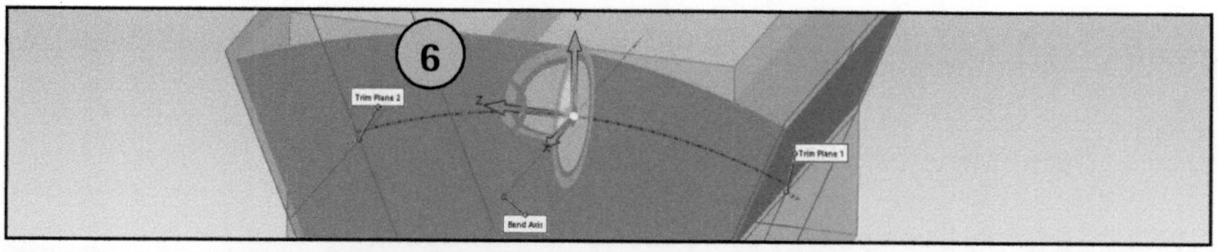

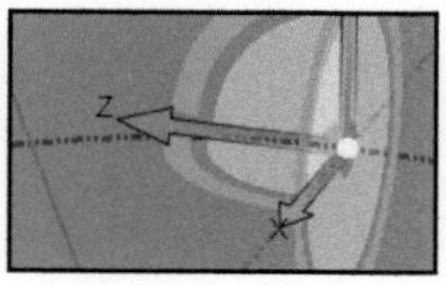

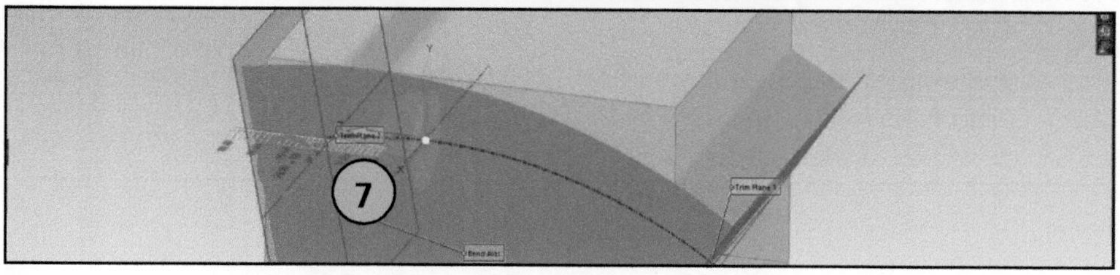

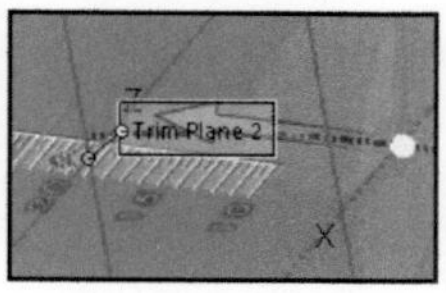

- Activate the vector display using the **Triad's** ring (8).
- Adjust the angle as desired (9).
- **Close dialog box** (10).

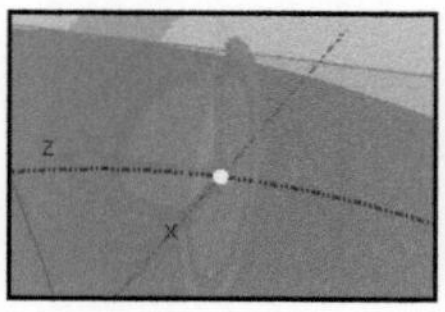

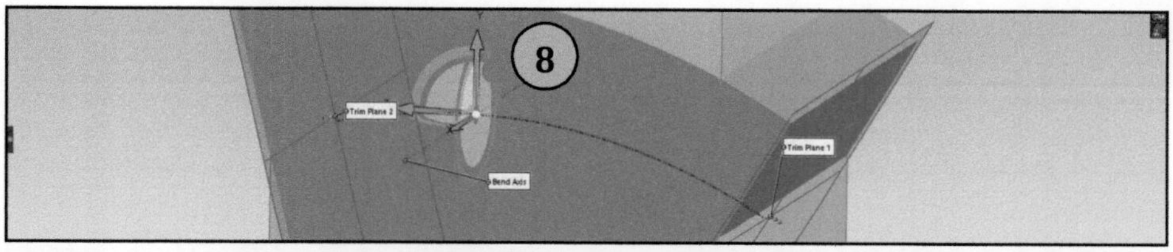

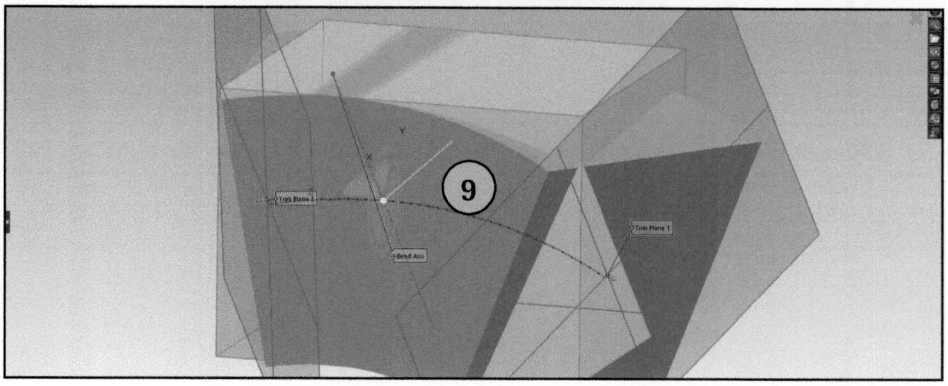

8.10.2.3 Data backup

Save as New / Enter a name of your choice.

Save as New

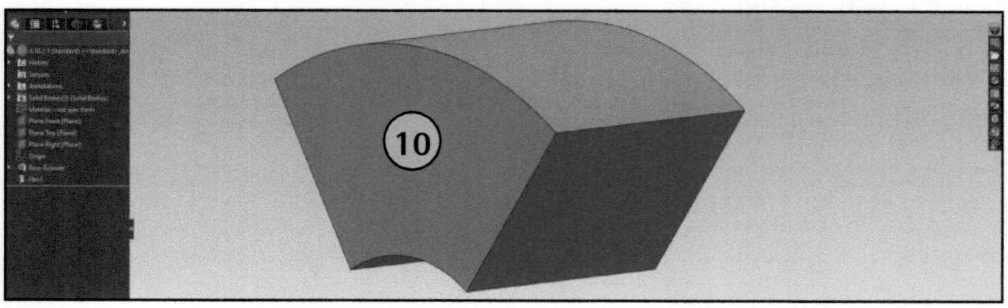

8.10.3 Model changes using feature "Flex", option "Twisting"

8.10.3.1 Open the working file

Open

Open (Menu bar) / Component from the book-DVD / **OK**.

8.10.3.2 Editing a component using the "Bending" option

Flex

Option Twisting

Flex option **Bending** (Menu bar/ **Insert/Feature**)
Select the loaded component (1).
Select the **Twisting** option (2), **Angle 90°** (3, 4).

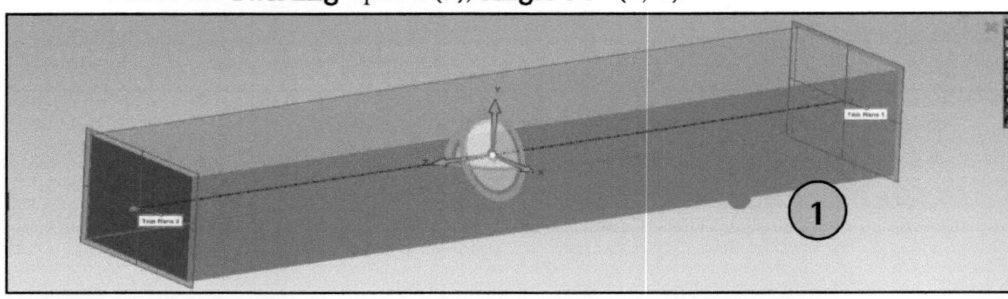

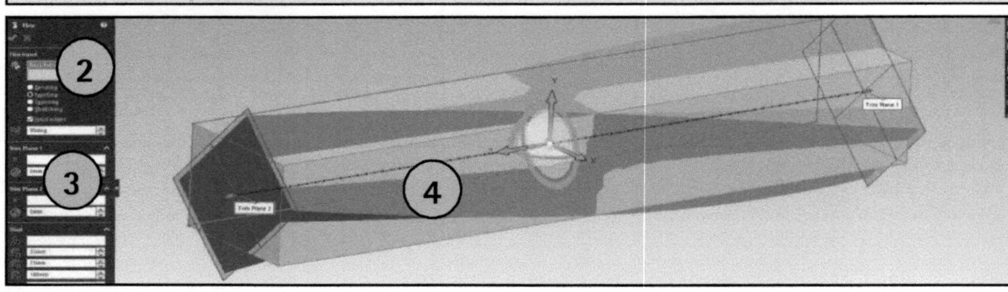

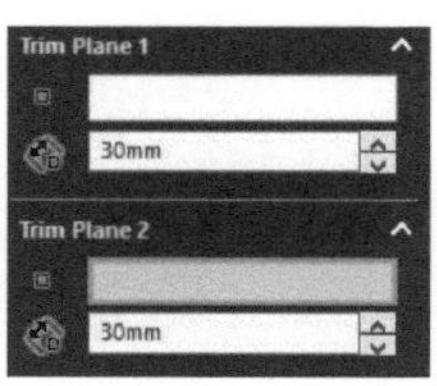

- **30** mm distance for **Trim plane 1** and **Trim plane 2** (5, 6).
- **Close dialog box** (7).

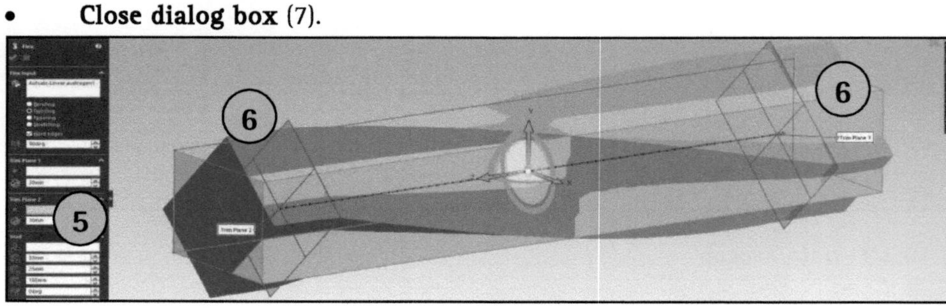

8.10.3.3 Data backup

Save as New

Save as New / Enter a name of your choice.

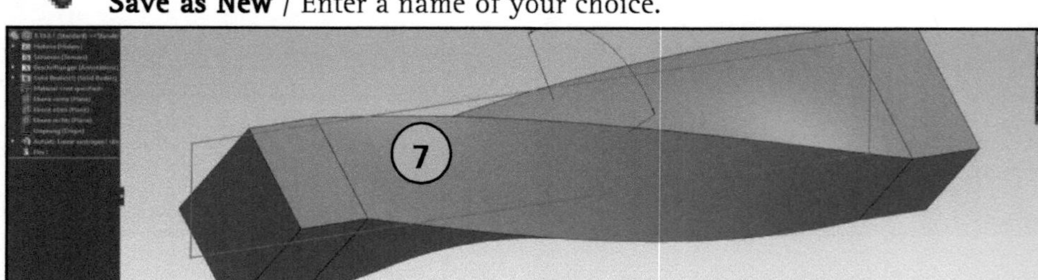

8.10.4 Model changes using feature "Flex", option "Tapering"

8.10.4.1 Open the working file

Open (Menu bar) / Component from the book-DVD / **OK**

Open

8.10.4.2 Editing a component using the "Tapering" option

Flex option **Tapering** (Menu bar/ **Insert/Feature**)
Select the loaded component (1).
Select the **Tapering** option (2), set the distance to **0.5** mm (3, 4).

Flex

Option Tapering

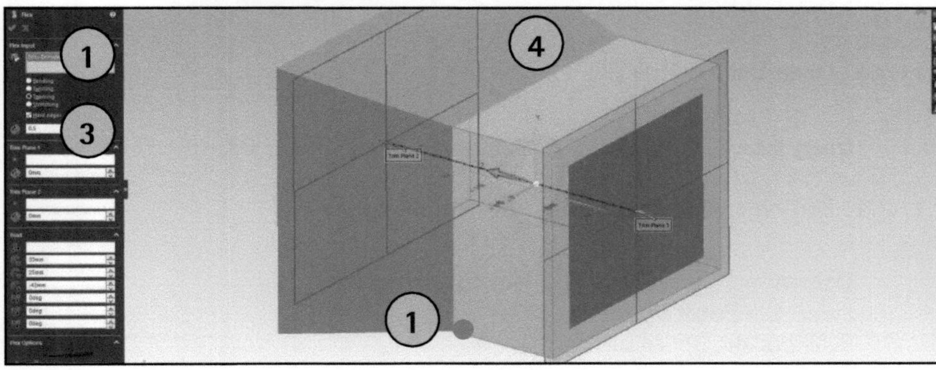

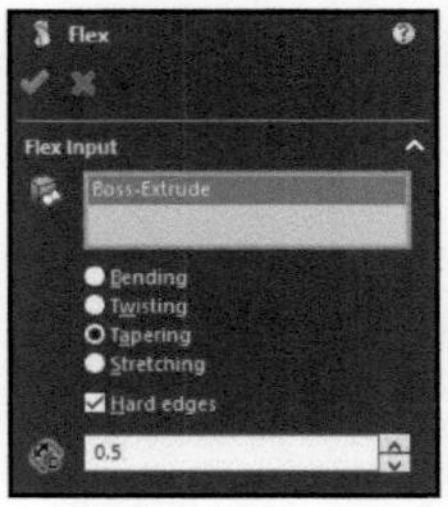

- **30** mm distance for **Trim plane 1** and **Trim plane 2** (5, 6).
- **Close dialog box** (7).

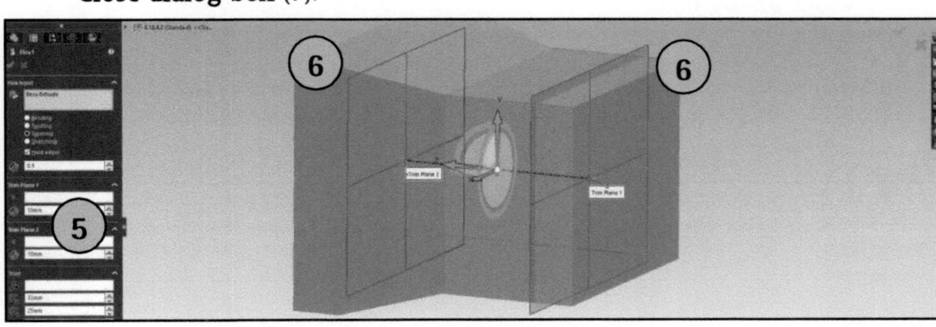

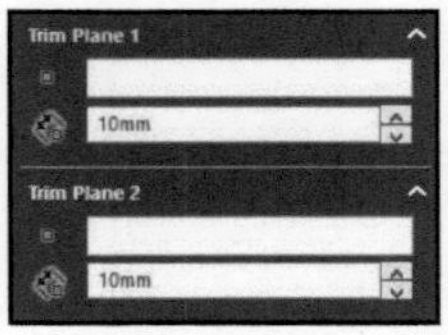

8.10.4.3 Data backup

Save as New / Enter a name of your choice.

Save as New

8.11 Deformation functions on a basic body, using feature "Deform"

8.11.1 Feature "Deform", basics

In the deformation function, the surfaces of target bodies are deformed using the surfaces of tool bodies.

You can select one of the pre-made, customizable tool bodies, such as a polygon or a sphere, or use your own tool body.

The surfaces of the target body are approximated to the surfaces of the tool body.

8.11.2 Model changes using feature "Deform", option "Point"

8.11.2.1 Open the working file

Open

Open (Menu bar) / Component from the book-DVD / **OK**.

8.11.2.2 Editing a component using the "Point" option

Deform

Option Point

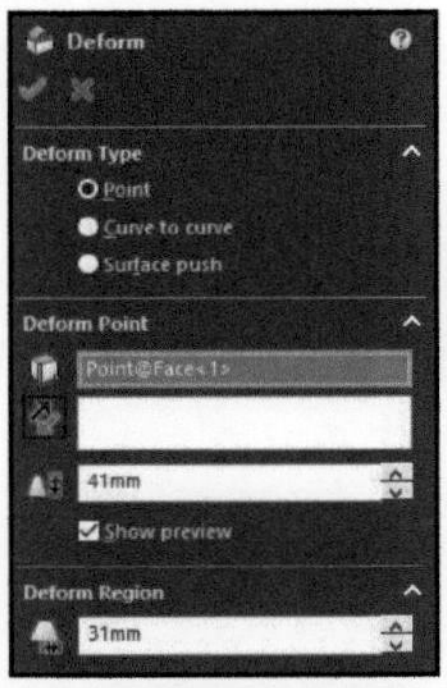

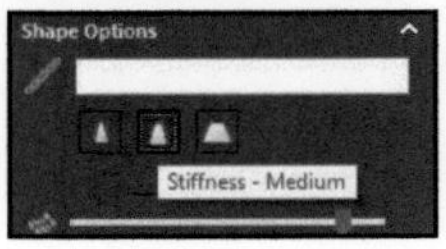

Deform option Point (Menu bar/ **Insert/Feature**)
Select the **Point** option (1).
Select of the upper surface (2).
Deformation distance **41** mm, Deformation Radius: **31** mm,
Show preview (3), **Stiffness Medium** (4).
Close dialog box.

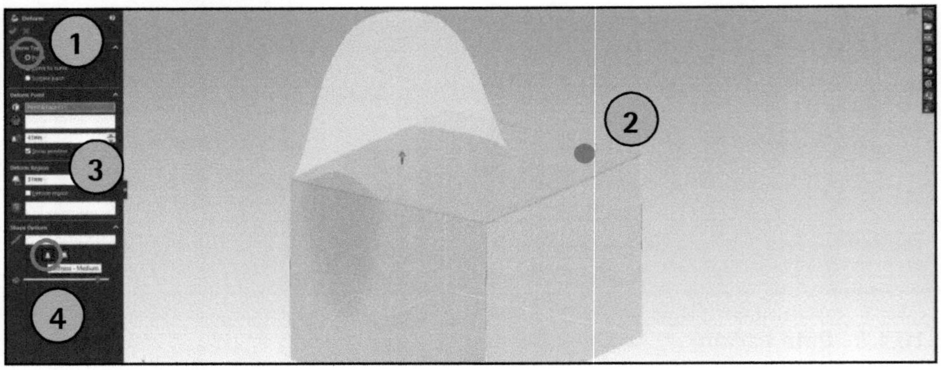

- **Stiffness Minimum** (5), **Stiffness Maximum** (6)

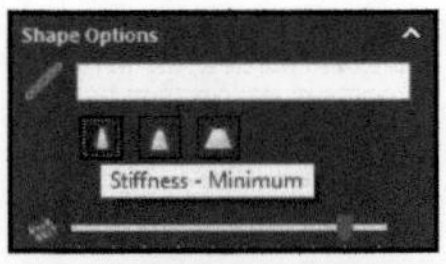

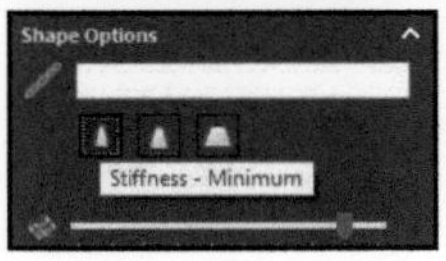

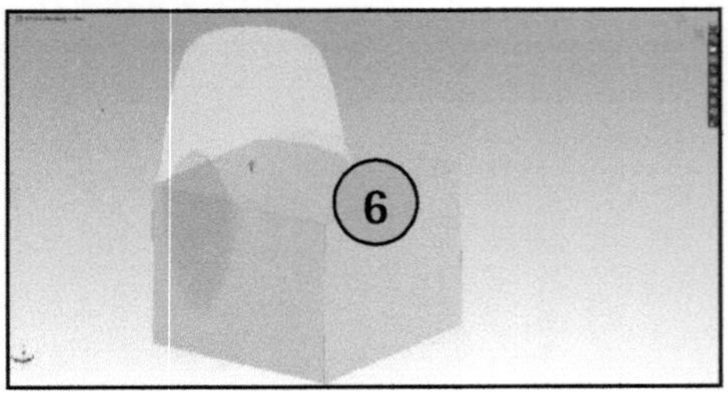

8.11.2.3 Data backup

Save as New

Save as New / Enter a name of your choice.

8.11.3 Model changes using feature "Deform" Option "Point", selection "Edge"

8.11.3.1 Open the working file

Open (Menu bar) / Component from the book-DVD / **OK**.

Open

8.11.3.2 Editing a component using the "Point" option, selecting "Edge"

Deform option Point (Menu bar/ **Insert/Feature**)
Select the **Point** option (1).
Select **Point** (2) and **Edge** (3).
Deformation distance **50** mm, Deformation Radius **50** mm (4).
Show preview (4), **Stiffness Medium** (5).
Close dialog box

Deform

Option Point

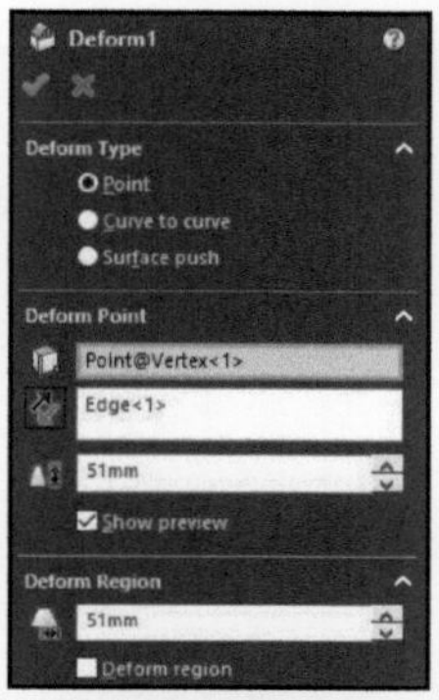

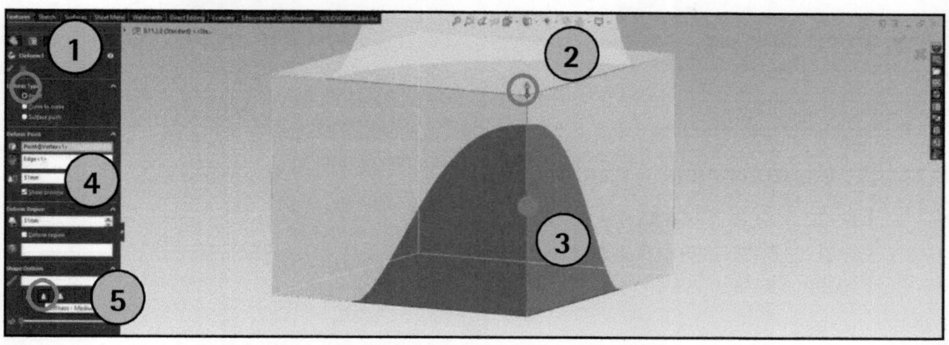

- **Stiffness Minimum** (6), **Stiffness Maximum** (7).

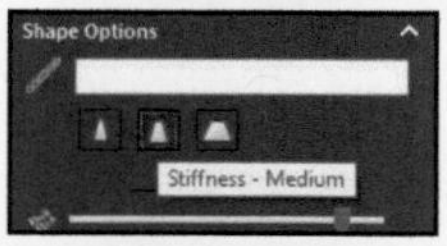

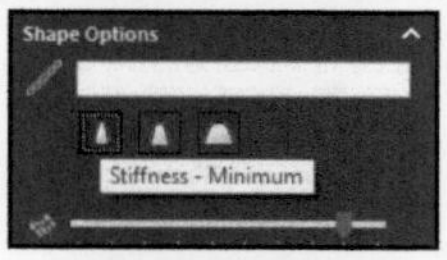

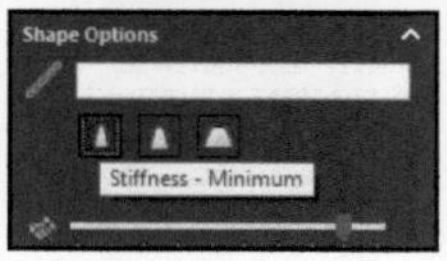

8.11.3.3 Data backup

Save as New / Enter a name of your choice.

Save as New

8.11.4 Model changes using feature "Deform" Option "Curve to Curve"

8.11.4.1 Open the working file

Open

Open (Menu bar) / Component from the book-DVD / **OK**.

8.11.4.2 Create a new work plane

- Create a new **Work Plane**, distance **40** mm (1, 2).

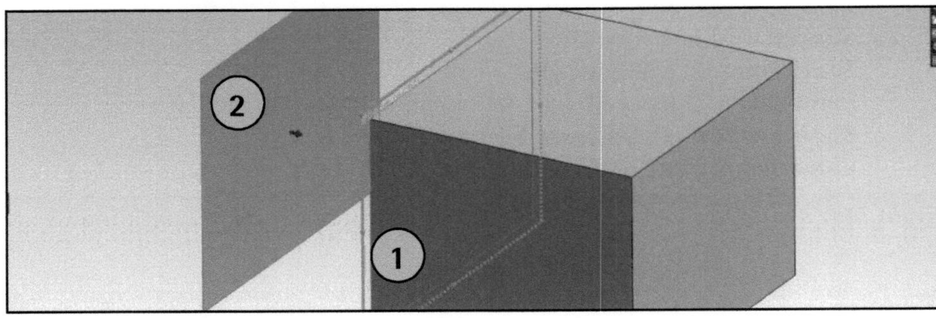

8.11.4.3 Construction of a transition curve

Sketch

Centerpoint Arc

- Create a new **Sketch**.
- Create a **Centerpoint Arc** (3), freely selecting the dimensions (4).
- **Finish Sketch**.

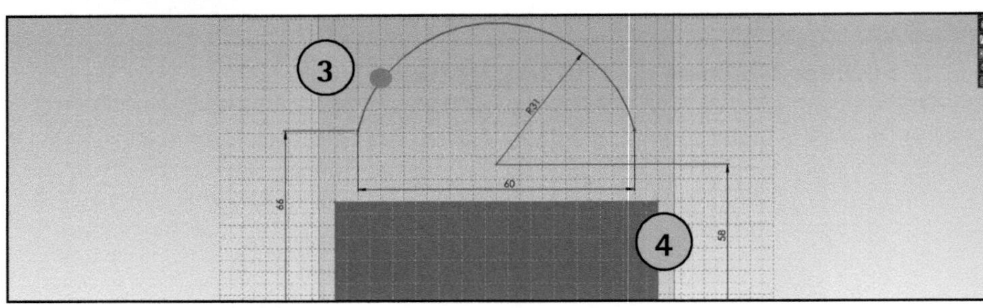

8.11.4.4 Editing a component using the "Point" option, selecting "Edge"

Deform

Option Curve to Curve

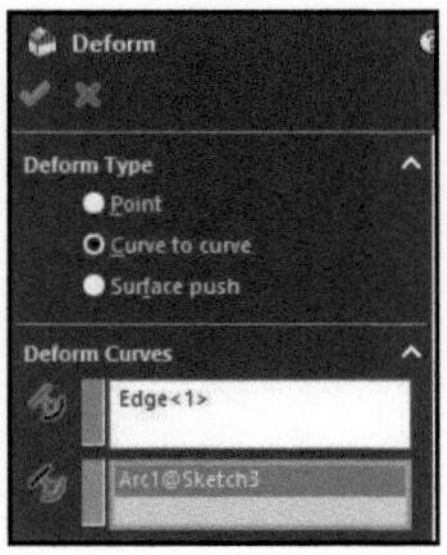

Deform option **Point** (Menu bar/ **Insert/Feature**)
Select the **Curve to Curve** option (5).
Select **Initial Curve** (6) and **Target Curve** (7).

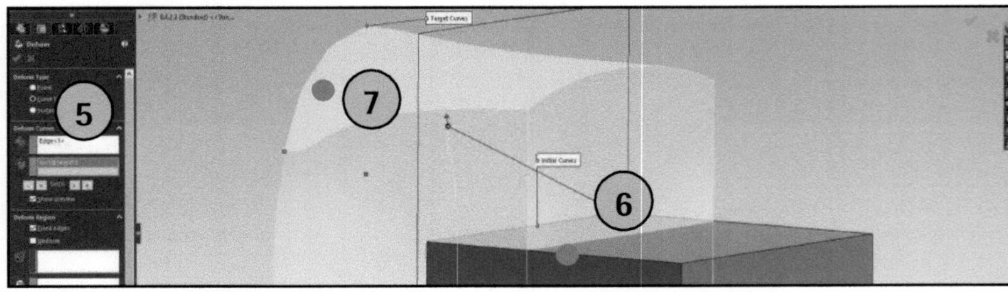

- Select **Bodies to be deformed** (7, 8).
- **Show preview** (9), **Stiffness Medium** (10).
- **Close dialog box**

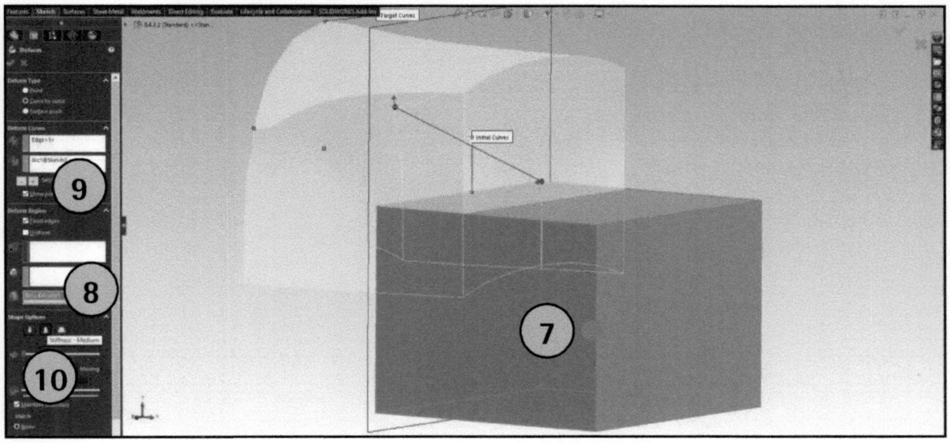

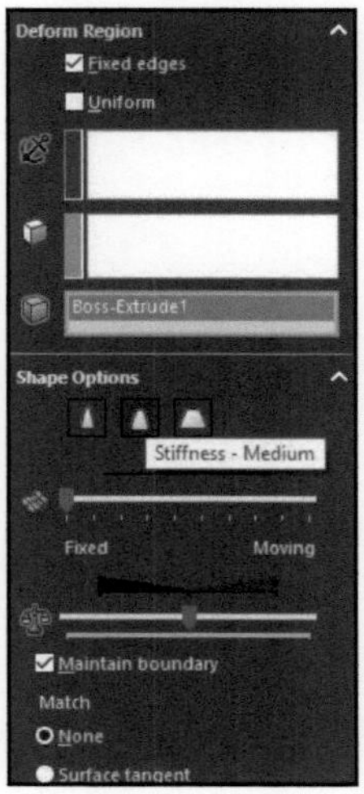

8.11.4.5 Data backup

Save as New / Enter a name of your choice.

Save as New

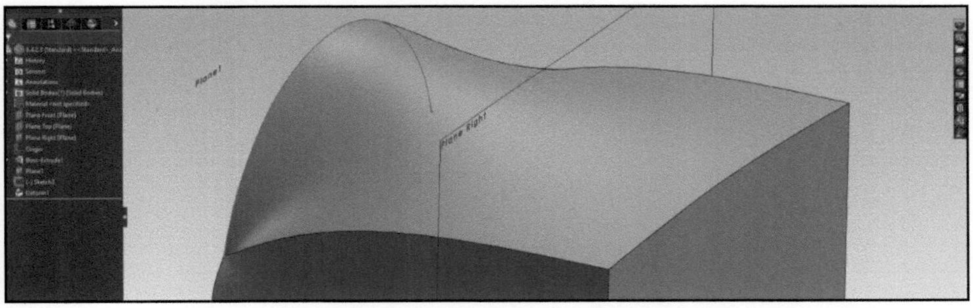

9

Dassault Systèmes

3DEXPERIENCE©

SOLIDWORKS Design

2026

Parts and Components

Create and Customize

Create Components

Drive Shafts

Housings

Drill Plates

9 Create Components

9.1 Parts and Components, preliminary remarks

When designing a part, you create sketches, create three-dimensional elements using feature tools, and then combine these elements to create parts.

The shape of the sketch is controlled by constraints, which are automatically applied by default during sketching, and the size of the sketch is controlled by dimensions. You can leave some parts of the sketch geometry undimensioned if you want to change the size later.

9.1.1 Dimensions, an overview

Dimensions allow you to add value annotations to 3D models or 2D design geometry by measuring characteristics such as the size, position, and orientation of elements.

For example, you can measure the length of a line, the distance between points, or the angle a line makes with the horizontal or vertical plane. Dimensions are linked to their 3D model or 2D datum entities so designs can be easily modified.

Solid Edge includes a full range of dimensioning features for documenting parts, assemblies, and drawings.

9.1.2 Parametric dimensions

With parametric dimensions, the geometry resizes when you change the dimension value. You can sketch freely without worrying about the correct size of the geometry. When you edit a sketch dimension, its position adjusts when the sketch geometry updates.

When you rotate the view of your sketch, the dimensions reorient themselves so they're easy to read. Parametric dimensions can be defined to display parameter values, parameter names, or expressions.

When sketching, the size of the geometry is automatically calculated. If the size meets your requirements, you can accept it. However, you typically add dimensions to specify the correct size.

You can roughly sketch the geometry and create a feature from it. Later, you can return to the sketch to edit it and add dimensions to precisely specify the feature size.

A key advantage of parametric dimensions is their control. You can define dimensions with parameters in a spreadsheet, control dimensions with equations to maintain proportions between geometric elements, or define dimensions as constant values.

9.1.3 Creation of components, command selection for creation

- The template file **Engelke2026.PRTDOT** on the book DVD should be used to create the components..
- The template file **Engelke2026.asmdot** on the book DVD should be used to create the assemblies.
- Create a separate directory for each subchapter.
- Use the **Extrude** or **Revolve** function for component base bodies.
- Holes and slots should always be created using the **Hole Wizard** function.
- Holes, as central holes in cylinders, are always created by selecting the circular area as the center point of the circular area.
- Circular ring surfaces, for example in bushings, to represent bores with extrude, should be avoided.
- For turned parts and shafts, the construction from individual cylinders with the basic body function extrude is preferable, as these are also dimensioned accordingly for manufacturing purposes.
- For creating complex revolved bodies with hollow internal elements, the Revolve function is preferable.
- **Chamfers** and **Fillets** are applied via the corresponding commands and should therefore not be used as sketch elements in the sketch for the rotation commands.
- Use the **Shell** function for wall thicknesses as often as possible.
- Regularly distributed elements, such as holes on a bolt circle, should be created individually and distributed using the **Circular Pattern**, **Linear Pattern** or **Mirror** function.
- Physical threads are created using the **Thread** function.
- Assign a material to the components using the **Edit Material** function.
- Data backup of individual components using **Save as New**.

9.1.4 Creation of the components manufacturing fundamentals

The following creation specifications are intended only as a directive:

- Bright steel / non-ferrous products according to DIN EN 10278, tolerance field h9.
  The surface treatment of the bare surfaces remains in the raw state; the further surface qualities of the mechanically machined surfaces must be specified in the drawing derivation in accordance with the function..
- Non-specified fitting dimensions must be dimensioned according to the function, selecting according to DIN EN ISO 286-1/2 and fitting selection according to DIN 7157.
- Missing dimensions must be added as appropriate.
- Additional surface treatments such as cadmium plating, hard chrome plating, galvanizing, etc. must be taken into account when determining the fitting dimensions/deviations.
- Permissible dimensional deviations according to ISO 2768-1, Medium quality, form/positional deviations according to ISO 2768-2, K quality.
- Request more precise form and position tolerances according to DIN EN ISO 1101 if required.

Engelke2026.
PRTDOT
Engelke2026.
asmdot
Extrude
Revolve
Hole izard
Fillet
Chamfer
Shell
Circular
Pattern
Linear
Pattern
Mirror
Thread
Edit
Material
Edit Scene
Save as New

Project XVI

Create Components
Drive shafts

Page 368 to 395

- Component creation “Coupling Bolt”
- Component creation “Drive Shaft”
- Component creation “Mounting Bolt”
- Component creation “Drive Shaft”
- Component creation “Gear Shaft”
- Component creation ”Worm Shaft”

9.2 Component creation "Coupling bolt"

9.2.1 The design sketch for the component creation

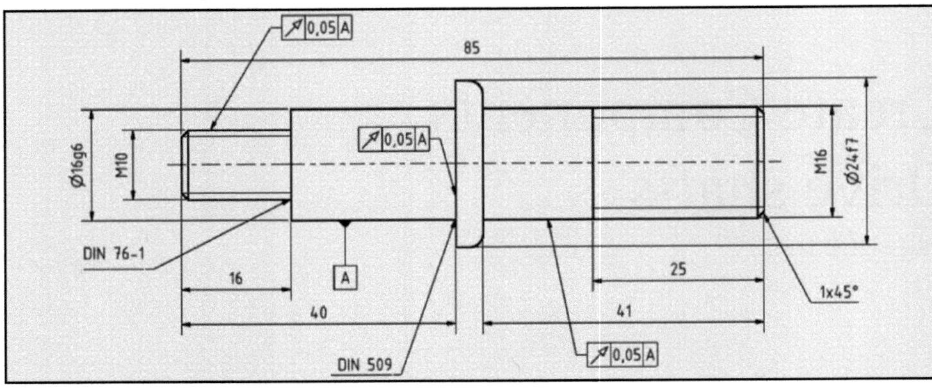

9.2.2 The coupling bolt, the creation

New

Engelke2026.
PRTDOT

Circle

Extrude

View Selektor

9.2.2.1 Opening your own template file

- Menu Bar **New** /  /  click **Engelke2026.PRTDOT** / **OK**

9.2.2.2 Creating the basic component

- Create a cylinder using **Extrude**, with **Circle Ø24** mm, height of **4** mm, **Plane Right** (1).
- Create additional cylinders using fearure **Extrude** with:
  Circle Ø16 mm, height of **41** mm (2).
  Circle Ø16 mm, height of **24** mm (3).
  Circle Ø10 mm, height of **16** mm (4).

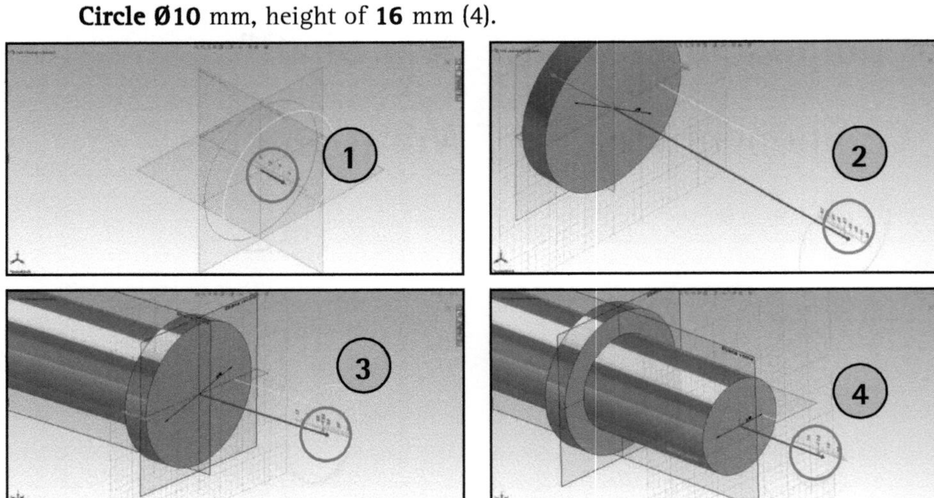

9.2.2.3 The coupling bolt, assign material

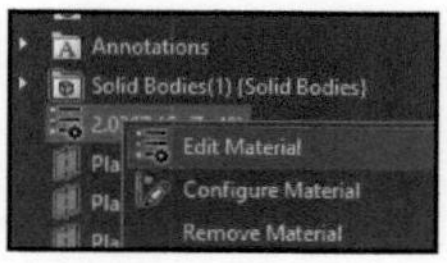

Edit Material

Edit Material (FeatureManager)
Right-click on **Material** to display the context menu for **Edit Material**.
Select **SOLIDWORKS Materials / Steels / Chrome Stainless Steel** (12, 13).
Click **Apply** and then **Close** (5).

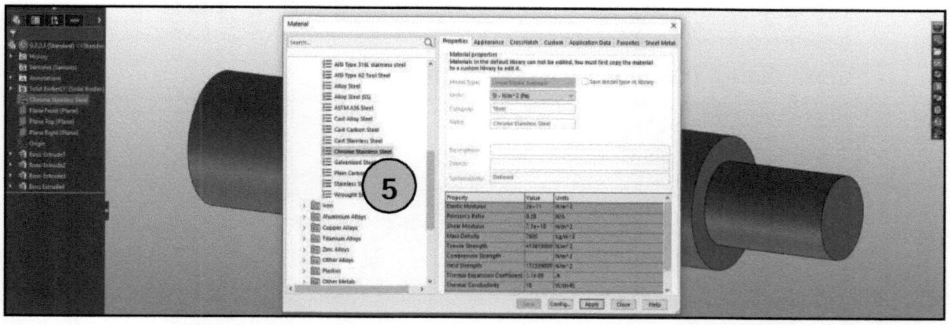

9.2.3 The coupling bolt, using "Stud Wizard"

9.2.3.1 External thread assignment, long extension M16 using "Stud wizard"

Stud Wizard

Stud Wizard (Features tab)
Select an edge of a cylindrical face to create the stud (6).
Standard: **ISO**, Size **M16** (7).
Select **Blind** for End Condition (8).
Thread length along the stud from the starting edge **25** mm (8).
Actvate option **Undercut** (9).
Close dialog box (10).

Stud Wizard

9.2.3.1 External thread assignment, long extension M10 using "Stud wizard"

Stud Wizard (Features tab)
Select an edge of a cylindrical face to create the stud (11).
Standard: **ISO**, Size **M10** (12).
Select **Blind** for End Condition (13).
Thread length along the stud from the starting edge **12** mm (13).
Actvate option **Undercut** (14).
Close dialog box (15).

Fillet

9.2.3.2 The coupling bolt, using „Fillet“

Fillet (Features tab)
Select the cylinder edge as shown (16).
Break with a value of R **2** mm (17).

Save as New

9.2.3.3 Data backup

Save as New / Enter a name of your choice.

9.3 Component creation "Drive Shaft"

9.3.1 The design sketch for the component creation

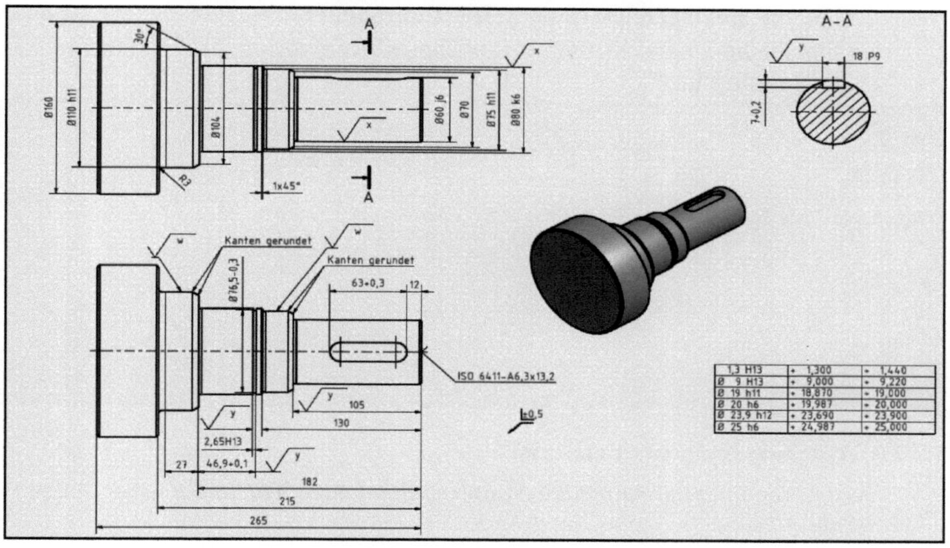

9.3.2 The "Drive Shaft", the creation

9.3.2.1 Creating the basic sketch

- Menu Bar **New** /  /  click **Engelke2026.PRTDOT / OK**
- On the **Front Plane**, create a **Line** path according to the sketch shown (1).

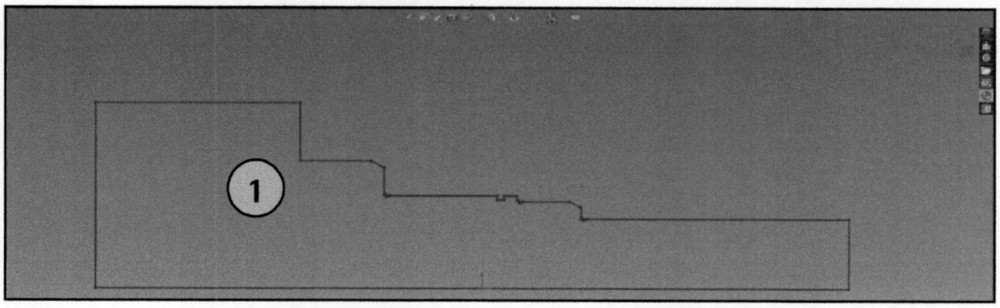

New

Engelke2026. PRTDOT

Line

- Assign the displayed dimensions using **SmartDimension** (2).

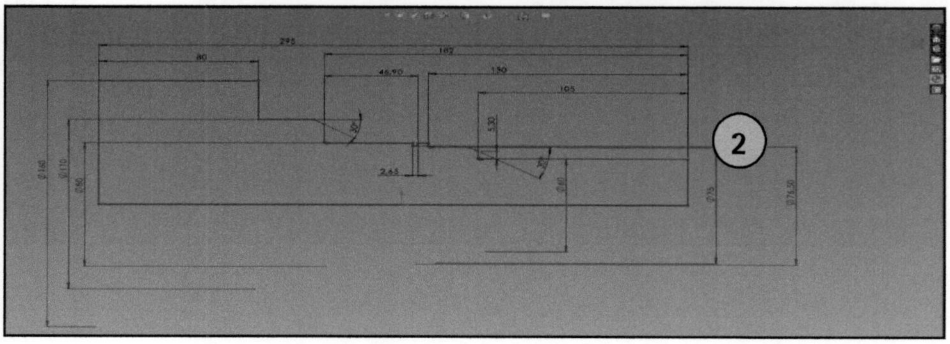

Smart Dimension

9.3.2.2 Revolved volume, the creation

Revolve

Revolved (**Features** tab)
Click the area **Sketch1**, using **Select Contours** (3).
Click the horizontal line to set it as the axis of rotation (4).
Close dialog box

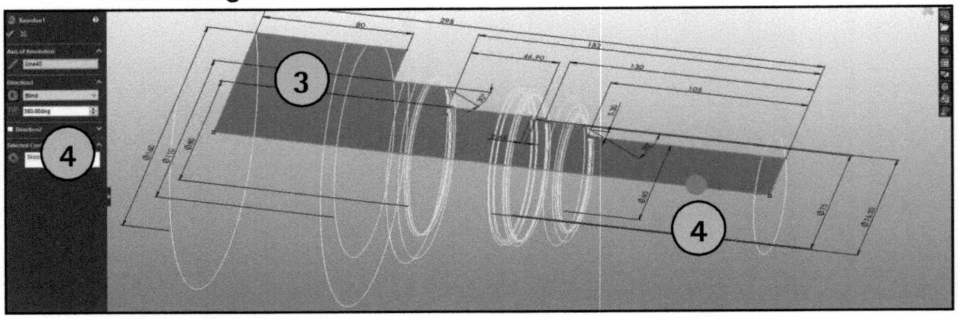

9.3.2.3 Assigning component material

Edit Material

- Assign the material **Annealed Stainless Steel AISI 347** to the drive shaft (5, 6).

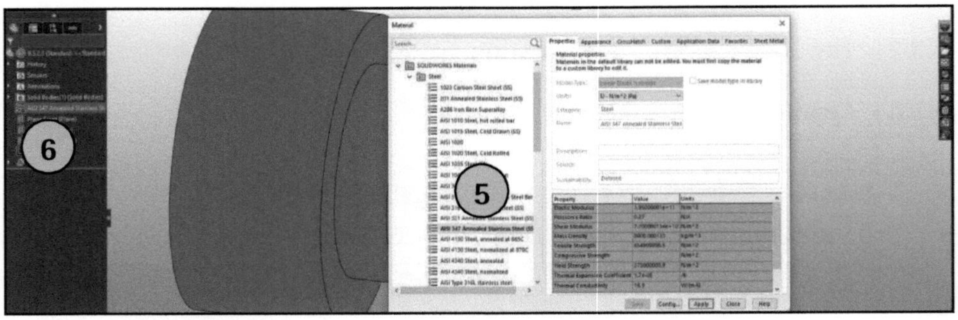

9.3.2.4 Chamfers for edge breaking 1 mm x 45°

Chamfer

Chamfer (**Features** tab)
Select the elements shown for edge breaking (7).
Break the edges with a value of **1** mm x **45°** (8).

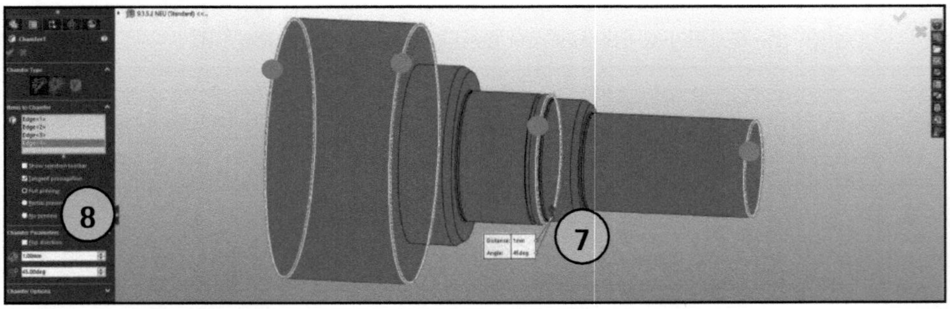

9.3.3 Creating the keyway slot

9.3.3.1 Tangential working plane for the basic sketch of the keyway slot

Plane (Reference Geometry toolbar)
Select the **Front Plane** as a reference (9), distance **30** mm (10).

New Plane

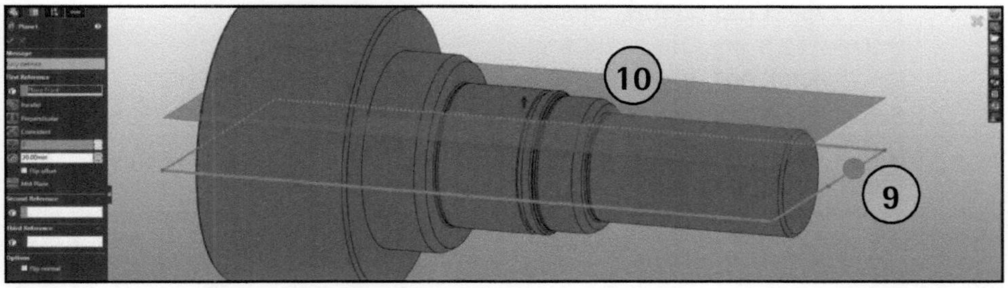

9.3.3.2 Basic sketch for the keyway slot

- Create the sketch shown using a **Line** (11) and a **Circle** (12) on the newly created plane.

Sketch

Normal To

Line

Circle

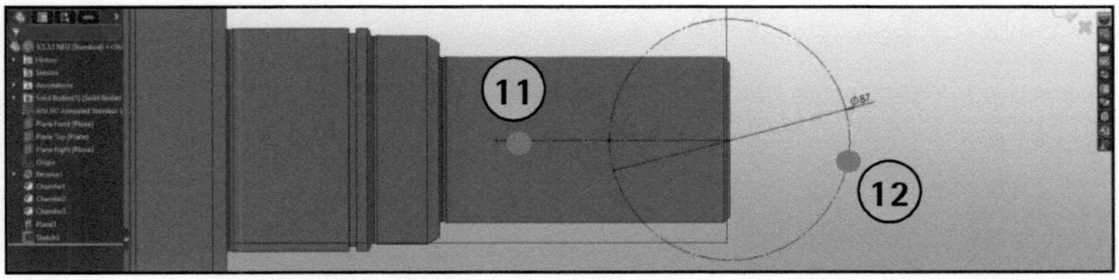

9.3.3.3 Keyway slot, the creation

Hole Wizard (**Features** tab)
Type options: **DIN**, **Blind 5** mm, Drill type: **Slot**.
Size **Ø18** mm Slot length **45** mm (13).
Show custom sizing, no drill bit **180°**
Select the **Positions / 3D Sketch** tab (13).
Click the visible **Plane** (14).
Select the center point shown for the slot (15).
Possible change of position of the keyway slot using the **Tab** key.
Close dialog box (5).

Hole Wizard

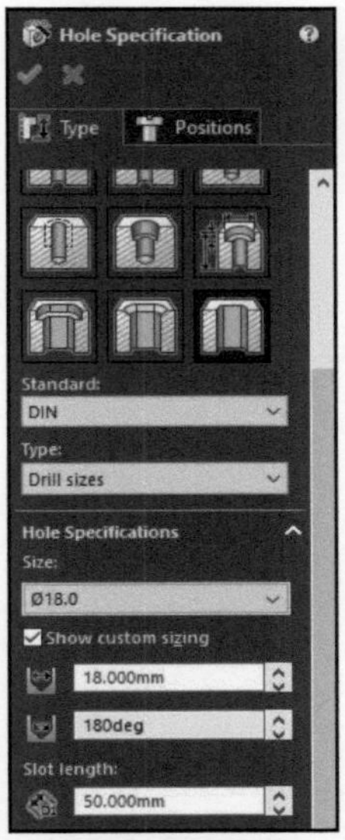

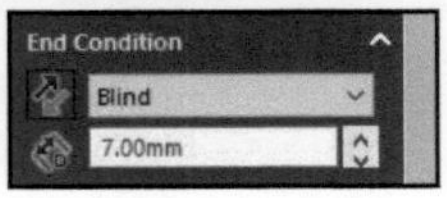

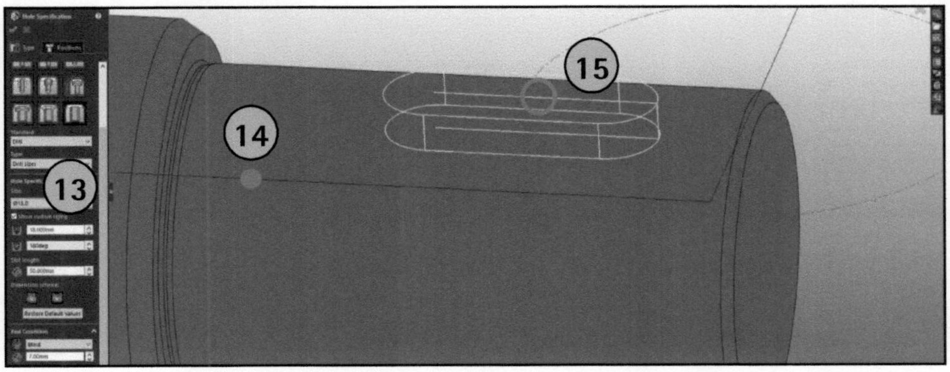

9.3.4 Creating center holes

9.3.4.1 Create centering hole on the keyway side

Hole Wizard

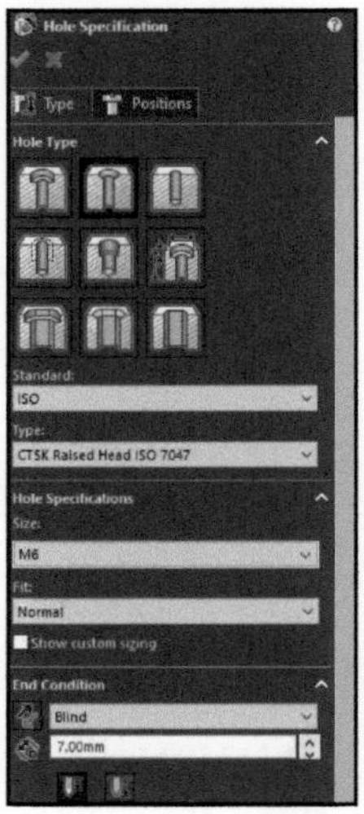

Hole Wizard (Features tab)
Click the **Type** tab.
Drill Type: **Countersink**, Standard: **ISO**
Outer-Ø**12.6** mm, Inner-Ø**6.6** mm,
Countersink **90°**, depth **7** mm, drill bit **118°**, option **Blind** (16).
Select the **Positions / 3D Sketch** tab.
Quick Snaps (Sketch tab) / **Center Point Snap** (17).
Close dialog box (18).

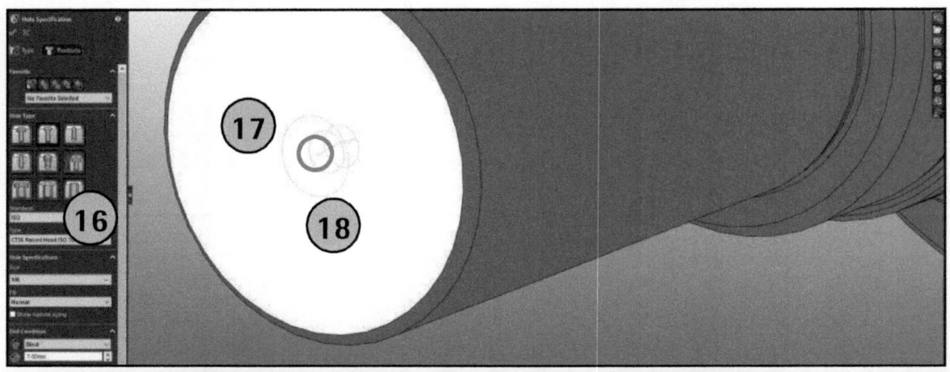

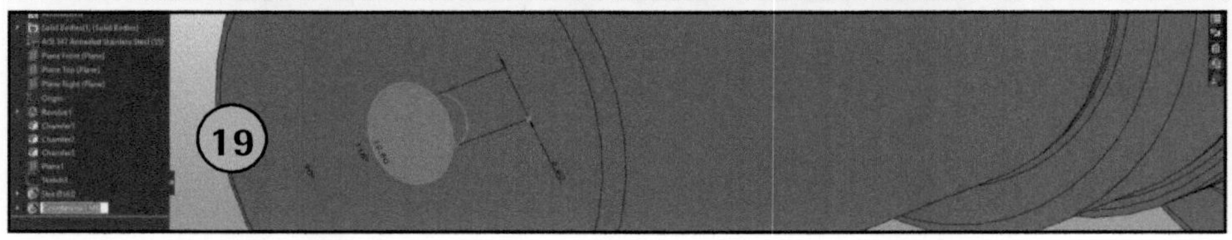

9.3.4.2 Create centering hole on the other shaft side

- Proceed accordingly with the centering bore on the other side of the shaft. (20, 21).

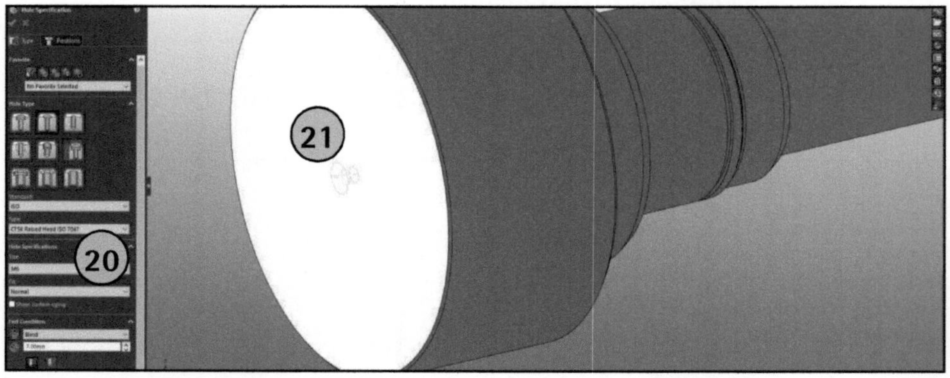

9.3.4.3 Data backup

Save as New

Save as New / Enter a name of your choice.

9.4 Component creation "Mounting bolts"

9.4.1 The design sketch for the component creation

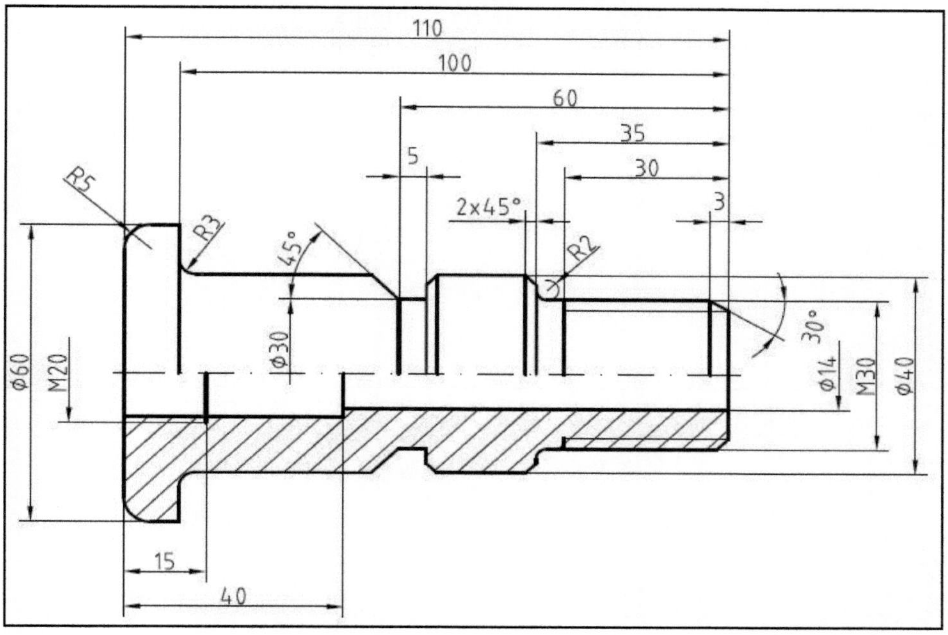

9.4.2 Creating the base body

9.4.2.1 Opening your own template file

- Menu Bar **New** /  /  click **Engelke2026.PRTDOT / OK**

New

Engelke2026.
PRTDOT

Line

Smart
Dimension

9.4.2.2 The basic sketch construction

- Select the **Front Plane**.
- Create a **Line** profile according to the design sketch (1).
- Enter the dimensions as shown (2).
- **Close dialog box**

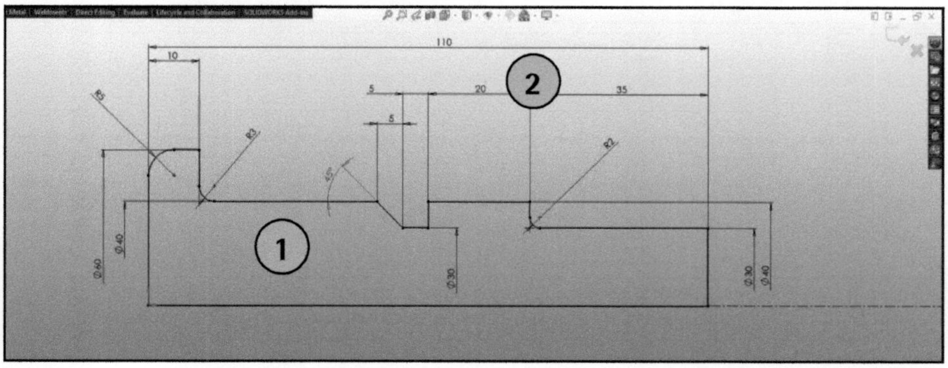

Revolve

9.4.2.3 The creation of the basic body, using feature "Revolve"

Revolved (**Features** tab)
Click the area **Sketch1**, using **Select Contours** (3).
Click the horizontal line to set it as the axis of rotation (4).
Close dialog box (5)

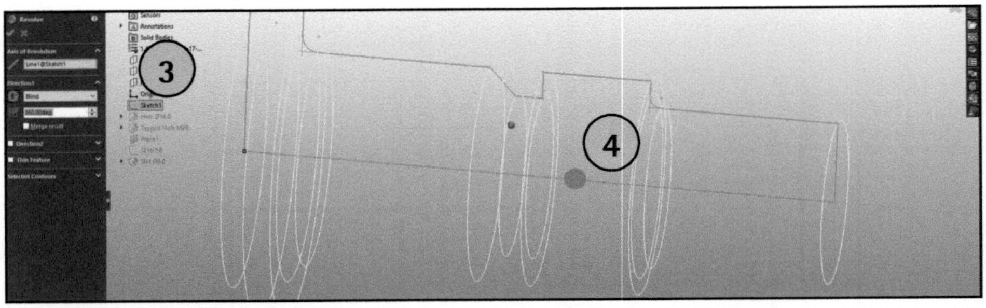

9.4.3 Edge breaking using "Chamfer", the creation

Chamfer

9.4.3.1 Creating the thread end chamfer

Chamfer (**Features** tab)
Select the **Angle/Distance** option (6).
Distance: **3** mm, Angle: **60°** (6) / select **Keep feature** (6).
Enable **Full preview** (6).
Click the edges for the chamfer (7).
Close dialog box.

9.4.3.2 Creating the chamfers for the wave shoulder

Chamfer

Chamfer (**Features** tab)
Select the **Angle/Distance** option (8).
Distance: **2** mm, Angle: **45°** (8) / select **Keep feature** (8).
Enable **Full preview** (8).
Click the edges for the chamfer (9, 10).
Close dialog box.

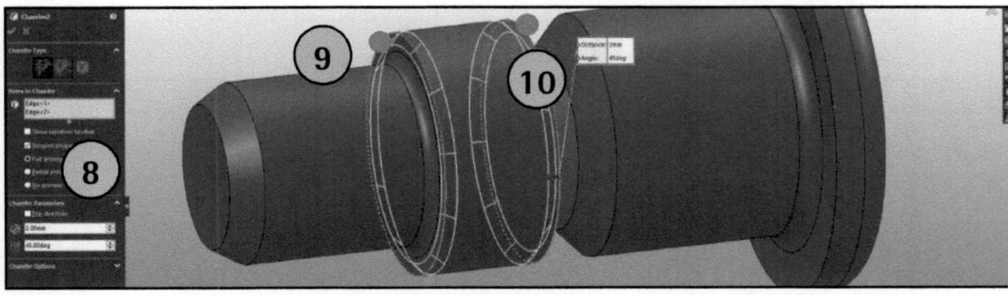

9.4.4 The central counterbore

Hole Wizard

Hole Wizard (**Features** tab)
Click the **Type** tab.
ISO, **Head socket screw ISO 4762**, **M12**.
Custom sizing: Bore diameter **14** mm, depth: **Through all**
Tiefe Grundloch **40** mm, Bohrungs-**Ø20** mm (11).
Select the **Positions / 3D Sketch** tab.
Select the external cylinder (12).
Close dialog box (13).

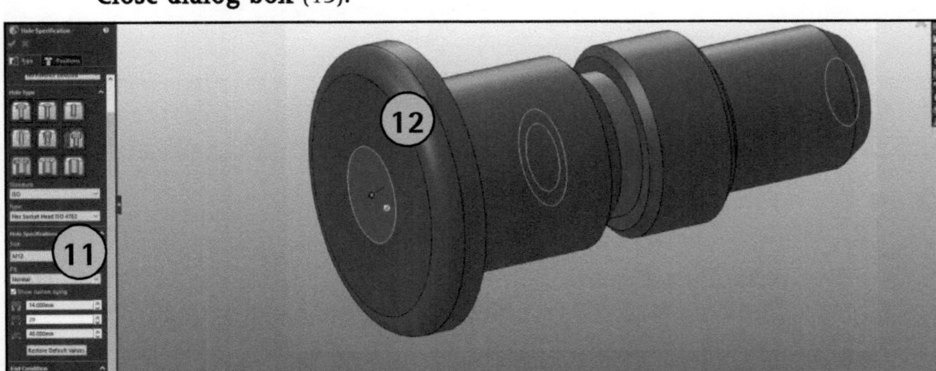

9.4.5 Creating a keyway slot

9.4.5.1 Creating a tangent plane

View Selektor

Plane

- Make the component sketch visible.
- Rotate the component using the **View Selection** function.

Plane (Reference Geometry toolbar)
Select the upper cylinder face (14), select the sketch point shown (15).
Click **Tangent** in the **FeatureManager design tree** (16).
Close dialog box

9.4.5.2 Creating the basic sketch for the keyway slot

Sketch

Normal To

Line

Line (**Sketch** tab)
Select the new **Plane 1** (17).
Create the **Line** construction to define the center point for the keyway (18).
Close dialog box / Finish Sketch

9.4.5.3 Keyway slot, the creation

Hole Wizard

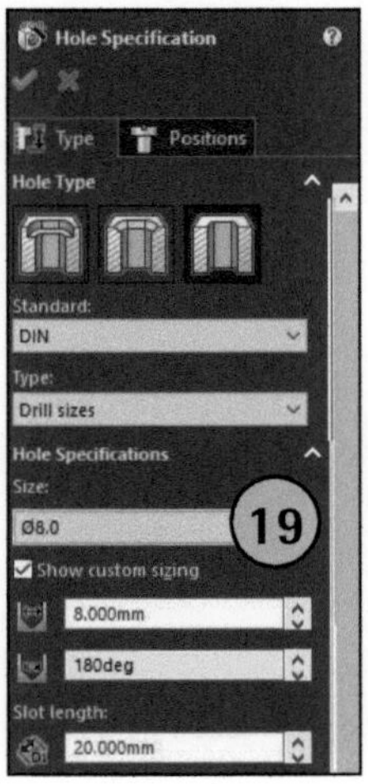

Hole Wizard (**Features** tab)
Type: **Blind 5** mm, Drill type: **Slot** Size **Ø8** mm, Slot length **20** mm.
Show custom sizing, no drill bit **180°** (19).
Select the **Positions / 3D Sketch** tab, click the visible **Plane** (20).
Select the center point shown for the slot (21).
Close dialog box.

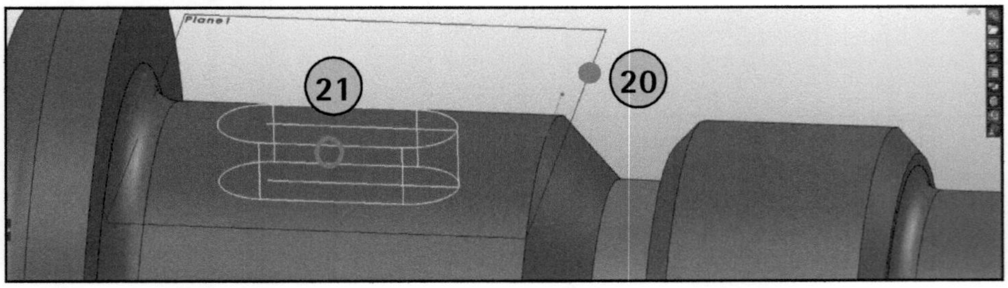

9.4.6 Physical thread assignment

9.4.6.1 Physical external thread, using feature "Thread"

Thread (Features tab / **Hole wizard)**

Select metric thread size **M30x2** (22).

Thread Location:

Select the upper cylinder edge as the thread position (23).

End Condition:

Option Up to Selection,

Select the bottom edge of the cylinder as the end condition (24).

Option **Cut Thread, Red** preview (10).

Option **Trim with start face** und **Trim with end face** (25).

Close dialog box (26).

Thread

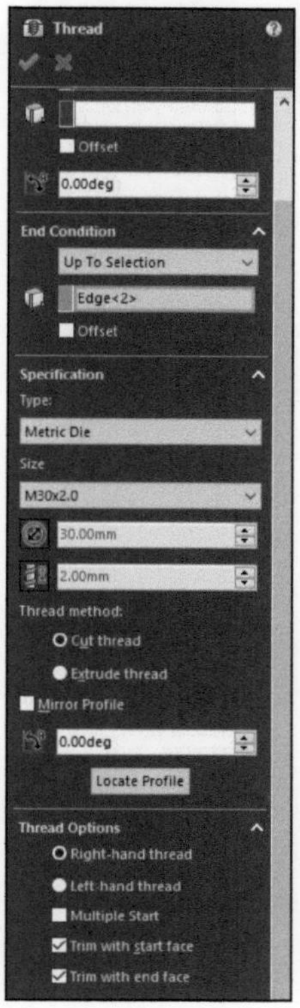

Thread

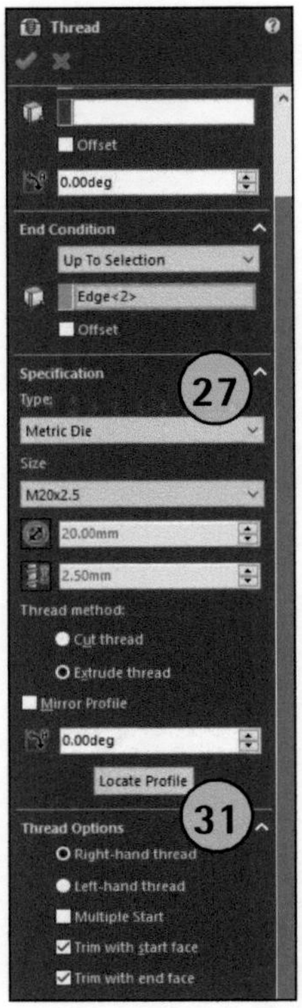

9.4.6.2 Physical internal thread, using feature "Thread"

Thread (**Features** tab / **Hole wizard**)
Select metric thread size **M20x2.5** (2).
Select the upper cylinder edge as the thread position (28).
Select the bottom edge of the cylinder as the end condition (29).
Option **Extruded thread, Green** preview (30).
Option **Trim with start face** und **Trim with end face** (31).
Close dialog box (32).

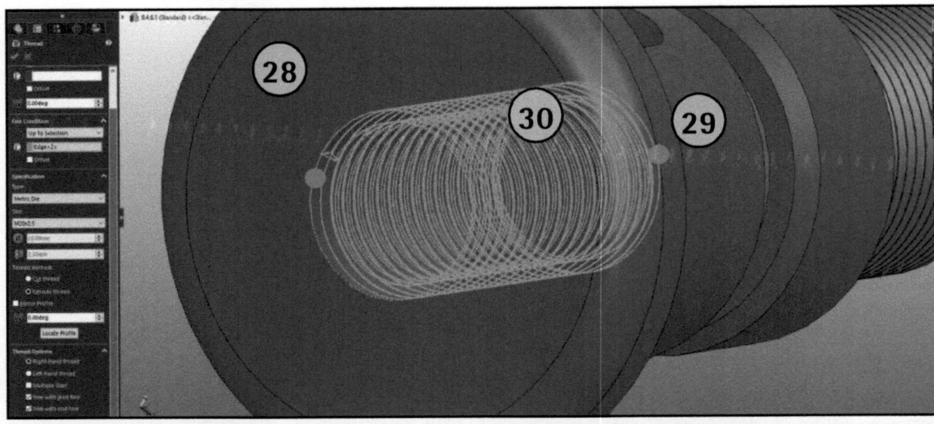

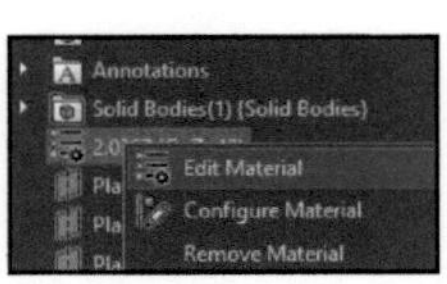

Edit Material

9.4.7 Assigning component material

- Assign the material **SOLIDWORKS DIN Steel (Stainles) 1.4401** (**X5CrNiMo17-12-2**) to the **Mounting bolt** (33).

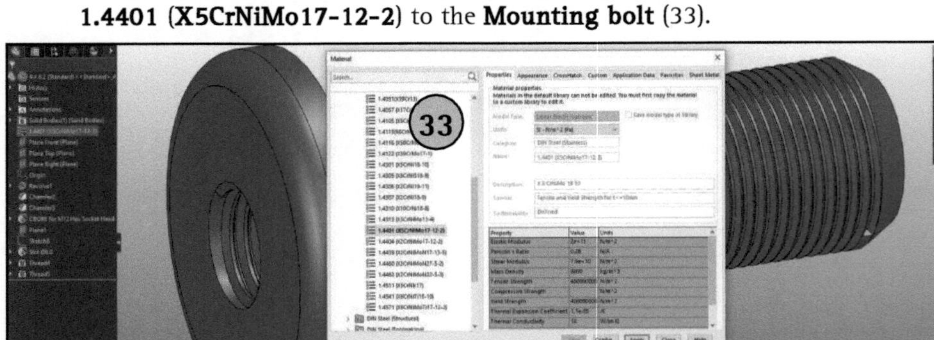

Save as New

9.4.7.1 Data backup

Save as New / Enter a name of your choice.

9.5 Component creation "Drive Shaft"

9.5.1 The design sketch for the component creation

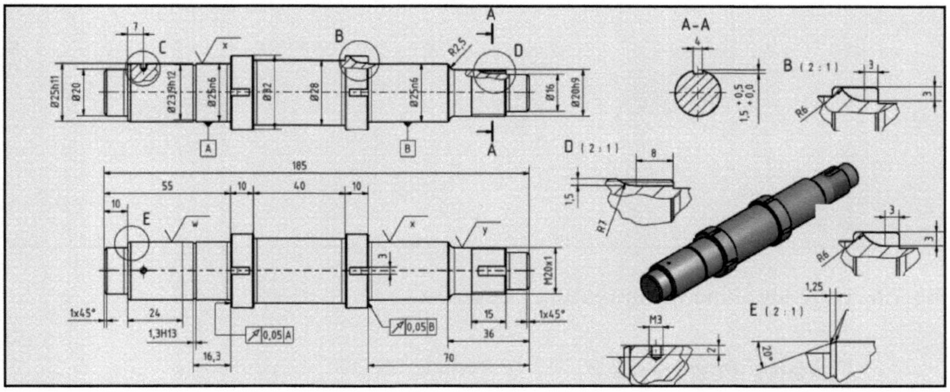

9.5.2 The drive shaft, component creation

9.5.2.1 Opening your own template file

New

Engelke2026.
PRTDOT

- Menu Bar **New** /  /  click **Engelke2026.PRTDOT / OK**

9.5.2.2 Creating the basic sketch

Line

Smart
Dimension

- On the **Front Plane**, create a **Line** path according to the sketch shown (1).
- Assign the displayed dimensions using **SmartDimension** (2).

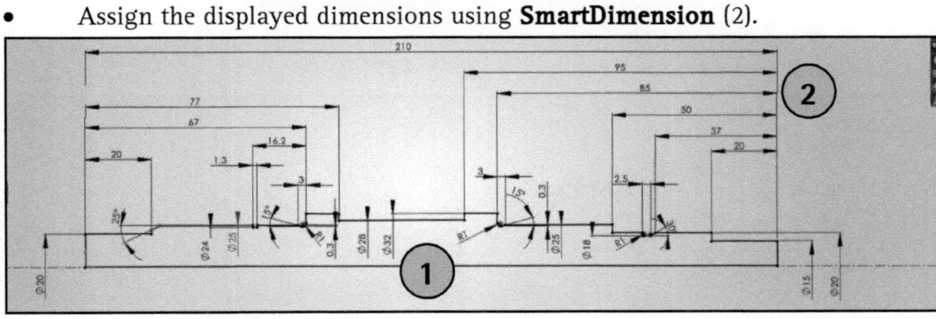

9.5.2.3 Revolved volume, the creation

Revolve

Revolved (**Features** tab)
Click the area **Sketch1**, using **Select Contours** (3).
Click the horizontal line to set it as the axis of rotation (4).
Close dialog box

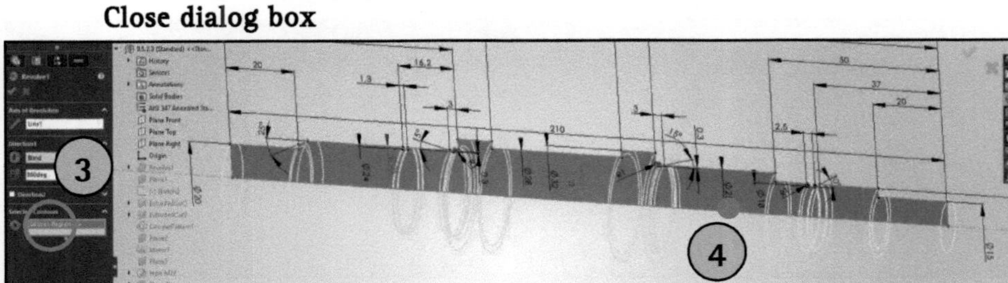

Edit Material

9.5.2.4 Assigning component material

- Assign the material **Annealed Stainless Steel AISI 347** to the drive shaft (5, 6).

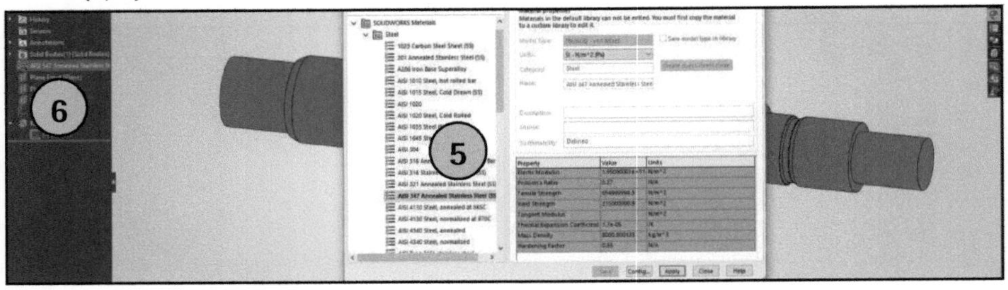

Chamfer

9.5.2.5 Edge breaking using feature "Chamfer"

Chamfer (**Features** tab)

Select the elements shown for edge breaking.
Break the edges with a value of **2.5** mm x **45°** (7, 8).

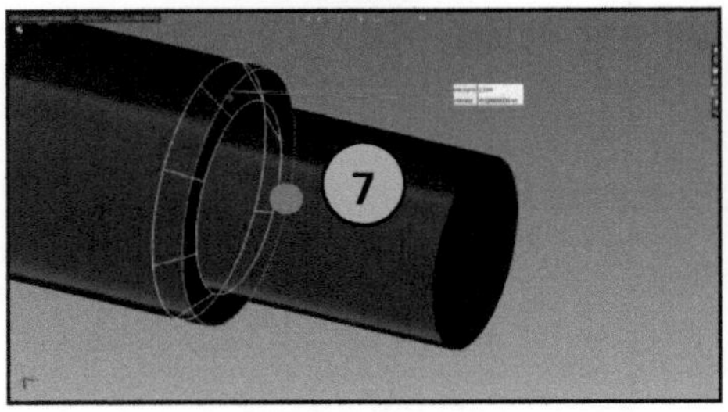

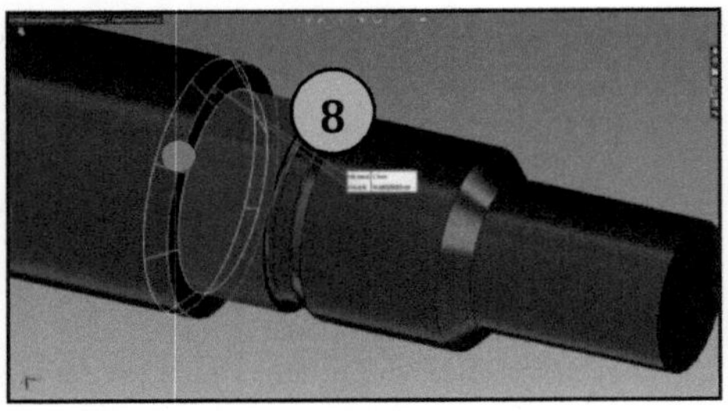

Chamfer

- Select the elements shown for edge breaking.
Break the edges with a value of **1** mm x **45°** (9, 10).

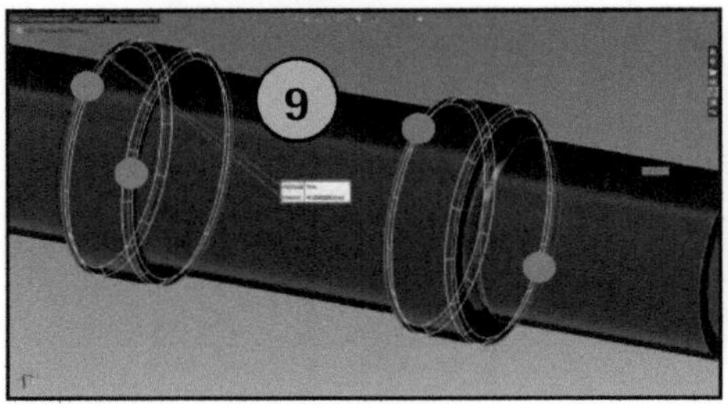

Fillet

9.5.2.6 Edge breaking using feature

Fillet (**Features** tab)
Edit the shown edge with a fillet of R=**0.5** mm (11).

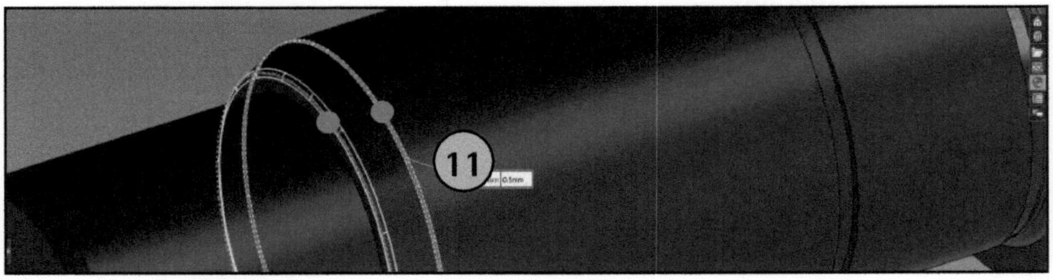

9.5.3 Locking plate slot, the creation

9.5.3.1 Basic sketch for locking plate slot

Plane

Tangent

- Create a **Tangent Work Plane** to the cylinder (12).

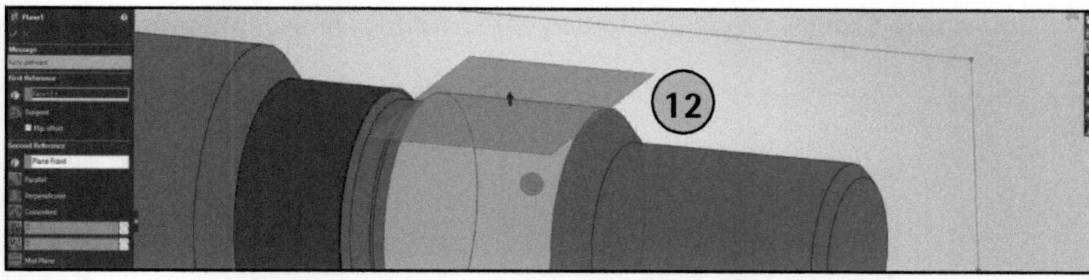

- On a new **Sketch**, create one basic construction each according to the illustration. (13, 14).

Line

Offset

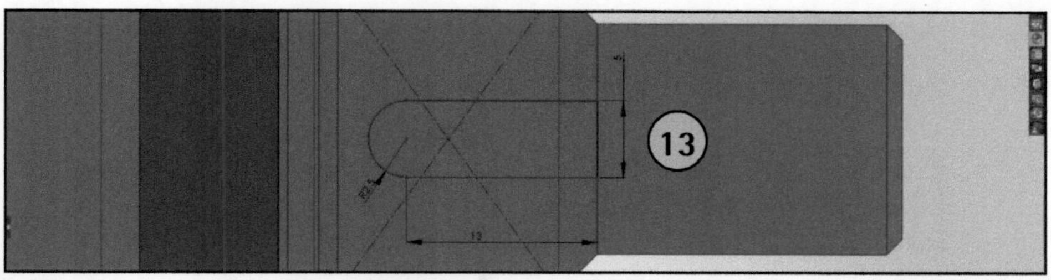

Line

Offset

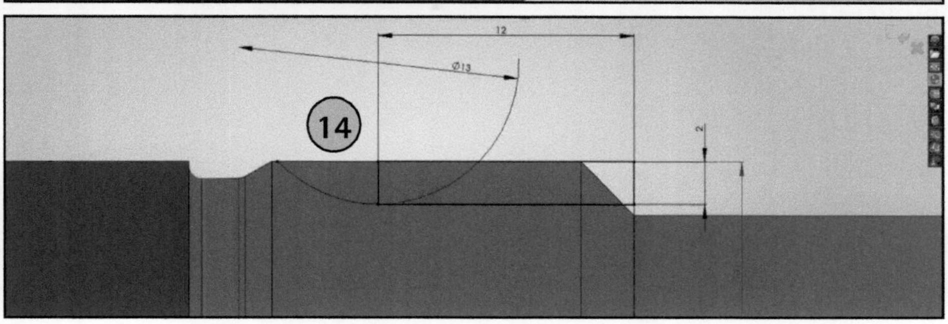

9.5.3.2 Locking plate slot using feature „Extruded Cut"

Extruded Cut (**Features** tab)

Generate an **Extruded Cut** by selecting sketch contour (15, 16).

Extruded Cut

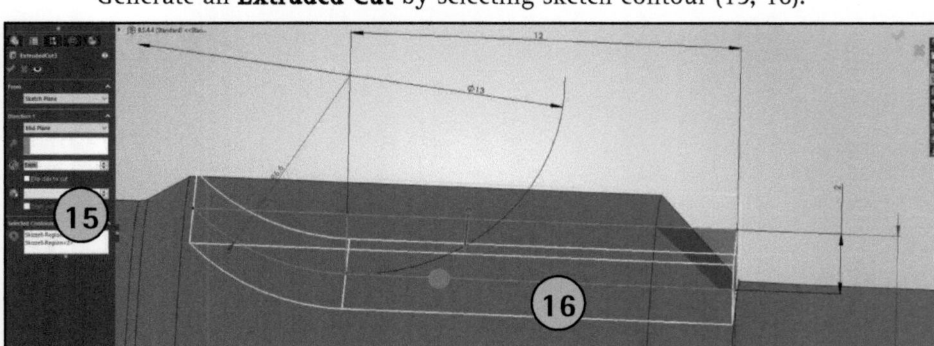

9.5.4 Shaft grooves, the creation

9.5.4.1 Basic sketch for shaft groove

Line

Offset

- Use the created **Tangent Work Plane** to the cylinder.
- On a new **Sketch**, create one basic construction each according to the illustration (17).

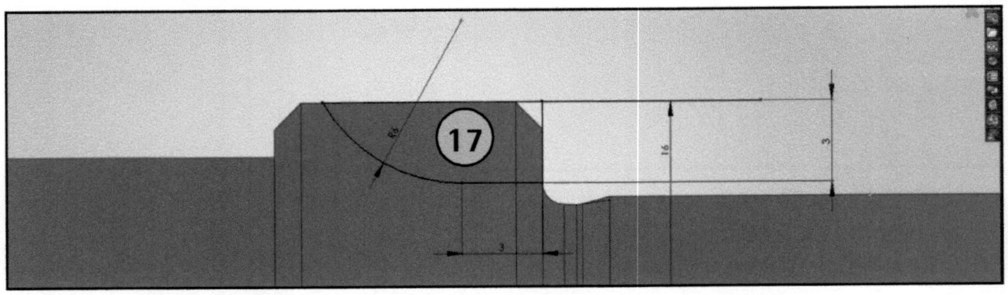

9.5.4.2 Shaft grooves using feature „Extruded Cut"

Extruded Cut

Extruded Cut (**Features** tab)
Generate an **Extruded Cut** from this by selecting the sketch contour, **Direction Mid Plane**, groove width **3** mm (18, 19).

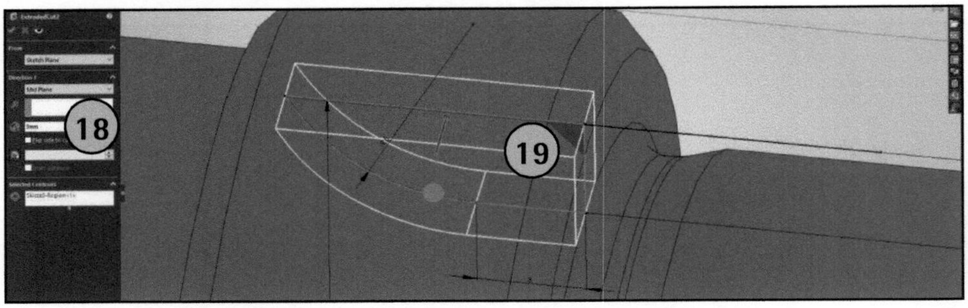

9.5.4.3 Distribution of shaft groove using "Circular Pattern"

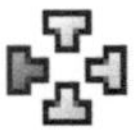
Circular Pattern

Circular Pattern (**Features** tab)
Using the **Circular Pattern** function, create a **90°** offset of the shaft groove, **4** pieces (20, 21).

9.5.4.4 Distribution of shaft groove using feature "Mirror"

- Create an additional **Work Plane** through the base body using the **Reference Plane**, selecting the left (22) and right (23) sides of the base body, and choosing the **Mid Plane** option (24).

Plane

Mid Plane

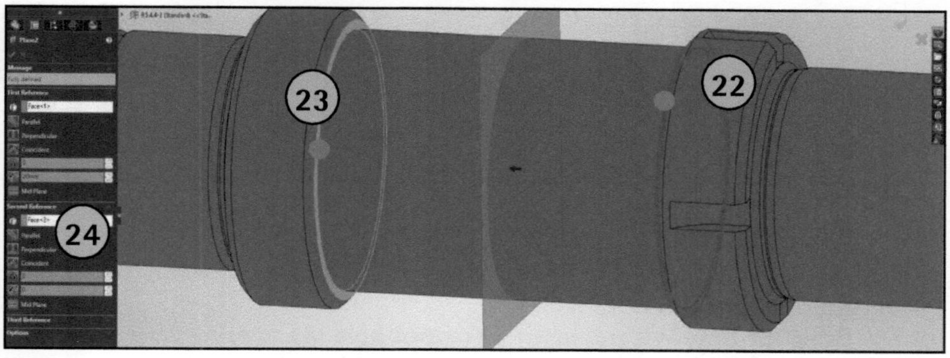

Mirror (**Features** tab)
Select the feature created using **Circular Pattern** (25) and **Mirror** the four grooves across the created **Work Plane** (26, 27).

Mirror

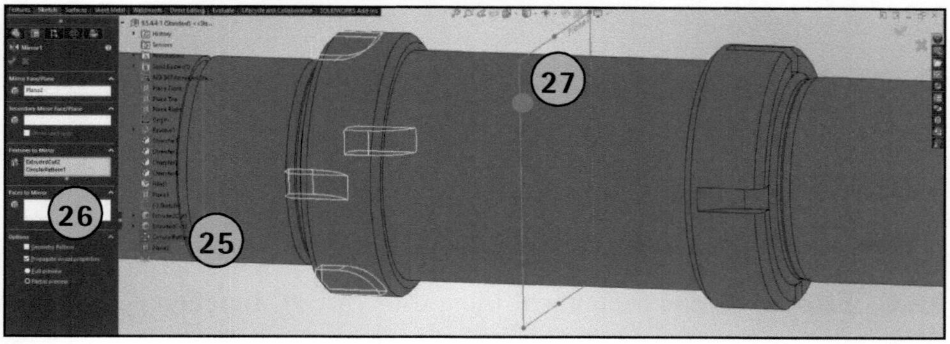

9.5.5 Inserting a tangential transverse bore

9.5.5.1 Creating an additional tangential work plane

- Create a **Tangent Work Plane** to the **Plane Front** (28, 29).

Plane

Tangent

Line

Offset

9.5.5.2 Basic sketch for the transverse drilling

- On a new **Sketch**, create a **Point** construction according to the illustration, with a distance of **11.5** mm on the created **Work Plane** (30, 31).

9.5.5.3 Inserting a tangential transverse bore, the creation

Hole Wizard

Hole Wizard (**Features** tab)
Using the **Hole Wizard**, insert a **Trapped hole M3** mm, **Blind** option, depth **6** mm, drill angle **118°** (32, 33).

9.5.6 External thread assignment using the "Thread" function

Thread

Thread (**Features** tab / **Hole wizard**)
Select the front cylinder edge as the thread position (34).
Select the rear cylinder edge as the end condition. (35).
Thread M10 x 1.5, option **Cut Thread**, **Red** preview (36).

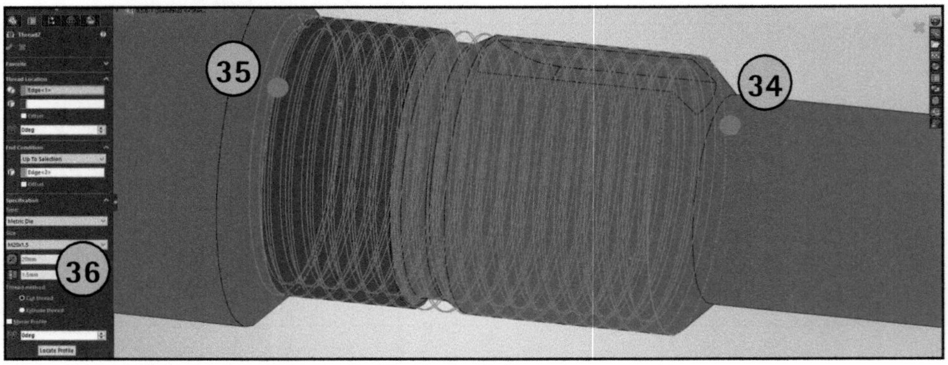

9.5.6.1 Data backup

Save as New

Save as New / Enter a name of your choice.

9.6 Component creation "Gear Shaft"

9.6.1 The design sketch for the component creation

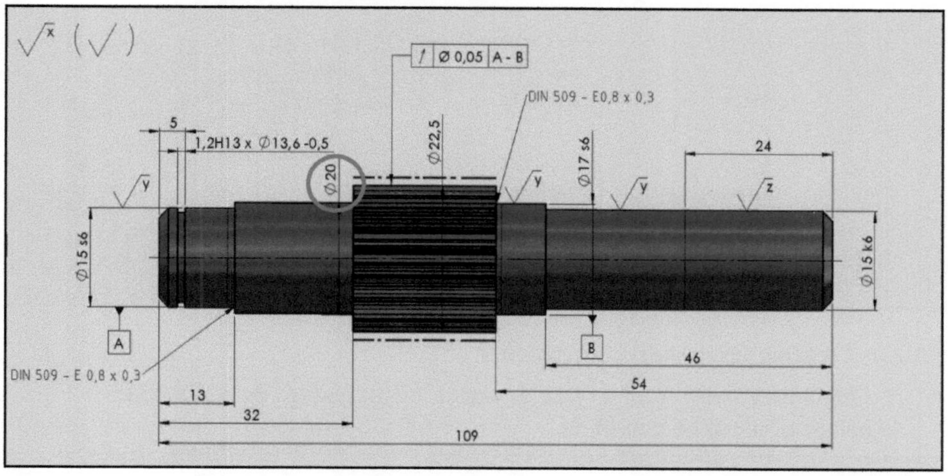

9.6.2 Gear creation using the SOLIDWORKS toolbox

New

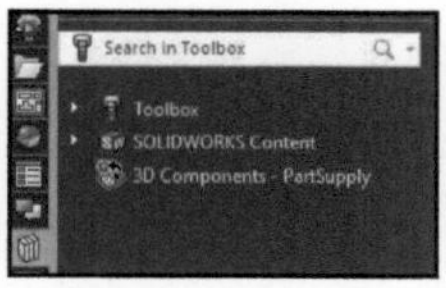

9.6.2.1 Opening your own template file

- Menu Bar **New** /  /  click **Engelke2026.PRTDOT / OK**

9.6.2.2 Gear creation

 **Design Library** /  **Toolbox** /  **DIN** (DIN)
 **Power Tansmission** /  **Gear** /  **Spur Gear** (1)
Select: **Create Part**
Enter the following data for the gear definition:
Module: **1.25**, Number of Teeth: **16**, Face Width: **33** mm,
Hub Style: **Typ A**, Nominal Shaft-Ø: **0.2** mm (1, 2).
Click **OK** to close the **PropertyManager**.

Design Library

Toolbox

DIN

Power Trans-
mission

Gears

Spur Gear

- **Save** the gear created in the background in your own project folder, once with the **Toolbox name** and once with your own name.

Save as New

Edit Material

9.6.2.3 Assigning component material

- Material allocation **AISI 316 Annealed Stainless Steel** using material processed (3, 4).

9.6.2.4 Creating drive shaft attachments

Sketch

Extrude

- Create a cylinder from a circular sketch using feature **Boss-Extrude** height **8** mm **Ø17** mm (5, 6).

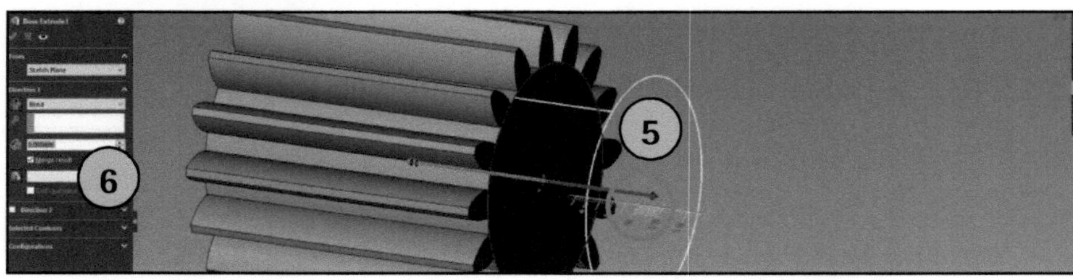

Sketch

Extrude

- Create a cylinder from a circular sketch using feature **Boss-Extrude** height **46** mm **Ø15** mm (7, 8).

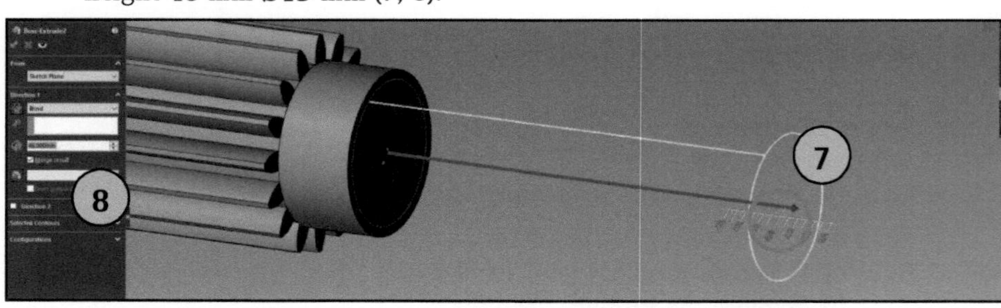

Sketch

Extrude

- Create a cylinder from a circular sketch using feature **Boss-Extrude** height **19** mm **Ø17** mm (9, 10).

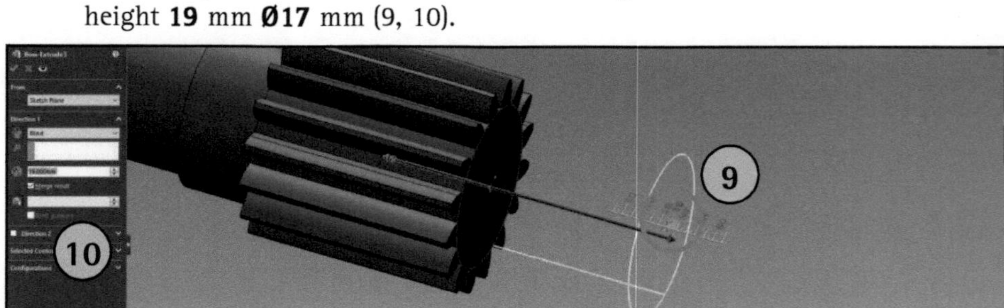

- Create a cylinder from a circular sketch using feature **Boss-Extrude** height **8** mm **Ø15** mm (11, 12).

Sketch
Extrude

- Create a cylinder from a circular sketch using feature **Boss-Extrude** height **1.2** mm **Ø13.6** mm (13, 14).

Sketch
Extrude

- Create a cylinder from a circular sketch using feature **Boss-Extrude** height **3.8** mm **Ø15** mm (15, 16).

Sketch
Extrude

9.6.3 Edge break using "Chamfer", the creation

- Edge chamfer, **1** mm x **45°** (17, 18).

Chamfer

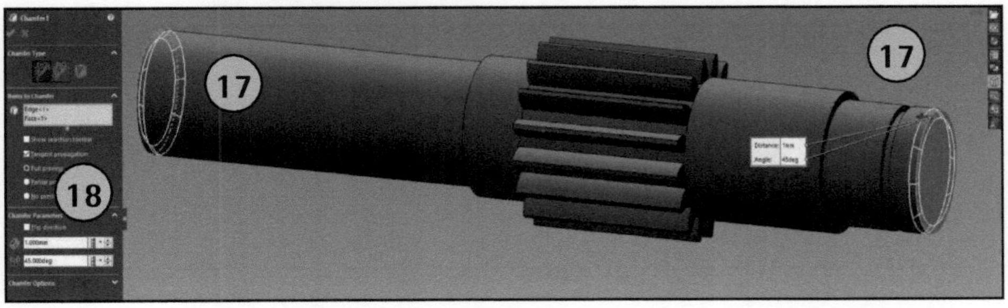

9.6.3.1 Data backup

Save as New / Enter a name of your choice.

Save as New

9.7 Component creation "Worm Shaft"

9.7.1 The design sketch for the component creation

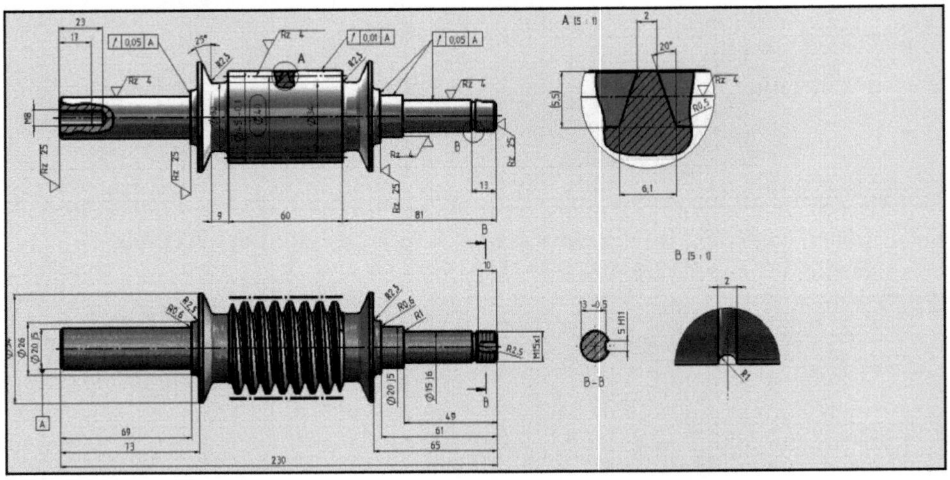

9.7.2 "Worm Shaft", the basic creation

 New

 Engelke2026.
PRTDOT

 Sketch

 Line

 Smart
Dimension

9.7.2.1 Opening your own template file

- Menu Bar **New** /  /  click **Engelke2026.PRTDOT / OK**

9.7.2.2 A closed surface of Rotation using command "Line"

- Sketch the line shown, disregarding line length, and ensure a precise finish at the origin point.
- The dimensions assigned using **SmartDimension** with resizing generate an automatic geometry change.

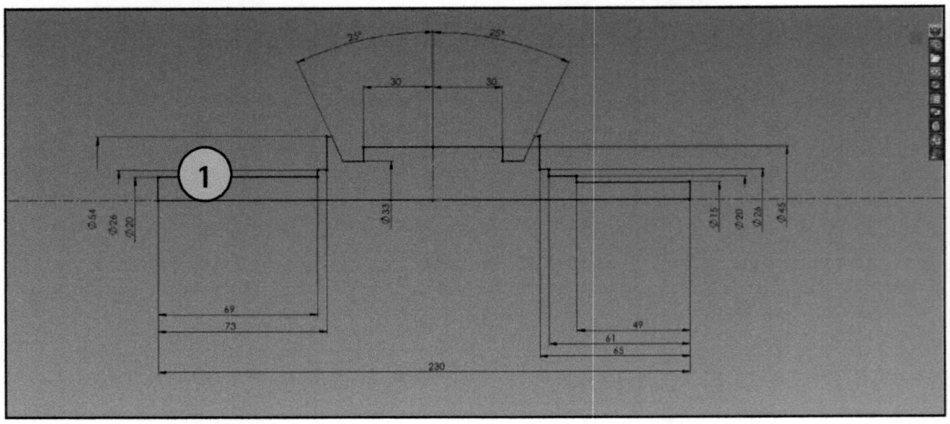

9.7.2.3 Revolved volume creation

Revolved (Features tab)
Click the area **Sketch1**, using **Select Contours** (2, 3).
Click the horizontal line to set it as the axis of rotation (4).
Close dialog box.

Revolve

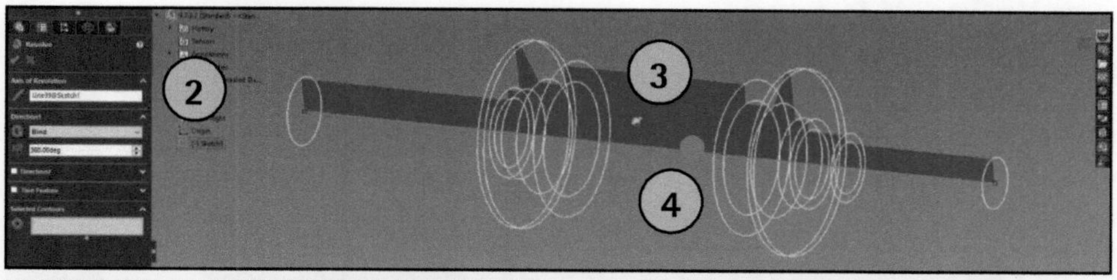

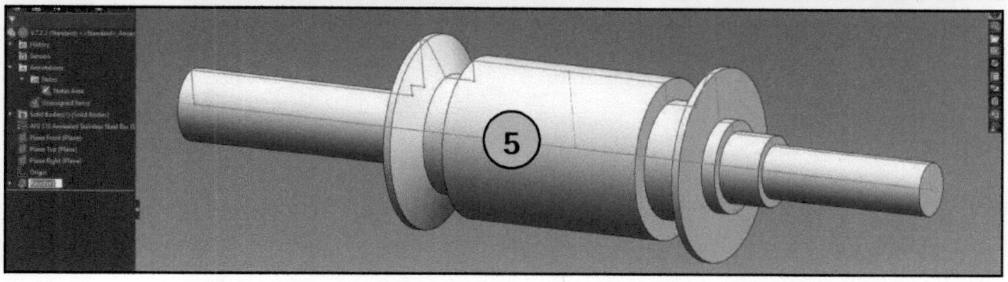

9.7.2.4 Assigning component material

- Material allocation **AISI 316 Annealed Stainless Steel** using material processed (6, 7).

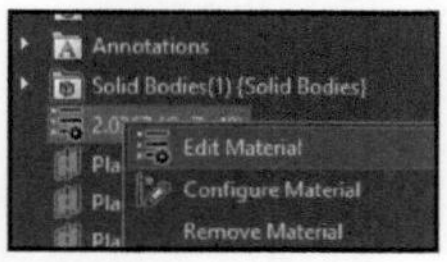

Edit Material

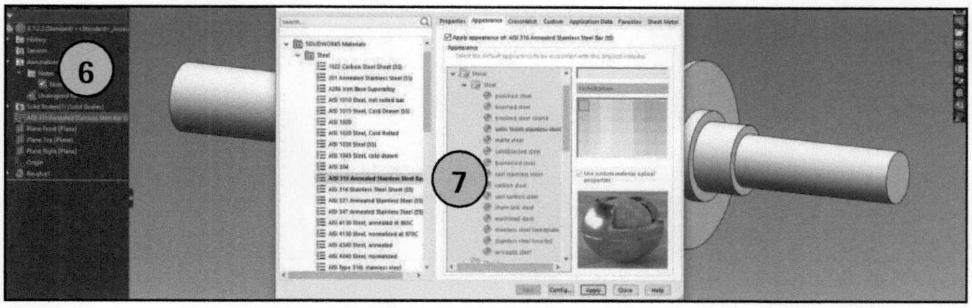

9.7.2.5 Edge breaking using feature "Chamfer"

- Edge chamfer, **1** mm x **45°** (8, 9).

Chamfer

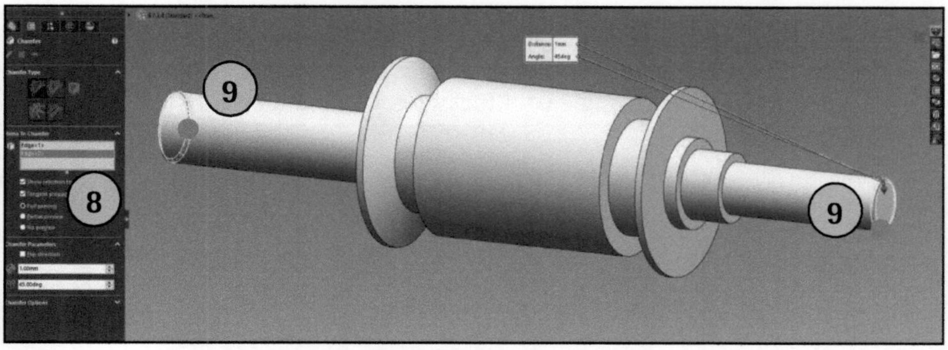

9.7.2.6 Edge breaking using feature "Fillet"

Fillet

- Edge breaking using feature **Fillet**, Radius **0.6** mm (10, 11)

Fillet

- Edge breaking using feature **Fillet**, Radius **1** mm (12, 13).

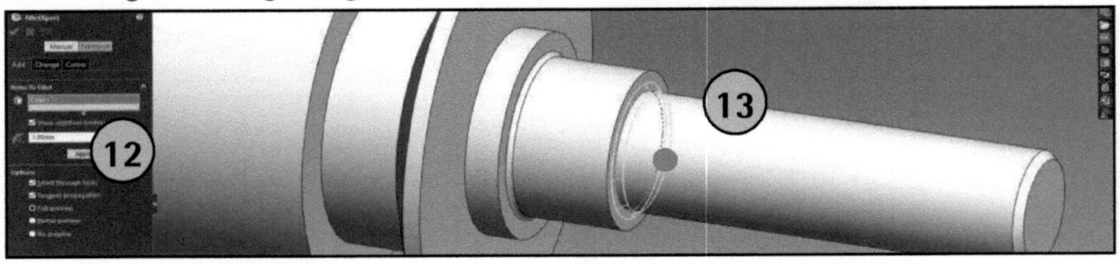

9.7.3 External thread assignment using the "Thread" function

Thread

Thread (**Features** tab / **Hole wizard**)
Select the front cylinder edge as the thread position (14).
End condition: Length **Blind 10** mm (15).
Thread M14 x 1.5, option **Cut Thread**, **Red** preview (16).

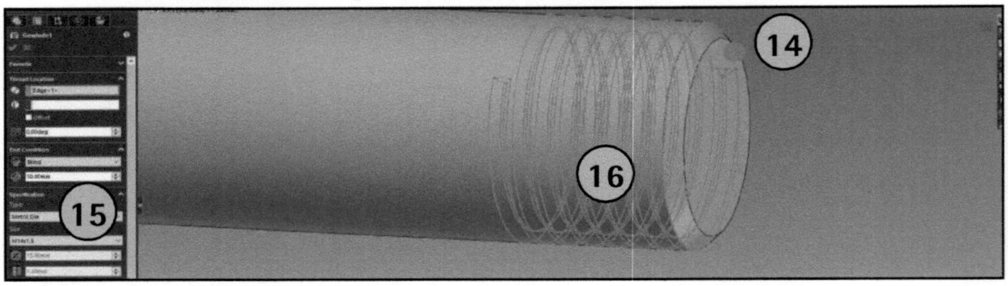

9.7.4 Worm Shaft using "Helix/Spiral" and "Cut Sweep"

9.7.4.1 "Helix" construction as a basis

Helix / Spiral

Helix/Spiral (**Insert** command tab / **Curve**-Flyout)
Pitch and Revolution (5), **Constant pitch**, Pitch: **7.5** mm
Revolution: **8**, Start Angle **0°**, **Clockwise**, **Close dialog box** (17, 18).

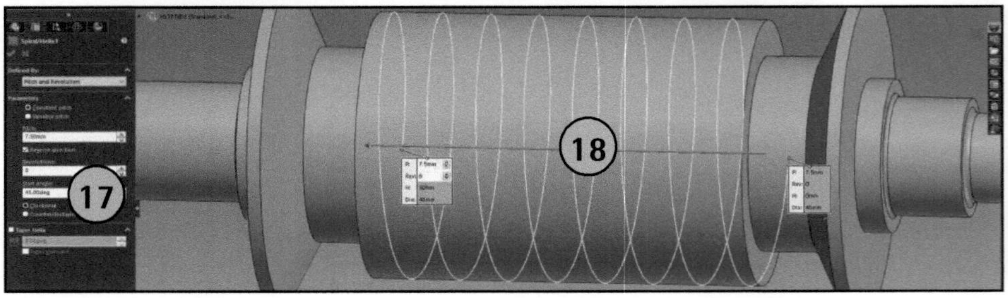

9.7.4.2 Sketch for circumferential worm shaft profile

Sketch
Line
Circle
Offset Entities
Trim Entities

- Create the sketch shown on the **Top Plane** using **Line, Circle, Offset** and clean up the sketch using **Trim** (19).

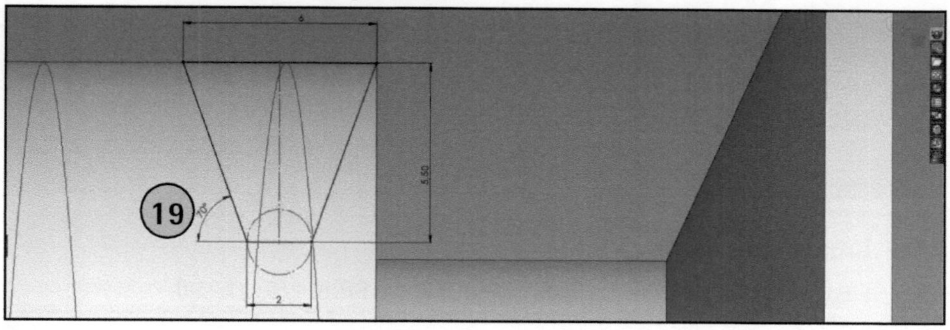

9.7.4.3 Creating a worm shaft structure using "Cut Sweep"

Cut Sweep

- Generate the worm shaft structure using **Cut Sweep** with the spiral as the basic sketch (20, 21, 22).

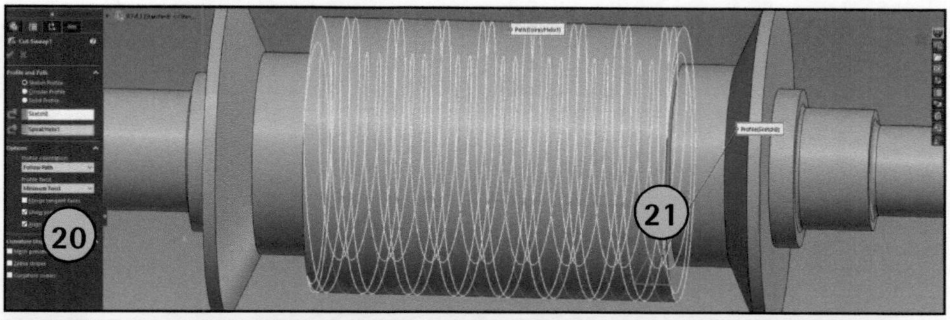

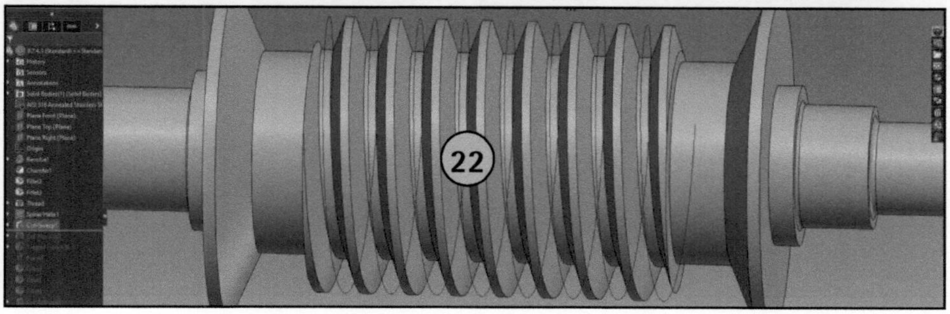

9.7.5 Relief groove for the physical thread

Sketch
Line
Circle
Trim Entities

- Create the sketch shown on the **Front Plane** using **Circle** and **Line.**
- Clean up the sketch using **Trim** (23).

Extruded Cut

- Select the created sketch and use the feature **Extruded Cut** to create the extrusion (24, 25).

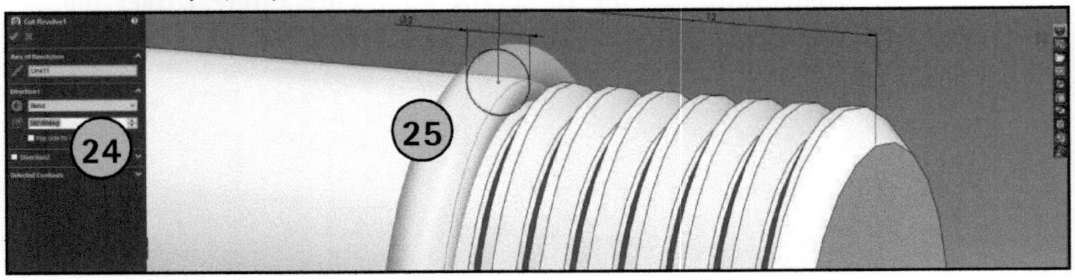

9.7.6 Break more edges

Fillet

- Edge breaking, radius 2.5 mm, using feature **Fillet** (26, 27, 28).

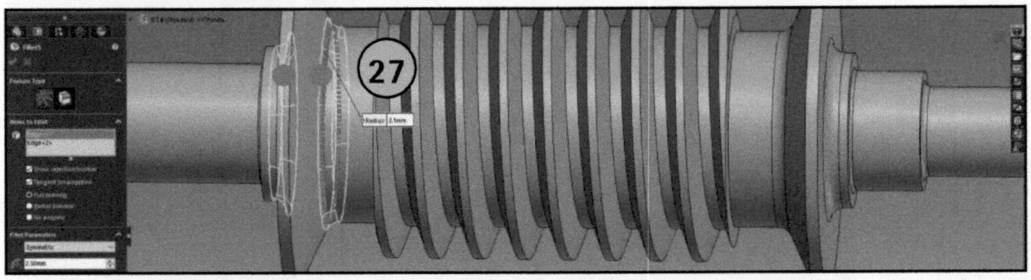

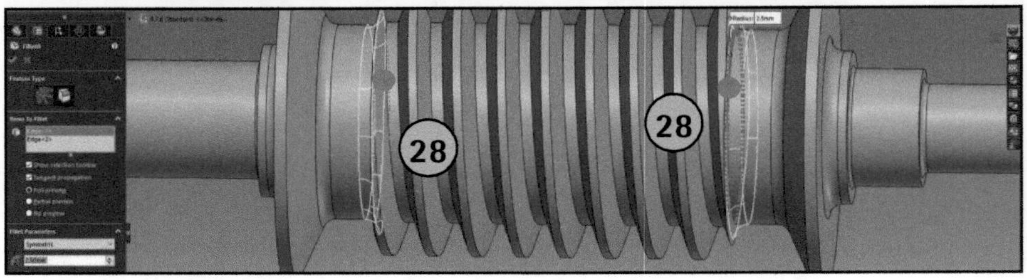

9.7.7 Central mounting hole

Hole Wizard

Using the **Hole Wizard**, insert a **Trapped hole M8** mm, **Blind** option, thread depth **17** mm, depth **23** mm, drill angle **118°** (29, 30).

9.7.8 Groove for locking plate

9.7.8.1 Create work plane for groove

Plane

- Create a **Work Plane** parallel to the displayed **Top Plane** at a distance of **7.5** mm (31, 32, 33).

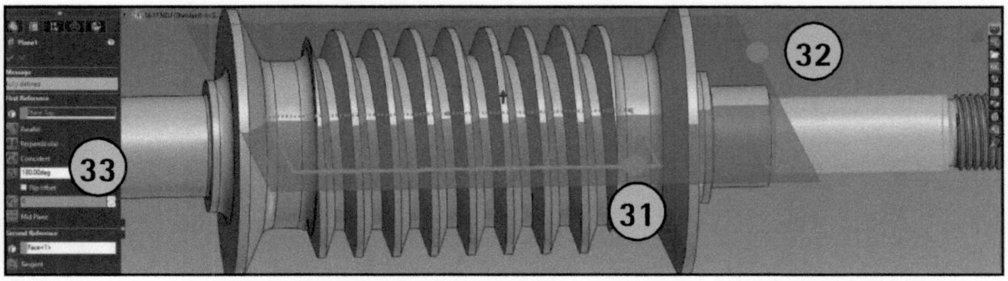

9.7.8.2 Groove for locking plate, the creation

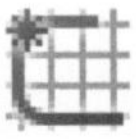

Sketch

- Create a **Sketch** design for the groove (34).

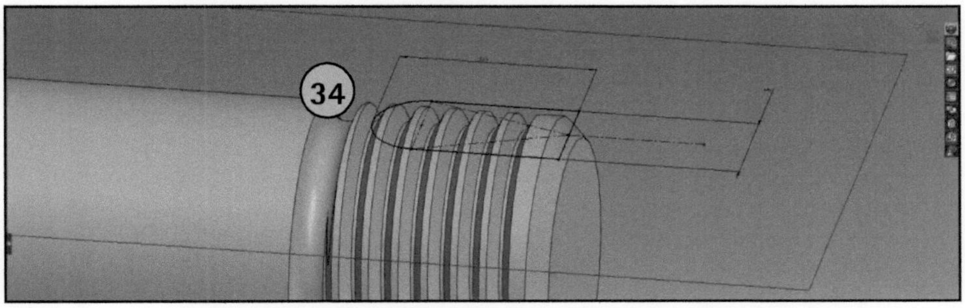

Extruded Cut

- Create the cutout using the **Extruded Cut** feature (35, 36)

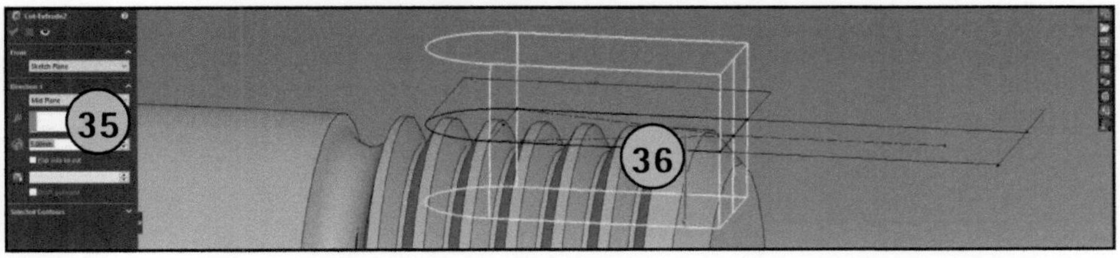

9.7.8.3 Data backup

Save as New

Save as New / Enter a name of your choice.

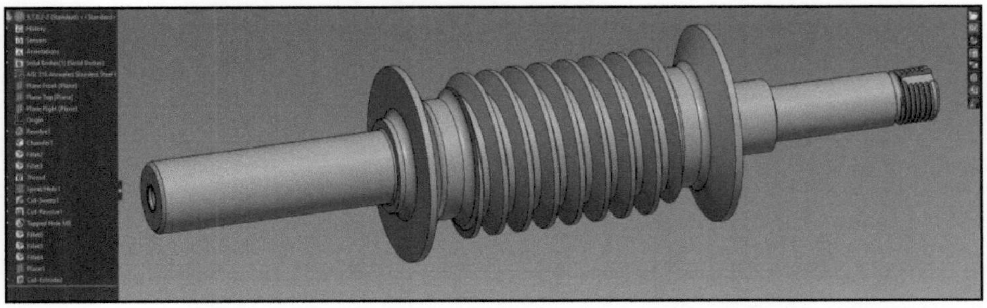

Project XVII

Create Components Housings

Page 398 to 410

- Component creation “Housing Dome”
- Component creation “Bearing Housing”
- Component creation
  “Housing for Bevel Gear”

9.8 Component creation "Housing Dome"

9.8.1 The design sketch for the component creation

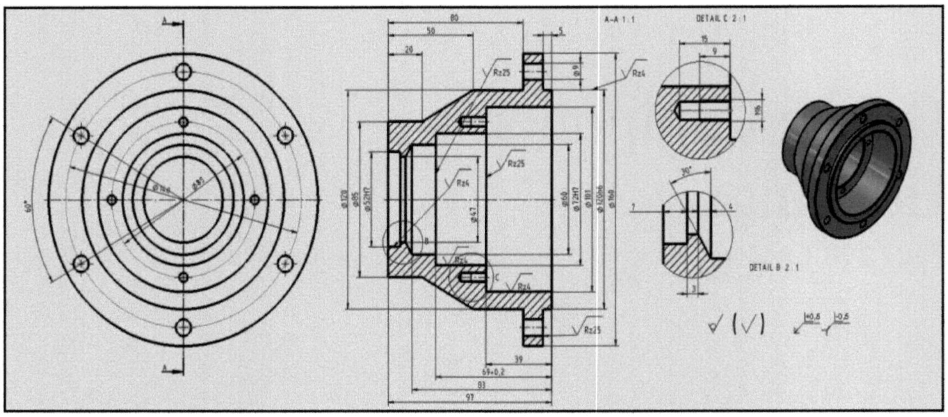

9.8.2 Creating the basic component

9.8.2.1 Opening your own template file

New

Engelke2026.
PRTDOT
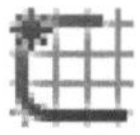
Sketch

Line

Smart
Dimension

Revolve

- Menu Bar **New** /  /  click **Engelke2026.PRTDOT / OK**

9.8.2.2 Creating and adapting basic body

- Create a line layout according to the sketch shown on the **Front Plane** (1).
- Assign the displayed dimensions using **SmartDimension** (2).
- Create a solid of revolution using the **Revolve** function, select the sketch from the expanding **FeatureManager** design tree, and the axis of revolution will be automatically detected (3, 4).

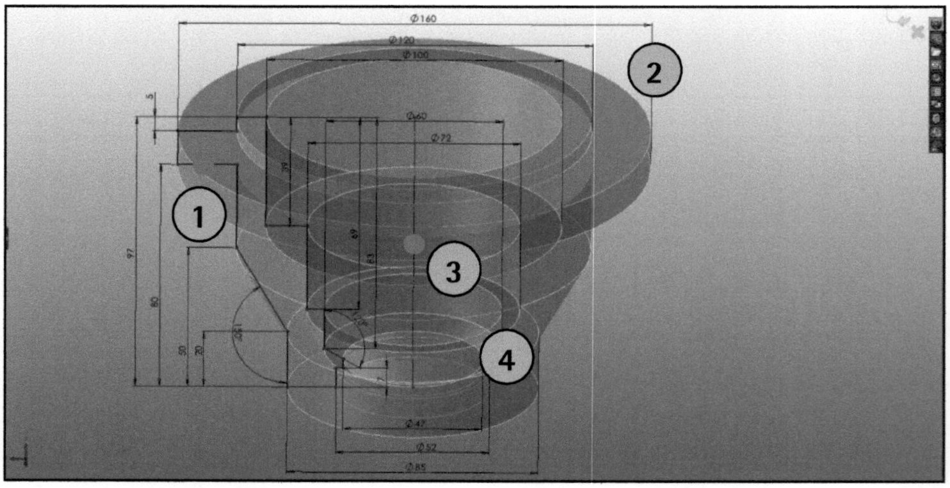

Fillet (Features tab)
Edit the shown edges using the feature **Fillet** R=**0.5** mm, selecting with the **Window selection** function (5, 6).

Fillet

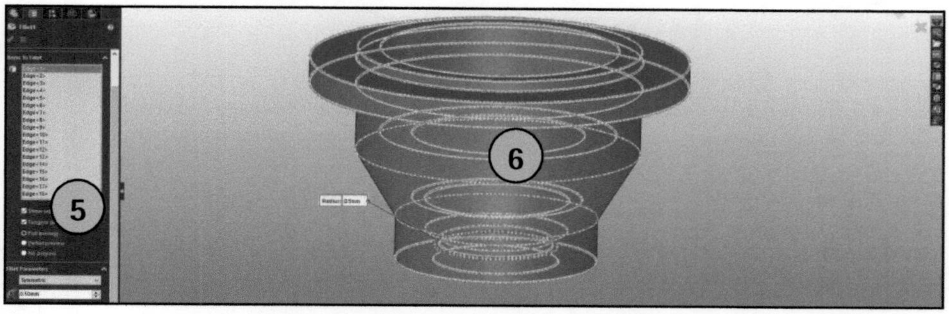

- Assign the material **Commercial Bronze, UNS C22000** to the housing using **Edit Material** (7, 8).

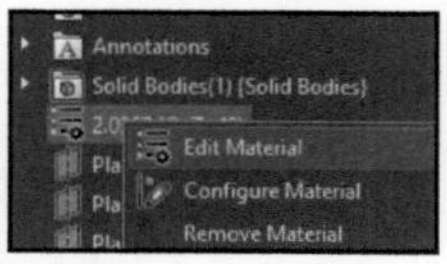

Edit Material

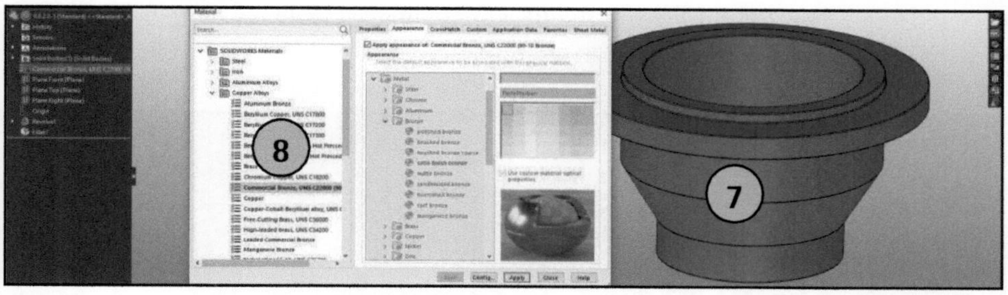

9.8.3 Creating flange holes

- Using a new **Sketch**, create a **140** mm diameter **Circle** on the inner ring (9).
- Place a **Point** at the axis intersection (10).

Sketch

Line

Circle

Point

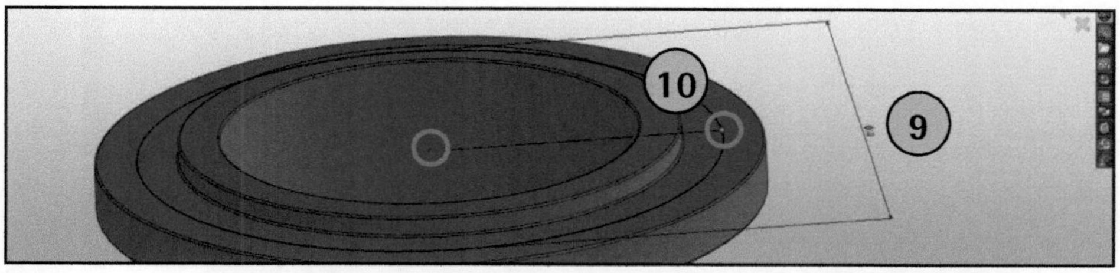

- At the created **Point**, use the **Hole Wizard** to drill a **Through Hole Ø9** mm (11, 12).

Hole Wizard

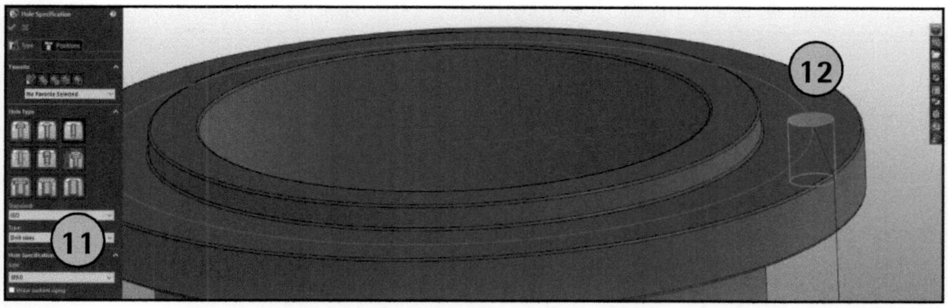

Circular Pattern

- Using the **Circular Pattern** function, create a **60°** offset of the bore, number **6,** selecting the inner cylinder as the base cylinder (13, 14).

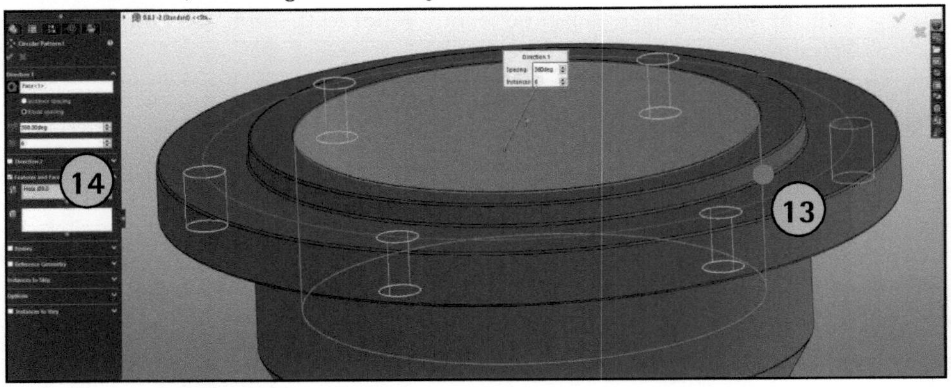

Sketch

Line

Circle

Point

9.8.4 Creating mounting holes

- Using a new **Sketch**, create the **85** mm diameter **Circle** on the inner ring (15).
- Place a **Point** at the axis intersection (16).

Hole Wizard

- At the point, use the **Hole Wizard** to create a threaded hole **M6**, thread depth **9** mm, drilling depth **15** mm (17, 18).

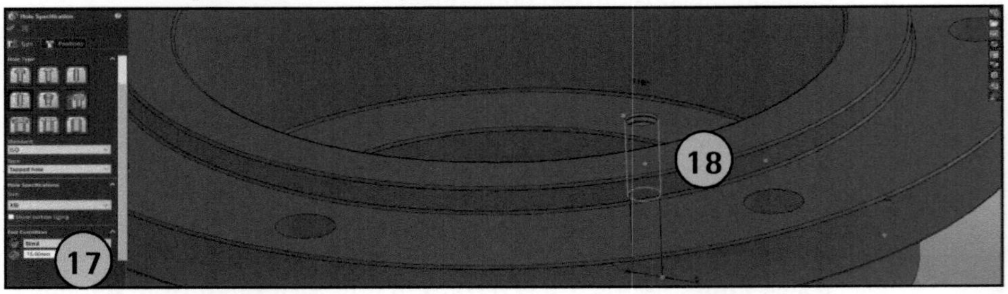

Circular Pattern

- Using the **Circular Pattern** function, create a **90°** offset of the bore, number **4**, selecting the inner cylinder as the base cylinder (19, 20).

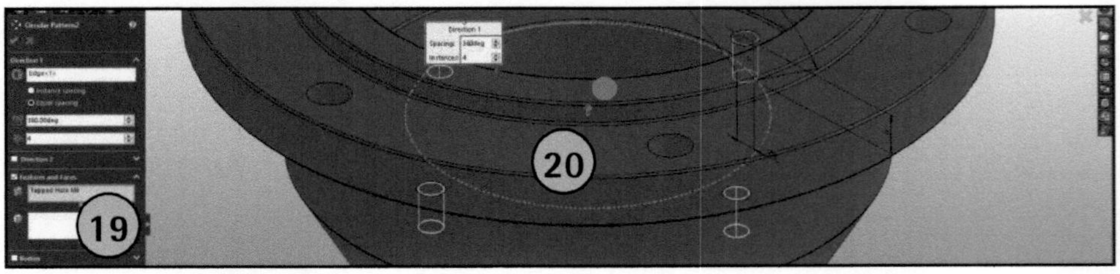

Save as New

9.8.4.1 Data backup

Save as New / Enter a name of your choice.

9.9 Component creation "Bearing Housing"

9.9.1 The design sketch for the component creation

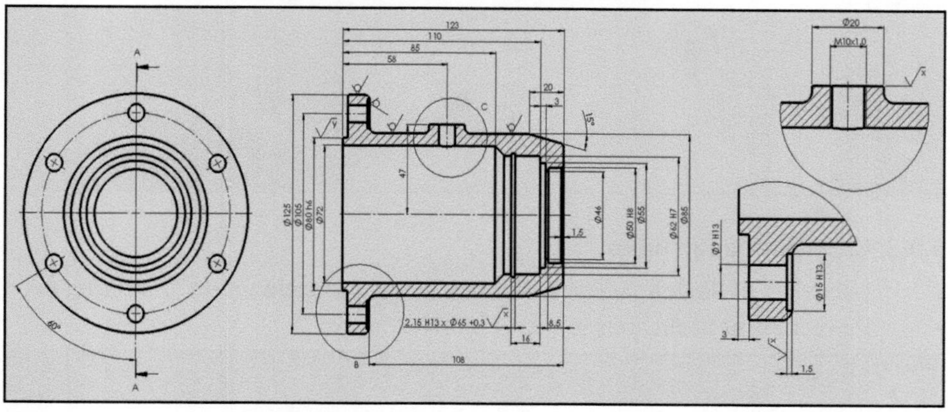

9.9.2 Creating the basic component

9.9.2.1 Opening your own template file

- Menu Bar **New** /  /  click **Engelke2026.PRTDOT / OK**

9.9.2.2 Creating and adapting basic body

Create a line layout according to the sketch shown on the **Front Plane** (1).
Assign the displayed dimensions using **SmartDimension** (2).
Create a solid of revolution using the **Revolve** function, select the sketch from the expanding **FeatureManager** design tree, and the axis of revolution will be automatically detected (3, 4).

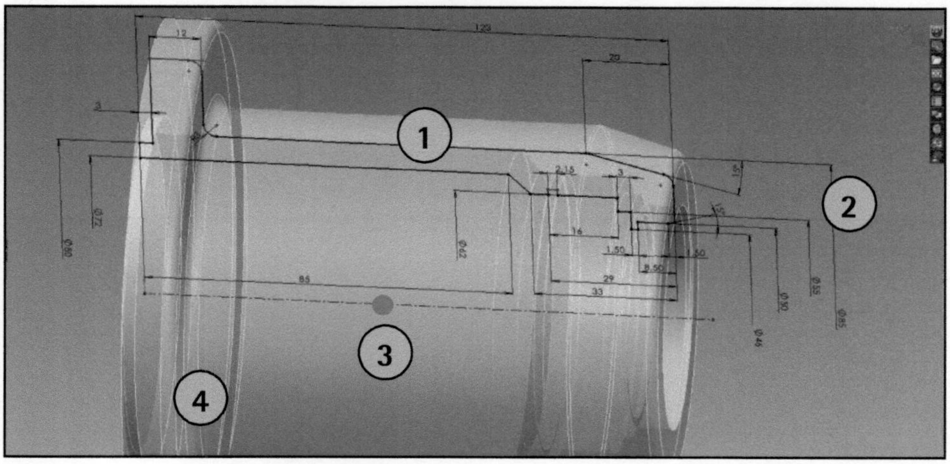

New

Engelke2026.
PRTDOT

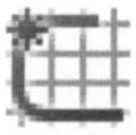
Sketch

Line

Smart
Dimension

Revolve

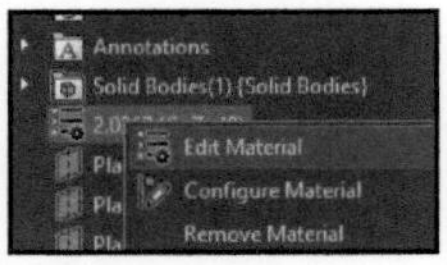

Edit Material

- Assign the material **Cast Stainless Steel** to the housing using **Edit Material** (5).

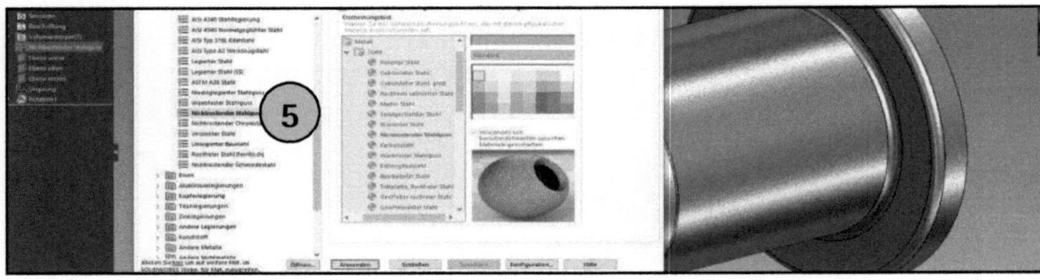

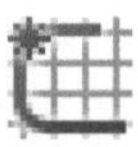

Sketch

Line

Circle

Point

9.9.3 Creating flange holes

- Using a new **Sketch**, create a **105** mm diameter **Circle** on the inner ring (6).
- Place a **Point** at the axis intersection (7).

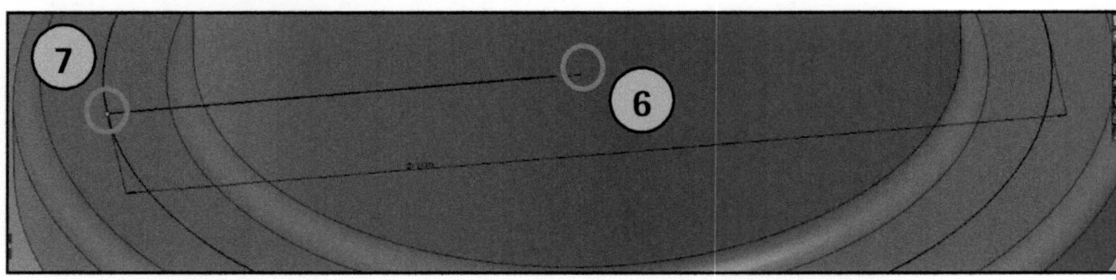

Hole Wizard

- Drill a **Cylindrical countersink Ø15** mm at this **Point 1.5** mm deep, **Through hole Ø9** mm (8, 9).

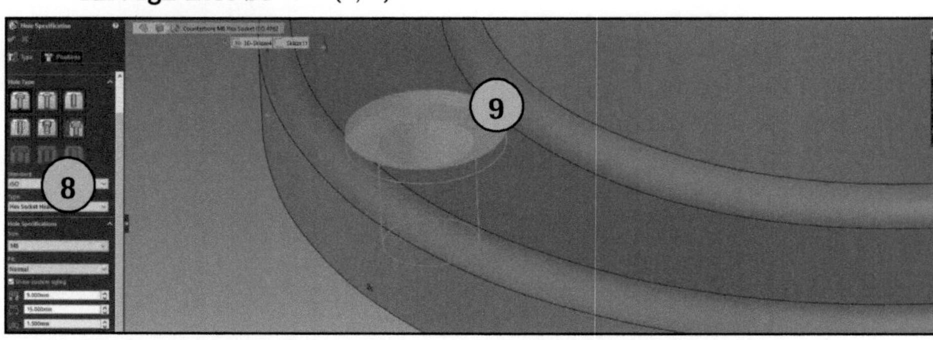

Circular Pattern

- Using the **Circular Pattern** function, create a **60°** offset of the bore, number **6**, selecting the outer cylinder as the base cylinder (10, 11).

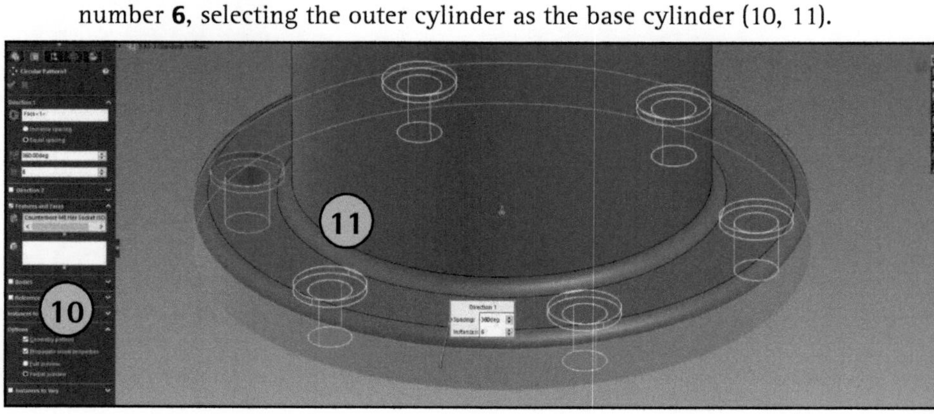

9.9.4 Insert threaded connection as an attachment

Plane

Tangent

- Create a **Tangent Work Plane** to the **Top Plane** (12, 13).

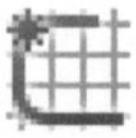
Sketch

Circle

Smart Dimension

- On a new **Sketch**, create a basic structure according to the illustration (14)

Extrude

- Generate from this, using the **Extrude** feature height of **4.5** mm, the **Mid Plane** option, and the **Merge result** option (15, 16).

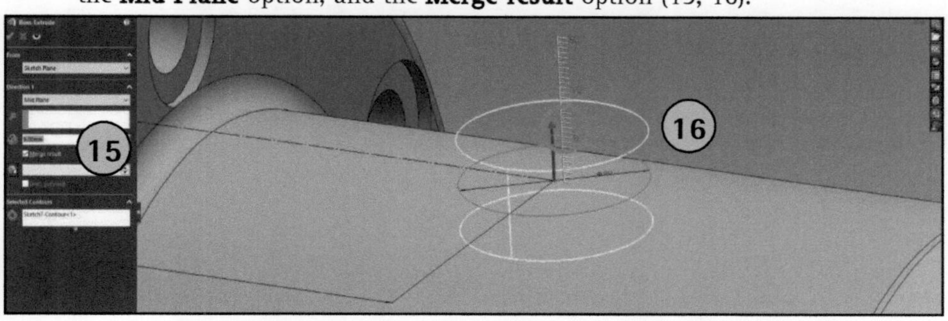

Hole Wizard

- Use the **Hole Wizard** to insert a central threaded hole **M10 x 1** mm, **Blind** option (17, 18).

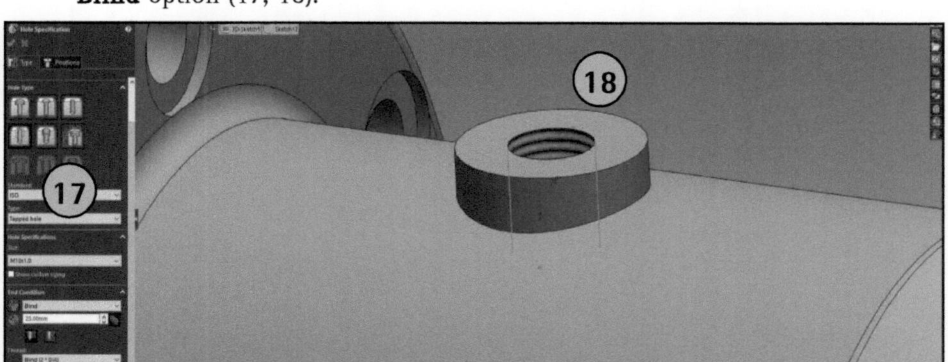

Fillet

- Edit the shown edge with a **Fillet** of R=**3** mm (19, 20).

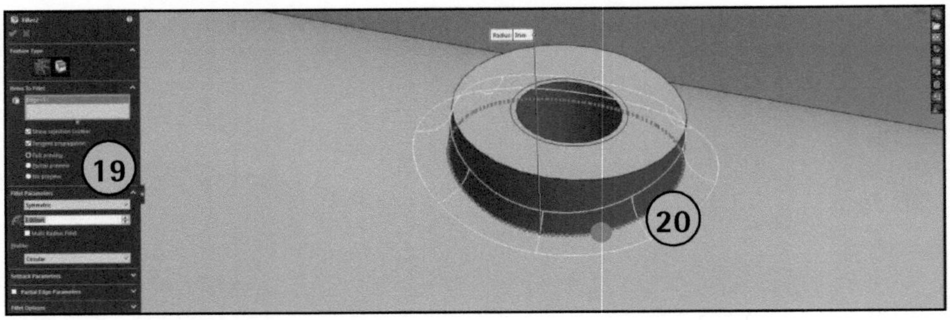

Save as New

9.9.4.1 Data backup

Save as New / Enter a name of your choice.

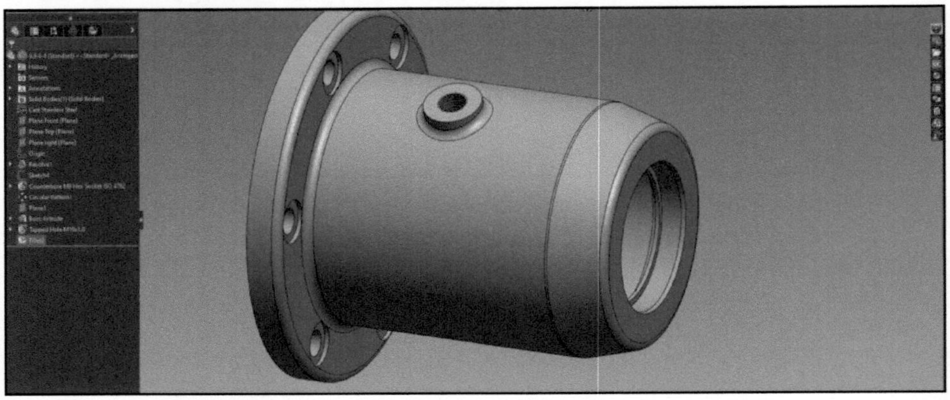

9.10 Component creation "Housing for Bevel Gear"

9.10.1 The design sketch for the component creation

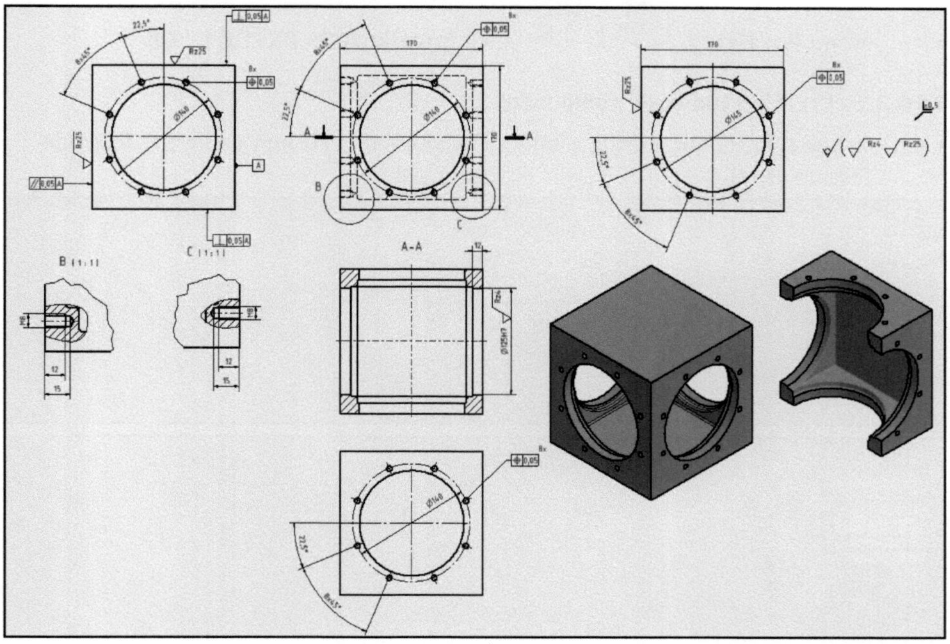

9.10.2 The component representation for component creation

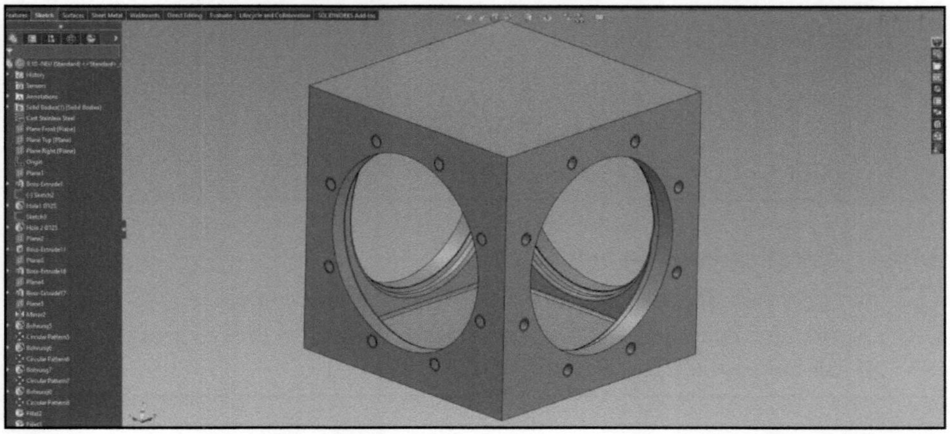

9.10.3 Bevel gear housing, the creation

9.10.3.1 Opening your own template file

New

Engelke2026.
PRTDOT

- Menu Bar **New** /  /  click **Engelke2026.PRTDOT** / **OK**

9.10.3.2 Creating the basic component

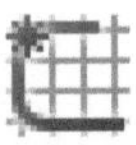
Sketch

Line

Smart
Dimension

Extrude

- Create a basic body design with a thickness of **170** mm using the **Extrude** feature (1, 2).

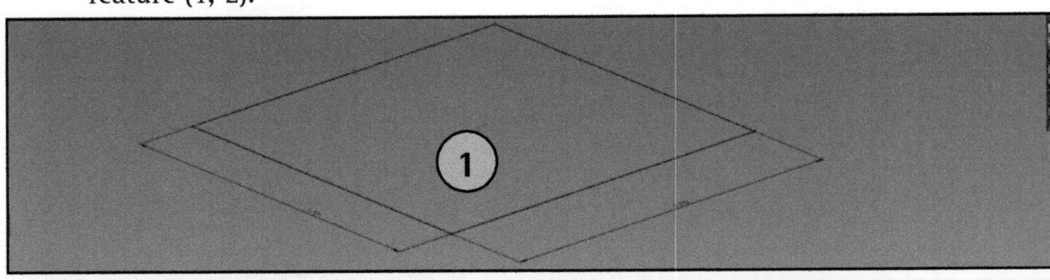

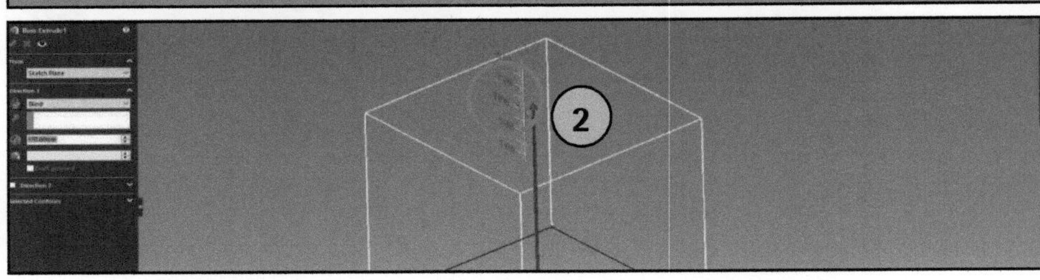

- Assign the material **Cast Stainless Steel** using **Edit Material** (3, 4).

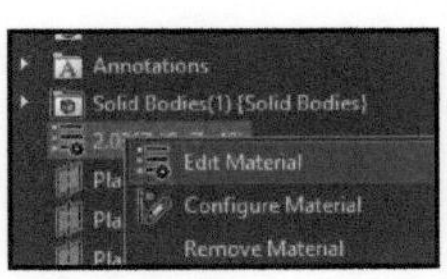

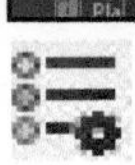
Edit Material

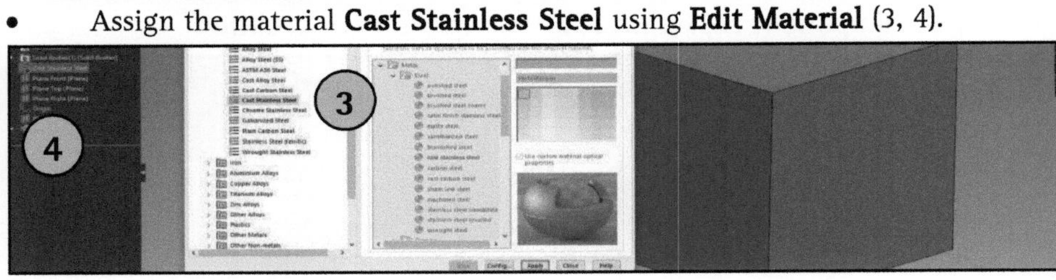

9.10.4 Creating housing holes

Sketch

Hole Wizard

- Create a new **Sketch** and place a **Point** on the **Line** endpoint. (5).
- At the Line endpoint, use the feature **Hole Wizard** to drill a through hole **Ø125** mm, option **Through all** (6, 7).

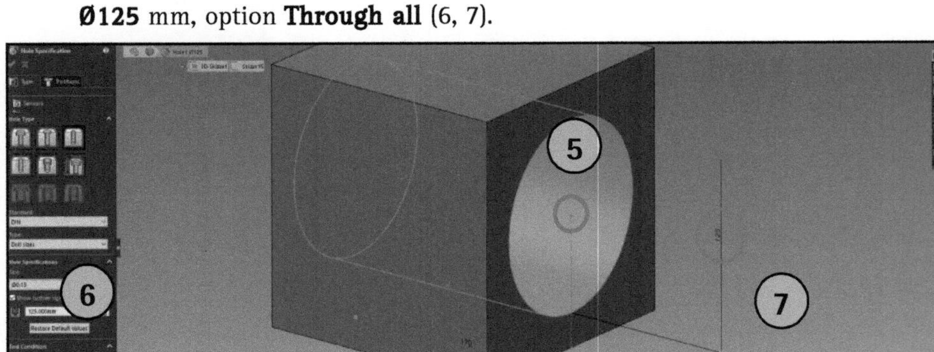

- Proceed accordingly with the other side of the cube (5, 6, 7).

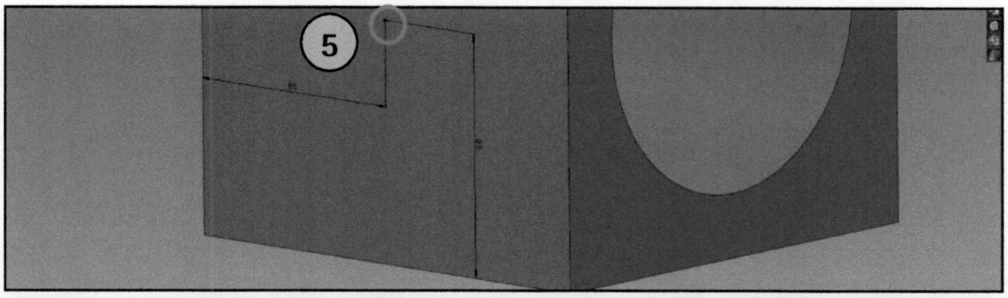

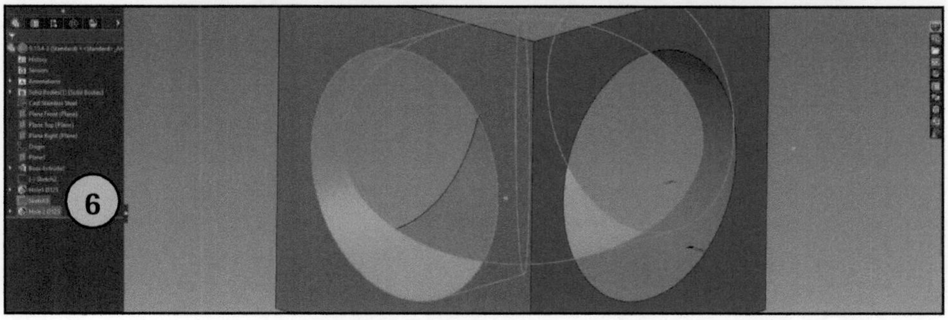

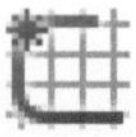
Sketch

Hole Wizard

9.10.5 Create the inner body

9.10.5.1 Create the main inner body

- Create a new **Parallel Plane** inside the cuboid, **12** mm from the outer wall of the cuboid (8, 9).

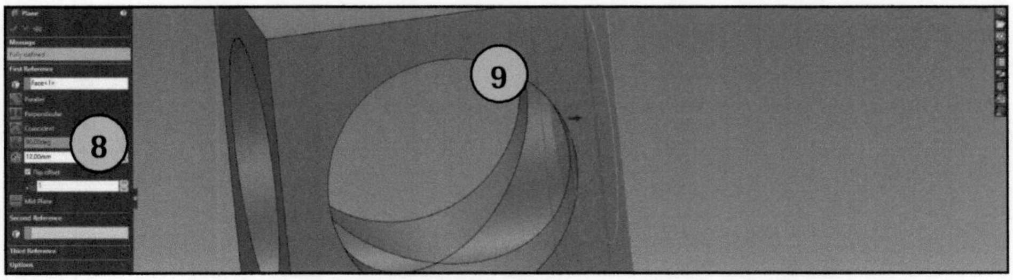

Plane

Parallel

- Create a sketch area of **146** mm x **146** mm on this new **Plane** (10).
- From the constructed sketch, create an inner body using **Extruded Cut** by selecting a sketch contour, depth **146** mm (11, 12).

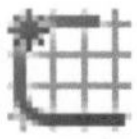
Sketch

Extruded Cut

9.10.5.2 Inner attachment surfaces, the creation

Sketch

Extruded Cut

- Create a circular sketch surface with a diameter of **130** mm on the inner wall of the cuboid (13).
- Create attachment surface with a depth of **8** mm using **Extruded Cut** (14,15).

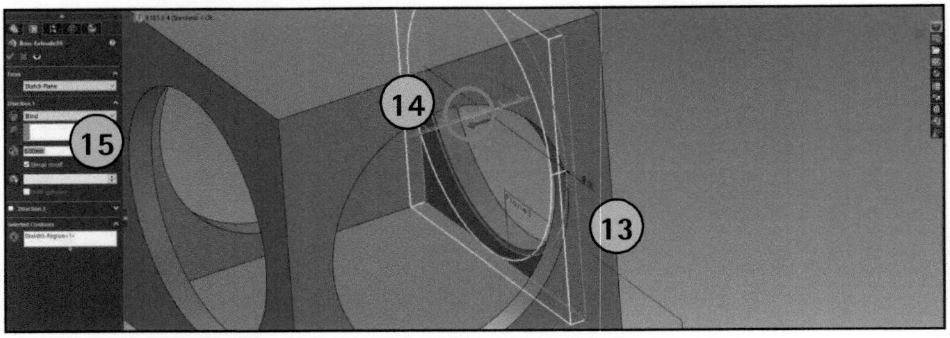

Sketch

Extruded Cut

- Proceed with the attachment surface accordingly (13, 14, 15).

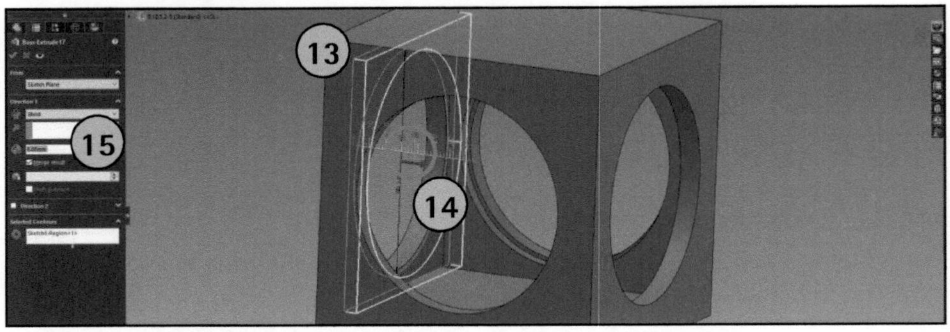

Plane

Mid Plane

Mirror

- The opposite attachment surface is transferred to the other side of the housing using the **Mirror** function, mirror **Plane Right** (16, 17, 18, 19).

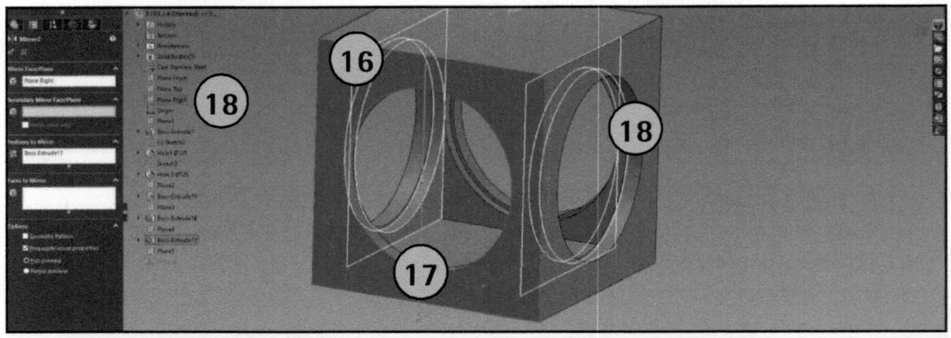

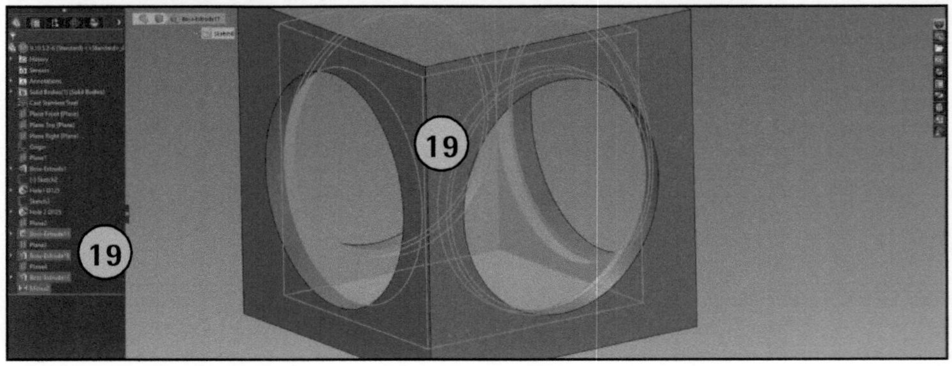

9.10.6 Creating connection holes

- Using a new **Sketch**, create a **140** mm diameter **Circle** on the inner ring (6).
- Place a **Point** at the axis intersection (20).
- At the point, use the **Hole Wizard** to create a threaded hole **M8**, thread depth **12** mm, drilling depth **16** mm (8).

Sketch

Line

Circle

Point

Hole Wizard

- Using the **Circular Pattern** function, create a **45°** offset of the bore, number **8**, selecting the inner cylinder as the base cylinder (22).

Circular Pattern

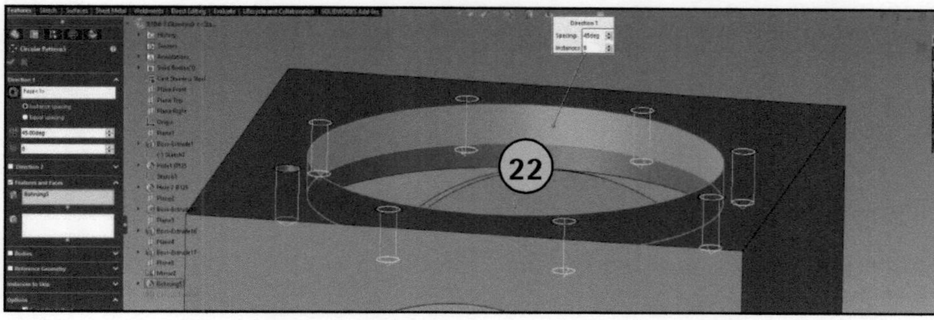

- Proceed with the two other cube faces (hole circle **Ø140** mm) accordingly (23, 24).

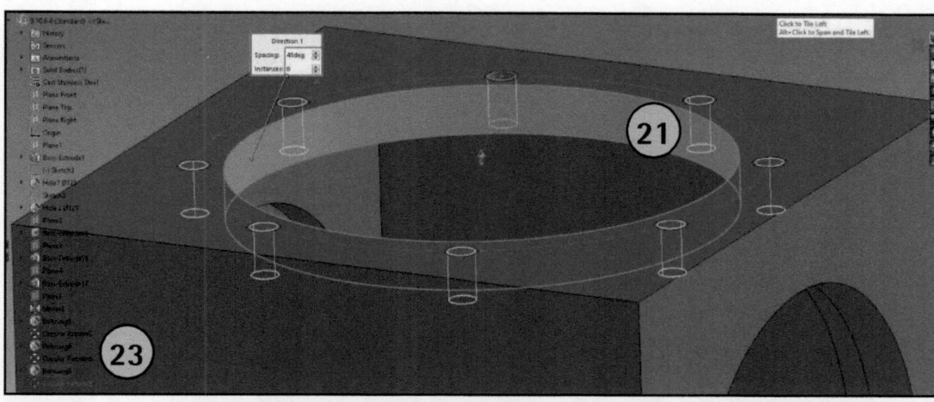

Sketch

Line

Circle

Point

Hole Wizard

Circular Pattern

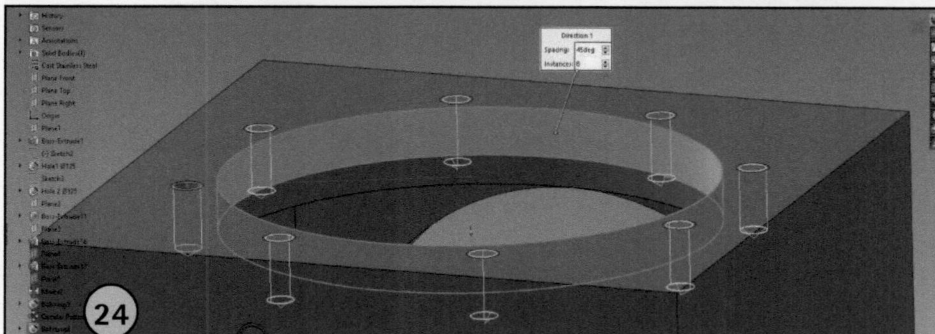

Sketch

Line

Circle

Point

Hole Wizard

Circular Pattern

- Using a new **Sketch**, create a **145** mm diameter **Circle** on the inner ring (6).
- Place a **Point** at the axis intersection (25).
- At the point, use the **Hole Wizard** to create a threaded hole **M8**, thread depth **12** mm, drilling depth **16** mm (26).
- Using the **Circular Pattern** function, create a **45°** offset of the bore, number **8,** selecting the inner cylinder as the base cylinder (27).

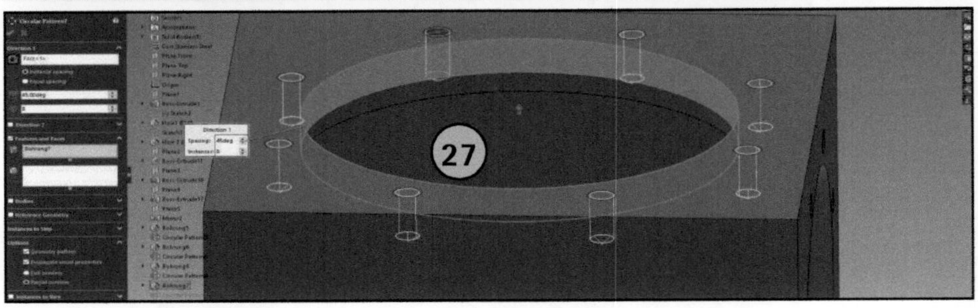

9.10.7 Edge breaking using feature "Fillet"

Fillet

- Edge breaking of all angular cuboid inner contours and bore turning contours with radius **2** mm using feature **Fillet** (28, 29).

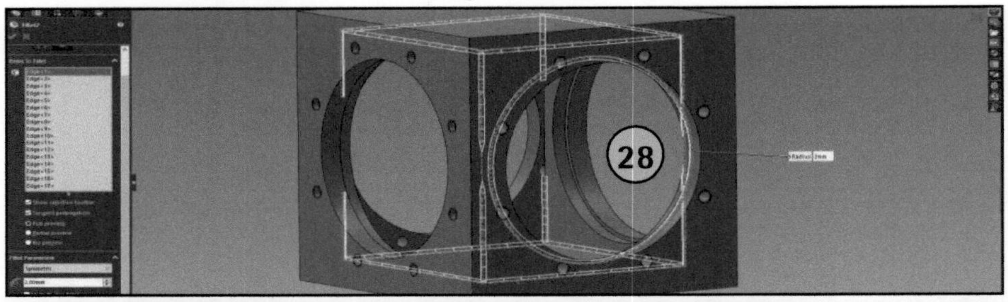

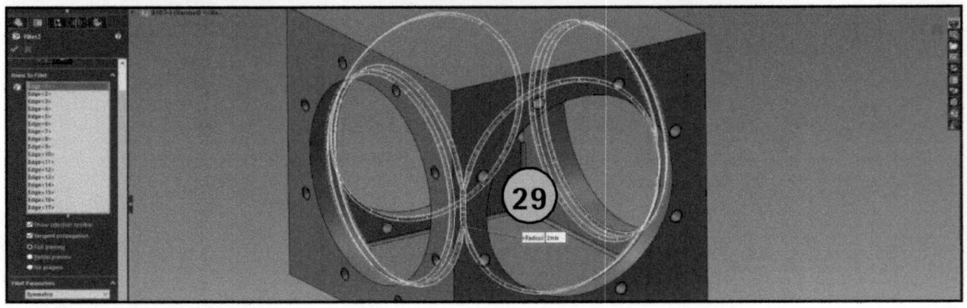

9.10.7.1 Data backup

Save as New

Save as New / Enter a name of your choice.

Project XVIII

Create Components
Drill plates

Page 413 to 440

- Component creation “Bearing Cover”
- Component creation “Bearing Base Part”
- Component creation “Base Plate”
- Component creation
  “Gear Switching Element”
- Component creation “Housing Cover”
- Component creation “Brake Disc”

9.11 Component creation "Bearing Cover"

9.11.1 The design sketch for the component creation

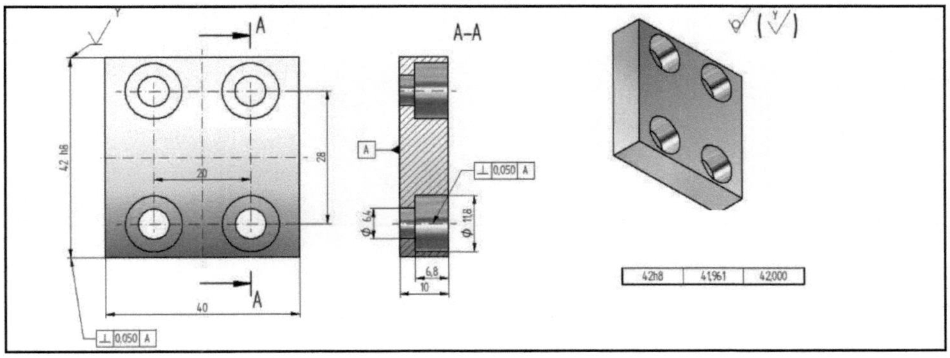

9.11.2 Bearing Cover, the creation

9.11.2.1 Opening your own template file

New

Engelke2026.
PRTDOT

Sketch

Extrude

- Menu Bar **New** /  /  click **Engelke2026.PRTDOT / OK**

9.11.2.2 Creating the basic component

- Create a basic body design with a thickness of **10** mm using the **Extrude** feature (1, 2)

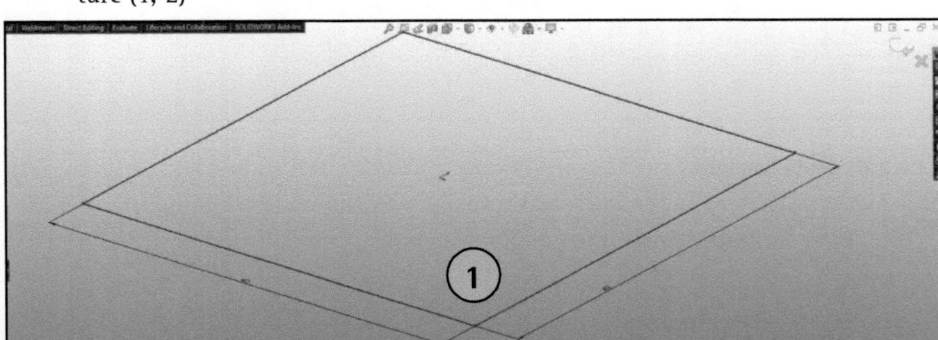

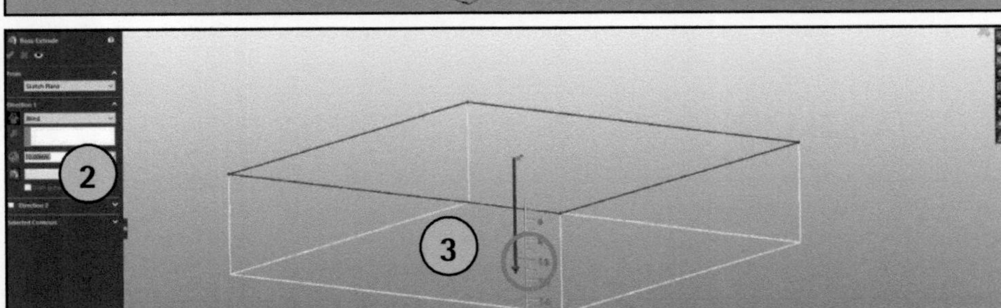

Edit Material

- Assign the material **DIN Steel Stainless 1.4401** using **Edit Material** (3, 4).

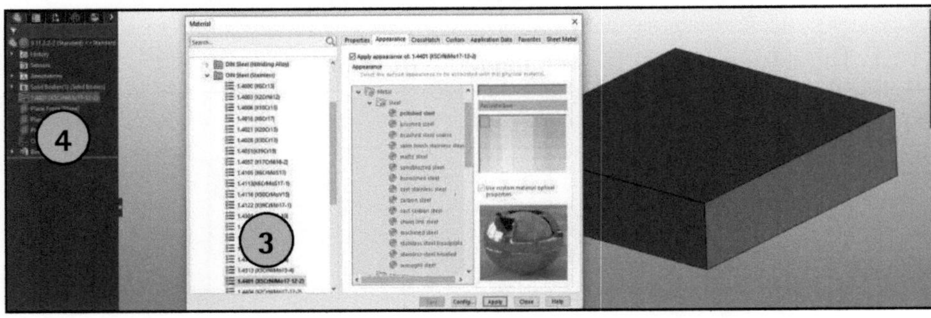

9.11.2.3 Creating connection holes

Sketch

Hole Wizard

- On a new **Sketch**, create one basic construction.
- Place a **Point** at the axis intersection (5).
- Drill a **Cylindrical countersink Ø11.8** mm at this **Points 6.8** mm deep, **Through hole Ø6.4** mm (6, 7) ein.

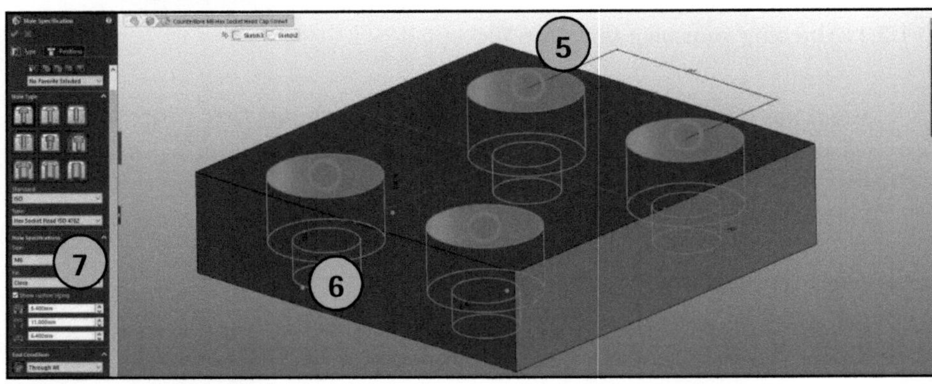

9.11.2.4 Data backup

Save as New

Save as New / Enter a name of your choice.

9.12 Component creation "Bearing Base Part"

9.12.1 The design sketch for the component creation

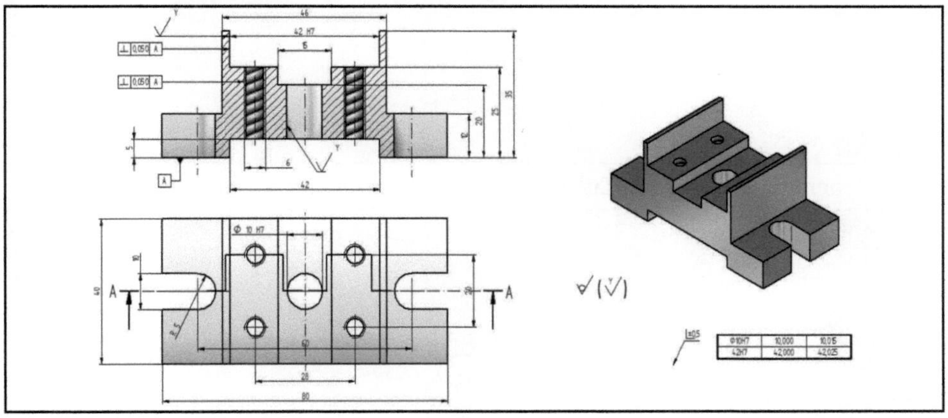

9.12.2 Bearing base part, the creation

9.12.2.1 Opening your own template file

New

Engelke2026.
PRTDOT

- Menu Bar **New** /  /  click **Engelke2026.PRTDOT / OK**

9.12.2.2 Creating the basic component

Sketch

Extrude

- Create a basic body design with a thickness of **35** mm using the **Extrude** feature (1, 2, 3)

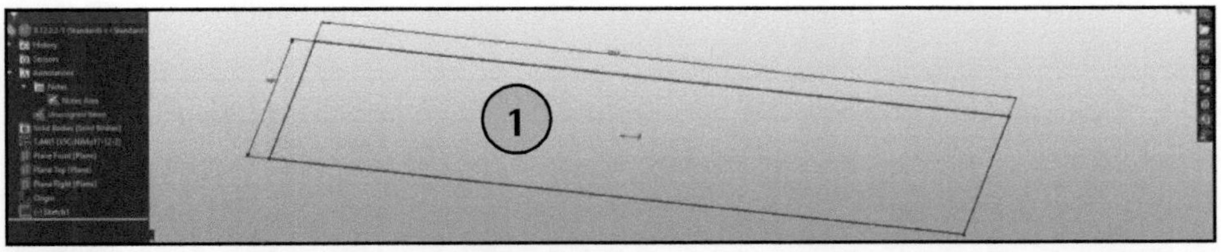

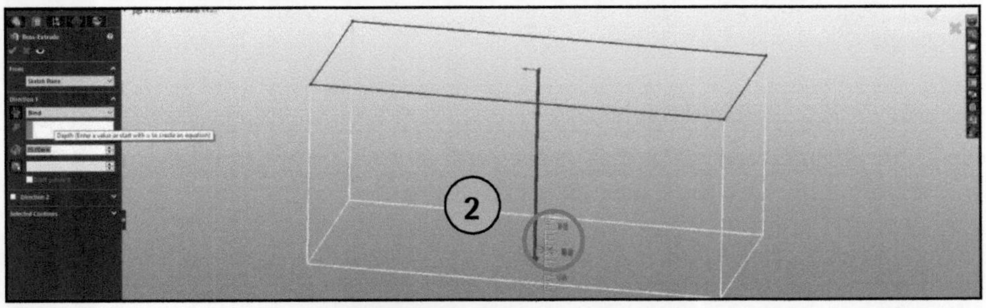

Sketch

Extruded Cut

- Generate an **Extruded Cut** by selecting sketch contour **Through All** (4, 5).

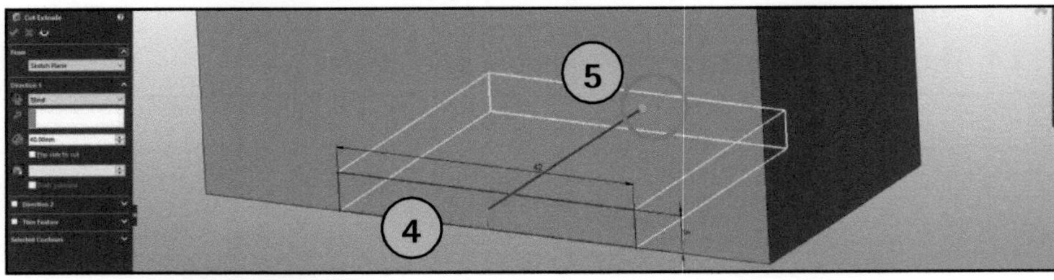

Sketch

Extruded Cut

- Generate an **Extruded Cut** by selecting sketch contour **Through All** (6, 7).

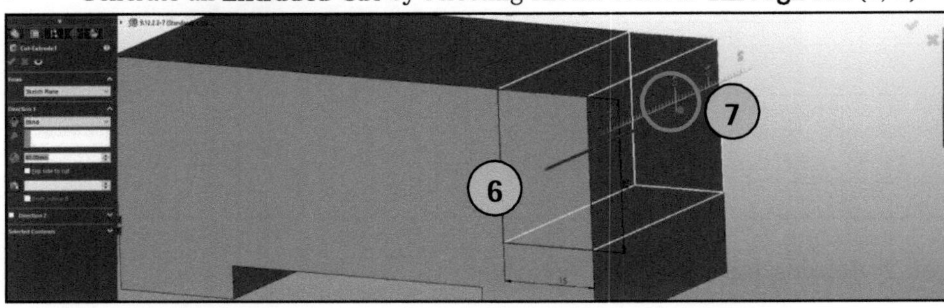

Plane

Mid Plane

Mirror

- The second recess is placed on the other side of the housing using the **Mirror** function mirror **Top Plane** on center (8, 9).

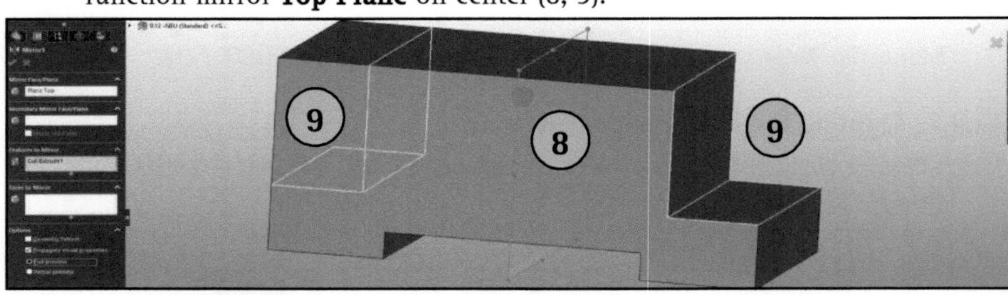

Sketch

Extruded Cut

- Generate an **Extruded Cut** by selecting sketch contour **Through All** (10, 11).

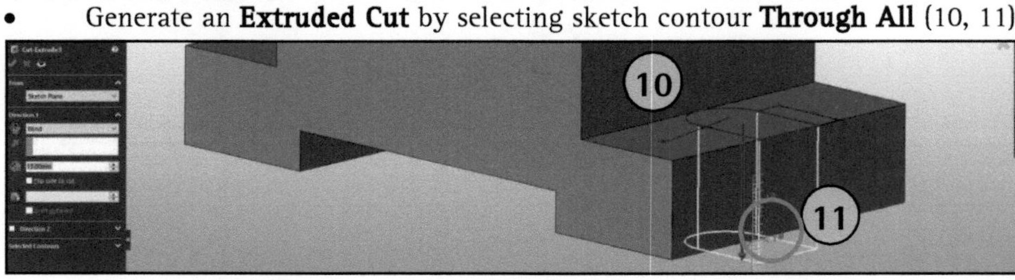

Plane

Mid Plane

Mirror

- The second recess is placed on the other side of the housing using the **Mirror** function mirror **Top Plane** on center (12, 13).

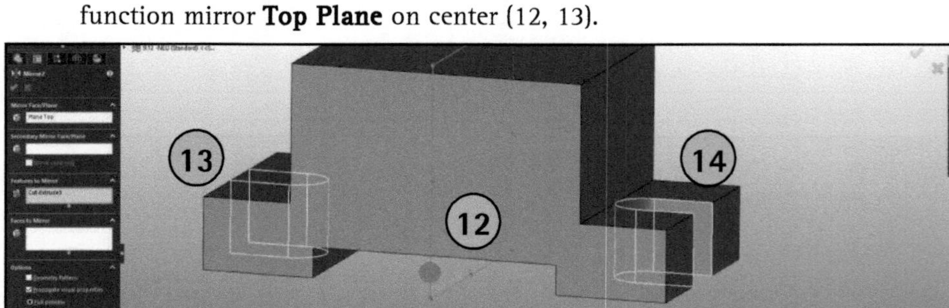

- Generate an **Extruded Cut** by selecting sketch contour **Through All** (15, 16).

Sketch

Extruded Cut

9.12.2.3 Create central hole

- Using a new **Sketch** on the inner surface, create a **Through hole Ø10** mm with the **Hole Wizard** (17, 18).

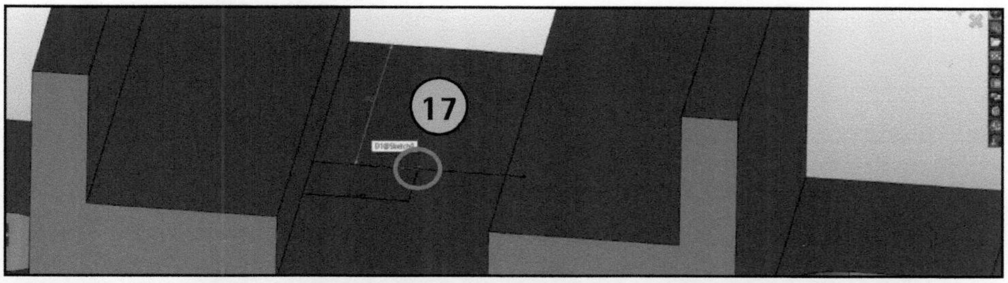

Sketch

Hole Wizard

9.12.2.4 Create mounting holes

- Using a new **Sketch** with the **Hole Wizard**, create **Trapped Holes M6** Option **Through All** (19, 20).

Sketch

Hole Wizard

Hole Wizard

9.12.2.5 Assigning component material

Edit Material

- Assign the material **DIN Steel Stainless 1.4401** using **Edit Material** (21).

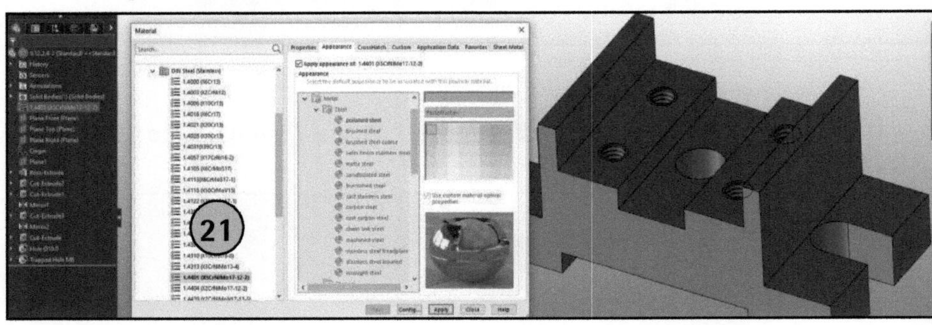

9.12.2.6 Physical thread unsing feature "Thread"

Thread

- The **Thread** function allows you to create a physical thread profile **M6 x 1** by selecting the upper and lower bore edges, the **Extrude Thread** option, **Trimming the start and end faces**, and creating the bore (22, 23, 24).

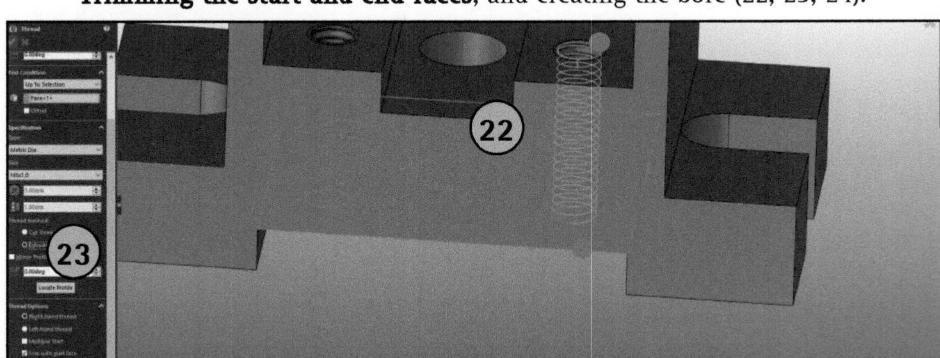

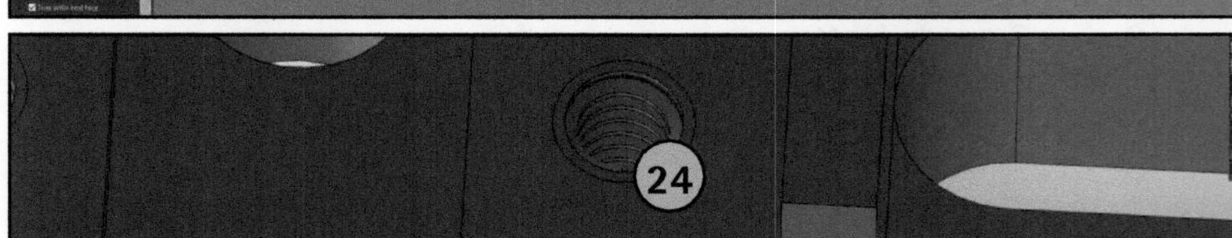

- The additional hole is placed on the other side of the component using the **Mirror** function mirror **Right Plane** (25, 26, 27).

Plane

Mid Plane

Mirror

- The additional hole is placed on the other side of the component using the **Mirror** function mirror **Top Plane**

Plane

Mid Plane

Mirror

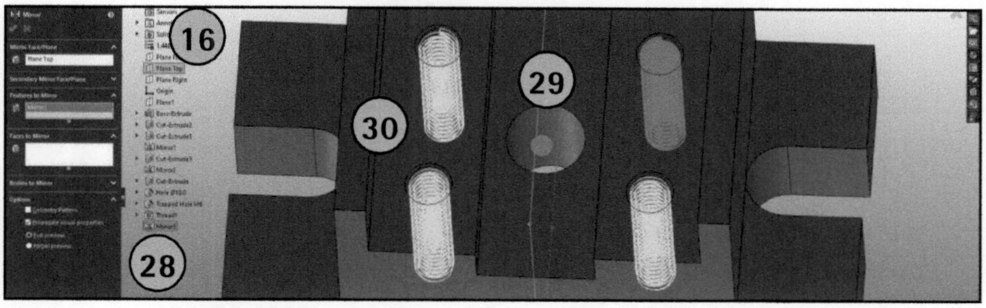

9.12.2.7 Data backup

Save as New / Enter a name of your choice.

Save as New

9.13 Component creation "Base Plate"

9.13.1 The design sketch for the component creation

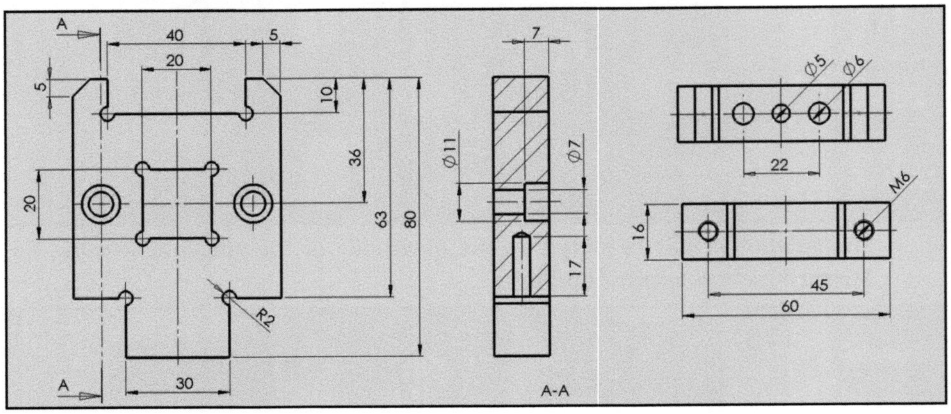

9.13.2 Base plate, the creation

9.13.2.1 Opening your own template file

New

Engelke2026. PRTDOT

- Menu Bar **New** /  /  click **Engelke2026.PRTDOT** / **OK**

9.13.2.2 Creating the basic component

Sketch

Extrude

- Create a basic body design with a thickness of **16** mm using the **Extrude** feature (1, 2).

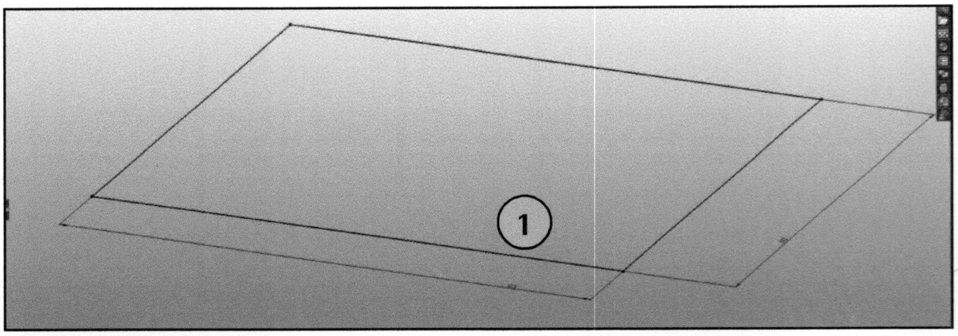

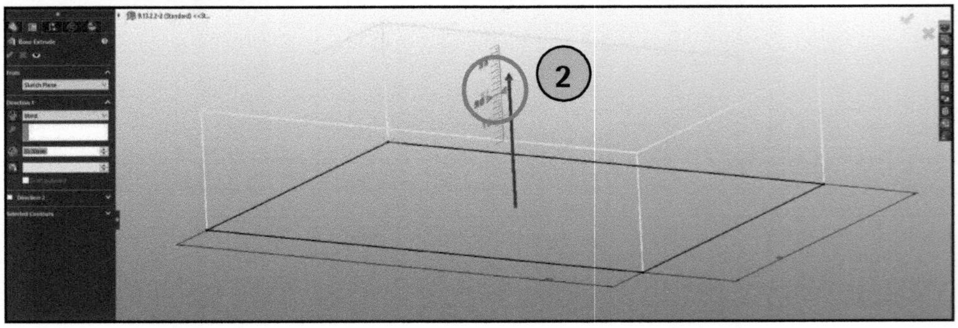

- Generate an **Extruded Cut** by selecting sketch contour **Through All** (3, 4).

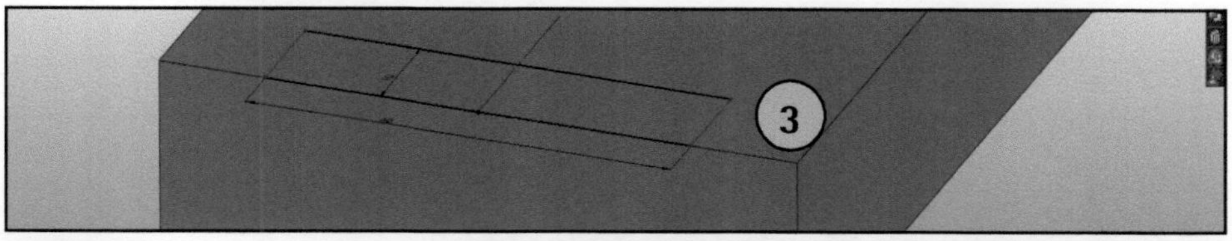

Sketch

Center Rectangle

Extruded Cut

- Generate an **Extruded Cut** by selecting sketch contour **Through All** (5, 6).

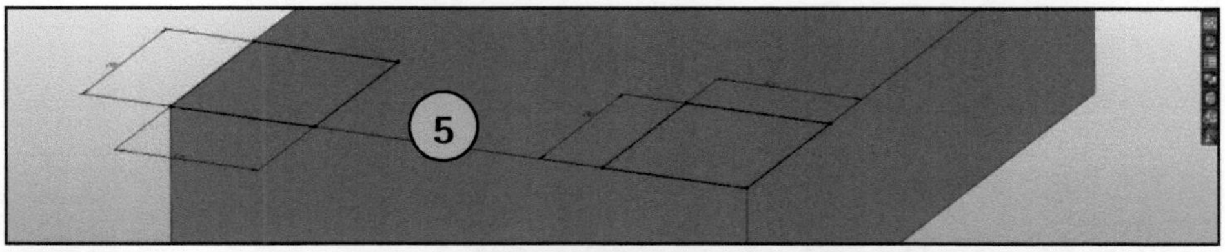

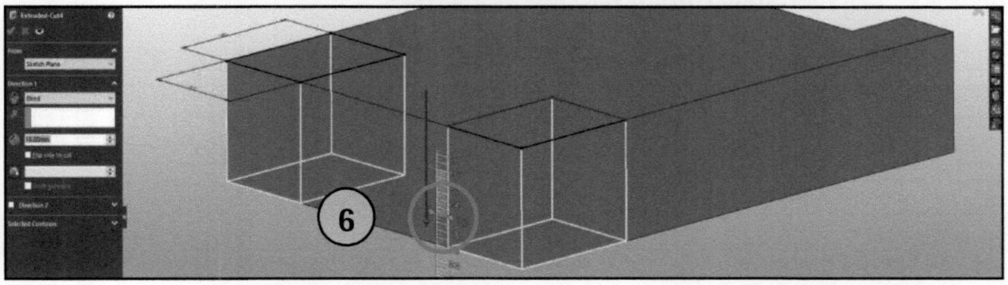

Sketch

Center Rectangle

Extruded Cut

- Generate an **Extruded Cut** by selecting sketch contour **Through All** (7, 8).

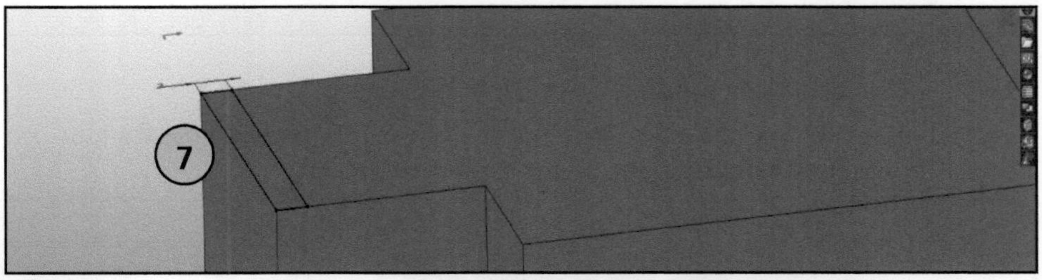

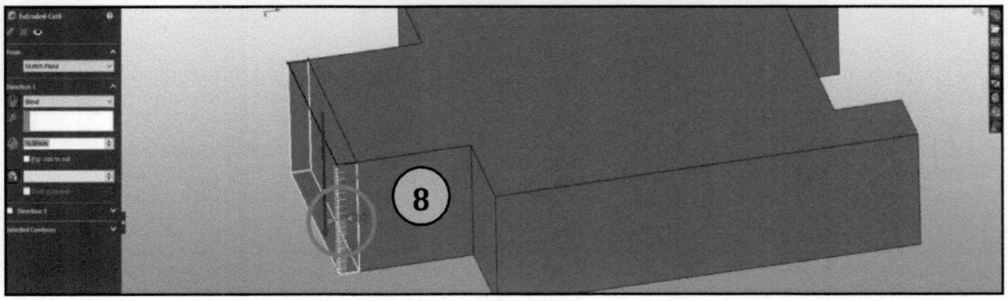

Sketch

Center Rectangle

Extruded Cut

Sketch

Center Rectangle

Extruded Cut

- Generate an **Extruded Cut** by selecting sketch contour **Through All** (9, 10).

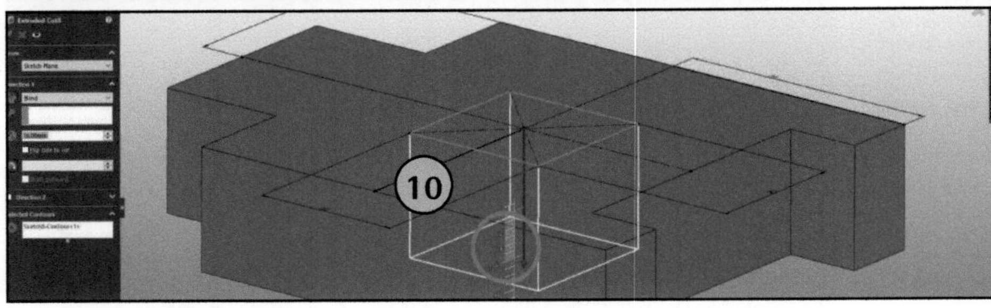

9.13.3 Edge Breakings

9.13.3.1 Edge Breakings using features "Chamfer"

Chamfer

- Select the back edges for edge breaking, edge chamfer, **5** mm x **45°** (11).

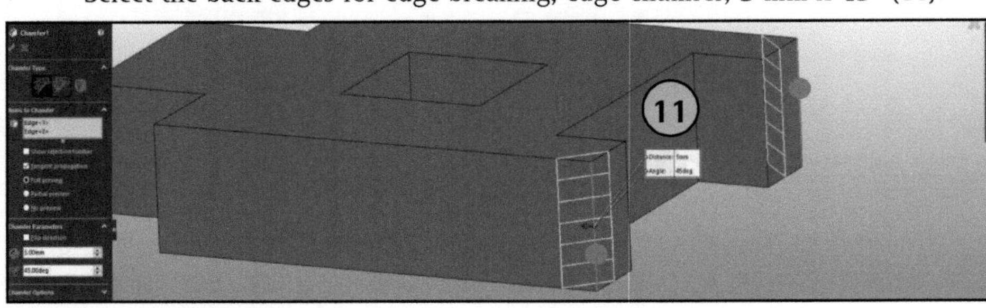

9.13.3.2 Edge Breakings using features "Hole Wizard"

Sketch

Hole Wizard

- Using a new **Sketch** on the inner surface, create a **Through hole Ø2** mm with the **Hole Wizard** at the points as shown (12, 13).

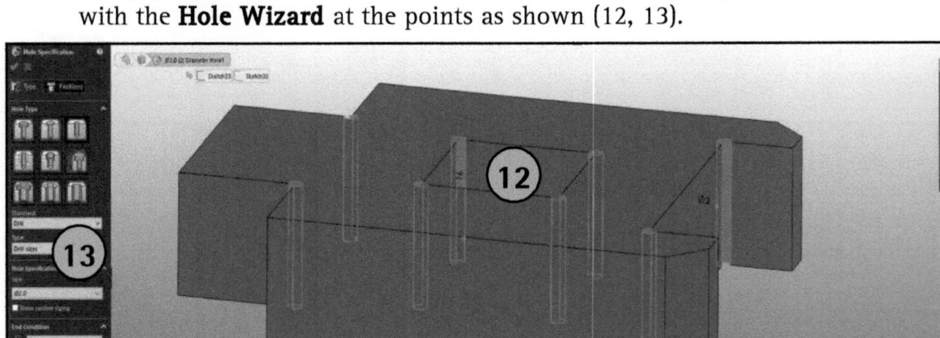

9.13.4 Create mounting holes

9.13.4.1 Mounting holes on the top side of the component

- Create an auxiliary construction on a new **Sketch** using **Offset** and **Line**.
- Place a **Point** on each of the construction intersection points.
- Drill a **Cylindrical countersink Ø11** mm at this **Point 7** mm deep, **Through hole Ø7** mm (14, 15).

Sketch

Line

Offset

Point

Hole Wizard

9.13.4.2 Mounting holes on the front side of the component

- Create an auxiliary construction on a new **Sketch** using **Offset** and **Line**.
- Place a **Point** on each of the construction intersection points (16).
- At the points, use the **Hole Wizard** to create a threaded hole **M6**, thread depth **10** mm, drilling depth **12** mm (17, 18).

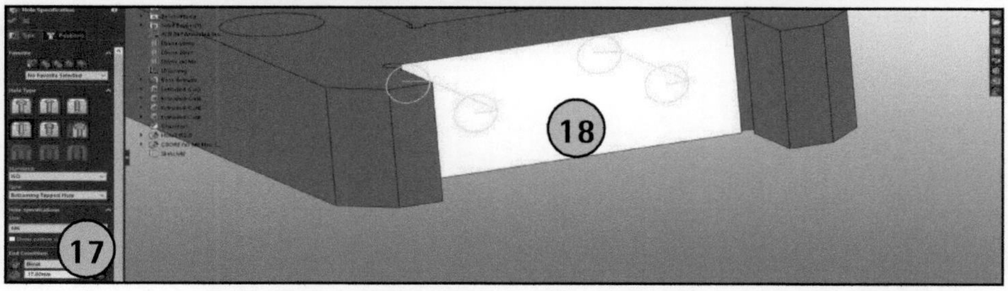

Sketch

Line

Offset

Point

Hole Wizard

- Create an auxiliary construction on a new **Sketch** using **Offset** and **Line**.
- Place a **Point** on each of the construction intersection points (19).
- At the middle **Point**, use the **Hole Wizard** to create a **Hole Ø5** mm, drilling depth **17** mm (20, 21).

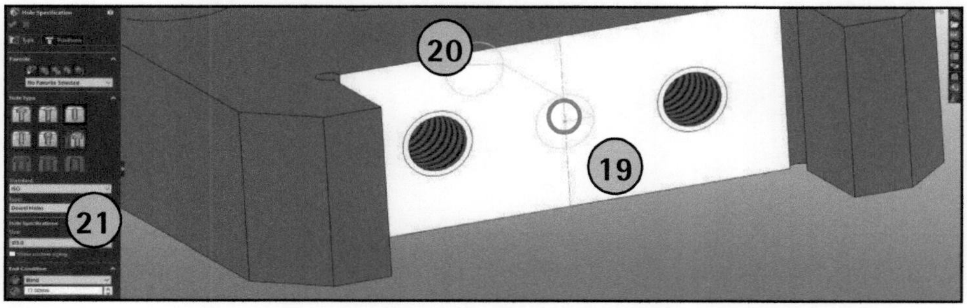

Sketch

Line

Offset

Point

Hole Wizard

Sketch
Line
Offset
Point
Hole Wizard

9.13.4.3 Mounting holes on the back side of the component

- Create an auxiliary construction on a new **Sketch** using **Offset** and **Line**.
- Place a **Point** on each of the construction intersection points (22).
- At the points, use the **Hole Wizard** to create a threaded hole **M6**, thread depth **10** mm, drilling depth **12** mm (23, 24).

Edit Material

9.13.4.4 Assigning component material

- Assign the material **Annealed Stainless Steel AISI 347** using **Edit Material** (25).

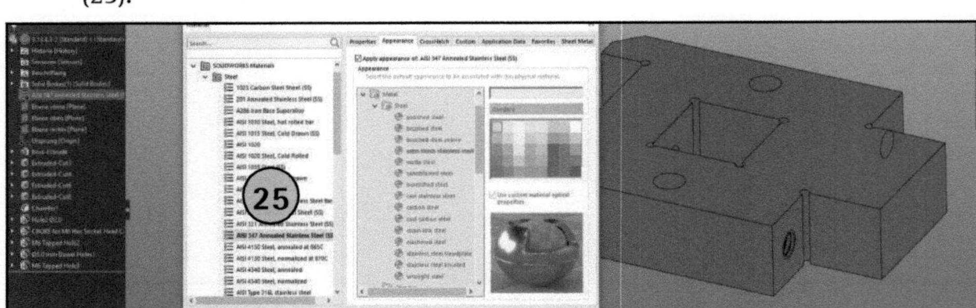

Save as New

9.13.4.5 Data backup

 **Save as New** / Enter a name of your choice.

9.14 Component creation "Gear Switching Element"

9.14.1 The design sketch for the component creation

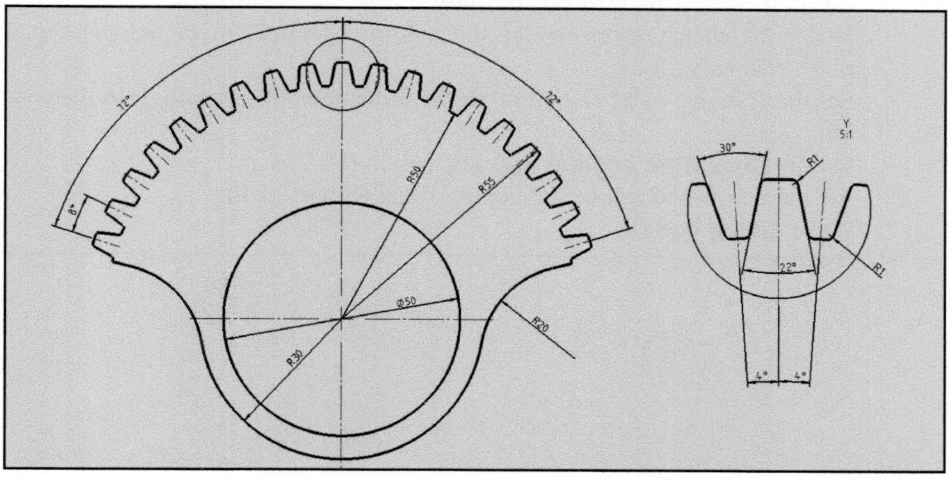

9.14.2 Interlocking tooth row, the creation

9.14.2.1 Opening your own template file

- Menu Bar **New** /  /  click **Engelke2026.PRTDOT / OK**

9.14.2.2 Basic sketch for the interlocking tooth

- Construct the sketch as shown on the **Front Plane**.
- Attention to cleanly trimmed edges and transition points.
- The dimension values should be rounded to whole numbers, ensure that the dimensions shown are fully adopted.
- The tooth mid-axis is to be executed as a construction line (1).

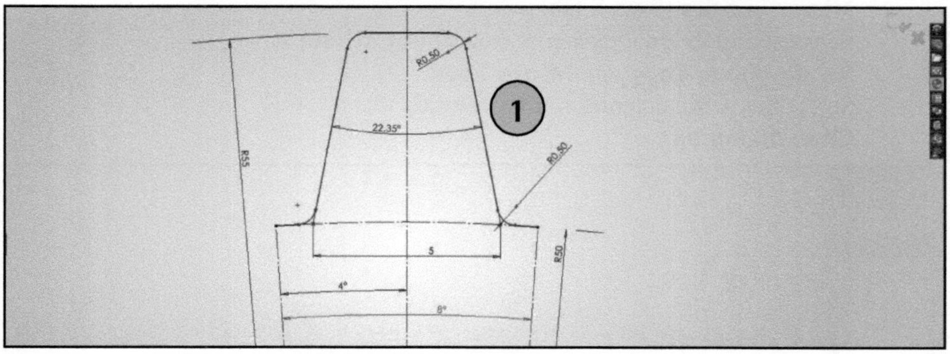

New

Engelke2026.
PRTDOT

Sketch

Line

Smart
Dimension

Circle

Trim Entities

Circular Sketch Pattern

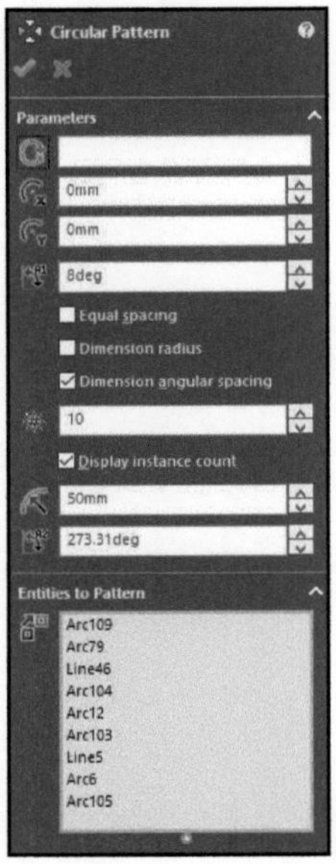

9.14.2.3 Create the left interlocking tooth row using the "Circular Sketch pattern"

Circular Sketch pattern (Sketch tab)
Select the sketch elements for the pattern by clicking on the individual tooth elements (2).
Set the distance to **8°** to define the total distance in the pattern in degrees. (3).
Set the **Dimension angular spacing** option (4).
Set the number of referenced copies of the pattern to **10.**
Close dialog box (5).

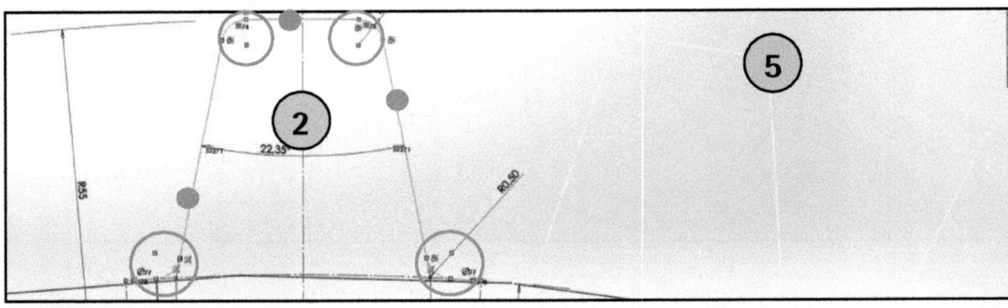

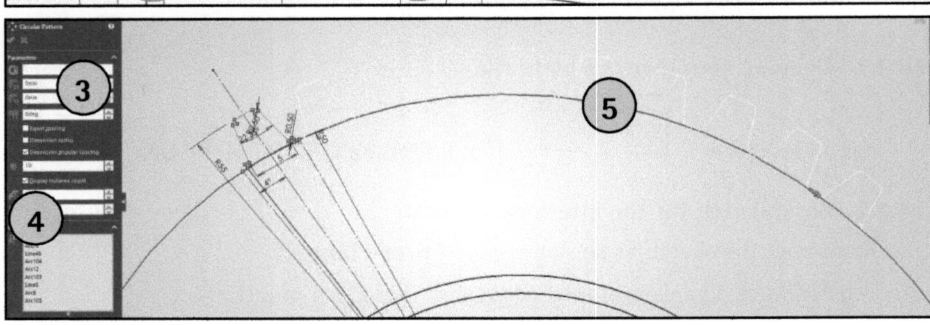

Mirror Entities

9.14.2.4 Creating the right interlocking tooth row using "Mirror Entities"

Mirror Entities (Sketch tab)
Select the individual elements from the sketch (6).
Set the option **Copy** and **Mirror about.** (7).
Select the vertical center line as the axis (8).
Close dialog box.

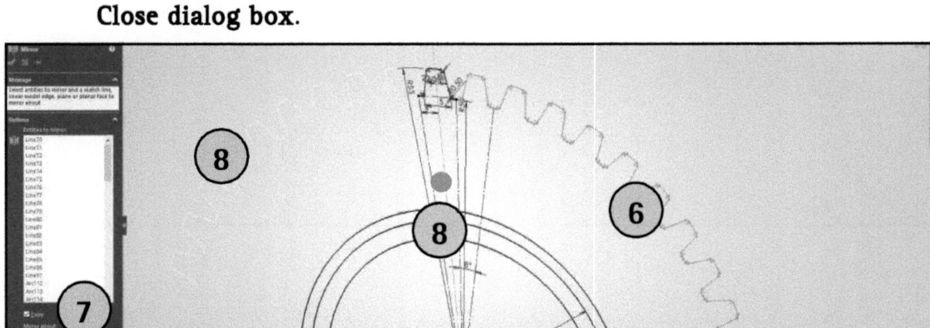

9.14.2.5 Completing the sketch construction

- Using the **Line**, quick snap **Endpoint** function, place a finishing line from the end of the interlocking tooth to the **Center Point** (9).

Line

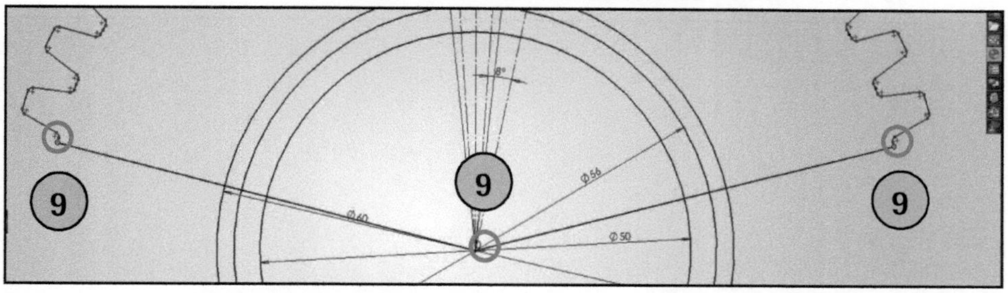

- Clean up the circle area according to the representation using the **Trim** function (10).
- **Finish Sketch**.

Trim Entities

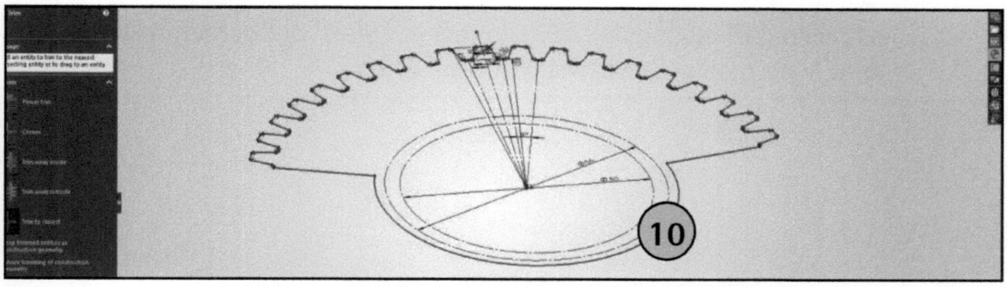

9.14.3 Volume generation of the „Gear switching element"

- Activate the **Sketch1** entry in the **FeatureManager**.
- Select the **Contour Select Tool** option from the **Context menu** (11).
- Click the inner contour (12).
- Create a basic body design using the **Extrude** feature (13).
- Click on the arrow and drag with the scale set to **10** mm, **Mid Plane** option (14, 15).

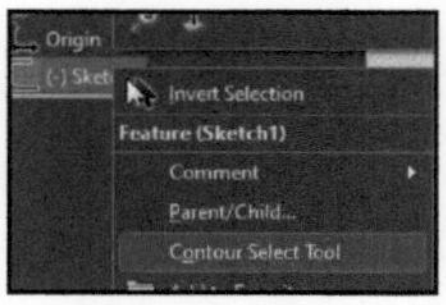

Extrude

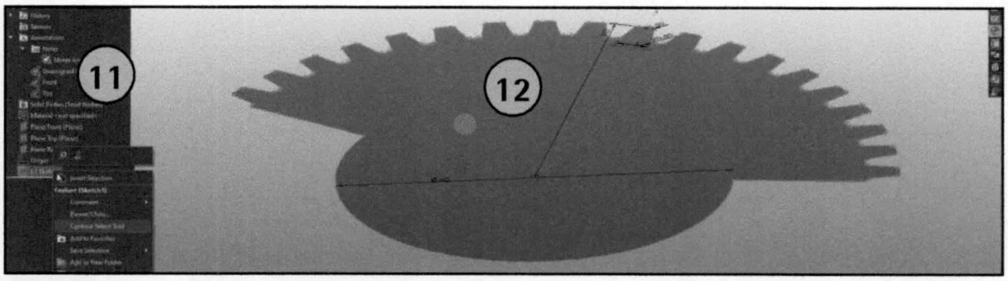

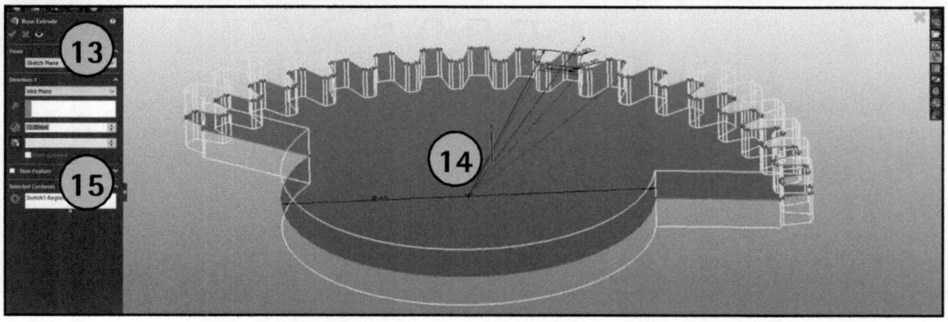

9.14.4 Drilling the central hole in the gear switching element

Hole Wizard

- Using the cylinder outer circle on the surface, create a **Through hole Ø50** mm with the **Hole Wizard** (16, 17).

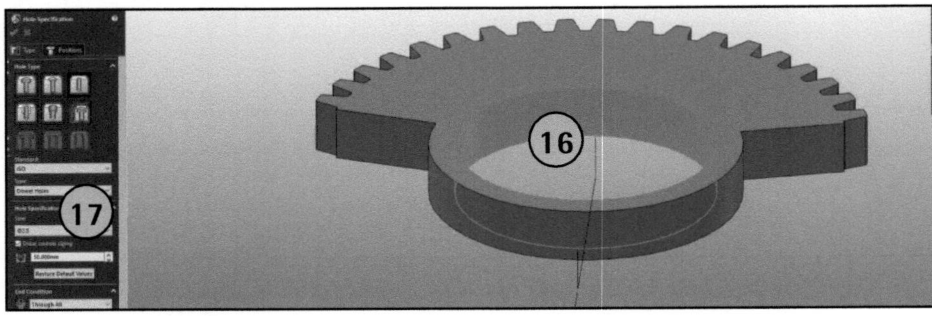

9.14.5 Edge breaking using feature "Fillet"

Fillet

- Edge breaking of all angular cuboid inner contours and bore turning contours with radius **20** mm using feature **Fillet** (18, 19).

9.14.6 Assigning component material

Edit Material

- Assign the material **Annealed Stainless Steel AISI 347** using **Edit Material** (20).

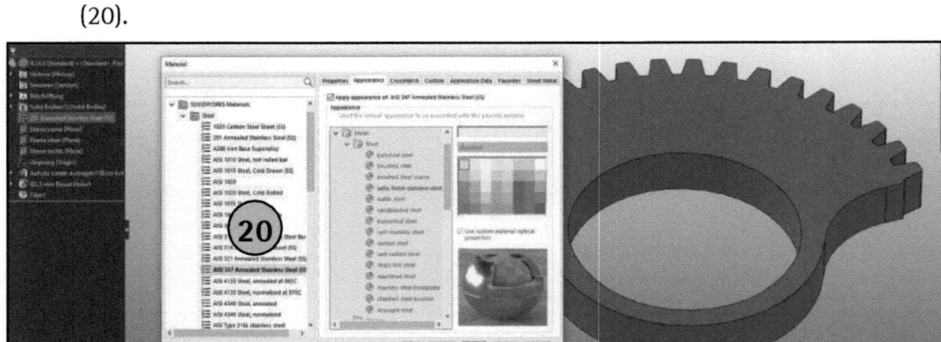

9.14.6.1 Data backup

Save as New

Save as New / Enter a name of your choice.

9.15 Component creation "Housing Cover"

9.15.1 The design sketch for the component creation

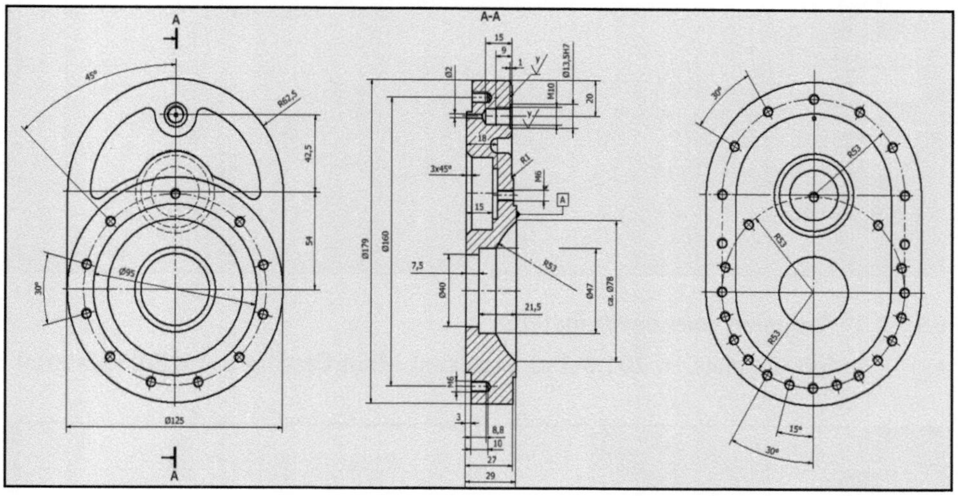

9.15.1.1 "Housing Cover", component representations

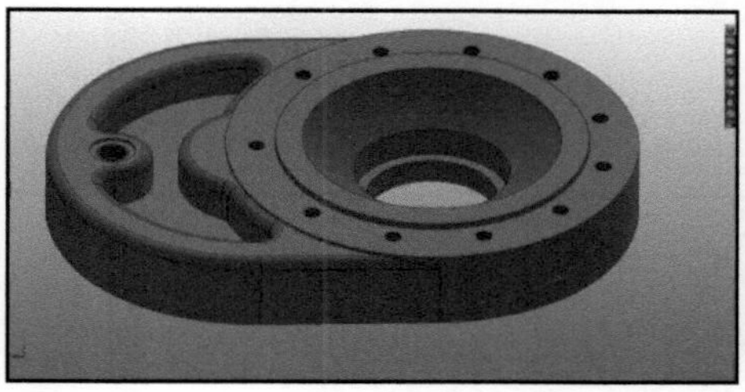

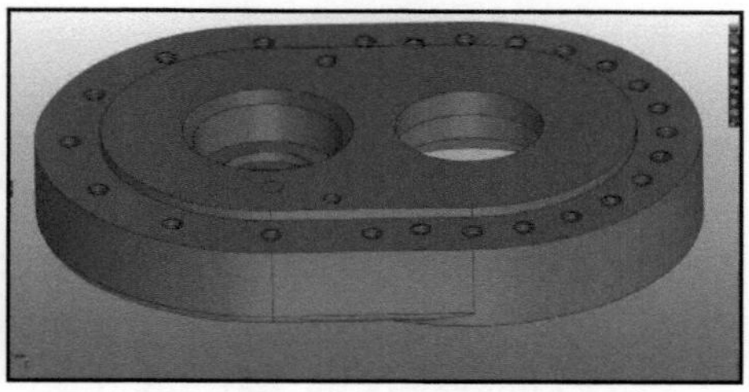

9.15.2 "Housing Cover", the creation

9.15.2.1 Opening your own template file

New

Engelke2026.
PRTDOT

- Menu Bar **New** /  /  click **Engelke2026.PRTDOT / OK**

9.15.2.2 Creating the basic component

Sketch

Line

Smart
Dimension

Circle

Trim Entities

- Construct the **Sketch** as shown on the **Front Plane**.
- Attention to cleanly trimmed edges and transition points.
- The dimension values should be rounded to whole numbers, ensure that the dimensions shown are fully adopted (1).

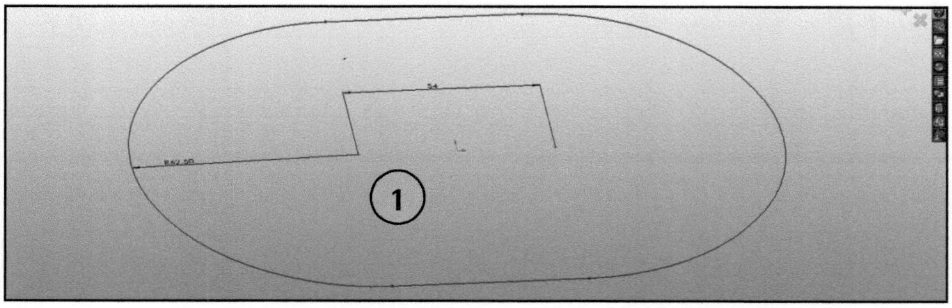

Extrude

- Create a basic body design using the **Extrude** feature (2).
- Click on the arrow and drag with the scale set to **10** mm, **Mid Plane** option (3).

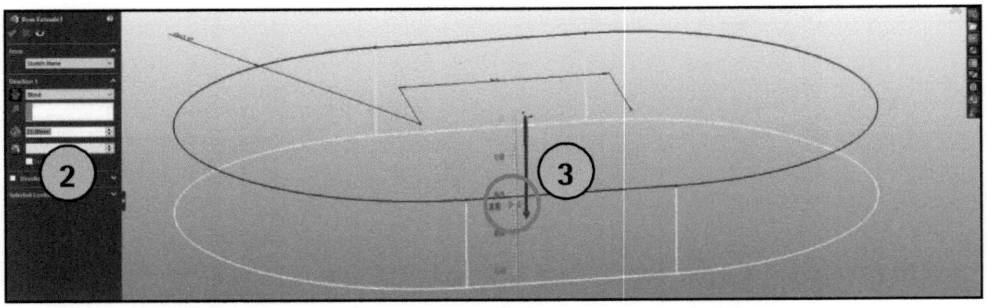

9.15.2.3 Assigning component material

Edit Material

- Assign the material **201.0-T43 Insulated Mold Casting** using **Edit Material** (4).

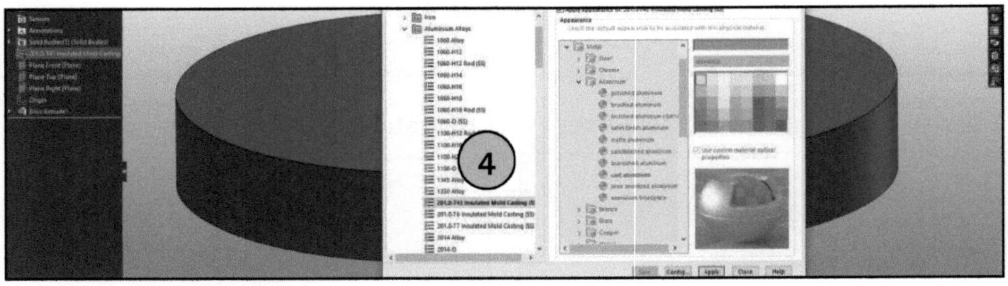

9.15.2.4 Attachment surfaces, the creation

Sketch

Circle

Extrude

- On a new **Sketch**, create a solid with a height of **1** mm and a diameter of **125** mm using the **Extrude** function (5, 6).

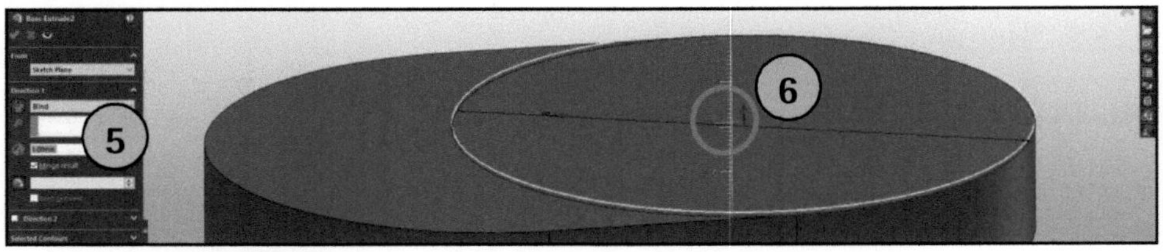

Sketch

Circle

Extrude

- On a new **Sketch**, create a solid with a height of **3** mm using the **Extrude** function (7, 8).

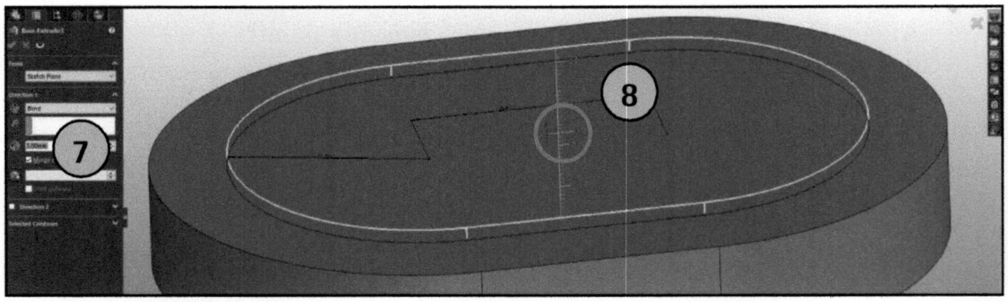

- On a new **Sketch**, create a solid with a height of **2** mm and a diameter of **95** mm using the **Extrude** function (9, 10).

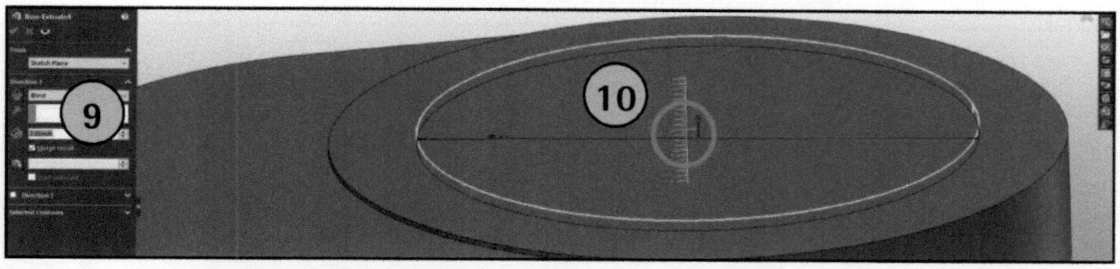

Sketch

Circle

Extrude

- On a new **Sketch**, use the **Extruded Cut** function with a depth of **12** mm to generate a volume difference (11, 12, 13).

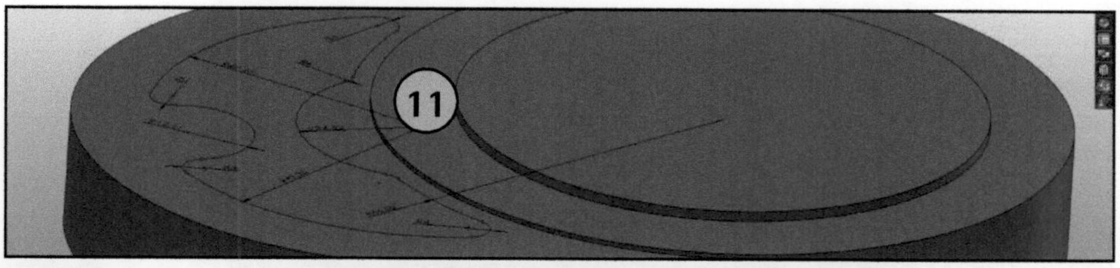

Sketch

Extruded Cut

9.15.2.5 Creating Housing Holes

- Using the **Hole Wizard**, drill a **Counterbore Ø47** mm, **21.5** mm deep, with a **Through hole Ø40** mm, at the central point (14, 15).

Hole Wizard

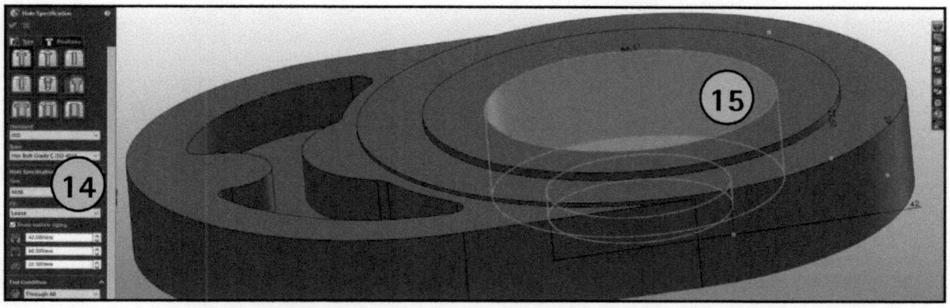

- Using the **Hole Wizard**, drill a **Counterbore Ø40** mm, **15** mm deep, with a **Through hole Ø28** mm, at the central point (16, 17).

Hole Wizard

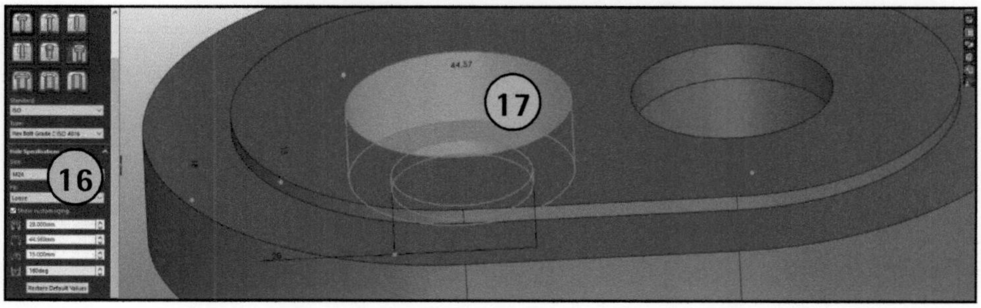

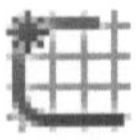
Sketch

Line

Circle

Point

9.15.2.6 Creating a lubricating oil bore

- Create a new **Sketch** and place a **Point** at the axis intersection. (18).

Hole Wizard

- Using the **Hole Wizard**, drill a **Threaded base hole M10**, **9** mm deep, at the point (19, 20).

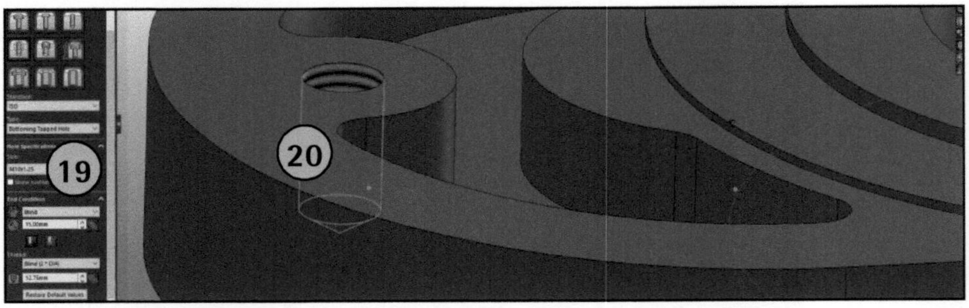

Hole Wizard

- Using the **Hole Wizard**, drill a **14** mm diameter **Counterbore**, **1** mm deep, at the central point (21, 22).

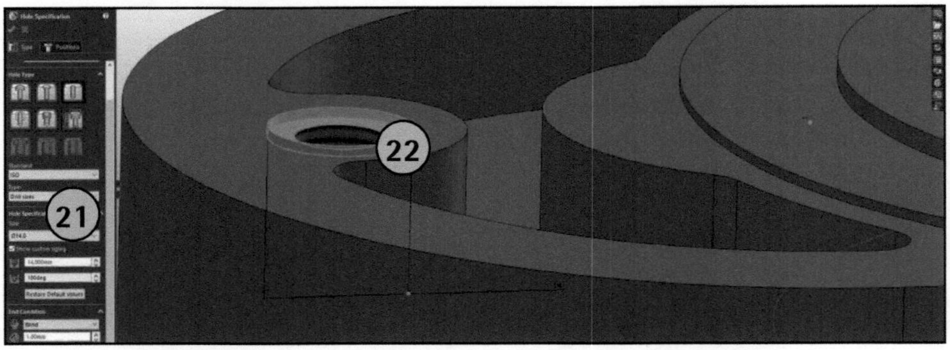

Hole Wizard

- Using the **Hole Wizard**, drill a **2** mm diameter **Through hole** at the central point (23, 24).

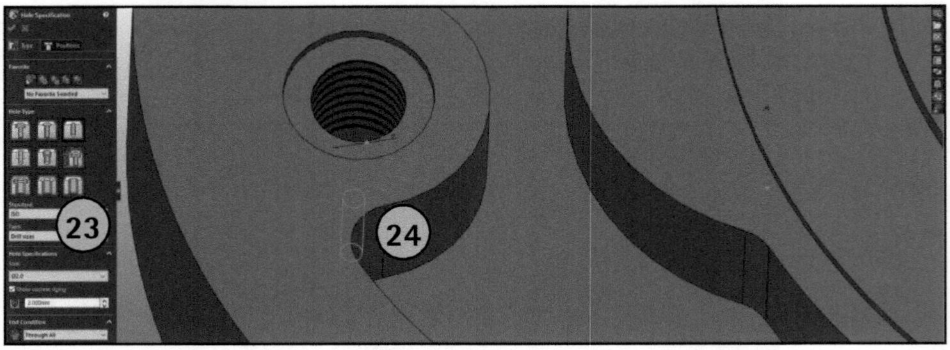

9.15.2.7 Creating connection holes

- Create a new **Sketch** and place one **Point** at each of the construction intersections (25).

Sketch

Hole Wizard

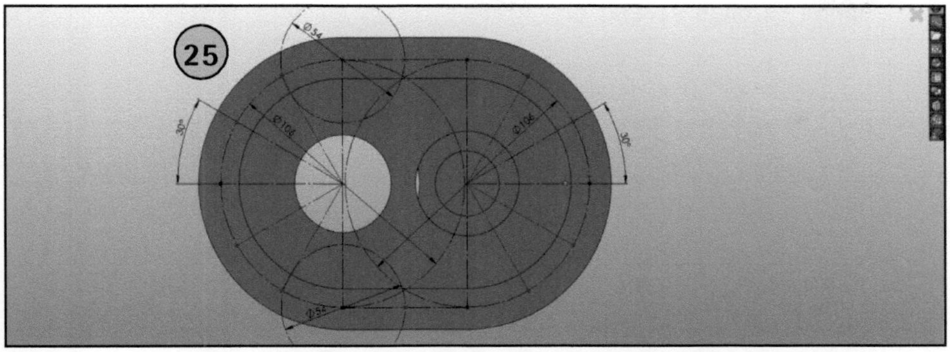

- At the points, use the **Hole Wizard** to create a **Threaded hole M6**, thread depth **8** mm, drilling depth **10** mm (26, 27).

Sketch

Hole Wizard

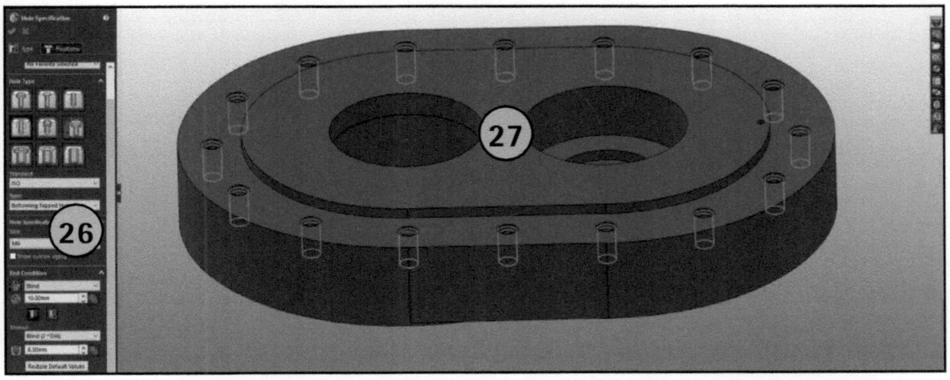

- Create a new **Sketch** and place one **Point** at each of the construction intersections (28).
- At the points, use the **Hole Wizard** to create a **Threaded hole M6**, option **Through All** (29, 30).

Sketch

Hole Wizard

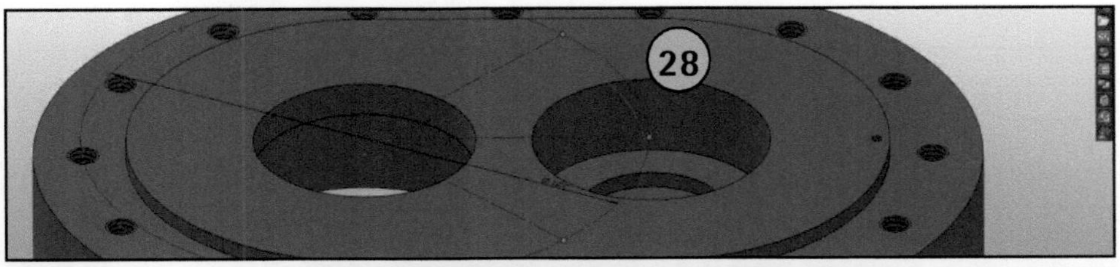

Sketch

Hole Wizard

- Create a new **Sketch** and place one **Point** at each of the construction intersections (31).
- At the points, use the **Hole Wizard** to create a **Threaded hole M6**, option **Through All** (32, 33).

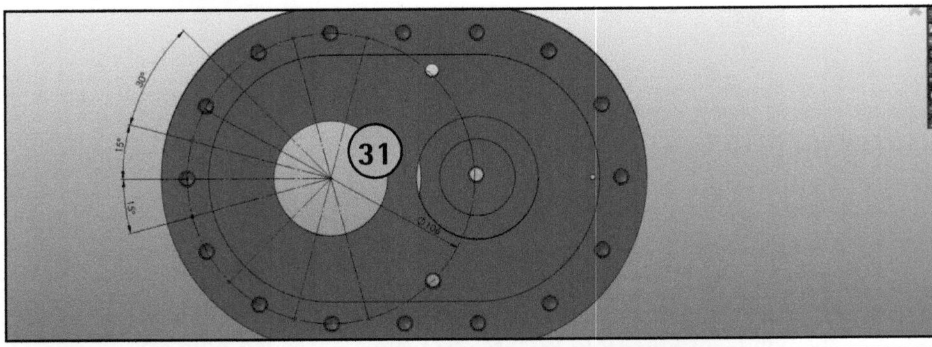

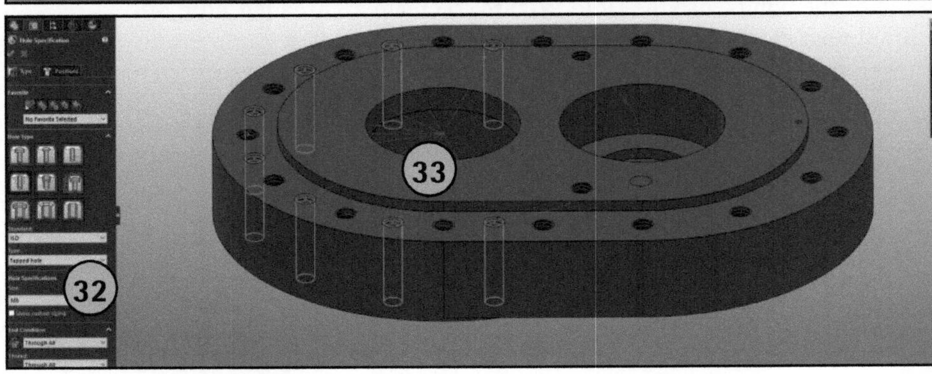

9.15.2.8 Component creation "Housing Cover", final edits

Plane

Sketch

Cut Revolve

- Create a **Parallel Work Plane** to the **Front Plane** (33).
- To create the rotation, you generate a line sketch construction on the new **Work Plane** (34).
- Select the created **Sketch** and use **Cut Revolve** to create the revolving section (35, 36).

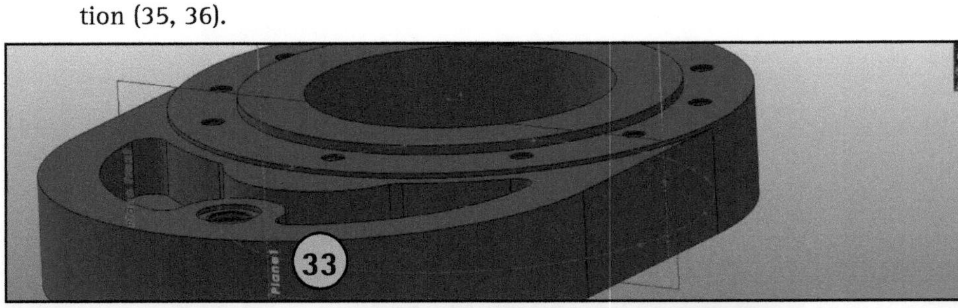

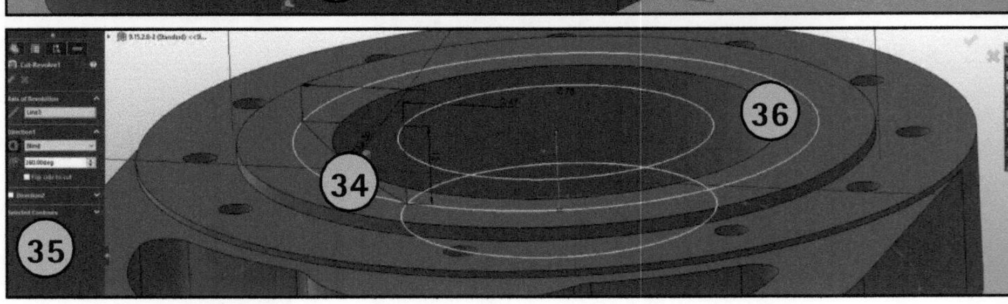

- Edge breaking, **3 mm x 45°**, using feature **Chamfer** (37).

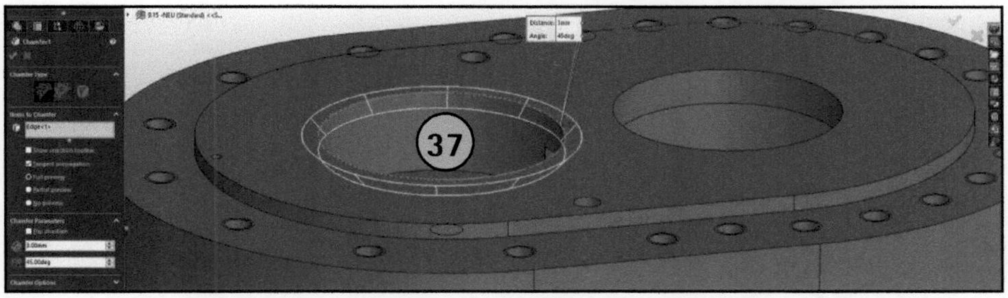

Chamfer

- Edge breaking, radius **3** mm, using feature **Fillet** (38, 39).

Fillet

9.15.2.9 Data backup

Save as New / Enter a name of your choice.

Save as New

9.16 Component creation "Brake Disc"

9.16.1 The design sketch for the component creation

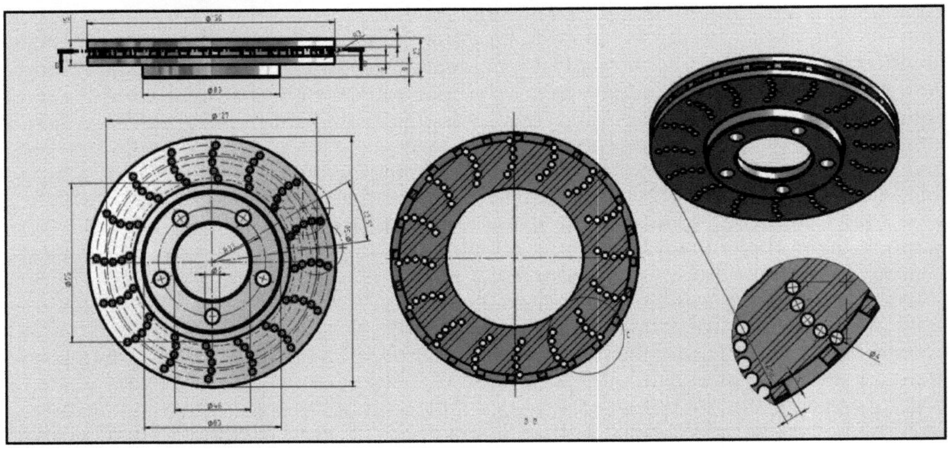

New

Engelke2026.
PRTDOT

9.16.2 The basic body, the creation

9.16.2.1 Opening your own template file

- Menu Bar **New** /  /  click **Engelke2026.PRTDOT** / **OK**

Sketch

Circle

Extrude

9.16.2.2 Creating cylindrical basic bodies

- Construct the **Sketch** as shown on the **Front Plane**.
- Create a basic body design cylinder with outer diameter **150** mm and height **5** mm using the **Extrude** feature (1).

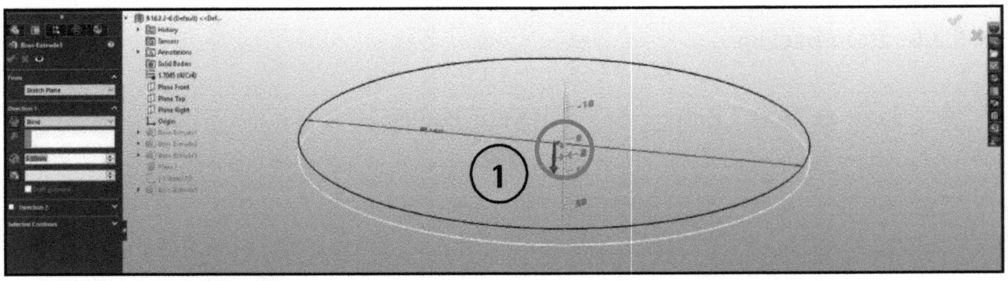

- Create a basic body design cylinder with an outer diameter of **140** mm and a height of **5** mm using the **Extrude** feature on the component surface (2).

Sketch

Circle

Extrude

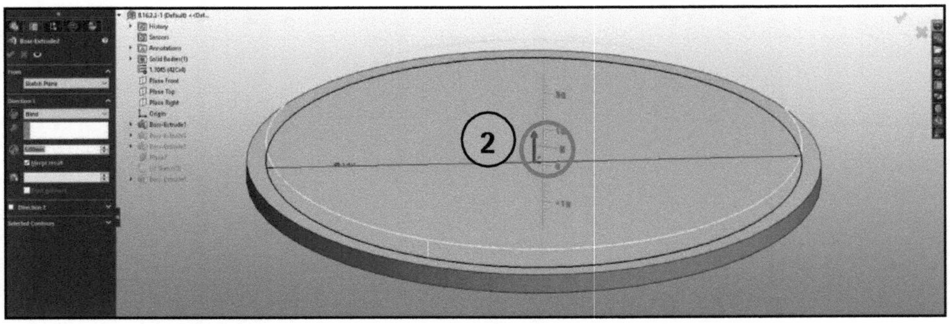

- Create a basic body design cylinder with an outer diameter of **150** mm and a height of **5** mm using the **Extrude** feature on the component surface (3).

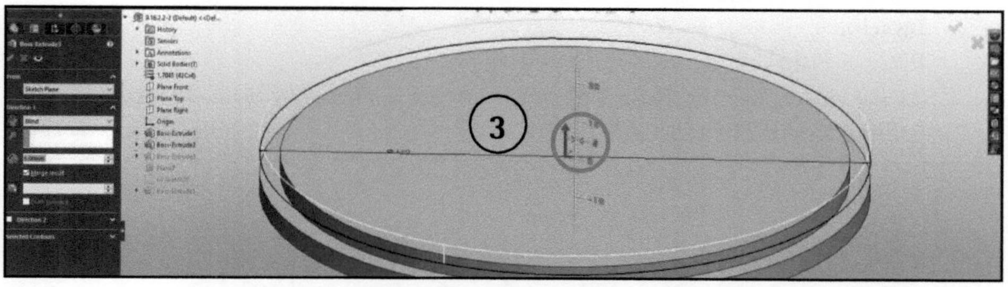

Sketch

Circle

Extrude

- Create a basic body design cylinder with an outer diameter of **83** mm and a height of **8** mm using the **Extrude** feature on the component surface (4).

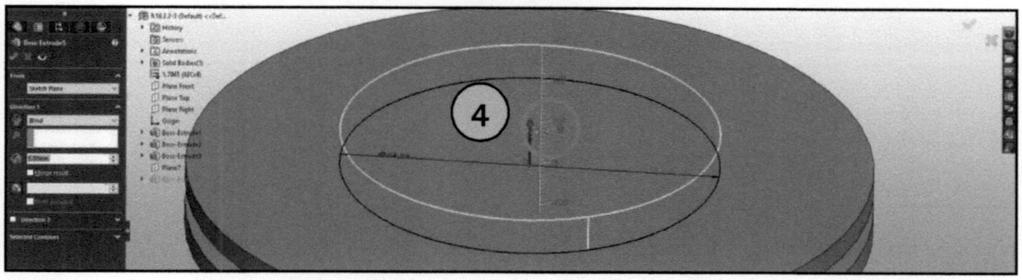

Sketch

Circle

Extrude

9.16.2.3 Assigning component material

- Assign the material **DIN Steel Nitriding Alloy 1.7045** using **Edit Material** (5).

Edit Material

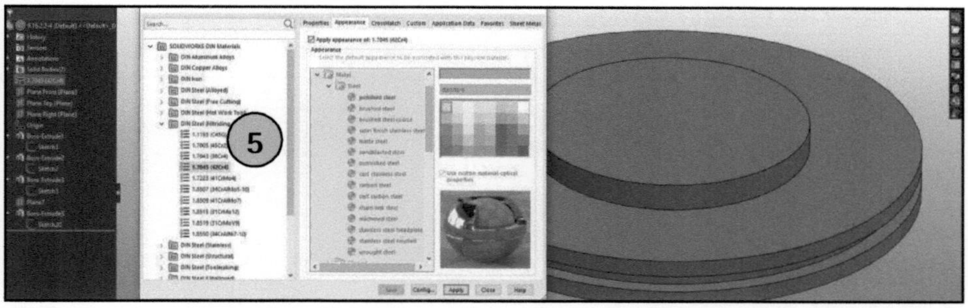

9.16.3 Creating central bore

- Using the central point on the component surface, create a **Through hole Ø46** mm with the **Hole Wizard** (6, 7).

Hole Wizard

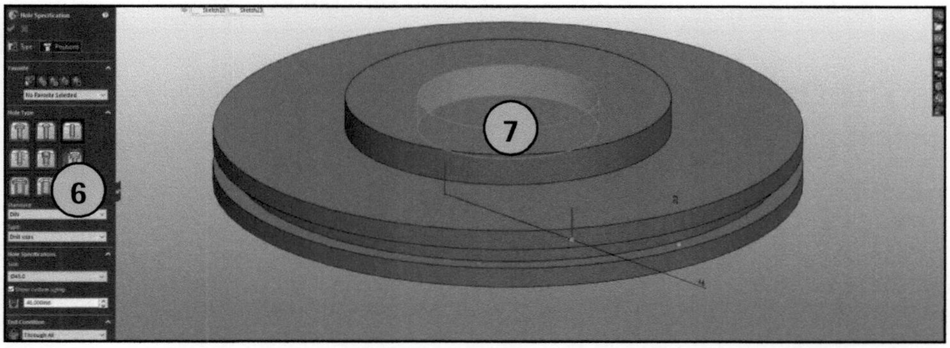

9.16.4 Creating connection holes

Sketch

Circle

Line

Point

Hole Wizard

- Using a new **Sketch**, create a **65** mm diameter **Circle** on the component surface (6).
- Place a **Point** at the axis intersection (8).
- At the point, use the **Hole Wizard** to create a **Through hole Ø5 mm**, drilling depth **Through All** (9, 10).

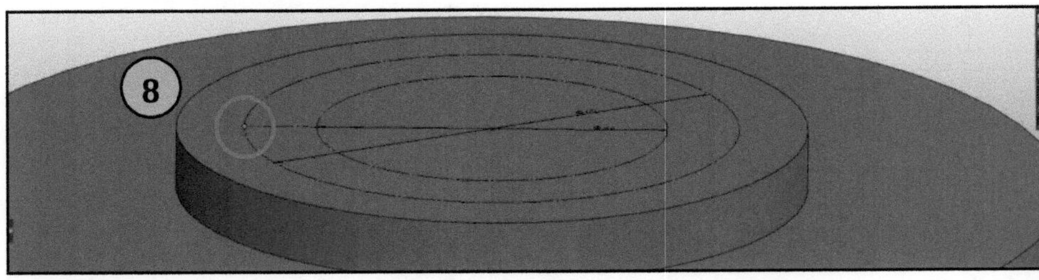

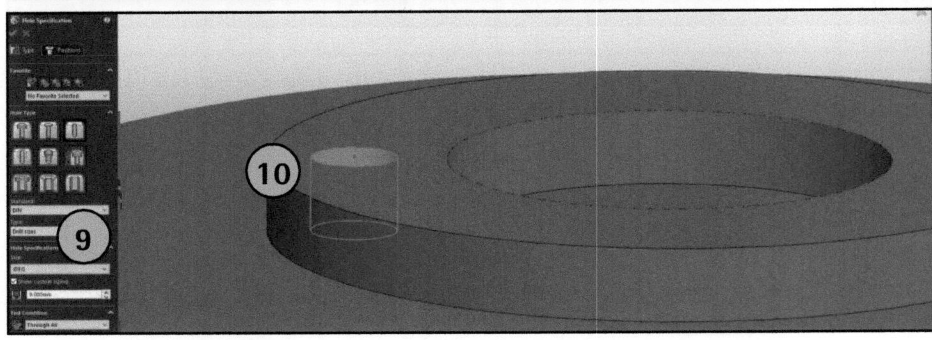

Circular Pattern

- Using the **Circular Pattern** function, create a **72°** offset of the bore, number **5**, selecting the inner cylinder as the base cylinder (11,12).

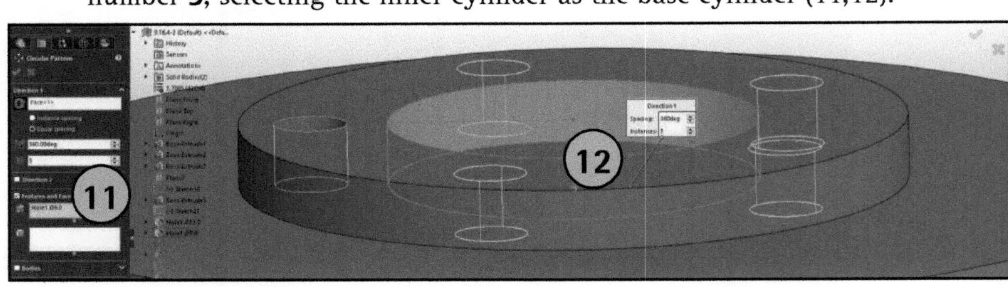

9.16.5 Creating central counterbore

Hole Wizard

- Using the central point on the inner surface create a **Cylindrical countersink Ø95** mm at this **Point 0.3** mm deep, **Through hole Ø83** mm (13, 14).

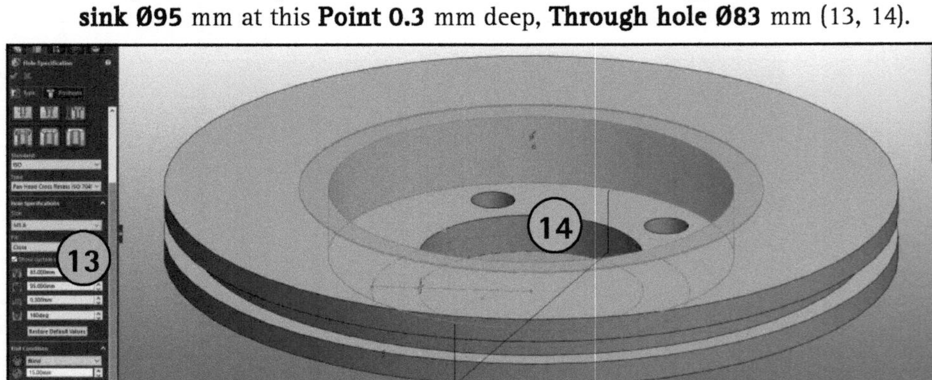

9.16.6 Creating vent holes

- Using a new **Sketch**, create **Circle** on the component surface (6).
- Place a **Point** at the axis intersection (15).
- At the points, use the **Hole Wizard** to create a **Through hole Ø4 mm**, drilling depth **Through All** (16, 17).

Sketch

Circle

Line

Point

Hole Wizard

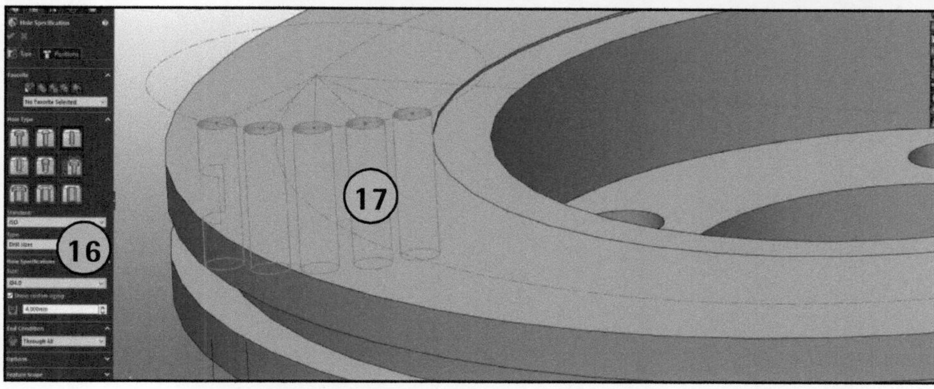

- Using the **Circular Pattern** function, create a **22.5°** offset of the bore, number **16**, selecting the inner cylinder as the base cylinder (18, 19).

Circular Pattern

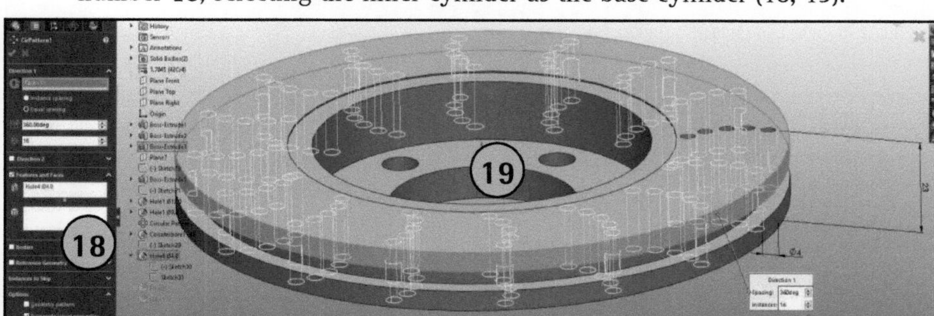

9.16.7 Edge rounding on the base body

- Edge breaking, radius **1** mm, using feature **Fillet** (38, 39).

Fillet

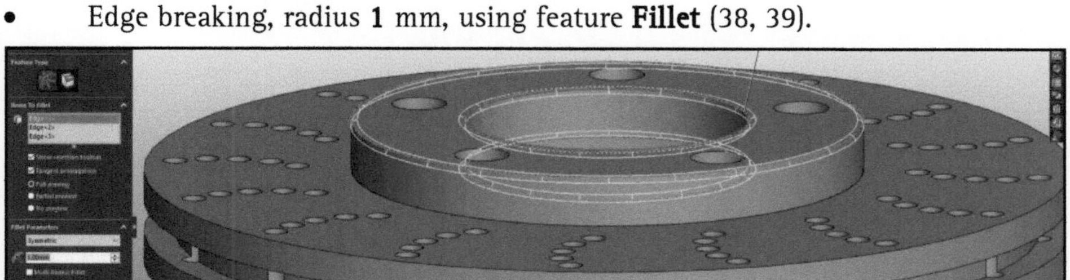

Fillet

- Edge breaking, radius **1** mm, using feature **Fillet** (38, 39).

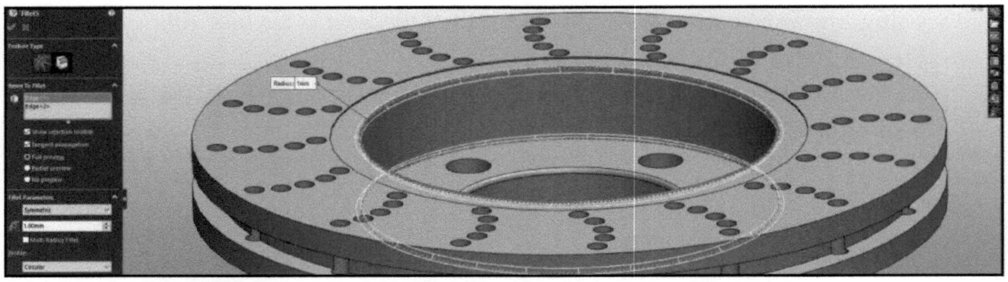

Save as New

9.16.8 Data backup

Save as New / Enter a name of your choice.

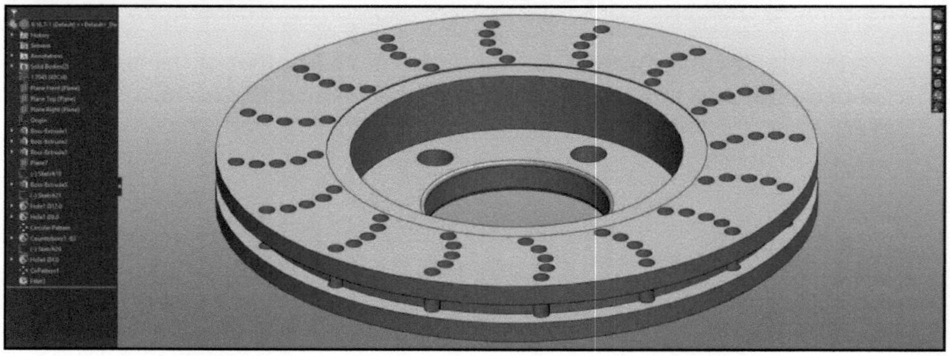

10

Dassault Systèmes
3DEXPERIENCE©
SOLIDWORKS Design
2026

Parts and Components

Create and Customize

The Book DVD
Order option

10 The book DVD, order option

10.1 The book DVD, basics

This book is published by BOD because it's not profitable for specialist publishers to publish high-quality CAD books for a smaller audience.

To make this book available to a smaller audience at a reasonable cost, I have decided not to print it in color.

10.2 The book DVD, price and ordering options

For the buyers of this book, I offer the possibility to order a DVD with all created component data for the version SOLIDWORKS Design 2026 and the color PDF edition of this book
The book DVD can be ordered via email to **engelke.cad@web.de**.
A purchase confirmation for buying the book must be included in the email as an attachment to the order. Delivery of this DVD version is free of charge.

10.3 The book DVD, contents at a glance

10.3.1 The book DVD, SOLIDWORKS Design 2026, files for the learning units

The book DVD contains the working files described in chapters 2 to 9 in the chapter directories on this book DVD.

10.3.2 The book DVD, SOLIDWORKS Design 2026, PDF file

The complete paper edition of the book is included on the book DVD in a color edition, in PDF format, to mitigate the disadvantages of the grayscale edition of the book.

10.3.3 The book DVD, list of contents, short overview

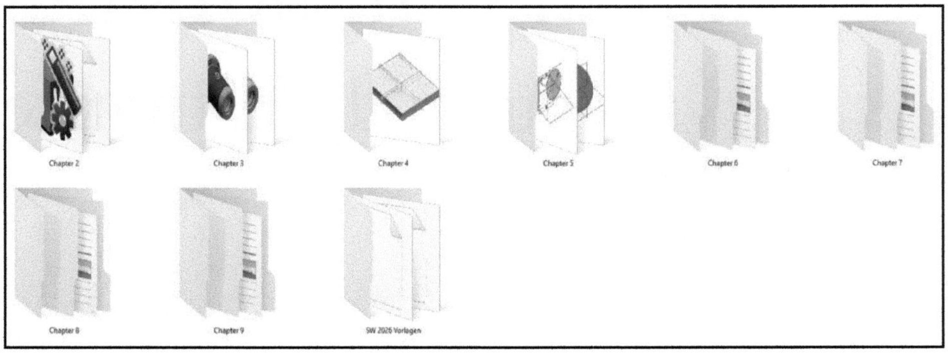

Dassault Systèmes
3DEXPERIENCE©
SOLIDWORKS 2026

Parts and Components
Create and Customize

Book Index

Numerics

.ASMDOT extension 19, 365
.DRWDOT extension 19
.PRTDOT file extension 19, 365
2D sketch cannot be converted to 3D sketch 259
2D-basic sketch the creation 259, 264
360° rotation 146
3D curves in Microsoft Excel 268
3D Piping Form element feature Planes 3D Sketch, Lofted-Boss 259
3D Piping with Thin feature 262, 263
3D Sketch for the Pipe Bend path 265
3D Sketch for the pipeline path the creation 260
3D Sketch tab 182
3D Sketch 260, 265
3D Sketching Functions 98
3D Solids an introduction 9
3D Solids and Solid Edge 2026 11
3D solids based on other objects 11
3Dconnexion 3D Mouse Access to special additional functions 48
3Dconnexion 3D Mouse Assembly mode 48
3Dconnexion 3D Mouse Drawing Mode 48
3Dconnexion 3D Mouse Part Modeling Mode 48
3DDashboard 16
3DExperience 29

- A -

Access to all SOLIDWORKS functions at the touch of a button 48
Acrylik and Neoprene 71
Activate created Section Views 68
Activating the work planes 41
Add Curves 282, 284
Add Points 282, 284
Add Relation 223, 270, 294, 318, 325
Additional sketch Circle on the lower working Plane2 257
Additional sketch Circle on the upper work Plane1 257
Additional work plane above 253, 256, 285
Additional work plane below 257
Additional work plane reference Plane Front 260
Additional work plane reference Plane Right 260, 262
Additional work plane reference Plane Top 265
Additional work planes 260
Adjust the position of the cone attachment 348
Adjusting document properties 44
Adjusting system properties 42
Adjusting the angle of the base body 346
Adjusting the basic body 302
Adjusting the basic dimensions assigning Driven 337
Adjusting the Button Size Command Bar 39
Adjusting the graphics area 40
Adjusting the high of the base body 347
Adjusting the hollow body height 349
Adjusting the thread representation 183, 196
Advanced Hole tool 175
Allocation of materials to components 70
Ambient occlusion 31
Annealed Stainless Steel AISI 316 388, 391
Annealed Stainless Steel AISI 347 372, 382, 424, 428
Annotations/Properties/Shaded cosmetic threads 183
Appearance on components 73
Appearance select Faces 74
Appearance select Feature 73
Appearance 30
Appearance-Surface finish 72
Apply wall thickness using the Thicken feature 276, 278, 281
Archimedean Solids 10
Assemblies 16
Assembly files 19
Assign display filter Shaded cosmetic threads 330
Assigning a background display 41
Assigning a background image 76
Assigning a Decal 75
Assigning component material 199, 220, 235, 241, 245, 372, 382, 388, 391, 418, 424, 428, 430, 437
Assigning relationships in sketches 91
Assistant for Copying User Settings 45
Attachment surfaces the creation 430
Automatic adjustment of planes and axes 110
Axis of rotation as a line sketch 271
axis of rotation 149
Axis/Two Planes 269
Axonometric representations according to DIN ISO 5456-3 64

- B -

Base area using function Center Rectangle 297
Base plate, the creation 420
basic body Cone 344
Basic body cube change of position 325
Basic body cylinder using circular are 143
Basic body processing the Helix/Spiral feature 222
basic body Pyramid 345
basic body using feature Revolve 376
Basic constructions of the shaft element 178
Basic geometric primitive body Cuboid 129
basic geometry drawing representation 189
basic geometry specifications 206, 209, 212, 218, 221, 250, 253
Basic planes 110
Basic profile curves for a Boundary Surface, the creation 277
Basic profile curves for a Lofted Surface 275
basic profile curves for a surface shape 287
Basic sketch center axes 191
basic sketch construction 130, 134, 190, 375
Basic sketch for locking plate slot 383
Basic sketch for shaft groove 384
basic sketch for the drilling, version 1 191
basic sketch for the end circles using 3D Sketch 265
Basic sketch for the interlocking tooth 425
Basic sketch for the keyway slot 237, 373
basic sketch for the lower pipeline 260
Basic sketch for the transverse drilling 386
Basic sketch horizontal parallel lines 192
basic sketch line extensions on Front Plane 261
basic sketch line extensions on Plane2 261
basic sketch Sketch Fillet 261
basic sketch transition guidelines 264
Basic sketch vertical parallel lines 191
Basic sketch with function Rectangle over center version 2 193
Basic sketch with function Rectangle over center 193
basic sketch269
Basic sketch 285
Basic solid Cone geometric description 13
Basic solid Cube geometric description 12
Basic solid Cuboids geometric description 12
Basic solid Cylinder geometric description 12
Basic solid Ellipsoid of revolution geometric description 13
Basic solid Pyramid geometric description 14
Basic solid Sphere geometric description 13
Basic solid Torus geometric description 13
Basic solid Truncated Cone geometric description 13
Basic solid Truncated Pyramid geometric description 14
Basics of construction geometric relationships 126
Basics of construction 125
Bearing base part the creation 415
Bearing Cover the creation 413
Bevel Gear component representations 244
Bevel Gear Creation using the SOLIDWORKS toolbox 244
Bevel gear housing, the creation 406
Bevel gear the creation 245
Bevel Gear the outer contour editing 246
Bevel Gear 245
Blind for End Condition 184
Bodies to be deformed 361
book DVD contents at a glance 442

book DVD files for the learning units 442
book DVD list of contents, short overview 442
book DVD order option 442
Book DVD PDF file 442
book DVD price and ordering options 442
book DVD 20, 442
Boolean Difference, operation type Subtract Rectangle-Circle-Difference using Extrude feature 297
Boolean Difference, operation type Subtract using Trim function 295
Boolean Difference, operation type Subtract 291
Boolean form elements 290
Boolean Intersection, operation type Combine using Trim function 296
Boolean Intersection, operation type Combine 291
Boolean Operation Combine Bodies Distance Shaft using Combine Bodies feature 305
Boolean Operation Combine Bodies Operation type Add Subtract and Common 302
Boolean Operation Combine Bodies using Split 308
Boolean operation dynamic preview mode 290
Boolean Operation Multibody Part Creating one part using Combine Bodies feature 310
Boolean Operation Multibody Part the creation 310
Boolean Operation Multibody Part 310
Boolean Operations Combine Bodies operation type Subtract 307
Boolean Operations for basic bodies Operation type Add and Subtract 298
Boolean Operations for basic bodies Operation type Subtract using Extruded Cut 300
Boolean Operations for Surfaces Base Areas using Trim feature 294
Boolean operations for surfaces basic sketch 294
Boolean Operations for Surfaces Editing with Sketch functions 295
Boolean operations 291
Boolean Split 291
Boolean Union operation type Add using Trim function 295
Boolean Union operation type Add 291
Bottoming Tapped Hole 183
Boundary Surface the creation 277
Boundary Surface 277
Bounding Entities 278
Brass 71
Breadcrumbs 20
Break Link to original assembly 310
Break more edges 394
Button Size Large 39
Button Size Medium 39
Button Size Small default 39

- C -

Callouts and Handles 23
Callouts 21, 23
Cartoon 31
Cast Stainless Steel 71, 402, 406
Catalan Solids 10
Center Point Snap 182, 374
Center Point 427
Center Rectangle 130, 140, 190
Centerpoint Arc 150, 360
central counterbore 377
Central mounting hole 394
chamber basic sketch 224
Chamfer change distance assignment 333
Chamfer using the feature Cut Revolve 225
Chamfer 372, 435
Chamfers for edge breaking 372
Change of position using the Horizontal relation 318
Change of position using the Merge relation 318
Change of position using the Parallel relation 319
Change of position using the Symmetric relation 319
Change of position using the Tangent relation 320
Change the position of the hole center point on corner point 341
Change the specified bore diameter to the core diameter 226, 228
Changing Circular Pattern 332
Changing edge breaking Chamfer and Thread Stud 333
Changing Linear Pattern 331
Changing orthogonal views together 66
Changing the background of a scene 76
Changing the component color 73
Changing the dimensions of the basic sketch 324
Changing the edge breaking Chamfer 333
Changing the hole size using Instant3D 340
Changing the Perspective 58
Changing the polygon prism 326
Changing the polygon size using the base sketch 326
Changing the position of the hole shifting the center point using sketch 339
Changing the position of the hole shifting the center point 339, 340
Changing the rotation angle using Edit Feature 343
Changing the rotation angle using Instant3D 343
Check sketch for feature usage 35
Checking the data backup of the created Section View 67
Chrome Stainless Steel 199, 369
Circle 143, 156
Circular Pattern feature, the creation 214
Circular Pattern 217, 243, 384, 400, 402, 409, 438
Circular Sketch pattern 426
Click File/Save to This PC 45
Close dialog box 130
Close dialog box/Finish sketch 133
closed surface of Rotation using command Line 390
closed surface of rotation using lines with vector data 178
Closing the base area using Planar surface 278
Collinear relation 320, 325
Collinear 223
Color assignment of the graphics area 40
Color tones for highlighting 80
Combine Bodies Add basics 302
Combine Bodies Add the creation 303
Combine Bodies Common the creation 304
Combine Bodies Cuboid and cylinder operation type Add 302
Combine Bodies Subtract the creation 303
Combine Bodies using feature Split 308
Combine 302, 307, 311
Command input using the keyboard 50
Command shortcuts 50
Command SOLIDWORKS Welcome dialog 29
Command Tabs Tools 46
CommandManager Direct Editing 25
CommandManager Evaluate 25
CommandManager Features 25
CommandManager for components 24
CommandManager Sheet Metal 25
CommandManager Sketch 25
CommandManager SOLIDWORKS Add-Ins 25
CommandManager Surface 25
CommandManager Weldments 25
CommandManager 20, 23
Commands for Boolean operations 290
Commercial Bronze, UNS C22000 399
Completing the sketch construction 427
Component adjustments using Triad 346
Component creation Base Plate 420
Component creation Bearing Base Part 415
Component creation Bearing Cover 413
Component creation Bearing Housing 401
Component creation Brake Disc 436
Component creation Coupling bolt 368
Component creation Drive Shaft 371, 381
Component creation Gear Shaft 387

Component creation Gear Switching Element 425
Component creation Housing Cover final edits 434
Component creation Housing Cover 429
Component creation Housing Dome 398
Component creation Housing for Bevel Gear 405
Component creation Mounting bolts 375
Component creation Worm Shaft 390
Component files 19
Component Preparation 70
component representation for component creation 405
Compression spring a Swept/Boss feature 219
Compression spring Form element feature Helix/Spiral Swept Boss 218
Cone element with draft angle Form element feature Chamfer, Draft, Shell 250
Cone, geometric description 153
Cone, using rotation of a triangular area made of lines 154
ConfigurationManager 20, 22, 29
Conical adaptations 206
Construction of a transition curve 360
Construction point for the working plane 236
construction template historical representation rules 6
Context menus 21
Context Toolbars 23
Contour Select Tool 427
Controlled dimensions 79
Converted Body 299
Converting Features to Bodies the creation 301
Converting Features to Bodies 298, 299
Coordinate systems 80
Copper Alloys 2.0367 CU ZN 40 179
Copper 70
Copy and Mirror 426
Copy hole in component 341
Copying the hole to front side of the cuboid 342
Corner Rectangle 132
cosmetic threads 196
counterbore holes DIN 974-1 198
Counterbore 431
Counterbore, Hex Socket Head Cap EN ISO 4672 210
Countersink DIN 74 and DIN EN ISO 15065 for countersunk screws 173
Countersink DIN 974-1 for cylinder head screws 173
Countersink DIN 974-2 for hexagon head screws 173
countersunk holes DIN 74 197
coupling bolt assign material 369
coupling bolt the creation 368
coupling bolt using Fillet 370
coupling bolt using Stud Wizard 369
Create a basic sketch for Trim Surface 279
Create a central plane between planar surfaces 215
Create a new sketch 222
Create a new work plane 360
Create a Pyramid using Draft 160
Create a Tangent Work Plane 383, 384, 385
Create a Trim Surface using Surface-Extrude 280
Create basic component 300, 302
Create centering hole on the keyway side 374
Create centering hole on the other shaft side 374
Create central hole 417
Create Components 364
Create cut rotation 241
Create mounting holes 417, 423
Create tangential working plane 187
Create tangential working 236
Create the differentiating surface bodies 280
Create the left interlocking tooth row using the Circular Sketch pattern 426
Create the main inner body 407
Create work plane for groove 395
Creating 3D solid primitive body 124
Creating 3D volume primitive solids 11
Creating a cone element using Shell 252
Creating a drill plate 189
Creating a feature rules and options 80
Creating a hollow body using Shell 271
Creating a keyway slot 378
Creating a new template file for components 39
Creating a tangent plane 378
Creating a worm shaft structure using Cut Sweep 393
Creating an additional tangential work plane 385
Creating an Extrude feature 131, 141
Creating and adapting basic body 398, 401
Creating basic cylinder 221
Creating center holes 374
Creating central bore 437
Creating central counterbore 438
Creating connection holes 409, 414, 433, 438
Creating cylindrical basic bodies 436
Creating drive shaft attachments 388
Creating flange holes 399, 402
Creating housing holes 406
Creating lubrication oil bore 432
Creating mounting holes 242
Creating mounting holes 400
Creating one part using Combine Bodies feature 311
Creating sketches of the three basic profile curves 285
Creating solids from 2D geometry 11, 124
Creating the base body 375
Creating the base surface for differential extrusion 297
Creating the basic body 209, 212, 256
Creating the basic component 368, 398, 401, 406, 413, 415, 420, 429
Creating the basic profile curves 286
Creating the basic sketch for the keyway slot 378
Creating the basic sketch 140, 145, 253, 294, 371, 381
Creating the chamfers for the wave shoulder 377
Creating the circular area 151
Creating the curve sketch 268
Creating the frame geometry 286
Creating the halved circular area 149
Creating the inner body 306
Creating the keyway slot 373
Creating the outer body 306
Creating the right interlocking tooth row using Mirror Entities 426
Creating the thread end chamfer 376
Creating the work plane on a cylindrical surface selecting a sketch point 119
Creating vent holes 439
Creating work plane Plane on a cylindrical Surface 118
Creating work planes Mid Plane 112
Creating work planes Parallel Plane 111
Creating work planes Plane centered between two Sides 115
Creating work planes Plane through Point 113
Creating Work Planes 111
Creation of components command selection for creation 365
Creation of the components manufacturing fundamentals 365
Creation of the hollow body using Shell 255, 258
Creation of work planes Plane with defined Offset 114
Creation work planes Angular Plane axis-related 120
Creation work planes Angular plane offset distance 121
Creation work planes Plane with Angle input 116
Creation work planes Plane with multiple defined Offsets 117
cross-sectional area for the pipe body 262
cross-sectional area the creation 262
CTRL key + mouse wheel 61
Cube geometric description 139
Cube over geometry changes 324
Cube Sketch function Center Rectangle using Extrude 140
cuboid as a basic geometry using feature Extrude 209
Cuboid construction using a line sketch 134
Cuboid Line sketch construction with dimension entries 134
Cuboid Sketch function Center Rectangle using Extrude 130, 132
Cuboid using Corner Rectangle sketch construction 132

Cuboid with top Form element feature Draft Shell Fillet 206
Cuboid with top Form element feature Rib Mirror Circular Pattern 215
Cuboid, geometric description 129
cursor view changes 135
Curve line as Curve Through XYZ Points from a text list 268
curve path 275, 277
Curve Through XYZ Points 268
Curve to Curve option 360
Curve using the Spline function 279
Customizing the CommandManager 39
Cut Revolve 225, 247
Cut Sweept 224
Cut Thread Red preview 227, 230, 392
Cut-Extrude 339
Cylinder geometric description 142
Cylinder Rotation over a stationary rectangular area 145
Cylindrical countersink 402, 414, 423, 438

- D -

Data backup of the customized template file 45
Data backup 131
Decals 30, 75
default settings 42
Deform 358, 359
Deformation functions on a basic body using feature Deform 358
Deformation functions on a basic body using feature Flex 353
Design fundamentals 78
Design Library 30, 234, 240, 245, 387
design sketch for the component creation 233, 239, 244, 368, 371, 375, 381, 387, 390, 398, 401, 405, 413, 415, 420, 425, 429, 436
Differentiating surface bodies using Trim Surface 280
Dimension angular spacing 426
Dimension entries in 2D sketches horizontal and vertical 103
Dimensional change for a sketch Centerpoint Straight Slot using SmartDimension 316
Dimensional change for a sketch Circle using SmartDimension 316
Dimensional change of a sketch Center Rectangle using SmartDimension 316
Dimensional change 316
Dimensioning in 2D sketches angular dimensioning 104
Dimensioning in 2D sketches Baseline Dimension 107
Dimensioning in 2D sketches circular dimensioning 105
Dimensioning in 2D sketches Diameter dimension using center 105
Dimensioning in 2D sketches Diameter dimensioning across centerline 106
Dimensioning in 2D sketches distance dimensioning 104
Dimensioning in 2D sketches quadrant-circle distance dimensioning 105
Dimensioning in 2D sketches Radian measure 106
Dimensioning in 2D sketches radius dimensioning 105
Dimensioning in 2D sketches 103
Dimensioning in 3D sketches 99
Dimensioning methods 79
Dimensions 79, 126, 364
DimXpertManager 29
DIN Steel 1.2312 40CrMnMoS8 225
DIN Steel 1.7225 42CroMo4 235, 241, 245
directional arrow X 339
Disable Trim Surface 281
Display of Managers 28
Display Style 69
Display using RealViewGraphics 56
Display without RealViewGraphics 56
Displaying models in Normal To view 65
DisplayManager 29
Distance Shaft volume creation 306
Distribution of shaft groove using Circular Pattern 384
Distribution of shaft groove using feature Mirror 385
Dowel hole in the center of the component 195
Dowels hole depth Through all 195
Draft angle adjustment by entering the angle value 328
Draft angle for the base cuboid using Manual Draft 207
Draft angle for the basic body 251
Draft angle for the cylinder using Manual Draft 206
Draft volume generation 163
Draft 206, 251
drag arrow in the center of the rectangle 136, 141
drag arrow 133
drawing as a design template in technology 6
Drawing files 19
Drawing methods in mechanical engineering 7
Drawings 16
Drill plate Form element feature Hole Wizard Linear Pattern 209
drill plate the basic body 190
Drill type Slot 188
Drilling technical basics 173
Drilling the central hole in the gear switching element 428
Drilling the through hole 182
drive shaft attachments 235
drive shaft component creation 381
Drive Shaft the creation 371
Driven assignment 337
Driven dimensions 79
DVD can be ordered via email to engelke.cad@web.de 442
DVD version is free of charge 442
Dynamic Feature Editing 336
Dynamic Preview 83

- E -

Edge break using Chamfer the creation 389
Edge breaking of the base body 250
Edge breaking using Chamfer 238, 242, 376
Edge breaking using feature Chamfer 382, 391
Edge breaking using feature Fillet 185, 382, 392, 410, 428
Edge Breakings using features Chamfer 422
Edge Breakings using features Hole Wizard 422
Edge rounding on the base body 439
Edit Appearance 73
Edit Feature Draft option 328
Edit Feature 329, 330, 331, 332
Edit Material 70, 179, 245
Edit Polygon 327
Edit sketch plane reverse side 197
Edit Sketch Plane 197, 198
Edit Sketch 226, 228, 326
Editing a component using the Bending option 354, 356
Editing a component using the Point option selecting Edge 359, 360
Editing a component using the Point option 358
Editing a component using the Tapering option 357
Ellipse 165
Enable Annotations 183
End chain 135, 148
End condition for Extrude Boss/Base 83
Error message 34
Error messages and possible solutions 34
extension .sldprt 131
External thread assignment using Stud wizard 369
External thread assignment using the Thread function 386, 392
External thread using Stud Wizard position change 184
External thread with physical thread profile specification 229
Extrude and Draft volume creation 160
Extrude feature change length 136
Extrude feature with depth change 133
Extrude Mid Plane 403
Extrude 156, 190, 406, 413, 431
Extruded Cut 226, 241, 300, 383, 395, 407, 416, 421, 431
Extruded thread green preview 228
extrusions to Mid Plane 136

- F -

Faces to Remove 207, 255, 258, 272
Feature Deform 358
Feature Extrude Boss change polygon height 326
Feature Extrude-Boss change dimension assignment 324
Feature Flex option Bending 353
Feature Flex option Stretching 353
Feature Flex option Tapering 353
Feature Flex option Twisting 353
Feature Flex 353
Feature Hole Wizard Change Hole size and Hole type 329
Feature Hole Wizard change Hole type 330
Feature Select 20, 21
Feature toolbars 26
Feature-based solids 124
FeatureManager Design Tree 20, 70
FeatureManager 22, 27
File Explorer 30
Fillet Feature the creation 208
Fillet 370, 399, 410, 435, 439
final chamfer the creation 224
Final sketch the creation 254
Finish sketch 130
Flange ring with mounting holes Form element feature Hole Wizard Circular Pattern 212
Flex option Bending 354, 356
Flex option Tapering 357
Flip Direction 282, 284
Flyout Apply Scene 31
Flyout Display Style 31, 32
Flyout Heads-Up View Toolbar 31
Flyout Hide all Types 31
Flyout Previous View 32
Flyout Section View 31, 32
Flyout View Orientation Heads-up View Toolbar 41
Flyout View Orientation 31, 33
Flyout View Settings 31
Flyout Zoom to Area 32
Flyout Zoom to Fit 32
Form element feature Thread the creation 226, 228, 230
Form element feature Thread using core diameter 226
Form element feature Thread with physical thread using outer diameter 228
Form element features 202
Form element function Chamfer 202
Form element function Circular Pattern 203
Form element function curved construction Deform 205
Form element function curved construction Dome 205
Form element function curved construction Flex 205
Form element function curved construction Freeform 205
Form element function Draft 202
Form element function Fillet 202
Form element function Helix/Spiral 203
Form element function Linear Pattern 203
Form element function Loft 204
Form element function Rib 203
Form element function Shell 203
Form element function SOLIDWORKS Toolbox 204
Form element function Sweep 204
Form element function Thread 203
Four countersunk holes DIN 74 axle element 2 reverse side 197
Four countersunk holes DIN 974-1 axle element 3 198
Four M10 threaded holes axle element 1 196
Freeform adjustment of the cover surface 282
Freeform adjustment of the front surface 284
Freeform Fittings adjustments 282
Freeform Surface the creation 282
Freeform 282
Freestanding geometry 35
Front Plane 401
Full preview 185
Fully defined sketches are black 78, 90
Fundamentals for basic constructions Work Planes 110

- G -

Gear creation using the SOLIDWORKS toolbox 234, 240, 245, 387
Gear Shaft component representations 233
Gear Shaft creation using the SOLIDWORKS toolbox 233
Gear Shaft editing of the basic geometry 235
Gear Shaft specification 233
Geometric basic primitive body Cone and Truncated Cone 153
Geometric basic primitive body Cube 139
Geometric basic primitive body Cylinder 142
Geometric basic primitive body Pyramid and Truncated Pyramid 158
Geometric basic primitive body Rotational ellipsoid 164
Geometric basic primitive body Sphere and Spherical Cap 147
Geometric basic primitive body Torus 167
Geometric basics 124
Geometric Fundamentals 78
Geometric Primitive Solids and SOLIDWORKS 2026 12
Geometry changes using Instant3D Truncated cone to cone 344
Geometry changes using Instant3D Truncated pyramid to pyramid 345
Geometry of thickness zero 36
German Institute for Standardization DIN 8
Groove for locking plate the creation 395
Groove for locking plate 395

- H -

Handles 21, 23
Heads-up View Toolbar 20, 31, 56, 66
Helix construction as a basis 392
Helix/Spiral feature 218, 219, 222, 392
Help window area 30
Help 20
Hemisphere and Spherical Cap 147
Hidden Lines Removed 32, 69
Hidden Lines Visible 32, 69
Hide option in the FeatureManager 179
Hide/Show all Types 31
Highlight object selection 82
history of drawing as a design template 4
history of geometry 2
history of perspective 5
history of technical standardization 8
Hole changes in the component 339
Hole Wizard basics 174
Hole Wizard change Hole size 329
Hole Wizard change Hole type 330
Hole Wizard edit feature for holes 175
Hole Wizard End Condition 175
Hole Wizard feature End condition 173
Hole Wizard feature hole types 173
Hole wizard feature type Counterbore 210, 213
Hole Wizard Threaded Holes 174
Hole Wizard 377, 399, 406, 417
Holes as a SOLIDWORKS Hole Wizard function 173
hollow body axis as an alignment element of the base surface 269
hollow body base using sketch feature Polygon 269
Hollow body Form element feature Curve through XYZ Points 268
horizontal arrow of the Triad 348
Horizontal relation 318
Housing Cover component representations 429
Housing Cover the creation 429
how do I use the book 54

- I -

Inner attachment surfaces the creation 408
Insert cylindrical countersink 235
Insert Line and choose As Sketched 178
Insert threaded connection as an attachment 403
Inserting a tangential transverse bore 385, 386
Instant3D changing the dimension of the cuboid height 337
Instant3D changing the dimensions of the cuboid surfaces 337

Instant3D Cube over geometry changes 337
Instant3D Features 51
Instant3D Functionality 51
Instant3D Live Section Planes 52
Instant3D model changes 336
Instant3D Rulers 52
Instant3D Unit Adjustment 336
Instant3D 246, 306, 314
Insulated Mold Casting 430
Interlocking tooth row the creation 425
Internally Spur Gear 240
Internally toothed Spur Gear component representations 239
Internally toothed Spur Gear Creation using the SOLIDWORKS toolbox 239
Internally toothed Spur Gear the outer contour editing 241
intersection point 195
Introduction to design concepts 16
Invalid solution found 90

- J -

Johnson Solids 10

- K -

Keep relations parameters 305
Kepler-Poinsot Solids 10
Keyway slot according to DIN 6885-1 175
Keyway slot creating the basic sketch 187
Keyway slot the creation 188, 236, 237, 373, 378

- L -

left mouse button 61
Length adjustment of the inner body 306
Line construction sketch snap function Point 86
Line construction sketch snap function Point-Centerpoint 87
Line construction sketch snap function Point-Midpoint 86
Line construction sketch snap function Point-Perpendicular 87
Line construction sketch snap function Point-Tangent Point 87
Line construction sketch snap function Tangent 87
Line properties to For Construction 319
Line 134
Linear Pattern feature the creation 211
Linear Pattern change 331
Linking error 36
List of form element functions 202
Locking plate slot the creation 383
Locking plate slot using feature Extruded Cut 383
Lofted Boss 254, 257
Lofted Surface the creation 275, 287
Lofted-Boss 266
Log in to the 3DEXPERIENCE platform 16
lower basic body 258

- M -

M C Escher 5
Magnified Selection access using the context menu 60
Magnified Selection accessed using the keyboard 60
Magnified Selection 60
Mahogany and 1060-Alloy 71
Make Multibody Part 310
Manual Fillet 208
master of the impossible perspective 5
Material allocation 70
Material assignment 179, 181
Materials Overview 70
Menu Bar 20, 22, 24, 39
Merge relation 318
Merge result 403
Mesh density 282
Mid Plane 384, 385, 430
middle mouse button 59
Mirror Entities 426
mirror Right Plane 408, 419
mirror Top Plane 416
Mirror 217, 385, 408, 416, 419
Model Changes example lists 314
Model changes modifying features 324
Model changes using feature Deform Option Curve to Curve 360
Model changes using feature Deform Option Point selection Edge 359
Model changes using feature Deform option Point 358
Model changes using feature Flex option Bending 354
Model changes using feature Flex option Tapering 357
Model changes using feature Flex option Twisting 356
Model Changes 314
Modifying Features in Instant3D 51
Modifying sketches changes in position regarding relationship 314, 318
Modifying sketches changing positions 314, 317
Modifying sketches geometry changes 314, 316
Modifying the basic body using the Extrude option Draft 328
Molded surfaces 285
Mounting holes on the back side of the component 424
Mounting holes on the front side of the component 423
Mounting holes on the top side of the component 423
Mouse Functions 47
Mouse Gestures 49
Mouse with three buttons 47
Mouse with wheel 47
Move display 61
Move Entities 223, 305
Move Face option Rotate 346
Move Face option Translate 348, 349
Move Face 347
moving the Sketch2 305
Multibody Part, basics 310
Multiple Views linking orthogonal views 66
Multiple Views Single View and Four View 66
Multiple Views Two View Vertical and Two View Horizontal 66
Multiple Views Viewports 66
Multiple Views 66

- N -

Neutral plane 207, 251
New SOLIDWORKS Document program functions 19
No solution found 90
Normal To 65, 187

- O -

Offset Entities 192, 246
Older than paper 2
Open SOLIDWORKS Connected 16
Open the component file from the book DVD 111
Open the working assembly file 310
Open the working file and make adjustments 250
Open the working file 20, 55, 298
Opening the SOLIDWORKS template file for parts 39
Opening your own template file 130, 132, 140, 406
Operation type Add, using Extruded-Boss 298
Operation Type click Add 304, 311
Operation Type click Subtract 307
Operation type Subtract using Extruded Cut 300
Option Cut Thread, Red preview 379, 386
Option Extruded thread Green preview 380
orientation center of polygon to the main axis, 270
orientation Polygon to Curve relation Pierce 269
Origin point for repositioning 305
Origin point 135, 154, 269
Outer contour editing diameter change of the attachment cylinder 246
Outer contour editing length change 246
Over defined sketch 34
Over defined sketches are yellow 90
Overview of sketch construction for parallel lines 192

- P -

Pan Context menu 61
Parallel Plane 407, 434

Parallel relation 319, 321
Parametric dimensions 364
part user interface 20
Parts and Components 364
Parts 16
PartSupply 30
Pattern Arrangement Changing Linear Pattern and Circular Pattern 331
Pattern-Axis 214
Perimeter Circle 265
perspective representation 5
Perspective view 146
Perspective 31
Physical external thread using feature Thread 379
Physical internal thread using feature Thread 380
Physical thread assignment 379
Physical Thread Profile Form element feature Thread 226
physical thread with the function Thread 175
Pipe Bend creation using feature Lofted-Boss 266
Pipe Bend Form element feature Planes 3D Sketch Lofted-Boss 264
Pitch and Revolution 219, 222, 392
Place a Point at the intersection of the axes 242
Planar Surface 278
Plane option Mid Plane 215
Plane Top Plane Front, Plane Right 41
Plane 79, 126, 187, 236
Platonic solids 9
Point at the axis intersection 414, 432
Point on intersection points 423, 424
Point option 358, 359
Point 400
Polygon 269
Position change for a Center Rectangle 317
Position change for a Centerpoint Straight Slot 317
Position change for Circles 317
Positioning basic sketches 305
Positioning the basic sketches, 305
Power Transmission 234, 240, 245, 387
Powerful commands optimized constructions 172
Preserve reference geometry and sketches 301
Press the spacebar 63
Previous View 31
Primitives bodies 124
profil sketch construction 219
Program Adjustments 15
Program Basics 15
program startup 3DEXPERIENCE© SOLIDWORKS 2026 for Makers 16
PropertyManager 20, 22, 27
Pyramid geometric description 158
Pyramid 159

- Q -

Quick Access Tools 24
Quick Snap Quadrant Snap 236
Quick Snaps Intersection Snap 195
Quick Snaps 182

- R -

RealViewGraphics 31
RealViewGraphics 56
Reassign component material 70, 179
Rectangle position change alignment to a guideline using the Parallel relation 321
Rectangle position change alignment to center line using the Colinear relation 320
rectangular basic sketch259
Rectangular cone element Form element feature Planes, Lofted-Boss Shell 253
Rectangular funnel element Form element feature Lofted Surface Thicken 275
Reference Geometry 269
Reference Plane Front 67
Reference Plane Top 68
Reference Triad 21
Relation Coincident 270
relation Equal 294
Relation Pierce 270
Relationship assignment Collinear 96
Relationship assignment Concentric 96
Relationship assignment Concident 92
Relationship assignment Equal 94
Relationship assignment Horizontal or Vertical 91
Relationship assignment Intersection 97
Relationship assignment Midpoint 93
Relationship assignment Parallel 92
Relationship assignment Perpendicular 93
Relationship assignment Points merge 91
Relationship assignment Symmetric 94
Relationship assignment Tangent 95
Relationships 80
Relief groove for the physical thread 393
Resetting the Perspective 58
Resizing circular objects to the same size 294
Resulting Bodies 308
revolve sketch 223
Revolve volume creation 146
Revolve 398
Revolved volume creation 145, 149, 152, 155, 166, 169, 306, 343, 372, 376, 381, 391
Rib feature mirrored rib construction 217
Rib feature multiple ribs over Circular pattern 217
Rib feature one rib the creation 216
Rib feature the basic rib 216
Roll View 62
Rotate view around one edge 61
Rotate view 61
Rotational ellipsoid geometric description 164
Rotational ellipsoid Rotation of half an elliptical surface 165
Round to Square Form element feature Planes Lofted-Boss Shell 256
Round to Square the creation 257
Rules for written execution in the book 54

- S -

Save as New 131
Save as the View orientation 186
Save as type Part Templates *.prtdot45
Saving system settings 46
Scenes 30
scroll the mouse wheel 60
Search 20
Section View adjust the level variably 68
Section View for design control 186
Section View on Plane 67
Section Views in models 67
Select Contours 179
Select Initial Curve and Target Curve 360
Select the Body to Subtract 303, 307
select the component from the book's DVD 20, 55
Select the Cuboid and the Cylinder 304
Select the Main Body 303, 307
Select the Plane Right 132
Select the Top Plane 130
Select View Orientations Normal To using the CTRL key 65
Selectable flyouts in the Features toolbar 26
Selected bodies and Cut Bodies 308
Selection Breadcrumbs 23
Selection Tools 82
Setting Plane Display for the active document 44
Setting System options Sketch/Relation/Snap 42
Setting the Button Size using Options/Customize 40
Setting the Detailing for the active document 44
Setting the Image Quality for the active document 44
Setting the options from the Default Templates tab 43

Setting the options from the FeatureManager tab 43
Setting the options from the General tab 43
Setting the options from the Performance tab 43
Setting Units for the active document 44
Shaded cosmetic threads 229, 330
Shaded with Edges 32, 69
Shaded 32, 69
Shadows in Shaded Mode 31, 56
shaft element Chamfers and Fillets 185
shaft element external thread 184
shaft element Holes and Threading 182
Shaft element Keyway slot, 187
Shaft element using a line construction 178
shaft element with a line construction using SmartDimension 180
Shaft grooves the creation 384
Shaft grooves using feature Extruded Cut 384
Shell 207, 252, 255, 258, 272
Shortcut bars 23
Show preview 206
Show Section cap 186
Simple Hole DIN EN 20273 173
Simple hole with physical thread profile 226
Sketch conflicts 35
Sketch creation within volume generation 143, 145
Sketch creation 86
Sketch definitions 90
Sketch dimensioning horizontal and vertical 136
Sketch dimensioning horizontal 132
Sketch dimensioning vertical 133
Sketch Dimensions 102
Sketch entry under Extruded Cut 228
Sketch Fillet 190
Sketch for circumferential worm shaft profile 393
Sketch function Center Rectangle 130
Sketch geometry Polygon, change number of corners 326
sketch position change 325
Sketch relationships in 3D sketches 99
Sketch Relationships 90
Sketch Snap Functions 81
Sketch using Offset and Line 423
sketch will be placed on the face 197
Sketches 125
Sketches 78
Smart Dimension 132
SmartDimension with resizing 180
snap symbol 135
Solid bodies 310
SOLIDWORKS 2026 Geometric basics 125
SOLIDWORKS Content 30
SOLIDWORKS Design 2026 program start 16
SOLIDWORKS Design 2026 program startup 16
SOLIDWORKS Design 2026 start screen 17
SOLIDWORKS Design 2026 User Interface Overview 20
SOLIDWORKS Design 2026© controls functions and customization 55
SOLIDWORKS Document symbolism 19
SOLIDWORKS Document Window Extensions 22
SOLIDWORKS Document Window 22
SOLIDWORKS main window 38
SOLIDWORKS menus 24, 42
SOLIDWORKS terms, basics 16
SOLIDWORKS users and 3Dconnexion 3D Mouse 48
SOLIDWORKS© Design 2026, Program basics 16
SOLIDWORKS® Toolbox 204
Sphere geometric description 147
Sphere using a rotation of a halved circular area 148
Split document window 38
Split 308
Splitting the Base Body 308
Spur Gear 234, 387
start screen Home Recent Learn and Alerts 17
start screen Learn 17
start screen New SOLIDWORKS Document Advanced 18
start screen New SOLIDWORKS Document Standard 18
Status Bar 21
Steel Nitriding Alloy 1.7045 437
Steel Stainless 1.4401 X5CrNiMo17-12-2 380, 414
Stiffness Medium 358, 359, 361
Stud Wizard using outer diameter 229
Stud Wizard 175, 229, 333, 369
Style Spline 286
Sub define sketches are blue 78
Surface Extrude 281
Surface finish for components 72
Surface finish Machined und Burnished 72
Surface finish Sandblasted und Casted 72
Surface modeling Boundary Surface Different profile surfaces corner-determined 277
Surface modeling Freeform Editing Form element feature Surface Extrude Freeform 282
Surface modeling Molded surfaces 3D-Sketch basic profile curves 285
Surface modeling Molded surfaces Differentiate curve surface over trim surface 279
Surface-Extrude 280
Sweept path 220
Sweept profile 220
Sweept-Boss 263, 271
Swept Boss 220
Switching on the isometric view 41
Symmetric relation 319

- T -

Tangent in the FeatureManager design tree 187, 378
Tangent relation 320
Tangent Work Plane 403
Tangential working plane for the basic sketch of the keyway slot 373
Tapering option 357
Task Pane Tabs 29
Task Pane 20
Task Window Area 29
Technical Drawing 4
Technical Drawings a Cultural History 2
Technical principles for basic constructions drilling 173
Technical tasks 16
template files basics 18
text file for the XYZ points 268
The basic body the creation 436
the user interface advanced views 24
Thicken 255, 276, 278, 281, 284, 288
Thickness both Sides 216
Thin feature 263, 266
thread as a cosmetic thread 175
Thread Stud set a Undercut 333
Thread 226, 228, 379, 386, 392
Threaded base hole 173, 183, 432, 433
Threaded hole creating Circular Pattern feature 243
Through hole using the Hole Wizard 182
Toolbars 22
Toolbox 26, 30, 234, 240, 245, 387
Torus Rotation of a circular area around a central axis 168
Torus, geometric description 167
transitional body using Lofted Boss, the creation 254
Transparent Flyout FeatureManager 27
Trapezoidal thread using the feature Cut Sweep 224
Trapezoidal thread 221, 223
Triad ring 355
Trim Entities Option Trim to closest 151
Trim Surface 279, 280
Trim Tools 308
Trim with end face 227, 228, 230, 379, 380
Trim with start face 227, 228, 230, 379, 380
Trimming the start and end faces 418
Truncated Cone geometric description 153

Truncated cone to cone, adapting the base body 344
Truncated Cone using feature Extrude and Draft 156
Truncated pyramid to pyramid adapting the base body 345
Truncated Pyramid using Extrude feature option Draft 162
Truncated Pyramid, geometric description 158
Turn on the Decal element 75
Twisting option 356

- U -

Unalloyed 1.8159 51CrV4 220
Under defined sketches are blue 90
UnderCut 229, 333, 369
Unit System 21
Unsolvable sketch 34
Up to Next for End Condition 229
upper basic body 257
Use Large Buttons with Text 24
user interface, definitions of terms 22
User interface, overview 20
Using Mouse Gestures 49

- V -

vertical arrow of the Triad 347
vertical center line as the axis 426
View changes Roll View 62
View changes rotating position 61
View mode Shadow, settings using Edit Scene 57
View Orientation Dimetric 64
View Orientation Heads-up View Toolbar 42
View Orientation in component Mode 42
View Orientation Isometric 64
View Orientation option Shaded with Edges 42
View Orientation Trimetric 64
View Orientations according to DIN ISO 128-30 63
View Orientations Bottom 63
View Orientations Front 63
View Orientations Right 63
View Orientations Top 63
View position changes 61
View Selector 33, 184
View Setting Perspective 57
View Setting Shadows 56
View size changes 58
Views and Settings 55
Visibilities Decals On 75
Visibility On 75
Volume generation of the Gear switching element 427
Volume Generation 144

- W -

Wall defects 36
wall thickness using the Thicken feature 284, 288
Windows Functions 22
Wireframe 32, 69
Working Planes 110
Worm Shaft the basic creation 390
Worm Shaft using Helix/Spiral and Cut Sweep 392

- Y -

Y-arrow of the Triad 354

- Z -

Z-direction on the Triad 283, 284, 355
Zoom to Area 31, 58
Zoom to Fit 31, 59
Zooming in and out 59